Christ Jesus, the True Israel

Christ Jesus, the True Israel

Progressive Covenantalism on Israel, Christ, and the Church

BRENT E. PARKER

Foreword by Stephen J. Wellum

WIPF & STOCK · Eugene, Oregon

CHRIST JESUS, THE TRUE ISRAEL
Progressive Covenantalism on Israel, Christ, and the Church

Copyright © 2024 Brent E. Parker. All rights reserved. Except for brief quotations in critical publications or reviews, no part of this book may be reproduced in any manner without prior written permission from the publisher. Write: Permissions, Wipf and Stock Publishers, 199 W. 8th Ave., Suite 3, Eugene, OR 97401.

Wipf & Stock
An Imprint of Wipf and Stock Publishers
199 W. 8th Ave., Suite 3
Eugene, OR 97401

www.wipfandstock.com

PAPERBACK ISBN: 978-1-6667-3074-6
HARDCOVER ISBN: 978-1-6667-2262-8
EBOOK ISBN: 978-1-6667-2263-5

JANUARY 4, 2024 2:50 PM

Scripture quotations are from the ESV® Bible (The Holy Bible, English Standard Version®), copyright © 2001 by Crossway Bibles, a publishing ministry of Good News Publishers. Used by permission. All rights reserved.

To Kandace,
my loving and supportive wife,
you are God's precious gift to me (Prov 18:22),
and a constant reminder of God's love and grace.

CONTENTS

Foreword by Stephen J. Wellum | *ix*

Preface | *xiii*

Acknowledgments | *xv*

List of Abbreviations | *xvii*

Chapter 1
Introduction | 1

Chapter 2
The Nature, Characteristics, and Challenges of Typology | 15

Chapter 3
The Hermeneutics of Covenant Theology | 80

Chapter 4
The Hermeneutics of Dispensationalism | 115

Chapter 5
The Israel-Christ-Church Relationship: Israel as a Type of Christ | 157

Chapter 6
The Israel-Church Relationship via Christ: Implications for Ecclesiology | 236

Chapter 7

Challenging Texts For Progressive Covenantalism: Overcoming Potential Defeaters | 316

Chapter 8

Conclusion | 336

Bibliography | 339

Author Index | 381

Bibliography | 397

FOREWORD

WITHIN EVANGELICAL THEOLOGY, a number of biblical-theological systems vie for attention as Christians throughout the ages have wrestled with how to put together the whole counsel of God. Since Scripture is what it claims to be, namely, *God's* authoritative word written through the agency of human authors over time, it is the task of biblical and systematic theology to think through how the "parts" of God's unfolding revelation fit with the "whole" in a coherent and consistent manner.

In current discussion, although there are a variety of biblical-theological systems, two views tend to dominate the discussion: covenant theology in its paedobaptist variety and varieties of dispensational theology. Although these two views agree on many points, there remain important differences, and inevitably views that disagree with them are distinguished by setting themselves over against these dominant views. Given that differences among us are significant (despite our agreement), we ought to continue to work hard to resolve our theological disagreements. If we are not careful, there is a tendency to retreat to our systems and not to engage other views. But if *sola Scriptura* means anything, we should not be satisfied with retreat or simply with more four views books that describe our theological differences. Instead, we should desire to defend our views in light of alternatives by testing our theological systems according to the teaching of Scripture.

In regard to resolving differences between covenant and dispensational theology, there are a number of issues to consider. However, in this work, Brent Parker focuses on two of the most crucial areas that require further discussion: first, how each system understands the nature of typology, and second, how each system construes the Israel-Christ-church relationship. Unless headway is made on these two issues, resolution of our differences will not occur. Let me reflect further on the importance of these two areas for this entire discussion.

FOREWORD

First, discussion must occur on how biblical-theological systems understand the nature of typology. Although a lot of work has been done on "typology" over the years, we still do not agree. Books continue to be written that argue that there is no difference between typology and allegory, that "figural" is a better way to understand typology since typology is not a subset of predictive prophecy, and so on. In fact, in current debates regarding whether we should retrieve patristic and medieval exegesis, how we should interpret Scripture theologically, whether *prosopological exegesis* is valid or not, and whether reading the OT Christologically is legitimate exegetically, the nature of typology is central to all of these discussions.

As it pertains to resolving differences between dispensational and covenant theology, along with various mediating positions, no headway will be made unless a forthright discussion occurs regarding how we understand the nature of typology and how typology "works" in Scripture. For example, in dispensational theology, "typology" is employed but in diverse and inconsistent ways. The entire Levitical system may be viewed as a type, or various prophets, priests, and kings are types of Christ, but Israel, as an ethnic-national people is not. By contrast covenant theology has no problem viewing Israel as a type of the church, but not in a way that the church, as the new covenant people of God, is by nature different than Israel of old. Covenant theology is quick to identify the church as the "new Israel" or conversely, to speak of Israel as the "church." But they continue to think of the relationship between the two as the same *essentially*; the only differences are a number of *administrative* changes, hence the reason why Israel and the church are both viewed as a mixed community constituted by a believing and unbelieving people.

What this book contributes to the discussion is that it addresses the diverse debates regarding typology head-on, and in my view, with rare understanding, skill, and precision. Brent Parker not only navigates various debates on typology; he also proposes and defends a classic, traditional view of typology. Parker rightly argues that typology is best understood as a feature of divine revelation and a subset of predictive prophecy. Not prophecy in the sense of direct verbal predictions, but prophecies in a more "indirect" sense that builds on God-intended patterns, which are gradually unveiled as later OT authors reinforce those patterns, with the goal of anticipating their fulfillment in Christ. In God's plan, revealed progressively through the covenants, various persons, events, and institutions (types) are designed by God to correspond to, and predictively prefigure, their intensified antitypical fulfillment in Christ. As this occurs, a trajectory unfolds through the covenants that NT authors rightly recognize as divinely intended, which now reach their fulfillment in Christ and the new covenant age.

FOREWORD

Typology understood this way best corresponds to the Pauline sense of "mystery" (e.g., Eph 1:9-10; 3:1-10), where God's plan is hidden in the past, but now, in light of Christ's coming, is made known and disclosed publicly for all to see. Given that typology is God-intended, types are discovered exegetically, not by "typological interpretation," but according to a proper sense of *sensus literalis*, i.e., exegesis of texts according to authorial intention first in their immediate context and then picked up by later authors in the OT and brought to fulfillment in Christ. Ontologically, types are *in* the text precisely because they are divine revelation. But epistemologically, types and typological patterns are discovered only as later OT authors pick up the pattern, and then in Christ, the veil is removed, and the pattern is finally seen as God had always planned and intended. Furthermore, Parker argues that types reach their fulfillment first in Christ before they are applied to Christ's people, the church. This is a point that is often overlooked, and as Parker persuasively argues, it is a crucial point that both covenant theology and dispensationalism fail to apply consistently.

Second, discussion must also occur on how biblical-theological systems understand the Israel-*Christ*-church relationship as unfolded through the biblical covenants. What Parker convincingly demonstrates is that both covenant and dispensational theology speak of the Israel-church relationship (albeit differently), but they do not consistently move from Israel to *Christ* to the church. In dispensational theology, Israel and the church are ontologically distinct, but Israel is never viewed as a type of Christ. In covenant theology, Israel and the church are united, but how Israel is first fulfilled in Christ with benefits to the church is not worked out consistently.

This is why Parker's work not only makes a contribution to our understanding of typology, and how the Israel-Christ-church relationship is unpacked through the covenants, it also offers further biblical and theological grounding to an alternative biblical-theological system known as *progressive covenantalism*. In 2012, and then updated in 2018, Peter Gentry and myself first proposed this view in *Kingdom through Covenant* (Crossway). What Parker has done is this book is to build on our work and to offer a further and more robust defense of our view of the Israel-Christ-church relationship in contrast to covenant and dispensational theology.

Overall, progressive covenantalism argues that we must think of the Israel-church relationship by unpacking two points. First, God has *one* people, yet Israel and the church are distinct due to their respective covenants. The church, then, is *new* redemptive-historically, not ontologically, because she is the people of the new covenant. Second, the Israel-church relationship must be viewed *christologically*, which is the crucial point that Parker so ably defends. In this sense, the church is *not* directly the "new

Israel" or her replacement, as covenant theology argues. Instead, in Christ Jesus, the church is God's new creation people, composed of *believing* Jews and gentiles because Christ is the last Adam and true Israel, the faithful seed of Abraham who inherits all of the promises by his work. In fact, because Christ is the antitypical fulfillment of Israel and Adam, *all* of God's promises are fulfilled in him, which are then applied to his people, namely, the church. In contrast to dispensational theology, this means that the church receives all of the OT promises, which includes what the land typified, i.e., the new creation, in and through Christ. Not one of God's promises fails, but all of them reach their fulfillment in Christ. Furthermore, in contrast to covenant theology, in union with Christ, the church is God's new covenant people, in continuity with the elect in all ages but different from Israel in its nature and structure. The church, in contrast to Israel, is constituted by a believing, regenerate people who are united to Christ by faith and partakers now of the new covenant, which includes our justification before God, the gift of the Spirit, and new hearts. What Parker does in this work is to offer more biblical-theological grounding to progressive covenantalism's view of the Israel-church relation, thus building on and augmenting *Kingdom through Covenant*.

This work first started as a dissertation under my supervision at The Southern Baptist Theological Seminary. As a dissertation, it was a stellar piece of work, and I am thrilled that it is now being published for more people to read and enjoy. Since its dissertation phase, it has been updated to include further work on this subject, but overall, the argument remains the same. Yet I am convinced that it makes a contribution to the ongoing resolution of differences between covenant and dispensational theology, and it helps provide further argumentation to the mediating biblical-theological system of progressive covenantalism.

Stephen J. Wellum
Professor of Christian Theology
Editor, *Southern Baptist Journal of Theology*
The Southern Baptist Theological Seminary
Louisville, Kentucky, USA

PREFACE

THIS PROJECT REPRESENTS THE fruit of my labors over the years to rightly understand the relationship between Israel and the church. I was raised Presbyterian, but during my youth I heard about the significance of God's promises to Israel on Christian radio and from prophecy conferences, hosted by nearby churches, I would attend now and then. The nation of Israel, the end times, and the return of Christ were hot topics and of particularly strong interest among some of my family members. My fascination with Israel and Israel's relationship to the church continued on in my college years as I began to read books and hear sermons by the well-known dispensationalist, John MacArthur.

A few years after college I went on to seminary to study the Bible and theology in more depth. One of the issues I was hoping to gain clarity on was this hot-button topic of the relationship between Israel and the church. How should we understand the people of God across the canon? Southern Seminary was a good place to think about and debate this subject since some of the professors were more dispensational in their approach, a few were more covenantal (Reformed Baptist), and others did not fit neatly into either but as it turned out, were in the process of formulating a mediating position. It was through courses with Stephen Wellum, Peter Gentry, Thomas Schreiner, and Brian Vickers that I became convinced of a *via media* that is now formally presented as *progressive covenantalism*.

The significant shift in how I interpreted and understood the Bible that resulted was not just influenced by how the New Testament authors cited and used the Old Testament, but how the biblical covenants were to be properly interpreted independently and also in relationship to each other. Every view has to contend with the biblical covenants in drawing conclusions regarding the Israel-church dynamic. The more I examined this question, the more dissatisfied I became with the approaches of both dispensationalism and covenant theology. I also observed a significant problem with how typology was appealed to and understood in this debate between these two marquee systems of evangelical theology.

As a relatively minor revision to my dissertation completed in 2017, not all of the recent writings and publications discussing the topics of covenant and dispensational theology, typology, Israel, and the church in these past six years could be included in this work. Nevertheless, some thirty new sources and references (including some from 2017) have been added to this present volume. The books by Benjamin Gladd (*From Adam and Israel to the Church: A Biblical Theology of the People of God*) and Benjamin Merkle (*Discontinuity to Continuity: A Survey of Dispensational & Covenantal Theologies*), published in 2019 and 2020 respectively, are particularly germane to the subject matter and I have added ample references to these works.

Not everyone will agree with the biblical theological approach and interpretative moves that I make. However, my hope is that proponents of covenant theology and dispensationalism will not only be challenged by this work but will appreciate the effort to present their views objectively and fairly. I also hope that readers will gain a better understanding of progressive covenantalism and how this perspective seeks to put together the Israel-Christ-church relationship biblically.

ACKNOWLEDGMENTS

Ecclesiastes 12:12 states, "Of making many books there is no end, and much study is a weariness of the flesh." These words accurately reflect the laborious nature of studying and writing a dissertation, and the subsequent work of revising my PhD dissertation (submitted to The Southern Baptist Theological Seminary) which is what this book is. Despite the arduous study, there are many joys in contemplating God's word and thinking through the contours of God's plan for his covenant people. Thankfully, this effort was not a completely solitary one as many others have offered their support and encouragement.

First, I have much appreciation and gratitude for my doctoral committee—Professors Steve Wellum, Tom Schreiner, Gregg Allison, and my external reader, Ardel Caneday. Professor Allison's seminar on ecclesiology helped me think more deeply on the nature and doctrine of the church. My appreciation is also extended to Professor Schreiner, who has influenced me significantly through his books and courses, as a faculty shepherd, and as my former pastor. Special thanks and gratitude are extended to Professor Wellum, my doctoral supervisor. His course on issues in biblical and systematic theology in 2007 spurred my aspirations to write on systems of theology. More than anyone else, Wellum's approach to hermeneutics, theological method, and the doing of biblical and systematic theology has cultivated and shaped my understandings of these areas, leaving an indelible imprint on me. His friendship over the years, even through difficult times, has also been a source of great comfort. I am so grateful for these professors and the other members of the Southern Seminary faculty, such as Peter Gentry and Brian Vickers, who have also been influential through their writings and courses.

ACKNOWLEDGMENTS

I would also like to acknowledge friends who have supported me and who have been helpful conversation partners along the way. In recent years Richard Lucas has been incredibly valuable given his keen interest and knowledge of theological systems and through our work together in advancing progressive covenantalism. Richard has also been an astute coworker and a dear friend as we edited a recent publication together for InterVarsity's Spectrum Multiview Book Series, entitled *Covenantal and Dispensational Theologies: Four Views on the Continuity of Scripture*. John Meade provided much friendship to me during his time as a PhD student as we dialogued about a host of theological and interpretative issues over the years. My former roommate Brian Bunnell has also been a good friend and has provided excellent insights into dispensationalism. Matt Claridge's feedback on my dissertation was extremely helpful as have been our conversations on typology over the years. Lastly, during ETS conferences and through email, my external reader, Professor Ardel Caneday has been a mentor for me, helping me grasp hermeneutical issues and offering many keen suggestions and comments for my dissertation. He has had a hand particularly in developing my understanding of typology and allegory. Many other colleagues in the PhD program have also offered challenging and thoughtful feedback.

Third, I am extremely grateful for my family. My parents, Bob and LaDeane, have been supportive of me through my seminary coursework and have continued to offer their prayers in completing this work. My loving and devoted wife, Kandace, has served me countless ways, patiently enduring my labors on this project even as I made little advance on it during a three-and-a-half-year stint as a full-time thermal engineer. She has sacrificed for me and cared for me in innumerable ways these years while simultaneously managing and nurturing our two young boys, Evan and Will, during the writing of the dissertation. Now six years later, she has continued to amaze me with her care and devotion with the addition of three more children: Andrew, Annette, and baby Glenn. I am blessed to have such a faithful and supportive wife.

Most of all, thanks and praise go to my great God and Savior, Jesus Christ. He is truly the obedient Son, the one who has fulfilled the Old Testament hopes and promises and the one who has ratified the glorious new covenant of which I am member through the blood of his cross. My prayer is that this book brings glory and honor to the Son and that it will edify the church in viewing Jesus as the focal point of all things, not least of all the relationship between the old covenant and new covenant people of God. *Soli Deo Gloria.*

LIST OF ABBREVIATIONS

ABD	*The Anchor Bible Dictionary*
ANE	Ancient Near East
ATR	*Anglican Theological Review*
AUSS	*Andrews University Seminary Studies*
BBR	*Bulletin for Biblical Research*
BDAG	Walter Bauer, William Frederick Danker, William F. Arndt, and F. Wilber Gingrich, *A Greek-English Lexicon of the New Testament and Other Early Christian Literature*
BECNT	Baker Exegetical Commentary on the New Testament
BibSac	*Bibliotheca Sacra*
BR	*Biblical Research*
BTB	*Biblical Theology Bulletin*
BTNT	Biblical Theology of the New Testament
BZNW	*Beihefte zur Zeitschrift für die neutestamentliche Wissenschaft*
CBQ	*Catholic Biblical Quarterly*
CJ	*Concordia Journal*
CQR	*Church Quarterly Review*
CTJ	*Calvin Theological Journal*
CTQ	*Concordia Theological Quarterly*
CTR	*Criswell Theological Review*
DBSJ	*Detroit Baptist Seminary Journal*
DTIB	*Dictionary for Theological Interpretation of the Bible*

LIST OF ABBREVIATIONS

EAJT	*East Asia Journal of Theology*
EJ	*Evangelical Journal*
EJT	*European Journal of Theology*
EmJ	*Emmaus Journal*
ERT	*Evangelical Review of Theology*
ESV	English Standard Version
EvQ	*Evangelical Quarterly*
GTJ	*Grace Theological Journal*
HBT	*Horizons in Biblical Theology*
ICC	International Critical Commentary
IJST	*International Journal of Systematic Theology*
Int	*Interpretation*
ISBE	*The International Standard Bible Encyclopedia*
JAOS	*Journal of the American Oriental Society*
JBL	*Journal of Biblical Literature*
JEPTA	*Journal of the European Pentecostal Theological Association*
JETS	*Journal of the Evangelical Theological Society*
JMT	*Journal of Ministry and Theology*
JSNT	*Journal for the Study of the New Testament*
JSNTSup	Journal for the Study of the New Testament Supplement Series
JSOT	*Journal for the Study of the Old Testament*
JSOTSup	Journal for the Study of the Old Testament Supplement Series
JSJSup	Journal for the Study of Judaism Supplement
JTI	*Journal of Theological Interpretation*
LHB/OTS	The Library of Hebrew Bible/Old Testament Studies
LNTS	Library of New Testament Studies
LXX	Septuagint
MAJT	*Mid-America Journal of Theology*
MSJ	*Master's Seminary Journal*

LIST OF ABBREVIATIONS

NAC	New American Commentary
NACSBT	New American Commentary Studies on the Bible and Theology
NDBT	*New Dictionary of Biblical Theology: Exploring the Unity & Diversity of Scripture*
NICNT	New International Commentary on the New Testament
NICOT	New International Commentary on the Old Testament
NIGTC	New International Greek Testament Commentary
NovT	*Novum Testamentum*
NovTSup	Supplements to Novum Testamentum
NSBT	New Studies in Biblical Theology
NTS	*New Testament Studies*
OTL	Old Testament Library
PNTC	The Pillar New Testament Commentary
PRJ	*Puritan Reformed Journal*
RBTR	*Reformed Baptist Theological Review*
RTR	*Reformed Theological Review*
SBET	*Scottish Bulletin of Evangelical Theology*
SBJT	*Southern Baptist Journal of Theology*
SJT	*Scottish Journal of Theology*
SNTSMS	Society for New Testament Studies Monograph Series
STR	*Southeastern Theological Review*
SWJT	*Southwestern Journal of Theology*
TDNT	*Theological Dictionary of the New Testament*
TDOT	*Theological Dictionary of the Old Testament*
TJT	*Toronto Journal of Theology*
TrinJ	*Trinity Journal*
TynBul	*Tyndale Bulletin*
VT	*Vestus Testamentum*
WBC	Word Biblical Commentary
WTJ	*Westminster Theological Journal*

LIST OF ABBREVIATIONS

WUNT	Wissenschaftliche Untersuchungen zum Neuen Testament
ZECNT	Zondervan Exegetical Commentary on the New Testament
ZNW	*Zeitschrift für die neutestamentliche Wissenschaft und die Kunde der älteren Kirche*

Chapter 1

INTRODUCTION

SINCE THE RISE OF the modern evangelical movement in the twentieth century, two overarching biblical-theological systems of theology—covenant theology and dispensationalism—have primarily characterized the evangelical landscape and scholarship. Covenant theology, with its long historical pedigree in the Reformed tradition and rooted in the Reformation, stresses God's covenantal dealings through the progressive unfolding of the Bible. With all the diverse themes of Scripture united under the structure or framework of covenant, covenant theology is known as a theological system of *continuity* in relating the Old Testament to the New, especially in conceiving of the church—"the new Israel"—as essentially the fulfillment of OT Israel.[1] The principal rival of covenant theology, dispensationalism, has become especially popular in the United States during the last century given its emphasis on prophecy, the rapture, and end times.[2] The dispensational tradition seeks to put the whole Bible together without the emphasis on a covenantal structure per se but by identifying God's dealings and arrangement with human beings along the stages or dispensations throughout history. Dispensationalism as a system features more *discontinuity* given the belief that God's arrangements and relationships with man have differed

---

1. Berkhof, *Systematic Theology*, 571; Woudstra, "Israel and the Church," 221–38; Clowney, *Church*, 42–44; Horton, *Christian Faith*, 730, states that the "New Testament church is complete only as it grows out of the Old Testament church, the Israel of God attains its eschatological form only with the inclusion of the nations."

2. Popular books, though by no means accepted by many dispensationalists, include the works of Hal Lindsey, such as *The Late Great Planet Earth*, and LaHaye's and Jenkins's *Left Behind* series.

from the past, present, and future resulting in an important distinction between Israel and the church as OT promises and prophecies to national and ethnic Israel still await fulfillment.³ While representatives of each system have been able to work together in terms of ministry, and both views share an understanding of the gospel, these two systems are nevertheless opposed on important matters such as hermeneutics, ecclesiology—especially the relationship between Israel and the church—and arguably the most identifiable area, eschatology with all the debates surrounding the rapture and the meaning of the millennium. The essential differences may be reduced to how covenantalists and dispensationalists carry out the task of biblical theology in understanding the biblical covenants and in terms of how they relate the various stages of development or covenantal shifts that takes place across the storyline of Scripture.⁴ More specifically and bound up with the doing of biblical theology is the subject of typology. It is the nature and identification of key typological patterns between the OT and NT that proves to be of consequential import to the covenantal-dispensational divide explored in this study.

THE IMPORTANCE OF TYPOLOGY IN THE COVENANT-DISPENSATIONAL DEBATE

Several years have passed since Edward Glenny offered his helpful, informative summary and survey of typology within evangelicalism. His survey reveals that the understanding of the nature and function of typology between covenant theology and the variety of dispensational theologies represents a key hermeneutical area separating the two systems.⁵ John Feinberg, a dispensationalist, agrees, as he has aptly stated that the fundamental and interrelated issues tied to the ongoing debate between covenantalists and dispensationalists on the topic of hermeneutics stem from "the relation of the progress of revelation to the priority of one Testament over the other, the understanding and implications of the NT use of the OT, and the understanding and implications of typology."⁶ In the same vein, Reformed

---

3. Blaising and Bock, *Progressive Dispensationalism*, 14–21; Ryrie, *Dispensationalism*, 143–68; Saucy, "Israel and the Church," 239–59; Vlach, *Has the Church Replaced Israel?*, 177–201.

4. For the critical importance of how the covenants are interpreted and related to each other in systems of theology, see Gentry and Wellum, *Kingdom through Covenant*.

5. Glenny, "Typology," 627–38. For another survey of typology in covenant and dispensational theology, see Ninow, *Indicators of Typology*, 65–75.

6. Feinberg, "Systems of Discontinuity," 74–75.

theologian Mark Karlberg surmises the importance of typology in the debate: "Resolution of lingering differences of interpretation among evangelicals depends, to a large extent, on a proper assessment of the nature and function of OT typology."[7] Baptist theologian David Dockery also believes that a "balanced and sane approach to typological exegesis can bring together those in the dispensational and covenant communities."[8]

Unfortunately, major hurdles need to be overcome. One significant difference on the subject of typology, as pointed out by Glenny, is to what degree the NT antitypes fulfill or annul the original OT types, especially in regard to the Israel-church relationship.[9] In other words, even if Israel is a type, does it follow that its role as a national and ethnic entity is eclipsed by the church in the new covenant era, or can the Israel typology be understood in a manner such that certain OT promises to Israel still remain as the pattern of realization pertains to only aspects of Israel? Glenny also raises the critical question that will receive much attention in the chapters ahead: "What part does Christ have in the correspondence between Israel and the Church? Or—to try to word this question more clearly—how does the Church's 'in Christ' relationship help explain the application to the Church of OT promises for Israel?"[10]

Furthermore, the dispute and fundamental differences regarding typology are not likely to abate, for on a broader scale, one's understanding of typology is tied to how one apprehends the unity of the canon, the unfolding of redemptive history (progressive revelation), the promise-fulfillment pattern, the study of the NT use of the OT, and cannot be disconnected from more basic issues such as one's view of the inspiration of Scripture, biblical history, and the sovereignty and providence of God.[11] Given the importance of typology for interpreting the Bible then, it is not surprising that the nature and defining characteristics of typology (e.g., the prospective

---

7. Karlberg, "Legitimate Discontinuities," 19. See also the attention typology receives in Karlberg, "Israel and the Eschaton," 117–30. Poythress, *Understanding Dispensationalists*, 117, also finds that further "reflection on problems with typology may therefore help to bring us together." He devotes a brief chapter to the subject of typology, challenging dispensationalism at crucial points.

8. Dockery, "Typological Exegesis," 162.

9. Glenny, "Typology," 638.

10. Glenny, "Typology," 638.

11. For the connection of typology to these crucial themes, see Goppelt, *Typos*; Lints, *Fabric of Theology*, 293–311; Goldsworthy, *Gospel-Centered Hermeneutics*, 242–43; Reventlow, *Problems of Biblical Theology*, 14–31; Johnson, *Old Testament in the New*, 55–57; Markus, "Presuppositions of the Typological Approach," 442–51; Legarth, "Typology and its Theological Basis," 143–55; Gundry, "Typology as a Means of Interpretation," 237–40.

quality or divine prefiguration aspect of typology), as well as the methodology for identifying types (e.g., are the only typological relationships those identified and designated as such by the NT authors?), continue to attract much attention from evangelical and non-evangelical scholars alike.[12] Even defining typology is a challenge, as Douglas Moo finds that "typology is much easier to talk about than to describe" and a unified understanding of typology is elusive since no one definition of typology is acceptable to all.[13] Despite these difficulties, investigating the impact of typology for systems of continuity and discontinuity is a worthwhile endeavor if there will be continued reform in how evangelicals do biblical theology and understand the Israel-church relationship.

A scholarly consensus on the defining characteristics of typology has not been reached; however, most evangelicals would agree that typology (1) involves the study of real and organic historical and theological correspondences of types—identifiable as OT persons, events, or institutions; (2) possesses a divinely intended quality with prophetic or prospective import (OT types and typological patterns point forward to later persons and events) that are progressively unpacked across successive epochs of biblical revelation culminating in NT counterparts (generally denoted as *antitypes* and routinely identified with Jesus Christ or the salvation or new covenant realities he secures); and (3) exhibits a significant resemblance, as well as an escalation (an *a fortiori* quality) or qualitative progression, that is detected between the type and antitype.[14] Even with these general characteristics in place, covenant theologians and dispensationalists of various stripes understand and use typology differently, especially at the crucial and central points of their respective systems and in conjunction with how they understand the relation between Israel and the church. Moreover, not only is typology employed and understood differently by dispensational and covenant theologians, but critical OT institutions and themes tied to

---

12. Generally there are two broad approaches to typology: the more traditional evangelical view and the post-critical neo-typology view. For a discussion of the two approaches, see chapter 2 and note Davidson, *Typology in Scripture*, 46–75. Ribbens, "Typology of Types," 84–85, describes these two approaches as *"prefiguration typology"* and *"correspondence* typology" and describes how they are responses to modern historical criticism.

13. Moo, "Paul's Universalizing Hermeneutic," 81; see also Davidson, *Typology in Scripture*, 4. Kaiser, *Uses of the Old Testament in the New*, 231, writes, "There is nothing approaching a consensus within the believing or scholarly communities either on the definition or the ways typology is to be used for biblical studies." The difficulties have been present for a long time as noted by Gundry who summarizes the studies of typology in the 1960s ("Typology as a Means of Interpretation," 233).

14. See chapter 2 below, esp. footnote 79; see Glenny, "Typology," 628–29.

INTRODUCTION

the biblical covenants are not identified or recognized as typological when they should be, or if certain OT-NT typological relationships are identified they are not properly formulated theologically.

Delineating the typological patterns through the OT and NT is important. Unpacking the typological role of Israel is vital for ecclesiology. Covenant theology does recognize Israel as type, but the relationship between Israel and the church is made too fast or held too tightly given the overarching covenant of grace framework without doing justice to the newness of the new covenant and the discontinuity that results from the coming of the new and true Israel—Jesus Christ. The church, contend advocates of paedobaptist covenant theology, consists of a "mixed" community of believers and unbelievers just like Israel of old. On the other hand, dispensationalists do not recognize Israel as a type of Jesus Christ, or if they do, the typological relationship is reduced to an analogy or illustration. For progressive dispensationalists, application or initial-fulfillment drawn between Israel and the church does not lead to reforming the strong separation between Israel and the church in their theological system. For dispensationalists, the OT promises and prophecies to Israel are not completely annulled or fulfilled by such typological patterns. However, this position also does not seem to do due diligence to how the Scripture presents Jesus as the antitypical fulfillment of the nation of Israel. Further, dispensationalism does not adequately address the entailment of Christ as antitypical Israel: the church is the eschatological people of God, the renewed or restored Israel as a consequence of her faith union with Christ, the true Israel.

Appropriating the typological connections rightly and viewing Israel and the church through the prism or focal point of Jesus Christ has significant bearing on the central ecclesiological features of both theological systems.[15] The Israel-Christ typological relationship is not unrelated to how the Abrahamic covenant is understood. Both covenant theology and dispensationalism fail to understand the typological aspects within the Abrahamic covenant. Covenant theologians reduce the national and typological elements rooted in the Abrahamic covenant to merely spiritual aspects. The strong continuity between Israel and the church in covenant theology means that the covenant sign of circumcision and the seed promise are not formulated rightly because the discontinuity of these features tied to the Israel-Christ-church framework is missed or is subsumed under a more governing, direct Israel-church connection. Hence the genealogical principle

---

15. These assertions regarding the nature and use of typology in both dispensational and covenant theology are discussed in Gentry and Wellum, *Kingdom through Covenant*, 107–158, 767–839. In regard to the Israel-church relationship, note also Moore, *Kingdom of Christ*, 116–20, 146–50.

remains unchanged across the canon as NT baptism directly replaces OT circumcision. Similarly, dispensationalists do not view the land promised to Abraham as typological, or any typological significance is minor as this "unconditional" promise must have actual or literal fulfillment to the nation of Israel either just before or during the millennial reign of Christ. The promise of land goes straight across the canon then, unchanged and directed to national, ethnic Israel alone with no alteration or transformation on the basis of Christ's first coming and fulfillment of the Abrahamic covenant.

Therefore, the focus of this project is to provide a study of the Israel-Christ-church relationship and demonstrate that this necessary framework, linking Israel to Christ foremost and drawing theological conclusions for the Israel-church relationship in light of the church's union with Jesus the true Israel, is missing at the central areas of covenant theology and dispensationalism. Furthermore, a study of the Israel-Christ-church relationship cannot proceed without presenting a proper understanding of the nature of typology, especially the aspect of fulfillment and escalation or heightening embedded within typological patterns. The type-antitype relationship always has a notable resemblance, but the heightening aspect or eschatological nature of the antitype means that there will also be a significant difference corresponding to the greater NT realities ushered in with the coming and work of Christ such that the antitype is the goal, fulfillment, or reality that the OT type anticipated.[16] Moreover, there is an added factor of how typological relationships are closely linked to the unfolding of the biblical covenants and are channeled through Jesus Christ who brings all that the covenants pointed to and promised; thus the OT types and patterns reach their eschatological fulfillment. The role of Israel as a type, then, must be carefully delineated in connection to Jesus Christ and the new covenant realities that he has inaugurated in the church. Rightly identifying and understanding these typological patterns brings about modifications that result in a shift to a new system, a tertium quid, the true interface between all forms of dispensationalism and covenant theology, a system called *progressive covenantalism*.[17]

---

16. The element of eschatological fulfillment in typological patterns is treated in chapter 2.

17. The terminology of progressive covenantalism has been employed before, see Lioy, "Progressive Covenantalism as an Integrating Motif," 81–107. More refinement and clarity is needed in Lioy's proposal for it seems to aim for a synthesis of sorts between covenantalism and dispensationalism as he affirms a covenant of works and a covenant of grace (84–89), but maintains that God's promises for Israel (including the land) are still operative (100, cf. 94). The understanding of progressive covenantalism used throughout this study follows that of Gentry and Wellum, *Kingdom through Covenant*; and Wellum and Parker, *Progressive Covenantalism*. See also Merkle, *Discontinuity*

INTRODUCTION

THESIS

Given the above discussion, I argue that OT Israel is a typological pattern in terms of the nature of typology as described by Richard Davidson and others, and that national Israel's antitypical fulfillment in Christ and the church necessarily entails that the essential ecclesiological tenets of covenant and dispensational theology on the Israel-church relationship are incorrect. With Israel as a type of Christ and derivatively of the church, the escalation and heightening characteristics intrinsic to typological patterns means that instead of interpreting the church-Israel relationship in strict continuity, as in the church replacing or having the same essential nature of OT Israel, the new humanity in Christ—the church—has a qualitative difference in possessing better spiritual realities as a regenerate community. On the other hand, instead of overly emphasizing the discontinuity of Israel and the church, as in keeping them too separated such that OT promises not mentioned in the NT must still await fulfillment for a national, ethnic Israel, the characteristics of the Israel-Christ typology reveal that the mediatorial and national role of OT Israel has reached its terminus and fulfillment in Jesus Christ, and derivatively to the church as the "renewed/new Israel." The main thrust of the argument is that the relationship between Israel and the church must be understood in direct orientation to the person and work of Christ. Jesus Christ is the antitype of Israel, and while Israel and the church are the one people of God and linked together typologically and analogically, the church-Israel relationship must always be triangulated through God's Son. All the promises to Israel are fulfilled in Christ, and he is the one who ushers in a new and better covenant that establishes a Spirit-filled and faithful international community—the church. The entailments of this relationship result in understanding the typological components of the Abrahamic covenant in coordination with Jesus Christ: the promise of the seed anticipates

---

to Continuity, 108–38, for a helpful overview of progressive covenantalism. The term "progressive" highlights how God's revelation progressively unfolds across the OT and NT while the term "covenantalism" underscores that the structure of God's plan—the storyline of Scripture—is revealed along the unfolding of the biblical covenants. The creation, Noahic, Abrahamic, Mosaic, and Davidic covenants all culminate and are fulfilled in Jesus Christ, the mediator and inaugurator of the new covenant. See also Brand and Pratt, "Progressive Covenantal View," 231–80. Brand and Pratt develop their form of progressive covenantalism independently from Gentry and Wellum, leaning especially on George Eldon Ladd, which in the end is very similar even if the stress on the covenants is not as prominent as in *Kingdom through Covenant*. Progressive covenantalism is loosely related to "New Covenant Theology" (NCT). Some of the works that use the NCT label should not be endorsed; however, the following are helpful treatments: Wells and Zaspel, *New Covenant Theology*; Reisinger, *Abraham's Four Seeds*; White, *Newness of the New Covenant*; White, *What Is New Covenant Theology?*

7

a regenerate covenant people where only those in faith union with Christ are to be baptized; the promise of the land anticipates a new heavens and earth that will be enjoyed by both Jewish and gentile believers in Christ, for he is the true seed, the heir and recipient of all the Abrahamic promises. In pursuing this topic, the hope is to have a more biblically faithful ecclesiology that is formed and cultivated from Christology by carefully tracing the typological links in the doing of biblical theology.

Given that covenant and dispensational theology represent whole biblical-theological approaches, not everything pertaining to each respective system can be addressed. Outside the scope of the present work are the important questions and discussions associated with eschatology, such as the rapture and millennial debates. These vital areas distinguish dispensational and covenant theologies, but such questions will not be in the purview of this study. Furthermore, both systems, especially covenant theology, have a long history of development and modification. While references are made to some of the key historical figures who advanced a form of either covenant or dispensational theology in the past, more modern forms of each system receive the primary focus.

METHODOLOGY

What does it mean to be biblical? How does one move from the text and development of themes and motifs at different stages in the canon and properly formulate a theological conclusion? Theological prolegomena are receiving significant attention in recent scholarship.[18] Moreover, the relationship of biblical theology to systematic theology and how the disciplines relate has also received substantial discussion.[19] Not least involved in these debates is how these disciplines are to be defined. Elaboration upon these issues is

---

18. Many proposals are offered, including Vanhoozer, *Drama of Doctrine*; Grenz and Franke, *Beyond Foundationalism*; Horton, *Covenant and Eschatology*; Naselli, "D. A. Carson's Theological Method," 245–74; Lints, *Fabric of Theology*; Meadors, ed., *Four Views on Moving beyond the Bible to Theology*; Stackhouse, *Evangelical Futures*; Webster, "What Makes Theology Theological?," 17–28.

19. Vos, *Biblical Theology*; Goldsworthy, *Christ-Centered Biblical Theology*; Gentry and Wellum, *Kingdom through Covenant*, 39–50; Carson, *Collected Writings on Scripture*, 111–49; Carson, "Systematic Theology and Biblical Theology," 89–109; Robertson, "Outlook for Biblical Theology," 65–91; Gamble, "Relationship between Biblical Theology and Systematic Theology," 211–39; Hasel, "Nature of Biblical Theology," 203–15; Gaffin, "Systematic Theology and Biblical Theology," 281–99; Bird, "New Testament Theology Re-Loaded," 265–91; Scobie, "Challenge of Biblical Theology," 31–61; Rosner, "Biblical Theology," 3–11. For a survey of approaches for the doing of biblical theology, see Köstenberger, "Present and Future of Biblical Theology," 3–25.

beyond what can be suitably addressed here. The definition of a whole-Bible biblical theology, according to Geerhardus Vos, "rightly defined, is nothing else than *the exhibition of the organic progress of supernatural revelation in its historic continuity and multiformity.*"[20] Brian Rosner's definition is more specific as he finds that biblical theology "proceeds with historical and literary sensitivity and seeks to analyse and synthesize the Bible's teaching about God and his relations to the world on its own terms, maintaining sight of the Bible's overarching narrative and Christocentric focus."[21] Since Scripture is the progressive revelation of God, biblical theology seeks to examine how the individual parts fit within the whole and how the inner-textual development occurs between earlier and later portions of Scripture.[22] Furthermore, biblical theology is not an end in itself but is a bridge discipline, sensitive to the movement and development along redemptive history and mapping the diversity within the unity of Scripture which is the necessary and first component of doing systematic theology. John Murray rightly states,

> Systematic theology will fail of its task to the extent to which it discards its rootage in biblical theology as properly conceived and developed. It might seem that an undue limitation is placed upon systematic theology by requiring that the exegesis with which it is so intimately concerned should be regulated by the principle of biblical theology. . . . The fact is that only when systematic theology is rooted in biblical theology does it exemplify its true function and achieve its purpose.[23]

---

20. Vos, "Idea of Biblical Theology," 15, emphasis original. For other helpful definitions, see Scobie, *Ways of Our God*, 47. Schreiner, *New Testament Theology*, 883, also helpfully finds that "biblical theology recognizes the stages of growth and development in God's revelation and unfolds God's revelation genetically." Gentry and Wellum, *Kingdom through Covenant*, 46, conclude that biblical theology "as a discipline attempts to exegete texts in their own context and then, in light of the entire canon, to examine the unfolding nature of God's plan and carefully think through the relationship between *before* and *after* in that plan, which culminates in Christ" (emphasis original). It is also important to note "that the distinctive contribution which biblical theology makes (and the key point of its value for systematic theology) is precisely this, that in its engagement with the text as a whole, its concern is to allow the text's own categories, concerns and emphases to speak." See Hart, "Systematic—In What Sense?," 345.

21. Rosner, "Biblical Theology," 10. See also Naselli's treatment of biblical theology and his helpful discussion of how evangelicals do biblical theology in DeRouchie et al., *40 Questions about Biblical Theology*, 19–27; 101–9.

22. Goldsworthy, *Christ-Centered Hermeneutics*, 68, 262. For discussion on the nature of progressive revelation, see Packer, "Evangelical View of Progressive Revelation," 143–58.

23. Murray, "Systematic Theology," 4:19–20.

In order for the discipline of systematic theology or dogmatics to inform what the whole Bible says about a given topic and arrive to correct theological constructions, rigorous exegesis and understanding the Bible's unfolding plan are necessary.[24]

The second component of systematic theology is to articulate a constructive worldview or metanarrative that thinks God's thoughts after him, seeking to answer what the whole Bible teaches regarding a given topic. In going about this process, the discipline of systematic theology does not treat the Bible as a loose collection of disembodied abstract propositions. Rather, as the synthetic and culminating discipline, systematic theology depends on exegesis, pays close attention to the structure and not merely the content of the storyline of Scripture, rests on Scripture as the *norming norm*, and incorporates insights from the church's reflections and studies during the last two millennia.[25] Therefore, John Frame's definition of systematic theology is fitting: systematic theology is "the application of God's Word by persons to all areas of life."[26]

Having briefly described the nature of the disciplines of biblical and systematic theology, the hermeneutical methodology may now be addressed. Since God's plan comes as a progressive revelation, the plotline of Scripture with its eschatological nature and christological focus must be accounted for. This requires that readers interpret Scripture within the Bible's own "intrasystematic" categories—i.e., on its own terms and self-presentation.[27] In other words, given the nature of the unfolding of revelation as presented in Scripture, biblical texts are to be interpreted within their textual, epochal, and canonical horizons.[28] The textual horizon seeks

---

24. Gentry and Wellum, *Kingdom through Covenant*, 47–49.

25. Williams, "Systematic Theology as a Biblical Discipline," 177–78, 184–85.

26. Frame, *Doctrine of the Knowledge of God*, 76. Carson's definition is also helpful: "By *systematic theology*, I refer to the branch of theology that seeks to elaborate the whole and the parts of Scripture, demonstrating their logical (rather than their merely historical) connections and taking full cognizance of the history of doctrine and the contemporary intellectual climate and categories and queries while finding its sole ultimate authority in the Scriptures themselves, rightly interpreted." Carson, *Collected Writings*, 118. Vanhoozer, "Systematic Theology," 885, offers this definition: "Systematic theology is faith seeking understanding—of God, the world and ourselves—through an ordered presentation of the doctrines implicit in the biblical testimony to the history of creation and redemption." See also Lints, *Fabric of Theology*, 316.

27. See Horton, *Covenant and Eschatology*, 1–19, 147–276. Horton presents a theological method within the framework of redemptive-history, "the organic unfolding of the divine plan in its execution through word (announcement), act (accomplishment), and word (interpretation)," and one in which the lens is eschatological since this is "the form and shape in which redemptive revelation comes" (*Covenant and Eschatology*, 5).

28. Lints, *Fabric of Theology*, 293–311; Clowney, *Preaching and Biblical Theology*,

to carefully apply the tools of exegesis in the immediate context of a text. The epochal and canonical horizons are needed to understand how the text fits within the broader context of the Bible. The epochal horizon specifically aids the reader in situating a text within the various stages of progressive revelation.[29] Each stage or epoch of the unfolding plan of God must be understood on its own terms as well as in relationship to the other stages and epochs that precede or succeed it.[30] The interpretative task, moreover, is to evaluate how a given text fits within the canon as a whole in light of all of

---

15–16.

29. Not all agree on what the stages or epochs of redemptive history are to include. Most generally on a macro-level scale, many evangelical scholars would agree with Beale, *New Testament Biblical Theology*, 5, who portrays the storyline "about God's purposes in creation, fall, redemption, and consummation," even as he concentrates on creation and new creation themes. This four-fold scheme is also recently defended by Wenkel, "Most Simple and Comprehensive Script," 78–90. However, zooming in on the storyline of Scripture is where massive differences appear. Ciampa, "History of Redemption," 254–308, presents a biblical-theological structure whereby the biblical narrative consists of a national Covenant-Sin-Exile-Restoration (CSER) embedded within a global CSER with the former as the key to the resolution of the global structure. Wright, *New Testament and the People of God*, 139–43, posits that the drama of Scripture is disclosed in five acts: (1) creation, (2) sin, (3) Israel, (4) Christ, and (5) church. Bartholomew and Goheen, *Drama of Scripture*, build on Wright by adding a sixth act all structured around the central motif of kingdom: (1) creation, (2) fall, (3) redemption initiated (Israel), (4) redemption accomplished, (5) the mission of the church, (6) redemption completed. Others see more stages to frame the storyline of Scripture. Goldsworthy, *Christ-Centered Biblical Theology*, 25, defends the Robinson-Hebert threefold structure of creation and especially Abraham to Solomon, the eschatology of the writing prophets, and the fulfillment of all things in Christ. However, Goldsworthy seems to identify several stages: creation to the fall, the flood, Abraham, Moses and the exodus, David, Solomon in conjunction with Jerusalem/Zion and the temple along with wisdom, exile and return, and then the coming of Christ and the new creation (*Christ-Centered Biblical Theology*, 114–67). Gentry and Wellum, *Kingdom through Covenant*, offer another proposal in asserting that the epochal structure of the Bible occurs along the covenants (creation, Noahic, Abrahamic, Mosaic, Davidic, and new), forming the framework or backbone of the entire metanarrative of Scripture. Similarly, Hafemann, "Covenant Relationship," 23, finds that the covenant relationship provides the structure that integrates the themes developed throughout redemptive history. On the plot-line of the Bible, see Carson, *Gagging of God*, 193–278.

30. This raises the important point of reading Scripture as a progressive revelation and paying close attention to the historical unfolding and the *before* and *after* sequences in Scripture. See Carson, "Theological Interpretation of Scripture," 191–92; Carson, "Systematic Theology and Biblical Theology," 98; cf. Gentry and Wellum, *Kingdom through Covenant*, 124–28. Lints, *Fabric of Theology*, 305, helpfully highlights the progressive links in the epochal horizon: "Theological construction must begin to wrestle with the fact that this progressive fulfillment lies at the heart of a theological framework. The meaning of past epochs is invested into later epochs in the Scriptures, and the meaning of those epochs is in turn invested into future epochs. This might be referred to as the 'epochal reach' of typology."

God's special revelation, and this constitutes the canonical horizon. Finally, the horizons are important for correcting presuppositions and modifying theology. Theologians and biblical interpreters must be careful not to overlay an extratextual grid upon Scripture because doing so will not result in the right interpretation. Such an external or foreign framework, indicative of an unbiblical worldview, misses the Bible on its own terms, categories, structures, and in turn leads to faulty exegetical conclusions and theological formulations.[31]

The study of the Israel-Christ-church relationship built off a careful focus on typological patterns will proceed via the theological task described. The Israel-Christ typological relationship is to be traced along the three horizons. Careful consideration is required to recognize the typological indicators in the textual horizon, for as Davidson writes,

> Some indication of the existence and predictive quality of the various OT types should occur already in the OT *before* their NT antitypical fulfillment—otherwise there would be no predictive element. Thus some inherent textual indicators identifying the OT types should be apparent already in the OT.[32]

Furthermore, many typological patterns enjoy further development along redemptive historical epochs until reaching their antitypical fulfillment in the NT, which draws upon the consideration of the canonical horizon. Once the typological aspects of the nation of Israel in relation to Christ are discerned, the theological task is to seek an ecclesiological formulation that does justice to the Israel-Christ-church relationship as a whole. My contention throughout is that this relationship has not been rightly worked out in paedobaptist covenant theology or in dispensational theology.

---

31. The terms and concepts of "intratextual" and "extratextual" are derived from Wellum, see Gentry and Wellum, *Kingdom through Covenant*, 45, 115n17. An intratextual approach is to read the Scripture according to its own categories, structures, literary forms, and self-description in order to direct and inform our theology. An extratextual reading is to read the Scripture with an ideological or philosophical grid and therefore foist an alien framework upon the Bible. This form of intratextuality is contrasted from the postliberal intratextuality where there is meaning, but no truth. See Vanhoozer, *Drama of Doctrine*, 171–73.

32. Davidson, "Nature [and Identity]," 15 (emphasis original) and note Davidson, "Eschatological Hermeneutic," 16–17; see also Ninow, *Indicators of Typology*; Beale, *Handbook*, 15–16; and see Beale, "Finding Christ in the OT," 30–38 as he presents two criteria of discerning types including typological anticipation in the immediate OT context and indicators within the wider canonical OT context.

INTRODUCTION

OVERVIEW AND STRUCTURE OF THE PRESENTATION

Seeking to challenge well affirmed systems of theology, such as covenant and dispensational theology, is no small task. Exposing the weaknesses of each system with regard to key ecclesiological areas grounded in typological relations is the centerpiece, but to do so, much groundwork needs to be laid.

Chapter 2 evaluates the nature of typology and provides a proposal for theologically characterizing biblical typology. Can a distinction be discerned between allegory and typology? Do typological relationships always entail fulfillment? How does typology help to address issues of continuity and discontinuity between the Old and New Testaments? The chapter also explores how types are identified as such and what constitutes as the criteria or textual warrant in determining a type.

In relating typology to systems of theology, the hermeneutical underpinnings of covenant theology and dispensational theology are presented in the next two chapters. Chapter 3 interacts and synthesizes the main features of paedobaptist covenant theology. While recognizing that different streams of covenant theology exist (e.g., Federal Vision or theonomy), the focus will not address these forms or the historical development of covenant theology. Instead, the main hermeneutical aspects of covenant theology representative of the whole are presented, followed by how covenant theologians put together the Israel-church relationship in terms of typology. Furthermore, how covenantalists differentiate and identify certain features of the Abrahamic covenant as typological—the land is considered typological while other facets involving the genealogical principle and circumcision are not—is briefly highlighted.

Chapter 4 follows the same pattern as chapter 3 but with emphasis on dispensationalism. There are varieties within dispensationalism, but space permits interaction with only the more revised and progressive forms of dispensationalism. The chapter surveys, just as in the previous chapter, how the Israel-church relationship is understood along with how typology functions within these systems of dispensationalism. Last, the typological aspects of the Abrahamic covenant that dispensationalists acknowledge is overviewed.

Chapter 5 serves as the cornerstone of this work. In this chapter I seek to make a convincing case that before relating OT Israel to the church theologically, theologians need to wrestle first with the relationship between Israel and Christ. The exegetical and biblical-theological portions of this chapter seek to show that Israel as a nation served as a type of Jesus Christ. Israel's identity, role, and institutions find their fulfillment in Jesus. With the nature of typology always entailing fulfillment, the Israel-Christ typological connection means that Israel's national and mediatorial role has come to an end with the coming of Jesus and therefore results in significant implications for all forms of dispensationalism. On the other hand, recognizing that Jesus is the "true Israel" does not necessarily mean that the church is of the same nature as OT Israel. The aspect of heightening or escalation intrinsic to typology means that the new covenant community, those in faith union with Christ, the new humanity, is not of the same nature as OT Israel because of the work of Christ, and thus there are critical ramifications for covenant theology.

Chapter 6 seeks to take the exegetical and biblical-theological conclusions from the previous chapter and move to theological formulation for ecclesiology. First, the church's relationship to Christ is explored by focusing on the characteristics of union with Christ. Next, the church as the antitype of OT Israel is examined. There are certain continuities and discontinuities between Israel and the church drawn from the nature of the Israel-Christ typological relationship, but neither covenant theology nor dispensational theology grasps all of these features rightly. In contrast to dispensationalism, the church, only through Christ, is the antitypical fulfillment of Israel—the ecclesiological fulfillment flows out of the christological fulfillment. The NT does not project a future restoration of national Israel and thus OT Israel is a typological pattern not unlike other commonly recognized OT types. Furthermore, in exploring the Israel-church typology, the escalation from Israel through Christ to the church is coordinate with how individual union with Christ is aligned with corporate union with Christ. The church is not like Israel of old in being a mixed community as posited in covenant theology but is the new man, new temple, and Spirit-filled covenant community with all of its members marked by faith.

Finally, in chapter 7, challenging texts to the thesis of this study are evaluated, particularly coming from the dispensational school of thought. These scriptural passages, posited as defeaters of the progressive covenantal understanding of the Israel-Christ-church typology, do not in the end support dispensationalism as many advocates would have us believe.

Chapter 8 offers a summary of the study and briefly posits that the theological conclusions should move theologians to a via media of these two prominent biblio-theological systems. The system buttressed in this study, the true interface between covenant theology and dispensationalism, is known as *progressive covenantalism*.

Chapter 2

THE NATURE, CHARACTERISTICS, AND CHALLENGES OF TYPOLOGY

IN THE INTRODUCTORY CHAPTER, the importance of typology was presented in relation to whole systems of theology along with some of the significant hermeneutical challenges associated with identifying and understanding typological patterns. As Oswald Allis observed over a half century ago, the study of typology is "very difficult; and it is easy to make mistakes, even serious mistakes, in dealing with it."[1] Despite the challenges, the exploration of the nature of typology is unavoidable, not only because the many typological connections between the Old and New Testaments demand interpretation, but typology is one of the primary ways of understanding how the NT relates to the OT and why Jesus Christ truly is the focal point of all biblical revelation (Luke 24:27, 44; John 5:39). In fact, Leonhard Goppelt's study of typology led him to conclude that typology "is the central and distinctive NT way of understanding Scripture ... [and] it is the decisive interpretation of Jesus, the Gospel, and the Church.... According to its NT core ... typology is theologically constitutive for an understanding of the Gospel."[2] To adjudicate properly covenant and dispensational theology,

---

1. Allis, *Prophecy and the Church*, 23.

2. Goppelt, "τύπος," 8:255–56. Goppelt further calls typology "the principal form of the NT's interpretation of Scripture and the way the NT understands itself in the light of redemptive history." Goppelt, *Typos*, xxiii; cf. 198. Similarly, E. Earle Ellis, citing W. G. Kümmel, asserts, "Typological interpretation expresses most clearly 'the basic attitude of primitive Christianity toward the Old Testament.'" See Ellis, *Prophecy and Hermeneutic*, 165. Other scholars who posit typology as central for relating the NT to the OT include Hamilton, "Typology of David's Rise to Power," 4–5 and Gundry,

the typological role of Israel in relation to Christ and the church must be evaluated and going about this task requires a sound theology of typology given the importance of typological patterns to the relationship of the OT to the NT.

In the following sections, the task is to thoroughly define and develop the substance of biblical typology. Before doing so, however, more recent discussions of figural reading—combining typology and allegory together—need to be addressed. If typology is shackled to a looser association of verbal analogies or allegorical interpretation and thereby not identified through grammatical-historical-canonical exegesis in conjunction to the *sensus literalis*, then seeking to correct whole systems of theology by zeroing in on typological structures will be of little value or superfluous. This study of typology proceeds in four steps. First, the contrast and distinction between typology and allegory is examined. Next, the nature of typology is then explored, specifically with respect to the Christ-centered focus of types, prophetic aspects of typology, and escalation or heightening intrinsic to the type-antitype correspondence. Third, the question of fulfillment in typological patterns is raised. Pinpointing the exact timing of typological fulfillment is difficult given how inaugurated eschatology[3]—the "already/not yet" realities in the new covenant era of the church—permeate the NT. Some typological patterns are completely annulled on the basis of Christ's coming while other typological relationships are transformed through Jesus' first coming but also possess actualization in the church age and await completion and culmination in the eschaton. The type-antitype relationship is not always a one-to-one correspondence in terms of the timing of fulfillment; the text must dictate the nature of the fulfillment in Christ and to what degree that extends into the new covenant age and the new heavens and new earth. Fourth and last, elucidating how types and typological patterns are identified, especially along the covenants, and a brief foray into

---

"Typology as a Means of Interpretation," 234, who calls typology "part of the warp and woof of scripture." LaRondelle, *Israel of God*, 38, may exaggerate the importance when he declares, "The whole New Testament is essentially characterized by the typological and eschatological application of the Old Testament." Others are not so convinced of the prominence of typology. See Reventlow, *Problems of Biblical Theology*, 20; and Hanson, *Jesus Christ in the Old Testament*, 172, 177.

3. Inaugurated eschatology is the NT's portrayal of how the kingdom of God has broken into this present evil age because of Christ's coming and atoning work such that disciples of Christ live between the times, currently enjoying blessings and spiritual benefits of the age to come "now" even as the full manifestation of the kingdom and God's redemptive work are "not yet," awaiting the return of Christ. See Ladd, *Presence of the Future*; Morgan and Peterson, *Kingdom of God*; Schreiner, *New Testament Theology*, 50–59, 96–116; Goldsworthy, "Kingdom of God," 615–20.

the topic of *sensus plenior* draws this theological proposal of the nature of typology to a close.

TYPOLOGY AND ALLEGORY: IS THERE A DISTINCTION?

The Case for Figural Reading: Blurring the Distinction

Any study of typology in recent days must also account for allegory and elucidate if any distinction should be maintained between the two. A current scholarly movement known as the Theological Interpretation of Scripture (TIS) classifies typology and allegory under the general heading of *figural reading*.[4] For most advocates of TIS, the distinction between typology and allegory is a modern convention and is not detectable in the writings of the early church fathers. O'Keefe and Reno explain, "Allegory and typology are part of the same family of reading strategies, often referred to by the fathers as 'spiritual,' that seek to interpret the scriptures in terms of the divine economy."[5] In addition, fueled by recent patristic research, most notably

---

4. Theological Interpretation of Scripture defies definition since it is not a monolithic movement; nevertheless, the movement generally is a negative response to modern critical and ideological approaches to biblical interpretation and instead seeks, in light of post-Enlightenment developments, to read and interpret the Bible with multiple lenses, which generally involves taking account of traditional pre-critical interpretations, especially patristic interpretations, reading within the Rule of Faith (early church creeds) and within one's ecclesial location (reading in the community), engaging the entire narrative of Scripture (canonical approach), and emphasizing the role of the reader including the need for the formation and virtue of the reader. For introductory work on TIS, see Treier, *Theological Interpretation of Scripture*; Vanhoozer, "'Exegesis I Know, and Theology I Know, but Who are You?,'" 289–306; Vanhoozer and Treier, *Theology and the Mirror of Scripture*, 158–91, 244–53; Green, "Practicing the Gospel in a Post-Critical World," 387-97; O'Keefe and Reno, *Sanctified Vision*; Fowl, *Theological Interpretation of Scripture*; Leithart, *Deep Exegesis*; Moberly, "What Is Theological Interpretation," 161–78. The movement has a biannual journal (*Journal of Theological Interpretation*) with the inaugural issue published in 2007 and a commentary series known as the Two Horizons Commentary

5. O'Keefe and Reno, *Sanctified Vision*, 90; cf. Seitz, *Figured Out*, 8–9. For an overview of "figural reading" see Treier, *Theological Interpretation of Scripture*, 46–51. The discussion of "figural reading" is complicated and confusing because scholars do not use the term consistently. According to Dawson, *Christian Figural Reading*, 15, "Auerbach and Frei present their formulations of allegorical reading in direct opposition to their presentation of Christian figural reading. Both argue that figural reading preserves and extends the literal meaning of the text. . . . Figurative interpretation is based on a conception of language as a series of tropes in which nonliteral meanings replace literal meanings; in contrast, figural reading generates a figurativeness that is not nonliteral." Note also Dawson's discussion, 84–97 and 143–49. See further, Frei,

by Frances Young, the once common hermeneutical distinctive between the Antiochene and Alexandrian schools in the fourth century—the latter school thought to exemplify allegorical interpretation and the former as champions of typology and the historical/literal context of interpretation—has been demonstrated to be anachronistic and reductionistic.[6] Young argues,

> In practice drawing a line between typology and allegory in early Christian literature is impossible, not just in Origen's work, where prophetic and symbolic types are fully integrated into his unitive understanding of what the Bible is about, but also, for example, in the tradition of Paschal Homilies beginning with the *Peri Pascha* of Melito.[7]

Her study of early patristic writings concludes,

Eclipse of Biblical Narrative, 7, 28–30; Auerbach, "Figura," 50–55. For other scholars, the typological and allegorical interpretation or "figural reading" would be classified as nonliteral exegesis, see Martens, "Revisiting the Allegory/Typology Distinction," 296–310. For Vanhoozer, "figural reading" is synonymous with typology and definitely incorporates history and biblical theology: typology or figural reading "is the mainspring of theo-dramatic unity, the principle that accounts for the continuity in God's words and acts, the connecting link between the history of Israel and the history of the church, the glue that unifies the Old and New Testaments." Vanhoozer, *Drama of Doctrine*, 223. Note also Hays, *Reading Backwards*, 1–3, 104–5; Hays, "Figural Exegesis and the Retrospective Re-cognition," 34–36, 43–44.

6. For example, Dockery, *Biblical Interpretation Then and Now* has a chapter entitled "The Alexandrian School: Allegorical Hermeneutics" and another labeled "The Antiochene School: Literal-Historical and Typological Hermeneutics"; cf. Kaiser and Silva, *Introduction to Biblical Hermeneutics*, 264–67; Allison, *Historical Theology*, 163–66. Others who maintain a strong distinction between allegory and typology in the early church include Daniélou, *From Shadows to Reality*, who proposed that both typology and allegory were nonliteral exegetical practices but the former was native to Christianity while the latter was foreign; Lampe and Woollcombe, *Essays in Typology*; and Alsup, "Typology," 682–85, esp. 684. Some evangelicals are more cautious of the distinction between the exegetical approaches of the Alexandrian and Antiochene schools; see Silva, "Has the Church Misread the Bible?," 47–61, esp. 48; Goldsworthy, *Gospel-Centered Hermeneutics*, 94–99, esp. 97; Moo, "Problem of *Sensus Plenior*," 181–82. For a more exhaustive discussion on why the distinction is misleading for the case of Origen, and for a more comprehensive bibliography, see Martens, "Revisiting the Allegory/Typology Distinction," 283–317; note also Childs, "Allegory and Typology," 305–10.

7. Young, "Alexandrian and Antiochene Exegesis," 337. For a defense of Origen and challenge to the critique that early Christian allegorical interpretation was not historical, see Martens, "Origen against History?," 635–56. Barr, *Old and New Interpretation*, 107, asserts, "Allegory cannot be described categorically as anti-historical in character, and we cannot make this into an ultimate distinction from typology."

THE NATURE, CHARACTERISTICS, AND CHALLENGES OF TYPOLOGY

> [The] differing results [between Alexandrian and Antiochene treatment of the biblical texts] were not the outcome of literal reading opposed to spiritual sense, for both knew, unlike modernists but perhaps not postmodernists, that the wording of the Bible carried deeper meanings and that the immediate sense or reference pointed beyond itself.[8]

The real difference in their methodology had more to do with the rhetorical and philosophical schools from which they preferred with the Alexandrians exhibiting "symbolic" *mimēsis* and the Antiochenes viewing the biblical text more along the lines of "ikonic" *mimēsis*.[9] Young writes,

> The modern affirmation of typology as distinct from allegory, an affirmation which requires the historical reality of an event as a foreshadowing of another event, its "antitype," is born of modern historical consciousness, and has no basis in the patristic material.[10]

Therefore, with a renewed emphasis on patristic exegesis and with studies showing that the early church fathers applied allegorical and typological

---

8. Young, "Alexandrian and Antiochene Exegesis," 352. See also Carter, *Interpreting Scripture*, 95, 99, 179. Frances Young has many studies of the patristics and the question of allegory and typology in their writings. Ultimately her thesis regarding what really separated the Antiochene and Alexandrian schools was not specifically typology versus allegory but *ikonic mimēsis* (Antiochene) and *symbolic mimēsis* (Alexandrian): "The difference lay in the Antiochene desire to find a genuine connection between what the text said and the spiritual meaning discerned through contemplation of the text. I use the terms 'ikonic' and 'symbolic' to distinguish that difference. . . . [The] representation (*mimēsis*) may be through genuine likeness, an analogy, 'ikon' or image, or it may be by a symbol, something unlike which stands for reality. The 'ikon' will resemble the person or event which it represents, but symbols are not representations in that sense; symbols are 'tokens' or 'signs' whose analogous relationship with what is symbolized is less clear." Young, *Biblical Exegesis*, 210; cf. 162–67, 175–76, 182–85. See also Young, "Typology," 29–48; Young, "Allegory and the Ethics of Reading," 103–20, esp. 114–16. In this latter treatment, after having "disposed of the mirage of typology," she offers seven categories of allegory (some Hellenistic, others ancient or biblical and rabbinic): rhetorical, parabolic, prophetic, moral, natural or psychological, philosophical, and theological. Young, "Allegory and the Ethics of Reading," 111. For other works germane to the subject of allegory and the early church, see Louth's essay "Return to Allegory" in his book *Discerning the Mystery*, 96–131; de Lubac, *Theological Fragments*, 129–96; Ayres, *Nicaea and Its Legacy*; Olsen, "Allegory, Typology, and Symbol, Part I," 161–89; and "Allegory, Typology, and Symbol, Part II," 357–84.

9. Young, "Alexandrian and Antiochene Exegesis," 344; Young, *Biblical Exegesis*, 210–12. It is important to note that ikonic *mimēsis* still includes forms of allegorical interpretation, the Antiochenes rejected only the type of allegory that "destroyed the textual coherence," according to Young, *Biblical Exegesis*, 176.

10. Young, *Biblical Exegesis*, 152–53.

interpretative techniques in figural readings without ever distinguishing them, TIS advocates urge that modern exegetes should follow suit.[11] For example, Benjamin Ribbens, depending on Young, argues that the modern understanding of typology should be replaced with the broader definition of ikonic *mimesis*, having three subcategories of christological, tropological, and homological typological patterns.[12] This broader understanding can then be correlated or equated with figural reading. Thus, Daniel Treier explains, with "the label 'figural reading,' perhaps we can make space for some of the ambiguity over typology while nevertheless suggesting that certain forms of allegorizing are inappropriate."[13]

Beside the resurgence of patristic studies and the question of the allegorical and typological distinction in early Christian interpreters, a second reason is offered for why modern interpreters should be more receptive to figural reading that includes certain forms of allegorical interpretation. The claim is that allegorical interpretation or figural reading is present within Scripture itself. Robert Louis Wilken avers that three Pauline texts (Eph 5:28-32 with the citation of Gen 2:24; 1 Cor 10:1-11; and Gal 4:21-31)

> provide a biblical foundation for the practice of allegory, i.e. that
> for Christians the Old Testament is to be read on more than one

---

11. For example, Gignilliat, "Paul, Allegory, and the Plain Sense," 135-46, follows Louth and Young, arguing that typology "is a form of allegorical reading or a subset of allegorical reading and is still a useful term but is not to be opposed to allegory. Typology *is* allegorical or figural reading" (140; emphasis original). For a brief historical overview of allegory and typology and what he dubs the "figurative sense" in twentieth century scholarship, see Childs, "Allegory and Typology," 299-305.

12. Ribbens, "Typology of Types," 81-95. Ribbens writes, "If ikonic *mimēsis*, consequently, forms the boundaries of typology, then symbolic *mimēsis* is not typology, because it derives correspondence entirely from outside the text – interpreting a word or phrase as a symbol of something outside of the narrative" ("Typology of Types," 88). For Ribbens, ikonic *mimēsis* includes a diverse group of types: christological types—certain OT persons, actions, or institutions that prefigure Christ and his redemptive work; tropological types—certain figures and actions are examples exemplifying moral or immoral activity; and homological types—a catchall subcategory of persons or events that correspond to similar persons and events, thus fitting a general pattern. Also appealing to ikonic and symbolic *mimēsis* in the discussion of typology is Treier, "Superiority of Pre-Critical Exegesis?," 95-97. Gignilliat seems to go in this direction as well since he finds that "Paul's figural reading of the Sarah/Hagar story is not like a certain type of Alexandrian exegesis that tears apart the narrative coherence of the text. Rather, Paul respects the textual coherence of the story, or the way the words go, while recognizing that it has the potential within the divine economy to function figurally as an eschatological indicator of God's future action in Christ." Gignilliat, "Paul, Allegory, and the Plain Sense," 141.

13. Treier, "Pursuing Wisdom," 19. As to what forms of allegorizing would be inappropriate, Treier never explains.

level. . . . It was St. Paul who taught the earliest Christian to use allegory. By giving us "some examples of interpretation," writes Origen, Paul showed us how to use allegory so that we "might note similar things in other passages."[14]

Galatians 4:21–31 is the most frequently cited text supporting allegorical interpretations since it is the one passage in the Bible where the word *allegory* (ἀλληγορούμενα) appears, as Paul links Sarah and Hagar to two covenants. Another passage that is purported to contain an allegorical interpretation is 1 Cor 9:9–10.[15] Wilken writes, "Used in the Scriptures as an interpretative device to discern a meaning that is not plainly given by the text," allegory pertains to the "christological" dimension of the OT, also called the *spiritual sense*, and is important for the life of the church, for "context needs to be understood to embrace the Church, its liturgy, its way of life, its practices and institutions, its ideas and beliefs."[16] Accordingly, the spiritual sense, which comprises of allegorical interpretations, would appear to possess scriptural warrant then since even the apostle Paul invoked OT

---

14. Wilken, "In Defense of Allegory," 200. Note also Martens, "Revisiting the Allegory/Typology Distinction," 297, 301–3. Elliot, "Allegory," 101, seems to agree with Wilken as he writes, "Paul's narrative examples and his use of the word ["allegorical"] (Gal 4:24)] gave the green light to future Christian allegorical interpreters of the Bible."

15. Barr, *Old and New*, 109, states that in this passage where a legal text is invoked regarding the muzzling of the ox, "the literal and original sense is explicitly repudiated by the apostle." Olsen, "Allegory, Typology, and Symbol, Part II," 360–64, also views allegory present in 1 Cor 9 and Gal 4. With reference to Gal 4:24, Richard Hays argues that the distinction between allegory and typology is not one that Paul himself recognizes. See Hays, *Echoes of Scripture*, 116. He still maintains a distinction: "*Typology* is a particular species of the genus *allegorical interpretation*, a species distinguished by its propensity for representing the latent sense of a text as *temporally posterior* to its manifest sense. In typology, the allegorical sense latent in the text's figures is discovered not by a reading that ascends from the material to the spiritual but by a reading that grasps the preliminary in relation to the ultimate." Hays, *Echoes of Scripture*, 215n87, emphasis original.

16. Wilken, "In Defense of Allegory," 199, 201, 209. For an appeal to the spiritual sense that builds off the literal sense but still incorporates allegorical interpretation, see Reno, "From Letter to Spirit," 463–74. The *quadriga*, the four-fold mode of reading the Bible—historical or literal, allegorical, anagogical, and tropological—is receiving revived interest and acceptance as multiple scriptural readings or senses are viewed as valid. See Storer, "Theological Interpretation and the Spiritual Sense," 79–96; Leithart, *Deep Exegesis*, 207. De Lubac is particularly recognized for drawing attention to the medieval *quadriga* and postulating a sacramental hermeneutic which did have a historical foundation, but he was convinced that spiritual or allegorical interpretation preserved the historicity of biblical accounts. For a helpful discussion of the hermeneutic of de Lubac and Daniélou, see Boersma, *Nouvelle Théologie and Sacramental Ontology*, 149–90. For an evangelical reception of the spiritual sense conjoined to the theme of wisdom, see Treier, "Pursuing Wisdom," 17–26.

texts in a manner that extended beyond the plain, literal meaning, resituating texts to meet his paraenetical or polemical purposes. Wilkin clarifies, "St. Paul gives an allegorical interpretation of passages from the Old Testament whose meaning is *not* on the face of it allegorical."[17]

Reaffirming the Allegory/Typology Distinction

The TIS movement has helpfully emphasized that exegesis is always spiritual and theological in contrast to the rationalistic, historical-critical procedures that have dominated the academy the past two centuries.[18] Drawing more attention to pre-critical interpreters and seeking to address the gap between biblical studies and theology are also efforts to be lauded, but the TIS stress on "figural reading" and diminishing the distinction between typology and allegory, even if such interpretative approaches were blurry in the first few centuries of the church, is problematic and leads to confusion.[19] Many salient points may be offered for rejecting the notion of "figural reading" and the merging of typology with allegorical reading.

First, Allegory and Typology are Distinct Literary Features

Before addressing the hermeneutical and interpretative issues associated with allegorizing or allegorical interpretation and typological interpretation, of critical importance is observing that the literary characteristics of allegory and typology differ in the Bible. Just as there are many figures of speech and nonliteral language—metaphors, hyperboles, sarcasm, synecdoche, and metonymy—so there are also parables, symbols, analogies, prophecies, allegories, and typologies in Scripture as well.[20] Allegory and

---

17. Wilken, "In Defense of Allegory," 202. For yet another rationale for the acceptance of allegorical interpretation, see Jewett, "Concerning the Allegorical Interpretation," 1–20. Jewett, thinks that the difference between typology and allegory comes down to semantics. For Jewett, the broader principle of avoiding arbitrary and fanciful interpretations beyond the strict grammatical exegesis rests on having a genuine organic relationship or analogy between the original text. Jewett, "Concerning the Allegorical Interpretation," 13, 18.

18. Treier, "Pursuing Wisdom," 24; Treier, *Theological Interpretation of Scripture*, 14.

19. It would go too far afield to address the positives but also the pitfalls of the TIS movement. For helpful surveys and critiques, see Carson, "Theological Interpretation of Scripture," 187–207; Porter, "What Is Theological Interpretation of Scripture?," 234–67; Trimm, "Evangelicals, Theology, and Biblical Interpretation," 311–30.

20. The list provided is by no means exhaustive. The subject of literary forms and

typology are distinguishable literary entities. Observed by many scholars, including TIS advocates, an allegory is "to mean something other than what one says."[21] Allegory as a literary form is an extended metaphor or a trope that functions to illustrate and tell a story or convey a truth by personifying abstract concepts.[22] More generally, according to Thiselton, allegory "is grounded in a linguistic system of signs or *semiotic* codes and presupposes resonances or parallels between *ideas* or *semiotic meanings*."[23] The most common example cited of a literary composition representing an allegory is John Bunyan's *The Pilgrim's Progress*.[24] However, allegory is also present in the Bible. Instructive examples in both the OT and NT are Ezek 17:1–10, Eccl 12:3–7, Ps 80:8–15, John 10:1–16, Eph 6:1–11, and arguably Matt 22:1–14.[25] In each of these biblical passages the literary features consist of

---

features is common fare in standard hermeneutics textbooks, see McCartney and Clayton, *Let the Reader Understand*, 127–37; Kaiser and Silva, *Introduction to Biblical Hermeneutics*, 139–64; Berkhof, *Principles of Interpretation*, 67–112; Ramm, *Protestant Biblical Interpretation*, 143–44.

21. Young, *Biblical Exegesis*, 176–77, 189–90; cf. O'Keefe and Reno, *Sanctified Vision*, 89; Wilken, "In Defense of Allegory," 198; Vanhoozer, *Is There a Meaning*, 113–14; see also Schodde, "Allegory," 1:95. Elliot, "Allegory," 100–103, problematically discusses allegory only as a method of interpretation.

22. Whitman, *Allegory*, 3–5; Yoshikawa, "Prototypical Use," 13; Thiselton, *Hermeneutics*, 72; LaRondelle, *Israel of God*, 26; Ramm, *Protestant Biblical Interpretation*, 24, 143–44, 217, esp. 223–25; Schodde, "Allegory," 95; Ninow, *Indicators of Typology*, 24n34; Hoskins, *That Scripture Might Be Fulfilled*, 30–31; Fairbairn, *Typology of Scripture*, 1:2. For a rationale as to why parables are not allegories, see Thiselton, *Hermeneutics*, 35–39.

23. Thiselton, *First Epistle to the Corinthians*, 730, emphasis original. Similarly, Moo, "Problem of *Sensus Plenior*," 181. Goppelt, *Typos*, 13, describes an allegory as "a narrative that was composed originally for the single purpose of presenting certain higher truths that are found in the literal sense, or when facts are reported for that same reason." Frye, *Great Code*, 85, asserts, "Typology is not allegory: allegory is normally a story-myth that finds its 'true' meaning in a conceptual or argumentative translation, and both testaments of the Bible, however oblique their approach to history, deal with real people and real events." Note also Frye, *Great Code*, 10. Fowl, "Who Can Read Abraham's Story?," 77–95, advances a looser notion of allegory that is unlike the common view of allegory, which typically treats words, phrases, or stories as ciphers for something else. Instead he follows John David Dawson in finding that "while allegory may rely on metaphor, etymology or personification in order to generate its counterconventional account, such substitutions are not in themselves an allegory (or allegorical interpretation) until they are extended into the narrative account." Fowl, "Who Can Read Abraham's Story?," 80. With such a broadened view, Fowl and Dawson wrongly understand typology as a species of allegory.

24. Thiselton, *Hermeneutics*, 38; Ramm, *Protestant Biblical Interpretation*, 24; Schodde, "Allegory," 95.

25. Schodde, "Allegory," 95; LaRondelle, *Israel of God*, 26–27; Thiselton, *Hermeneutics*, 73.

extended metaphors or figures that represent or symbolize certain truths or concepts. An allegory, to summarize, describes a larger narrative episode that has features laden with symbolic function.

On the other hand, typology is a special and unique phenomenon of Scripture, not a genre or literary device, whereby types are manifest through the unfolding of the divine plan, bound-up with redemptive-historical discourse. There are two related forms of typology based on the directional orientation of the typological patterns. The first and most commonly recognized form of typology, known as "horizontal typology," signifies where God has providentially intended certain OT persons, events, institutions, and actions to correspond to, foreshadow, and prefigure escalated and intensified NT realities in and through the person of Jesus Christ.[26] The attention to "horizontal typology" receives the primary focus in this study given the attention to unpacking the nation of Israel as a type through Scripture. A second categorization, but intrinsically and complementarily related to "horizontal typology," called "vertical typology," is directionally oriented to the correspondences between the heavenly and earthly spatial realms (e.g., the heavenly and earthly tabernacle, the priesthood; see Exod 25:40; Acts 7:44; Heb 8:5, 9:22–25). Charles Fritsch notes that horizontal typology "is deeply rooted in redemptive history which finds its goal and meaning

---

26. Many different definitions of biblical typology are offered, and many do not agree, as will be discussed later in this chapter. Richard Davidson defines typology, based from his semasiological analysis of τύπος and six passages where τύπος is hermeneutically significant in terms of the NT author's interpretation of the OT (Rom 5:14; 1 Cor 10:6, 11; 1 Pet 3:21; Heb 8:5; and Heb 9:24), "as the study of certain OT salvation historical realities (persons, events, or institutions), which God has specifically designed to correspond to, and be prospective/predictive prefigurations of, their ineluctable (*devoir-etre*) and absolutely escalated eschatological fulfillment aspects (Christological/ecclesiological/apocalyptic) in NT salvation history." Davidson, *Typology in Scripture*, 405–6; cf. Davidson, "Nature [and Identity]," 39. Cole, *He Who Gives Life*, 289, defines typology this way: "The idea that persons (e.g., Moses), events (e.g., the exodus), and institutions (e.g., the temple) can—in the plan of God—prefigure a later stage in that plan and provide the conceptuality necessary for understanding the divine intent (e.g., the coming of Christ to be the new Moses, to effect the new exodus, and to be the new temple)." Similarly, for Goppelt, *Typos*, 17–18, the concept of typology has many components including historical facts, divinely ordained representations of future realities, and heightening between type and antitype. Eichrodt, "Is Typological Exegesis an Appropriate Method?," 225, defines typology as "persons, institutions, and events of the Old Testament which are regarded as divinely established models or prerepresentations of corresponding realities in the New Testament salvation history." Terry, *Biblical Hermeneutics*, 246, over a hundred years ago stated, "In the technical and theological sense a type is a figure or adumbration of that which is to come. It is a person, institution, office, action, or event, by means of which some truth of the Gospel was divinely foreshadowed under the Old Testament dispensations. Whatever was thus prefigured is called the antitype."

THE NATURE, CHARACTERISTICS, AND CHALLENGES OF TYPOLOGY

in Christ; [*vertical* typology is rooted] in the view that God's redemptive purpose is realized on earth through material and temporal forms which are copies of heavenly patterns."[27] Vertical typology also involves historical realities and God's providential design as correspondences between heavenly and earthly orders involve intensification and escalation from "copy and shadow" (Heb 8:5) to the "true" (Heb 9:24).[28] The heavenly prototype or archetype (*Urbild*) has its "antitype" in the earthly, OT copy and shadow, which in turn serves as the OT type or mold (*Vorbild*) for its antitypical fulfillment in the NT (*Nachbild*).[29] In this way, vertical typology intersects with horizontal typology.

Unlike allegory, which features an episode having many elements of metaphor and imagery to convey a truth or idea, typological patterns in Scripture are more discrete as real phenomena—persons and events—correspond and anticipate future fulfillment in similar, yet different persons and events—primarily Jesus Christ and the redemption he accomplishes. OT types have their own independent meaning and justification that is a significant departure from most forms of allegory where the thing signified is bound up with the imagery. Moreover, there is a principle of analogy in typology just as there is in allegory, but not of surface imagery, which is wrapped in metaphor and encoded to resonate or parallel some other idea or concept. In addition, typology, unlike compositional allegory, has development and takes shape as later biblical authors build upon earlier written texts with the typological connections progressing along the stages of redemptive history. The typological patterns, then, are primarily discerned or detected through the progress of revelation (epochal and canonical horizons, though not excluding the textual horizon). Typology, then, is

---

27. Fritsch, "To 'Antitypon,'" 106. Ounsworth, *Joshua Typology*, 37–38, helpfully comments, "What makes the vertical typology in Hebrews 9 distinctive is that (a) it is directed to an eschatological purpose and (b) that it combines the vertical aspect with a two-fold horizontal one embracing both time and space, *Heilsgeschichte* and *Heilsgeographie*, as it were" (emphasis original). See also, Caneday, "God's Parabolic Design for Israel's Tabernacle," 103–24.

28. Davidson, *Typology in Scripture*, 352–58. See also, Fritsch, "To 'Antitypon,'" 100–107; Vos, *Teaching of the Epistle to the Hebrews*, 55–65; La Rondelle, *Israel of God*, 41–44; Ounsworth, *Joshua Typology*, 37–39, 53.

29. Unless otherwise noted, my terminology follows that of Davidson, *Typology in Scripture*, 420, who clarifies, "Since in Hebrews the functional movement (from OT reality to NT fulfillment) is the same as in other hermeneutical τύπος passages—even though the referents of τύπος and ἀντίτυπος are reversed—it seems proper for the sake of convenience and consistency to employ the term 'type' in its most common hermeneutical usage to refer to the OT prefiguration (whether person, event, or institution) and 'antitype' to denote the NT fulfillment."

grounded textually.[30] Typology actually shows more affinity with prophecy than it does with allegory. In fact, many scholars classify typology as a form of indirect prophecy. Beale, to cite just one example, observes how typology "indicates fulfillment of the indirect prophetic adumbrations of events, people and institutions from the Old Testament in Christ who now is the final, climactic expression of all God ideally intended through these things in the Old Testament."[31] These characteristics of allegory and typology clearly differ, and such observations should not be obliterated by confusingly lumping allegory and typology into a general category of *figural*.

The nature and characteristics of typology outlined are further elucidated next, but it is important at this juncture to address the relationship of typology to the τύπος word-group in Scripture. Frances Young does find the

---

30. Vanhoozer, "Ascending the Mountain," 788, rightly identifies "typology to be a form of theological interpretation that responds to something unique to the biblical text, a special rather than general hermeneutic that is particularly attentive to the divine authorial discourse and its organic unity." For helpful discussion on intertextuality, see Hays, *Echoes of Scripture*, 154–92, and Beale, *Handbook*, 39–40. The version of intertextuality appealed to in this analysis with respect to typology refers "to the procedure by which a later biblical text refers to an earlier text, how that earlier text enhances the meaning of the later one, and how the later one creatively develops the earlier meaning." Beale, *Handbook*, 40. Intertextuality is inner-biblical or intrabiblical exegesis. For intertextuality as understood by postmodern literary critics, see Vanhoozer, *Is There a Meaning*, 121, 125–26, 132–35.

31. Beale, "Did Jesus and His Followers Preach?," 396. See also Beale, *Handbook*, 17–18, 57–66. Beale finds that verbal prophecy is directly fulfilled while typological foreshadows are indirectly fulfilled. Beale, *Handbook*, 17. There are two types of prophecy: "one as direct prophecy by word, the other as indirect prophecy by foreshadowing event." Beale, *Handbook*, 18. For others who would classify typology as an indirect or implicit form of prophecy, see Robertson, "Outlook for Biblical Theology," 75; Kaiser, *Messiah in the Old Testament*, 34; Achtemeier, "Typology," 927; Brumm, *American Thought and Typology*, 27; Gentry and Wellum, *Kingdom through Covenant*, 130–32; Fritsch, "Biblical Typology," 215; Fairbairn, *Typology of Scripture*, 1:106–39; Yoshikawa, "Prototypical Use," 22–23, refers to typology as "circumstantial prophecy." Johnson, *Him We Proclaim*, 207, differentiates between verbal prophecy and embodied prophecy, the latter referring to typology which is promise through event and closely related to promise through word (prophecy). Roehrs, "Typological Use of the Old," 214–15, rejects the "direct" and "indirect" modes of prophecy but situates typology as a form of prophecy. For critical scholars who also link typology to prophecy, see Eichrodt, "Is Typological Exegesis an Appropriate Method?," 229, 234, and Hummel, "Old Testament Basis," 48–49. Ounsworth, *Joshua Typology*, 51, concludes his survey of the τύπος word-group in the NT and its historical background, stating: "It is not necessary to emphasise historical *event* to justify typology and distinguish it from allegory. What is necessary, rather, is an emphasis on divine causation or providence. Certainly, the OT presents God as being responsible for the events of salvation-historical significance, and the NT reads the OT thus; but also he is seen as ordaining the ongoing existence of institutions such as the priesthood and the monarchy, the temple and its cultic calendar and sacrifice."

term "typology" to have value; however, much of her research of the early church shows how typology and allegory shade into each other in an almost indistinguishable way:

> The word "typology" is a modern coinage. Nevertheless, it is a useful term, and may be employed as a heuristic tool for discerning and describing an interpretative device whereby texts (usually narrative but . . . not exclusively so) are shaped or read, consciously or unconsciously, so that they are invested with meaning by correspondence with other texts of a "mimetic" or representational kind. Typology, then, is not an exegetical method, but a hermeneutical key, and, taking our cue from places where the word "type" is explicitly used, we may be able justifiably to identify other examples of the procedure where the terminology is not explicit.[32]

In his recent study, Richard Ounsworth notes Young's research on Antiochene and Alexandrian exegetical schools and cites her quote above. In response, he follows,

> The strategy suggested by Young, allowing a definition to emerge from the New Testament's use of the τύπος word-group which has given its name to "typology," so that we can be confident that it is a definition that would have been recognizable to the first addressees of NT texts, even if in fact it was not offered.[33]

---

32. Young, *Biblical Exegesis*, 193. Near verbatim remarks may be found in Young, "Typology," 35. For the term "typology" as a modern word, Charity, *Events and their Afterlife*, 171n2, cites J. Gerhard (1582–1637) as one of the first theologians to distinguish allegory from typology. Later in the nineteenth century "comes the first word 'typologia' (Latin, c. 1840), 'typology' (English, 1844)." For a translation of J. Gerhard's distinction between typology and allegory, see Goppelt, *Typos*, 7. Interestingly enough, while TIS advocates appeal to Young in advocating figural reading, she still values a notion of typology, which she links to ikonic *mimesis*, and as such a distinction from allegory is maintained, for what she calls "ikonic exegesis requires a mirroring of the supposed deeper meaning in the text taken as a coherent whole, whereas allegory involves using words as symbols or tokens, arbitrarily referring to other realities by application of a code, and so destroying the narrative, or surface, coherence of the text." Young, *Biblical Exegesis*, 162. Martens, "Revisiting the Allegory/Typology Distinction," 291–92, summarizes Young: "Allegorists interpret violently because of their myopic fascination with individual words that are allowed to serve only as tokens and that are made to refer arbitrarily to other, unrelated realities. Young's distinction between typology and allegory brings with it something new to Origenian scholarship . . . the claim that texts alone and not events are being interpreted, and her emphasis upon whether the coherence of a passage was discerned or dismantled by the reader."

33. Ounsworth, *Joshua Typology*, 33; cf. 4. It should be noted that one of the significant problems of Ounsworth's work is his audience-centered hermeneutic. The true referent of a term can be found only by attending to what the author meant and not

From this point, Ounsworth canvasses the uses of τύπος within the NT as many others, particularly Davidson and Goppelt, have in more or less detail.[34] From these lexical studies, τύπος is acknowledged to denote an image, model, pattern, example, form, and imprint, but more broadly, "τύπος is understood to signify either the molding pattern (*Vorbild*) or the resulting pattern of another mold (*Nachbild*)," or in some instances both simultaneously.[35]

Conducting a focused study on the τύπος word group is an important consideration, after all, as highlighted, allegory (ἀλληγορέω) says one thing and means another. Having a terminological control is important and Davidson has convincingly demonstrated the essential characteristics of typology from his study of key passages (Rom 5:14; 1 Cor 10:6, 11; 1 Pet 3:21; Heb 8:5; and Heb 9:24). However, this is because τύπος in these contexts overlaps with what is commonly associated with typology. Young, Ounsworth, and Davidson run into trouble because they are attempting, in the words of H. Wayne Johnson,

> to answer hermeneutical questions about the nature of typology based on the lexicography of one word. This is asking too much for a number of reasons. First, it is questionable whether or not there is 'one basic meaning' for τύπος. The word is used to denote a mark (John 20:25), an idol or image (Acts 7:43), a pattern or model (Acts 7:44), an example (Phil 3:17 etc.) or type (Rom 5:14, clearly not an example). The diversity of English words used to render τύπος is not evidence of sloppiness in translation but an appreciation of the range of its meaning in various contexts.... Simply put, τύπος is not a technical term for 'type.' Neither is it a *sine qua non* for typology. Consequently, any attempt to establish the biblical definition of typology based purely on semasiological or lexical analysis is filled with problems.[36]

---

speculating about what the original audience understood.

34. Ounsworth, *Joshua Typology*, 34–40, 51; Davidson, *Typology in Scripture*, 115–90; Goppelt, "τύπος," 8:246–59; Fritsch, "Biblical Typology," 87–91; Baker, "Typology," 144–46; Woollcombe, "Biblical Origins and Development," 60–62; Currid, "Recognition and Use of Typology," 115–16; Brumm, *American Thought and Typology*, 20–22; Ellis, *Paul's Use of the Old*, 126.

35. Johnson, "Pauline Typology," 21; cf. Woollcombe, "Biblical Origins and Development," 61; Davidson, *Typology in Scripture*, 128–32; Ounsworth, *Joshua Typology*, 34–35.

36. Johnson, "Pauline Typology," 23, 25. Johnson rightly observes that τύπος is used in a variety of passages that have absolutely nothing to do with typology (Acts 20:25; Rom 6:17; Phil 3:17; 1 Thess 1:7; 2 Thess 3:9; 1 Tim 4:12). The range of τύπος is also nicely organized in BDAG, s.v. "τύπος."

In other words, as Johnson has helpfully articulated,[37] typology has less to do with the lexicography of a Greek term and should be understood as a hermeneutical and theological term or category that describes a unique feature that is the property of certain persons, events, and institutions that are recorded in Scripture. A proper understanding of typology in Scripture should examine critical passages where τύπος is employed to correspond to OT persons, events, and institutions (precisely the six passages where Davidson has already provided an excellent exegetical analysis), but there is a host of other passages that should be considered as well (e.g., Matt 2:15, 4:1–11, 12:39–42; John 6:32, 12:37–43, 15:1; 1 Cor 5:7b, 15:21–22, 45–49; Col 2:16–17; Heb 3–4, 7, 10; 1 Pet 2:4–10).[38] Therefore, the rendering of *typology* as a technical term is to describe a unique literary phenomenon of Scripture that is divergent from allegory because it accounts for the organic relationships between persons, events, institutions, and actions that occur at different stages in Scripture. Types possess a divine design in that they prefigure corresponding intensified realities (antitypes) in the new age inaugurated by Jesus Christ. Although different, both allegories and types are revelatory in nature, divinely authorized, and they are embedded in Scripture by the biblical authors rather than created by the literary genius of later writers of Scripture or subsequent interpreters.[39]

---

37. Johnson, "Pauline Typology," 25. Johnson, points out, "Even if there were 'one basic meaning' for τύπος, it would be unclear what relationship that meaning would have to a biblical definition of 'typology.' Vern Poythress has warned that 'no term in the Bible is equal to a technical term of systematic theology.'" Also bearing on this issue of etymology of terms is Barr, *Semantics of Biblical Language*. Rightly, Evans and Novakovic, "Typology," 986, assert that the use of typology "is not limited to the presence of the term *typos* and its cognates."

38. The list is by no means exhaustive. Hoskins, *That Scripture Might Be Fulfilled*, 27–30, points out other NT Greek terms related to typology, such as σκια (e.g., Col 2:17; shadow), παραβολὴ (e.g., Heb 9:9; symbol, figure), and ἀληθινός (e.g., John 6:32; true). Other scholars also mention ὑπόδειγμα (e.g., Heb 8:5; illustration, pattern, copy). For a list of Hebrew terms and phrases in the OT, see Fishbane, *Biblical Interpretation*, 352–53. He also notes that "there are many other cases of inner-biblical typology which are not signalled by technical terms at all. To recognize the typologies at hand, the latter-day investigator must be alert to lexical co-ordinates that appear to correlate apparently disparate texts.... Sometimes, moreover, motifs are juxtaposed, sometimes pericopae, and sometimes recurrent scenarios." Fishbane, *Biblical Interpretation*, 353.

39. I owe this insight to Ardel B. Caneday through personal correspondence.

Second, Complications Arise with the Notion of "Figural Reading," "Allegorical Interpretation" or "Typological Interpretation"

As argued, allegory and typology are distinct literary entities that a reader should recognize in Scripture and hence there is reason for rejecting figural reading or any other attempt to merge typology with allegory. Another rationale for avoiding the confusion, however, is that the move from identifying and recognizing the allegories or typologies already intended as such in Scripture to the position of crafting figural, allegorical, or typological interpretations, much as Christian interpreters have freely fashioned in the past and the present, results in unwarranted and arbitrary readings. Allegories and typologies are in Scripture, but, as Hans LaRondelle succinctly observes,

> It is a different story if an interpreter would *allegorize* a plainly historical narrative in the Bible. Such allegorizing transforms the narrative into a springboard for teaching an idea which is different from that intended by the Bible writer. Whenever an allegorical interpretation arbitrarily converts a historical narrative into teaching a spiritual or theological truth, such a speculative allegorizing is negatively called an "*allegorism*." It imposes a meaning on the Bible text that is not really there. It is added to the text by the interpreter only for the purpose of edification and finding spiritual truths and deep meanings.[40]

An allegorical interpretation requires an extra-textual grid or key, which is used to warrant an explanation.[41] With such an approach, a deeper spiritual or mystical sense or foreign aspect is introduced into the meaning

---

40. LaRondelle, *Israel of God*, 27, emphasis original. For a helpful discussion of the difference between typology and forms of first-century interpretative approaches such as allegorization, pesher, and midrash, see Evans and Novakovic, "Typology," 987; and Hamilton, "Typology of David's Rise to Power," 8–9.

41. Carson, "Mystery and Fulfillment," 404; Carson, "Theological Interpretation of Scripture," 199; Drane, "Typology," 206; Gentry and Wellum, *Kingdom through Covenant*, 129–30; Vanhoozer, *Is There a Meaning*, 119, states, "In locating meaning in an intelligible conceptual realm, allegorical interpretation gives stability to the 'spiritual sense': '*This* (word) means *that* (concept).' Allegorical interpretation sees the meaning of a text as constituted outside the text in another framework: the conceptual." Boyarin, "Origen as Theorist of Allegory," 45, observes that for the allegorist, "The role of the interpreter . . . is to perceive and then describe this clear and determinate message, to somehow divine the invisible 'magic language' that underlies or lies behind the visible language and then to translate it in the form of allegorical commentary. The allegorist reaches this level of interpretation through a process of contemplation."

of the text.[42] Vanhoozer writes, "Allegorizing becomes problematic... insofar as it resembles a general hermeneutical strategy by which later readers find new meanings in texts *unrelated* to the human authorial discourse."[43] The problem of allegorical interpretation then is not so much that the historicity of a certain passage is denied, though the historical features are often diminished or ignored, but that the interpretative moves are arbitrary as there is no possible way to detect the relationship between the text and the meaning ascribed to it.[44]

A plethora of allegorical interpretations in the early church fathers could be recalled, but perhaps a few will suffice. Tertullian, Cyril of

---

42. On this point, see Ramm, *Protestant Biblical Interpretation*, 223; Markus, "Presuppositions of the Typological Approach," 443–44; Beale, "Did Jesus and His Followers Preach?," 395; Currid, "Recognition and Use of Typology," 119; Moo, "Problem of *Sensus Plenior*," 181; Baker, *Two Testaments, One Bible*, 180–81; Nicole, "Patrick Fairbairn and Biblical Hermeneutics," 769; Osborne, "Type; Typology," 4:931. Lints, *Fabric of Theology*, 304n17, avers that "allegory involves a relationship stemming from some accidental or peripheral aspect of the original event, person, or institution." Woollcombe, "Biblical Origins and Development," 40, also asserts that "allegorism is the search for a secondary and hidden meaning underlying the primary and obvious meaning of a narrative. This secondary sense... does not necessarily have any connexion at all with the historical framework of revelation."

43. Vanhoozer, "Ascending the Mountain," 788; cf. Frei, *Eclipse of Biblical Narrative*, 82. France, *Jesus and the Old Testament*, 40, writes that allegorical interpretation "has little concern with the historical character of the Old Testament text. Words, names, events, etc. are used, with little regard for their context, and invested with a significance drawn more from the allegorist's own ideas than from the intended sense of the Old Testament. No real correspondence, historical or theological, between the Old Testament history and the application is required." Silva, "Has the Church Misread the Bible?," 58, agrees, for if the allegorical method was more generally about finding a deeper meaning in the text, then the distinction with typology would be less significant, but if "we narrow the meaning of *allegorical* so that it describes a playing down or even a rejection of historicity, then the distinction becomes valid, useful, and important." Silva, "Has the Church Misread the Bible?," 59–60, mentions other problems with allegorical interpretation, namely its attachment with a philosophical system which could be an alien framework, the issue of arbitrariness, and the problem of elitism as certain interpreters happen to have the spiritual acumen and maturity in possessing the key to unlock the allegorical or hidden connections from the text.

44. Vanhoozer, "Ascending the Mountain," 787, citing Thiselton, *First Corinthians*, 150, notes, "Absent the original context, there are no constraints—no air traffic control—with which to rein in flights of exegetical fancy: 'allegory (in general) rests on parallels between *ideas* and can become too often self-generated and arbitrary.'" Clearly Vanhoozer is in opposition to Young as she seeks to do away with the distinction between compositional allegory and allegorical interpretation. Young, "Allegory and the Ethics of Reading," 112. Contra Young, preserving the authorial intent and detecting an "undersense" from textual indicators in the text must be maintained to arrive at proper meanings tied to human authorial discourse, avoiding subjective readings without hermeneutical control.

Jerusalem, and John Chrysostom all connect the dove that Noah sent out from the ark with the descending of the Holy Spirit in the synoptic Gospels since the Spirit came down upon Jesus in the form of a dove when Jesus arose from his baptism. Origen finds symbolic significance in the dimensions of Noah's ark, and he also resorts to mystical and moral allegorizing when he compares the animals of the ark with those who are saved in the church. Moses praying with his arms outstretched during the battle with Amalek (Exod 17:8–13) was interpreted by Tertullian as a type of Christ on the cross since his arms were outstretched during the crucifixion, and Moses' staff, which transformed the bitter waters of Marah, was seen as the cross while the transformed waters pointed to baptism.[45] Philo's philosophical interpretative approach seems to be appropriated by Origen and Clement leading to allegorical readings. Symbolism is employed to interpret Pharaoh's daughter as a type of the church, the "life of Moses as an allegory of the soul's journey to spiritual perfection," and the waters of Marah refer to the "strictness of the virtuous life for beginners, which is gradually tempered by hope."[46] Justin and Irenaeus are just two of many church fathers with the exception, surprisingly, of the Alexandrian School for the most part, who view Rahab's scarlet cord as an illustrative resemblance of the blood of Christ since it recalls the Passover lamb.[47] The church fathers should be rightly esteemed for their high view of Scripture and defense of doctrinal truths, but clearly at times they applied mystical and foreign interpretive schemes in their readings of Scripture. For them, deeper religious truths or hidden meanings were to be unearthed as a principle of similitude and likeness was made, and the etymological significance of words led to allegorical readings based off lexical links and associative strategies.[48] However, such

---

45. For the examples cited, see Daniélou, *From Shadows to Reality*, 97–101, 104–10, 168–72. For a modern work that also allegorizes the OT in a similar manner at points, see Chase, *40 Questions about Typology and Allegory*, 255–90.

46. Daniélou, *From Shadows to Reality*, 220, 224–25. Carson, "Theological Interpretation of Scripture," 199, rightly says, "When Philo tells us that the respective meanings of the patriarchs Abraham, Isaac, and Jacob are the three fundamental principles of a Greek education, with the best will in the world it is difficult to see how this conclusion derives from the text of Genesis."

47. Daniélou, *From Shadows to Reality*, 247–49. Irenaeus also links the three spies that Rahab receives with the Father, Son, and Holy Spirit. Despite the fact that the text indicates that only two spies were sent by Joshua (Josh 6:22), the link to the Trinity is imaginative and depends on Greek philosophy. See Daniélou, *From Shadows to Reality*, 249.

48. O'Keefe and Reno, *Sanctified Vision*, 48–56, 66–67; cf. Martens, "Revisiting the Allegory/Typology Distinction," 310–12. Unfortunately, using lexemes as a springboard to other passages of Scripture just because the same word or imagery is present is certain to exemplify the word fallacies of the kinds catalogued in Carson, *Exegetical*

allegorisms, even if containing elements of truth, are unwarranted because the literal sense is obscured or distorted given the random symbolical associations or cleverly created correspondences at the level of semiotic code.

The danger is not just with "allegorical interpretations" however. Often scholars present the case for "typological interpretation." Clarification and caution are needed though, for Ardel Caneday convincingly argues,

> *Typological interpretation*, using the adjective to modify *interpretation*, creates confusion by focusing upon the *act of interpretation* rather than upon the *act of revelation*. . . . [T]ypology and allegory are fundamentally categories that belong to the *act of revelation*, not the *act of interpretation*. The reader discovers types and allegories that are already present in the text.[49]

The typological patterns belong in the domain of revelation because God casts and invests the types with foreshadowing significance in Scripture. The notion of "typological" and "allegorical" interpretations or "prosopological exegesis" subtly expresses a form of reader-response hermeneutics, but the task of the reader is to explicate the meaning of the text by attending to the authorial intent and their usage of literary forms, i.e., faithfully reading the text according to its genre and nature—reading

---

Fallacies. In fairness, the propensity to allegorize is not just found in the writings of the patristics.

49. Caneday, "Covenant Lineage Allegorically Prefigured," 68n5, emphasis original. See also Caneday, "Biblical Types," 136, 141–42, 147, and Caneday, "Muzzled Ox and the Abused Apostle," 20–21. Examples of scholars who speak of "typological interpretation" include LaRondelle, *Israel of God*, 35; Hamilton, "Typology of David's Rise to Power;" Chase, *40 Questions about Typology and Allegory*; and Goppelt, *Typos*. In his more recent work, Hamilton, *Typology*, 27, continues to use the phrase "typological interpretation" though he does focus more on authorial intent. Beale, "Did Jesus and His Followers Preach?," 401, and Beale, *Handbook*, 24, speaks of typology as an "exegetical method" because he is countering the view of R. T. France and David Baker who believe that exegesis is only concerned with uncovering the human author's original intent and meaning. While the association of typology as an interpretative scheme employed by readers should be avoided in light of Caneday's remarks, Beale's broader point is correct, for finding typological correspondences is part of the exegetical task since the framework of the canon and the "interpretation and elucidation of meaning of earlier parts of Scripture by latter ones" is necessitated given the divine author. In the end, Caneday and Beale are not far from each other: genuine typological patterns are discerned through grammatical-historical-canonical exegesis. For additional discussions on the relation of typology to exegesis or hermeneutics, see Davidson, "Nature [and Identity]," 12–17; Hoskins, *Jesus as the Fulfillment*, 23–25; Currid, "Recognition and Use of Typology," 121; Markus, "Presuppositions of the Typological Approach," 447–48.

historical narratives historically, poetry poetically, and law passages should be read legally.⁵⁰ Schodde rightly stresses that Protestant biblical interpretation rejected

> allegorizing and adhered to the safe and sane principle, practiced by Christ and the entire NT, of *Sensum ne inferas, sed efferas* ("Do not carry a meaning into [the Scriptures] but draw it out of [the Scriptures]"). It is true that the older Protestant theology still adheres to a *sensus mysticus* in the Scriptures, but by this it means those passages in which the sense is conveyed not *per verba* (through words), but *per res verbis descriptas* ("through things described by means of words"), as, e.g., in the parable and the type.⁵¹

---

50. Caneday, "Biblical Types," 142. The point is an important one as O'Keefe and Reno, *Sanctified Vision*, have a whole chapter dedicated to "typological interpretation" that concentrates on "typological exegesis" as an interpretative strategy in the early church. When typological interpretation is used to associate the civil rights movement of Martin Luther King to Israel's exodus or in terms of how patristic interpreters developed certain typologies retrospectively from the OT, then theologians have clearly departed from the identification of genuine typological patterns in Scripture to the imaginative and fanciful creation of typologies (or really analogies) that have absolutely nothing to do with what the text actually says. Others in the TIS movement paddle in the same stream as O'Keefe and Reno. Young, "Typology," 48, describes typology as "a 'figure of speech' that configures or reads texts to bring out significant correspondences so as to invest them with meaning beyond themselves." Leithart, *Deep Exegesis*, 44–52, 74, also describes typology as a reading strategy that is particularly susceptible to reader-response propensities given his understanding of how the meaning of texts change over time and how typological interpretation can be applied as a general hermeneutic. For an overview of his approach and the suggestion that Leithart's answer to avoiding false typological interpretations requires the judgment of the Church's Magisterium (as a liturgically and theologically attuned community of believers), see Levering, "Readings on the Rock," 707–31, esp. 722–27. See also Caneday's critique of Leithart in "Biblical Types," 138–39.

51. Schodde, "Allegory," 95, emphasis original. Vanhoozer, *Is There a Meaning*, 311, very helpfully states, "Interpreters err either when they allegorize discourse that is intended to be taken literally or when they 'literalize' discourse that is intended to be taken figuratively." There is an important distinction between literal and literalistic interpretation. Vanhoozer further writes, "Literal, that is to say, *literate*, interpretation grasps the communicative context and is thus able to identify the communicative act. We grasp the literal meaning of an utterance when we discern its propositional matter and its illocutionary force—that is to say, when we recognize what it is: a command, assertion, joke, irony, parable, etc. . . . Taking the Bible literally means reading for its literary sense, the sense of its communicative act. This entails, first, doing justice to the propositional, poetic, and purposive aspects of each text as a communicative act and, second, relating these to the Bible considered as a unified divine communicative act: the Word of God" (312). See also Ramm, *Protestant Biblical Interpretation*, 119–26.

Thus, the role of the reader is to identify types, symbols, and allegories that are in Scripture and not creatively invent them as the phrase "typological interpretation" suggests. Similarly, Ounsworth rightly affirms that typology appeals to Scripture "*as a record*, and therefore retains and relies upon the literal sense of scripture. . . . [T]he role of the literary record is not to encode the theological meaning but to reveal to the reader (or hearer) the mimetic correspondences that exist in reality."[52] The connection between two persons or events as mimetic correspondences is not established by the "creative act on the part of the interpreter so much as a discovery, a discernment of what intended (sc. by God) to be understood."[53] The same concern regarding "allegorical" and "typological" interpretation is also applicable to the term *figural reading*. The terminology suggests an accent on the reader's role of constructing figural correspondences from the text. While figural reading is sometimes used as a synonym for typology (e.g., Vanhoozer, Ribbens), the language indicates that it is the reader who crafts the figural connections.[54] The attention is diverted once again to the act of interpretation rather than the act of revelation. This leads not only to hermeneutical confusion and, depending on the one doing the figural reading, to treating the Scripture as a wax nose, carving and shaping out an array of superficial analogies and correspondences. Instead, reading the Bible faithfully means seeking to demonstrate the textual warrant and indicators for typological patterns. Such a constraint is necessary since there are "some interpreters ('hyper-typers') who see typology on almost every page of Scripture."[55]

---

52. Ounsworth, *Joshua Typology*, 52, emphasis original.

53. Ounsworth, *Joshua Typology*, 53. So also, Gundry, "Typology as a Means of Interpretation," 235, finds that there is a danger "whenever typology is used to show the Christocentric unity of the Bible, it is all too easy to impose an artificial unity (even assuming that there is a valid use of the basic method). Types come to be created rather than discovered, and the drift into allegorism comes all too easily." Similarly, Kaiser, *Uses of the Old Testament in the New*, 121, correctly argues that "types cannot be 'read into' or 'read back' in the OT from the NT in some sort of canonical *eisegesis*."

54. To be fair, while Vanhoozer, "Ascending the Mountain," 792, cf. 791, uses the language of figural reading he does claim that with typology, the interpreter "discovers the plain sense of the author. . . . It is only when we read the plain sense of the human author in canonical context that we discern the divinely intended 'plain canonical sense,' together with its 'plain canonical referent:' Jesus Christ."

55. Currid, "Recognition and Use of Typology," 121.

Third, Allegorical Interpretations Are Not Exemplified in the NT as Some Scholars Claim.

While some may claim Gal 4:21–31 and 1 Cor 9:9–11 as exemplars of "allegorical" interpretation, careful reading and analysis of the OT passages that are invoked in these Pauline passages provide a definitive conclusion that Paul did not devise allegories. A brief discussion of each of these passages shows that Paul did not engage in "allegorical" interpretation and therefore refutes the argument by Wilken and others that modern readers have the license to allegorize.

The use of Deut 25:4 in 1 Cor 9:9–10 seems puzzling as Paul appears to be lifting an ancient OT law about oxen and applying it to justify material benefits that ministers of the gospel, like Paul and Barnabas, should reap. While Deut 24–25 may appear to list a group of disconnected and unstructured laws, viable interpretations have been offered to explain why a command about oxen would appear in the context of Deut 25. Jan Verbruggen argues that "all these laws seem to deal with situations that show how one should deal with one's fellow man" and particularly, the law about oxen (Deut 25:4) should be understood about how to care for a neighbor's ox.[56] God is concerned for the welfare of oxen, but the law is originally for humans, particularly the economic responsibility of using someone's property. On the other hand, Caneday finds that Deut 25:4 in its original context is a proverbial saying that is attached to Deut 25:1–3, "a fitting aphoristic conclusion to reinforce the commandment that prohibits inhumane and abusive threshing of another human with excessive lashes."[57] If this is the case, Paul's use of Deut 25:4 reflects its original proverbial nature as he reprimands the Corinthians for their mistreatment of him in prohibiting him from benefitting from his own labors. Another interpretation is that Paul is using a *qal wahomer* argument (from lesser to greater; *a fortiori*) characteristic of rabbinic exegesis.[58] Accordingly, Paul argues that if the law

---

56. Verbruggen, "Of Muzzles and Oxen," 706. Johnson, *Old Testament in the New*, 44–46, also highlights the context of Deut 24–25. Johnson concludes that the literal sense was not excluded, but Paul used the passage analogically, giving it a further spiritual or moral sense even as the proverbial or figurative notion should not be excluded since the command about oxen may have been related to human interactions in the original context.

57. Caneday, "Muzzled Ox and the Abused Apostle," 23.

58. See Instone-Brewer, "Paul's Literal Interpretation," 139–53. Instone-Brewer argues that "ox" was a standard legal term for a servant or laborer in any species per the Talmud, Mishnah, and Targums. Paul derives a new halakah as "he mustered all his legal expertise, using legal terminology, quoting legal rulings, and employing legal exegetical techniques that a contemporary rabbi would have been proud of" ("Paul's

permits animals to eat of crops in fields where they work, how much more may human laborers, such as ministers, be worthy to share in the benefits of the harvest. With these three interpretative options, the use of Deut 25:4 in 1 Cor 9:9 is far from being an allegorical interpretation as postulated by TIS advocates or Pauline commentators, such as Richard Longenecker.[59] First Corinthians 9:9–11 is best categorized as an analogical use of Scripture. Paul applies a principle from an agricultural case with ethical import or Paul's use of the muzzled ox reflects its original proverbial nature which fittingly applies to his situation.[60]

The question of the legitimacy of allegorical interpretation has received by far the most attention with Gal 4:21–31. Paul writes with reference to Sarah and Hagar that "these things are spoken/written allegorically: for these women are two covenants" (Gal 4:24).[61] When instructing the Galatians to not live under the Law, Paul connects Hagar to the Mosaic covenant, the present Jerusalem, and slavery on the one hand, while implicitly associating Sarah with the Abrahamic covenant, the heavenly Jerusalem, and freedom through promise. Paul weaves together themes of Abrahamic sonship, barrenness, flesh versus Spirit, and slavery versus freedom in affirming that the Galatians are sons of the free woman (Sarah) and not of the slave woman (Hagar). The notoriously difficult passage has garnered a variety of explanations for Paul's hermeneutic. Some believe that what Paul is doing is actually typology, even though he uses the word "allegorically," but others think that Paul is employing an allegorical interpretation, and still others make the case for the presence of both typological and allegorical elements in Gal 4:21–31.[62]

Literal Interpretation," 153). The *qal wahomer* position is also advocated in Ciampa and Rosner, "I Corinthians," 718–22; cf. Garland, *1 Corinthians*, 409–12.

59. Longenecker, *Biblical Exegesis*, 109–10.

60. See Verbruggen, "Of Muzzles and Oxen," 710–11 and Caneday, "Muzzled Ox and the Abused Apostle," 22–24. Note also Beale, *Handbook*, 67–69; Kaiser, "Single Meaning, Unified Referents," 81–87.

61. For discussion of the only use of verb form ἀλληγορέω in the NT and LXX along with helpful elucidation of Paul's phrase, ἅτινά ἐστιν ἀλληγορούμενα, see Di Mattei, "Paul's Allegory," 104–9; Caneday, "Covenant Lineage Allegorically Prefigured," 53–55. While the verb can mean to "to speak allegorically" or "to interpret allegorically," Di Mattei, "Paul's Allegory," 106, finds in his survey of the ancient sources that "ἀλληγορέω is predominantly used by these authors in the sense 'to speak allegorically,' in which case it is usually the author or the personified text itself which speaks allegorically." This assessment is crucial as it undermines the notion that Paul constructed or cleverly devised the allegorical connection. Further, Caneday, "Covenant Lineage Allegorically Prefigured," 55, makes a good case for translating the clause as "these things are written allegorically" since the clause is bracketed by two explicit OT citations on either side.

62. The lack of a clear delineation and agreed upon definition of allegory complicates

The best treatment of Gal 4:21–31 is offered by Caneday. Specific types are presented in Gal 4:22–23 and 28–30, but in the main the passage is an allegory, but not an allegorical interpretation on the part of Paul. Caneday explains that it is

> unreasonable to think that Paul expects to convince his converts by grounding his argument in Gal 4:21–31 in nothing more than his adeptness to spin an impressive allegory from the Genesis narrative on the authority of a Christophany, his reception of the 'revelation of Jesus Christ' (1:12ff).[63]

While Paul makes the metaphorical connection between Hagar and Sarah to the two covenants, he finds grounding from the OT itself as the narrative of Gen 16–21 presents Abraham, Sarah, Hagar, Isaac, and Ishmael as historical figures that are divinely invested with symbolism and point beyond themselves to the salvation to come in the latter days.[64] Isaiah also

---

the matter of Gal 4:21–31, but generally, those in favor of viewing the passage in terms of typology include Ellis, *Paul's Use of the Old*, 51–53, 130; Goppelt, *Typos*, 139–40; Silva, "Galatians," 808; Foulkes, "Acts of God," 367–68; Roehrs, "Typological Use of the Old," 210–12. Those in favor of some form of an allegorical interpretation include Fowl, "Who Can Read Abraham's Story?," 82, 87–90; Longenecker, *Biblical Exegesis*, 110–13; Longenecker, *Galatians*, 199–200, 208–10; Hays, *Echoes of Scripture*, 116; Meyer, *End of the Law*, 116–19. Many others promote that both elements of allegory and typology are present: Schreiner, *Galatians*, 293–300, identifies 4:21–23 and 4:28–30 as typology and 4:24–27 as allegory; Moo, *Galatians*, 294–96; De Boer, "Paul's Quotation of Isaiah 54.1," 370–89; Cosgrove, "Law Has Given Sarah No Children," 221; Echevarria, *Future Inheritance of Land*, 135–36; Harmon, "Allegory, Typology, or Something Else?," 154–58; Lincoln, *Paradise Now and Not Yet*, 13–14; Di Mattei, "Paul's Allegory," 102–22, argues that Paul's hermeneutic uses the rhetorical this-for-that, the hallmark of allegorical principle, but the *historia* of Hagar and Sarah is not removed as Paul exemplifies a *haftarah* liturgical reading practice, a Jewish reading technique, which makes use of prophetic texts (Isa 54:1 in this case) to read the Torah (Gen 16–17, 21:10 in this case) eschatologically.

63. Caneday, "Covenant Lineage Allegorically Prefigured," 54; cf. 51.

64. Caneday, "Covenant Lineage Allegorically Prefigured," 55. The Genesis narrative features "historical persons divinely invested with symbolic significances that transcend their own experiences and times, converging together within an allegorical story, bearing significance that reconfirms the promise and engenders hope that the promise will be fulfilled in the latter days when Messiah, Abraham's true seed, is to be revealed. Thus, by quoting Isa 54:1 (in Gal 4:27), Paul is drawing the Galatians' attention to the fact that what they are now experiencing at the hands of those who trouble them with a different gospel was allegorically written long ago *in nuce* in the Genesis narrative that entails Abraham, Sarah (the desolate woman), Hagar (the woman with the husband), and the contrasting conceptions and births of two boys" (Caneday, "Covenant Lineage Allegorically Prefigured," 60). Caneday's assertions have been further buttressed by Emerson's study of the lexical and thematic connections between Hagar/Sarah and the Sinai episodes within the Pentateuch itself, particularly how Gen 16–17, 21 link to

notices these features in the Genesis account (see Isa 51:2 and 54:1, the latter explicitly cited by Paul in Gal 4:27) as the Isaianic intertextual development of the barren woman (Sarah) with Jerusalem provides Paul with the redemptive historical context and lens that sharpens the focus of the allegory already present in Genesis.[65] Furthermore, as Caneday helpfully observes, Paul expects his readers to recognize the allegory already there in the Pentateuch by bracketing his appeal at the beginning: "Do you not hear the Law [i.e., Scripture]?" (4:21) with a reprise, "But what does the Scripture say?" (4:30).[66] Caneday writes, "The Scriptures—Genesis and Isaiah—authorize his dual concluding appeal to the Galatians: (1) to cast out the Sinai covenant and its descendants, the Judaizers and those who preach 'another gospel,' and (2) to affirm that Gentile believers are children of promise."[67]

---

the narratives concerning the fall, Cain, and to wilderness/wandering narratives in the book of Exodus and Numbers, see Emerson, "Arbitrary Allegory, Typical Typology," 14–22. Emerson notices how the identification of Hagar as an Egyptian slave and how both she and Israel receive their promises from God in the wilderness lead to thematic connections between them. Further, Hagar's and Ishmael's wandering can be linked to Israel's wandering in the wilderness. Another connection may be based on wordplay of Hagar's name. Di Mattei, "Paul's Allegory," 119, suggests, "Paul . . . sees an elaborate allegory here in the Abrahamic narrative. Genesis' angel of God, who reveals himself to Hagar [Gen 16:9] to establish a 'covenant', allegorically speaks of the revelation at Hagra (i.e. Sinai at Arabia), whereupon the angels of God mediate a covenant, the Law, to Moses (Gal. 3:20). But as Hagar's 'covenant', allegorically is but temporarily established and does not alter God's predestined promise to a make a covenant with Sarah's future and promised son, so too the giving of the Law at Sinai; it does not abrogate the covenant promises made beforehand to Abraham (Gal 3.17)."

65. Caneday, "Covenant Lineage Allegorically Prefigured," 60; Harmon, "Allegory, Typology, or Something Else?," 152–53, 156. Harmon, though very similar, differs from Caneday in finding the allegory not so much in the Genesis narrative itself, but the allegory is through the correspondences "more fully revealed through the use of a theological and textual framework provided by Isaiah 54:1 and its surrounding context." Harmon, "Allegory, Typology, or Something Else?," 156. He ultimately concludes that typology and allegory are present, but the allegory is based on the external framework provided by the "extra-textual" lens of Isa 54:1. The problem with this view is that it suggests that Paul or Isaiah make an allegorical interpretation which is problematic for the reasons laid out above and as discussed in Caneday's article. For a helpful discussion of Isa 54:1 and Paul's use of this text, see Jobes, "Jerusalem, Our Mother," 299–320.

66. Caneday, "Covenant Lineage Allegorically Prefigured," 55–56. A chiasm is present, for between the initial (Gal 4:21) and reprising (Gal 4:30) interrogatives (A, A'), Paul twice affirms, "for it is written" (Gal 4:22 and 27; B, B'), with these authoritative appeals to Scripture enclosing the assertion (C), "These things are written allegorically" (Gal 4:24).

67. Caneday, "Covenant Lineage Allegorically Prefigured," 56. Like Caneday, Emerson, "Arbitrary Allegory, Typical Typology," 20, finds that Paul reads the Pentateuch carefully and when "he uses the term 'allegory,' it is not to indicate that he is moving from a textual reading to one that ignores the Pentateuch's plain sense, but only to note

Therefore, while typology involves discrete historical persons, places, events and institutions, Paul chooses the term "allegory" in Gal 4:21–31 probably because he is not meditating exclusively upon discrete figures and subjects from the Genesis accounts. Instead, his attention is upon the entire narrative of the Pentateuch concerning God's promises to Abraham and a complex set of themes regarding the obstacles to his promises (the episode of Hagar; themes of barrenness, slavery) and how those promises are ultimately fulfilled in Abraham's true offspring, Jesus Christ, and not through reliance on the Law-covenant at Sinai.[68] Paul does not forge the allegory or conjure an allegorical interpretation in the manner of Philo or Origen; rather, his argument is rooted in Scripture, which can be traced.[69] As Jobes rightly concludes, "Far from being an arbitrary allegorical assignment, the association of Hagar with the 'now' Jerusalem and Sarah with the 'above' Jerusalem follows logically from Paul's understanding of Isa 54:1 in light of Christ's resurrection."[70] The interpretative moves Paul makes may seem arbitrary, but Paul's warrant for this allegory, like the typological connections he finds elsewhere, is grounded in the Scriptures and integral to the mystery theme (μυστήριον) where concealed and enigmatic features in the OT are now revealed in light of further revelation as the progress of Scripture unfolds.[71]

---

that he is expounding on the full sense and interconnectedness of these related passages." Concurring is Harmon, "Allegory, Typology, or Something Else?," 155–56, as he also notes how Gen 16–21 has patterns that point forward to greater realities.

68. I owe this insight to Ardel Caneday through personal correspondence. In this way, the allegory that Paul appeals to has a similarity to typology but has a crucial difference. The similarities include the assumption of the historicity of the figures and intertextual development that can be discovered within the OT itself. Paul's use of Isa 54:1 in discussing the Hagar-Sarah allegory is instructive in the same way the writer of Hebrews uses Psalm 110:4 in the discussion of Melchizedekian typology (Heb 7:1–10). As a discrete individual, Melchizedek is a type (Gen 14:18–20), but the difference between typology and the allegory of Gal 4:21–31 is that Paul is noticing in a broader way the allegory present in the entire narrative as he deals with Hagar, Sarah, and the Abrahamic and Mosaic covenants. Paul is not concentrating on individual elements in the Genesis narrative as *types* in Gal 4:24–27.

69. Contra Moo, *Galatians*, 294, who implies that Paul commits eisegesis when he writes that "Paul's interpretation of the Sarah/Hagar story seems to go further in the direction of an imposition of a preconceived scheme onto a text than is typical of NT interpretation of the OT." Joel Willitts wrongly asserts that Paul creates the allegory. Willitts, "Isa 54,1 in Gal 4,24b," 198, 202.

70. Jobes, "Jerusalem, Our Mother," 317.

71. Caneday, "Covenant Lineage Allegorically Prefigured," 51–53; Harmon, "Allegory, Typology, or Something Else?," 158n51. Also arguing for a warranted allegory is Starling, "Justified Allegory," 227–45.

Fourth, Appealing to the Patristics Is Not Definitive in How to Understand Biblical Typology and Interpretation

The early church fathers have made a comeback in scholarly circles with more stress on how they interpreted Scripture and defended orthodox teachings.[72] Surely drawing attention to the Patristics and their reading of Scripture is a welcome development. The understanding of typology, and more generally, the hermeneutical approach to Scripture, should be informed by earlier interpreters, but their approach is not ultimately authoritative, nor are they as significant as the NT authors. Ribbens, for example, wishes to arrive at a definition of typology that embraces "the varied τύπος interpretations of the NT and Greek fathers and not, like prefiguration typology, exclude τύπος interpretations that do not fit a preconceived definition of typology."[73] This suggestion is wrongheaded because it elevates the fathers to the same level as the NT authors, and secondly, seeks to define typology from the τύπος-word group when the nature of typology should be derived from broader considerations from Scripture than just the use of τύπος. In this way, *typology* as a term should be defined in such a way to characterize unique biblical phenomena, drawn from, but not limited to, the τύπος-word group, whereby persons, events, and institutions serve as indirect prophecies or adumbrations of future realities. Moreover, even if the patristic fathers did not distinguish between allegory or typology, that does not mean that such a distinction is necessary, legitimate, and of critical hermeneutical importance. In fact, it is this point that later interpreters, the Protestant Reformers, provide a helpful corrective to the early church figurative approach.[74]

---

72. Besides the works of Frances Young cited earlier, see also Green, ed., *Shapers of Christian Orthodoxy*; Haykin, *Rediscovering the Church Fathers*.

73. Ribbens, "Typology of Types," 85.

74. Vanhoozer, "Ascending the Mountain," 789–90, aptly writes, "I am less inclined to take descriptions of Patristic exegesis as normative for biblical interpretation today. [Ayres] may be right historically about the difficulty of distinguishing allegory and typology, but I believe some such distinction is both necessary and legitimate. I therefore propose to 'reform' (not reject!) Patristic figural interpretation. . . . The way forward—call it 'good type'—is to recover not modern historicist assumptions but rather the Protestant Reformers' habit of following typological *trajectories* (i.e., the broad sweep of redemptive history), as opposed to compiling allegorical *inventories* (i.e., a list of detailed correspondences). Note that the focus in making inventories is on the multiple referents of individual words; by contrast, what comes to the fore in following trajectories is the importance of following the whole discourse." In his critique of the TIS movement, Carson, "Theological Interpretation of Scripture," 199–200, is in a similar orbit as Vanhoozer on this point: "Speaking of learning from past thinkers of pre-critical eras, one begins to grow in respect for the Reformers who thought their

Against the Roman Catholic abuses in allegorizing Scripture, Calvin and the Reformed scholastics rejected the multiple and various senses and championed the *sensus literalis*—the literal sense that is derived from the intention of the divine and human authors, seeking to do justice to the grammatical, historical, rhetorical/literary elements of the text including figures of speech. In this way, rather than advocating multiple senses as imposed by the exegete, the distinct and separate senses of the *quadriga* had to be grafted on to the text itself as "valid applications of or conclusions drawn from the literal sense."[75] More narrowly on the subject of allegorical interpretation, the "Reformed made a strict distinction between allegories and figures that were intrinsic to the text and therefore its literal sense and allegories imposed from without by the imaginative expositor."[76] Figurative or typological meanings should be indicated by the text and identified through the analogy of Scripture. The Reformer's hermeneutic and understanding of typology serve as a guide since these principles derive from the nature of the Bible—a divine and human unified discourse that progressively unfolds—and its role as having sole authority for matters of faith. Vanhoozer rightly expounds this point:

> We can now make explicit the logic governing best typological practice. The formal principle of Protestant spiritual interpretation derives from its confession of divine authorship: read the biblical parts in light of the canonical whole (i.e., as a unified divine discourse). Divine authorship also gives rise to the material principle of spiritual interpretation: read God's involvement in Israel's history as elements in a unified history or theodrama whose climax and end is Jesus Christ. Even more succinctly: read Scripture in redemptive-historical context. The typology the Protestant Reformers practiced ultimately presupposes neither *linear* nor *sacramental* but rather *redemptive* history, where type is related to antitype as anticipation is related to its

---

way clear of fuzzy notions of allegory to a greater dependence on 'literal' interpretation (without losing a sophisticated grasp of metaphorical language), and less of TIS support for unspecified allegory." Carter, *Interpreting Scripture*, 161–90, seems to expand the literal sense interpretation to include a spiritual sense (figural, allegorical). Note his unconvincing appeal to Patristic prosopological exegesis (191–223). For a clearer presentation on the literal sense, see Provan, *Reformation and the Right Reading of Scripture*, 81–106.

75. Muller, *Holy Scripture*, 479, cf. 472–78, 480–82.

76. Muller, *Holy Scripture*, 474; cf. Vanhoozer, *Is There a Meaning*, 118–19. For analysis of Calvin's rejection of allegorical interpretations even as he did accept some allegories in practice, and his appeal to typology, see Puckett, *John Calvin's Exegesis of the Old*, 105–24. See also Carter, *Interpreting Scripture*, 183–86.

realization, promise to fulfillment. The rule, then, is never to dislodge the spiritual sense given to persons, things, and events from the biblical narratives in which they are emplotted. In the words of Hans Frei: "figuration or typology was a natural extension of literal interpretation. It was literalism at the level of the whole biblical story and thus of the depiction of the whole historical reality." To be sure, not every piece of wood figures the cross. It is the redemptive-historical context that both enables and constrains the spiritual sense. *What spiritual significance things have is not a function of their sheer createdness but rather their role in the ongoing drama of redemption.*[77]

In summary, the distinction between allegory and typology is crucial, as blending the two and deriving allegorical or typological interpretations as the terminology of *figural reading* suggests leads to theological confusion and faulty interpretative moves. Faithful readers of Scripture treat Scripture as a unified revelation, discovering God's intent by explicating what biblical authors say and interpreting Scripture with Scripture. In this manner, rather than the focus being in front of the text, the reader discovers and draws out the typologies and allegories that are in the text. This brief survey of allegory and typology indicates that Woollcombe is correct when he asserts that the similarities between allegory, typology, and prophecy "are not so close as to justify ignoring the differences between them, and using one of the terms to cover them all."[78] Maintaining these distinctions, and more importantly, understanding biblical typology and elucidating the nature of the legitimate typological patterns, makes significant headway in understanding the relationship between the OT and NT, and in turn, formulate a whole-Bible theological system that carefully addresses the thorny issues of continuity and discontinuity.

THE HALLMARKS AND CHARACTERISTICS OF TYPOLOGY

Having dispensed with the controversy associating typology and allegory, unpacking the nature of typology in its own right is a challenge as typology is debated within broader biblical studies, but also divisions occur within evangelicalism since the conception of typology and its application impacts whole theological systems. In establishing the essential features of biblical

---

77. Vanhoozer, "Ascending the Mountain," 793, emphasis original. Cf. Vanhoozer, *Is There a Meaning*, 119. For Frei, see his *Eclipse of Biblical Narrative*, 2.

78. Woollcombe, "Biblical Origins and Development," 42.

typology, first an overview of the more traditional or evangelical view of typology is offered, and then a more in-depth presentation of areas of debate within evangelicalism, for example, the extent of fulfillment in typological relationships and the identification of types is explored.

The Traditional View of Typology

Aside from the typology-allegory distinction debate among church historians and TIS proponents, in biblical and theological studies there is a general scholarly consensus that typology involves the study of historical and theological correspondences within salvation history between types—identifiable as OT persons, events, or institutions—and their counterparts in the NT (antitypes) such that a significant resemblance as well as an escalation (an *a fortiori* quality), or qualitative progression, is detected between the type and antitype.[79] There are two particular areas of clarification that proponents of a more traditional view would advance in contrast to the "post-critical neo-typology view."[80] The first addresses the nature of the historical

---

79. Hoskins, *Jesus as the Fulfillment*, 19–20; Goppelt, *Typos*, 17–18; Davidson, *Typology in Scripture*, 94–96; Gentry and Wellum, *Kingdom through Covenant*, 129–36; Hugenberger, "Introductory Notes," 337; Carson, "Mystery and Fulfillment," 404–7; McCartney and Clayton, *Let the Reader Understand*, 162–64. For examples of this general definition, see Ellis, *Paul's Use of the Old*, 127–28; Harris, "Typological Trajectories," 283–84; Achtemeier, "Typology," 926–27; Alsup, "Typology," 682–83; Osborne, "Type; Typology," 930–31; Foulkes, "Acts of God," 366–67. For a summary of typology within progressive covenantalism, see Merkle, *Discontinuity to Continuity*, 114–17. For historical surveys of how typology has been understood by key interpreters throughout church history, see Davidson, *Typology in Scripture*, 15–114, and Meek, "Toward a Biblical Typology," 12–102.

80. The terminology of "post-critical neo-typology" comes from Davidson, *Typology in Scripture*, 111. In the mid-twentieth century, representatives of post-critical neo-typology sought "to bring together elements of the traditional typology with the findings of modern critical scholarship" (Hoskins, *Jesus as the Fulfillment*, 27). According to this approach, typology is basically the result of drawing analogies or correspondences within the uniform pattern of God's activity; it possesses no prospective aspect, and typology is understood as a theological reflection and not governed by hermeneutical regulations, thus the number of types is unlimited. Critical scholars who fit within this approach include von Rad ("Typological Interpretation," 174–92); Wolff ("Hermeneutics of the Old," 160–99); Lampe and Woollcombe (*Essays on Typology*); and Goulder (*Type and History in Acts*, 1–13). Young, "Typology," 34, seems to advance Goulder's view. Some evangelicals adopted aspects of post-critical perspective, with exception to the critical view of the historicity of the type and anti-type, see France (*Jesus and the Old Testament*, 39–42); and Baker (*Two Testaments, One Bible*, 179–89). For summaries of the post-critical approach, see Ninow, *Indicators of Typology*, 36–48, and Johnson, "Pauline Typology," 26–39 and for critiques, see Davidson, *Typology in Scripture*; Hoskins, *Jesus as the Fulfillment*, 21–31; Beale, "Did Jesus and His Followers

THE NATURE, CHARACTERISTICS, AND CHALLENGES OF TYPOLOGY

correspondences and the second involves the predictive or prospective element of typology.

The Historical Correspondences of Typology

Advocates of the traditional understanding of typology insist on the facticity of both the type and antitype as the typological OT persons, events, institutions, and settings/places are understood as historical realities.[81] The assumption is that while the Bible is not a textbook of history, the historical narratives, however selective in terms of what was decided to be written and how it was to be arranged, do bestow a true recording of history as the events occurred.[82] The historical dimension is important, for types are not abstract symbols or metaphors of spiritual ideas but genuine historical realities; real persons and events that have been recorded accurately to reflect the historical Jesus.[83] Adhering to special divine revelation in history contrasts sharply from most post-critical scholars where typology is planted within a framework of theologically informed history or historical traditions.[84]

A second clarification in regard to the nature of the correspondences is also important for proponents of a more traditional conception of biblical

Preach?," 395–402.

81. Davidson, *Typology in Scripture*, 96; Yoshikawa, "Prototypical Use," 23; Chase, *40 Questions about Typology and Allegory*, 65–68. Legarth, "Typology and its Theological Basis," 149, writes, "The message of the type is closely determined by the concrete historical reality of the type in question. It is precisely in a concrete historical reality that God reveals himself." Ounsworth, *Joshua Typology*, 52, notes historical reality validates typology as the "divinely-ordained culmination of the lives and history of the people of Israel, and its legitimacy springs from the record of that history, which is presupposed to be an accurate record."

82. For evangelical discussions of the historicity of events recorded in the Bible, see Goldsworthy, *Gospel-Centered Hermeneutics*, 217–33, 245; Carson, *Collected Writings on Scripture*, 25–26; Kaiser and Silva, *Introduction to Biblical Hermeneutics*, 107–19.

83. Hoskins, *Jesus as the Fulfillment*, 27; cf. Stek, "Biblical Typology," 160–61. Philpot, "See the True and Better Adam," 90–102, demonstrates that the Adam-Christ typological relationship demands that Adam is a historical person. Davidson, *Typology in Scripture*, 421, rightly observes that historical realities of the typological patterns are an indispensable part of the NT authors' presentation of typology.

84. For example, Goulder, *Type and History*, 182, claims that the more a passage or incident is completely or almost wholly accounted for on typological grounds, the less likely the passage is historically factual. The historicity of types is also unnecessary for von Rad, "Typological Interpretation," 188, who separated the historical facts from the biblical kerygma. Further, "Typological interpretation has to do only with the witness to the divine event, not with the correspondences in historical, cultural or archaeological details as the Old Testament and the New may have in common" (190).

typology. For the post-critical neo-typology school, the salvation historical correspondences are "brought about by the recurring rhythm of the divine activity"[85] or through the "structural analogies"[86] by which biblical writers re-actualize earlier events experienced as divine revelation into new situations.[87] Typology becomes the application of parallel circumstances, being "seen as a common human way of analogical thinking which in Scripture (and in the [neo-typological] approach) involves the recognition of correspondences within God's consistent activity in salvation history."[88] Analogies or illustrations from the OT do appear in the NT as was highlighted in the previous discussion of 1 Cor 9:9–10.[89] Typological models or patterns

85. Lampe, "Reasonableness of Typology," 29, and elsewhere describes typology similarly as the recognition of the pattern "of the continuous process of the acts of God." Lampe, "Typological Exegesis," 202; cf. Woollcombe, "Biblical Origins and Development," 49. Foulkes, "Acts of God," also stresses the repetition of God's acts in history. France, *Jesus and the Old Testament*, 39, states that "typology is essentially the tracing of the constant principles of God's working in history." Likewise, Baker, *Two Testaments, One Bible*, 180. Wright, *Knowing Jesus*, 114, views typology as a matter of analogy and the repeating patterns of God's activity in history.

86. Von Rad, *Old Testament Theology*, 2:363; cf. Stek, "Biblical Typology," 149. For summaries of von Rad's approach to typology alongside Stek's review, see Ninow, *Indicators of Typology*, 37–39, and Meek, "Toward a Biblical Typology," 67–69.

87. Barr, "Biblical Theology," 108, describes von Rad's work of separating out different groups of OT traditions, since there was no unified OT theology. Stek, "Biblical Theology," 153; cf.156–57, finds that for von Rad, "Typology belongs, therefore, not to the *historia revelationis*—because of the discontinuity of the divine acts of God in history no such history exists—but to the *historia theologiae* which arose in Israel and the church in response to a series of events experienced as a series of divine revelations climaxing in Jesus Christ. Here typology is understood as an element in which the human response to events experienced as divine revelation which evoke new religious forms and new theological reflection within a particular religious and theological tradition."

88. Davidson, *Typology in Scripture*, 74. Examples of Davidson's summation abound. Von Rad, *Old Testament Theology*, 2:364, states, "[Typology] rises out of man's universal effort to understand the phenomena about him on the basis of concrete analogies"; cf. Wolff, "Hermeneutics of the Old," 180. For Frye, *Great Code*, 226, the antitype begins in the reader's mind. For Lampe, "Reasonableness of Typology," 19, the NT authors "felt free to modify the details of the narrative tradition in order to bring out the meaning which it possessed for them when it was expressed in imagery derived from the Old Testament history." France describes the typological correspondence as both "historical (*i.e.* a correspondence of situation and event) and theological (*i.e.* an embodiment of the same principle of God's working)" with the consistent principle of God's working involving "two persons or events that present a recognizable analogy to each other." France, *Jesus and the Old Testament*, 41, emphasis original. See also Baker, *Two Testaments, One Bible*, 180; Wright, *Knowing Jesus*, 111–13.

89. Beale, *Handbook*, 67–71, also refers to Jezebel in Rev 2:20 and the reference of the rich in Rev 3:17–18 as other examples of analogy from the OT. Many direct links are drawn between the God of Israel and Jesus (such as the "I am" statements in the Gospel of John). Similarly, analogies between Israel and the church are drawn as

however, while involving resemblance and analogy, are much more. The historical correspondences possess the mark of divine design and are not essentially a natural analogy formed by human thought processes or ingenuity. Addressing the notion of typology as essentially that of similarity with OT facts comparable to NT events, Ellis asserts,

> For the NT writers a type has not merely the property of 'typicalness' or similarity; they view Israel's history as *Heilsgeschichte*, and the significance of an OT type lies in its particular *locus* in the Divine plan of redemption. When Paul speaks of the Exodus events happening τυπικῶς and written 'for our admonition' [in 1 Cor 10:11; cf. Rom 15:4], there can be no doubt that, in the apostle's mind, Divine intent is of the essence both in their occurrence and in their inscripturation.[90]

In other words, the correspondences between type and antitype, developing along the repetition of "promise-fulfillment" patterns through redemptive history, are designed, established, and governed by God as he molds unique details of history for his purposes.[91] Typological relationships are not conveniently forged by theological reflection or by cleverly pinpointing analogical features between earlier and later people and events; rather, grounded in God's providence and ordination, OT types are invested by God to resemble and foreshadow greater things to come. The scriptural presentation of types "are both divinely appointed to occur and divinely authorized

---

Israel is pictured as the bride of Yahweh (Jer 2:2; Hos 2:14–20) and the church is called the bride of Christ (2 Cor 11:2; Eph 5:32). For further discussion and examples, see Greidanus, *Preaching Christ*, 220–22.

90. Ellis, *Paul's Use of the Old*, 127, emphasis original; see also Terry, *Biblical Hermeneutics*, 247–48; Fairbairn, *Typology of Scripture*, 1:46; Fritsch, "Biblical Typology," 214–15; Goppelt, *Typos*, 18, 130; Hoskins, *Jesus as the Fulfillment*, 21; Johnson, *Walking with Jesus*, 73–74.

91. Gentry and Wellum, *Kingdom through Covenant*, 131–33; Lints, *Fabric of Theology*, 306; Carson, "Mystery and Fulfillment," 406; Chase, *40 Questions about Typology and Allegory*, 41–44. The notion of typology involving the identification of God's recurring activity in history is correct, but does not go far enough. Currid, "Recognition and Use of Typology," 128; cf. 121, rightly stresses that "typology underscores the doctrine of the sovereignty of God. It teaches that the Lord has sovereignly planned history with a unified purpose so that what God has done in the past becomes the measure of the future. He has simply designed history in such a way that certain patterns repeat themselves." Ounsworth, *Joshua Typology*, 40, writes, "What all these correspondences do have in common, however, is at least implicitly the notion that they are all determined by the divine will: it is of the nature of God's providence that he should . . . stamp salvation history and religious practices of his people with the character of his saving power, making them reflections of his heavenly glory. The correspondences are of the nature of things, revealed but not created by the way in which the Old Testament is written."

as written. Revelatory foreshadowing divine appointments of correlative NT persons, events, and institutions, and places is *what* we should accept as an apt description of biblical types."[92] Readers of Scripture must find textual warrant and exegetical evidence for identifying the divinely intended types present in the text since such patterns are embedded therein and are not fancifully derived from a reading strategy or hermeneutic.

The Debate on the Prospective Nature of Typology

The debate with respect to the divine intent of the typological correspondences goes hand in hand with one of the primary controversies in typological studies. Are OT types by nature prospective, being advance prefigurations, effectively foreshadowing later patterns in history, or are they retrospective in that later biblical authors, particularly the NT authors, looked back to OT texts in light of the work of Christ and through the empowerment of the Spirit and thereby forged typological connections? More simply, Moo asks, "Does the Old Testament type have a genuinely predictive function, or is typology simply a way of looking back at the Old Testament and drawing out resemblances?"[93]

A traditional conception of biblical typology affirms that the original prototypes and types in Scripture possess a prospective or prophetic-predictive quality leading to the antitype. God has orchestrated his sovereign plan such that through the progress of revelation, "certain Old Testament events, persons, and institutions would prefigure New Testament events, persons, and institutions."[94] OT types are prospective in that they are advanced presentations, predicting, and pointing forward to the antitypical fulfillment and eschatological realities in Christ.[95] On the other hand,

---

92. Caneday, "Biblical Types," 147 (emphasis original).

93. Moo, "Problem of *Sensus Plenior*," 196.

94. Hoskins, *Jesus as the Fulfillment*, 21; cf. 186–87. For others advancing typology as prospective/predictive/prophetic, refer to footnote 31 above and see Carson, "Mystery and Fulfillment," 405–6; Davidson, *Typology in Scripture*, 95, 401–8; Beale, "Did Jesus and His Followers Preach?," 395–98, 401; Goppelt, *Typos*, 17–18, 226–27; Fairbairn, *Typology of Scripture*, 1:145–50; Ramm, *Protestant Biblical Interpretation*, 227–28; Markus, "Presuppositions of the Typological Approach," 447, 450; Waltke, "Kingdom Promises as Spiritual," 277–78; Bock, "Single Meaning, Multiple Contexts," 118–20; Naselli, *From Typology to Doxology*, 126–27; Legarth, "Typology and Its Theological Basis," 145–46; LaRondelle, *Israel of God*, 47, 52–55; Ninow, *Indicators of Typology*, 93–97, 242–46; Lints, *Fabric of Theology*, 306; Vos, *Biblical Theology*, 146; Currid, "Recognition and Use of Typology," 120–21; McCartney and Clayton, *Let the Reader Understand*, 159–74.

95. This point does not mean that the particular OT people, institutions, events,

THE NATURE, CHARACTERISTICS, AND CHALLENGES OF TYPOLOGY

post-critical neo-typology advocates do not find types to be predictive or prophetic in any way. Instead, the biblical writers apprehended the typological relationship retrospectively. A type has no forward reference to the future nor is it predictive.[96] The retrospective aspect of typology is clearly emphasized in France's study:

> [The] antitype [is not] the fulfillment of a prediction; it is rather the re-embodiment of a principle which has been previously exemplified in the type. A prediction looks forward to, and demands, an event which is to be its fulfillment; typology, however, consists essentially in looking back and discerning previous examples of a pattern now reaching its culmination.... The idea of fulfillment inherent in New Testament typology derives not from a belief that the events so understood were explicitly predicted, but from a conviction that in the coming and work of Jesus the principles of God's working, already imperfectly embodied in the Old Testament, were more perfectly re-embodied, and thus brought to completion.[97]

Similarly, for Richard Hays's proposal for figural reading, the Gospel writers looked backwards in light of the cross and resurrection, "reading retrospectively under the guidance of the Spirit and discerning new significances that *no one* could have predicted."[98] In addition, the OT types could not be prospective or prefigure something future because that would entail an additional meaning that was hidden from the OT authors.[99] For

---

and actions that are typological lose value and significance in their own redemptive historical setting. On the significance of earlier events see Hays, *Echoes of Scripture*, 100.

96. Baker, *Two Testaments, One Bible*, 181; France, *Jesus and the Old Testament*, 41. Von Rad, "Typological Interpretation," 189–90, understands typology apart from prospective prophecy. See also Eichrodt, "Is Typological Exegesis an Appropriate Method?," 229.

97. France, *Jesus and the Old Testament*, 40. France also speaks of the characteristics of typology as incorporating numerous applications of Old Testament passages which have no forward reference. Jesus could use non-predictive passages in a way which implied or explicitly stated that they were "fulfilled" in his coming. France, *Jesus and the Old Testament*, 42.

98. Hays, "Figural Exegesis and the Retrospective Re-cognition," 40 (emphasis added). Hays later adds that the Gospels "presuppose and require the recognition that Jesus's fulfillment of scriptural prefigurations comes as a poetic surprise, a surprise that *reconfigures* our understanding of the precursor texts and transforms any conscious intention of the OT authors" (p. 43; emphasis original).

99. Baker, *Two Testaments, One Bible*, 181, 187–89; France, *Jesus and the Old Testament*, 41–42; cf. Foulkes, "Acts of God," 369–70. Hence, for the post-critical neo-typology position, typology is not a part of exegesis since true meaning and intention

still others, typology involves both prospective and retrospective aspects. Greidanus, for example, says the answer "is not an either-or but a both-and: some Old Testament types are predictive and others are not. I suspect that most types are not predictive, but specific persons or events are later seen to have typological significance."[100]

The problem with the debate regarding the prospective versus retrospective quality of typology has to do with what is meant by "retrospective." This is best illustrated by the recent studies of G. K. Beale. In his programmatic essay outlining the presuppositions of Jesus' and the NT authors' exegetical method, Beale classifies typology as indirect prophecy but at the same time suggests that the "New Testament correspondence would be drawing out retrospectively the fuller prophetic meaning of the Old Testament type which was originally included by the divine author."[101] In more recent writings, Beale argues for "retrospection" as an essential characteristic of typology, but not in the way that France and Baker do. For Beale, retrospection carries

> the idea that it was after Christ's resurrection and under the direction of the Spirit that the apostolic writers understood certain OT historical narratives about persons, events, or institutions to be indirect prophecies of Christ or the Church. A qualification ... [is that] there is evidence of the foreshadowing nature of the OT narrative itself, which then is better understood after the coming of Christ.[102]

---

of the original text can only be what the human author intended. Typology is more of a theological reflection or application. Moo argues that "typology is not an exegetical technique, nor even a hermeneutical axiom, but a broad theological construct with hermeneutical implications." Moo, "Paul's Universalizing Hermeneutic," 82; cf. 81. See also LaRondelle, *Israel of God*, 45–46, as he follows Foulkes and argues that typology "is the theological-christological interpretation of the Old Testament history by the New Testament, which goes beyond mere exegesis."

100. Greidanus, *Preaching Christ*, 253. Others who opt for a middle position include Osborne, "Type; Typology," 931; and Hamilton, "Typology of David's Rise to Power," 6, seems to go in this direction by concurring with Osborne "that more needs to be said about *how* and *when* these types would have been understood as pointing forward" (emphasis original). In his latest work, Hamilton, *Typology*, does not discuss typology as prospective or as indirect prophecy but finds that types are God-ordained and providentially ensured (see p. 26). Hays, "Figural Exegesis and the Retrospective Re-cognition," 40–43, allows for prospective or predictive prophecy but the vast majority of examples of figural reading are retrospective.

101. Beale, "Did Jesus and His Followers Preach?," 401. Similarly, Bock, *Proclamation from Prophecy and Pattern*, 291–92n124.

102. Beale, *Handbook*, 14–15; cf. 17–19, 23–24, 98; Beale, "Use of Hosea 11:1," 699; and Beale, "Finding Christ in the OT," 29–30. Similar to Beale on this score is D. A. Carson, who articulates that Hos 11 fits within a "messianic matrix" that points

THE NATURE, CHARACTERISTICS, AND CHALLENGES OF TYPOLOGY

Beale's comments indicate that there needs to be clarity in what is meant when the terms "prospective" and "retrospective" are applied in the discussion regarding biblical typology. As I will argue, the OT types and prototypes are by their very nature (ontologically) prospective since they are divinely designed by God, just as proponents of the traditional approach propose. However, when OT types were discerned to be typological from an epistemological point of view is a distinct issue. Certain types may be retrospective in the sense that the NT writers, and in turn subsequent Bible readers, recognize them through the benefit of later revelation and in light of the fulfillment in Christ. The original OT authors and audience did not have the complete revelatory picture, which means the ultimate significance was not revealed to them; they only had a vague perception of the anticipatory nature and import of OT types (1 Pet 1:10–12). Whether Abraham or Moses' audience, for example, understood the full import of Melchizedek in the context of Gen 14 to be typological of the Messiah may be difficult to discern, but given the inner-textual development of Melchizedek in Ps 110, there is additional revelation that God intended him to point forward to Christ (Heb 7). The Latter Prophets would have had much more clarity than Moses or Joshua just as the NT authors were granted significantly more insight into God's plan than the prophets would have had.

If OT types are retrospective in an ontological sense though, then they surely are not God-intended anymore, the type-antitype relationship becomes a mere analogy of human thinking and potentially arbitrary given the theological principles one uses to make such connections. The danger is that if typological patterns are retrospectively constructed by the reader, then one has entered onto the path of allegorizing. On the other hand, just because some types are recognized from a retrospective standpoint does not mean that the types themselves were not prospective and intended by God.[103] When the type is exegetically discovered to be a type either in the

---

forward to Jesus Christ even as Matthew (Matt 2:15) draws the "fuller meaning" from Hos 11:1 via the retrospective clarity that comes with the unfolding of salvation history. Carson, *Matthew 1–12*, 92–93.

103. Carson, "Mystery and Fulfillment," 405–6. For Carson, the divine intention of the types means that "when Paul (or, for that matter, some other New Testament writer) claims that something or other connected with the gospel is the (typological) fulfillment of some old covenant pattern, he may not necessarily be claiming that everyone connected with the covenant type understood the pattern to be pointing forward, but he is certainly claiming that God himself designed it to be pointing forward. In other words, *when* the type was *discovered* to be a type (at some point along the trajectory of its repeated pattern? only after its culmination?)—i.e. when it was discovered to be a pattern that pointed to the future—is not determinative for its classification as a type." See Carson, "Mystery and Fulfillment," 406, emphasis original.

immediate context or through inter-biblical development in the canon of Scripture, then the God-given typological pattern is warranted and as an advance presentation designed by God, fits within the promise-fulfillment structure of God's plan. Types are in the text, and readers do not construct typological patterns any more than later biblical authors confer something as a type, even though later authors may develop a pattern that provides more clarity in recognizing it as a type. Affirming typology as prospective by nature (ontology), while qualifying that some of the types are grasped or identified in hindsight, retrospectively in terms of epistemological justification, is a crucial issue that has unfortunately been a point of confusion.[104]

Having offered clarity on what I mean by "retrospective," there still remains the question of whether types are by nature prospective. In terms of passages that explicitly make typological references in the NT, the prospective aspect and divine intentionality of the type-antitype correspondence appear. Romans 5:14 (cf. 1 Cor 15:20–22, 45–49) and 1 Cor 10 serve as just two examples. In the former passage, Paul notes that Adam was a type *of the one to come*. "The reference to 'the coming one' (τοῦ μέλλοντος)," argues Schreiner, "should be understood from the perspective of Adam. In other words, from Adam's standpoint in history Jesus Christ was the one to come. . . ."[105] Adam is an advance presentation of Christ. God has superintended that the first man, Adam, would prefigure Christ. The prospective aspect is also clear in 1 Cor 10:6, 11. When the events "took place as types of us" (1 Cor 10:6) "in Israel's history God had already imbued them 'as types of'

---

104. I owe this insight to Stephen Wellum in our conversations around the time of the publication of the first edition of *Kingdom through Covenant* (2012). For Wellum's added treatment of this point in the second edition, see *Kingdom through Covenant*, 131–33, esp. 132n64. Others have picked up on Wellum's important distinction between prospective and retrospective. See DeRouchie et al., *40 Questions about Biblical Theology*, 83–84. Chase, *40 Questions about Typology and Allegory*, 59–62, also highlights this point but without reference to *Kingdom through Covenant*. Moo, "Problem of Sensus Plenior," 197, rightly concludes "that typology does have a 'prospective' element, but the 'prospective' nature of specific Old Testament incidents could often be recognized only retrospectively. . . . [T]he prospective element in many Old Testament types, though intended by God in a general sense, would not have been recognized at the time by the Old Testament authors or the original audience." See also Moo and Naselli, "Problem of the NT's Use of the Old," 729. Cf. Naselli, *From Typology to Doxology*, 127; Hoskins, *Jesus as the Fulfillment*, 25–26.

105. Schreiner, *Romans*, 285. Similarly Moo, *Romans*, 361, finds that the "future tense is probably used because Paul is viewing Christ's work from the perspective of Adam." For a helpful discussion of Rom 5:12–21 as divinely ordained prefiguration, see Johnson, "Pauline Typology," 64–68. That Adam is a type is grounded in how Gen 3:15 connects with Gen 1–2 and additionally, implicit confirmation is found in later OT indicators (Ps 8:4–8 [cf. Heb 2:6–8] and Dan 7:13–14).

Messiah and his latter-day people."[106] The episodes of Israel in the wilderness happened typologically or occurred typologically (τυπικῶς συνέβαινεν) and were written down for the instruction of Christians. Davidson's discussion of this text is significant:

> Paul is not saying that the events can now be seen to be τυπικῶς—as if they *became* τύποι as a result of some later occurrence or factor. Rather, Paul insists that in their very happening, they were happening τυπικῶς. The τύποι-quality of the events was inherent in their occurrence, not invented by the Pentateuchal historiographer or artificially given "typical" significance by Paul the exegete. The divine intent of the events clearly includes the τύπος-nature of the event. A providential design was operative, causing the events to happen τυπικῶς. The OT events enumerated by Paul are not presented as τύποι just because of the continuity of God's actions and purposes at all times, as true and fundamental as that is. There is involved also the Lordship of Yahweh, molding unique details of history.[107]

In analyzing 1 Cor 10:1–13, Rom 5:12–19, and Rom 4, Roehrs also finds that what

> happened in the Old Testament is not merely an illustration of how God acts consistently in certain or similar circumstances and at various times. The analogy is bound up in the determinate

---

106. Caneday, "Biblical Types," 148.

107. Davidson, *Typology in Scripture*, 268; see Caneday, "Biblical Types," 148–49; Fritsch, "Biblical Typology," 88–90; Johnson, "Pauline Typology," 68–74; Kaiser, *Uses of the Old Testament in the New*, 111–21; contra the minimalistic outlook of Drane, "Typology," 201, and Perriman, "Typology in Paul," 200–206. Perriman wrongly concludes from 1 Cor the following: "There is little evidence that Paul worked with a clear model of typological exegesis and in many cases it seems that the perceived correlations are illustrative or metaphorical rather than typological" ("Typology in Paul," 205). Johnson, *Him We Proclaim*, 204, rightly states that "Paul views Israel's desert experience as history-embedded foreshadowing of the church's privilege and trial in the new covenant." In addition, Schreiner and Caneday, *Race Set before Us*, 223, make a similar observation: "Paul holds the Israelites before the Corinthians, because he understands that God designed Israel's rebellion and their consequences as foreshadows or types to warn Christians and to deliver us to the promised land of salvation in the last day." They also helpfully observe that Paul restricts the foreshadowing in 1 Cor 10:12 since the church is faced with the same critical moments as Israel was, and so the typological relationship does not mean that the church will reenact Israel's rebellion. Schreiner and Caneday, *Race Set before Us*, 224. Israel's unfaithfulness and failure serve as a warning, and ultimately anticipate the perseverance and faithfulness of the new covenant people of God.

counsel of God, conceived before the foundations of the world and carried out in the course of time.[108]

While there is a recurring pattern or rhythm to God's consistent activity in redemptive history as the post-critical neo-typology advocates emphasize, this does not exhaust what typology is. Paul perceived the forward reference of the types because he found the intentionality and voice of God in the OT (e.g., Gal 3:8); the repeated typological patterns are found in Scripture, which is understood to be the product of divine self-disclosure.

For a passage more indirectly typological, Todd Scacewater has demonstrated that the typological link between the rejection of Isaiah's ministry and the rejection of Jesus' ministry presented in John 12:37–43 is of a prospective nature.[109] John 12:37–43 features two citations from Isaiah (Isa 53:1 in John 12:38 and Isa 6:10 in 12:40) and an allusion to Deut 29:2–4 (in John 12:37), a passage that is alluded to in Isa 6:9–10 as well. The allusion to Deut 29:2–4 is important in establishing a prototypical pattern, for even though Israel had seen the wonders and signs that God had accomplished in redeeming them from Egypt (Exod 6:6; Neh 9:10) under Moses' leadership, yet the people were stubborn, obstinate, and rebellious because of hardened hearts. The pattern of obstinacy continues alongside the motif of prophetic rejection (see Luke 11:47; Acts 7:52; 1 Thess 2:15; cf. Neh 9:26) with both themes coming together with the rejection of Isaiah and his message (Isa 53:1; 6:10).[110] These twin themes of prophetic rejection

---

108. Roehrs, "Typological Use of the Old," 206. Note also Carson, "Mystery and Fulfillment," 405: "Paul and some other New Testament writers understand [typological patterns] to point to the future. In other words, they are not merely convenient analogies on which later writers may draw, but recurrent patterns pointing forward to a culminating repetition of the pattern. This presupposes that God himself is directing the pattern toward the end; it does not presuppose that early observers in the cycle of patterns necessarily understood this anticipatory or predictive function." For the prospective nature of other NT passages explicitly typological (Heb 8:5, 9:24; 1 Pet 3:21), see Davidson, *Typology in Scripture*. If the two axes of typology, the revelatory-spatial and historical-temporal (vertical and horizontal typology), cohere and are inseparable, then types must be prospective, for the prophetic or anticipatory function derives not from the temporal axis but from the revelatory-spatial axis as God assigns and authorizes the types to be earthly copies and shadows of heavenly realities. So Caneday, "God's Parabolic Design for Israel's Tabernacle," 105–6, 119–20.

109. Scacewater, "Predictive Nature," 129–43; see also Tabb, "Johannine Fulfillment of Scripture," 495–505, esp. 501–3.

110. Scacewater, "Predictive Nature," 135–36. Köstenberger, "John," 477, explains that the "internal logic connecting both passages [Isa 53:1 and Isa 6:10] is that the people's rejection of God's servant depicted in Isa. 53 is predicated upon their spiritual hardening mentioned in Isa. 6:10." Tabb, "Johannine Fulfillment of Scripture," 502, also observes additional links in the broader context of these passages.

and spiritual rebellion in the midst of signs and wonders find intensified realization and fulfillment in Jesus' day as the Jews reject him, ultimately to the point of pursuing and being complicit in his death, despite the many signs he performed before them. The prospective or prophetic element of Israel's unbelief is evident because John says their unbelief was "in order that" the word of Isaiah might be fulfilled (John 12:38) and because Isaiah decreed (John 12:39-40) that God would judicially harden corporate Israel due to their predilection for idolatry.[111] While some view John 12:37-43 as an appeal to direct prophetic proof of Jesus' rejection—certainly the servant of Isa 53:1 is a prophetic figure—nevertheless, the focus of the citations is upon Isaiah and his rejected message, which should be understood as typological of the climactic servant-prophet whose mission and message would also be rejected (Isa 53:4-8).[112] Thus, Isaiah's ministry was designed by God to point forward to the rejection of a greater prophet, the servant of the Lord. Indeed, the people "could not" believe in Jesus (John 12:39), as Scacewater explains,

> because the typological pattern established by Isaiah *must* be fulfilled by the intended antitype, or the Scriptures would be broken. This demonstrates John's understanding that typology is predictive by nature.... This interesting interweaving of typology and direct prophecy suggests that John sees the two as closely related.[113]

In summary, God has stamped certain persons, events, and institutions to point forward as advance presentations of the greater realities tied to the person and work of Christ. Types are prospective by nature even if

---

111. For discussion as to why the ἵνα in John 12:38 should be understood as having telic force instead of be taken as resultant, and for the stronger claim as to why the Jews could not believe because (ὅτι) of what Isa 6:10 says (John 12:39), see Scacewater, "Predictive Nature," 132-34, 137-38; Tabb, "Johannine Fulfillment of Scripture," 501; and Carson, *John*, 447-48.

112. Köstenberger, "John," 478: "The typology extends not only to the linkage between Isaiah and his message, on the one hand, and Jesus and his message on the other, but also to the rejection of Isaiah's message by his contemporaries and the rejection of Jesus' message and signs ('arm of the Lord') by the same trajectory of people." Scacewater, "Predictive Nature," 142, nicely summarizes John's appropriation of Isaiah and Deuteronomy: "John's apologetic argument, proven from the OT Scriptures themselves is threefold: (1) the Scripture necessitated the rejection of Jesus because of the established typological pattern of prophetic rejection; (2) God's ensuring this rejection is righteous because of Israel's consistent obduracy; (3) Isaiah prophesied that the Servant (who is Jesus) would be the intended antitype of this typological pattern."

113. Scacewater, "Predictive Nature," 142-43 (emphasis original). For further on John's appropriation of OT texts and hermeneutical axioms as being primarily typological, see Carson, "John and the Johannine Epistles," 249-56.

Bible readers come to recognize or discover the God intended typological pattern retrospectively. Even with the retrospective epistemological recognition, the types are not retrospective by nature and thus typology should not be characterized as a common way of human thinking by constructing structural similarities or analogies. Lastly, more could be added to the examples of Adam (Rom 5:12), the events following the exodus (1 Cor 10:6, 11), and the rejection of Isaiah's message (John 12:37–43). The exodus, temple, sacrificial system, flood, offices of prophet, priest, king, along with Moses, David, Solomon, and more are all types of the good things to come (Heb 10:1; Col 2:17).

THE NATURE OF TYPOLOGICAL FULFILLMENT

The contours of biblical typology, as discussed, consist of genuine historical correspondences, featuring some detailed parallel between the type and anti-type, which are of a prospective nature because God designed OT types to prefigure and point forward to NT antitypes. Since the OT types are by nature prospective, there is a "must needs be" quality to the typological pattern as the OT pre-presentation implies that the NT antitypical presentation will occur.[114] This leads to another critical characteristic of typology: the aspect of *heightening* and *escalation* as the type looks forward to fulfillment.[115] The OT type and NT antitype are not on the same plane as there is an element of intensification or qualitative progression. Matthew 12, for example, provides the explicit *a fortiori* quality of typological patterns as Jesus says he is greater than the temple (v. 6), greater than Jonah (v. 41), and greater than Solomon (v. 42). Many other examples abound. As the true bread from heaven, Jesus is greater than the manna provided in the wilderness as those who feed on him will not perish (John 6:32–50). The Passover anticipates the supreme Passover Lamb (1 Cor 5:7).[116] Jesus is the second

---

114. Davidson, "Nature [and Identity]," 10; Davidson, *Typology in Scripture*, 223, 285, 309–10, 332, 352, 402.

115. See Gentry and Wellum, *Kingdom through Covenant*, 134–35, and Schreiner, *Hebrews*, 36–45, for a helpful discussion of the escalation of typological patterns. Cf. Goppelt, *Typos*, 18, 177, 199–202, 220; Foulkes, "Acts of God," 356; Davidson, "Eschatological Hermeneutic," 36–44; Hoskins, *That Scripture Might Be Fulfilled*, 23; Beale, *Handbook*, 14, 17. Davidson, "Nature [and Identity]," 7, rightly specifies that this aspect of typology is in "contradistinction to *paraenesis*, which is giving advice or warning using some example as a model, but with no higher correspondence." Goppelt, *Typos*, 126, makes this point as well. One possible exception of the movement from a lesser entity (the type) to a greater one (the antitype) would be the vertical typology presented in the epistle to the Hebrews.

116. Passover typology is developed throughout John's Gospel. See Hoskins,

Adam, the Messianic Davidic king, and the new Moses, which all entail a heightened realization of the OT type. The OT typical persons, events, institutions, and experiences were preparatory then, foreshadowing better and greater realities of the redemption and salvation of the new covenant age, the inaugurated kingdom of Christ, and the new creation.

Escalation and Fulfillment: The Christotelic and Eschatological Orientation of Typology

Undergirding this crucial component of escalation of typological patterns in Scripture is the nature of progressive revelation as God's plan unfolds with the OT's thoroughly eschatological outlook (Gen 3:15 being the starting place). The OT prototypes and types are preparatory, having their goal, end, climax, and terminus in Jesus Christ and/or the new covenant age he inaugurates. The heightening and escalation of typology in relation to the storyline of Scripture is thoughtfully summarized by Lints:

> First, there was a repetition of the promise-fulfillment pattern of redemptive history: God would be continually faithful to his people and to his promises. Second, there was a difference of degree between the former acts of God and the new ones: the fulfillment of God's promises would be even better than the recipients of the original promise had foreseen.[117]

Fritsch captures the point with this analogy:

> The idea of growth in the process of revelation from the less to the more, from the imperfect to the perfect, from the type to antitype is characteristic also of the realm of nature. The relation of the bud to the flower, the acorn to the oak, the embryo to

---

"Deliverance from Death by the True Passover Lamb," 285–99.

117. Lints, *Fabric of Theology*, 305. Cf. Stek, "Biblical Typology," 162. Hoskins, *Jesus as the Fulfillment*, 20, states, "Typology is often connected . . . along a trajectory involving promise and fulfillment. Such a movement is already evident in the Old Testament itself. . . . God's previous dealings with his people became patterns for his future dealings with his people. Thus Old Testament prophets 'looked for a new David, a new Exodus, a new covenant, a new city of God.' In doing so, they were anticipating the ultimate fulfillment of God's promises. Thus the future realities anticipated by the prophets would not merely serve to repeat the past, but would be greater than the patterns or types that preceded them." The brief citation in Hoskin's quote comes from von Rad, *Old Testament Theology*, 2:322–23. This notion of promise-fulfillment does not deny that there were partial fulfillments of the promises within the OT itself.

the child, and the child to the man all bear witness to a unifying principle amid laws of change.[118]

Redemptive history with its teleological trajectory—biblical history being linear and directed to its eschatological goal—serves as the theological underpinning of typology. Thus, the OT types, while having imperfections such as spiritual flaws or moral failings (OT typical persons; e.g., David) and lacking spiritual efficacy (OT typical institutions, events; e.g., the sacrificial system, the exodus; see Rom 3:21–26),[119] were stamped as indirect prophetic adumbrations anticipating a future, but in view of God's grand prophetic and covenantal promises, an intensified and escalated future with the coming of the messianic era as Christ "fills up" all that the OT types lacked.[120]

Typological patterns, then, have a christological and eschatological orientation. The escalation is intrinsic to the nature of the coming of Christ

---

118. Fritsch, "Biblical Typology," 214. On the organic nature of progressive revelation moving from seed-form to tree, see Vos, *Biblical Theology*, 7–8 and Lints, *Fabric of Theology*, 309. Contra Baker, *Two Testaments, One Bible*, 179–83; Baker, "Typology," 152–53, who recognizes the progression from the OT to the NT, but denies the heightening or escalating characteristic of typology. Baker fails to understand that typological patterns develop along the axis of redemptive history and he reduces them to mere analogical or theological correspondences. But this misses how typological structures are embedded within the fabric of redemptive history and are inextricably linked to the promise-fulfillment structure of Scripture. All explicit typological patterns in the NT possess this important attribute.

119. The imperfections of the OT types in comparison to the NT antitypes is indicated by the use of the word "shadow" in Heb 10:1 and Col 2:17 while the usage of the word "true" in association of NT antitypes denotes that which is true and genuine in completing what preceded it (so John 1:9, 6:32; Heb 8:2 and 9:24). For Rom 3:21–26, see Gentry and Wellum, *Kingdom through Covenant*, 727–29.

120. Moo and Naselli, "Problem of the NT's Use of the Old," 710–11; Beale, "Did Jesus and His Followers Preach?," 396. Harris, "Typological Trajectories," 284, uses the term *typological trajectory* "to describe the [NT] author's appropriation and development of typologies already established within the Old Testament to show their eschatological culmination in Christ." Rightly, Davidson, "Nature [and Identity]," 8, avers, "Christ and His work of salvation is thus the ultimate orientation point of OT types and their NT fulfillments." Similarly, Goldsworthy, *Gospel-Centered Hermeneutics*, 243, states, "The heart of the antitype in the New Testament is the person and work of Jesus Christ, and especially the resurrection." Unfortunately, Philpot, "Was Joseph a Type of Daniel?," 681–96, wrongly concludes that Daniel is the antitype of Joseph—a new Joseph—based on thematic, linguistic, and sequential event correspondences (following the methodology of Hamilton). While there is enough evidence that Daniel is analogous to Joseph in many ways, their placement in the OT storyline means that there is no significant escalation between Joseph and Daniel. There is no sense in which Daniel is some form of fulfillment of Joseph as a type. While there is much emphasis on typology in biblical scholarship, the category of analogy deserves to have its place.

and the ushering in of the last days which Christians now live (Heb 1:2; Acts 2:16–17). While not all typological patterns are directly Christocentric—the flood typology of 1 Pet 3:18–22 does not have its antitype in the person of Christ but to water baptism and cosmic judgment—all OT types have a *Christotelic* emphasis as they are qualified by their relationship to Jesus, his redemptive work, and the consummation of the new heavens and earth.[121] In other words, all typological patterns either converge or are channeled through Jesus Christ in some way. Jesus is the preeminent antitype of the OT types and shadows as shown by the examples previously discussed. Other typological relationships that are not specifically directed to the person of Christ, such as the flood-baptism typology, are established as a consequence of Christ's redemptive work. Noah was preserved through the waters of the flood, but believers experience a greater salvation when baptized into Christ, being rescued on account of Christ's resurrection and triumph over death (cf. Rom 6:3–5; Col 2:12).[122] Since Jesus brings about

---

121. LaRondelle, *Israel of God*, 44–45, states, "Because the covenantal communion with God is established through Christ only, all typology in the New Testament converges and culminates in Christ. Because Christ fulfills and completes Old Testament salvation history, New Testament typology originates, centers, and terminates in Christ." Similarly, Goppelt, *Typos*, 202. The term "Christotelic" comes from Enns, *Inspiration and Incarnation*, 154; and Enns, "Fuller Meaning, Single Goal," 213–15. Enns, *Inspiration and Incarnation*, 154, states, "To read the Old Testament 'christotelically' is to read it *already knowing* that Christ is somehow the *end* to which the Old Testament story is heading. . . . A grammatical-historical reading of the Old Testament is not only permissible but absolutely vital in that it allows the church to see the varied trajectories set in the pages of the Old Testament itself. It is only by understanding the Old Testament on its own terms . . . that the church can appreciate the impact that the death and resurrection of Christ . . . ." (emphasis original). The term "Christotelic" is perhaps more beneficial than "Christocentric" since it avoids reading Christ into every OT passage and instead accents how the OT points to the eschatological coming of Christ. See Beale, *Erosion of Inerrancy*, 86. I am adopting the term aside from Enns's view of Scripture which he believes entails elements of myth and legend as well as his problematic proposal for the NT use of the OT whereby the apostles committed eisegesis, manipulating OT texts and sometimes ignoring the original OT context. For an in depth critique of Enns's approach, see Beale, *Erosion of Inerrancy*.

122. For a helpful discussion of the flood-baptism typology, see Schreiner, *New Testament Theology*, 744–45, and Yoshikawa, "Prototypical Use," 449–90. Another example of how the typological pattern does not converge directly in the person of Christ is 1 Cor 10 as Israel's experiences in the wilderness occurred typologically as warnings to the church. Yet even here with the Israel-church typology, the correspondence is drawn in light of the significance of Christ's new covenant work since the end of the ages (1 Cor 10:11) pivots upon the manifestation of Christ (2 Tim 1:9–10). That the typological pattern is channeled through Christ is seen in the reference to the pre-existent Christ (1 Cor 10:4) and the correspondences to the Lord's Supper and baptism (1 Cor 10:2–4), which are again brought about as ordinances of the new covenant in light of the fulfillment of Christ's soteriological work. See Davidson, *Typology in Scripture*, 282–83.

a new redemptive-historical epoch marked by the new covenant, the empowering presence of the Holy Spirit, the inauguration of the kingdom, the dawning of the new creation, and the fulfillment of God's promises (2 Cor 1:20), all OT typological patterns feature an intensified character and heightened realization. The OT types reach their aim and goal in the age of fulfillment.[123] Further, the arrival and ratification of the promised new covenant (Jer 31:29-40; Ezek 36:24-38; Luke 22:20; 1 Cor 11:25; 2 Cor 3; Heb 8-10) requires that all of the typological features of the previous covenants have been inaugurated or superseded since the new covenant is the goal and terminus of the OT covenants.[124] The mediatorial work of Christ is greater than any of the OT mediators, for through him all of God's people now have direct knowledge of the Lord and are taught by God (cf. Isa 54:13 and Jer 31:34 with John 6:45 and 1 Thess 4:9, note also 1 John 2:20, 27), experience the outpouring of the eschatological Holy Spirit with the Law written on the heart, and they enjoy complete forgiveness of sins.

The eschatological orientation of typological patterns is somewhat more complicated than the observation that all typological patterns in the Bible are directed toward and converge in Christ. Davidson's research has led him to conclude that there is a three-fold eschatological substructure of biblical typology. The antitypical fulfillment of OT typology involves one or more of the three NT eschatological manifestations of the kingdom: the inaugurated, appropriated, and consummated kingdom.[125] Davidson describes the eschatological fulfillment of typology with three aspects this way:

---

123. For the notion of "fulfillment" in the NT as one that involves a sense of completion or consummation such that the OT prediction or promise is brought to its designed end, see BDAG, s.v. "πληρόω"; Moo and Naselli, "Problem of the NT's Use of the Old," 710-11; Carson, *Matthew 1-12*, 27-29, 142-44; Baker, *Two Testaments, One Bible*, 208-9.

124. Naturally, the universal structures of the creation and Noahic covenants continue on in this age, but even these covenants point to the new creation freed from sin that will come to fruition based upon the new covenant. See Gentry and Wellum, *Kingdom through Covenant*. Williamson, "Covenant," 427, summarizes, "In some sense previous divine covenants culminate in the new covenant, for this future covenant encapsulates the key promises made throughout the OT era . . . while at the same time transcending them. Thus the new covenant is the climactic fulfilment of the covenants that God established with the patriarchs, the nation of Israel, and the dynasty of David. The promises of these earlier covenants find their ultimate fulfilment in the new covenant, and in it such promises become 'eternal' in the truest sense." For further development, cf. Williamson, *Sealed with an Oath*, 182-207.

125. Davidson, *Typology in Scripture*, 398-99; Davidson, "Nature [and Identity]," 7-8; Davidson, "Eschatological Hermeneutic," 36-42.

(1) "inaugurated," connected with the first Advent of Christ (as Adam is a type of Christ, Rom 5); (2) "appropriated," focusing on the time of the Church living in the tension between the "already" and the "not yet," (as in 1 Cor 10 the Exodus experiences are 'types' *typoi* of the Christian church); or (3) "consummated," linked to the Apocalyptic Day of the Lord and the Second Coming of Christ and beyond (as the Noahic Flood is a type of the destruction of the world in 2 Pet 3:6–7).[126]

Although Davidson does not claim specifically that all typological patterns are directed or channeled through Christ, he does argue that the one eschatological fulfillment in three manifestations is brought to basic realization in Christ's first advent when the age to come irrupted into this present evil age.[127] The ecclesiological appropriation occurs because the church is in union with Christ and shares in the one who is the principal antitype.

Davidson's categories are helpful, then, as the explicit typological patterns follow along the inaugurated eschatological framework of the NT, permitting the interpreter to determine which types have become obsolete and which are initially fulfilled and yet have continuing and ongoing fulfillment in this present age as the presence of the future overlaps with the continuity of the realities of the creation covenant and the post-fall structures of the Noahic covenant.[128] Given the inaugurated eschatological structure for typological fulfillment, the biblical texts must dictate, on a case by case basis, whether the type is completely annulled or fulfilled in Christ's first advent, or inform the reader whether there may be additional fulfillment and appropriation in the church and in the eschaton (the new heavens and new earth). For example, the whole sacrificial system of the OT has been rendered completely obsolete and fulfilled in the sacrifice of Christ (John 1:29, 36; Rom 8:3; 1 Cor 5:6–8; 1 Pet 1:18–19; Heb 9–10; Rev 5:6–10, 13:8). The only possible appropriation is that on the basis of Christ's atoning sacrifice Christians can now offer acceptable spiritual sacrifices in their priestly ministry and service (Heb 13:15; 1 Pet 2:5; cf. Rom 15:16). Every indication from the NT is that Christ's once and for all perfect sacrifice means that the sacrificial practices of OT Israel under the Mosaic covenant are done away with now and forever. Some more traditional dispensationalists argue that memorial or even actual ceremonial non-atoning sacrifices will be offered

---

126. Davidson, "Nature [and Identity]," 7–8.
127. Davidson, "Eschatological Hermeneutic," 40.
128. See footnote 3 above. Cf. Ladd, *Theology of the New Testament*, 61–67; Gentry and Wellum, *Kingdom through Covenant*, 648–54, 735–42; Hoekema, *Bible and the Future*, 13–22.

in the future millennium.¹²⁹ But such a position misses how the sacrificial system as a whole, tied to the old covenant, being typological and prophetic as specified by the biblical text (e.g., Isa 53) and disclosed through the covenants in the storyline, terminates in Christ's sacrificial death on the cross.¹³⁰ To return to the shadows of the OT cultic practices and posit them in the future is to fail to read the Bible in a redemptive historical manner, missing how such themes are developed progressively through the covenantal epochs and reach their goal and end in the finished work of Christ.¹³¹

A second illustration of how a type is fulfilled in Christ but with further realization or "spill-over" in the church and the consummation is in order. Tracing out the temple typology through the canon reveals that Christ is the antitypical fulfillment and replacement of the temple (Matt 12:6; Mark 14:58; John 1:14, 51; 2:14-22; 4:20-24; Heb 10:19-22; note also Matt 27:51-53 and Ezek 47:1-12; Joel 3:18; Zech 13:1, 14:8 with John

---

129. Pentecost, *Things to Come*, 517-31; Hullinger, "Function of the Millennial Sacrifices, Part 1," 40-57, Hullinger, "Function of the Millennial Sacrifices, Part 2," 166-79; Whitcomb, "Christ's Atonement and Animal Sacrifices in Israel," 201-17; Fruchtenbaum, *Israelology*, 810-13.

130. Rightly, Allis, *Prophecy and the Church*, 246-48; Hoekema, *Bible and the Future*, 204-5.

131. Merkle, "Old Testament Restoration Prophecies," 23, rightly observes the problem with dispensationalists who read Ezek 40-48 literalistically in arguing for the reinstitution of animal sacrifices in the millennium: "[A]ffirming that the restored people of Israel will rebuild the temple, reinstate the priesthood, and restore animal sacrifices, minimizes the complete and perfect work of Christ.... To go back to the shadows and images of the Old Testament is to neglect the centrality of Christ's finished work on the cross." Merkle also points out that God has already given his people a memorial of Christ's sacrifice—the Lord's Supper (p. 25n26). Why this new covenant meal, which is the continuing rite of the new covenant, would be replaced by animal sacrifices in the millennium is an argument with no warrant from the NT. The Lord's Supper will cease upon Christ's return (1 Cor 11:26), but gives way to the messianic banquet, the marriage supper of the Lamb (Luke 22:15-18; Rev 19:7-9) and not to the OT cultic practices of sacrificing animals. Furthermore, to argue for the reinstitution of the animal sacrifices in the future millennium but not the reinstitution of the Mosaic covenant is to rip the sacrifices out of their covenantal setting and context. Yet the consummation of the kingdom at Christ's return is still tied to the new covenant age (God's final covenant is the new covenant; 2 Cor 3:11), and so again this dispensational perspective fails since the sacrifice of Christ has been offered making the old covenant, and its sacrifices, obsolete (Heb 8:6-13; cf. Heb 7:11-12; 9-10). Hamilton, *Typology*, 73-90 demonstrates through textual analysis of 1 Sam 2:27-35; Isa 61:6, 66:19-21; Jer 33:14-26; and Zech 6:9-15 that the offices of king and priest would merge in a future Davidic king, ending the Aaronic priesthood with anticipation of the priestly office expanding to include gentiles. From the OT itself there is evidence to refute a future reconstitution of an Aaronic or a Levitical priesthood tasked with offering memorial sacrifices during the millennium.

THE NATURE, CHARACTERISTICS, AND CHALLENGES OF TYPOLOGY

7:37–39; and Ps 118:19–27 and Dan 2:34–35 with Matt 21:42–44).[132] With the eclipse of the temple through Jesus, however, the typological temple pattern is appropriated to the church, since the people of God are united to the true temple through the Holy Spirit. Temple imagery is applied to believers corporately (1 Cor 3:16–17; 6:19; 2 Cor 6:16; Eph 2:19–22; 1 Pet 2:4–10).[133] The pattern takes further shape and additional realization in the new heavens and new earth with God's presence fully realized as Jesus, the perfect temple, dwells with his people for eternity (Rev 21:22). In this way, typological patterns are always either completely fulfilled with the coming of the Christ, the primary and pervading antitype, or they are initially inaugurated by Christ with further fulfillment through the church, living in the "already" and "not yet" tension of the kingdom in the new covenant era. Finally, some typological patterns may have further realization as the temple example showed, with the second coming of Christ and the consummation of God's kingdom. Even when the type has ongoing or continuing fulfillment (the antitype fulfilling it in this age or in the eschaton), it is important to observe that there is always a transformation from the type to the antitype, hence the escalation embedded within typological relationships, because of the shifts that have occurred in light of Jesus Christ. Therefore, while Davidson's categories of inaugurated, appropriated, and consummated are helpful, it is important to note that with the arrival of the anitype, there is no return of the type. The shadow gives way to the substance, and that substance may take on additional realization in the church and in the new heavens and earth.

In summary, the heightening and escalation of the typological patterns have their focal point in the person and work of Jesus Christ as he secures a new order that realizes all that the OT types prefigured and foreshadowed. The NT antitype is greater than the OT type not just because of the better spiritual realities tied to the antitype, but also because of the greater glory that is realized now since all that the types pointed forward to have been fulfilled in the unprecedented and climactic acts of God through Jesus Christ. Hoskins rightly concludes,

> [T]he antitype abundantly fills the role of the type in way that makes the type unnecessary and effectively obsolete. . . . In

---

132. See Beale, *Temple and the Church's Mission*; Beale, *New Testament Biblical Theology*, 617–22; Beale and Kim, *God Dwells among Us*. Cf. Hoskins, *Jesus as the Fulfillment*; McKelvey, "Temple," 806–11; Holwerda, *Jesus and Israel*, 59–83; Clowney, "Final Temple," 156–89; Dalrymple, *Understanding Eschatology*, 56–99; Gladd, *From Adam and Israel to the Church*, 91–94, 132–39.

133. First Corinthians 6:19 may refer to individual bodies of believers as temples. But note Piotrowski, "One Spirit, One Body, One Temple."

short, as the goal or fulfillment of the Old Testament type, the New Testament antitype fulfills and surpasses the patterns and predictions associated with the Old Testament type and in doing so takes the place of the type.[134]

Typological Fulfillment: Continuity and Discontinuity

One final area remains in the discussion regarding the relationship between the type and antitype. The characteristic of escalation in typological patterns for theological systems of continuity and discontinuity is critically significant. With some degree of resemblance or likeness between the type and antitype and grounded in the promise and fulfillment theme, typological patterns help establish the continuity of Scripture. The organic unity of Scripture is maintained between the parallels and links of OT types and that to which they point—the NT antitypes. Continuity between the OT and NT is preserved as the antitypes of the new covenant era reference back to the OT types and thus connect OT themes, covenants, and promises to the NT fulfillment, thereby bridging the gap between the testaments. Therefore, if Israel can be demonstrated to be a type of Christ and derivatively of the church, then some degree of continuity is present and that proves problematic for dispensational theology that dismisses or truncates any notion of Israel as a typological pattern.

On the other hand, typological relationships also pronounce and disclose significant areas of discontinuity in the unified plan of God. The escalation and qualitative progression of typology embraces discontinuity between Christ and the realities of new covenant era with those typological features of the OT economy. The OT types associated with the OT covenants are brought to their fulfillment either completely or partially because of the massive changes that have been inaugurated by Christ.[135] If the role and function of Israel, including Israel's promises, are typologically fulfilled,

---

134. Hoskins, *Jesus as the Fulfillment*, 23; cf. 29.

135. See Gentry and Wellum, *Kingdom through Covenant*, 133–35. On the discontinuity of typological patterns, Carson, "Mystery and Fulfillment," 410, succinctly writes, "Where the polarity moves from the lamb of *yom kippur* to the sacrifice of the Messiah [Lev 16; Isa 53; Heb 8–10], from removal of yeast at a festival to universal moral exhortation [1 Cor 5:7–8], from a rock to Christ [1 Cor 10:4], then once again the broad appeal to the unity of the unfolding revelation embraces important elements of *dis*continuity. And this, Paul is convinced, is what responsible reading of the Old Testament Scripture warrants. But on this reading, the gospel that Paul preaches, though it grows out of the Old Testament and in this sense is organically tied to and authorized by the Old Testament, is that to which the Old Testament points, in such a way that the pointers, at least in some cases, fall away" (emphasis original).

even partially, in the first advent of Christ, then once again the dispensational scheme collapses as such would not entail a return to the shadows of the OT with national Israel receiving the kingdom and territorial promises during the millennium and beyond. Rather, the typological pattern converges and culminates in Christ resulting in significant changes because Israel's roles and promises terminate in Christ and the new covenant era he has ushered in. Further, if OT Israel is truly a typological pattern, then it cannot have a direct relationship to the church as the inaugurated eschatological fulfillment that is the framework of all typology requires a degree of discontinuity. In this manner, the old covenant community pointed to a greater covenant community filled by the Spirit and in faith union to the Messiah. The church, then, is not of the same nature as Israel of old because she is an organism that lives in the greater realities of what the chief antitype—Jesus Christ—has accomplished. As the eschatological people of God, the new covenant community—the church—has a nature and structure different from Israel if these typological patterns are unpacked rightly across the canon and thus proves problematic for covenant theology.

IDENTIFYING TYPES: THE TEXTUAL WARRANT FOR TYPOLOGY

Another vital area in the study of biblical typology is the question of exegesis: how are typological patterns discerned, and are there hermeneutical controls for evaluating and confirming typology? The many disagreements regarding the textual warrant for typology are not surprising given how prophecies and typologies correlate with the "mystery" (μυστήριον) motif.[136] Paul can say on the one hand that Christ and the gospel were formerly predicted and promised in the OT and now confirmed and fulfilled (e.g., Rom 1:2; 3:21; 15:8; Gal 3:8) and yet on the other hand, he presents these as formerly hidden in the OT but now revealed in light of Christ's coming (e.g., Rom 16:25–27).[137] Caneday explains, "The same scriptures which revealed

---

136. The "mystery" theme, which frequently appears in Pauline literature (Rom 11:25; 16:25; 1 Cor 2:1, 2:7, 4:1, 13:2, 14:2, 15:51; Eph 1:9, 3:3–4, 3:9, 5:32, 6:19; Col 1:26–27, 2:2, 4:3; 2 Thess 2:7; 1 Tim 3:9, 16), is generally about how something, usually the saving purposes of God, has been hidden in the past but is now revealed and manifested. For a thorough study, see Carson, "Mystery and Fulfillment," 412–36; and Beale and Gladd, *Hidden but Now Revealed*. The "mystery" theme is key to answering why those who had the OT scriptures could be indicted for not understanding the Scriptures and at the same time did not have the eyes of faith to grasp the Christ to whom the Scriptures pointed (John 3:10–11; 5:39–40; 1 Cor 2:1–10).

137. For discussion linking typology to the "mystery" theme, see Yoshikawa,

in advance, both prophetically and typologically, the coming of messiah, also concealed mysteries which could only be solved by later revelation. What was promised was simultaneously hidden in some substantial way."[138] There is an obscurity and opaqueness to typology, but as more and more time elapses in the progress of revelation, there is also clarity.[139] Recognizing and tracing types requires wisdom and much exegetical care. The next section explores the hermeneutical controls and textual warrant in validating typological structures by first briefly surveying wrong approaches.

Maximalist and Minimalist Approaches in Discerning Typological Relationships

Scholars who reject the prospective nature of typology and primarily understand typology in terms of the consistency of God's activity (the postcritical neo-typology school), as delineated, generally argue that typology is not regulated by hermeneutical norms. For both Baker and France, typological connections are the result of the theological reflection of the relationship between persons, events, and institutions in Scripture, but are not

---

"Prototypical Use," 28–34; Gentry and Wellum, *Kingdom through Covenant*, 131–32; Lampe, "Reasonableness of Typology," 29–30; Caneday, "Christ as Paul's Bifocal Optic."

138. Caneday, "Christ as Paul's Bifocal Optic," 22–23. Yoshikawa, "Prototypical Use," 32, notes, "Uncovering a type requires seeing connections that are not overtly stated, thus, discerning true biblical types is far more difficult than prophecies. And if prophecies suffer from misinterpretations and misidentifications, it is no surprise, then, that typology would suffer at the hands of those with 'typomania.'"

139. Fritsch, "Biblical Typology," 220, observes, "The type becomes more clear and understandable as the time for its fulfillment in the antitype draws near." Paul can understand the gospel as being both predicted in past times and now fulfilled while also hidden in the past and now revealed because they are part of an interlocking web. Carson, "Mystery and Fulfillment," 426–27, explains, "[M]uch of the Old Testament's promise is expressed . . . in one kind or another of typology, and fulfilled in the antitype: the Passover lamb versus the Messiah as the Passover lamb, cleaning the house of yeast in preparation for the Feast of Unleavened Bread and permanently abandoning the 'yeast' of all malice and evil, and so forth. Moreover, Paul certainly does not insist that when the stipulations regarding the Passover lamb were first written down, both writer and readers understood that they were pointing to the ultimate 'lamb,' the Messiah himself. So it would be fair to say that such notions were still hidden—hidden in plain view, so to speak, because genuinely there in the text (once one perceives the trajectory of typology), but not yet revealed. And that, perhaps, is why a 'mystery' *must* be *revealed*, but also why it *may* be revealed *through the prophetic writings* . . . and this is why the gospel itself, not to say some of its chief elements, can be simultaneously seen as something that has been (typologically) predicted and now fulfilled, and as something that has been hidden and has now been revealed" (emphasis original).

governed directly by exegesis.[140] With typology reduced to drawing mere analogies and resemblances, the number of types is unlimited, as Baker summarizes, "There is no exhaustive list of types and no developed method for their interpretation. On the contrary, there is great freedom and variety in the outworking of the basic principle that the Old Testament is a model for the New."[141]

Coming from a different hermeneutical framework, but no less maximalist in terms of postulating typological patterns, are those who swim in the stream of covenant theologian Johannes Cocceius (1603–1669). The Cocceian School (especially exemplified among Puritans) had no adequate hermeneutical controls and excessively raided the OT for types.[142] Modern scholars, like James Jordan and Peter Leithart, as well as certain TIS advocates with their penchant for figural reading, may generally be classified in this camp.[143]

---

140. Baker, *Two Testaments, One Bible*, 181–82; France, *Jesus and the Old Testament*, 41–42. Both recognize that exegesis is a prerequisite to typology but understand typology in terms of "theological reflection" and "application." Von Rad, "Typological Interpretation," 191, emphatically states, "As regards the handling of this sort of typological interpretation in the case of individual texts, no pedagogical norm can or may be set up; it cannot be further regulated hermeneutically, but takes place in the freedom of the Holy Spirit." The problem with this is pinpointed by Beale, *Handbook*, 25, who observes, "Even those rejecting typology as exegesis employ exegetical language to describe typology."

141. Baker, *Two Testaments, One Bible*, 182. Von Rad, "Typological Interpretation," 190, also thinks the number of types is unlimited. France, *Jesus and the Old Testament*, 43, is more cautious and would likely deny that there are unlimited typological connections, but he does see the typological method as fluid and loose as some types are more or less explicit, while others are implicit having no more than an echo or illustration of a general truth (see *Jesus and the Old Testament*, p. 76).

142. Critiques are offered by Fairbairn, *Typology of Scripture*, 1:9–14; note also Ninow, *Indicators of Typology*, 28. Davidson, *Typology in Scripture*, 34–35, provides some examples of how this school viewed typical every OT event which bore superficial resemblance to Christ.

143. Hugenberger, "Introductory Notes," 335, associates James Jordan with typological maximalism, citing an example where Jordan identifies "the attempted Sodomite rape of the Levite in Judges as a type of Christ's sufferings." Hyper-typing tendencies also may be observed in Leithart, *Deep Exegesis*. A more modest and helpful maximalist is Goldsworthy, *Gospel-Centered Hermeneutics*, 245–57, and *Christ-Centered Biblical Theology*, 170–89. Goldsworthy is immensely instructive in terms of biblical theology and in putting the OT and NT together. However, Goldsworthy's "macro-typology" superstructure allows him to go "beyond the usually identified elements of typology." Goldsworthy, *Gospel-Centered Hermeneutics*, 251. For a recent critique of Goldsworthy's approach to biblical theology and his proposed macro-typology, see Gentry, "Significance of Covenants," 9–33, esp. 24–30. A notable historical figure within the Cocceian school was Herman Witsius. For his discussion of typology, see Witsius, *Economy of the Covenants between God and Man*, 2:188–230.

On the other hand, because of the excesses of the typological maximalists of whatever stripe, Hugenberger writes that there are those who "appear distrustful of typology largely because of the apparent subjectivism of this approach, its unfalsifiable and contradictory results, and the indisputable record of interpretative excess."[144] Those reacting in this way would not necessarily invalidate biblical typology altogether but would only acknowledge typological patterns explicitly revealed in the NT. Advocates of a minimalist approach to typology follow in the footsteps of Bishop Herbert Marsh (1757–1839), who constricted typological patterns to those explicitly mentioned by Jesus or the apostles.[145]

Identifying Types: Exegetical Criteria

The maximalist and minimalist perspectives for identifying types are illegitimate. First, the maximalist position, as elucidated throughout this chapter, fails to understand the nature of typology. Typology is not a theological reflection of analogies of biblical figures, but belongs to scriptural revelation and possesses characteristics of divine design, prefiguring heightened and escalated antitypes in the fulfillment Christ has wrought. Further, the notion of the number of types being unlimited is excessive; readers are not to forge types, for to do so is to go down the path of allegorizing in arbitrarily making typological links. However, since typology has a prophetic sense, Beale is correct to classify typology within the exegetical task.[146] The number of types is limited as a consequence, for only the biblical texts can establish the presence of a type.

On the other hand, while the minimalist approach correctly wants to ensure that foreign meanings are not read into OT texts, the position is too restrictive. Many of the typological relationships are directly explicated by

144. Hugenberger, "Introductory Notes," 335.

145. See Marsh, *Lectures on the Criticism and Interpretation of the Bible*, 373. For Fairbairn's critiques of Marsh, see Fairbairn, *Typology of Scripture*, 1:19–24. A modern day representative of the Marsh school is Legarth, "Typology and its Theological Basis," 148, as he argues that typology can be utilized "only in cases where the NT authors do so." As will be explored in chapter 4, many dispensationalists are also situated within the Marshian school.

146. Beale, "Did Jesus and His Followers Preach?," 401; Beale, *Handbook*, 24–25. Berkhof, *Principles of Biblical Interpretation*, 145, also emphasizes, "Accidental similarity between an Old and New Testament person or event does not constitute the one a type of the other. There must be some Scriptural evidence that it was so designed by God." Cf. Vos, *Biblical Theology*, 145–46. In contrast to Baker, Ninow, *Indicators of Typology*, 88, notes that if typology is based on sound exegesis, then it has to be guarded with a controlled hermeneutical procedure.

the NT authors, but their appeal to types are not exhaustive. As Fairbairn argues, the explicit typological connections in the NT are paradigmatic of the "principles of which others of a like description are to be discovered and explained."[147] Moreover, later OT writers already begin to draw out the typological implications of previous OT texts (e.g., the latter OT prophets already develop persons, institutions, and events that anticipate fulfillment in the future), thereby evaporating any claim that the NT authors are unique in recognizing typological connections because of their charismatic gifting and authority as apostles.[148] In fact, some inherent and internal textual indicators identifying types are already apparent or present in the OT; further, how else would the NT authors convince their readers of their interpretations of the OT texts unless the types were recognizable from the OT itself?[149]

147. Fairbairn, *Typology of Scripture*, 1:23. Rightly, Naselli notes the implications of Heb 9:5 in DeRouchie at al., *40 Questions about Biblical Theology*, 87, and Hamilton, "Typology of David's Rise to Power," 9, finds that the problem with restricting the typological patterns to only those explicitly cited in the NT is that NT does not cite all the instances of OT types identified as such within the OT itself.

148. For specific examples of indications of typology already in the OT, see Bird, "Typological Interpretation within the Old Testament," 36–52; Streett, "As It Was in the Days of Noah," 33–51; Ninow, *Indicators of Typology*, 98–241; Anderson, "Exodus Typology in Second Isaiah," 177–95. More generally on the discussion of typology within the OT, see Hummel, "Old Testament Basis," 38–50; Fishbane, *Biblical Interpretation*, 350–79; and Reventlow, *Problems of Biblical Theology*, 28–29. Harris, "Typological Trajectories," 291, notes how the author of Hebrews "draws out truths that are adumbrated from within the Old Testament texts themselves."

149. Davidson, "Eschatological Hermeneutic," 16–18. See also Evans and Novakovic, "Typology," 986. This point of recognizing the typological nature within the OT is critical, for sometimes just the presence of thematic linkages can be pressed too far in what is labelled as typology. For example, Naselli, *From Typology to Doxology*, 130–41, commendably presents the thematic links between Isa 40 and Job 38–41 and Rom 11; see also Naselli's summary in DeRouchie et al., *40 Questions about Biblical Theology*, 321–25. However, he is not convincing in asserting that Paul's use of Isa 40:13 and Job 41:3a are typological in Rom 11:34–35. Rather than viewing these as typological, the discrete citations and allusions of Isa 40:13 and Job 41:3a are straightforwardly applied in Paul's doxology regarding the wisdom and knowledge of God, and tied to how no one can understand what God is doing in the world. These specific verses are about God's wisdom and his sovereign freedom in executing his plan; no one is his counselor, and no one earns recompense from God, but neither Isa 40:13 or Job 41:3a are prophetic or point to an intensified (heightened, escalated) realization to come—they are both applied in a doxological setting regarding God's character. Throughout time and through Scripture, God's character and nature are constant; hence, texts about God's attributes cannot be typological because there can be no intensification or escalation with the character of God. This does not deny the biblical theological role of Isa 40 and Job 38–41, but application of OT texts can be cited in an analogous or straightforward way as was discussed earlier. Therefore, I am not convinced that "the situation of Israelites in Isaiah 40 and the situation of Job in Job 41 typologically connect with the situation of the Israelites in Romans 9–11" (DeRouchie et al., *40 Questions about Biblical Theology*,

Avoiding the extremes of the maximalists and minimalists naturally leads to the question of the criteria for recognizing types. What are the evidences that an OT person, office, event, and institution prefigure and correspond in some salvifically significant detail to a heightened antitypical fulfillment realized in Jesus Christ? The following points from Davidson and Beale are instructive.[150]

First, the immediate OT context may indicate that the author himself recognized the foreshadowing significance of a person, event, or institution. Deuteronomy 18:15–18 forecasts a greater prophet like Moses in the future. Psalm 2 and a host of other OT passages feature Davidic typology in projecting a greater David to come (e.g., Jer 23:5; Ezek 34:23, 37:24; Isa 9:5–6, 11:1–5; Hos 3:5; Amos 9:11; Zech 8:3). The early chapters of Genesis present Adam as a covenantal head and anticipate a new Adam, a seed, who will undo the fall (Gen 3:15). Similarly, Exod 15:14–17 and Num 23–24 feature internal indicators of a greater exodus to come and Jonah 2:2 and 2:6 indicate that Jonah's prayer in the fish points to death and resurrection.

Second, moving beyond the immediate context, Beale suggests that "types may be discernible in the central theological message of the literary unit and not in the minute details of a particular verse."[151] For example, Jeremiah's portrayal of the lament and grief over the Assyrian and Babylonian exile, metaphorically presented as Rachel weeping for her children (Jer

---

324). If the larger context of the citations is considered, perhaps a correspondence or analogy between the situations of the Israelites in Isa 40 and of Job with the situation of the Israelites in Rom 9–11 could be established, but the situation of the Israelites in Rom 9–11 is not the antitype of Isa 40 or of Job 38–41. This does not appear to be the point of Rom 11:34–35.

150. Davidson, "Nature [and Identity]"; Beale, *Handbook*, 19–23; Beale, "Finding Christ in the OT," 30–43. Hamilton, "Was Joseph a Type of the Messiah?," 52–77, also provides three criteria for the evidence of a type: linguistic correspondence, sequential event correspondence, and redemptive historical import. In his latest work, *Typology*, 19–26, Hamilton presents two essential features of typology: 1) historical correspondence, which encompasses the biblical authors' re-use of significant terms, quoting phrases or lines, repeating sequences or events, and the similarity of covenantal import, and 2) escalation—the repeated similarities draw attention to the increasing importance of the pattern. For the latter work, one concern is that Hamilton does not emphasize the prophetic aspect of typology in his characterization of typology. Per Davidson and others, there must be some indication that the OT type is divinely designed such that the force of predictive foreshadowing, the prophetic/eschatological warrant, is evident in the OT itself. At points Hamilton does mention the anticipatory import and the direction of future fulfillment when he presents the typological patterns through his book, but that this prospective and predictive aspect is not part of his definition of typology leaves the door open for viewing many things, including mere analogies, as types.

151. Beale, *Handbook*, 23.

31:15), possesses a prophetic and prototypical announcement when one considers how this verse is couched within the messianic and eschatological setting of Jer 31–34 as a whole. Matthew's appeal to this passage (Matt 2:17–18) is understandable for the tears of the exile begun in Jeremiah's day and associated with restoration hopes (Jer 31:15–20) have climaxed with the tears of the mothers of Bethlehem (Ramah, located not far from Bethlehem), coinciding with the arrival of the Son, who brings the new covenant and the people back from exile (Jer 31:31–34).[152]

Third, if the immediate or broader literary context does not explicitly disclose a particular type, though textual hints and clues are present that the original OT author grasped some measure of the typological import of the larger-than-life features, the later OT intertextual development at the epochal level reveals and deepens the typological significance and thus provides the clarifying textual warrant. Paying close attention to the redemptive historical trajectory and observing the repetitions of earlier OT references in later OT prophetic contexts indicates the presence of a typological pattern. Melchizedek, discussed earlier, is an example of a figure who receives more clarity as a type in Ps 110 than in the context of Gen 14. The repetition of the flood theme in the latter prophets (Isa 24:18, 28:2, 43:2, 54:8–9; Dan 9:26) and the development of Israel's promised land (Isa 51:2–3; Ezek 36:35, 47:1–12; Joel 2:3; Zech 14:8–11; cf. Pss 2; 37; 72) are also cases in point.[153] More examples could be given, but the lucidity of the typological correspondences emerges through the progress of revelation as later OT writers build upon and recapitulate past themes, further projecting the anticipatory import of certain OT persons, events, and institutions. The NT authors also benefit in having additional revelation with the coming and resurrection of Christ. They observe the fulfillment in Christ and shed further light and clarity on the typological roles of OT types and their corresponding antitypes.

Fourth, as Beale observes, if the OT itself shows that a later person carries on the typological function of an earlier person, "who is clearly viewed as a type of Christ by the NT, then this later OT person is also likely a good candidate to be considered to be a type of Christ."[154] For example, the

---

152. Carson, *Matthew 1–12*, 95; Davies and Allison, *Matthew 1–7*, 266–69; Hays, *Reading Backwards*, 41–43.

153. For the universalism of the land promise as a typological pattern in contrast to the dispensational view, which affirms a literalistic fulfillment of Palestine to ethnic Israel in the future, see Beale, *New Testament Biblical Theology*, 750–72; Johnston and Walker, *Land of Promise*; Davies, *Gospel and the Land*; Martin, *Bound for the Promised Land*; and Holwerda, *Jesus and Israel*, 85–112.

154. Beale, *Handbook*, 21; Beale, "Finding Christ in the OT," 39–41.

covenantal headship and role of Adam is carried through other covenant mediators and ectypal installments, such as Noah, Abraham, Isaac, Jacob, the nation of Israel, and David. Adam and David are clearly viewed as typological of Christ (Gen 1–3; 5:1–2; Ps 8:4–8; and Dan 7:13–14 for Adam; Ps 2, other Davidic psalms, etc., for David), but given how the other partners of God's covenants carry out Adam's role of kingly dominion, they too serve a typological function. Another example, and linked to Adam, is the "seed" theme which typologically points to Christ and the church. The seed promise goes through Abraham and develops through the patriarchs, narrows down to the Davidic king, and culminates in Christ (Gal 3:16). Therefore, the patriarchs, Isaac and Jacob, key individuals through whom the seed theme progresses, along with all the Davidic kings in terms of office, are all part of this typological pattern that points to Christ.[155] Joshua, who takes the mantle of Moses (Num 27:16–18; Moses is clearly a type of Christ), and the whole institution of the prophets derived from Moses (and earlier figures such as Adam, Abraham [Gen 20:7], and Isaac; see Ps 105:9, 12–15 which likely refers to Abraham and Isaac as anointed ones and prophets), should also be recognized as types.

Other principles could be added, but these four points provide the guard rails for ascertaining whether an OT historical person, event, or institution prefigures a corresponding NT antitype. Three other points should also be kept in mind. First, the redemptive historical import of types coincides with the unfolding of the biblical covenants. Types are not merely

---

155. Whether Joseph is typological of Christ is difficult to ascertain. Hamilton, "Was Joseph a Type of the Messiah?," argues that he is based on linguistic and sequential event correspondence and redemptive historical considerations. Groningen, *Messianic Revelation in the Old*, 165–67; Johnson, *Him We Proclaim*, 215, also considers Joseph a messianic type, while Chase, *40 Questions about Typology and Allegory*, 133–34, 257, contends that Joseph and the Joseph narrative are typological and allegorical. The problem with appealing to linguistic correspondences and historical event sequences is that these only establish analogies between Joseph and David (e.g., both having the Spirit, being handsome in appearance, etc.), but this does not reveal any prophetic aspect characteristic of typological patterns. The same point applies to Philpot, "Was Joseph a Type of Daniel?" One has to be careful not to press the details of the narrative too far; this is a problem that plagues Hamilton's other article on typology as well, i.e., "The Typology of David's Rise to Power." More promising is Hamilton's appeal to redemptive historical import as Joseph may be situated in the broader theme of the seed of the woman contending against the seed of the serpent. However, some uncertainty remains because David comes from the line of Judah, not of Joseph, and later OT and NT writers do not seem to draw significant attention to Joseph in terms of identifying him as a prefiguration of the Messiah even if he is the subject of discussion (e.g. Acts 7). For probably the best treatment of Joseph as a type, see Emadi, "Covenant, Typology, and the Story of Joseph," 1–24. Emadi presents Joseph within the covenantal storyline and argues for textual warrant from the Genesis narrative itself.

THE NATURE, CHARACTERISTICS, AND CHALLENGES OF TYPOLOGY

sprinkled throughout the OT that arbitrarily appear here and there. The typological patterns are embedded in the eschatological orientation of the OT itself which moves along the covenants. Since the covenants are fundamental to the plot structure of the Bible, they serve as the framework that the typological patterns move along and develop in pointing to Christ.[156] Tracing the advance of a plausible typological pattern in relation to the covenants assists the reader in validating both the presence and meaning of the type and antitype relationship. How one puts together the covenants will have significant impact in how one interprets typological patterns as will be explored with how covenant and dispensational theologians interpret typological patterns that stand at the core of their respective theological systems.

Second, when dealing with an OT type it is important to note that not all the details and aspects of that particular person, event, and institution are typological.[157] Only what is central theologically and specifically prophetic and divinely designed is typological. David is a type of Christ, but not every detail of his circumstances and life events are. Fascinating analogous features may be present in a particular OT type that coordinate with the NT antitype, but that does not necessarily mean that these specific details are also typological. Isaac is a type in terms of the broader seed theme, but caution is needed when one considers Abraham's "sacrifice" of Isaac in Gen 22. Abraham's willingness to not spare his son points to God's offering of his Son (Rom 8:32); the ram that is sacrificed as a substitute for Isaac is a type as it serves as a prelude to the sacrificial system which is fulfilled in Christ's atoning sacrifice, but Isaac's carrying the wood and his near sacrifice as a burnt offering should not be construed as typological.[158]

---

156. Gentry and Wellum, *Kingdom through Covenant*, 135–36; and see Gentry, "Significance of Covenants," 22–33, for how this approach differs from other biblical theological methodologies. Chase, *40 Questions about Typology and Allegory*, 54–55, brings up how types flow from a covenantal stream, but while citing other scholars, he never attributes this idea to Wellum, nor does he develop the covenantal import when identifying types. Also seeking to discern types through a covenantal framework is Schrock, "What Designates a Valid Type?," 3–26. Schrock's approach is similar to mine; nevertheless, Schrock's acceptance of ikonic *mimēsis* (14), which still entails allegorization (see footnotes 8–9 in this chapter), and his unconvincing example of Rahab's scarlet thread as a type organically linked to the covenantal structure of Passover (11–12, 25), leaves one with questions regarding his overall proposal. Goldsworthy, *Christ-Centered Biblical Theology*, 187, rightly states, "The redness of Rahab's cord is not a type of Christ's blood."

157. Rightly, Goppelt, *Typos*, 10; Greidanus, *Preaching Christ*, 257; Ramm, *Protestant Biblical Interpretation*, 229–31; LaRondelle, *Israel of God*, 48.

158. Contra Leithart, *Deep Exegesis*, 42; and Tidball, *Message of the Cross*, 42–46, who wrongly press the details so that the wood that Isaac carries, the binding of Isaac, and his willing submission are all considered typological features of Christ's suffering at

The texts indicate not only what is typological but also to what degree that extends to the details of the type or episode in question just as a careful reading uncovers the areas of similarity and contrast and the nature of the fulfillment between the type and antitype.

Third and related to the two points above, in considering typology it is worth reiterating that OT persons, events, and institutions have meaning in their own redemptive-historical context while also being preparatory and revelatory of the greater antitypical fulfillment to come. Each of these persons, events, and institutions are significant and meaningful in their own immediate, textual horizon, but as shadows and copies (Col 2:17, Heb 8:5; 10:1) they point to greater and heavenly realities, the substance of which is the antitype. Instead of saying that typology functions on two levels of meaning, which confusingly suggests one typological level and a subsequent, second level of typology, it is better to recognize that OT types have their own meaning and spiritual significance in their context while they also anticipate the promises, blessings, and good things to come with the Messiah (epochal, canonical horizon).[159] The type is not of the same substance as the antitype but signifies the spiritual vitality provided in Christ alone such that while the OT saints did not receive what was promised, "only together with us should they be made perfect" (Heb 11:40 NIV).[160]

Typology and Sensus Plenior

Lastly, since the presence and meaning of a typological pattern become more transparent through the textual development in the epochal and canonical horizons, the question of the relationship between the human and divine author and the issue of *sensus plenior* naturally arises.[161] Was the

---

the cross. For a more sensible approach to the Aqedah of Isaac, see Greidanus, *Preaching Christ*, 314, and Stanley, "Wood, Sand and Stars," 301–30, esp. 325.

159. Renihan, *Mystery of Christ*, 33–34, discusses two-level typology. The main point that Renihan makes seems appropriate, but the original historical meaning is not "the first level of typology."

160. See Caneday, "God's Parabolic Design for Israel's Tabernacle," 105–6 for the shadow to heavenly reality relationship. Note also Renihan, *Mystery of Christ*, 36–39, who points to John Owen and Particular Baptists who rightly recognized that the type is not the same substance of the antitype.

161. Space does not permit a developed analysis of the hermeneutical debates that arise from the dual authorship of Scripture. Bock lays out four schools of thought: the full human intent, the divine intent-human words, the historical progress of revelation and Jewish hermeneutic school, and the canonical approach. See Bock, "Evangelicals and the Use of the Old," 209–23, and 306–19. For the full human intent position such that the divine and human author's intent always overlap with only a single intent

anticipatory and indirectly prophetic import of OT persons, events, and institutions hidden from the earlier OT authors only to be revealed by the divine author in later OT authors and NT writers? If so what about the grammatical-historical hermeneutic that locates meaning in the human author's intention? Or does the later development of typology annul the OT author's willed meaning, as Leithart postulates, "Typology is deliberate foreshadowing, and the change in meaning from expectation to conclusion is the change from promise to fulfillment. The original text changes meaning when brought into relation to other texts."[162]

A complete analysis of these topics cannot be managed here, but some brief comments are in order. First, the concept of *sensus plenior* can be helpful depending on how it is defined and whether it is conceived to be part of the literal sense.[163] Based on the previous discussion of Scripture having

---

based on what the human author was conscious of, see Kaiser, "Single Meaning, Unified Referents," 45–89. For the divine-intent human words position that posits a single meaning based on the human author, but with related submeanings, implications or development of that one meaning intended by God, see Johnson, *Old Testament in the New*, 49–51. Representative of the view that NT authors used contemporary Jewish interpretative principles are Longenecker, *Biblical Exegesis*; Enns, "Fuller Meaning, Single Goal," 167–217. Advocates of a canonical approach where biblical texts are interpreted in the ultimate literary context—the whole canon, such that the intention of OT texts become deeper and clearer as the canon expanded, include Waltke, "Kingdom Promises as Spiritual," 263–87; others who affirm a canonical approach but incorporate elements from other schools are Moo and Naselli, "Problem of the NT's Use of the Old," 734–36; Hoskins, *Jesus as the Fulfillment*, 25–26; Beale, "Did Jesus and His Followers Preach?," 391–95, 400–1; Poythress, "Divine Meaning of Scripture," 241–79; and Oss, "Canon as Context," 105–27. Bock himself is eclectic, combining features of the divine intent-human words and Jewish hermeneutic school. Bock, "Single Meaning, Multiple Contexts," 105–51.

162. Leithart, *Deep Exegesis*, 64. Enns, "Fuller Meaning, Single Goal," 167–217, also represents a position where the NT authors perceived new meanings in the OT texts that are not necessarily close to the meanings intended by the original authors.

163. The often cited definition of *sensus plenior* (SP) comes from the Catholic scholar who wrote frequently on the subject. See Brown, *Sensus Plenior of Sacred Scripture*, 92: "The sensus plenior is that additional, deeper meaning, intended by God but not clearly intended by the human author, which is seen to exist in the words of a biblical text (or group of texts, or even a whole book) when they are studied in the light of further revelation or development in the understanding of revelation." See also Bavinck, *Reformed Dogmatics*, 1:396–97, who describes the SP even though the term was not specifically used until the twentieth century. For Brown, the SP takes into account the *words* of a text but not the *things* written about in the text. Therefore, typology, or the "typical sense" as he describes it, differs and is distinct from the SP (in the typical sense, the *things* that take on a deeper meaning are the typological persons, events, and institutions in Scripture). Moo and Naselli, "Problem of the NT's Use of the Old," 730–31, follow Brown's definition. For many evangelicals, this distinction is not retained as the SP characterizes the fuller meaning intended by God but in some

only one sense, the *sensus literalis*, if *sensus plenior* is defined as an additional sense then such would have to be rejected. However, in evangelical discussions, the *sensus plenior* is that fuller divine meaning that transcends the understanding of the human author, being another dimension or level of the meaning, but not a completely different meaning or sense.

Some scholars, such as France and Baker, locate the literal meaning strictly to the grammatical-historical study of the human author's willed intent found in the original context. The grammatical-historical method is required by the doctrine of inspiration, for God has caused his words to be written by human authors in various times, cultural settings, and in diverse situations, and they wrote to be understood by their audiences.[164] But the problem with strictly limiting interpretation in this approach, noted by S. Lewis Johnson, is that Scripture is not just a human product but a divine one as well.[165] The identity between God's words and the words of the biblical authors means that interpreters must understand the human author's intent to ascertain God's intent. However, the grammatical-historical approach is not sufficient if it is only left to the immediate literary context; the meaning of a text within the canonical context must be accounted for since the Bible is unified, the Holy Spirit being the author of the whole, and so should be read as one book. With revelation unfolding progressively—the literary corpus of the canon increasing over time—the OT authors would not have known where the whole revelation was going, nor the total scope

---

degree unknown by the human author which would include typology. Glenny, "Divine Meaning of Scripture," 499–500, rightly points this out: "Typology by definition involves an extension of the concept found in the original affirmation (a pattern). This is of course a fuller divine meaning. Moo [and Naselli and Brown] differentiates the two by describing the *sensus plenior* as the deeper meaning of words and typology as the deeper meaning of things. Since words represent things, the distinction is difficult to maintain." Some Roman Catholic scholars did not ascribe the SP to the literal sense since that sense was viewed strictly as the human author's intention. For Brown, the SP was not a "second literal sense" but rather a deepening—"an approfondissement"—of the one and only literal sense of the text. Brown, *Sensus Plenior of Sacred Scripture*, 113, 145. On the other hand, other Catholic scholars, such as Jean Daniélou, rejected the SP entirely since they linked the human authorial intent with the literal sense, and then everything beyond the literal sense was understood to be the spiritual or typical sense.

164. Packer, "Infallible Scripture and the Role of Hermeneutics," 349–50; cf. Poythress, "Divine Meaning of Scripture," 277–79. However, the doctrine of inspiration does not require that the human and divine authorial intent are of a singular, undivided meaning as in Kaiser's single intent approach. For a critique of this approach, see Compton, "Shared Intentions?," 23–33.

165. Johnson, *Old Testament in the New*, 56. Johnson interacts specifically with France. Hays, "Figural Exegesis and the Retrospective Re-cognition," 43–44, also appeals to the divine author but his retrospective approach ultimately severs the human author (authorial intent) from the divine author.

to which his writing was ordained, and therefore would not have exhaustively understood the meaning, implications, and possible applications of all that they wrote (see 1 Pet 1:10–12).[166] The later parts of Scripture draw out and develop earlier texts that are consistent with the OT authors' understanding and yet adds clarity to the anticipatory import of their writings.[167] The *sensus plenior* is helpful then in recognizing the added dimensions of meaning, specifically the divine author's intent in light of the entire canon.[168] This fuller sense also coincides with the "mystery" motif referred to

---

166. Beale, "Did Jesus and His Followers Preach?," 393; Gentry and Wellum, *Kingdom through Covenant*, 111; Hoskins, *Jesus as the Fulfillment*, 26; McCartney and Clayton, *Let the Reader Understand*, 164–67. Moo and Naselli, "Problem of the NT's Use of the Old," 735, write, "The human authors may have had inklings that their words were pregnant with meanings that they did not yet understand, but they would not have been in a position to see the entire context of their words." On 1 Pet 1:10–12, Glenny, following Grudem, argues that v. 11 should be understood to mean that the prophets were inquiring as to "who or what time." Glenny, "Divine Meaning of Scripture," 486, perceptively adds that "1 Pet 1:12 states that it was made known to the OT prophets that they were not ministering the things concerning Christ's sufferings and subsequent glory to themselves but to the NT people of God. That would be hard to comprehend if they understood all of it themselves." Another passage in support of a concept of SP is Dan 12:6–9.

167. Beale, "Did Jesus and His Followers Preach?," 393; Gentry and Wellum, *Kingdom through Covenant*, 111–12; Hoskins, *Jesus as the Fulfillment*, 26; Compton, "Shared Intentions?," 31. Moo, "Problem of *Sensus Plenior*," 206, writes, "God knows, as He inspires the human authors to write, what the ultimate meaning of their words will be; but it is not as if he has deliberately created a *double entendre* or hidden a meaning in the words that can only be uncovered through a special revelation. The 'added meaning' that the text takes on is the product of the ultimate canonical shape—though, to be sure, often clearly perceived only on a revelatory basis."

168. Vanhoozer, *Is There a Meaning*, 263–65; Oss, "Canon as Context," 116–17, 121; Glenny, "Divine Meaning of Scripture," 497–99; Beale, "Did Jesus and His Followers Preach?," 400; Moo and Naselli, "Problem of the NT's Use of the Old," 734–37; Carter, *Interpreting Scripture*, 183–85, 188. Vanhoozer, "Intention/Intentional Fallacy," 329, writes that acknowledging the Scripture as the word of God "calls for recognition of dual authorship where the divine intention appropriates, superintends, or supervenes on the human intention. . . . As with any action, we can adequately identify what has been done in Scripture only by considering its action as a *whole*. The divine intention most comes to light when God's communicative acts are described in *canonical* context." Where the divine author's meaning has little or no relationship to the meaning of the human author then the problem with figural and allegorical readings resurfaces. For a discussion and critique, see Poythress, "Divine Meaning of Scripture," 243; and Williams, *Far as the Curse Is Found*, 80–82. Williams's rightly states, "*Sensus Plenior* interpretation must be a development of what is said via authorial intention. The fuller sense should be just that, a fuller sense of what is already present, not an entirely other sense, as one finds in allegorical interpretation. While it is fair to see an oak within an acorn, it is not fair to see a cow within an acorn. But we must not lose sight of the author and his intention" (*Far as the Curse Is Found*, 81–82, emphasis original).

previously—simultaneously there are elements of the gospel grounded and predicted in the OT even though hidden until the advent of Christ. Therefore, God's fuller meaning, though never less than nor detached from the intended meaning of the human author, as "revealed when the text is exegeted in its canonical context, in relation to all that went before and came after, is simply extension, development, and application of what the writer was consciously expressing."[169]

The study of typology then, involves the *sensus plenior* of OT persons, events, institutions, and offices. The earlier OT authors would not have grasped the complete prefigurative import even though they would have recognized something of the "larger than life" features of the OT type.[170] Later revelation adds clarity to the prophetic expectation of the OT type and this is "open to verification, since the texts relevant to each type and antitype are within the canon."[171]

SUMMARY

Typology is a crucial area for resolving the debates of systems of theologies. The theological proposal offered here has sought to carefully distinguish it

---

169. Packer, "Infallible Scripture," 350. See also Johnson, *Old Testament in the New*, 50; Bock, "Evangelicals and the Use of the Old," 309, 315–16. Elsewhere, Packer, "Biblical Authority, Hermeneutics and Inerrancy," 147–48, puts it this way: "Since God has effected an identity between their words and his, the way for us to get into his mind, if we may thus phrase it, is via theirs. Their thoughts and speech about God constitute God's own self-testimony. If, as in one sense is invariably the case, God's meaning and message through each passage, when set in its total biblical context, exceeds what the human writer had in mind, that further meaning is only an extension and development of his, a drawing out of implications and an establishing of relationships between his words and other, perhaps later, biblical declarations in a way that the writer himself, in the nature of the case, could not do. . . . The point here is that the *sensus plenior* which texts acquire in their wider biblical context remains an extrapolation on the grammatico-historical plane, not a new projection on to the plane of allegory" (emphasis original).

170. Perhaps if Brown had considered SP to include typology and held to a different view of inspiration, then he might not have abandoned it in the end. In his later writings he noticed that the SP as he conceived it was almost never appealed to and used, even by scholars who accepted it. See Brown, "The Problems of *Sensus Plenior*," 460–69, esp. 462 and 464. Brown, "Hermeneutics," 618, found that the SP "is seldom verified and so is of little use in justifying or explaining NT, patristic, liturgical, or ecclesiastical exegesis. It is interesting to note that the proponents of the SP tend to confine their discussion of this sense to the theoretical plane, seldom appealing to it in their works of exegesis." For further discussion, see Dunn, "Raymond Brown and the Sensus Plenior," 531–51.

171. Hoskins, *Jesus as the Fulfillment*, 26.

from allegorization while offering adequate textual and hermeneutical controls for identifying type-antitype relationships. The antitype is either the complete or partial fulfillment of the type such that one should not expect a return of the type. Chapter 5 will seek to demonstrate that the nation of Israel is a typological pattern, though not in every detail or category, which finds its fulfillment in Christ. Before examining that typological relationship, the next two chapters offer the hermeneutics of covenant and dispensational theology, and how they understand the role of Israel in terms of typology and fulfillment through the unfolding of the covenants.

Chapter 3

THE HERMENEUTICS OF COVENANT THEOLOGY

COVENANT OR REFORMED THEOLOGY is a system of theology that stresses the continuity of the Bible as the "architectonic structure" or matrix providing the context for recognizing the unity of the Bible amid its diversity is the covenant.[1] According to Robert Letham, the covenant received more detailed attention in the sixteenth century with the initial impetus arising because of the Anabaptist challenge to infant baptism.[2] A defense of infant baptism was provided through the unity of the covenant with the practice of circumcision for Abraham's offspring being analogous to baptism. In Reformed federal or covenant theology, three covenants are set forth which undergird this system. R. Scott Clark explains,

> Those three covenants are (1) the pretemporal covenant of redemption (*pactum salutis*) between the Father and the Son, (2) a historical covenant of works between God and Adam as the federal head of humanity (*foedus operum*), and (3) a covenant

---

1. Horton, *Introducing Covenant Theology*, 13.
2. Letham, *Work of Christ*, 50. To be sure, early forms of covenant theology are present in the church fathers as they expressed their understanding of the transmission of sin, the inclusion of the gentiles in the church, the discontinuity between the old and new covenants, and in their discussions of Christian ethics, see Clark, "Christ and Covenant," 406. For a historical treatment of the doctrine of the covenant in the Westminster Assembly and through the patristic, medieval, early and post-Reformation periods, see Woolsey, *Unity and Continuity in Covenantal Thought*.

of grace with the elect, in Christ, administered through a series of covenants from Adam to Christ.[3]

The inter-Trinitarian covenant of redemption or counsel of peace, whereby the Father elects a people in the Son who is the guarantor and mediator of their redemption with saving faith applied by the Spirit, will not receive attention since the other two overarching theological covenants specifically concern the issue of continuity and discontinuity, centering as they do on the covenants established in history.[4] The covenant of works and the covenant of grace are the two main constructs for how covenant theologians understand the unity of the Bible and unfold the progress of revelation. I concentrate on these two covenantal constructs and later address how these concepts shape the covenantalist's ecclesiology and understanding of Israel.

Before unpacking the covenants of works and grace, two points should be noted. First, there are a variety of forms of covenant theology—Presbyterian and Dutch Reformed, Seventh Day Adventist, Federal Vision, and the New Perspective of Paul.[5] Reformed Baptist covenant theology or *1689 Federalism* also posits a covenant of works and covenant of grace, but their understanding of covenant theology diverges at significant areas from paedobaptist covenant theology.[6] Since Baptists are in general agreement on the topic of baptism and the church as a regenerate community, Reformed

---

3. Clark, "Christ and Covenant," 407. For a brief overview of these three overarching covenants, see Merkle, *Discontinuity to Continuity*, 146–51.

4. For helpful studies on the covenant redemption, see Fesko, *Trinity and the Covenant of Redemption*; VanDrunen and Clark, "Covenant before the Covenants," 167–96; and Berkhof, *Systematic Theology*, 265–71. For a more popular level description, see Brown and Keele, *Sacred Bond*, 23–39. For a treatment by a key historical Dutch Reformer, confer Witsius, *Economy of Covenants between God and Man*, 1:165–202. Interestingly, some Reformed theologians challenge the inter-trinitarian covenant of redemption, see Robertson, *Christ of the Covenants*, 54. For another critique and rejection of the covenant redemption, see Williamson, "Pactum Salutis."

5. For example, a Seventh Day Adventist form of covenant theology is offered by LaRondelle, *Our Creator Redeemer*. Federal Vision advocates include Douglas Wilson, Peter Leithart, and Richard Lusk. Their understanding of the covenant is presented in such works as Wilson, *"Reformed" Is Not Enough*; and Beisner, *Auburn Avenue Theology, Pros and Cons*. Proponents of the New Perspective on Paul are E. P. Sanders, James Dunn, and N. T. Wright. For example, see Sanders, *Paul and Palestinian Judaism*; and Wright, *What Saint Paul Really Said*. Note also the overview and critique of the Federal Vision in McGowan, *Adam, Christ and Covenant*, 79–107.

6. Denault, *Distinctiveness of Baptist Covenant Theology*; Renihan, *Mystery of Christ*; Johnson, *Kingdom of God*; Blackburn, *Covenant Theology*. *1689 Federalism* differs from some modern Reformed Baptists who maintain the many administrations of the one covenant of grace while advocates of the former equate the covenant of grace solely with the new covenant. For an overview of the covenants from a Reformed Baptist perspective, see Renihan, *Mystery of Christ*.

Baptist covenant theology will not receive attention in this study. Rather, the focus is particularly centered upon traditional paedobaptist covenant theology of a Presbyterian and Dutch Reformed heritage and how their form of covenant theology shapes their understanding of Israel typology as well as their ecclesiological conclusions regarding Israel and the church.

Second, there are competing views as to the nature and definition of covenant. The role and presence of oaths and the question as to whether covenants normalize existing relationships or create new relationships are just some of the issues that have arisen in recent scholarship.[7] Furthermore, classifying covenants as conditional or bilateral (sometimes referred to as suzerain-vassal) and unconditional or unilateral (sometimes referred to as royal grant) surfaces frequently in the discussions where covenants are defined.[8] Defining God-human covenants is also disputed depending on how narrow or broad one casts the biblical data. Williamson and Stek suggest a narrow definition of covenant such that formal oaths were indispensable to the covenant that formalized existing relationships but did not establish them (thus they reject any notion of a covenant with Adam or creation). On the other hand, traditional covenantalists have described covenants in broader terms. For example, Williams finds that insisting on a single definition for *covenant* is inappropriate. He explains, "A covenant is a relationship between persons, begun by the sovereign determination of the greater party, in which the greater commits himself to the lesser in the context of mutual loyalty, and in which mutual obligations serve as illustrations of that loyalty."[9] Likewise, Brown and Keele argue that a general definition is nec-

---

7. Advocates for understanding covenants to include the presence of a self-maledictory or solemn oath include Williamson, *Sealed with an Oath*, 38–43; and Stek, "'Covenant' Overload," 25–26, 39. However, others have demonstrated that while the oath is important, it is ancillary to the covenant itself: Dumbrell, *Covenant and Creation*, 17, 19–20; Collins, *Genesis 1–4*, 113. For debate regarding whether covenants confirm existing relationships see Niehaus, "Argument against Theologically Constructed Covenants," 259–73; Bartholomew, "Covenant and Creation," 25; and Hugenberger, *Marriage as a Covenant*, 175. A mediating position between Dumbrell's and Niehaus's description is best: covenants may formalize existing relationships, but in some contexts the covenant constitutes the relationship or gives rise to a new level of the relationship.

8. Hahn, *Kingship by Covenant*, 28–31; Gentry and Wellum, *Kingdom through Covenant*, 166–68, 662–66; Waltke, "Phenomenon of Conditionality," 123–39. For other pertinent works defining covenant in light of ancient Near Eastern treaties, see Weinfeld, "Covenant of Grant in the Old Testament," 184–203; Freedman, "Divine Commitment and Human Obligation," 419–31.

9. Williams, *Far as the Curse Is Found*, 45–46. Robertson, *Christ of the Covenants*, 4–15, also appeals to a broad description of covenant pointing to the concept of "bond" or "relationship" with "a pledge to life and death" in order to defend his definition of covenant as "a bond in blood sovereignly administered." Similarly, Collins, *Genesis 1–4*,

essary, and accordingly, find that "a covenant is a solemn agreement with oaths and/or promises, which imply certain sanctions or legality."[10] With these general descriptions of the concept of the covenant, I turn now to focus on how covenant theologians put together the storyline of Scripture through their understanding of the covenants.

COVENANT OF WORKS

Many scholars have rejected the notion of a covenant with Adam or the concept of a creation covenant. Some of these critics, even from Reformed and covenantal backgrounds, note that covenant terminology does not occur until Gen 6:18 where the Hebrew word בְּרִית (berît) first appears; furthermore, the Bible does not explicitly call the arrangement with God and Adam a covenant.[11] Anthony Hoekema, echoing the view of theologian John Murray, also challenges the idea of a pre-fall covenant because "the word *covenant* in Scripture is always used in a context of redemption. God establishes his covenant with fallen man, in order to provide a way whereby fallen humankind can be redeemed from sin."[12] Third, while the early

---

1:13, infers a general description for the notion of *covenant*. McComiskey, *Covenants of Promise*, 63, argues that the "basic idea underlying the concept of *běrît* is that of a relationship involving obligation." Similarly, Kline, *By Oath Consigned*, 16. Dumbrell, *Covenant and Creation*, 20, determines from the secular biblical examples that "covenants presupposed a set of existing relationships to which by formal ceremony they gave binding expression. They operated between two parties, though the status of the parties varied considerably." For covenant theologians defining covenants in light of ancient Near Eastern suzerain-vassal treaties, see Kline, *By Oath Consigned*, 14–22; Fesko, *Last Things First*, 78–81; Horton, *Introducing Covenant Theology*, 23–34, 74; Horton, *Christian Faith*, 44–45n19. For other definitions, all using a broader concept of covenant than that of Williamson or Stek, see Berkhof, *Systematic Theology*, 264; Bavinck, *Reformed Dogmatics*, 2:568; Turretin, *Institutes of Elenctic Theology*, 1:574; Murray, *Covenant of Grace*, 5–7; Murray, *Collected Writings*, 4:217. For an excellent compilation of how covenant was defined by seventeenth century classic covenant theologians, see Ward, *God and Adam*, 89–91.

10. Brown and Keele, *Sacred Bond*, 17; cf. Horton, *Introducing Covenant Theology*, 10; McManigal, *Encountering Christ in the Covenants*, 3–4; McKay, *Bond of Love*, 11–14. For a more technical study, see Hugenberger, *Marriage as a Covenant*, 171–74.

11. Williamson, *Sealed with an Oath*, 57–58, 72; Wright, *Knowing Jesus*, 80; Hoekema, *Created in God's Image*, 119.

12. Hoekema, *Created in God's Image*, 121; cf. Murray, *Collected Writings*, 2:49. Hoekema and Murray challenge the expression of the "covenant of works" but approve of the concepts behind the covenant of works, such as acknowledging Adam as a representative or federal head. Following Murray is McGowan, *Adam, Christ and Covenant*, 111–28, as he advances a headship theology rather than a covenant of works. See also Klooster, "Biblical Method of Salvation," 149. Similar to Klooster, Stek, "'Covenant'

chapters of Genesis contain commands and conditions, no oath, solemn obligation, or covenant ratification ceremony is necessary for the concept of a *berît*.[13]

Nevertheless, the covenant of works, sometimes labeled as the covenant of creation, nature, or law, is an old Reformed doctrine and essential to federal theology. Not only is this doctrine present in the past luminaries of the Reformed traditions, but recent studies of the Genesis narrative (Gen 2:15-17; 6:17-18; 9:8-17), along with indications from the rest of Scripture (e.g., Rom 5:12-21, 8:20; 1 Cor 15:20-23, 45-49; Heb 2:5-18), have confirmed that Gen 1-2 is a covenantal context with Adam as the federal head of humanity.[14] In terms of the theological content and formulation of the covenant of works, Charles Hodge offers an apt description:

> God having created man after his own image in knowledge, righteousness, and holiness, entered into a covenant of life with him, upon condition of perfect obedience, forbidding him to eat of the tree of knowledge of good and evil upon the pain of death. According to this statement, (1.) God entered into a covenant with Adam. (2.) The promise annexed to that covenant was life. (3.) The condition was perfect obedience. (4.) Its penalty was death.[15]

Overload," 40, argues, "Covenants served rather to offer assurances, bolster faith, and reinforce commitments. In a world not invaded by sin, there would be no need for adding oaths to commitments, no need for 'covenants'.... Biblical covenants were ad hoc emergency measures occasioned by and ministering to human weaknesses..." Berkouwer, *Sin*, 207-9, disputes the notion of a covenant of works wanting to avoid that man's original relation with God was strictly legal or could be merited by obedience. Other critiques are summarized in Golding, *Covenant Theology*, 105-9.

13. Williamson, *Sealed with an Oath*, 39, 43, 58; Hoekema, *Created in God's Image*, 120; Klooster, "Biblical Method of Salvation," 149-50.

14. For recent defenses of a covenant of works aimed toward covenant theologians who challenge the doctrine like those listed in n12, see Estelle, "Covenant of Works in Moses and Paul," 89-135; Bolt, "Why the Covenant of Works Is a Necessary Doctrine," 171-89; and Horton, *Introducing Covenant Theology*, 89-92, as he draws upon exegetical and theological considerations from traditional Reformed theologians such as Mastricht, Olevianus, and Cocceius. While not necessarily affirming all the aspects of the covenant of works, other studies have also shown the existence of a creation covenant or covenant with Adam: Gentry and Wellum, *Kingdom through Covenant*, 184-98, 666-85; Dumbrell, *Covenant and Creation*, 11-26, 31-39; Hafemann, "Covenant Relationship," 40-42; and Smith, "Structure and Purpose in Genesis 1-11," 307-19, esp. 310-11.

15. Hodge, *Systematic Theology*, 2:117; cf. Berkhof, *Systematic Theology*, 215-17, who has a similar breakdown of the covenant of works but has a fifth element regarding the sacrament or seal of the covenant of works. Brown and Keele, *Sacred Bond*, 45, define the covenant of works as "God's commitment to give Adam, and his posterity in

Hodge's description indicates that the covenant of works is a conditional covenant of love and law. Adam, created in a state of innocence and "in a state of positive righteousness—with all of its requisite natural and moral abilities to fulfill the commission entrusted to him," was situated in a probationary test or trial period such that his obedience and covenant loyalty and love would have merited him the right to eat from the tree of life, implicitly meaning that God would confirm him in everlasting peace and righteousness.[16] The covenant was legal in nature, for the stipulation entailed the penalty of death for disobedience (Gen 2:17). Since Adam was not just the natural head of a humanity, but the federal head or legal representative of all mankind, his transgression broke the covenant and the guilt associated with Adam's actions were imputed to his children. The covenant of works is important not only for hamartiology but also for the principle of corporate solidarity with persons being either in union with Adam or in Christ. The active obedience of Christ, with Christ perfectly satisfying the law of God in his life as a representative of his people, and the law/gospel distinction

---

him, eternal life for obedience or eternal death for disobedience." Bavinck, *Reformed Dogmatics*, 2:567, writes, "It was called 'covenant of nature,' not because it was deemed to flow automatically and naturally from the nature of God or the nature of man, but because of the foundation on which the covenant rested, that is, the moral law, was known to man by nature, and because it was made with man in his original state and could be kept by man with the powers bestowed on him in creation, without the assistance of supernatural grace. Later, when the term occasioned misunderstanding, it was preferentially replaced by that of 'covenant of works'; and it bore this name inasmuch as in this covenant eternal life could only be obtained in the way of works, that is, in the way of keeping God's commandments." For detailed discussion of the covenant of works, see Witsius, *Economy of Covenants*, 1:41–161; and Cocceius, *Doctrine of the Covenant*, 27–57. Significant statements on the covenant of works are in the *Westminster Confession of Faith*, chapter 7, sections 1 and 2, and chapter 19, section 1.

16. Horton, *Christian Faith*, 420–21; cf. Horton, *Introducing Covenant Theology*, 83–84. Though not all covenant theologians agree that Adam was placed on probation. McKay, *Bond of Love*, 16, states that the probationary notion is "highly speculative," but he does acknowledge that it is the majority opinion among covenantalists. See also Blocher, "Old Covenant, New Covenant," 255–59. Another debated is the presence of grace in the covenant of works. Both Horton and Reymond, *New Systematic Theology*, 405n23, 431–33, challenge Daniel Fuller (particularly *Gospel and Law*) and John Murray. The latter, according to Horton and Reymond, incorrectly views divine covenants as always entailing elements of grace; hence, Murray rejects the covenant of works. On the other hand, Reymond and other covenant theologians refute Fuller's views because of his claim that God's grace is operative in all of God's dealings with man, including the pre-fall situation with Adam. Most covenant theologians understand the original relationship with humanity to be a voluntary condescension rather than one of grace. The grace of God is expressed only after the fall while justice serves as the governing principle that unifies the pre-fall and redemptive covenants. Besides Murray, other covenantalists have argued for the gracious character of the covenant of works, such as Herman Bavinck, Charles Hodge, R. L. Dabney, Geerhardus Vos, and Blocher.

that weaves through both the OT and NT, both receive their foundation in Reformed theology through the doctrine of the covenant of works.

The Perpetuity of the Covenant of Works

As to the perpetuity of the covenant of works, there is debate among advocates of covenant theology. Hodge, Berkhof, and Reymond affirm that the covenant of works is in one sense abrogated but in another sense not abrogated.[17] On the one hand, the eternal principles of justice continue to be in force as created man always owes God perfect obedience. Further, the curse on disobedience and sin remains even as the conditional promise, though not attainable after the fall, remains (Lev 18:5; Rom 2:6–14, 10:5; Gal 3:12). The covenant of works is no longer in force, however, in that the probationary period with Adam is over—all mankind was on probation in Adam and as a result are children of wrath by nature, no longer born in a natural and innocent state. Moreover, the means of life rested in Adam's obedience, but following the fall, man cannot render perfect love and obedience to God and must find life through the second Adam, Christ, who has fulfilled the obligations to God and is the ground of man's approbation before God. Christ keeps the requirements of the covenant of works. On the other hand, not all covenantalists are convinced of this perspective on the covenant of works. Letham, for example, argues that the *effects* of the covenant of works remain, for the pre-fall covenant was broken and now abolished.[18] Man is still under obligation to obey God as his creature and not in covenantal terms. Letham writes,

> There is no sacrament of this covenant left, no promise of life, only a sentence of death, and so no probationary period. There was no way back to the garden after Adam was cast out, no chance—even hypothetical—to take his place and try again. Given this there can be no active covenant.[19]

---

17. Hodge, *Systematic Theology*, 2:122; Berkhof, *Systematic Theology*, 218; Reymond, *New Systematic Theology*, 439–40. Cf. Ward, *God and Adam*, 140–45; Witsius, *Economy of Covenants*, 1:151.

18. Letham, "Not a Covenant of Works," 143–77, esp. 148. Cf. Bavinck, *Reformed Dogmatics*, 3:65.

19. Letham, "Not a Covenant of Works," 149. Letham advances that it is the law of God which was given in the covenant of works that remains as the law transcends and outlasts that covenant.

According to Letham then, the covenant of works is not perpetual; rather, it is the law of God which was given in the covenant with Adam that remains.

The Covenant of Works and the Mosaic Covenant

The question of the perpetuity of the covenant of works also relates to an area of internal debate among paedobaptist covenant theologians: was the Mosaic covenant in some sense a republication of the covenant of works? There is even much disagreement as to how standard this republication thesis was in the history of reformed thought.[20] The seventeenth century was no stranger to the controversy on the nature of the Mosaic or Sinaitic covenant, as both John Ball and Francis Turretin observed four positions in their day: (1) the Mosaic covenant as a covenant of works; (2) the covenant was considered neither a covenant of works or grace but subservient to the covenant of grace; (3) the Mosaic covenant was a mixture of the covenant of grace and works; and finally (4) the Mosaic covenant was posited in the covenant of grace but promulgates the law.[21]

For most modern advocates of the republication thesis, which falls generally under the third view listed, the Mosaic covenant is a legal, conditional covenant that shares in the substance of the covenant of grace in terms of individual salvation (post-fall salvation is always by grace through

---

20. Horton, *Introducing Covenant Theology*, 97, follows what he describes as Meredith Kline's "defense of the classic federal view, which identified Israel's national covenant (Sinai) with law (indeed, the republication of the covenant of creation), and personal election and salvation with the covenant of grace (Abraham)." Further, Kline's position, argues Horton, is "an elaboration of a significant Reformed consensus in the past." On the other hand, Letham, who rejects the perpetuity of the covenant of works and the notion of the Mosaic covenant as a republication of the covenant of works, acknowledges that Kline's position has formal similarities in Reformed orthodoxy, but it was a "minority report" and never "adopted by any Reformed confession." Letham, "Not a Covenant of Works," 152–69, esp. 169. Also advancing a similar position in line with Letham is Venema, "Mosaic Covenant," 57–76. Those aligned with Meredith Kline and Michael Horton in arguing that many within Reformed orthodoxy affirmed a doctrine of republication include Clark, "Christ and Covenant," 403–28; Karlberg, *Covenant Theology*, 17–58; Fesko, "Calvin and Witsius on the Mosaic Covenant," 25–43; and Brown and Keele, *Sacred Bond*, 105. See also Golding, *Covenant Theology*, 164–69.

21. See Turretin, *Institutes of Elenctic Theology*, 2:262; and Beach, *Christ and the Covenant*, 301–2. John Ball's categorizations are laid out in Letham, "Not a Covenant of Works," 153–60. Cf. Ward, *God and Adam*, 126–39. Turretin and Ball appear to affirm the fourth position. See also Vos, *Reformed Dogmatics*, 2:128–31. According to Denault, *Distinctiveness of Baptist Covenant Theology*, 18–23, the famous Puritan, John Owen, advanced the second position.

faith and not through obedient law keeping) and yet features a works principle reiterated from the covenant of works, which Israel was required to obey in order to receive the temporal covenantal blessings and retention of the land of Canaan (Lev 18:5, 26–28; 20:22).[22] Israel was a corporate Adam, recapitulating Adam's creation, fall, and also situated under probation, required to obey God's commands to remain in the land and retain its national identity and status (Exod 20:12; 19:5, 7–8). Instead, Israel received covenant curses for disobedience in the form of judgment and exile. These features of the Mosaic covenant typologically and pedagogically point to Christ's obedience to the law as he fulfilled the stipulations of the covenant of works, meriting the blessings of salvation, and led his people to the everlasting rest of the eternal promised land.[23]

Other covenantalists reject the republication thesis as they understand such a perspective to be at odds with consistently maintaining two separate covenants, the prelapsarian covenant of works and the postlapsarian covenant of grace with the Mosaic covenant *substantially* being a covenant of grace while only *accidentally* distinct from the other administrations of the covenant of grace.[24] Venema explains,

---

22. Horton, *Introducing Covenant Theology*, 31–34, 47, 90, 94, 97–104, 130–31; Brown and Keele, *Sacred Bond*, 106–16; McManigal, *Encountering Christ in the Covenants*, 64–78; Kline, *Kingdom Prologue*, 320–23; note also Kline, *By Oath Consigned*, 22–25. Hodge, *Systematic Theology*, 2:375, after placing the Sinaitic covenant within the covenant of grace, also highlights two other aspects: "First, it was a national covenant with the Hebrew people. In this view . . . the promise was national security and prosperity; the condition was the obedience of the people as a nation to the Mosaic law; and the mediator was Moses. In this aspect it was a legal covenant. It said, 'Do this and live.' Secondly, it contained, as does also the New Testament, a renewed proclamation of the original covenant of works. It is as true now as in the days of Adam . . . that rational creatures who perfectly obey the law of God are blessed in the enjoyment of his favour; and that those who sin are subject to his wrath and curse."

23. Proponents of the republication thesis view the Mosaic covenant as having the substance of the covenant of grace because it was a post-fall covenant with a history of grace (Abraham and the patriarchs) leading up to it, because it featured elements of grace (e.g., the sacrificial system), and because it ultimately pointed to the perfect law-keeper and redeemer, Jesus Christ.

24. Venema, "Mosaic Covenant," 92. For Letham's reasons for rejecting the notion of republication, see "Not a Covenant of Works," 147–48. Letham argues that Israel was already in covenant with Yahweh through the promises of the Abrahamic covenant and the law was given to the people by God's free grace. Noting God's redemption of Israel from Egypt (Exod 20:2–3), Letham, "Not a Covenant of Works," 147, asserts the "process was not 'do this and live' but 'you are my people; therefore you shall do this, and in doing this you shall live.'" Bavinck, *Reformed Dogmatics*, 3:220–22, also argues that the covenant at Sinai was essentially no other than that with Abraham and carried the same benefits as the Abrahamic. He writes that the Mosaic covenant of grace "is but an explication for the one statement to Abraham: 'Walk before me, and be blameless'

> If what belongs to the substance of the covenant of works does not belong to the substance of the covenant of grace *in any of its administrations*, it is semantically and theologically problematic to denominate the Mosaic administration as *in any sense* a covenant of works.[25]

Furthermore, Venema and Letham are unconvinced with the understanding of typology that is postulated by adherents of the republication thesis. Venema particularly highlights the problem of typology:

> From the vantage point of this understanding of the nature of biblical typology, it is difficult to make sense of the claim that the Mosaic administration functioned typologically as a kind of covenant of works, at least at the stratum of Israel's inheritance of temporal blessings. In order for this to be the case, a disjunction has to be posited between Israel's inheritance of temporal blessings and her inheritance of spiritual blessings. In the usual view of Reformed covenant theology, however, the temporal blessings promised Israel are regarded typologically as a foreshadowing of the full spiritual blessing of fellowship with God in a renewed creation. The promise to Israel of blessing and life in the land of promise represented in the state of her immaturity a picture of the fullness of salvation in the life to come.

[Gen. 17:1], and therefore no more a cancellation of the covenant of grace and the foundation of the covenant of works than this word spoken to Abraham" (p. 222). Similarly, Berkhof, *Systematic Theology*, 298, writes, "The Sinaitic covenant included a service that contained a positive reminder of the strict demands of the covenant of works. . . . But the covenant at Sinai was not a renewal of the covenant of works; in it the law was made subservient to the covenant of grace." See also Robertson, *Christ of the Covenants*, 172–75; and Frame, *Systematic Theology*, 72–73.

25. Venema, "Mosaic Covenant," 92, emphasis original. Venema adds that in positing a principle that substantially belongs to the covenant of works economy to the Mosaic administration, "the Mosaic economy is viewed as though it included features at some level of administration that belong to the substance of a different covenant, namely, the prelapsarian covenant of works." Ibid., 93. Perhaps this concern is not misplaced as Johnson, *Kingdom of God*, 24, a Reformed Baptist, writes, "It is interesting to note that some within Presbyterian covenant theology have stepped closer to the Baptist position by confessing that the Mosaic Covenant was a republication of the covenant of works. This admission significantly advocates a higher degree of *discontinuity* between the old and new covenants because the Mosaic covenant no longer is considered a manifestation of the covenant of grace." Of course even those advocating the republication thesis would still affirm the Mosaic covenant as a covenant of grace, so Horton, *Introducing Covenant Theology*, 54–55, though Horton is ambiguous about how exactly the Mosaic is a covenant of grace when he states, "The covenant of grace is uninterrupted from Adam after the fall to the present, while the Sinai Pact, conditional and typological, has now become obsolete (Heb. 8:13), its mission having been fulfilled (Gal. 3:23—4:7)." Horton, *Introducing Covenant Theology*, 75.

Canaan was a "type" of the "city that has foundations, whose designer and builder is God" (Heb. 11:10, ESV). Moreover, in Kline's view of the typology of the Mosaic covenant, two radically opposed inheritance principles are posited, each of which is said to operate at a distinct level of Israel's life, the earthly and the spiritual. In the case of Israel's earthly inheritance, the operative principle is one of (meritorious) works; in the case of Israel's spiritual inheritance, the operative principle is that of grace alone. The problem with this conception is that the typology of Mosaic economy does not foreshadow or prefigure, at least at the level of Israel's existence as a nation in the land of promise, the blessings that are granted freely and graciously to the new covenant people of God. The blessings are different in kind; and the principles for the inheritance of these blessings are radically different. To put the matter differently, because the Mosaic administration actually consists of two levels of covenant administration, one of works and the other of grace, it cannot function at both levels as a typological promise of the new covenant, which is essentially and exclusively a covenant of grace.[26]

While the debate within covenant theology showcases an internal tension with how the Mosaic covenant is best understood within the conception of the two overarching covenants of works and of grace, all covenantalists interpret the moral law within the Mosaic covenant as functioning to instruct Israel for her need of a perfectly obedient Son and to arouse the consciousness of sin and one's inability to obey God's commands. Moreover, despite the debate over the principle of works in the Mosaic covenant, all covenantalists agree that the features of the Mosaic administration, such as the tabernacle, temple, priesthood, sacrifices, and the promised land, functioned typologically of the spiritual blessings of the new covenant economy.[27] To complete the overview of how covenantalists

---

26. Venema, "Mosaic Covenant," 90–91. See also Letham, "Not a Covenant of Works," 170–71; and Robertson, *Christ of the Prophets*, 364–65n6.

27. While Venema opposes the typological argument of the covenant of works being republished in the Mosaic by Kline, Horton, and others, he affirms that because "the Mosaic administration of the covenant includes everything that belongs to the substance of the covenant of grace, it communicated the same grace of Christ, albeit in the form of anticipatory types and shadows, as is communicated in the new covenant in Christ. The promises and obligations of the Mosaic economy are substantially the same as the promises and obligations of the new covenant economy." Venema, "Mosaic Covenant," 93. For further on how the Mosaic covenant as a covenant of grace was typological of salvation realities in Christ, see the WCF 7.5.

understand the progress and development of the storyline of Scripture, the crucial role of covenant of grace is explored next.

COVENANT OF GRACE

The defining mark as a system of continuity for covenant theology is inexorably linked to the understanding of the unified and overarching covenant of grace, which stands as the framework for the whole progress of revelation after the fall. Genesis 3 through Revelation unfolds God's plan of redemption in history as God, now appearing as Redeemer and Father, promises a Savior who will undo the curses of sin in graciously rescuing a people, all of which is ultimately realized in Jesus Christ's obedience and atoning work.[28] While the historical inauguration of the covenant of grace occurs with the gracious promise of a seed, a second Adam, who will crush the head of the serpent (Gen 3:15) and is then the basis for all the post-fall divine-human covenants (Noahic, Abrahamic, Mosaic, Davidic, and the new), the covenant of grace is grounded in and flows out of the covenant of redemption from eternity past, historically unfolding the way of salvation throughout the testaments in terms of justification by faith alone in the mediator of this covenant, Jesus Christ.[29] The gospel, which is the revelation of the covenant

---

28. Discussions of the covenant of grace may be found in Berkhof, *Systematic Theology*, 272–83; Hodge, *Systematic Theology*, 2:362–77; Turretin, *Institutes of Elenctic Theology*, 2:174–247; Bavinck, *Reformed Dogmatics*, 3:193–232; Reymond, *New Systematic Theology*, 503–37; Murray, *Collected Writings*, 4:223–40; Golding, *Covenant Theology*, 121–63; Brown and Keele, *Sacred Bond*, 57–71. See also the WCF chapter 7, sections 3 and 5. A helpful definition of the covenant of grace is provided by Turretin, *Institutes of Elenctic Theology*, 2:175: "This covenant of grace is a gratuitous pact entered into in Christ between God offended and man offending. In it God promises remission of sins and salvation to man gratuitously on account of Christ; man, however, relying upon the same grace promises faith and obedience. Or it is a gratuitous agreement between God offended and man offending, concerning the bestowal of grace and glory in Christ upon the sinner upon condition of faith." Cf. Witsius, *Economy of Covenants*, 1:165; Cocceius, *Doctrine of the Covenant*, 71–72.

29. According to Bavinck, *Reformed Dogmatics*, 3:215–16, "All the grace that is extended to the creation after the fall comes to it from the Father, through the Son, in the Holy Spirit. The Son appeared immediately after the fall, as Mediator, as the second and final Adam who occupies the place of the first, restores what the latter corrupted, and accomplishes what he failed to do. And the Holy Spirit immediately acted as the Paraclete, the one applying the salvation acquired by Christ. All the change that occurs, all the development and progress in insight and knowledge, accordingly, occurs on the side of the creature. . . . The Father is the eternal Father, the Son the eternal Mediator, the Holy Spirit the eternal Paraclete. For that reason the Old Testament is also to be viewed as one in essence and substance with the New Testament. . . . Although Christ completed his work on earth only in the midst of history and although the Holy Spirit

of grace, is the same throughout the storyline of Scripture, and therefore, there is one covenant of grace. To maintain the unity of the covenant of grace while also recognizing the different covenants throughout the OT and NT, covenantalists make a fundamental distinction between the substance and administrations of the covenant of grace. Furthermore, the nature of the covenant of grace is distinguished with respect to internal and external aspects, often referred to as the "dual aspect" of the covenant of grace. Each of these subjects, though vastly important, is summarized next.

The Substance and Administrations of the Covenant of Grace

By maintaining a distinction between the substance or essence and the administrations or dispensations of the covenant of grace, paedobaptist covenantalists understand a significant unity across the OT and NT that has direct ramifications for ecclesiology, especially as such a construction grounds a direct continuity between Israel and the church and establishes the basis for infant baptism. First, the substance of the covenant of grace, which accounts for the unity of the testaments and was already alluded to, is God's sovereign initiative to dispense grace to sinful man so that the Lord will be God to his people through the mediatory work of Christ, comprising of the same promises made to Adam after the fall (Gen 3:15), to Noah (Gen 6:9; 7:1; 9:9, 26–27), to Abraham (Gen 17:7), and through Moses (Exod 3:15; 19:5; Deut 29:13), David (2 Sam 7:14), and lastly, having its fullness in the new covenant (Jer 31:33; Heb 8). The promised benefits of the covenant of grace, namely reconciliation and communion with God, was granted to OT and NT believers alike. Brown and Keele write, "The covenant of grace was administered by type and shadow . . . during the times of the patriarchs . . . and of the nation Israel, as believers put their trust in God's promise to send the Messiah."[30]

---

was not poured out till the day of Pentecost, God nevertheless was able, already in the days of the Old Testament, to fully distribute the benefits to be acquired by the Son and the Spirit. Old Testament believers were saved in no other way than we. There is one faith, one Mediator, one way of salvation, and one covenant of grace." On this point, see also Reymond, *New Systematic Theology*, 528–35; Hodge, *Systematic Theology*, 2:366–73. For the covenant of redemption as the basis of the covenant of grace, see Vos, "Doctrine of the Covenant," 252.

30. Brown and Keele, *Sacred Bond*, 59. The unity and substance of the covenant of grace through the different dispensations or administrations is maintained for a variety of reasons including the identity of the mediator (Jesus Christ) being the same in both the OT and NT, the summary expression of the covenant that God will be the covenant Lord to his people occurs throughout Scripture, the same condition of faith is required throughout, and the way of salvation is the same in the sense of the

Nevertheless, according to the wisdom of God the same covenant of grace was dispensed in diverse manners. Turretin explains that the covenant of grace

> had various forms and as it were faces, on account of the varied economy of the mystery of Christ (who is its foundation), which God so willed to administer as to propose it at first somewhat obscurely and then more clearly; first in the promise and then in the fulfillment.[31]

Clearer manifestations of the covenant of grace are revealed through redemptive history, but the *protoevangelium* (Gen 3:15), Noahic, Abrahamic, Mosaic, Davidic, and new covenants are all administrations of the covenant of grace. Although these covenants differ in their accidental properties (nonessential parts) and are diverse and particular in terms of mode, they all profoundly agree in their substance.[32]

---

gospel being promised (as in the OT) or completed and manifested (NT). See Berkhof, *Systematic Theology*, 277–80; Turretin, *Institutes of Elenctic Theology*, 2:192–205; Witsius, *Economy of Covenants*, 1:292–306; Hodge, *Systematic Theology*, 2:364–73; and Robertson, *Christ of the Covenants*, 45–52.

31. Turretin, *Institutes of Elenctic Theology*, 2:216. Similarly, Witsius, *Economy of Covenants*, 1:308 (cf. 291), writes, "The difference of the testaments consists in the different manner of dispensing and proposing the same saving grace, and in some different adjuncts and circumstances. Whatever was typical in that dispensation, and denoted imperfection, and an acknowledgment that the ransom was not yet paid, belongs to the Old Testament. Whatever shews that the redemption is actually wrought out, is peculiar to the New Testament." Karlberg, *Covenant Theology*, 22, highlighting the unity of the covenant of grace in Heinrich Bullinger (1504–1575), observes that the "common formulation of the essential nature of the Covenant of Grace is imbedded within the Reformed tradition. The employment of scholastic terminology is clearly evident, viz., the terms 'substance' and 'accidents.' In substance there is unity; in accidents (the historical administrations of the single Covenant of Grace) there is diversity."

32. See Calvin, *Institutes of the Christian Religion* 2.10.2, 429, 448–49; Berkhof, *Systematic Theology*, 279–85; Witsius, *Economy of Covenants*, 1:291–306; Turretin, *Institutes of Elenctic Theology*, 2:192–205, 216–40; Bavinck, *Reformed Dogmatics*, 3:216–28; Murray, *Covenant of Grace*, 27–32. Robertson, *Christ of the Covenants*, 28 (cf. 34), writes, "The cumulative evidence of the Scriptures points definitely toward the unified character of the biblical covenants. God's multiple bonds with his people ultimately unite into a single relationship. Particular details of the covenants may vary. A definite line of progress may be noted. Yet the covenants of God are one." Note also Venema, "Covenant Theology and Baptism," 215–17. Reformed Baptist covenant theologians differ among themselves on the topic of the administrations of the covenant of grace. According to Denault, *Distinctiveness of Baptist Covenant Theology*, 71, seventeenth-century Reformed Baptists understood a progressive revelation of the covenant of grace before its establishment. Thus, the "Abrahamic Covenant, the Sinaitic Covenant and the Davidic Covenant were not the Covenant of Grace, nor administrations of it; however, the Covenant of Grace was revealed under these various administrations." See

While all of the post-fall covenants are part of the unified covenant of grace, one covenantal administration plays a foundational role. According to Reymond, "Once the covenant of grace had come to expression in the spiritual promises of the Abrahamic covenant, the Abrahamic covenant became salvifically definitive for all ages to come."[33] The Abrahamic covenant is the most normative covenant for the NT economy. Berkhof writes,

> [The] Sinaitic covenant is an interlude, covering a period in which the real character of the covenant of grace, that is, its free and gracious character, is somewhat eclipsed by all kinds of external ceremonies and forms.... In the covenant with Abraham, on the other hand, the promise and the faith that responds to the promise are made emphatic.[34]

The Abrahamic is the model covenant for how God works out the covenant of redemption through the progress of revelation as the Abrahamic is tightly viewed in relation to the new covenant. Berkhof explains that the Abrahamic covenant "is still in force and is essentially identical with the 'new covenant' of the present dispensation."[35]

The accent upon the Abrahamic covenant in the covenant of grace does not mean that paedobaptist covenant theologians do not see a qualitative difference between the Abrahamic and new covenant. The new covenant does not abrogate or cancel the Abrahamic, but fills out, extends, and expands it. The new covenant is really "new" in how it is distinguished

---

Renihan, *Mystery of Christ*, 170–75 for his discussion of the new covenant as the covenant of grace. On the other hand, Chantry, "Covenants of Works and of Grace," 108, argues that all the biblical covenants after the fall are administrations of the covenant of grace.

33. Reymond, *New Systematic Theology*, 512. Reymond adds, "So significant are the promises of grace in the Abrahamic covenant, found in Genesis 12:1–3; 13:14–16; 15:18–21; 17:1–16; 22:16–18, that it is not an overstatement to declare these verses, from the covenantal perspective, as the most important verses in the Bible" (p. 513). Also highlighting how the concrete form of the covenant of grace is found in the Abrahamic covenant is Murray, *Collected Writings*, 4:223–24; Golding, *Covenant Theology*, 122; Berkhof, *Systematic Theology*, 295–97.

34. Berkhof, *Systematic Theology*, 296–97. See also Horton, *Introducing Covenant Theology*, 37, 54–57, 60, 70, 75, 106, as he views the Abrahamic covenant as an unconditional covenant of promise in contrast to the Mosaic (covenant of law). While the Mosaic is still part of the covenant of grace, the Abrahamic covenant is presented as having the basis and direct connection to the new covenant.

35. Berkhof, *Systematic Theology*, 633; cf. Bromiley, *Children of Promise*, 23–24; Brown and Keele, *Sacred Bond*, 86–87; and Murray, *Covenant of Grace*, 27. Hodge, *Systematic Theology*, 2:373, also, appealing to Gal 3:13–28 and Rom 3:21, argues, "The covenant under which we live and according to the terms of which we are to be saved, is the identical covenant made with Abraham."

from the old covenant: it is designed and received by all nations, dispensed with the highest level of grace with sin definitively dealt with, results in the democratization of the teaching and priestly offices (or the end of individuals as covenant mediators), marks out a new age with the Holy Spirit poured out on all flesh, and is the permanent and final arrangement before the restoration of all things.[36] In sum, the new covenant completes all the promises, preparatory types, shadows, and adumbrations of the OT economy, especially with reference to the institutions of the Mosaic covenant.[37] Nevertheless, the new covenant is not new in terms of substance given the organic unity of the covenant of grace but is new in form or mode only even as greater blessings are realized.[38]

---

36. Other reasons may be offered for the "newness" of the new covenant. See Hodge, *Systematic Theology*, 2:376–77; Berkhof, *Systematic Theology*, 299–300; Murray, *Covenant of Grace*, 31–32; Witsius, *Economy of Covenants*, 1:308; Turretin, *Institutes of Elenctic Theology*, 2:232–33; Bavinck, *Reformed Dogmatics*, 3:223–24; Robertson, *Christ of the Covenants*, 57–63, 275–86, 293–96; McManigal, *Encountering Christ in the Covenants*, 101–8; Beale, *New Testament Biblical Theology*, 730–40; Neill, "Newness of the New Covenant," 127–55; Booth, *Children of Promise*, 63–66; Williams, *Far as the Curse Is Found*, 210–16; cf. Gentry and Wellum, *Kingdom through Covenant*, 87–88. Most covenantalists also recognize continuity between the old and the new because the old covenant is not condemned; rather, it is Israel's covenant breaking that leads to a new covenant. Further, the law of the old covenant is not abrogated, and neither does Jer 31 call for a new law; the substance of covenant law is continuous through the old and the new covenants according to covenant theologians. Reformed Baptist covenant theologians part ways with this understanding on the nature of the new covenant, see Denault, *Distinctiveness of Baptist Covenant Theology*, 63–67; White, "Newness of the New Covenant (Part I)," 144–68; and White, "Newness of the New Covenant (Part II)," 83–104.

37. Not all covenantalists would agree that the new covenant is "new." Some refer to the new covenant in terms of "renewal" (e.g., Kline, *By Oath Consigned*, 75). More recent works by covenant theologians have sought to explicate each of the historical covenants within the covenant of grace (e.g., McManigal, *Encountering Christ in the Covenants*; Brown and Keele, *Sacred Bond*; Robertson, *Christ of the Covenants*). However, covenantalists typically framed the Bible into a three-fold structure: (1) Adam to Abraham, (2) Abraham to Moses, and (3) Moses to Christ. Examples of this approach include Hodge, *Systematic Theology*, 2:373–76; Turretin, *Institutes of Elenctic Theology*, 2:220–25; while Witsius, *Economy of Covenants*, 1:313–17; and Berkhof, *Systematic Theology*, 292–300, also discuss the Noahic covenant. See also Clowney, *Preaching and Biblical Theology*, 16; and Vos, *Biblical Theology*. Graeme Goldsworthy rightly criticizes this approach because it does not allow the OT to speak for itself and provide its own epochal structures. Specifically, the move from Moses to David and the eschatological perspective of the latter prophets is neglected. See Goldsworthy, *Christ-Centered Biblical Theology*, 87, 113. Gladd, *From Adam and Israel to the Church*, is a recent example as little attention is paid to David and the role of the Davidic covenant.

38. On this point, see especially Borg, "New Covenant (Jeremiah 31:31–34)," 16–34.

The Dual Aspect of the Covenant of Grace

Alongside the unity of the covenant of grace is another important theological consideration that will be surveyed briefly: the parties of the covenant of grace. For most covenant theologians, the covenant of grace is conceived as being both unconditional—God unilaterally establishes the covenant and meets the conditions himself through grace in Christ—and conditional—based on the suretyship of the last Adam (who fulfills the covenant of works). In addition, the covenant is conditional in that the satisfaction of covenant stipulations are met as those who receive the promises of the covenant possess the necessary responses of faith and repentance but in a relative and instrumental sense for God provides the gift of faith.[39]

This understanding of the covenant naturally leads to a topic of more difficulty in regard to the parties or dual aspect of the covenant. According to most Reformed theologians, membership in the covenant of grace is defined as comprising the elect in Christ, but in other respects is delineated as consisting of believers and their children.[40] With the conditionality of the covenant of grace in terms of individual faith, repentance, and covenant loyalty, the covenant of grace is not confined to the elect because this would not allow for covenant breakers.[41] Regenerate and unregenerate are in the covenant of grace as distinctions have been made between an external/internal covenant, or between essence and administration, or spiritual and natural, or legal versus a communion of life.[42] However construed, as

---

39. See Berkhof, *Systematic Theology*, 280–81; Murray, *Collected Writings*, 4:225–34; Venema, "Covenant Theology and Baptism," 211. Witsius, *Economy of Covenants*, 1:281–91; Turretin, *Institutes of Elenctic Theology*, 2:184–89; and Bavinck, *Reformed Dogmatics*, 3:229–30, all emphasize the unconditional and unilateral nature of the covenant of grace but also acknowledge the duties and obligations but in a manner that comports with the operations of grace which are unconditional. For a general overview, see also Wellum, "Baptism and the Relationship," 105–7. Horton, *Introducing Covenant Theology*, argues that the ANE covenantal forms permit classifying the Noahic, Abrahamic, Davidic, and new covenants as royal grant covenants and unconditional while the Mosaic covenant reflects a suzerain-vassal treaty and is thus conditional (e.g., 40–50, 68–69, 74–75). Nevertheless, the new covenant has a variety of conditions (182–86) that are real and yet graciously provided via Christ's fulfillment of God's standards (105, 184–85).

40. Discussion of the dual aspect of the covenant of grace may be found in Berkhof, *Systematic Theology*, 284–89; Bavinck, *Reformed Dogmatics*, 3:228–32; Golding, *Covenant Theology*, 128–30.

41. Golding, *Covenant Theology*, 128. For covenant breaking in the new covenant community, see Pratt, "Infant Baptism in the New Covenant," 169–74.

42. Golding, *Covenant Theology*, 128; Berkhof, *Systematic Theology*, 284–87; Bavinck, *Reformed Dogmatics*, 3:231; Denault, *Distinctiveness of Baptist Covenant Theology*, 43.

THE HERMENEUTICS OF COVENANT THEOLOGY

Bavinck notes, some are *in* the covenant, but not *of* the covenant, for the covenant of grace passes through history and through different dispensations and "is never made with a solitary individual but always also with his or her descendants."[43] The one unified covenant of grace in its essence, argues Horton, is unchangeable and inviolable because of the mediatorial work of Christ, but as an administration involves conditions:

> [It] is a covenant made with believers and their children. Not everyone in the covenant of grace is elect: the Israel below is a larger class than the Israel above. Some Israelites heard the gospel in the wilderness and responded in faith, while others did not—and the writer to the Hebrews uses this as a warning also to New Testament heirs of the same covenant of grace (Heb. 4:1–11).[44]

In summary, covenantalists posit that the substance of the covenant of grace remains the same throughout the unfolding of the biblical covenants and the principle of covenant membership, a dual aspect, is present through each administration of the covenant of grace, including the new covenant. The Reformed theological grid of a covenant of works and covenant of grace naturally is foundational for paedobaptist covenant ecclesiology such as the mixed nature of the people of God, the notion of the visible and invisible church, and the correlation of baptism with circumcision in the OT.[45] The genealogical principle—"to you and your offspring"—is constant throughout every administration of the covenant of grace, but germane for the purposes of this study are the clear implications that these theologically constructed covenants have in leading to a very tight relationship between Israel and the church.

---

43. Bavinck, *Reformed Dogmatics*, 3:231–32. For a helpful description of how unregenerate are in the covenant of grace in terms of responsibility, having a claim to the promises and being subject to the warnings of the covenant, and granted influential benefits of the Spirit, but only standing in the covenant in terms of a legal relationship, see Berkhof, *Systematic Theology*, 289.

44. Horton, *Introducing Covenant Theology*, 182.

45. For discussion of how the paedobaptist teaching of the covenant of grace relates to these areas of ecclesiology from a historical standpoint, see Denault, *Distinctiveness of Baptist Covenant Theology*, 39–54. Note also, Gentry and Wellum, *Kingdom through Covenant*, 84–105.

ISRAEL AND THE CHURCH IN COVENANT THEOLOGY

Flowing straightforwardly from the unified covenant of grace that incorporates every covenant after Adam's fall, covenant theologians stress the oneness of the people of God and the continuity between OT Israel and the church of the NT. There is one church embracing the people of God under both the old and new covenants.[46] Berkhof expresses a representative view of the relationship between Israel and the church from a covenantal perspective:

> The New Testament Church is essentially one with the Church of the old dispensation. As far as their essential nature is concerned, they both consist of true believers, and of true believers only. And in their external organization both represent a mixture of good and evil. Yet several important changes resulted from the accomplished work of Jesus Christ. The Church was divorced from the national life of Israel and obtained an independent organization. In connection with this the national boundaries of the Church were swept away. What had up to this time been a national Church now assumed a universal character.[47]

Covenant theologians understand the unity of the people of God either in terms of replacement or fulfillment.[48] Some covenantalists argue that the NT church actually *replaces* OT Israel since Israel has forfeited its national identity by disobedience and faithlessness.[49] Others refrain from

---

46. Some covenantalists do agree with dispensationalists that the NT church begins at Pentecost; see Karlberg, "Israel and the Eschaton," 128; and Klooster, "Biblical Method of Salvation," 159. Nevertheless, while the pouring out of the Spirit at Pentecost marks a new and glorious era, the content of saving faith and union with Christ remain the same throughout redemptive history. See Gaffin, "Pentecost: Before and After," 3–24.

47. Berkhof, *Systematic Theology*, 571. Besides the universal character that marks a contrast with Israel of old, Berkhof also notes the missionary role and spiritual worship of the church that are other changes for the church in the NT era.

48. Besides the discussion by Berkhof, for more on the relationship between OT Israel and the NT church, see Bavinck, *Reformed Dogmatics*, 4:277–79, 4:665–67; Hodge, *Systematic Theology*, 3:548–52; Clowney, "New Israel," 207–20; Horton, *Christian Faith*, 729–33; Horton, *Introducing Covenant Theology*, 129–35; Reymond, "Traditional Covenantal View," 17–68; Ridderbos, *Paul*, 333–41, 360–61; Beale, *New Testament Biblical Theology*, 651–749; Robertson, *Israel of God*, 33–51; Woudstra, "Israel and the Church," 221–38; Holwerda, *Jesus and Israel*, 27–58, 147–84; Hoekema, *Bible and the Future*, 194–201, 215–16; Venema, *Promise of the Future*, 261–77; Booth, *Children of Promise*, 71–95; cf. Merkle, *Discontinuity to Continuity*, 159–63.

49. For example, Waltke, "Kingdom Promises as Spiritual," 274, writes, "National

the language of *replacement* and repudiate the accusation of supersessionism by delineating the continuity as one of fulfillment and redefinition.⁵⁰ Regardless, as the embodiment and successor to Israel, the NT church is the "true" or "new" Israel. Israel's promises and status are transferred to the NT church.⁵¹ Even if Rom 11 teaches a mass conversion of Jews in the future, a national and political restoration of Israel is not in purview, for all the prerogatives, promises, and prophecies to OT Israel are translated to the church.⁵²

The covenant of grace serves as the grounding for the continuity of the church throughout the OT and NT, but covenantalists also establish this position by a variety of biblical and theological arguments. The main points below are by no means exhaustive but highlight some of the important reasons covenant theologians understand the church as a singular, unified body and covenant community throughout redemptive history.

Israel and its law have been permanently replaced by the church and the New Covenant." Bavinck, *Reformed Dogmatics*, 4:667, states, "The community of believers has in all respects replaced carnal, national Israel. The Old Testament is fulfilled in the New" (cf. 296). Karlberg, "Significance of Israel," 263, 269, advances a similar line of thinking. Note also Zorn, *Christ Triumphant*, 22–49, esp. 30. Other scholars also use the language of replacement. See for example, LaRondelle, *Israel of God*, 101, cf. 130–31; and France, *Jesus and the Old Testament*, 67. Cf. Bright, *Kingdom of God*, 228.

50. For example, Horton, *Christian Faith*, 730–31, writes, "The church does not replace Israel; it fulfills the promise God made to Abraham that in him and his seed all the nations would be blessed. . . . Israel is not replaced by the church, but is the church *in nuce*, just as the church is the anticipation of the kingdom of God." Likewise, see Williams, *Far as the Curse Is Found*, 251–52. For Pratt, "To the Jew First," 174, the Reformed position is not replacement theology but is a "unity theology." Pratt further establishes the unity of Israel and the church by appealing to Reformed understanding of the invisible and visible church. On this topic, see also Storms, *Kingdom Come*, 177–227, esp. 195–96.

51. Zorn, *Christ Triumphant*, 30–38.

52. Fairbairn, *Interpretation of Prophecy*, 246, writes, "Unquestionably, there is no explicit announcement to [the re-establishment of the Jewish old economy] in the whole range of the historical and epistolary writings of the New Testament. The infliction of divine judgment upon the mass of the Jewish people, was very distinctly proclaimed by our Lord himself, with the destruction of their city and temple, and the scattering of the community at once from the kingdom of God, and from the land of their fathers. But in not so much as one passage does he unequivocally indicate for them a re-gathering to their paternal home, or a reinvestment with their former relative distinctions and privileges; far less is there any statement to imply, that the temple-worship should be again set up as the common religious centre and resort of Christendom." There is a minority voice within covenant theology for making a case for a "remarkable 'fluidity'" on the future and restoration of Israel, see VanGemeren, "Israel as the Hermeneutical Crux," 132–44; and VanGemeren, "Israel as the Hermeneutical Crux (II)," 254–97. There were also diverse views regarding unfulfilled prophecy and Israel's restoration among the Puritans.

Much attention is made to how the NT authors apply the Greek word for church (ἐκκλησία), sometimes translated "congregation" or "assembly," to the new covenant people of God when the exact same word is used in the Septuagint (LXX) to translate the Hebrew term for assembly (קָהָל). The term "church" is an OT word as it is used for the assembly of the old covenant people of God (Deut 4:10; 9:10; 10:4). The NT church looks back to the "church in the wilderness" (Acts 7:38; 1 Cor 10:1–11; Heb 12:18–28).[53] The OT church or assembly was a prototype of the NT church, and yet the terminology of ἐκκλησία designates the essence of the church throughout both the OT and NT.

Second, the OT titles and designations for Israel are applied in the NT to the church, and as such, contend covenantalists, provide rationale for a significant degree of continuity between Israel and the church. Williams succinctly describes a variety of images of Israel applied to the church:

> The image of Jesus as the bridegroom (Mark 2:18–20) and the church as the bride of Christ (2 Cor. 11:2) develop the Old Testament image of Israel as the wife of God (Isa. 54:5–8; 62:5; Jer. 2:2). Other Old Testament imagery for the people of God that is carried over into the New and applied to the church includes the church as the branches of a vine (John 15), a flock led by a shepherd (Luke 12:32; John 10:1–8), the elect (Rom. 11:28; Eph. 1:4), a priesthood (1 Peter 2:9; Rev. 1:6), the remnant (Rom. 9:27; 11:5–7), the true circumcision (Rom. 2:28–29; Phil. 3:3; Col. 2:11), and Abraham's seed (Rom. 4:16; Gal. 3:29).[54]

Descriptions of the church as the "saints," the "beloved," and the "called" could also be added as these find their origin as references to Israel too.[55] In addition, a majority of covenant theologians understand that the church is called the "Israel of God" by Paul in Galatians 6:16.[56] Taken to-

---

53. McKay, *Bond of Love*, 198; Berkhof, *Systematic Theology*, 571–72; Clowney, "New Israel," 209–11; Clowney, *Church*, 30–32; Williams, *Far as the Curse Is Found*, 247–48; Woudstra, "Israel and the Church," 222; Zorn, *Christ Triumphant*, 11–12. Horton, *Christian Faith*, 719–20, notes the progress of the assembly as "a progression from 'people of God' (as promise) to *ekklēsia* (fulfillment)." See also Bavinck, *Reformed Dogmatics*, 4:277–79; 296–97; and Reymond, *New Systematic Theology*, 805–10.

54. Williams, *Far as the Curse Is Found*, 249. See also Ridderbos, *Paul*, 330–35; Reymond, *New Systematic Theology*, 526–27; McKay, *Bond of Love*, 325; Woudstra, "Israel and the Church," 233–35. For a fuller treatment, note Beale, *New Testament Biblical Theology*, 669–79. For the analogies of family, bride, and city, see Horton, *Christian Faith*, 724–29.

55. Ridderbos, *Paul*, 332–33. For a more complete analysis of OT descriptions of Israel applied to the church, see Minear, *Images of the Church*, 66–104.

56. Robertson, *Israel of God*, 38–46; Weima, "Gal. 6:11–18," 90–107; Beale, "Peace

gether, these OT titles and descriptors of Israel that are reapplied to the NT church demonstrate that the church constitutes the true Israel.

Another key factor for understanding the continuity of the people of God is how the NT portrays the blessings, privileges, and promises to Israel as now being inherited by the church.[57] The promises of the Abrahamic covenant come to fruition through Christ with the church as the heir of the Abrahamic blessings.[58] All the benefits of the new covenant, including the eschatological outpouring of the Holy Spirit, pass over to the church. According to Ridderbos, because of Christ's work of fulfillment,

> all the privileges Israel as God's people was permitted to possess recurs with renewed force and significance in the definition of the essence of the Christian church: being sons of God (Rom. 8:14ff.; Eph. 1:5); being heirs according to promise (Gal. 3:29; 4:7); sharing in the inheritance promised to Abraham (Rom. 8:17; cf. 4:13; Col. 1:2); being heirs of the kingdom of God (1 Cor. 6:9, 10; 15:50; Gal. 5:21). For this reason the church may rejoice in the hope of the glory of God (Rom. 5:2; 8:21; 2 Cor. 3:7ff., 18; Phil. 3:19), the splendor of the presence of God among his people, once the privilege of Israel (Rom. 9:4).[59]

Fourth and lastly, the restoration and renewal prophecies of a nationalistic Israel regathered to the promised land are generally understood to have been provisional, or literally fulfilled in Israel's history, or were spiritually and symbolically or typologically fulfilled in the church through Christ's redemptive work. Other restoration prophecies are interpreted by covenantalists to come to complete fruition with the cosmic renewal of the new heavens and earth.[60] The restoration prophecies are not to be taken in a

---

and Mercy," 204–23; Beale, *New Testament Biblical Theology*, 722–24; Woudstra, "Israel and the Church," 234–35; Hoekema, *Bible and the Future*, 197; Venema, *Promise of the Future*, 274–77.

57. For discussion of these areas, confer Horton, *Christian Faith*, 717–23, 729–33; Williams, *Far as the Curse Is Found*, 252–54; Clowney, "New Israel," 211–16, 219–20; Ridderbos, *Paul*, 336–41. Many other themes could be discussed as well including election, the church as God's dwelling (i.e., temple), the vital union in Jesus as covenant head, and the theme of worship in the assembly of God's people.

58. Hodge, *Systematic Theology*, 3:549–51; Davis, "Who Are the Heirs of the Abrahamic Covenant?," 149–63; cf. McComiskey, *Covenants of Promise*, 17–21.

59. Ridderbos, *Paul*, 336–37.

60. For discussion of the OT prophecies and promises regarding Israel's restoration, see Beale, *New Testament Biblical Theology*, 680–749; Hoekema, *Bible and the Future*, 206–12, esp. 209–11; Fairbairn, *Interpretation of Prophecy*, 270–83; Robertson, *Christ of the Prophets*, 453–502, esp. 486–98; Hendriksen, *Israel in Prophecy*, 16–31; Riddlebarger, *Case for Amillennialism*, 68–80; Strimple, "Amillennialism," 84–100. For how

literalistic fashion, for the prophets project the future in the historical structures and imagery to which they were accustomed. Fairbairn highlights this principle: "Situated as the prophets generally were, it was quite natural, and, in a sense, necessary, that they should speak of the better things to come in language and imagery derived from such as were known and familiar to their minds."[61] One example often presented by covenant theologians is the citation of the prophetic words of Amos 9:11–12 in the Jerusalem council described in Acts 15. The appropriation of Amos' prophecy in the present era with the inclusion of gentiles serves as evidence that the "body of believers in Christ stand in unbroken continuity with the covenant community of the Old Testament."[62] The OT prophecies concerning Israel's restoration, land, temple, and the city of Jerusalem with a Davidic king ruling over the nations are all fulfilled in Jesus Christ, the church, or await a final fulfillment with the rejuvenation of the world at the consummation.[63]

In sum, the establishment of the NT church, according to covenant theologians, is the fulfillment of the Abrahamic promises. The prophesied future kingdom of Israel is inaugurated through Christ. The ushering in of the kingdom by Jesus ends Israel's exile, secures salvation, and brings about the inclusion of the gentile nations. The joining together of Jew and gentile in the church (Eph 2:11–22) means there will be no restoration of Israel as a nationalistic entity. Israel and the church are essentially one and differ only in terms of organized, visible representations. Closely connected to the theological arguments for the continuity of Israel and the church within the framework of the covenant of grace is how typology is understood. This final and crucial discussion of how typology is used in the ecclesiology of covenant theology will draw this hermeneutical overview to a close.

---

certain OT prophecies are applied to the church by NT authors, see Allis, *Prophecy and the Church*, 134–66.

61. Fairbairn, *Interpretation of Prophecy*, 273; cf. 270–71. Likewise, Woudstra, "Israel and the Church," 232; Johnson, *Him We Proclaim*, 223–26; Berkhof, *Principles of Biblical Interpretation*, 151–52.

62. McKay, *Bond of Love*, 200; and see Robertson, "Hermeneutics of Continuity," 89–108, as he devotes his whole chapter to unpacking Amos 9:11–12 in Acts 15:15–18.

63. Berkhof, *Systematic Theology*, 713, finds, "The books of the prophets themselves already contain indications that point to a spiritual fulfillment, Isa. 54:13; 61:6; Jer. 3:16; 31:31–34; Hos. 14:2; Mic. 6:6–8.... It is remarkable that the New Testament, which is the fulfilment of the Old, contains no indication whatsoever of the re-establishment of the Old Testament theocracy by Jesus, nor a single undisputed positive prediction of its restoration, while it does contain abundant indications of the spiritual fulfilment of the promises given to Israel, Matt. 21:43; Acts 2:29–36, 15:14–18; Rom. 9:25, 26; Heb. 8:8–13; I Pet. 2:9; Rev. 1:6; 5:10."

COVENANT THEOLOGY AND TYPOLOGY

The interpretation of typological patterns in covenant theology has a deep and diverse history. A historical overview and discussion of the nature of typology within covenant theology is offered as context before focusing on how the nation of Israel functions as a type. Much of how typology is understood correlates well with the proposal for typology offered in chapter 2, but differences emerge when considering how Israel is a type given the theological framework of the covenant of works and grace.

Historical Overview

For modern day covenant theologians, influential for their understanding of typology was the mid-nineteenth century Presbyterian scholar Patrick Fairbairn (1805–74),[64] who wrote a classic treatment of biblical typology and was one of the first to develop a formal list of principles for identifying and interpreting types.[65] Fairbairn avoided the penchant for allegorical interpretations. The Cocceian school—derived from Johannes Cocceius (1603–1669)—had no adequate hermeneutical controls and a potentially limitless number of OT types or analogies could be interpreted since no essential principles for identifying types were in place.[66] Those who would generally fall into this camp include Witsius[67] and Jonathan Edwards,[68] among other Puritans.[69] However, Fairbairn set rules for drawing

---

64. Fairbairn, *Typology of Scripture*. For summary and discussion of Fairbairn's understanding of typology, see Stek, "Biblical Typology," 133–62; Nicole, "Patrick Fairbairn and Biblical Hermeneutics," 767–76. According to Groningen, *Messianic Revelation in the Old*, 161, "Patrick Fairbairn can be considered the spokesman for the Reformation tradition."

65. Fairbairn, *Typology of Scripture*, 1:140, notes that the typological views "of our elder divines [had no] fixed or definite rules being laid down for guiding us to the knowledge and interpretation of particular types."

66. Critiques are offered by Fairbairn, *Typology of Scripture*, 1:9–14. Note also Ninow, *Indicators of Typology*, 28. Davidson, *Typology in Scripture*, 34–35, provides some examples of how this school viewed typical every OT event which bore superficial resemblance to Christ: "Adam's awakening out of sleep typified Christ's resurrection; Samson's meeting of a lion on the way prefigured Christ's meeting of Saul on the road to Damascus."

67. For Witsius' discussion of typology, see *Economy of the Covenants between God and Man*, 2:188–231.

68. See Kloosterman, "Use of Typology in Post-Canonical Salvation History," 59–96.

69. Davis, "Traditions of Puritan Typology," 11–46; Brumm, *American Thought and Typology*.

typological relations such that through proper hermeneutics, typological relations could be found and identified without necessarily needing them to be explicitly cited as such in the NT.⁷⁰ Haphazard, subjectively analogous, accidental, or imaginative connections were to be disregarded. Without following all of Fairbairn's rules for understanding typology, most modern day covenantalists would be aligned with his moderate approach in evading the excesses of allegorical interpretation or the overly conservative interpretative scheme that limits typological patterns to only those the NT formally announces or identifies as such.⁷¹

The Nature of Typology in Covenant Theology

In covenant theology, typology is one aspect of a theology of the progression of God's acts of salvation that is directed toward Jesus Christ and the redemption he accomplishes. All redemptive history moves forward to Christ and his work and is fulfilled in Christ and the church.⁷² Richard Lints asserts,

> The typological relation is the central means by which particular epochal and textual horizons are linked to later horizons in redemptive revelation. It links the present to the future, and it retroactively links the present with the past. It is founded on the organic connection of God's promises with his fulfillment of those promises.⁷³

For most covenantalists, including but not limited to Vos, Berkhof, Beale, Clowney, Lints, Waltke, Karlberg, Currid, Poythress, and Stek,

---

70. Stek, "Biblical Typology," 134–40, 151–54. For Fairbairn's rules for identifying types, see Fairbairn, *Typology of Scripture*, 1:141–67; or the summary offered by Ninow, *Indicators of Typology*, 29–30.

71. Ninow, *Indicators of Typology*, 30, 30n67. See also Hugenberger, "Introductory Notes," 233–34; Gundry, "Typology as a Means of Interpretation," 233–40, esp. 236–37. Clowney, *Preaching and Biblical Theology*, 111–12, finds that "the lack of hermeneutical method can shut us up to recognizing types only where the New Testament itself explicitly recognizes them. Such caution is admirable. But a better grasp of biblical theology will open for us great riches of revelation."

72. Ninow, *Indicators of Typology*, 68; Glenny, "Typology," 629; Waltke, "Kingdom Promises as Spiritual," 279. On this point, see also Goldsworthy, *Gospel-Centered Hermeneutics*, 242–43; LaRondelle, *Israel of God*, 44; and Merkle, *Discontinuity to Continuity*, 143–45.

73. Lints, *Fabric of Theology*, 304. Similarly, Karlberg, "Significance of Israel," 261, highlights "the fact that typology deals with the relation between distinct yet inseparable epochs of redemptive revelation." See also Vanhoozer, *Drama of Doctrine*, 221–24.

typology involves OT historical persons, events, or institutions that are divinely designed, having a prophetic function that anticipates greater and heightened realization in the NT, namely in Jesus Christ and the church.[74] Furthermore, for covenant theology, the antitype supersedes and fulfills the type, which is generally understood to be a symbol or shadow of spiritual truth possessing significance for the original reader but is then developed into a discernible pattern in redemptive history as one moves across the canon.[75] There is recognition among covenantalists that some types, while initially fulfilled in Christ and the church, still await complete fulfillment in the consummated state given the structure of inaugurated eschatology.[76] For example, the land promise is a type that awaits full manifestation in the new heavens and earth at Christ's return.[77] Lastly, typological patterns are legitimately identified through hermeneutical procedure as textual controls and warrant must be applied for establishing typological patterns not explicitly spelled out in the NT.[78]

---

74. Lints, *Fabric of Theology*, 304–10; Berkhof, *Principles of Biblical Interpretation*, 145–47; Vos, *Biblical Theology*, 144–48; Clowney, "Interpreting the Biblical Models," 90–95; Currid, "Recognition and Use of Typology," 118–21; McCartney and Clayton, *Let the Reader Understand*, 162–67; Stek, "Biblical Typology," 159–62; Beale, *Handbook*, 13–27; Karlberg, "Significance of Israel," 260–63; Waltke, "Kingdom Promises as Spiritual," 276–79; Venema, *Promise of the Future*, 286–95; Robertson, "Outlook for Biblical Theology," 74–76; Johnson, *Him We Proclaim*, 199–238; Greidanus, *Preaching Christ*, 250–60. For a thorough treatment of typology from a covenantalist perspective, see Johnson, "Pauline Typology," 26–90.

75. See Lints, *Fabric of Theology*, 305; Hugenberger, "Introductory Notes," 341; Berkhof, *Principles of Biblical Interpretation*, 146; Beale, *Handbook*, 15–18; Venema, *Promise of the Future*, 287.

76. Waltke, "Kingdom Promises as Spiritual," 279; Karlberg, "Legitimate Discontinuities," 18–19.

77. Hoekema, *Bible and the Future*, 211–12, 278–79; Waltke, *An Old Testament Theology*, 558–87, esp. 560, 580–83; Beale, *New Testament Biblical Theology*, 750–72; Reymond, "Traditional Covenantal View," 41–47, 56; Robertson, *Israel of God*, 3–31; Holwerda, *Jesus and Israel*, 101–12; Riddlebarger, *Case for Amillennialism*, 70–75; Strimple, "Amillennialism," 90–91.

78. Berkhof, *Principles of Biblical Interpretation*, 145; Vos, *Biblical Theology*, 145–46; Currid, "Recognition and Use of Typology," 118–21; Clowney, "Interpreting the Biblical Models," 90–94, and see a summary of Clowney's approach in Hugenberger, "Introductory Notes," 339–41. Note also Beale, *Handbook*, 19–25.

Israel-Church Relationship in Covenant Theology and in Typological Perspective

With this overview of the nature of typology in Reformed thought in place, it is important to focus on the function of typology in covenant theology as it relates to Israel and the Abrahamic covenant. As discussed, covenant theology places a strong emphasis on the continuity of the church; that is, there is one church of God throughout both the Old and New Testaments because of the foundational role of the covenant of grace worked out through the administrations of the covenants. There is a continuity between Israel and the church in a variety of ways as both covenant communities are comprised of believers and unbelievers (i.e., a mixed community), the continuity in covenant signs (i.e., circumcision spiritually signifies the same realities as baptism), as well as uniformity of the salvation experience of old and new covenant believers with some modifications made for the final realities that Christ has achieved.

Interwoven with this view of Israel and the church within the covenant of grace is typology. The nation of Israel, its experiences, and the OT economy as a whole were symbolic, preparatory, and typical for covenant theologians.[79] Promises and prophecies made to Israel are fulfilled typologically in the church; there is no room for any future restoration of national Israel subsequent or alongside Christ's return. Some covenantalists, though, like Witsius, Venema, Riddlebarger, and Holwerda do see a future salvation and ingathering of Israel into the church based upon Rom 9–11; certainly others, like Bavinck, Berkhof, Hoekema, Hendriksen, and Robertson, do not.[80] Karlberg puts it this way: "If one grants that national Israel in OT revelation was truly a type of the eternal kingdom of Christ, then it seems that, according to the canons of Biblical typology, national Israel can no

---

79. For a helpful summary, note Glenny, "Typology," 631.

80. Witsius, *Economy of the Covenants*, 2:413–21; Riddlebarger, *Case for Amillennialism*, 180–94; Venema, *Promise of the Future*, 127–39; Venema, "'In This Way All Israel Will Be Saved,'" 19–40; Holwerda, *Jesus and Israel*, 168–75; see also VanGemeren, "Israel as the Hermeneutical Crux (II)," 288–90. The following covenant theologians understand Rom 11:26 to refer to ethnic Israel, but the salvation of elect Jews occurs throughout the new covenant era: Bavinck, *Reformed Dogmatics*, 4:668–72; Berkhof, *Systematic Theology*, 698–700; Hoekema, *Bible and the Future*, 145–47; Hendriksen, *Israel in Prophecy*, 34–52; Strimple, "Amillennialism," 112–18; Reymond, *New Systematic Theology*, 1025–30. Robertson, "Is There a Distinctive Future for Ethnic Israel?," 209–27, also held to this view originally, but more recently, in Robertson, *Israel of God*, 167–92, he views the "all Israel" in Rom 11:26 to refer to the whole church, both Jew and gentile. This is also the view of John Calvin and is well presented by Wright, *Climax of the Covenant*, 231–57.

longer retain any independent status whatever."[81] Along the same lines, Waltke asserts,

> Jesus taught in several places that the true people of God are not to be found in national Israel but in the Christian community that replaced it (cf. Mark 12:1–9; Matt 15:13). His apostles continued his teachings. They emphatically taught that the Old Covenant with its types has been done away forever in favor of the superior and eternal New Covenant that governs the church (Jer 32:40; 50:5; Ezek 16:60; 37:26; Heb 8:1–13).... Biblical typology as taught by Christ's apostles disallows the notion that the material types of the Old Covenant will be reintroduced into this history after the church upon whom the end of the ages has come (cf. Heb 7:18).[82]

Clowney also follows suit as he avers that the "church in both the N.T. and the Old *is* the people of God, yet O.T. Israel is also a model, a type, in its earthly form, of the spiritual and heavenly reality of the church."[83] Robertson writes,

> If the new covenant people of God are the actualized realization of a typological form, and the new covenant now is in effect, those constituting the people of God in the present circumstances must be recognized as the "Israel of God." As a unified people, the participants of the new covenant today are "Israel."[84]

Therefore, although some covenantalists emphasize typological correspondences between Israel and Jesus (or describe Jesus as the "true

---

81. Karlberg, "Significance of Israel," 259; cf. Fairbairn, *Interpretation of Prophecy*, 255.

82. Waltke, "Kingdom Promises as Spiritual," 279; cf. Venema, *Promise of the Future*, 290–91.

83. Clowney, "Interpreting the Biblical Models," 92, emphasis original. Robertson, *Christ of the Covenants*, 289, argues that Israel did not function merely as type, but its typological role is significant. "The old covenant nation of Israel typologically anticipated the new covenant reality of the chosen people of God assembled as a nation consecrated to God." For a basic overview of Israel as a type of the church, see Mathison, *Dispensationalism*, 38–39.

84. Robertson, *Christ of the Covenants*, 289.

Israel")[85] or directly link Israel with Jesus,[86] typological connections are also maintained directly between Israel and the church in terms of fulfillment or less frequently, as replacement. Yet at the same time, the overarching covenant of grace administered through the covenants also keeps Israel and the church in direct continuity. This issue raises two significant problems when considering the nature of these typological relationships for the ecclesiology of covenant theology.

First, there is a substantial question of how covenant theologians put together the typological relationship between Israel and the church. If OT Israel is typological of the church, then that would entail a qualitative progression and escalation between Israel and the church given how covenant theologians understand the characteristics of typology (and given the nature of typology as presented in chapter 2). If the "superior and eternal New Covenant that governs the church" is in effect, to use Waltke's phrase, should there not be an escalated and heightened reality when it comes to the essential nature and structure of the new covenant community, the church, in comparison to OT Israel? Perhaps covenant theologians could offer that the escalation of the Israel-church typological relationship corresponds to the areas of the newness of the new covenant and fulfillment of the promises of Israel to the church. However, even with the contrast to the national, political, and theocratic Israel of old with the church encompassing all nations, possessing a greater distribution and empowering presence of the Holy Spirit, and having sin finally dealt with through the cross of Christ, covenantalists still argue that the NT church is one with Israel. The dual aspect of the covenant is still operative in the new covenant era, for there are covenant breakers in the new covenant community just as there were in the nation of Israel.[87] The church, just like Israel, is a mixed community of believers and unbelievers. In regard to essential nature then, there is no

---

85. Beale, "Did Jesus and His Followers Preach?," 392, 395–97; Beale, *Handbook*, 53, 95–102; Beale, *New Testament Biblical Theology*, 406–29, 651–56, 920–21; Holwerda, *Jesus and Israel*, 27–58; Strimple, "Amillennialism," 87–90; Riddlebarger, *Case for Amillennialism*, 37, 68–70; Williams, *Far as the Curse Is Found*, 223–29, esp. 225. Horton, *Introducing Covenant Theology*, frequently refers to Christ as the true Israel (e.g., 90). See also Donaldson, *Last Days of Dispensationalism*, 53–59. Cf. Dumbrell, *Search for Order*, 178–79.

86. Poythress, *Understanding Dispensationalists*, 126–29; Clowney, "New Israel," 218–20; Johnson, *Him We Proclaim*, 207–17.

87. On the other hand, Williams, *Far as the Curse Is Found*, 214, says that with the forgiveness of sins in the new covenant, sin "will no longer be a problem. Covenant breach will come to an end. While the new covenant shares much of the substance of the Mosaic covenant, it differs radically in its ability to effect the goal of covenant intimacy and obedience."

typological relationship between Israel and the church, and, therefore, covenant theology cannot consistently frame Israel as a type of the church since the covenant communities are essentially the same given the basic continuity between the two.[88] The entailment of understanding the new covenant as just another administration of the one covenant of grace theologically requires that the Israel-church typological relationship can only be applied in a truncated or inconsistent manner when one compares how other typological patterns are presented and understood by covenant theologians where the antitype always possesses a greater nature, intensification, and eschatological reality (such as the exodus, temple, sacrifices, priesthood, and land as portrayed in Reformed theology).

How covenantalists typologically link Israel with Jesus is scripturally appropriate, but a second problem emerges in light of the implications of the Israel-Christ typological relationship. If Jesus fulfills Israel's promises and roles and the church is really the "true Israel" because of his manifold work on the cross, should not this new covenant community, now in direct union with Christ as their covenant head, a people now marked with the universal distribution of the Holy Spirit (Num 11:27–29; Ezek 36:25–27; Joel 2:28–32; John 7:28–39; Acts 2; Rom 8:9–11; Eph 1:13–14), known as the new humanity, the new creation, and God's new temple, be different from OT Israel in terms of structure and nature? Covenant theologians will explain the Israel-Christ typological relationship but generally do not address the theological entailments of that to their understanding of the nature of the church as she relates to Christ.[89] Jesus is presented in terms of

---

88. For example, the tension is observable when Mathison, *Dispensationalism*, 39, writes that national Israel was typological of the NT visible church: "The nation of Israel included both believers and unbelievers. The visible church . . . also includes believers and unbelievers. The relationship between Old Testament national Israel and the New Testament visible, professing church is not a relationship of equivalence but of type and antitype, or shadow and reality." Cf. Pratt, "To the Jew First," 174–75. But how exactly is Israel typological of the church given Mathison's claim since the two covenant communities consist of believers and unbelievers? Since both are mixed communities the comparison is between shadow and shadow, not between shadow and reality. The difference between Israel and the church is only in political and national terms according to Mathison, *Dispensationalism*, 38, but such does not comport with the nature of typological fulfillment in Christ, nor fit with the changes to the nature and structure of the church because of him.

89. One exception is Beale, who writes that "all who identify with [Jesus] become adopted as true Israel (which, recall, is a corporate Adam) and . . . inherit the promises as such. . . . Accordingly, Christ as true Israel and the last Adam represents the church, so that the church becomes true eschatological Israel and part of the end-time Adam. Thus, far from being a narrow name, 'true Israel' really is a name that connotes true humanity." Beale, *New Testament Biblical Theology*, 749, cf. 654–56. Beale's quote comes from a chapter where he presents the church as the transformed and restored

corporate solidarity as he embodies Israel's hopes and fulfills Israel's roles and tasks.[90] Nevertheless, if Jesus represents Israel and typologically is the true Israel, then what implications does this have for the nature of the NT community, the church, which is described as being in faith union with Christ?

The covenantal framework also impacts the interpretation of the Abrahamic covenant in terms of what is typological. In his discussion of typology, Clowney notes that the metaphors of the church in the NT involve "a transformation of figures drawn from the O.T. At times the transformation is by way of contrast: for example, the change from the Passover meal to the Lord's Supper, or from circumcision to baptism as the initiatory rite of the people of God."[91] While circumcision is called a "figure" by Clowney, it is not genuinely identified as typological, at least as typology is defined and presented by covenantalists, since covenantalists argue that essentially the same spiritual meaning of circumcision comes across in the NT in the

---

eschatological Israel because Israel's identity and restoration promises are fulfilled in Christ and the church. However, if the church is the transformed and eschatological Israel, how could the covenant communities remain the same in terms of nature? The restoration of the remnant of Israel as seen in the fulfillment of Christ and in the church, as postulated by Beale, theologically requires the NT community of Jesus to be a completely regenerate covenant people.

90. Beale, *Handbook*, 53, 96–99; Beale, *New Testament Biblical Theology*, 192–93; Holwerda, *Jesus and Israel*, 34; cf. Horton, *Christian Faith*, 721.

91. Clowney, "Interpreting the Biblical Models," 92. The significant debate regarding paedocommunion shows another area of confusion in regard to typological patterns. Some covenantalists argue that since children were involved in the Passover meal and because children in the new covenant era have already received the initial rite of the new covenant—baptism—then children should also be permitted to participate in the Lord's Supper. See the collection of essays in Strawbridge's *Case of Covenant Communion*. Arguing against paedocommunion are Venema, *Children at the Lord's Table?* and the essays presented in Waters's and Duncan's *Children and the Lord's Supper*. As most covenant theologians rightly argue, the Passover and the Lord's Supper do not have the same essential meaning, as the Passover was a type of Christ's sacrificial death that is commemorated in the Lord's Supper and further, 1 Cor 11:27–32 restricts the recipients to those who are capable of examining themselves. If only paedobaptists would apply the same hermeneutic to the topic of circumcision and infant baptism they would avoid the tension that paedocommunion advocates are trying to avoid: passive subjects who receive the rite of infant baptism but active (believing) subjects are the only recipients of the continuing rite, the Lord's Supper. As Jewett rightly points out, "Having embraced their children in the covenant by giving them baptism, Paedobaptists exclude them from that same covenant by refusing them participation in the covenant meal. Having reasoned from inclusive circumcision to inclusive baptism, they turn about and go from an inclusive Passover to an exclusive Eucharist." Jewett, *Infant Baptism & the Covenant of Grace*, 205.

form of infant baptism.[92] Moreover, the genealogical principle ("to you and your seed") is never handled in a typological way in covenant theology as covenantalists appeal to the "unconditional" nature of the Abrahamic covenant with the result that the physical or biological children of God's people are always included in the covenant community throughout redemptive history. Hence, entrance into the covenant is granted to believers and their children in the Reformed tradition, but such direct association between physical circumcision in the OT and baptism in the new must assume that the circumcision of the flesh was not typological of greater spiritual realities of the new covenant—circumcision of the heart for all members of the new covenant (Jer 31:28–34)—which is fulfilled with Christ having regenerate offspring (Isa 53:10–11, 54:1, 3; Eph 2:5–6; Col 2:12–13; Phil 3:3; Gal 4:26, 31; Titus 3:4–7).[93]

92. Clowney, *Church*, 280–84; Booth, *Children of Promise*, 96–119; Collins, "What Does Baptism Do for Anyone? Part I," 1–33. Collins, "What Does Baptism Do for Anyone? Part II," 74–98. See also Gibson, "Sacramental Supersessionism Revisited," 191–208. Note Fritsch, "Biblical Typology," 96. See also Beale's treatment in *New Testament Biblical Theology*, 802–16. Beale identifies physical circumcision as a type of spiritual circumcision and the physical rite of baptism (808–9). But again, how can physical circumcision have typological fulfillment in physical baptism when they have the same essential meaning and are equivalent (as even Beale recognizes later, 816)? Like the Israel-church typological relationship, covenant theologians construe the typological relationship of circumcision to baptism in terms of the widening of the people who receive the sign of the covenant (baptism now applied to women and gentiles), but again, this fails to adequately understand the eschatological heightening and escalation of biblical typology which requires discontinuity in terms of the nature of the type-antitype correspondence. For further critique, confer Wellum, "Baptism and the Relationship," 153–60.

93. For critique of the paedobaptist assertion that the genealogical principle remains unchanged into the Messianic new covenant, see White, "Last Adam and His Seed," 60–73. Robertson, *Christ of the Covenants*, 289–90; Brack and Oliphint, "Questioning the Progress in Progressive Covenantalism," 207–9; and Gibson, "On Abraham, Covenant, and the Theology of Paedobaptism," 26–27, argue that the genealogical principle extends to the new covenant because Jer 32:39 teaches that the children of covenant participants are included in the promise and blessings of the covenant. However, within the broader context of Jer 32:36–44, Jer 32:39 describes the benefits the new covenant people of God receive in terms of restoration. The returning remnant (Jer 32:37) will dwell in safety and they will be his people (Jer 32:38; cf. Exod 19:5). Further, these will have one heart and one way and they will fear the Lord forever (Jer 32:39). This will be for their good and the good of their children after them. The everlasting covenant made with them also means that God will not turn away from them and the fear placed in their hearts means that they will not turn away from him (Jer 32:40). Far from seeing this text as proof of the genealogical principle in the prophecy of the new covenant, the passage as a whole teaches the opposite. The new covenant members will all have the fear of the Lord on their hearts (reminiscent of circumcision of the heart) and not turn away from the Lord. The benefits for God's people are not just economic prosperity (Jer 32:42–44), but also that in the end it will be good for them and their

On the other hand, while circumcision and the genealogical principle are not regarded as typological in the Abrahamic covenant, covenant theologians understand the land promise as typological of the inheritance of heavenly rest. Why do covenantalists view the land as typological but other features of the Abrahamic as not typological? First, given the continuity between Israel and the church within the framework of the covenant of grace, the land promise logically could not be preserved independently for national, ethnic Israel in the future. Such a literal fulfillment of the land promise strikes against the overarching covenant of grace and the unity of the one people of God in covenant theology.[94] Covenant theologians, therefore, treat the land promise as typological in one of two ways. First, some covenantalists link the land back to Eden and observe the expansion of the land promise in OT prophecies in arguing that the land points to a new heavens and new earth.[95] Second, the conditionality of the Mosaic covenant is appealed to in regard to the promised land as lack of faithful loyalty to the Lord leads to covenantal curses and expulsion from the land (Lev 18:25–28; 26:14–26).[96] While the land promises may seem unconditional, Reymond criticizes dispensationalists on this point:

> Moses stated that the physical progeny's obedience to God's law was a basic requirement for inheriting and *continuing to possess* the land (Deut 4:25–31; 28:15–68). While the land promises may appear at times to be unconditional, they always contained

---

children. Thus, there is no indication that children are automatically in the covenant community, the passage only confirms God's goodness to the children of those who are truly his people, wholly devoted to him.

94. For example, Hoekema, *Bible and Future*, 211, writes, "For [Israel] *the land of Canaan* was the land God had given to his people as their dwelling place and their possession. But the Old Testament is a book of shadows and types. The New Testament widens these concepts. . . . In New Testament times the land which is to be inherited by the people of God is expanded to include the entire earth" (emphasis original).

95. Robertson, *Israel of God*, 3–31; Beale, *New Testament Biblical Theology*, 750–72; Waltke, *Old Testament Theology*, 534–87. Holwerda, *Jesus and Israel*, 85–112, does not link the Abrahamic promise of land back to Eden, but does trace the theme through the OT and into the NT. Pratt, "To the Jew First," 183, summarizes the Reformed eschatological position on the land of Canaan as being fulfilled in the new heavens and earth.

96. Horton, *Introducing Covenant Theology*, 47, comments on this issue of retention of the land of promise: "Dispensationalism . . . treat[s] the land promise as eternal and irrevocable, even to the extent that there can be a difference between Israel and the church in God's plan. . . . [This fails] to recognize that the Hebrew Scriptures themselves qualify this national covenant in strictly conditional terms." "The principle of law is the basis for remaining in the earthly land; the principle of promise is the basis for entering and remaining in the heavenly land" (p. 101).

the tacit requirement of obedience that had to be met for the promises to materialize and to come to lasting fruition.[97]

In sum, the prominence of the Abrahamic covenant and its direct continuity to the new covenant means that very few features of it are considered typological in covenant theology. In contrast, the Mosaic covenant with its conditions or understood as a covenant of works, with the exception of the moral law, is primarily typological.[98]

SUMMARY

The hermeneutics of covenant theology require that the Israel-church relationship be one of unity and direct continuity. Covenant theologians cast this continuity through the framework of the theological covenants of works and grace, with all post-fall covenants having the same substance and essence. Israel is typological of Jesus and the church, but the Israel-church typology is one of correspondence and not escalation or qualitative progression normative of typological patterns because of the aforementioned hermeneutical commitments, even as covenantalists highlight the era of fulfillment that arrives with Christ.

In framing the biblical covenants into a unified covenant of grace, there is a legitimate question as to whether covenant theologians allow each covenant to be self-defining and properly unfold within its redemptive historical context.[99] Further, Paul, upon reflecting on the OT era, does not postulate one covenant with many administrations. Instead, he speaks of the *covenants* of promise that are now fulfilled in Christ (Gal 4:24; Eph 2:12; Rom 9:4; cf. Heb 8:7–13).[100]

---

97. Reymond, "Traditional Covenantal View," 56, emphasis original.

98. Horton, *Introducing Covenant Theology*, 59–60, states, "Like Paul, the writer to the Hebrews contrasts the typological covenant of law (Sinai) with the covenant of promise (Abrahamic). While the old covenant has passed away, the Abrahamic covenant has not." See discussion above on the foundational role of the Abrahamic covenant. The stress of the typological nature of the Mosaic covenant is not all encompassing, for covenantalists do consider the Sabbath as a type having fulfillment in Jesus and experienced with believers entering God's rest in an already, not yet fashion (Heb 3–4), but the Sabbath command must still be observed with the only change being the day—Sunday (e.g., Beale, *New Testament Biblical Theology*, 775–801).

99. Covenant theologians are directly challenged on this score by Gentry and Wellum, *Kingdom through Covenant*, 94, 666–712; Wellum, "Baptism and the Relationship," 126–27; Zens, "Is There a 'Covenant of Grace?,'" 50.

100. Gentry and Wellum, *Kingdom through Covenant*, 655; Zens, "Is There a 'Covenant of Grace?,'" 45.

The typological relationship between Israel, Christ, and the church in covenant theology needs recalibration. As Murray so helpfully states,

> It would not be, however, in the interests of theological conservation or theological progress for us to think that the covenant theology is in all respects definitive and that there is no further need for correction, modification, and expansion. Theology must always be undergoing reformation. The human understanding is imperfect. However architectonic may be the systematic constructions of any one generation or group of generations, there always remains the need for correction and reconstruction so that the structure may be brought into closer approximation to the Scripture and the reproduction be a more faithful transcript or reflection of the heavenly exemplar. It appears to me that covenant theology, notwithstanding the finesse of analysis . . . needs recasting.[101]

In chapters 5 and 6 I offer an alternative approach to how covenant theologians construct the Israel-Christ-church typological relationship in a manner beyond what Murray would have conceded. However, first, the Israel-church relationship and nature of typology within the other significant school of theology, dispensationalism, is addressed.

---

101. Murray, *Covenant of Grace*, 4–5.

Chapter 4

THE HERMENEUTICS OF DISPENSATIONALISM

As a system of theology, dispensationalism and its varieties are relatively new on the scene of church history as it was first advanced by the British Plymouth Brethern leader, John Nelson Darby (1800–1882).[1] Throughout the late nineteenth and early twentieth century, dispensationalism became a popular millennialist movement, particularly in the United States, as dispensational teachings were disseminated through the Niagara Bible Conference (1883–1897) and the well-known and popular *Scofield Reference Bible* (first published in 1909), which contained the annotations of C. I. Scofield (1843–1921) and currently remains in publication as the *New Scofield Reference Bible*.[2] In the post–World War I era, dispensationalism "enjoyed its greatest

---

1. For an overview of dispensationalism with particular attention on Darby, see Bass, *Backgrounds to Dispensationalism*, 7, 17, 48–63. For a historical survey, see Svigel, "History of Dispensationalism," 69–100. For the rise of dispensational premillennialism, see Weber, "Dispensational and Historic Premillennialism," 1–22. Many dispensationalists acknowledge John Nelson Darby as the originator or key figure in formulating dispensational thought, so Blaising, "Doctrinal Development in Orthodoxy: Part 1," 133–40; Saucy, "Contemporary Dispensational Thought," 10; Bateman, "Dispensationalism Yesterday and Today," 21, 45n5; cf. Helyer, *Witness of Jesus*, 99–102. Still, many dispensationalists would probably agree with Charles Ryrie's assertion, in Ryrie, *Dispensationalism*, 77 (cf. 70–76), that Darby "had much to do with [the] systematizing and promoting of dispensationalism. But neither Darby nor the Brethren originated the concepts involved in the system." See Bigalke and Ice, "History of Dispensationalism," xvii-xlii, esp. xix-xxii.

2. For a historical overview of the Niagara Bible Conference and the *Scofield Reference Bible*, see Blaising, "Dispensationalism," 16–23; Ryrie, "Update on

success among the Baptists, the Reformed Episcopalians, and especially the Presbyterians," as well as among the newly formed Pentecostal denominations that adopted dispensationalism except the common dispensational view of the cessation of charismatic gifts.[3] To this day, dispensationalism continues to be a popular and evangelical movement in the United States as dispensational seminaries and schools have thrived and the emphasis on prophecies, the nation of Israel, the rapture, and the millennium continue to receive attention through books, movies, and other media.

The name "dispensationalism" is derived from the noun "dispensation," a translation of the Greek word οἰκονομία (Eph 1:10; 3:2; 1 Cor 9:17; Col 1:25; 1 Tim 1:4), meaning administration, stewardship, or the management of a household.[4] Although dispensationalism cannot be defined based on the term or concept of dispensation,[5] dispensations as distinguishable economies or periods of time during which God dispenses or administers his plan of redemption differently from other eras are important to dispensationalists and their system as a whole.[6] According to Ron Bigalke and Mal Couch, "[d]ispensationalism is that biblical system of theology which views the Word of God as unfolding distinguishable economies in the outworking of the divine purposes for the nation of Israel in a distinct and separate manner from His purpose for the church."[7] For covenant theologians the role of covenant is paramount for structuring the unity of the Bible, but

> unlike covenantalists, [dispensationalists] do not believe that the "covenant" establishes the framework of the biblical story.

Dispensationalism," 18–19; cf. Weber, "Dispensational and Historic Premillennialism," 11–17. For a brief biography of Lewis Sperry Chafer and his importance to the dispensational movement, see Parle, *Dispensational Development*, 11–30.

3. Weber, "Dispensational and Historic Premillennialism," 16–17.

4. Ryrie, *Dispensationalism*, 27–36, esp. 30–33; Blaising and Bock, *Progressive Dispensationalism*, 11, 106–11; Kreider, "What Is Dispensationalism?," 20–27; Toussaint, "Biblical Defense of Dispensationalism," 82–84; Couch, "Dispensational Hermeneutics," 18–19; Fruchtenbaum, *Israelology*, 318–23; cf. Grenz, *Millennial Maze*, 94.

5. See Feinberg, "Systems of Discontinuity," 68–69. Vlach, "What Is Dispensationalism Not?," 52, agrees with Feinberg that "acknowledging the word *oikonomia* does not make one a dispensationalist, nor does defining this term reveal the essence of dispensationalism."

6. Ryrie, *Dispensationalism*, 34–35; Toussaint, "Biblical Defense of Dispensationalism," 82–83; Kreider, "What Is Dispensationalism?," 21; Blaising and Bock, *Progressive Dispensationalism*, 14; Pugh, "Dispensationalism," 232–33; and Cone, "Dispensational Definition," 145–63.

7. Bigalke and Couch, "Relationship between Covenants and Dispensations," 18. See Ryrie, *Dispensationalism*, 34, for another summary of the importance of the various stages and dispensations. For a more expansive definition of dispensationalism, see Blaising, "Contemporary Dispensationalism," 5–6.

This does not mean that dispensationalists deny the importance of covenants . . . but that they believe that covenants are subsidiary to another structural construction.[8]

This epochal construction or dispensational framework varies among dispensational scholars depending on how the distinguishable stages within the progress of revelation are identified and understood to relate to each other.[9] For traditional, classic dispensationalists following Scofield, including many modern, revised dispensationalists, there are seven distinct dispensations: Innocency, Conscience, Human Government, Promise, Mosaic, Grace, and Kingdom/Millennium.[10] For contemporary progressive dispensationalists, the number of dispensations varies from two to four, to as many as seven.[11] While the emphasis on progressive revelation and the distinguishable dispensations within the Bible is not the primary characteristic of dispensationalism or unique to dispensationalism—dispensationalists

---

8. Kreider, "What Is Dispensationalism?," 20. Interestingly, Blaising and Bock, *Progressive Dispensationalism*, 16, state, "The dispensations are structured by various covenants God has made or promised." They also describe dispensations relating to covenants or conceptually overlapping. Ibid., 127–128. Similarly, note Bigalke and Couch, "Relationship between Covenants and Dispensations," 27–36. Cf. Pugh, "Dispensationalism," 232–36. For the differences between covenant theology and dispensationalism, see Ryrie, *Dispensationalism*, 213–27; and Lightner, "Covenantism and Dispensationalism," 62–74.

9. Donaldson, *Last Days of Dispensationalism*, 4, critiques dispensationalism on this point: "How can the dispensations be distinguishable and at the same time indistinguishable to the point of there being a multiplicity of views within dispensational scholarship regarding their number? It seems these *definite* and *distinguishable* dispensations must be really *indefinite* and *indistinguishable*" (emphasis original). Many scholars differ in how to identify the epochs or stages of redemption, however. See my discussion in chapter 1.

10. See the charts in Blaising and Bock, *Progressive Dispensationalism*, 118–19 (cf. 24–26). Cf. Helyer, *Witness of Jesus*, 106. The seven-fold scheme of Scofield is incorporated by some revised or modified dispensationalists, see Ryrie, *Dispensationalism*, 58–65; Toussaint, "Biblical Defense of Dispensationalism," 85–90; Pentecost, *Thy Kingdom Come*, 323; Benware, *Understanding End Times Prophecy*, 86–88. However, Cone, "Dispensational Definition," 150–63, argues for twelve dispensations. See also Parle, *Dispensational Development*, 119–25.

11. Barker, "Scope and Center," 293–328, esp. 295, argues for two major dispensations: the old covenant era and the new covenant era. For Blaising and Bock, *Progressive Dispensationalism*, 120–23, four primary dispensations appear in biblical history: patriarchal, mosaic, ecclesial, and zionic (millennial and eternal), while Kreider, "What Is Dispensationalism?," 28–36, affirms seven. For progressive dispensationalists, the dispensations are not understood "simply as *different* arrangements between God and humankind, but as *successive* arrangements in the *progressive* revelation and accomplishment of redemption." Blaising and Bock, *Progressive Dispensationalism*, 48, emphasis original.

themselves have acknowledged that other Christians and Christian traditions recognize distinct epochs or dispensations in God's overall plan and control of the world—the content and meaning of each dispensation is important.[12] Dispensationalism stresses more discontinuity than covenant theology does in regard to the relationship between Israel and the church and arrives at significantly different conclusions regarding eschatological issues, particularly the nature of the millennium, largely due to how they identify the dispensations and interpret the relationship between them in the progress of revelation.[13]

The above discussion is a brief historical and general overview of dispensationalism. In what follows, the essential aspects or core beliefs of dispensationalism are offered, followed by a description of the recent expressions of dispensationalism. Next, the dispensational understanding of the essential covenants—Abrahamic, Davidic, and new—are examined since their understanding of these covenants have direct bearing on the system's ecclesiology and eschatology. Lastly, like the examination of covenant theology in chapter 3, the dispensational hermeneutical approach to typology is examined with particular emphasis on how typology functions in relation to the nation of Israel.

THE ESSENTIAL TENETS OF DISPENSATIONALISM

Defining the core beliefs of dispensationalism is a challenge given the varieties of characteristics offered by dispensational scholars. Moreover, the idea of dispensationalism immediately arouses the notion of a pre-tribulational rapture and other chronological events of the end leading to Christ's premillennial reign. However, just as recognizing dispensations is not unique to dispensationalism, the pre-tribulational rapture, while affirmed

---

12. For discussion by dispensationalists on how non-dispensationalists, either past or present, recognize epochs or dispensations in the storyline of Scripture, see Ryrie, *Dispensationalism*, 45; Bateman, "Dispensationalism Yesterday and Today," 22–23; Feinberg, "Systems of Discontinuity," 69–70; Vlach, "What Is Dispensationalism Not?," 52; Cone, "Dispensational Definition," 145–46. See also Poythress, *Understanding Dispensationalists*, 9–13; Grenz, *Millennial Maze*, 95; and Bass, *Backgrounds to Dispensationalism*, 16–17.

13. Ryrie, *Dispensationalism*, 20–23. Ryrie argues that with the unifying principle of the covenant of grace, soteriology is the philosophy of history for covenant theologians. Instead, for dispensationalism the unifying principle is eschatological, theological, and doxological leading to what he argues is a broader philosophy of history. Also, according to Ryrie, *Dispensationalism*, 22, "Only dispensationalism does justice to the proper concept of the progress of revelation."

by most dispensationalists, is also not essential to the position.¹⁴ Similarly, premillennialism is not a defining mark of dispensationalism since not all premillennialists are dispensationalists.

In the past thirty years, determining the core tenets of dispensationalism has also been compounded by the modifications to the system offered by progressive dispensationalists (mid-1980s to present) and to what extent these developments impact the distinctives of dispensationalism. Some of the advocates of a more traditional or normative dispensational perspective find the modifications by progressive dispensationalists to be a departure from the tradition.¹⁵ Despite the difference between normative and progressive dispensationalism (see the next section), there is enough of a family resemblance to observe common dispensational features, or as Michael Svigel concludes, "Though we can speak in terms of *dispensationalism* as a definable and distinguishable theological movement, we must in some ways also speak of *dispensationalisms* as distinct varieties within a larger species."¹⁶ Exploring the different expressions or forms of dispensationalism indicates that the Israel-church distinction is at the heart of dispensationalism. This commonality in dispensationalism is demonstrated by how dispensationalists have characterized their system of theology, even though many other features are offered.

Key spokesmen in dispensational scholarship have sought to define or describe the main characteristics of dispensationalism. Probably the most recognized description of the essentials, or the *sine qua non*, was offered by Charles Ryrie. He lists three marks to the system: the distinction between Israel and the church, an approach to hermeneutics where the Bible is

---

14. See Kreider, "What Is Dispensationalism?," 39; cf. 19. Saucy, *Case for Progressive Dispensationalism*, 8-9, writes, "While most dispensationalists probably hold to a pretribulation rapture of the church . . . many would not desire to make this a determining touchstone of dispensationalism today." Cf. Grenz, *Millennial Maze*, 99, 228n43. Ryrie, *Dispensationalism*, 173, believes pretribulationism is normative for dispensationalism. For its importance to most dispensationalists, see Hart, *Evidence for the Rapture*; and Blaising, "Case for the Pretribulation Rapture," 25-73. Grenz, *Millennial Maze*, 107, asserts that "the pretribulation rapture is demanded by the dispensational system itself."

15. See Bigalke and Ice, "History of Dispensationalism," xxix-xxxix. Also note the essays in the same volume. Likewise, Nichols, "Dispensational View of the Davidic Kingdom," 213-39, finds that it is questionable to call progressive dispensationalism part of the dispensational tradition. Cautions toward progressive dispensationalism are also voiced by Ryrie, *Dispensationalism*, 193-210; and Thomas, "Hermeneutics of Progressive Dispensationalism," 79-95.

16. Svigel, "History of Dispensationalism," 93, emphasis original; cf. also 87-89. Also, in his conclusion, Bateman, "Dispensationalism Tomorrow," 309, finds "hope we can put to rest the charge that progressive dispensationalists are not dispensationalists."

interpreted in a consistently literal or plain manner, and that the underlying purpose of God in the world is his glory.[17] John Feinberg, a well-known systematic theologian, presents six core principles he believes are common to all forms of dispensationalism: (1) a belief that there are multiple senses to terms like "Jew" and "seed of Abraham"; (2) a literal hermeneutic whereby OT teachings or prophecies are taken on their own terms and are still in force unless the NT explicitly or implicitly cancels these prior promises; (3) an understanding of the covenants and their unconditional promises that require a future fulfillment to national Israel; (4) a distinct future for ethnic Israel as a nation; (5) a belief that the church is a distinct organism in the NT era; and (6) a philosophy of history that emphasizes both the soteriological or spiritual aspects and the social, economic, and political implications of God's kingdom work.[18] Progressive dispensationalists Craig Blaising and Darrell Bock provide a list of features that are the common strands of the tradition: (1) authority of Scripture; (2) dispensations; (3) uniqueness of the church; (4) practical significance of the universal church; (5) significance of biblical prophecy; (6) futurist premillennialism; (7) imminent return of Christ; and (8) a national future for Israel.[19] Other proposals for the core beliefs of dispensationalism have also been offered.[20]

---

17. Ryrie, *Dispensationalism*, 46–48. Ryrie, "Update on Dispensationalism," 21–22, complains that progressive dispensationalism reduces Israel and the church to a mere "distinction" instead of a "clear distinction." However, while it seems progressives have incorporated inaugurated eschatology (some progressives more than others) into their understanding of the kingdom of God and have a more unified view of the dispensations and the covenants, they still affirm a strong distinction between Israel and the church as well as a future restoration of ethnic Israel. See Blaising and Bock, *Progressive Dispensationalism*, 267–70; Saucy, *Case for Progressive Dispensationalism*, 28–29, 187–218; Saucy, "Israel and the Church," 239–59; Allison, *Sojourners and Strangers*, 87–89, esp. 88n57.

18. See Feinberg, "Systems of Discontinuity," 71–85. These six distinctives are also summarized in Feinberg, "Dispensationalism and Support for the State of Israel," 109–12; cf. Vlach, "What Is Dispensationalism?," 20–21.

19. Blaising and Bock, *Progressive Dispensationalism*, 13–21. See also their definition and characteristics of progressive dispensationalism in Blaising and Bock, "Dispensationalism, Israel and the Church," 378–84. Cf. Vlach, "What Is Dispensationalism?," 21.

20. See Bass, *Backgrounds to Dispensationalism*, 13–47. DeWitt, *Dispensational Theology in America*, 44–52; esp. 52; cf. 53–76, argues that the essentials of dispensationalism, rather than distinctives, are (1) the literal interpretation of all Scripture; (2) progressive revelation; (3) dispensations as the eras of salvation history; (4) the church as a Pauline revelation; (5) distinctions between historic Israel, the church, and the future kingdom; (6) the church as free from the law under grace; and (7) the pretribulational rapture of the church.

Some of the characteristics of dispensationalism offered by these important representatives are not unique to the system. Ryrie's list includes the glory of God, but this has been questioned by not just whether this was a distinctive within the historical consciousness of the dispensational tradition, but the claim is also undermined by the fact that covenant theologians and other non-dispensationalists affirm the doxological theme of Scripture.[21] Further, acknowledging dispensations cannot be part of the essence of dispensationalism as was noted, nor can the authority of Scripture as non-dispensational evangelicals also affirm a high view of Scripture.

There is also much discussion on the role of hermeneutics and Ryrie's principle of a consistent literal interpretation as a distinctive of dispensationalism. On the one hand, Blaising questions whether a literal interpretation characterized earlier dispensationalists, such as Darby and Scofield.[22] In addition, Blaising and others have noted the development of hermeneutics in the past few decades as historical-grammatical exegesis has benefitted from biblical theology and historical-literary studies, and they have also observed that the reduction of the differences in systems of theology to literal versus spiritual interpretation is misleading.[23] Furthermore, non-dispensationalists utilize the historical-grammatical hermeneutic and therefore also employ, depending on definition, a literal hermeneutic.[24]

---

21. Bateman, "Dispensationalism Yesterday and Today," 36. See also Blaising, "Development of Dispensationalism," 267–69; Blaising, "Dispensationalism," 27. Feinberg, "Systems of Discontinuity," 84–85, disagrees with Ryrie's distinctive but finds that dispensationalists and non-dispensationalists do have different emphases in what God is doing with history. However, Cone, "Dispensational Definition," 148–50, argues that God's doxological purpose is a dispensational distinctive.

22. Blaising, "Dispensationalism," 26; Blaising and Bock, *Progressive Dispensationalism*, 37; cf. Bateman, "Dispensationalism Yesterday and Today," 37. Stallard, "Literal Interpretation" 7–12, challenges Blaising on this point. He traces the interpretative method of some early dispensationalists and finds that "*literal interpretation of prophecy is kept intact* among these kinds of dispensationalists, a point that may be lost among those who downplay the role of literal interpretation in the current debate." Stallard, "Literal Interpretation," 11, emphasis original. See also Parle, *Dispensational Development*, 31–43.

23. Blaising, "Development of Dispensationalism," 269–71; Blaising and Bock, *Progressive Dispensationalism*, 35–37, 51–53; Bateman, "Dispensationalism Yesterday and Today," 37.

24. For discussion of the issue of literal interpretation and the confusion of dispensational understandings of literal interpretation, see Poythress, *Understanding Dispensationalists*, 82–96, and Donaldson, *Last Days of Dispensationalism*, 7–17. See also Feinberg, "Systems of Discontinuity," 74. Saucy, *Case for Progressive Dispensationalism*, 20, writes, "An analysis of non-dispensational systems, however, reveals that their less-than-literal approach to Israel in the Old Testament prophecies does not really arise from an a priori spiritualistic or metaphorical hermeneutic. Rather, it is the result

Thus, Blaising concludes that a "consistently literal exegesis is inadequate to describe the essential distinctive of dispensationalism."[25] On the other hand, some dispensationalists are not willing to abandon a consistent literal hermeneutic as an essential feature as they find the hermeneutic of progressive dispensationalism problematic.[26] Recently, without seeking to mediate a resolution, Nathan Holsteen observes that Blaising's and Bock's grammatical-historical-literary-theological approach is not the same as Ryrie's, but nevertheless, "the unifying factor in dispensationalism is indeed a systemic commitment to literal interpretation."[27] Holsteen's claim is that the variations within dispensationalism are unified by the pursuit of a literal hermeneutic, but that the diversity of approaches arises as to when, where, how, and why dispensationalists adapt literalism.[28] Nevertheless, many non-dispensational evangelicals are committed to the *sensus literalis* and interpret the Bible accordingly. Dispensationalists such as Feinberg, Bateman, Vlach, and Blaising are more on target in their conclusions that the key issue is not a literal hermeneutic or the question of consistency.[29] More germane to the hermeneutical differences between dispensationalists and non-dispensationalists are the presuppositions in interpretation and particularly how interpreters prioritize one testament over the other, understand the NT use of the OT and typology, and more generally how interpreters comprehend the progress of revelation and integrate the relationship between earlier and later texts at the canonical level.[30]

---

of their interpretation of the New Testament using the same grammatico-historical hermeneutic as that of dispensationalists." Ladd, "Historic Premillennialism," 18–29, raises concerns over Ryrie's literal hermeneutic in how the NT uses the OT. Donaldson, *Last Days of Dispensationalism*, 17–21, and Mathison, *Dispensationalism*, 6–8, contend that dispensationalists themselves do not entirely interpret the Bible in a consistently literal way.

25. Blaising, "Development of Dispensationalism," 272; cf. Blaising, "Dispensationalism," 30–33. See also Bock, "Why I Am a Dispensationalist," 388–90.

26. Ice, "Dispensational Hermeneutics," 29–49; Thomas, "Hermeneutics of Progressive Dispensationalism," 82–84. Ryrie, *Dispensationalism*, 100, finds progressives "distancing themselves from the consistent literal hermeneutics of normative dispensationalism by introducing 'complementary hermeneutics.'" Cf. Johnson, "Traditional Dispensational Hermeneutic," 63–84.

27. Holsteen, "Hermeneutic of Dispensationalism," 112–16, quote from p. 113. Holsteen defines a literal hermeneutic as "an approach to Scripture that finds the meaning of the text in the plain or normal sense of the text in its context" (113). For the importance of literal interpretation to dispensationalism, see DeWitt, *Dispensational Theology in America*, 54–56, 77–100.

28. Holsteen, "Hermeneutic of Dispensationalism," 115.

29. See also Stallard, "Literal Interpretation," 18.

30. See Bateman, "Dispensationalism Yesterday and Today," 37–38; Feinberg,

Therefore, while a consistent literal hermeneutic is not a distinctive feature of dispensationalism, hermeneutical presuppositions factor significantly in the dispensational system as they do in any biblical or systematic theology. These hermeneutical commitments, particularly in what dispensationalists describe as a literal interpretation of the OT promises and prophecies, impinge upon the other *sine qua non* that Ryrie identifies and which is clearly a distinctive of all varieties of dispensationalism.[31] The crucial mark of dispensationalism is the distinction between Israel and the church such that OT promises and prophecies to Israel must be fulfilled during the millennial reign of Christ (Rev 20:4–6).[32] OT prophecies and promises, such as the possession of the promised land as described in the Abrahamic covenant, must come to pass as God will fulfill national Israel's hopes and blessings materially in a future age that logically occurs during the millennium. This hallmark of the Israel-church distinction is not only recognized as such by the dispensational spokesmen described, but that it is an essential tenet of dispensationalism is confirmed by the vast volume of literature by dispensationalists on the topic of Israel and the church.[33] Israel

---

"Systems of Discontinuity," 73–79; Vlach, "What Is Dispensationalism?," 22–24; Blaising, "Biblical Hermeneutics," 79–105, esp 81–83; Stallard, "Literal Interpretation," 13–26; and Harless, *How Firm a Foundation*, 58–61. Stallard, "Literal Interpretation," 27–36, points out that refinement in exegesis may cause rapprochement, but more foundational is theological method, how biblical theology is understood, and how biblical theology leads to systematic theological formulations. While Stallard is correct to emphasize theological method, his reduction of the non-dispensational theological method with the prioritization of the NT over the OT is eclipsed by the fact that some non-dispensational theologians seek to demonstrate from the OT itself, employing a literal interpretation, the flaws of dispensationalism. Further, as Wellum demonstrates, it is evident that dispensationalists do prioritize the NT over the OT on certain matters. Gentry and Wellum, *Kingdom through Covenant*, 139–40.

31. Stallard, "Literal Interpretation," 34, offers the following as a replacement to Ryrie's *sine qua non* of a consistent literal hermeneutic: "The preservation of the literal interpretation of the Old Testament at all points of theologizing in the light of progressive revelation."

32. Saucy, *Case for Progressive Dispensationalism*, 91, describes the "primary tenet of dispensationalism" as being "the final fulfillment of the prophetic hope including the restoration of national Israel." Cf. Blaising, "Development of Dispensationalism," 273; Pugh, "Dispensationalism," 233–34.

33. On the importance of the Israel-church distinction for dispensationalism, see Ryrie, *Dispensationalism*, 46–47, 148–50, 172. The literature on the Israel-church relationship by dispensationalists is massive. For progressive dispensationalist treatments, see n17 in this chapter, and Saucy, "Progressive Dispensational View," 155–208; Saucy, "Israel as a Necessary Theme," 169–81; Burns, "Israel and the Church," 263–303. For more traditional dispensationalists on the subject of the distinctive role and future of national Israel, see Walvoord, "Does the Church Fulfill Israel's Program?," 17–31, 118–24, 212–22; Pentecost, *Thy Kingdom Come*; House, "Future of National Israel,"

will be restored as a national entity in the future under the reign of Jesus Christ as the Davidic king and thereby exercise her mediatorial role to the nations in the promised land.[34] The emphasis between Israel and the church is clearly one of discontinuity, for even in the affirmation of one people of God, the church and Israel still have distinct purposes and roles in the outworking of the kingdom of God for all forms of dispensationalism, even as the details may differ depending on the variation of dispensationalism in question. Distinguishing Israel and the church consistently with the future existence of national, political, and ethnic Israel "is probably the most basic theological test of whether or not a person is a dispensationalist."[35]

To summarize, all dispensationalists reject what they describe as "supersessionism" or "replacement theology." Although Christ may be identified with Israel, such a relationship does not transcend or remove the idea of national Israel.[36] The church does not supersede the nation of Israel even as they share a similar identity as the people of God. The Israel/church distinction is the defining mark of dispensationalism. Undergirding this essential tenet are hermeneutical presuppositions regarding the progress of revelation, typology, the NT use of the OT, and understanding OT covenant promises and prophecies to Israel unconditionally and "literally."[37] Probably the best treatment of what constitutes the foundational beliefs of dispensationalism is the one offered by Vlach. After evaluating the core principles

---

463–81; Fruchtenbaum, "Israel and the Church," 113–30; Benware, *Understanding End Times Prophecy*, 103–20. Note also Vlach, *Has the Church Replaced Israel?* and Feinberg, "Israel in the Land," 183–94.

34. For Israel's mediation to the nations in the future, see Saucy, *Case for Progressive Dispensationalism*, 259, 306–23; Saucy, "Progressive Dispensational View," 170–74, 198. Not all dispensationalists would agree with the description of Israel having a *mediatorial* role to the nations in the millennium and beyond. Some prefer to describe Israel's future restoration and role in terms of prominence or being a channel of blessing or having a functional role of service to the nations.

35. Ryrie, *Dispensationalism*, 46. Blaising and Bock, *Progressive Dispensationalism*, 267, observe that the NT never presents the inaugurated kingdom blessings "as a *replacement* of the specific hopes of Israel. Instead, they are argued as *compatible or complementary* to the hopes of Israel" (emphasis original). Further, "[r]edeemed Jews and Gentiles will share equally in the completed blessings of the Spirit. . . . The same redeemed Jews and Gentiles will be directed and governed by Jesus Christ according to their different nationalities. The national identities and political promises of Israel and the Gentiles in the last dispensation testifies in turn to this aspect." Blaising and Bock, *Progressive Dispensationalism*, 50.

36. Vlach, "What Does Christ as 'True Israel' Mean," 43–54; Blaising, "Premillennial Response," 145–46; cf. Saucy, "Is Christ the Fulfillment of National Israel's Prophesies?"

37. See Feinberg, "Hermeneutics of Discontinuity," 109–28, as he addresses these points from a dispensational perspective.

offered by Ryrie, Feinberg, and Blaising and Bock, Vlach adds clarity by elucidating six points that comprise the essence of dispensational theology:

1. Progressive revelation from the NT does not interpret OT passages in a way that cancels the original authorial intent of the OT writers as determined by historical-grammatical hermeneutics....
2. Types exist, but national Israel is not a type that is superseded by the church....
3. Israel and the church are distinct, thus the church cannot be identified as the new or true Israel....
4. There is both spiritual unity in salvation between Jews and Gentiles and a future role for Israel as a nation....
5. The nation Israel will be saved, restored with a unique identity, and function in a future millennial kingdom upon the earth....
6. There are multiple senses of "seed of Abraham"; thus, the church's identification as "seed of Abraham" does not cancel God's promises to the believing Jewish "seed of Abraham."[38]

Vlach's second point on typology will receive further attention in the following chapter. In chapters 5 and 6, I demonstrate that national Israel is indeed a type of Christ and derivatively, of the church, and that accordingly, there is no future role of national Israel in the plan of God. The sharp distinction between Israel and the church, along with the other essential points, also will be undermined by my analysis. While the six points summarize key dispensational tenets, there are still significant differences among contemporary dispensationalists. An overview of two main forms is offered to appreciate the modifications implemented in some quarters of dispensational thinking.

MODERN FORMS OR EXPRESSIONS OF DISPENSATIONALISM

Over the past thirty years and up into the contemporary discussion of dispensational theology, two varieties of dispensationalism have stood out in garnering continuing attention and academic support.[39] Beginning in the

---

38. Vlach, "What Is Dispensationalism?," 24–35.

39. What has become known as classical dispensationalism, or Scofieldism, will not be included in this study since very few or any dispensational scholars advance this position today. For overviews of classical dispensationalism, see Blaising and Bock,

mid-twentieth century, a form of dispensationalism arose out of the classical dispensationalism of Darby and Chafer. Referred to or identified as "revised," "normative," or "essentialist" dispensationalism, this more traditional form has been advocated by Ryrie, John Walvoord, Dwight Pentecost, and Alva McClain and has received ongoing support from Elliott Johnson, Robert Thomas, Michael Stallard, H. Wayne House, Thomas Ice, and others.[40] As already noted, developments in dispensational theology have resulted in the rise of progressive dispensationalism advocated by Blaising, Bock, Robert Saucy, Bruce Ware, and others.[41] While the family resemblances are enough to categorize progressive and revised dispensationalism together, they differ on important areas, including hermeneutics, the kingdom, the appropriation of inaugurated eschatology, and there is a contrast in the conception of the discontinuity between Israel and the church.

The Hermeneutical Divide of Traditional and Progressive Dispensationalism

Traditional or revised and progressive dispensationalists both seek to interpret the Bible in a literal fashion, employing a grammatical-historical hermeneutic. There are notable differences, however, as revised dispensationalists advocate a stricter literal hermeneutic. According to Mappes and House, more traditional dispensationalists practice a

> common, consistent hermeneutical historical-grammatical-literal (*sensus literal*) method of interpretation to *discern the intention of the human author by examining what the author*

Progressive Dispensationalism, 23–31; Helyer, *Witness of Jesus*, 103–9; and Blaising, "Contemporary Dispensationalism," 6–8.

40. The "revised" dispensational label is from Blaising and Bock, but Ryrie and others do not use this label for themselves and instead opt to describe their view as "normative" or "traditional" dispensationalism. In the discussion that follows I use the two terms interchangeably. For recent works defending this form of dispensationalism, see Thomas, "Traditional Dispensational View," 87–136; Mappes and House, "Biblical and Theological Discussion," 5–56; House, "Traditional Dispensationalism and the Millennium," 3–27; Bigalke, *Progressive Dispensationalism*; Johnson, "Traditional Dispensational Hermeneutic."

41. Blaising, "Contemporary Dispensationalism," 11, states that progressives believe in one divine plan of holistic redemption for all peoples and that this "holistic redemption is likewise partially and progressively realized in biblical history through a succession of divine-human dispensations. . . . The term *progressive dispensationalism* is taken from this notion of progressive revelation and accomplishment of one plan of redemption" (emphasis original). Cf. Blaising and Bock, "Dispensationalism, Israel and the Church," 380.

affirms in the historical context of his writing and then correlate all the material related to a topic in a compressive manner. Rather than re-interpret the OT or practice a complementary hermeneutic, traditional dispensationalists seek to understand the *literal meaning of a text by its immediate historical-textual parameters* and then understand how this meaning relates to God's overall program. This system of interpretation allows the immediate historical context of a passage to define and limit textual meaning.[42]

This plain or normal interpretative approach of literalism does allow for symbols, metaphors, and figures of speech. Stress is placed on the objectivity of the interpreter who does not read his or her theological system into the text and additionally, emphasis is placed on the static or fixed nature of meaning.[43] On the issue of the expansion of meaning in the progress of revelation or with how later authors appropriate earlier texts, traditional dispensationalists find that meaning "is stable in spite of the perspective gained by further revelation."[44] There is only one single meaning as that meaning is fixed in the context of its original historical setting no matter how the NT uses the OT. Mappes and House write,

> Traditional dispensationalists support the single historical, human/Divine authorial meaning for any given text. Some traditional dispensationalist [sic] support a controlled form of *sensus plenior* or *reference plenior*, though any fuller NT explanation is

---

42. Mappes and House, "Biblical and Theological Discussion," 8–9, emphasis original. Johnson, "Traditional Dispensational Hermeneutic," 65, explains that the "*literal* interpretation entails those meanings which the author intended to communicate in the expressions of the text (grammar) in the original setting (historical). *Literal* thus works with a text within the frame of an author and his communication" (emphasis original). See also Ryrie, *Dispensationalism*, 91–93; Ice, "Dispensational Hermeneutics," 30–31; and Couch, "Dispensational Hermeneutics," 13–17.

43. Thomas, "Hermeneutics of Progressive Dispensationalism," 85–89. Mappes and House, "Biblical and Theological Discussion," 12–13, write, "Once the human authorial meaning is determined, then that meaning becomes fixed in time and does not change."

44. Johnson, "Traditional Dispensational Hermeneutic," 67. Mappes and House, "Biblical and Theological Discussion," 13, find that "[s]ince the OT provides the foundational building block for NT theology, the traditional dispensationalist argues that the OT literal interpretation must be preserved in light of later progressive revelation." In arguing against progressive dispensationalists, Thomas, "Hermeneutics of Progressive Dispensationalism," 89, strikingly states, "According to traditional hermeneutical principles, such a 'bending' [of the text] is impossible because the historical dimension fixes the meaning of a given passage and does not allow it to keep gaining new senses as it comes into new settings." See also Feinberg, "Hermeneutics of Discontinuity," 120, 123–24.

only an extension and development of the OT authorial verbal meaning and thus always governed by the initial pattern of authorial meaning.⁴⁵

Application of this hermeneutic is significant particularly for understanding OT prophecies and promises to national Israel. As Grenz observes, "The literalist hermeneutic leads dispensationalists to anticipate that prophecies concerning Israel (and perhaps the surrounding nations) will be fulfilled sometime in the future basically as they were originally given."⁴⁶ Thus, normative dispensationalists claim that consistency in utilizing a plain or literal hermeneutic requires the literal fulfillment of Israel's promises and prophecies be met with Israel's future possession of the promised land and reception of all the national blessings.

Progressive dispensationalists also advocate a literal hermeneutic as they contend that their form of dispensationalism "is not an abandonment of 'literal' interpretation for 'spiritual' interpretation. Progressive dispensationalism is a development of 'literal' interpretation into a more consistent historical-literary interpretation."⁴⁷ Noting the syntactical, rhetorical, history of interpretation, and literary studies, progressives call their approach the "historical-grammatical-literary-theological"

---

45. Mappes and House, "Biblical and Theological Discussion," 10–12, emphasis original. Cf. Ryrie, *Dispensationalism*, 95–96. Feinberg, "Hermeneutics of Discontinuity," 127–28, concludes, "Where a promise or prediction is expanded or amplified, the amplification does not preclude the original addressees as a part of the referent (fulfillment) of that promise. *Expansion* does not require *exclusion*. Exclusion from any promise must be based upon some explicit or implicit statement of subsequent Scripture" (emphasis original). In addition to Feinberg, treatment of the NT use of the OT or the relationship between the testaments in revised dispensationalism is addressed by Thomas, "New Testament Use of the Old," 165–88; Ice, "Dispensational Hermeneutics," 38–41; Fruchtenbaum, *Israelology*, 842–45; House, "Traditional Dispensationalism and the Millennium," 6–10; and Zuck, *Basic Bible Interpretation*, 260–70. Overall, traditional dispensationalists reject that the NT reinterprets OT prophecies and predictions to Israel as having fulfillment with the church. Where OT predictions are literally fulfilled requires clear indication in the NT, but other aspects of "fulfillment" include analogical correspondence or application.

46. Grenz, *Millennial Maze*, 101. Grenz further finds that classical dispensationalists (which for him stands for dispensationalists prior to progressives, i.e., revised dispensationalists) take their literal hermeneutic to an extreme in advancing, based on Ezekiel, the rebuilding of the temple in Jerusalem and the reinstitution of the sacrificial system as a memorial of Christ's sacrifice. On the subject of the rebuilding of the temple prophesied in Ezek 40–48, see Hullinger, "Realization of Ezekiel's Temple," 375–95. For discussion of future animal sacrifices, see chapter 2, n129 and n131. Cf. Benware, *Understanding End Times Prophecy*, 334–36. Some, but not all, progressive dispensationalists also affirm these views.

47. Blaising and Bock, *Progressive Dispensationalism*, 52.

method.⁴⁸ Progressive dispensationalists do affirm the stability of textual meaning, the dual authorship of Scripture, and deny their approach allegorizes texts or creates multiple meanings or neglects the author's original intent.⁴⁹ While the commitment to grammatical-historical interpretation is maintained, their hermeneutic is more sophisticated than that of revised dispensationalists in that it is not strictly grammatical-historical. Progressives are more sensitive to the successive stages of Scripture in not treating them as discrete, distinct arrangements and are more complex in how they interpret OT promises through the canonical horizon.

Probably the most significant interpretative feature of progressive dispensationalism, and a point of much debate among dispensationalists, is the appeal to a complementary hermeneutic. Blaising and Bock describe the complementary concept:

> According to this approach, the New Testament does introduce change and advance; it does not merely repeat Old Testament revelation. In making complementary additions, however, it does not jettison old promises. The enhancement is not at the expense of the original promise.⁵⁰

The original authorial intent with applications or implications of that meaning is not eschewed in this dispensational framework, but the progress of revelation brings complementary aspects of meaning as additional elements of the text's message take added shape.⁵¹ Progressive

---

48. Blaising and Bock, *Progressive Dispensationalism*, 77. Cf. Helyer, *Witness of Jesus*, 111–12, and Holsteen, "Hermeneutic of Dispensationalism," 115–16, as they note other developments that impacted their hermeneutic.

49. See Bock, "Hermeneutics of Progressive Dispensationalism," 85–118, esp. 90–96. Contra Thomas, "Hermeneutics of Progressive Dispensationalism," 86–91.

50. Blaising and Bock, "Dispensationalism, Israel and the Church," 392–93. Bock, "Why I Am a Dispensationalist," 390, explains that the "'complementary' hermeneutic of progressive dispensationalism meant that what the NT gives us comes in alongside what God has already revealed in the OT. God can say more in his development of promises from the OT in the NT, but not less. He can also bring fresh connections in the development of promises as more revelation fills it out. It is this dynamic of the multitemporal dimension of promise that some dispensationalists have underplayed, while covenant theologians have overplayed the NT element. . . . Progressives argue that the NT indicates a complement of the OT promise, with more fulfillment also to come within the ethnic structures the OT had already indicated. This means that in both views the Church can exist as a distinct institution in the plan of God and yet can share in promises originally given to Israel. . . ." For critiques of this complementary hermeneutic by more traditional dispensationalists, see Ryrie, *Dispensationalism*, 205–6; Thomas, "Hermeneutics of Progressive Dispensationalism," 89–93; Baker, "Is Progressive Dispensationalism Really Dispensational?," 349–54.

51. Blaising and Bock, *Progressive Dispensationalism*, 64, 68; Bock, "Hermeneutics

dispensationalists, then, offer a multilayered reading of the text in accounting for the near context and in consideration to the inter-textual literary connections that occur in the more distant contexts.[52] The three levels of reading are the historical-exegetical level (the immediate context), the biblical-theological level (context of the whole book where the text is found), and the canonical-systematic level (reading a text in light of the whole canon).[53] This approach to biblical texts overcomes the problems in more traditional forms of dispensationalism that do not allow the NT to develop the progress of a promise given how the OT is prioritized. Further, this hermeneutic avoids the criticisms of the revised dispensational hermeneutic that has been described as a "flat" reading or interpretation of Scripture.[54] From these differing hermeneutical commitments arise other dissimilarities between progressive and revised dispensationalists, particularly in how each conceives of the kingdom of God and the Israel-church relationships. These areas are briefly treated next.

The Kingdom and Inaugurated Eschatology in Dispensational Views

Crucial modifications to the dispensational system made by progressives and contested by more traditional or revised dispensationalists are observable in regard to the theme of the kingdom of God and inaugurated eschatology (already-not yet framework).[55] According to Blaising and Bock,

---

of Progressive Dispensationalism," 90, 96–98; Saucy, "Progressive Dispensational View," 158. Bock, "Current Messianic Activity," 71, explains, "Does the expansion of meaning entail a change of meaning? This is an important question for those concerned about consistency within interpretation. . . . The answer is both yes and no. On the one hand, to add to the revelation of a promise is to introduce 'change' to it through addition. But that is precisely how revelation progresses, as referents are added to the scope of a previously given promise. . . . Progress and expansion can emerge as more pieces of the promise are brought together into a unified whole or as more of its elements are revealed. These additions can occur without undercutting a consistency of meaning, which is necessary for texts to be understandable and hermeneutics to be stable."

52. See Bock, "Son of David," 445–47; Blaising, "Biblical Hermeneutics," 81–83; and Saucy, "Progressive Dispensational View," 157–60. See also Merkle, *Discontinuity to Continuity*, 80–83.

53. Blaising and Bock, *Progressive Dispensationalism*, 100–101; Bock, "Son of David," 445n9. Saucy is not as explicit in *Case for Progressive Dispensationalism*, but a complementary hermeneutic with fuller meaning understood to reside at the canonical level appears in Saucy, "Progressive Dispensational View," 156–65.

54. Poythress, *Understanding Dispensationalists*, 87–96.

55. Bailey, "Dispensational Definitions of the Kingdom," 201–21, helpfully traverses the concept of the kingdom held by key figures in the dispensational tradition,

The theme of the kingdom of God is much more unified and more central to progressive dispensationalism than it is to revised dispensationalism. Instead of dividing up the different features of redemption into self-contained "kingdoms," progressive dispensationalists see one promised eschatological kingdom which has both spiritual and political dimensions.[56]

Writing almost a decade earlier, Saucy articulated that a newer form of dispensationalism agreed with historic premillennialists in finding it

> preferable to interpret this age as the first phase of the fulfillment of the one promised Messianic kingdom. The present age involves the spiritual aspects of the Messianic kingdom.... The remainder of the promises including those concerning Israel and the nations will find their fulfillment following the second advent.[57]

The eschatological kingdom is present in the person of king Jesus who displays, through his appearing and in his messianic and salvific work, the characteristics of the kingdom, but the kingdom is also a present reality through the church, the first institutional appearance of kingdom citizens.[58] The not yet aspects of the kingdom, the fullness of the kingdom, await Christ's return when all of national Israel's promises will come to fruition and God's enemies will be judged (occurring in the millennial and

---

from Darby to the present (e.g., Bock).

56. Blaising and Bock, *Progressive Dispensationalism*, 54; cf. Blaising, "Contemporary Dispensationalism," 12–13; Bock, "Reign of the Lord Christ," 37–67. Saucy, *Case for Progressive Dispensationalism*, 28, states, "Contrary to traditional dispensationalism, [the mediatorial kingdom, ultimately fulfilled through the reign of Christ] does not entail separate programs for the church and Israel that are somehow ultimately unified only in the display of God's glory or in eternity. The present age is not a historical parenthesis unrelated to the history that precedes and follows it; rather, it is an integrated phase in the development of the mediatorial kingdom. It is the beginning of the fulfillment of the eschatological promises."

57. Saucy, "Contemporary Dispensational Thought," 11; cf. Saucy, "Progressive Dispensational View," 156. See also Saucy, *Case for Progressive Dispensationalism*, 81–110. Saucy differs with other progressives on the nature of the presence of the kingdom. See esp. Saucy, *Case for Progressive Dispensationalism*, 101. On the other hand, Bock, "Reign of the Lord Christ," 44, 46, 65–66, argues that Christ is presently reigning through the church and the fact that his exaltation gives him claim and sovereignty over all. The only difference now between his current reign and his future reign is the visibility of his rule.

58. See Blaising and Bock, *Progressive Dispensationalism*, 232–83. Cf. Bock, "Reign of the Lord Christ," 65; Bock, "Son of David," 440–57. For other progressive dispensational discussion of the kingdom, see Turner, "Matthew among the Dispensationalists," 697–716; and Saucy, *Kingdom of God*.

consummative phases of the kingdom). The progressive dispensational understanding of the kingdom, therefore, is an inaugurated eschatology that is similar to George Eldon Ladd's version, although it differs from Ladd's in placing many aspects of the OT promises to Israel into the future manifestation of the kingdom.[59] The use of inaugurated eschatology is especially exemplified in their view that Christ is presently reigning as the Davidic king and currently seated on David's throne.[60] This point receives more attention with the discussion of the Davidic covenant.

Most traditional or revised dispensationalists made modifications to their conception of the kingdom by rejecting the classical distinction between the kingdom of God and the kingdom of heaven held by their predecessors.[61] Nevertheless, unlike progressives, the kingdom is not a singular unified theme, and if the kingdom is present in the current dispensation, aside from God's sovereign rule, it is only manifested in a spiritual or mystery form.[62] Traditional dispensationalists also reject inaugurated

---

59. For an overview of the progressive dispensational appropriation of inaugurated eschatology for their theology of kingdom eschatology and ecclesiology, see Moore, *Kingdom of Christ*, 39–44, 140–43. See also the discussion of the already-not yet framework in Blaising and Bock, *Progressive Dispensationalism*, 97–98; Bock, "Current Messianic Activity," 69–70. For the application of inaugurated eschatology specifically to the Davidic kingdom and messianic hope, see Bock, "Reign of the Lord Christ," 37–67. Inaugurated eschatology is also applied to the new covenant, consult Ware, "New Covenant," 68–97, and Saucy, "Israel as a Necessary Theme," 176–80. Differences with Ladd's form of inaugurated eschatology are pinpointed in Bock, "Reign of the Lord Christ," 54.

60. See Blaising and Bock, *Progressive Dispensationalism*, 175–87, 257; Bock, "Reign of the Lord Christ," 47–55; Bock, "Son of David," 443–55; and though having differences with Blaising and Bock in terms of Christ's current, active Davidic reign, Saucy, *Case for Progressive Dispensationalism*, 59–80, esp. 70–76, also affirms inaugural fulfillment of the Davidic messianic promise. For discussion of the differences on the kingdom between Saucy and Bock, see Bock, "Current Messianic Activity," 62–64.

61. Bailey, "Dispensational Definitions of the Kingdom," 213, finds that "Ryrie's works reflect the developing decline of the importance of what was once considered a basic distinction within dispensationalism, namely, the clearly defined bifurcation of the kingdom of heaven and the kingdom of God."

62. Ryrie, *Dispensationalism*, 180–83; Walvoord, "Biblical Kingdoms," 75–91, esp. 76–82; Pentecost, *Things to Come*, 446–75; and Benware, *Understanding End Times Prophecy*, 185–95. For an overview of the kingdom programs of more traditional dispensationalists, see Fruchtenbaum, *Israelology*, 381–414; Blaising and Bock, *Progressive Dispensationalism*, 39–46; cf. Bailey, "Dispensational Definitions of the Kingdom," 209–16. Some more traditional dispensationalists do not find any presence of the kingdom during the era of the church. For example, Toussaint, "Israel and the Church," 231, submits that the "term *kingdom* always refers to the promised yet future fulfillment of Israel's Old Testament covenants, promises, and prophecies. The kingdom was not present when Christ Jesus was here and it is not here even in 'mystery form' in this church age. It is totally future, awaiting fulfillment in the Millennium and eternity."

eschatology and specifically the already-not yet framework that appears in progressive dispensational writings.[63] Adherents to this form of dispensationalism, moreover, are unified with earlier or classical dispensationalists in maintaining the offer, rejection, total postponement, and complete future fulfillment of the Davidic kingdom.[64] Jesus offered the Davidic kingdom to Israel; however, it was contingent upon their response and given their rejection, the kingdom was postponed.[65] Accordingly, Jesus is not currently ruling from the Davidic throne but will do so in his reign during the millennium.[66]

The Israel-Church Relationship in Dispensational Perspectives

Given the revised dispensationalist view of the kingdom with the fulfillment of Israel's promises as well as the earthly mediatorial kingdom postponed until after Christ's return, the presence of the church is a parenthesis or intercalation in relation to God's program with Israel.[67] Mappes and House write,

---

Alva McClain's view of an interregnum seems similar to the position of Toussaint.

63. For critiques of progressive dispensationalism on this score, consult Ryrie, *Dispensationalism*, 196–200; Johnson, "Prophetic Fulfillment," 183–201; Johnson, "Traditional Dispensational Hermeneutic," 74–76; House, "Traditional Dispensationalism and the Millennium," 11–12; Baker, "Is Progressive Dispensationalism Really Dispensational?," 354–61.

64. See Nichols, "Dispensational View," 219–31, and the sources cited there. Note also Bass, *Backgrounds to Dispensationalism*, 31–33; Bailey, "Dispensational Definitions of the Kingdom," 219.

65. Toussaint and Quine, "No, Not Yet," 131–47; Bigalke, and Gunn, "Contingency of the Davidic Reign," 179–204; Pentecost, *Things to Come*, 449–56; Pentecost, *Thy Kingdom Come*, 207–14, 225–34; cf. DeWitt, *Dispensational Theology in America*, 69, 315–21. Turner, "Matthew among the Dispensationalists," 701, finds this position mistaken: "The absence of a political kingdom, a millennium, as it were, should not be equated with a hiatus in God's saving rule. Rather, the kingdom message summons those who hear it to turn their lives in the direction announced by Jesus with the expectation that God's reign is beginning and will be even more extensive and intensive in the future."

66. Mappes and House, "Biblical and Theological Discussion," 14–15; House, "Traditional Dispensationalism and the Millennium," 10–11; Walvoord, *Millennial Kingdom*, 199–207; Ryrie, *Dispensationalism*, 196–200. Some traditional dispensationalists describe Christ's present reign as a Melchizedekian priest over Christians.

67. Ryrie, *Dispensationalism*, 146–47, 156; Walvoord, *Millennial Kingdom*, 227–30; DeWitt, *Dispensational Theology in America*, 68, 199; Benware, *Understanding End Times Prophecy*, 105. The distinction between Israel and the church extends into the future age. See Campbell, "Church in God's Prophetic Program," 149–61.

There is only one people of God soteriologically in the sense that everyone in any time period is saved by God's grace; thus they mutually share in some of God's promises. There are, however, two distinct peoples/programs of God historically and teleologically in accomplishing God's purpose of glorification.[68]

Israel is an object of unique privilege and blessing because of her national election and because God entered into unconditional covenants that featured physical and material promises. The church, however, is structured differently with its distinct dispensational placement and purpose in the age of grace. Important to this conception of the church is the *mystery* theme. According to Ryrie, "the church as a living organism in which Jew and Gentile are on equal footing is the mystery revealed only in New Testament times and able to be made operative only after the cross of Christ."[69] While blessings to gentiles are predicted in the OT, the co-equality and inclusion of Jews and gentiles in the one body of Christ, the church as an organism indwelt by Christ, was not revealed previously and shows that the church is something new and different from national Israel.[70] Lastly, although Jews and gentiles share in salvation, given the traditional dispensational understanding of two peoples with two purposes, Israel and the church as distinct anthropological groups will continue throughout eternity.[71]

In contrast to the more traditional dispensationalists, progressives—in conjunction with their understanding of the one promised kingdom having initial fulfillment with Christ's first coming and the formation of the church—view the church as in some manner including and extending

---

68. Mappes and House, "Biblical and Theological Discussion," 15. For an overview of the revised/classical position on Israel and the church with the church as an interruption or insertion into history, see Hoch, *All Things New*, 257–60.

69. Ryrie, *Dispensationalism*, 145. Ryrie argues that the church's distinctiveness is based on its character (Christ's indwelling and Jew-gentile composition), its time (revealed as a mystery, exists as a result of Christ's resurrection and ascension, and begins at Pentecost with the baptizing work of the Holy Spirit), and its difference with Israel (use of the words *Israel* and *church* show that there is no blurring between these entities). See Ryrie's discussion in *Dispensationalism*, 144–50. See also Fruchtenbaum, "Israel and the Church," 116–18 and the summary in DeWitt, *Dispensational Theology in America*, 201.

70. Ryrie, *Dispensationalism*, 144–45. For other traditional dispensationalists who appeal to the church as something new and different from Israel on the basis of the church as a mystery, unknown and not formerly revealed until this present era, see Pentecost, *Things to Come*, 134–38; Walvoord, *Millennial Kingdom*, 231–47, esp. 232–37; Couch, "Dispensational Hermeneutics," 21–24, 27; Benware, *Understanding End Times Prophecy*, 116; cf. DeWitt, *Dispensational Theology in America*, 70–71, 202–13.

71. Vlach, "What Is Dispensationalism?," 29.

national Israel.[72] Being the Messiah's people, the church is the inaugurated form of the future kingdom of God and is described as a "sneak preview" or "functional outpost" of the kingdom.[73] Moreover, rather than there being two peoples of God with separate programs or understanding the church as a parenthesis in God's plan, there is one people of God as the church overlaps with Israel to a degree and is deemed a vital phase of the kingdom program, fitting within the one plan of holistic redemption.[74] Stated differently, in contrast to traditional dispensational expressions, Bock writes, "Progressives give more attention to how fulfillment takes place in the messianic work of the exalted Christ in the present, while also highlighting how God's ultimate reconciliation will one day bring together the creation into a

---

72. Hoch, *All Things New*, 260, describes the progressive dispensationalism position with the subtitle: "The Church Includes and Extends Israel." One problem is exactly how the term "church" is understood. Saucy, *Case for Progressive Dispensationalism*, 210, explains, "If the church ultimately signifies all of God's people who are in Christ, then surely the saved Israel will become a part of this body. By contrast, if 'church' applies only to the present age, then it would seem not to encompass that future Israel that will turn to God in faith. In either case, the church is not thereby identified with 'Israel.'" Saucy, *Case for Progressive Dispensationalism*, 209, asserts that "one never finds the term 'church' applied to those beyond the present age. Nowhere is the term as such, i.e., 'the church' applied either to the saints during the kingdom reign or in heaven either presently or in the future." However, Saucy's observation, though strictly true, fails to recognize that other terms or descriptions for the church demonstrate that it is the eschatological community that extends through eternity. The end of the ages has come upon the church (1 Cor 10:11), and it is the church that is comprised of kingdom priests who will reign with Christ (Rev 1:4–6; 5:9–10; cf. 1 Pet 2:9).

73. Blaising and Bock, *Progressive Dispensationalism*, 285–86; cf. 255–62. For the description of the church as a "sneak preview" of the future or of the kingdom," see Bock, "Reign of the Lord Christ," 46, 53. Saucy, "Church as the Mystery of God," 155, recognizes the church "as [the] functional outpost of God's kingdom." Saucy describes the unity of the one people of God and how the church and Israel share in salvation and participate in God's singular kingdom plan, but there are still distinctives as each have unique roles in the outworking of the kingdom. Saucy, *Case for Progressive Dispensationalism*, 218.

74. Blaising, "Contemporary Dispensationalism," 11–12; Blaising and Bock, *Progressive Dispensationalism*, 47; Helyer, *Witness of Jesus*, 111. See also Saucy, *Case for Progressive Dispensationalism*, 188–90, 208–10, 218; Saucy, "Progressive Dispensational View," 180–93; Bock, "Hermeneutics of Progressive Dispensationalism," 93. According to Blaising, "Contemporary Dispensationalism," 11–12, progressives differ from their predecessors by not viewing "the church as a separate group of the redeemed alongside Israel, whether as a different *kind* of people (i.e., heavenly as opposed to earthly, as in classical dispensationalism) or a different and exclusive class in the same order of redemption (as in revised dispensationalism). There will be diversity among the redeemed due to the personal and corporate aspects of humanity. . . . The church is not an ethnic or national category of humanity along the same order as the terms Israel and Gentiles. Consequently, the church is not a distinguishable group from the redeemed Jews and redeemed Gentiles in eternity" (emphasis original).

restored and total fullness and wholeness."[75] Progressive dispensationalists affirm greater continuity between Israel and the church than their more traditional counterparts—this is also seen in how they recognize that the church is comprised of a remnant of Israel. The presence of believing Jews within the body of Christ indicates a connection to OT Israel.[76] Furthermore, the manifestation of the church marks an initial fulfillment of OT promises and prophecies originally for national Israel. The church participates in and is a recipient of certain OT expectations and covenants in this present stage of the eschatological kingdom, not least of all the new covenant work of the Holy Spirit (e.g., Eph 1:13–14).[77] Nevertheless, the church is not the new or true Israel. Imagery of OT Israel is applied to the church, but the term *Israel* is never conferred upon the church and the eschatological hopes of Israel, including national restoration, await fulfillment in the future manifestation of the kingdom—the millennium and the consummated state.[78] Although progressives agree with non-dispensationalists that the "mystery" of the unity of Jews and gentiles in Christ is a fulfillment of OT prophecies regarding the gentiles becoming part of the people of God (Eph 3:3–6; cf. Isa 2:4; 12:3–4; 42:6; 49:6; Zech 9:9–10; Mic 4:3) and is therefore not completely unknown as traditional dispensationalists contend, this mystery does not negate the realization of all the prophecies or the future role of Israel.[79] In

75. Bock, "Hermeneutics of Progressive Dispensationalism," 94. For critique of the progressive dispensational view of the Israel-church relationship, see Johnson, "Prophetic Fulfillment," 193–96.

76. Hoch, *All Things New*, 261; Saucy, "Progressive Dispensational View," 182–84, 189; Blaising and Bock, *Progressive Dispensationalism*, 256, 280–81, 295; Burns, "Israel and the Church," 273.

77. Hoch, *All Things New*, 262; Saucy, "Progressive Dispensational View," 184–88; Blaising and Bock, *Progressive Dispensationalism*, 49, 174–211, 257–62. Saucy, "Israel and the Church," 252, writes, "That OT prophecies were being fulfilled in the reality of the church is a common theme of NT teaching."

78. Saucy, "Progressive Dispensational View," 188–202; Saucy, *Case for Progressive Dispensationalism*, 194–213; 221–323; Blaising and Bock, *Progressive Dispensationalism*, 267–70; Burns, "Israel and the Church," 273–89; Bock, "Reign of the Lord Christ," 55–61; Hoch, *All Things New*, 263–318. Cf. Richardson, *Israel in the Apostolic Church*.

79. Saucy, *Case for Progressive Dispensationalism*, 163–67. See also Saucy, "Church as the Mystery of God," 127–55, esp. 147–51. In these writings, Saucy understands the content of the mystery of Eph 3:6 as entailing two senses. First, added dimensions of the messianic salvation now revealed were not specified in the OT. Thus there is new truth concerning this fulfillment with the church whereas the OT had projected salvation coming to the gentiles when Christ was reigning over a restored Israel. Second, Paul's use of mystery signifies that the salvation in Christ has dawned in actuality whereas previously this messianic activity was only predicted. For a revised dispensational critique of this view, see Ryrie, *Dispensationalism*, 154–56. Bock, "Current Messianic Activity," 81 (cf. 80–85), finds that the mystery of Eph 3:6–9 is completely new "since

the eternal state, the church is not another "people-group" among national Israel; rather, as Blaising and Bock explain,

> Redeemed Jews and Gentiles will share equally in the completed blessings of the Spirit. The church in this [present] dispensation testifies to this aspect of redemption. The same redeemed Jews and Gentiles will be directed and governed by Jesus Christ according to their different nationalities. The national identities and political promises of Israel and the Gentiles in the last dispensation testifies in turn to this aspect of redemption.[80]

DISPENSATIONAL UNDERSTANDINGS OF THE COVENANTS

The differences between more traditional dispensationalists and progressives also appear in their understandings of the covenants. Naturally, however, all dispensationalists differ from covenant theologians in not advocating for the theological constructs of the covenant of works and grace. The main focus for this overview of covenants within dispensational thought will be upon the Abrahamic, Davidic, and new covenants since their interpretations of these covenants are pivotal for their understanding of the Israel-church distinction (ecclesiology) and eschatology.[81] The covenant of creation or covenant with Adam receives little attention in dispensational writings, and although it is not ignored altogether,[82] such a lack of treatment

---

the OT nowhere declares either the indwelling of Gentiles by the Messiah or the total equality of Jews and Gentiles in one new body." Recently, Beale and Gladd, *Hidden but Now Revealed*, 159–73, esp. 164–66, have convincingly argued that the mystery of Eph 3:6 concerns *how* gentiles become part of end-time Israel in the latter days and that the mystery is not specifically about the equal membership of the body of Christ. The OT already projected gentiles becoming part of the nation of Israel as Saucy acknowledges, but the mystery concerns *how* gentiles become part of the new or renewed Israel—not by following the customs and markers of the Mosaic Law but by identifying with Christ, the true Israel. It is through the gospel that gentiles are fellow partakers in Christ. For similar conclusions to those of Beale and Gladd, see Grindheim, "What the OT Prophets Did Not Know," 531–53.

80. Blaising and Bock, *Progressive Dispensationalism*, 50. See also Blaising, "God's Plan for History," 195–218, esp. 202–14, for a discussion on the differences between classic, revised, and progressives on the eternal state.

81. For examples, Pentecost, *Things to Come*; Walvoord, *Millennial Kingdom*; and Saucy, *Case for Progressive Dispensationalism*; all focus on these three covenants in their studies. Cf. Merkle, *Discontinuity to Continuity*, 36–40, 61–64, 88–92, who summarizes the covenants in dispensational thought.

82. Harless, *How Firm a Foundation*, 69–91, identifies a pre-fall Edenic covenant

raises the specter that dispensationalists are not linking national Israel back to Adam and the pivotal creation account in the doing of biblical theology. The Mosaic covenant, which is a significant area of debate within covenant theology, is also not as significant for dispensationalism as this covenant (or dispensation of Law) is interpreted as fulfilled or abrogated.[83] Therefore, a brief sketch of the Abrahamic, Davidic, and new covenants is in order.

The Abrahamic Covenant

For all dispensationalists, like covenant theologians, the Abrahamic covenant is foundational as a covenant and within their system of theology.[84] According to dispensationalists, the Abrahamic covenant is a unilateral or unconditional covenant, and some will also describe it as a royal grant covenant having affinities with ANE parallels.[85] The promissory or unconditional nature of the covenant, highlighted by God unilaterally cutting the covenant as Abram slept (Gen 15:1–21), is not negated by the fact that

---

and a post-fall Adamic covenant. Both are described as suzerain-vassal covenants featuring stipulations, beneficiaries, and clear points of establishment (Gen 2:16, 17; Gen 3:1–19, respectively). Cf. Walvoord, *Millennial Kingdom*, 78, as he mentions these two covenants in contrast to a covenant of works. Merrill, *Everlasting Dominion*, 238–40, describes the Adamic covenant in Gen 1:26–28 as a royal grant type. Blaising and Bock, *Progressive Dispensationalism*, 129, 216, give scant attention to the creation account and do not link national Israel back to Adam. Likewise, Marsh, "Dynamic Relationship," 262, in his discussion of the covenants the covenant of creation is absent (he rejects it for unspecified reasons, 263n25). Saucy, *Case for Progressive Dispensationalism*, 40, 44, briefly relates the Abrahamic covenant to the early chapters of Genesis, but again, there is no attempt to connect the nation of Israel back to Adam in any developed manner. Instead of referring to a covenant of creation, some dispensationalists speak of a dispensation of innocence and conscience with respect to the first three chapters of Genesis.

83. See Blaising and Bock, *Progressive Dispensationalism*, 194–99; Pentecost, *Thy Kingdom Come*, 85–94.

84. For treatment of the Abrahamic covenant by progressive dispensationalists, see Blaising and Bock, *Progressive Dispensationalism*, 53, 130–40, 187–93; Saucy, *Case for Progressive Dispensationalism*, 39–58; Bock, "Covenants," 172–77. For traditional/revised dispensational discussions, see Pentecost, *Thy Kingdom Come*, 51–81; Walvoord, *Millennial Kingdom*, 139–93; Gromacki, "Fulfillment of the Abrahamic Covenant," 77–119; Bigalke, "Abrahamic Covenant," 39–84; Fruchtenbaum, *Israelology*, 334–44, 572–81; Benware, *Understanding End Times Prophecy*, 35–54; Marsh, "Dynamic Relationship," 265–66. Note also Harless, *How Firm a Foundation*, 105–29; Essex, "Abrahamic Covenant," 191–212.

85. Some dispensationalists appeal to the study of Weinfeld, "Covenant of Grant in the Old Testament," 184–203. Whether royal grants were of a fixed form and unconditional is a matter of debate. See Knoppers, "Ancient Near Eastern Royal Grants," 670–97.

Abraham was obligated to serve and obey God—his obedience occasioned the blessings but the promises instituted by God are subject to his divine commitment.[86] This unconditional nature of the covenant is important for dispensationalists because the Abrahamic covenant is everlasting (Gen 13:15; 17:7, 13, 19; 1 Chr 16:16–17; Ps 105:9–10) and features physical and spiritual promises that establish the enduring or irrevocable role of the nation of Israel and her perpetual title to the promised land in God's plan.

More specifically, the promises to Abraham envelop three crucial elements: the seed, the land, and the universal blessing to all nations.[87] Most dispensationalists agree that the Abrahamic covenant is partially fulfilled through the church (or at the very least the church participates in the Abrahamic promises) as Christ is the singular seed who brings universal blessings to peoples and believers in and through Christ become Abraham's spiritual seed.[88] Further, all dispensationalists concur that the promise to Abraham of being made into a great nation and the promised land for the physical (and faithful) offspring of Abraham—the ethnic nation of Israel—await fulfillment in the future, namely the millennium.[89]

There are, however, differences between progressives and more traditional dispensationalists in terms of how they perceive the Abrahamic

---

86. Blaising and Bock, *Progressive Dispensationalism*, 132–34; Johnson, "Covenants in Traditional Dispensationalism," 125; Essex, "Abrahamic Covenant," 209–10; Walvoord, *Millennial Kingdom*, 149–58; Pentecost, *Things to Come*, 74–82. Cf. Feinberg, "Systems of Discontinuity," 79–80; DeWitt, *Dispensational Theology in America*, 312–14.

87. Other promises to Abraham, such as having a great name, how God will bless or curse those who bless or curse Abraham, and many others are also highlighted by dispensationalists. Blaising and Bock, *Progressive Dispensationalism*, 130; Bock, "Covenants," 174–77; Harless, *How Firm a Foundation*, 118–21; Gromacki, "Fulfillment of the Abrahamic Covenant," 79–84. Nevertheless, the seed, the land, and blessings for all peoples take center stage as most dispensationalists recognize, e.g., Saucy, *Case for Progressive Dispensationalism*, 42–46; Pentecost, *Things to Come*, 73.

88. Saucy, *Case for Progressive Dispensationalism*, 49–50, 57–58; Blaising and Bock, *Progressive Dispensationalism*, 189–93; Bock, "Covenants," 172; Ryrie, *Dispensationalism*, 161; Bigalke, "Abrahamic Covenant," 47–52; Gromacki, "Fulfillment of the Abrahamic Covenant," 114–16. Walvoord, *Millennial Kingdom*, 145–46; Pentecost, *Thy Kingdom Come*, 79–80; and Benware, *Understanding End Times Prophecy*, 50–52, all fail to identify Christ as the seed of Abraham though they do recognize that gentiles become Abraham's spiritual seed through Christ and so are heirs of the promise of Gen 12:3.

89. Saucy, *Case for Progressive Dispensationalism*, 44–46, 50–57; Blaising and Bock, *Progressive Dispensationalism*, 189, 193–94; Bock, "Covenants," 172–75; Walvoord, *Millennial Kingdom*, 174–93; Pentecost, *Things to Come*, 90–94; Johnson, "Covenants in Traditional Dispensationalism," 138–39; Thomas, "Traditional Dispensational View," 88–89. For specific emphasis on the promise of land, see Townsend, "Fulfillment of the Land Promise," 320–37; Kaiser, "Land of Israel and the Future Return," 209–27.

covenant developing in the progress of revelation. According to Bigalke, "Traditional dispensationalism interprets the spiritual promises or blessings as extending to the church, but the covenants are not fulfilled in the Church Dispensation."[90] In addition, the three essential aspects of the Abrahamic covenant (the seed promise, land, and universal blessings) form the basis of three sub-covenants of which they also find their fulfillment: the Davidic (national seed theme), the Palestinian or Land covenant (Deut 29–30), and the new covenant (universal blessings).[91] Progressives, in contrast, understand the Abrahamic covenant as having a more christological focus with Jesus inaugurating the fulfillment of this covenant (Gal 3) as he mediates the blessings to Israel and the nations.[92] Moreover, progressives reject the notion of a Palestinian covenant as they find no evidence for it, and they understand the new covenant as "*the form* in which the Abrahamic covenant has been inaugurated in this dispensation and will be fulfilled in the future. The Davidic covenant is both an aspect of Abrahamic blessings and *the means* by which the blessings are now inaugurated and will be bestowed in full."[93]

---

90. Bigalke, "Abrahamic Covenant," 52. Cf. Pentecost, *Things to Come*, 89–90. Johnson, "Covenants in Traditional Dispensationalism," 136–39, does refer to the covenant as partially fulfilled during Israel's history, but its exhaustive fulfillment is future. Cf. Walvoord, *Millennial Kingdom*, 192.

91. Bigalke, "Abrahamic Covenant," 43–45; Pentecost, *Things to Come*, 71–72 (cf. 95–99 for the Palestinian covenant); and Benware, *Understanding End Times Prophecy*, 52–54. See Benware's diagram of the covenants on p. 53 and his discussion of the Abrahamic "sub-covenants" on pp. 55–78. Cf. Harless, *How Firm a Foundation*, 131–49, for a discussion of the land covenant.

92. Blaising and Bock, *Progressive Dispensationalism*, 189–93; Saucy, *Case for Progressive Dispensationalism*, 49, 57. Despite this inaugural fulfillment wrought in Christ, Bock, "Covenants," 172–73, still argues that a second feature or track of the Abrahamic covenant is the prominent role for the ethnic nation of Israel, and Saucy, *Case for Progressive Dispensationalism*, 57–58, also finds the inauguration of the covenant in Christ's redemptive work, but the promises of land and the "great nation," are future as these "blessings promised to Israel are nowhere reinterpreted as presently belonging to the church." Cf. Saucy, "Progressive Dispensational View," 166–67.

93. Blaising and Bock, *Progressive Dispensationalism*, 53, emphasis original; cf. 156–58. See also Saucy, *Case for Progressive Dispensationalism*, 122–23. For reasons rejecting the Palestinian covenant, see Bock, "Covenants," 211n1. For summaries and critiques of the progressive dispensational interpretation of the Abrahamic covenant by traditionalists, see Bigalke, "Abrahamic Covenant," 52–53; and Gromacki, "Fulfillment of the Abrahamic Covenant," 110–11.

The Davidic Covenant

Some of the most vociferous debates among dispensationalists is centered on the Davidic covenant and the kingdom, as has already been noted in regard to the latter topic.[94] It is specifically at these points where the appropriation of inaugurated eschatology and complementary hermeneutics by progressive dispensationalists lead to significant areas of dispute with revised dispensationalists. Before highlighting more of these disagreements with regard to the Davidic covenant, the areas of agreement are observed.

All dispensationalists understand the Davidic covenant as an unconditional or unilateral covenant, and like the Abrahamic, some will identify it as a royal grant. While the covenant is everlasting and eternal, enjoyment of the promises is conditioned on the obedience and faithfulness of the Davidic kings.[95] Although there is some variation in describing the promises to David (2 Sam 7; 1 Chr 17), most dispensationalists agree that the promises entail a great name for David, a place and rest for national Israel, a house or dynasty for David (posterity), and an everlasting throne and kingdom.[96] Moreover, dispensationalists understand the Davidic covenant to enlarge or elaborate upon the Abrahamic covenant in terms of narrowing the focus of the seed promises.[97] Lastly, the exhaustive fulfillment of the Davidic cov-

---

94. For treatment of the Davidic covenant by progressive dispensationalists, see Blaising and Bock, *Progressive Dispensationalism*, 159–71, 175–87; Saucy, *Case for Progressive Dispensationalism*, 59–80; Bock, "Covenants," 177–89, 195–203; Bock, "Current Messianic Activity," 65–85. For more traditional dispensational understandings, see Pentecost, *Thy Kingdom Come*, 137–56; Walvoord, *Millennial Kingdom*, 194–207; Johnson, "Covenants in Traditional Dispensationalism," 127–31, 139–44; Cragoe, "Davidic Covenant," 99–134; Rogers, "Davidic Covenant in the Gospels," 458–78; Rogers, "Davidic Covenant in Acts–Revelation," 71–84; Fruchtenbaum, *Israelology*, 345–54, 583–86; Benware, *Understanding End Times Prophecy*, 61–71. Note also Harless, *How Firm a Foundation*, 151–65; Merrill, *Everlasting Dominion*, 434–42; Grisanti, "Davidic Covenant," 233–50.

95. Blaising and Bock, *Progressive Dispensationalism*, 163–65; Saucy, *Case for Progressive Dispensationalism*, 65–66; Pentecost, *Things to Come*, 103–4; Johnson, "Covenants in Traditional Dispensationalism," 129–30; Harless, *How Firm a Foundation*, 152–53; Benware, *Understanding End Times Prophecy*, 62–63.

96. Blaising and Bock, *Progressive Dispensationalism*, 159–61; Bock, "Covenants," 179–81; Saucy, *Case for Progressive Dispensationalism*, 60; Walvoord, *Millennial Kingdom*, 195–96; Pentecost, *Things to Come*, 101–3; Benware, *Understanding End Times Prophecy*, 62–63; Cragoe, "Davidic Covenant," 99–100.

97. As noted, traditional dispensationalists connect the Abrahamic land promises to the Palestinian covenant and view the seed promise developing in the Davidic covenant (e.g., Pentecost, *Thy Kingdom Come*, 140). On the other hand, progressive dispensationalists see more connections and development between the Abrahamic and the Davidic covenants. Saucy, *Case for Progressive Dispensationalism*, 63, writes, "Both Abraham and David are personally promised a 'great name' (2Sa. 7:9; cf. Ge 12:2) and

enant occurs when Jesus returns to earth, Israel experiences full national and political restoration, and Jesus' reign is displayed over all.

Aside from those general areas of agreement, dispensationalists part ways in regard to the fulfillment of the Davidic covenant. More traditional dispensationalists, while recognizing that Jesus is the messianic son of David, assert that the Davidic promises concerning a kingdom, throne, and reign will be fulfilled in the future as no partial or inaugurated fulfillment has occurred with Christ's first coming.[98] The Davidic covenant must be fulfilled to the nation of Israel in a literalistic manner, but the kingdom is postponed since Israel rejected the offer and did not receive Jesus.[99] Further, Jesus is enthroned in heaven as the vindicated Lord and Christ on account of his resurrection and ascension (Acts 2:14–36), but he is not on the throne of David (on earth), but on the throne of God.[100] Lastly, NT citations of Ps 110 only indicate Jesus' role as the Melchizedekian priest, but this priesthood is not a provision of the Davidic covenant.[101] Traditional dispensationalists critique progressives for blurring the distinction of the universal kingdom with the Davidic kingdom and thereby compromise the distinction between Israel and the church since progressives conceive of the church as the realm of Christ's current Davidic rule.[102]

In contrast, progressive dispensationalists understand the Davidic covenant as having inaugural fulfillment as the Davidic dynasty (house)

---

the Lord's blessing (2Sa 7:29; cf. Ge 12:2). In the long range, they will have kings among their offspring (2Sa 7:12–16; cf. Ge 17:6, 16) and a land or a 'place' for the nation (2 Sa 7:10; cf. Ge 12:7). The aim of universal blessing, so important to the Abrahamic promise, is clearly associated later on with the Davidic promise (Ps 72:17; cf. Ge 12:3). . . ." Similarly, Blaising and Bock, *Progressive Dispensationalism*, 166–68.

98. Walvoord, *Millennial Kingdom*, 197–207; Pentecost, *Things to Come*, 113–15; Pentecost, *Thy Kingdom Come*, 146–48; Benware, *Understanding End Times Prophecy*, 63–65; Cragoe, "Davidic Covenant," 104–12; Harless, *How Firm a Foundation*, 158–62; Johnson, "Covenants in Traditional Dispensationalism," 142.

99. Cragoe, "Davidic Covenant," 105–6; Johnson, "Covenants in Traditional Dispensationalism," 141–42; Pentecost, *Thy Kingdom Come*, 232–33; Rogers, "Davidic Covenant in the Gospels," 470–72, 476–77.

100. Walvoord, *Millennial Kingdom*, 203; Ryrie, *Dispensationalism*, 198–99; Benware, *Understanding End Times Prophecy*, 65–69; Rogers, "Davidic Covenant in Acts-Revelation," 74, 81–82. These dispensationalists understand the use of Pss 16, 110, and 132 in Acts 2 to only confirm that Jesus is the Davidic Messiah, but such uses of these passages say nothing about Christ's current rule on David's throne. For a critique of this view, see LaRondelle, *Israel of God*, 41–43.

101. Johnson, "Covenants in Traditional Dispensationalism," 130–31, 144; Cragoe, "Davidic Covenant," 108, 113–15; Ryrie, *Dispensationalism*, 199.

102. Johnson, "Prophetic Fulfillment," 191; Cragoe, "Davidic Covenant," 113, 115–16; Walvoord, "Biblical Kingdoms," 89.

culminates in Christ. Blaising and Bock rightly observe that the Davidic titles applied to Jesus, his anointing at his baptism, and his resurrection (which fulfills the promise of raising up a Davidic descendant) are all tied back to the Davidic covenant.[103] The Davidic kingdom is a present reality then, and Christ is sitting on the throne of David, which is not to be distinguished from the throne of God or from the language of being seated at the right hand of God.[104] As Blaising and Bock convincingly demonstrate, the description of Christ's enthronement is drawn from Davidic promises and additionally, the description of the Melchizedekian priesthood in Ps 110 is part of the Davidic office and is linked to Ps 132 (and derivatively to the Davidic covenant of 2 Sam 7) by Peter in Acts 2.[105] There is a difference among progressives in terms of Christ's reign on the throne, however. Saucy advances that Christ's session on the Davidic throne carries no present function in terms of an active reign as Christ's rule is only exercised with his second coming.[106] For Blaising and Bock, it is Christ's present activity that guarantees the fulfillment of all the Davidic promises in the future.[107] Specifically, Bock's survey of a whole constellation of titles, roles, and images associated with the rule and authority of the Davidic king, from shepherding to defeating enemies and conquering cosmic forces to the messianic activities of granting forgiveness and distributing the Spirit, has shown that Christ is currently exercising his regal rule as the ideal Davidic king.[108]

The New Covenant

The diversity of positions on the fulfillment of the new covenant, especially among more traditional dispensationalists, reveal the challenges dispensationalists have in applying a strict, consistent, literal grammatical

---

103. Blaising and Bock, *Progressive Dispensationalism*, 175–77; cf. Saucy, *Case for Progressive Dispensationalism*, 67–69.

104. Blaising and Bock, *Progressive Dispensationalism*, 177–78, esp. 182–85; Bock, "Reign of the Lord Christ," 49–51, 62–64; Bock, "Current Messianic Activity," 76–77; and Saucy, *Case for Progressive Dispensationalism*, 69–72.

105. Blaising and Bock, *Progressive Dispensationalism*, 182–84; Bock, "Reign of the Lord Christ," 49, 51; Bock, "Covenants," 199–200.

106. Saucy, *Case for Progressive Dispensationalism*, 72–76, 80, 101, 106. Saucy repeatedly states that Christ's present reign is not functioning in terms of an actual messianic rule. Saucy is followed by his son on this point: Saucy, *Kingdom of God*, 343–47. For critiques of these views, see Bock, "Covenants," 218n20, 222–23n34. Cf. Moore, *Kingdom of Christ*, 40–42.

107. Blaising and Bock, *Progressive Dispensationalism*, 162, 180.

108. Bock, "Covenants," 195–202.

hermeneutic as they contend with how new covenant promises or provisions to Israel are used by the NT authors with reference to the church.[109] Dispensationalists generally agree that the new covenant is an eternal, unconditional, or unilateral covenant (and some describe it as a grant covenant) and that Jesus Christ is the mediator of this covenant.[110] Nevertheless, the number of proposals regarding the relationship between the new covenant and the church indicates the strain of maintaining the Israel-church distinction, which lies at the heart of dispensationalism.

Among more traditional dispensationalists, at least three to four differing views of the new covenant may be discerned.[111] First, prominent dispensationalists have argued that there are two new covenants, one for Israel and one for the church.[112] OT and NT texts refer to the new covenant with Israel, which will be completed in the millennial kingdom. Other NT passages (1 Cor 11:25; 2 Cor 3:6) address a new covenant that is enjoyed by the church in the present age.

---

109. For presentations of the nature or fulfillment of the new covenant by progressive dispensationalists, see Blaising and Bock, *Progressive Dispensationalism*, 151–59, 199–210; Saucy, *Case for Progressive Dispensationalism*, 111–39; Bock, "Covenants," 189–94; Ware, "New Covenant," 68–97; Allison, *Sojourners and Strangers*, 70–78, 124; Hoch, *All Things New*, 75–135; Thorsell, "Spirit in the Present Age," 397–413. For the variety of views within revised dispensationalism, see Pentecost, *Things to Come*, 116–28; Pentecost, *Thy Kingdom Come*, 164–77; Walvoord, "New Covenant," 186–200; Walvoord, *Millennial Kingdom*, 208–20; Ryrie, *Dispensationalism*, 200–205; Johnson, "Covenants in Traditional Dispensationalism," 131–34, 144–53; Benware, *Understanding End Times Prophecy*, 71–78; Stallard, *Dispensational Understanding of the New Covenant*; Cone, *Introduction to the New Covenant*; Master, "New Covenant," 93–110; Compton, "Dispensationalism and the New Covenant," 3–48; Decker, "Church's Relationship to the New Covenant," 290–305, 431–56; Harless, *How Firm a Foundation*, 167–84; Pettegrew, "New Covenant," 251–70; cf. Merrill, *Everlasting Dominion*, 530–34, 545–46.

110. Although even here there seems to be division as some dispensationalists describe the new covenant as a suzerain-vassal covenant, e.g., Beacham, "Church Has No Legal Relationship," 117–19.

111. Compton, "Dispensationalism and the New Covenant," 6–9, surveys four views among dispensationalists while Decker, "Church's Relationship to the New Covenant," 431–47, and Cone, "Hermeneutical Ramifications," 5–22, review three positions. Cf. the three views in Stallard, *Dispensational Understanding of the New Covenant*, and Fruchtenbaum, *Israelology*, 354–69.

112. Walvoord, *Millennial Kingdom*, 214–19; Ryrie, *Dispensationalism*, 202–4, esp. 204. Walvoord, "Does the Church Fulfill Israel's Program?," 219–20, changed his view to positing one new covenant with application to the church, but he later reverted back to his original position; see Walvoord, "New Covenant," 198–99. Ryrie appears to have followed the same pattern, so Compton, "Dispensationalism and the New Covenant," 6–7n12. Master, "New Covenant," 108, seems to articulate something similar to this position. For critique of the two covenant position, see Thorsell, "Spirit in the Present Age," 401–10; Compton, "Dispensationalism and the New Covenant," 38.

A second position is that the new covenant is for Israel alone, and as the sole and exclusive covenant partner, Israel will receive the fullness of the new covenant in the eschaton.[113] The new covenant is actually not applied to the church in any manner in the NT. The salvation blessings in the church age are only similar to those promised to Israel under the new covenant. There is no indirect or direct relationship to the new covenant for the church; the similarities are only due to the fact that the church is in relationship with the same new covenant mediator, Jesus Christ.

A third view popular among traditional dispensationalists with some variation is that there is one new covenant, but in some manner the church participates in the blessings or benefits of the new covenant ratified by Christ.[114] Important for this view is that the church's experience of the blessings and provisions of the new covenant (soteriological in nature), as well as the ratification of the new covenant in the death of Christ, in no way mean that the new covenant is fulfilled either partially or in terms of inauguration. With Israel as the covenant partner of the unconditional and prophesied new covenant, fulfillment must occur with the second coming of Christ.

Lastly, the new covenant is understood to be inaugurated or operative in the current age with church members participating in the initial realization of the spiritual blessings.[115] The full appropriation of the new covenant is directed to national Israel. This position overlaps somewhat with the progressive dispensational perspective on the new covenant.

Turning to progressive dispensationalism, progressives recognize there is one new covenant, and it is established by the work of Christ. Although the new covenant in the OT context has Israel as the covenant partner, Saucy observes, "The fact that the prophetic statements are addressed only to Israel cannot logically be understood to *exclude* others from

---

113. Beacham, "Church Has No Legal Relationship," 107–44; Cone, "Hermeneutical Ramifications," 17–21; Master, "New Covenant," 108; Marsh, "Dynamic Relationship," 269–74. For critique of this view, see Compton, "Dispensationalism and the New Covenant," 39–40.

114. Pentecost, *Thy Kingdom Come*, 174–76; Decker, "Church's Relationship to the New Covenant," 447–56; Harless, *How Firm a Foundation*, 174–77; Benware, *Understanding End Times Prophecy*, 75–77; Compton, "Dispensationalism and the New Covenant," 47–48. Although disagreeing on some details, both Johnson, "Church Has an Indirect Relationship," 164–75, and Decker, "Church Has a Direct Relationship," 194–222, agree that the church does not fulfill any aspect of the new covenant promises to Israel, but the new covenant still applies to the church. For critique of the single covenant, multiple participants perspective, see Cone, "Hermeneutical Ramifications," 10–17.

115. Pettegrew, "New Covenant," 265–68; Alexander, "New Covenant—An Eternal People," 169–206, esp. 197–98.

participating even though they are not a part of Israel. The texts never say that the covenant would relate only to Israel and not others."[116] The new covenant is extended to gentiles since it restates or brings to fulfillment the promises of the Davidic and Abrahamic covenant as the universal blessing to all families (Gen 12:3) and the promise of reconciliation with the nations (e.g., Isa 55:3–5) come to initial fruition through the death of Christ, which also enacts the new covenant.[117] The participation of gentiles in the new covenant does not mean that they become part of a "new Israel." The new covenant promises involving the restoration of national Israel and the physical and material blessings, including the hope of Israel becoming a great nation (Gen 12:2), are provisions of the new covenant that await future fulfillment.[118]

What is vital for the progressive dispensational understanding of the new covenant, as with the other promissory covenants, is their use of inaugurated eschatology.[119] The spiritual aspects or blessings of the new covenant—forgiveness of sins, indwelling of the Holy Spirit, the transformation of the heart leading to faithfulness, and a new relationship to God for all covenant participants—are now inaugurated in this age through the mediation of Christ and the agency of the Holy Spirit. The not-yet aspects include the physical or territorial and political promises as those will be consummated for national Israel in the millennium (Rom 11:25–27). However, progressives also recognize that spiritual blessings of the new covenant are not yet. Blaising and Bock, for example, observe that moral and spiritual perfection (freedom from sin), full adoption of sonship (Rom 8:23), and the resurrection of the body are associated with Christ's return.[120]

---

116. Saucy, *Case for Progressive Dispensationalism*, 114, emphasis original; cf. Bock, "Covenants," 190, 219n24.

117. For the relationship between the new covenant and the Abrahamic and Davidic covenants in conjunction with the inclusion of the gentiles in the new covenant blessings, see Blaising and Bock, *Progressive Dispensationalism*, 155–58; Saucy, *Case for Progressive Dispensationalism*, 121–23, 131–32. Cf. Ware, "New Covenant," 72–73. Progressives also connect the new covenant to the Isaianic servant who brings salvation to the nations.

118. Saucy, *Case for Progressive Dispensationalism*, 124–25, 127–32, 134–35; similarly, Blaising and Bock, *Progressive Dispensationalism*, 158, 202, 205, 210–11; Ware, "New Covenant," 92–93. Cf. Vlach, *Has the Church Replaced Israel?*, 15/–60.

119. See Ware, "New Covenant," 93–96; Blaising and Bock, *Progressive Dispensationalism*, 206–11; Bock, "Reign of the Lord Christ," 48–49; Saucy, *Case for Progressive Dispensationalism*, 134–38; Saucy, "Israel as a Necessary Theme," 177–79; Thorsell, "Spirit in the Present Age," 410–13. See also Vlach, *Has the Church Replaced Israel?*, 158–59. Cf. Lucas, "Dispensational Appeal to Romans 11," 239–40.

120. Blaising and Bock, *Progressive Dispensationalism*, 208–10. Ware, "New Covenant," 95–96, arrives to the same conclusion that the new covenant spiritual aspects

Therefore, according to progressives, the spiritual promises of the new covenant have an already and a not-yet realization, while the material or physical promises to national Israel are entirely yet to be fulfilled. One of the thrusts of chapter 5 is to demonstrate that this asymmetrical conception of the new covenant in terms of inaugurated eschatology is off the mark. Israel's restoration commences with the coming of Christ and the land of promise is confirmed as a typological pattern given the indications within the OT itself and based on the developments of the inheritance and rest themes in the NT.[121] Taken together, the evidence strongly suggests that the entire new covenant is ratified by Christ's work on the cross and all of the new covenant provisions and promises have a present fulfillment and a future realization equally shared by all those in union with Christ, Jew and gentile Christians alike.

THE NATURE OF TYPOLOGY IN DISPENSATIONAL THEOLOGY

The previous elucidation of dispensational approaches to interpretation (whether strictly "literal" or utilizing complementary hermeneutics) and how that shapes the dispensational understandings of the kingdom, the covenants, and the Israel-church relationship provide the framework for their rendering and approach to typology. Dispensationalists recognize typological patterns in Scripture, but at the outset it is evident that national Israel is either not typological of Christ or the church (the antitypes), or Israel is typological if typology is redefined to consist of only correspondence and analogy (see chapter 2) or reframed such that antitypes are only partial or incomplete fulfillments of the type. Saucy captures this precisely when he writes,

---

are not yet: "The goal [of covenant fidelity] will surely be achieved in the end. At present, however, the struggle with the world, the flesh, and the devil goes on, but it does so with the resources of a new-covenant provision to enable holiness and obedience. . . . [S]uch new-covenant faithfulness will occur fully when Christ comes again and brings to completion the new covenant, which is now inaugurated in a preliminary way."

121. Intriguingly, Blaising and Bock, *Progressive Dispensationalism*, 153–54, identify the connection between the resurrection from the dead with the inheritance of the promised land (e.g., Ezek 37:14), but they posit these blessings to the future. On the other hand, Beale, *New Testament Biblical Theology*, 751, 761–62, 768, argues for the inaugurated fulfillment of the land through the physical resurrection of Christ as the inbreaking of the new creation. Beale thoroughly lays out how the land promises are universalized within the OT and NT in addition to the NT textual warrant for the already-not yet features (750–72). Cf. Lucas, "Dispensational Appeal to Romans 11," 241.

> If a type is understood as a *shadow* pointing forward to the *reality* of its antitype, then Israel is not a type.... On the other hand, if a type is more loosely defined simply as a general historical and theological correspondence, then the many analogies between Old Testament Israel and the New Testament people of God may well be explained by seeing Israel as a type without necessitating its cessation as a nation and the fulfillment of the promises related to its future.[122]

Despite similarities, the particular notions of typology differ among more traditional forms of dispensationalism and progressive dispensationalism.[123]

Typological Perspectives within Traditional or Revised Dispensationalism

There is some variation among more traditional dispensationalists on the topic of typology. Some articulate a view of typology that resonates with the presentation in chapter 2. Namely, in contrast to allegorization, typology, rooted in the literal sense of Scripture, is the study of persons, events, and institutions that are historically grounded, characterized by a genuine correspondence or resemblance with their antitypical counterpart and are divinely designed, possessing a prophetic character (prefiguration or element of foreshadowing).[124] Among many of this group of traditional dispensationalists, positive appeal is made to Patrick Fairbairn's classic study and textual warrant, either explicit or implicit, is required in the identification of types. Roy Zuck and others follow the Marshian principle that typological patterns are only those so designated by the NT, but some reject this extreme for a moderate approach similar to Fairbairn's.[125] What is not as clear

---

122. Saucy, "Progressive Dispensational View," 161–62, emphasis original. On this point, see also Vlach, *Has the Church Replaced Israel?*, 116–17.

123. For overviews of how typology functions in dispensationalism, see Merkle, *Discontinuity to Continuity*, 31–34, 57–60, 83–86; Glenny, "Typology," 632–35; Ninow, *Indicators of Typology*, 72–75; cf. LaRondelle, *Israel of God*, 48–52.

124. Pentecost, *Things to Come*, 50–53; Campbell, "Interpretation of Types," 248–55; Zuck, *Basic Bible Interpretation*, 169–82; Tan, "Symbols and Types," 71–84, esp. 80–84; Rigalke, "Abrahamic Covenant," 64. Cf. Feinberg, "Hermeneutics of Discontinuity," 120–21; and Walvoord, "Christological Typology (1948)," 286–96, esp. 286–87, 404–17, and Walvoord, "Christological Typology (1949)," 27–33.

125. Zuck, *Basic Bible Interpretation*, 175–76. See also Feinberg, "Systems of Discontinuity," 79; Marsh, "Dynamic Relationship," 259. Against Bishop Marsh's view and in line with Fairbairn are Tan, "Symbols and Types," 82; Campbell, "Interpretation of Types," 251–53; and Walvoord, "Christological Typology (1948)," 290–91. Walvoord

in these writings is the escalation in the typological pattern or the nature of the fulfillment between the type and the antitype. For Paul Feinberg and Zuck, typology involves a heightening or escalation as antitypes are on a higher plane compared to their corresponding types, but they differ in that Zuck describes this heightening in terms of fulfillment whereas Feinberg treats typology as a separate category from the fulfillment of prophecies or predictions.[126] Therefore, within one group of more traditional dispensationalists, a type is understood as a shadow, a form of prophecy, that reaches its reality and fulfillment in the greater antitype.[127] With this understanding of typology and given the commitment to dispensational presuppositions, Israel is not a type as Paul Tan seems representative in stating that certain things "should not be interpreted under [the] type-antitype relationship. The different peoples of God (Israel and the Christian church) are not identical concepts."[128]

On the other hand, another group of revised or more traditional dispensationalists take a different approach. Rather than viewing types as shadows pointing to an antitypical reality or fulfillment, these "[d]ispensationalists do not think types necessarily are shadows, and they demand that both type and antitype be given their due meanings in their own contexts while maintaining a typological relation to one another."[129] For this conception of typology, the type may have a prophetic element or be divinely designed to correspond to the antitype, nevertheless, typology is an application of historical persons, events, and institutions for illustrative or analogical purposes with no sense of fulfillment as the "NT antitypes

does not fit in the Marshian camp because he identifies Joseph as a type of Christ and lists Benjamin and Aaron's rod that budded as types. Zuck describes Joseph as an illustration of Christ, but not as a type. In fact, Walvoord and Chafer seem to go in the direction of the Coccesian school. Chafer and Walvoord would be outliers as Glenny, "Typology," 632, rightly notes that the commitment to literal interpretation in revised dispensationalism resulted in identifying far fewer OT types than those offered by classic dispensationalists. For a discussion of Chafer's, Ryrie's, and Blasing and Bock's approaches to typology, see Parle, *Dispensational Development*, 43–50.

126. Zuck, *Basic Bible Interpretation*, 173–74; Feinberg, "Hermeneutics of Discontinuity," 120–22 (for the feature of escalation in Feinberg's position, see p. 121). Pentecost, *Things to Come*, 50, also notes how the antitype transcends the type. A degree of escalation is also detected in the way Tan, "Symbols and Types," 83–84, describes messianic typologies in conjunction with OT prophecies.

127. Zuck, *Basic Bible Interpretation*, 173–74, 176, 178, is the clearest in positing the type as a shadow and a form of prophecy with the antitype as the heightening fulfillment of the type. Note also Tan, "Symbols and Types," 81; and Bigalke, "Abrahamic Covenant," 64.

128. Tan, "Symbols and Types," 81.

129. Feinberg, "Systems of Discontinuity," 78.

neither explicitly nor implicitly cancel the meaning of the OT types."[130] These particular dispensationalists can identify national Israel as a type of either Christ or the church because the escalation and fulfillment aspects (also dubbed as the "vanishing principle" where the antitype cancels the meaning of the type) of typology are absent.[131] Fulfillment may be present in a few other typological patterns (e.g., the sacrificial system). Given these hermeneutical commitments, Matthew's use of Hos 11:1 (Matt 2:15) can be taken in two different ways. Matthew's citation can be interpreted as merely an analogy or illustration between Jesus' life and the exodus events of national Israel, or, since the meaning of the original type is never substituted or cancelled by the antitype, a typological connection is present in Matt 2:15, but such a link does not nullify Israel's future role.[132] As this

130. Feinberg, "Systems of Discontinuity," 79. Feinberg follows David Baker in rejecting prefiguration since that may alter the meaning of the original OT context, although he does argue that types "look to the future, but not in a way that makes their meaning equivalent to the antitype" (78–79). Paul Feinberg, "Hermeneutics of Discontinuity," 121, seems to advocate a similar position as he mentions prefiguration as a feature of typology, but he rejects any prediction-fulfillment element and pairs typology with analogy. Walvoord, "Christological Typology (1948)," 286, should also be grouped with this perspective, although he is more free in finding OT types. Walvoord's study of christological typologies reduces to mere illustrations of spiritual truths with a few exceptions (e.g., OT sacrifices). Similarly, Brown, "Is Typology an Interpretative Method?," 82–85, 101–2, affirms God's purposeful design of the type-antitype correspondence, but rejects the prospective or prophetic element (with the exception of the OT sacrifices), dismisses antitypical fulfillment of the type, and describes typological relationships in terms of their explanatory and illustrative purposes. In this study, Brown wrongly pits typology against corporate solidarity when they should not be separated, and he provides unconvincing exegesis of the hermeneutically significant τύπος passages, failing also to develop how the nature and characteristics of typology interface with many other texts lacking the τύπος term (with exception to a few passages related to the land promise). Aside from Fairbairn, Goppelt, and Davidson, Brown does not engage other important works that feature helpful conclusions regarding typology (like the works by D. A. Carson, Paul Hoskins, Friedbert Ninow, and others; see chapter 2).

131. Feinberg, "Systems of Discontinuity," 72, does describe Israel as a type of the church. For how Jesus can be thought of as the "true Israel" (or antitype of Israel) but in a way that only secures national Israel's future restoration, consult Vlach, "What Does Christ as 'True Israel' Mean," 43–54; cf. Brown, "Is Typology an Interpretative Method?," 101–2. If the arrival of the antitype consists of the completion and fulfillment of the type, then Israel is not a type, for unconditional promises to Israel must be fulfilled and the NT still affirms Israel's future, so Feinberg, "Systems of Discontinuity," 79–83; Vlach, *Has the Church Replaced Israel?*, 104–7; and Vlach, "Have They Found a Better Way?," 12–17.

132. Feinberg, "Hermeneutics of Discontinuity," 122, interprets Matthew use of Hos 11:1 as an analogy. Vlach, *Has the Church Replaced Israel?*, 91–93; Vlach, "What Does Christ as 'True Israel' Mean," 48; indicates a typological correspondence is present between Jesus and Israel in Matt 2:15, but such does not deny Israel's unique eschatological place in God's plan. It is not difficult to postulate the promised land as an

example shows, the NT writers' use of certain OT passages does not necessarily cancel the original meaning as the application of the OT text differs from what the original author may have foreseen. This indicates that there is a double fulfillment; the NT authors can use OT texts with application to the church and do so while maintaining the integrity of the OT's meaning and unconditional promises for national Israel.[133]

Typological Perspectives within Progressive Dispensationalism

The appropriation of complementary hermeneutics and inaugurated eschatology by progressive dispensationalists means that typology is framed differently than by those proposed by more traditional dispensationalists. Nevertheless, the theological conclusions regarding national Israel end up in the same place. Whereas progressives are more willing to identify national Israel as a type of Jesus and the church, this typological fulfillment is only a partial one because the literal promises and prophecies directed to Israel must have an ultimate fulfillment in the future.[134]

Bock is the most visible in laying out a progressive dispensational understanding of typology.[135] Under the rubric of typological-prophetic, Bock offers two categories of typological fulfillment and then offers a separate category called *authoritative illustration* or *simple typology* which also figures into his rendering of typology. The first category is typological-*prophetic* fulfillment. Under this heading, Bock discusses texts where "there is a short-term historical referent, and yet the promise's initial fulfillment is such that an expectation remains that more of the pattern needs 'filling up' to be completely fulfilled."[136] Such expectations would have already been detected by the Jewish readers as passages such as Isa 65–66, the servant

---

analogy or as a type within this framework; see Walvoord, "Christological Typology (1948)," 296 (land of Canaan as analogy), and Brown, "Is Typology an Interpretative Method?," 64–76 (land as type but maintaining its significance for Israel in the future).

133. Feinberg, "Systems of Discontinuity," 77; cf. Feinberg, "Hermeneutics of Discontinuity," 118–19. Feinberg, "Systems of Discontinuity," 79, affirms that the NT antitype can cancel the meaning of the OT type but only where the NT tells us. Likewise, Vlach, *Has the Church Replaced Israel?*, 115–17. Bigalke, "Abrahamic Covenant," 66–67, finds the principle of double fulfillment faulty and prefers double reference.

134. Glenny, "Typology," 634–35. Note again the citation of Saucy referenced above (n122), expressed also in Saucy, *Case for Progressive Dispensationalism*, 31–32.

135. Blaising and Bock, *Progressive Dispensationalism*, 102–3; Bock, *Proclamation from Prophecy and Pattern*, 49–51, 291–92n124; Bock, "Scripture Citing Scripture," 255–76, esp. 271–74; Bock, "Single Meaning, Multiple Contexts," 118–21.

136. Bock, "Scripture Citing Scripture," 271; and "Single Meaning, Multiple Contexts," 119.

figure of the latter part of Isaiah, and short-term, partially realized promises (such as the "day of the Lord") anticipate an ultimate fulfillment or completion in the future. In these OT passages, an aspect "demands fulfillment beyond the short-term event and thus points to the presence of pattern. The prophetic character of the text resides in this 'needs to be fulfilled' feature in the pattern."[137] The second category under typological-prophetic is *typological*-prophetic. Typological patterns with this characterization still have a forward-looking element embedded in the pattern and are prophetic since God designed the correspondence; however, the pattern is not anticipated by the language of the immediate context but only becomes a decisive pattern when the fulfillment makes it apparent.[138] Matthew's use of Hos 11:1 (Matt 2:15) and the righteous-sufferer and regal psalms are listed as examples. Overall, with the broad typological-prophetic category, Bock elucidates typology as featuring identifiable patterns that have a prophetic orientation. Given that the typical event or person anticipates completion and fulfillment, moving to consummation, an escalation is present between the type and antitype.[139]

In addition, Bock also has a separate category for illustration or "simple typology" where there is no prophetic import. Past OT examples that do not have a forward-looking element are used for illustrative purposes in the NT, having an exhortative function for the present.[140] Fitting this description according to Bock are 1 Cor 10:1–13, where the Corinthians are to learn from the past examples of bad behavior, and the use of Ps 95 in Heb 3–4. In sum, the "problem is that typology ... involves a spectrum of usage, some of which is prophetic and some of which is not, so it is not a defining characteristic of the category as a whole, but comes to us in distinct ways."[141] Therefore, given this view, national Israel could fit in either the

---

137. Bock, "Scripture Citing Scripture," 272.

138. Ibid., 272–73. See also Bock, "Single Meaning, Multiple Contexts," 119–20; cf. 121.

139. See Blaising and Bock, *Progressive Dispensationalism*, 103, where Bock writes, "Escalation means that [Christ] fulfills [the typological pattern] to a greater degree than others before Him, pointing to His unique and often culminating position within the pattern." Bock, *Proclamation from Prophecy and Pattern*, 291–92n124, also states that although typology is often identified retrospectively, it is still prophetic (prospective) because the pattern is worked out by God in his plan. Holding to a similar view to Bock's, but without the explicit distinguishing categories under typological-prophetic, is Glenny, "Israelite Imagery of 1 Peter 2," 157–58.

140. Bock, "Scripture Citing Scripture," 273–74; Bock, "Single Meaning, Multiple Contexts," 120–21.

141. Bock, "Single Meaning, Multiple Contexts," 121. See Powers, "Prefigurement and the Hermeneutics of Prophetic Typology," 184–219, 296–306, who holds a similar

typological-prophetic general heading or the "simple typology" category because neither the analogous or illustrative nature of the latter nor the multiple fulfillments of the former would exhaust or abrogate the ultimate fulfillment of the promises to national Israel in the future. The original contextual meaning of Israel's promises and prophecies must be maintained even if the complementary development by later texts through the progress of revelation apply such promises to Christ and the church.[142]

Lastly, Blaising has also discussed typology in relation to the kingdom and the church.[143] For Blaising, typology is to be framed within a holistic eschatology that he describes as a new creation eschatology involving the redemption of all dimensions of created reality. Thus, a holistic anthropology and soteriology has multifaceted dimensions including personal, familial, ethnic, tribal, and national levels of human existence that will be redeemed and brought forward into the consummation.[144] Crucial for Blaising is his

---

view to Bock's. Although Powers does not sub-divide the typological-prophetic category as Bock does, Powers finds two major classifications of typology: analogical/theological and prophetic typology: "The key element in the analogical/theological approach to typology . . . is the absence of any textual indicators of prefiguration in the intended meaning of the OT human author." Ibid., 191, 297. Prefiguration in the sense of divine foreordination, but not prediction from the OT author's stance, is observed from a retrospective vantage point for analogical typology as later biblical authors find or forge links between events and persons of their time and those of earlier history. Examples of this form of typology, according to Powers, are 1 Cor 10:1–13 (like Bock) and 1 Pet 2:9–10 (see pp. 201–5, 298). For Powers, OT Israel fits into this analogical/theological category because the present application and illustrative use of Israel's blessings to the church does not nullify the future fulfillment of provisions directed to national Israel (206–7; 298). The other category, prophetic typology is like analogical/theological typology in having historical correspondence, divine intent, and escalation, but prophetic typology possesses a genuine predictive element that is part of the OT intended meaning. The escalation in prophetic typology narrows to one antitype that completely fulfills the promise associated with the initial event (299–300; cf. 208–19).

142. Bock recognizes that some NT texts cancel previous revelation or provide a substitution, but a complementary relationship between texts and themes is to be maintained, for "the additional inclusion of some in the promise does not mean that the original recipients are thereby excluded. *The expansion of promise need not mean the cancellation of earlier commitments God has made.*" Blaising and Bock, *Progressive Dispensationalism*, 103, emphasis original.

143. Blaising, "Typology and the Nature of the Church."

144. Blaising, "Typology and the Nature of the Church," 5–6. Cf. Blaising, "Critique," 120–24. In this poor critique of *Kingdom through Covenant*, Blaising charges Gentry and Wellum with asserting that typology is the means of establishing the divine plan (116–17) when Gentry and Wellum make no such argument. Instead, they observe that the escalated realities that come with what Christ has accomplished by inaugurating the kingdom and the dawning of the new creation are precisely what the storyline of Scripture provides as God's plan is progressively unfolded. Blaising also makes the extraordinary claim that Gentry and Wellum hold to a form of mysticism

appeal that the consummated order is multinational as the future, eternal kingdom features interrelating nations, tribes, and ethnicities. Therefore, while the historical Israelite blessings have limited application within the church, "the typology moves from OT Israel to the eschatological Israel" because the eschatological kingdom includes nations, including the nation of Israel.[145] Blaising's view of typology is not as defined as Bock's, but it is clear that Israel is not a type that culminates in Christ and the church.

Summary of the Dispensational Views on Typology

For covenant theology, as outlined in chapter 3, there was a fairly uniform understanding of the nature and function of typology in terms of historical correspondence, divine design, indirect prophecy, and escalation. For dispensationalism on the other hand, typology is frequently ill-defined, and its characteristics are malleable as the subject is treated in a way that the core distinction between Israel and the church is kept intact. If typology consists of the elements (correspondence, prefiguration, escalation, fulfillment) as described in chapter 2, then Israel and the promised land are not types. However, Israel or the land could be typological if typology (or a separate category of typology) is characterized by the mere repetition of patterns that serve analogous or illustrative purposes. The lack of consensus on the subject of typology, as well as the inconsistent or arbitrary use of typology, pose significant problems for dispensationalism.

---

that is a variant of metaphysical personalism (124–25), but such a claim is wide of the mark as these typological patterns are not mystically dissolved into the reality of Christ's person. Rather, Jesus is the focal point of the covenant promises and typological patterns because he is the agent of the new creation, which includes a physical new heavens and earth, and he is the one who initiates the fulfillment of the promises through his work.

145. Blaising, "Typology and the Nature of the Church," 9; cf. 10–14. With this proposal, it is very difficult to see how there is one people of God. The church is a singular entity comprised of people from every nation as one congregation, one new humanity in Christ, but Blaising's multi-national kingdom typology has many peoples of God who keep their national status. Blaising fails to see that the incorporation of gentiles into the church is the expansion of the people of God from what was an ethnic, political nation (Israel) to an international, transnational community that is one body. Blaising, "Critique," 116, agrees with Baker that typological patterns do not always involve escalation. Israel can be confirmed as a type by either reducing typology to analogy or by removing escalation as an intrinsic feature of typology.

SUMMARY

This discussion of dispensationalism demonstrates that the Israel/church distinction drives this system of theology. Unlike covenant theologians who operate with the theological covenants of works and grace, dispensationalists posit a variety of dispensations (conceived of differently) where the covenants, and particularly the Abrahamic covenant, take on prominent emphasis. For more traditional or revised dispensationalists, covenant promises and prophecies are to be fulfilled to national, ethnic Israel in the future even as the NT applies such promises to the church. Nevertheless, such NT teachings only reveal that the covenant blessings are extended to the church. Progressive dispensationalists utilize a complementary hermeneutic and rightly acknowledge the presence of an inaugurated eschatological framework and so they allow for more unity between Israel and the church in arguing that the initial or partial fulfillment of Israel's promises are directed to the church in this present age. However, the inclusion of the church in Israel's promises does not nullify the original context and the original recipients as a future realization awaits national Israel. The dispensational approaches to typology are variable. Sometimes typology is understood as featuring a predictive/prophetic import, escalation, and a notion of fulfillment between the type and antitype, but then Israel is rejected as a type. If typology is defined as primarily analogical, or if a separate category of typology exists that features illustrative uses of OT persons and events, then Israel can be a type of Christ and the church. These observations strongly suggest that the dispensational notions of typology are not adequately drawn from the text of Scripture but are formed based on their commitments regarding ethnic, national Israel.[146]

Such difficulties with the nature of typology are not surprising given the dispensational hermeneutical presuppositions and their understandings of the covenants. According to dispensationalists, a literal reading of the prophecies and covenant promises requires the realization of such promises to national Israel. Nevertheless, as argued in chapter 2, typology is not analogy and typological patterns are identified through textual warrant. In the next chapter I demonstrate that Israel is a typological pattern—a shadow that points to greater realities. As a corollary, the implication of chapter 5 is that dispensationalists are reading the promises to Israel in a literalistic manner and are not being sensitive to inner-canonical development of the covenant promises across the storyline of Scripture. In other

---

146. Though dispensationalists have written much more on typology since LaRondelle's analysis, his observations regarding the arbitrary use of typology within dispensationalism still stands. See LaRondelle, *Israel of God*, 48, 51.

words, the nation of Israel and her promises cannot be cordoned off from the larger biblical-theological structures that come before the inception of Israel and that continue and develop through Israel's history. National Israel cannot be treated as an island or as a separate entity with unique purposes since scriptural evidence shows that Israel is rooted back in creation structures and is inseparably part of the sonship motif that looks forward to a faithful, obedient, Davidic king who is the last Adam and the Abrahamic heir. This supreme representative of Israel ushers in the new covenant era and establishes a greater covenant community—a faithful covenant people who are the true recipients of the promises, experiencing better salvific realities—a renewed, eschatological Israel that national Israel anticipated and foreshadowed.

Chapter 5

THE ISRAEL-CHRIST-CHURCH RELATIONSHIP

Israel as a Type of Christ

DURING THE LATE TWENTIETH century, both covenant and dispensational theologies have incorporated needed modifications given the forcefulness of the NT's presentation of inaugurated eschatology.[1] Despite these welcome changes, the battle lines remain with respect to the issue of the relationship between Israel and the church. As demonstrated in chapter 3, the unity of the covenant of grace and God's plan of redemption leads covenant theologians to a position of strong continuity; the nature of the church is essentially one with Israel of the OT with the relationship being one of substitution or fulfillment or even replacement. Thus, covenant theologians view the church as the "new Israel." Even if there is a mass conversion of Jews in the future (Rom 11), all the prerogatives, promises, and prophecies to OT Israel are translated to the church. On the other hand, as was surveyed in chapter 4, dispensationalists maintain a sharp distinction between Israel and the church with God's promises and plans for national Israel still awaiting literal fulfillment during the millennium. The church is not the "new Israel" even as the church participates in the new covenant in one way or another and receives OT designations for Israel.

---

1. See Moore, *Kingdom of Christ*, 30–65, for how inaugurated eschatology with the "already/not-yet" realities of the kingdom of God popularized by George Eldon Ladd has impacted dispensational and covenant theologies.

For dispensationalists, covenant theologians are deemed guilty of "supersessionism," and so covenant theology is often labeled with the popular, pejorative moniker of "replacement theology."[2] In contrast, non-dispensational theologians have sought to highlight the dangers of dispensationalism, given what they view as a faulty understanding of the Israel-church relationship, particularly warning of "Christian Zionism" or "separation theology" and its impact on the political state of affairs associated with the modern State of Israel.[3] The issues of replacement theology and Zionism, primarily revolving around the relationship of the biblical covenants, the nature of the land promises, and the question of the restoration of Israel in Palestine as an ethnic entity, has also received much attention in theological and political writings surrounding the Israeli-Palestinian conflicts.[4] Given the back and forth of polemical writings between covenant and dispensational theologians there is significant doubt that evangelicalism will ever come to a consensus on this issue.[5]

In chapter 1, the crux of the matter that needs resolution is the Israel-Christ-church relationship as a whole and the way forward is to be found in a mediating position called *progressive covenantalism*. Most of the writings by covenant and dispensational theologians have, for the most part, sought to address directly the relationship between Israel and the church, but the

---

2. See Vlach, *Has the Church Replaced Israel?* And Vlach, "Various Forms of Replacement Theology," 57–69. For Vlach, anyone who does not believe in both a future salvation and restoration for Israel in the future is a supersessionist, thus anyone who does adhere to some form of dispensationalism would be considered a supersessionist. For other dispensational writings on the topic of replacement theology, see Blaising, "Future of Israel," 435–50; House, "Church's Appropriation of Israel's Blessings," 77–110. Much of these discussions are based on the important work of Soulen, *God of Israel and Christian Theology*; and Fackre, *Ecumenical Faith in Evangelical Perspective*, 147–67, as they describe various forms of replacement theology. See also Kaiser, "Assessment of 'Replacement Theology,'" 9–20.

3. Church, "Dispensational Christian Zionism," 375–98; Sizer, *Christian Zionism*, 106–205; Chapman, *Whose Promised Land?*, 241–66; Burge, *Jesus and the Land*, 110–31; Wright, "Jerusalem in the New Testament," 53–77, esp. 73–75. For a dispensationalist response, see Feinberg, "Dispensationalism and Support for the State of Israel," 104–31.

4. For a collection of Messianic Jewish and Palestinian Christian discussions on these topics, see Munayer and Loden, *Land Cries Out*; Loden et al., *Bible and the Land*. For further writings from a Christian Palestinian perspective see Ateek, "Earth Is the Lord's," 75–80; and from a Jewish perspective, Orlinsky, "Biblical Concept of the Land of Israel," 27–64.

5. See for example, Donaldson, *Last Days of Dispensationalism*; Mathison, *Dispensationalism*; Gerstner, *Wrongly Dividing the Word of Truth*; and for dispensational responses, see Karleen, "Understanding Covenant Theologians," 125–38; Turner, "'Dubious Evangelicalism?' A Response to Gerstner," 263–77.

methodological approach of progressive covenantalism is first to analyze the relationship between Israel and Israel's Messiah—Jesus Christ—and then address the relationship between Christ and the church before making theological conclusions regarding the Israel-church relationship. Stephen Wellum has made the argument that for dispensationalists, national (OT) Israel is not typological of Christ or does not function in the same way other typological patterns do, as such would diminish the strong distinction between Israel and the church and undercut the notion of Israel receiving restoration and nationalistic promises in the future millennium. On the other hand, covenant theology does view "Christ as the 'true Israel,' but it moves *too quickly* from Israel to the church without first thinking how Israel as type leads us to Christ as the antitype, which then has important ecclesiological implications."[6] In other words, covenant and dispensational theology do not consistently appropriate the typological relationship between Israel and Christ, and derivatively through Christ, the Israel-church typology.

In this chapter, I seek to explore the latter issue of typology as characterized and developed in chapter 2 with respect to the Israel-Christ relationship foremost, in order to confirm that progressive covenantalism offers a better way of handling the biblical data. First, if the restoration promises to Israel along with their prophesied national and mediatorial roles find their typological fulfillment in Jesus, and by extension, the church, then the system of dispensationalism should be abandoned. Progressive covenantalism argues this precisely: the NT presents Jesus as the fulfillment of Israel and all the OT covenant mediators, for he ushers in the promises to Israel (restoration and return from exile, the Land, etc.), embodies their identity, and completes Israel's role, calling, and vocation. All the institutions (the sacrificial system, tabernacle, temple, Sabbath, feasts, the Law), identity markers

---

6. Gentry and Wellum, *Kingdom through Covenant*, 156–57, emphasis original; and for Wellum's remarks concerning the dispensational rejection of Israel and the land as legitimate types, see pp. 152–55. The main thrust of Wellum's argument is that covenant and dispensational theologians misunderstand the Abrahamic covenant by conceiving of it as unconditional at key areas pertaining to their systems (the land for dispensationalists and the genealogical principle—"to you and your offspring"—for covenant theologians) and fail to do justice to how the covenants interrelate, missing how both of these issues, the land and the genealogical principle, function typologically across the covenants as they reach their terminus in Christ (141–47). The land and the genealogical principle do not work out canonically the way dispensationalists and covenant theologians claim. In this way covenantalism and dispensationalism employ the same hermeneutic, just in different areas. A very similar position to Gentry's and Wellum's with less emphasis on typology is Brand and Pratt, "Progressive Covenantal View," 231–80.

(e.g., circumcision),[7] offices (prophet, priest, king), and key events (e.g., the exodus) of Israel find their culmination in the life, death, resurrection, and ascension of Christ.[8] As Patrick Fairbairn correctly surmised over a century ago, the Israelite nation, "with their land and their religious institutions, were, in what distinctively belonged to them under the old covenant, of a typical nature, the whole together, in that particular aspect, has passed away—it has become merged in Christ and the Gospel dispensation."[9] Jesus is the "true Israel" in that he typologically fulfills the promises directed to the nation of Israel. As the last Adam, Jesus is the one who brings to completion the covenants, inaugurates the kingdom, and establishes the prophesied new covenant with his blood.

Second, once the typological relationship between Israel and Christ is established, the theological formulation can proceed by exploring Christ's relation to his people before devising theological conclusions regarding Israel and the church. If Jesus is the antitypical fulfillment of Israel and all the OT covenant mediators, what implications are there for the community—the church—in faith union with this Messiah? Given the eschatological realities associated with the inauguration of kingdom breaking into this present evil age through the salvific work of Christ, including the ratification of the new

---

7. Wright, *New Testament and the People of God*, 237, cf. 365–69, identifies boundary markers or badges as circumcision, Sabbath, and kosher laws that particularly distinguished Jews from gentiles in the first century. For the early Christian church, the identifying symbol was the cross (367–68). For identity markers, see also Burge, *Jesus and the Land*, 19; Beale, *New Testament Biblical Theology*, 424. Beale rightly argues that the only identity marker for the NT people of God is Jesus (308, 873–78).

8. Goldsworthy, *Gospel-Centered Hermeneutics*, 253–56, has correctly summarized how the OT stages, epochs, and structures move to their fulfillment in Christ as all things are summed up in him (Eph 1:10). Bruce, *This Is That*, 21, has also rightly captured the significance of Jesus Christ as the apex of redemptive history: "In Jesus the promise is confirmed, the covenant is renewed, the prophecies fulfilled, the law is vindicated, salvation is brought near, sacred history has reached its climax, the perfect sacrifice has been offered and accepted, the great priest over the household of God has taken his seat at God's right hand, the Prophet like Moses has been raised up, the Son of David reigns, the kingdom of God has been inaugurated, the Son of Man has received dominion from the Ancient of Days, the Servant of the Lord, having been smitten to death for his people's transgression and borne the sin of many, has accomplished the divine purpose, has seen light after the travail of his soul and is now exalted and extolled and made very high."

9. Fairbairn, *Interpretation of Prophecy*, 255. Schreiner, *New Testament Theology*, 173, similarly states, "Jesus is the true Israel who fulfills what God always intended when he chose Israel to be his people. He is the obedient Servant of the Lord who always does the will of the Father. He brings victory and freedom to his people not by waging war but by suffering in their place. . . . Jesus is also the true and better David who fulfills the promises that a new David would come who would free Israel from exile and bring salvation to the ends of the earth."

covenant, a significant development in the people of God has occurred. The coming of Christ introduces a profound epochal shift entailing structural changes to the covenant community. The momentous redemptive-historical progression in light of Christ and Pentecost should, in turn, impinge on how the nature of the church's relationship to Israel is understood. The church, made up of Jew and gentile believers in covenantal union with Christ, does not have the same essential nature as OT Israel in contrast to how paedobaptist covenant theologians construe the nature of the church and the continuity of "signs and seals" (the Passover and circumcision having direct continuity to the Lord's Supper and baptism, respectively). The church is a new redemptive-historical reality—the heavenly, eschatological, Spirit-empowered, new covenant community, which is the new creation (2 Cor 5:17; Gal 6:15) and new humanity in Christ (Eph 2:15).[10] Therefore, the church is linked to Israel only indirectly through its bond with Jesus. William Kynes explains,

> The relationship between the church and Israel ... is neither one of direct succession nor radical disjunction, but one of mediated continuity. One may describe the church as the 'true Israel,' but its continuity with the rejected Israel is found in the representative figure of Jesus, who bridges salvation-history even while fulfilling it.[11]

---

10. As Christ followers, Jewish and gentile believers alike are those upon "whom the end of the ages has come" (1 Cor 10:11). The eschatological and heavenly nature of the church is also indicated by passages such as Eph 2:5–6; Col 1:12–14, 3:3; and Heb 12:22–24, 13:14. On the other points of the definition of the church offered above, see Carson, "Evangelicals, Ecumenism, and the Church," 358–67; Carson, *Showing the Spirit*, 150–55; O'Brien, "Church as a Heavenly and Eschatological Entity," 88–119; Wellum, "Beyond Mere Ecclesiology, 183–212; Schreiner, *New Testament Theology*, 675–754; Fung, "Some Pauline Pictures of the Church," 89–107, esp. 105–7. Gladd, *From Adam and Israel to the Church*, 133, highlights that the "church is the restored people of God, the eschatological true Israel. Despite Adam and the nation of Israel being created in God's image, they did not enjoy the *eschatological* image of God. Through the success of Christ's earthly ministry, his work on the cross, and his resurrection as the last Adam, God begins the process of creating a new humanity" (emphasis original). Unfortunately, Gladd's correct observations are difficult to square with his covenant theology. His comments indicate that the church and Israel are not essentially the same, and given Christ's effective work and the church as the eschatologically restored people of God, how is the church not a regenerate community, a new humanity as the restored image of God?

11. Kynes, *Christology of Solidarity*, 202. Stephen Motyer, "Israel, New," 618–19, agrees as he also understands that the Israel-church relationship must be understood christologically. He suggests that the label "renewed Israel" would be a more fitting designation for the church than "new Israel." Also articulating this Israel-Christ-church relationship is Dodd, *According to the Scriptures*, 133, when he writes, "It is in [Christ]

Likewise, Alistair Donaldson correctly concludes that the NT

> displays, not a radical discontinuity from Israel, but rather a progression in the development of God's redemptive purpose—a development that has moved forward from the shadows and types of the Old Testament to the reality of Christ's better ministry. Inherent in this progressive development there is continuity and discontinuity. There is continuity in that the redemptive story progresses according to God's purpose, but discontinuity in that the nature of the people of God is of a greater nature than before, and the shadowy forms of Israel and her way of life have given way to the intended greater realities.[12]

Covenant theologians will argue for the Israel-church typological relationship, but the greater nature of the new covenant community is distorted resulting in the nullification of the intrinsic escalation of this typological relationship.[13] If the church continues to be a mixed community comprised of covenant breakers and keepers like Israel of old, then there is very little typological development between Israel and the church.

This chapter seeks to demonstrate that Jesus typologically fulfills OT Israel with some explorations of how the church, through Christ, inherits the promises of Israel and may be recognized as the renewed Israel. Lastly, the theological conclusions of this endeavor, particularly for dispensationalism, are offered. In the next chapter the Christ-church relationship will be discussed before the typological connections between Israel and the church are examined leading to theological summations for the Israel-Christ-church relationship as a whole. Before exploring these crucial topics, it is important to examine the terminology of "true Israel."

---

that what is essential in the prophecies of the true Israel (the Servant of the Lord, the Son of Man) found fulfillment. In Him the whole Israel of God was incorporate. Its destiny was wrought out in His experience. In Him the people of God was judged, died, and rose to newness of life. Thus whatever may be predicated of the Church is predicated of it only as its members are incorporate in Christ as their 'inclusive representative.'"

12. Donaldson, *Last Days of Dispensationalism*, 61.

13. Bruno, "Review of *Kingdom through Covenant*," 504–5, rightly recognizes, "While dispensationalism has an insufficient view of typology, paedobaptist covenant theology has an under-realized view of typological fulfillment, for in the new covenant there is no gap between the sign (baptism) and the thing signified (circumcision of heart)."

THE TERMINOLOGY OF "TRUE ISRAEL" AND THE IDENTITY OF ISRAEL

Germane to the discussion of the Israel-Christ typological relationship is the usage of the terminology of Jesus as the "true Israel." The case that will be made is that Jesus is the "true Israel" in the sense that eschatological fulfillment has come in Christ as he embodies the identity, vocation, and prophesied roles of corporate Israel. Jesus is the last Adam, the true servant, the true Son, the ultimate prophet, the final priest, and the reigning, exalted king (David's greater son). He is the faithful Israelite, perfectly obeying God in contrast to the disobedience that characterizes much of Israel throughout OT history. Identifying Jesus as the "true Israel" is a shorthand way, while recognizing that the term *Israel* is not applied to Jesus in the NT, of concisely describing who Jesus is as the antitypical Israel in realizing and completing the destiny, roles, function, and promises of national Israel in the plan of God.

Such terminology is often attacked in dispensational circles. Michael Vlach argues that the language of "true Israel" is a "combination of terms [that] is not found in the Bible. Jesus does not call himself 'true Israel' and neither do the other NT writers."[14] Many others bank on word studies on the use of *Israel* in the NT, asserting that the term always refers to the national, ethnic, covenant people of the OT and thus drawing the theological conclusion that OT Israel is not typological since Israel never loses its status as a national entity in the future of God's eschatological plan.[15] More recently, Stephen Voorwinde challenges the venerable Bauer-Danker lexicon (BDAG) for lexically associating *Israel* (Ἰσραήλ) with the patriarch Jacob and for having a separate entry for entitling the term to Christians.[16] For Voorwinde, *Israel* refers only to the people or nation of Israel ethnically since the term never possesses any metaphorical reference: "The New Testament never calls the church 'Israel.' It is never referred to as 'the new Israel' or 'the true Israel,' nor even as 'spiritual Israel.' Nor is a Gentile Christian

---

14. Vlach, "What Does Christ as 'True Israel' Mean," 47. Vlach further comments that calling Jesus the "true Israel" gives the impression that the nation of Israel is not truly Israel anymore. However, the issue is how terms are defined and how the redemptive historical trajectory of the Bible is understood. Jesus can be referred to the "true David" because he fulfills the Davidic covenant as the Messiah even though the NT never uses this label for him.

15. For example, see Saucy, *Case for Progressive Dispensationalism*, 194–207; Saucy, "Israel and the Church," 244–49; Blaising, "Premillennial Response," 146–48; Ryrie, *Dispensationalism*, 148–50; Kaiser, "Assessment of 'Replacement Theology,'" 11. See also Richardson, *Israel in the Apostolic Church*, 7, 71, 83n2.

16. Voorwinde, "How Jewish Is *Israel*?," 61–90. See also BDAG, s.v. "Ἰσραήλ."

ever called an 'Israelite.'"[17] Such assertions by Voorwinde could equally be applied to Jesus.

The problem, however, with Voorwinde's analysis against BDAG in concluding that there are no metaphorical uses for the term *Israel* is that he commits word fallacies in his lexical study.[18] He makes false assumptions about technical meaning driven from his own theology when good cases can be made for the term *Israel* extending beyond a nationalistic, ethnic sense in Gal 6:16, Rev 7:4, and 21:12.[19] More importantly, even if Voorwinde and others are correct about the ethnic limitations to the term *Israel* in the NT, the identity of Israel is not exclusively bound to the term *Israel*. Many other titles, designations, and imagery characterize and describe Israel and her vocation.[20] Quite simply, Israel may be referred to as God's treasured possession (Deut 7:6), called to serve and worship him alone (Exod 7:16; Deut 4:39; see the book of Psalms), and to be a kingdom of priests and a holy nation (Exod 19:6). Having received its name from Jacob (Gen 32:28; and often called *Jacob* later in the OT, see especially in Isaiah, Jeremiah, and Micah), Israel is known as the seed or offspring of Abraham (Gen 12, 15, 17; Ps 105:6; Isa 41:8, 51:2; Jer 33:26; and such was formative in Israel's future hope, e.g., Mic 7:18–20), and becomes God's elect, covenant nation through his sovereign choice (Deut 4:37; 7:7; 10:15; Jer 33:24) and covenantal faithfulness to Abraham (Exod 19:4; Deut 7:8). The defining and catalyzing event for Israel as a nation is their miraculous redemption from slavery in Egypt. The exodus serves as a crucial archetype for Israel's future characterized as a *new exodus*.[21] Furthermore, the exodus

17. Voorwinde, "How Jewish Is *Israel*?," 80, cf. 85.

18. See Carson, *Exegetical Fallacies*, 45. One could make the case for a prejudicial use of evidence, which Carson also describes as a word-study fallacy (54), in Voorwinde's proposal. Furthermore, Voorwinde criticizes BDAG based on his study of *Israel* in the NT but fails to recognize that BDAG also takes into account the use of Greek terms in early Christian literature.

19. See Harvey, *True Israel*, 225–56; cf. Schreiner, *New Testament Theology*, 751, 858. On the difficulty of answering who a Jew is from political and religious perspectives, see Holwerda, *Jesus and Israel*, 27–30; and Katanacho, *Land of Christ*, 16–26.

20. For helpful discussions, note Duguid, "Israel," 391–97; Scobie, *Ways of Our God*, 469–80; LaRondelle, *Israel of God*, 81–98. See also chapter 3, footnote 55 above. Gladd, *From Adam and Israel to the Church*, 52–54, discusses Israel in connection to Jacob and in spiritual terms as the covenant community.

21. Examples abound: Isa 11:10–16, 40:3–11, 43:2, 49:8–12, 51:1—52:15, 64:1–3; Jer 16:14–15; 23:5–8; Ezek 11:15–20; Mic 4:6–7, 7:15–20; Hos 2:14–15; Zech 10:6–12. The paradigmatic exodus of Israel from Egypt with the themes of redemption, slavery, captivity, liberation, Passover, new creation, etc., typologically point to a greater new exodus, an eschatological event whereby Israel's sin and rebellion are dealt with, Zion is restored, and salvation is extended to the ends of the earth. For an overview, see Watts,

is also the context where Israel is summoned as the son of God (Exod 4:22; Deut 14:1; Jer 31:20; cf. Israel as the children of God in Isa 1:2, 4; Hos 1:10; 11:1). As the firstborn son, Israel is to serve the Lord (e.g., Exod 4:23) and is denoted with the title *servant* or referred to as "my servant" in the second half of the book of Isaiah and elsewhere (cf. Jer 30:10; 46:27–28).[22] Other covenantal imagery describes who Israel is in relationship to Yahweh: Israel is the wife (Isa 54:5; and as an adulterous wife in Ezek 16; Hos 1–3) or bride (Jer 2:2; cf. Jer 31:32) of the Lord. Agrarian imagery is applied to Israel too, for God is the shepherd to his sheep (Isa 40:11; Ps 100:3) or flock (Ezek 34; Ps 77:20) and Israel is described as a *vine* planted but judged by the Lord for its fruitlessness (Ps 80:8; Isa 5:1–7; 27:2–6; Jer 2:21, 12:10–11; Ezek 15:1–8; 19:10–14; Hos 10:1–2; 14:7).

Moreover, from a biblical-theological tracing of Scripture's storyline, Israel is thematically and intertextually linked not just to the patriarchs but to Adam, corporately recapitulating his status and roles.[23] As another "Adam," or new Adam, Israel is called God's son as Adam was (Luke 3:38). Themes of blessing, fruitfulness, and multiplication first directed to Adam are repeated to the patriarchs and advanced through Israel (see Gen 17:2; 28:3; 35:11; 47:27; 48:3–4; Exod 1:7; Lev 26:9; Deut 7:13; 30:9; Ps 107:38; Isa 51:2).[24] Just as Adam enjoyed the presence of God in the arboreal temple of Eden, so Israel had the tabernacle and later the temple as the place where God's presence was supremely manifested.[25] With the Adam-Israel

---

"Exodus," 478–87.

22. Wright, *Knowing Jesus*, 130, observes that Israel as God's "firstborn" implies the expectation of other nations becoming sons. On the role of servanthood, see Dempster, "Servant of the Lord," 128–78; and Goldingay, "Servant of Yahweh," 700–7.

23. For an excellent sketch of the biblical narrative of creation to new creation, see Beetham, "From Creation to New Creation," 237–54.

24. Gentry and Wellum, *Kingdom through Covenant*, 261–64; Beale, *Temple and the Church's Mission*, 94–96; Smith, "Structure and Purpose in Genesis 1–11," 307–19; Beetham, "From Creation to New Creation," 245–46; Hamilton, *Typology*, 51–54; Wright, *Climax of the Covenant*, 21–23. Wright, *New Testament and the People of God*, 263, observes that at crucial turning points in the storyline—"Abraham's call, his circumcision, the offering of Isaac, the transition from Abraham to Isaac and from Isaac to Jacob, and in the sojourn in Egypt—the narrative quietly insists that Abraham and his progeny inherit the role of Adam and Eve. There are, interestingly, two differences which emerge in the shape of this role. The command ('be fruitful . . . ') has turned into promise ('I will make you fruitful . . . '), and possession of the land of Canaan, together with supremacy over enemies, has taken the place of Adam's dominion over nature." See also Waltke, *Old Testament Theology*, 297.

25. Fesko, *Last Things First*, 125–26, helpfully summarizes, "God placed Adam in the garden, which was a source of sustenance and the location of the temple, and so too God placed Israel, his son, in a land flowing with milk and honey (Exod. 13:5). . . . G. K. Beale notes that 'Israel's land is explicitly compared to the Garden of Eden (see Gen.

identification and connections of temple themes, the land of promise should be connected to the Garden of Eden, and Adam's expulsion from the garden with Israel's exile out of the land of promise.[26] Additionally, the significant offices of prophet, priest, and king exemplified within Israel's leadership structure go back to Adam, the prototypical prophet, priest, and king. Israel corporately was to be kingly in subduing the promised land and ruling over her enemies, priestly in being ceremonially clean and devoted to the Lord, and corporately prophets by receiving God's word and obeying the law-covenant. These three offices coalesce in another son of God, another Adam, and significant representative of Israel—David.[27] Lastly, Israel as a nation cannot be understood theologically apart from its being the means by which the promised seed (Gen 3:15) would emerge in reversing the effects of the fall and triumphing over the serpent, namely through a royal deliverer.[28] These sonship themes and the corporate solidarity between Israel with individual covenantal representatives such as Adam, Jacob, and David cannot be sidelined.

Therefore, theologians must address more than the usage of the term *Israel* and must attend to the redemptive historical development of Israel's

---

13:10; Isa. 51:3; Ezek. 36:35; 47:12; Joel 2:3) and is portrayed as very fruitful in order to heighten the correspondence to Eden (cf. Deut. 8:7–10; 11:8–17; Ezek. 47:1–12) . . . When the ultimate goals of the covenant made with Israel are considered, the same protological elements reappear. . . . Israel was to take the redemptive knowledge of God to the ends of the earth in the same way that Adam was to spread the image and worship of God throughout the earth (Isa. 49:6)." Wood, "Regathering," 190, also observes the "Edenic" conditions in the blessings section of Lev 26, with v. 12 promising that God will walk among the Israelites in a similar way as he walked with Adam and Eve in the Garden (Gen 3:8). Gladd, *From Adam and Israel to the Church*, 39–40, demonstrates that the creation of Israel at Mt. Sinai, which is like Eden and the tabernacle in being temple-like with gradations of holiness, is important for tying Israel back to Adam and for understanding Israel as the corporate image of God. See also Beale, *Temple and the Church's Mission*, 66–80; Beale, *New Testament Biblical Theology*, 617–22; Wenham, "Sanctuary Symbolism in the Garden," 399–404; Alexander, *From Eden to the New Jerusalem*, 13–60. Against the consensus, Block, "Eden: A Temple?," 3–29, argues that the author of Gen 1–3 does not present Eden as a temple. Nevertheless, he does admit that tabernacle and temple were "constructed as miniature Edens" (6).

26. See Hamilton, *Typology*, 53–54 and Beetham, "From Creation to New Creation," 246–47. Gladd, *From Adam and Israel to the Church*, 43 observes that the promised land is a gigantic temple where God dwells with his people as Exod 15:15–17 shows.

27. Priestly functions are attributed to David when he brings the ark to Jerusalem (2 Sam 6:14, 17–18; cf. 8:18) and he exercised the gift of prophecy as well (for example, 2 Sam 23:1–7; Ps 22; Acts 2:30). See Bruce, *This Is That*, 72.

28. For helpful works discussing the seed theme and for the individual and corporate aspects of the term *seed*, see Alexander, "Royal Expectations," 191–212; Alexander, "Messianic Ideology in Genesis," 19–39; Alexander, "Seed," 769–73; Hamilton, "Seed of the Woman," 253–73.

identity, roles, and vocation when seeking to derive biblical-theological conclusions regarding Israel's relation to Jesus and subsequently, the church. Stated differently, the titles, metaphors, corporate solidarity, and imagery of Israel, as well as Israel's service to the Lord and identity through covenant structures (the Law, tabernacle/temple, priestly-sacrificial system, feasts, Sabbath, circumcision, etc.) have to be taken into account through the progress of revelation (developed through the biblical covenants: creation, Noahic, Abrahamic, Mosaic, Davidic, and new covenant) to the person and work of Christ if proper theological conclusions are to be drawn with respect to his relationship to Israel. The case to be demonstrated is that Jesus really is the "true Israel" in that he not only represents Israel, but fulfills Israel's identity, calling, and promises in inaugurating the new age, ratifying the new covenant, and bringing forth the dawning of the eschatologically restored Israel—the church.

CHRIST AS THE TRUE ISRAEL: ISRAEL IN TYPOLOGICAL PERSPECTIVE

In examining how Jesus Christ recapitulates Israel's role and purpose, I will explore themes associated with Israel that were embedded with eschatological and restoration elements. Most notably, the typological pattern of sonship emerges. The NT unequivocally presents Jesus as the divine Son, but he is the culmination and goal of what God's sons through redemptive history anticipated. Jesus is presented as the antitypical Adam (Rom 5:12–21; cf. 1 Cor 15:21–22, 45–49), the covenantal head of the new humanity, restoring them to the dignity and role for which they were created by undoing the curse (Heb 2:5–18; cf. Ps 8). Furthermore, Christ is the true seed of Abraham (Gal 3:16) and the promised, ideal David (Acts 2:24–36; 13:32–37; Rom 1:3–4; Heb 1:1–14; 5:5). The correspondence is not just in terms of identity, for he fulfills the eschatological goals and promises associated with each of these covenantal figures. For example, already in Matthew's genealogy (Matt 1:1–17) and the opening chapters of Luke's Gospel (e.g., Luke 1:32–33, 54–55, 67–79; 2:29–32, 38), the reader receives significant indications that the climax of Israel's story, the end of exile with the emergence of the kingdom, the promises to Abraham and David, are being fulfilled through Jesus (cf. Rom 15:8–13).[29] The nation of Israel belongs to

---

29. For the theme of fulfillment in the structure of Matthew's genealogy, see France, *Gospel of Matthew*, 28–33; Davies and Allison, *Matthew 1–7*, 149–90; Kennedy, *Recapitulation of Israel*, 72–100; Menninger, *Israel and the Church*, 74–77. Matthew's genealogy concerns eschatology, for Jesus is the son of David and the son of Abraham

the stream of sonship, which culminates in Christ. After addressing this critical typological pattern, other roles and titles of Israel, such as "servant" and "Yeshurun," and lastly the imagery of the vine also has significance for developing a full orbed understanding of the typological relationship between Israel and Christ.

Israel-Christ Typological Pattern Evidenced through Sonship

The significant theme of sonship is the clearest textual indication of the Israel-Christ typological pattern. Focusing on this broad theme of sonship concentrates on three areas: the direct sonship link between Israel and Christ, Jesus as the antitypical offspring of Abraham, and Jesus as the greater Jacob and Son of Man. The *Son of Man* title is informative for understanding the broader Israel-Christ typological relationship even though the Son of Man figure is not explicitly a typological pattern, but is situated more generally in the realm of prophecy.

Israel-Jesus Typology through the Sonship Theme

Perhaps the most recognizable typological correspondence between Israel and Christ is found in Matt 2:15. In explaining Jesus' departure and return from Egypt (via his family) in avoiding Herod's wicked plot to destroy him, Matthew cites Hos 11:1 ("out of Egypt I called my son") as being fulfilled.[30]

---

and the phrase "book of Genesis" (Matt 1:1; Gen 2:4; 5:1 LXX) clearly concerns the hope of new creation. Cf. Wright, *New Testament and the People of God*, 385. The four women included in the genealogy are gentiles, suggesting that God's promise of universal blessing to Abraham, which includes the nations, is fulfilled in Jesus (cf. Matt 28:18–20). The literary structure of fourteen generations, likely explained by *gematria*, also highlights that Jesus is the rightful heir of the Davidic promises (the numerical value of David's name sums to fourteen). Matthew is indicating that Jesus is the *telos* of salvation history as Israel's promises are fulfilled in him. For an overview of Luke 1, see Hays, "Liberation of Israel," 103–6. Hays concludes that the "two major effusions of praise in Luke 1 (Mary's and Zechariah's) link God's new saving work to the promises made to *Abraham* and *David* in Israel's scripture. By the end of the first chapter of the Gospel, Luke has given the reader abundant clues that his story of Jesus is to be read as the narrative continuation of Israel's story and as the liberating climax toward which that story had moved" (106, emphasis original). For further on the eschatology and climax of Israel's redemption in the Lucan infancy narrative, see Pao and Schnabel, "Luke," 254–57; Strauss, *Davidic Messiah*, 86; Fuller, *Restoration of Israel*, 204–7; and Wilson, "Luke and the New Covenant," 156–77, esp. 168–71. Contra Marsh, "Dynamic Relationship," 268–69.

30. Matt 2:15 is one of eleven "formula-quotations" that highlights the theme of fulfillment in Matthew (cf. Matt 1:22; 2:5, 17, 23; 4:14; 8:17; 12:17; 13:35; 21:4; 27:9).

The citation seems obscure since Hos 11:1 merely recollects Israel's original exodus (cf. Exod 4:22) and is not in itself a prediction that the messiah would come out of Egypt; however, when the broader context of Hos 11 is considered, Hosea himself not only recalls the history of Israel's exodus, idolatry, and God's judgment, but he also anticipates a future restoration, a new exodus, from "Egypt" (Hos 11:10–11; cf. 11:5).[31] Nicholas Piotrowski concludes that the

> retrospective look at the exodus in Hos 11:1 serves as a foil; it is preparatory for the future predictions in Hos 11:5 and 11:11. ... Thus, though Hosea looks back to the exodus in 11:1, *this retrospect has a future orientation insofar as that past event is the warrant for future hope.* Hence the logic of Hosea is this:

For helpful discussion of the role of typology in many of these "formula-quotations," see France, "Formula Quotations of Matthew 2," 233–51. Hamilton, "'Virgin Will Conceive': Typological Fulfillment," 228–47, also considers the importance of typological fulfillment in Matthew's prologue (232–34), including Hos 11:1 in Matt 2:15 (243), but he unnecessarily pits typological fulfillment against the elements of indirect prophecy. Clearly, Hos 11:1 is not a direct prediction of the Messiah coming out of Egypt, but the prospective aspects of the Israel-Christ new exodus connection is present in the context of Hos 11 and the book as a whole. Kirk, "Conceptualising Fulfillment in Matthew," 77–98, opts for a narrative perspective of the formula quotations where Matthew understood Jesus as "embodying the stories and scriptures of Israel, thereby showing himself to be the true Israel" (90, cf. 93–94), but he fails to see how the narrative embodiment he correctly pinpoints is more intimately related to, indeed, is worked out through typological patterns and prophecies embedded in the OT that point forward to the Messiah.

31. For a convincing analysis of the use of Hos 11:1 in Matt 2:15 as typological, see Beale, *New Testament Biblical Theology*, 406–12; Beale, "Use of Hosea 11:1," 697–715; Carson, *Matthew 1–12*, 91–93; Davies and Allison, *Matthew 1–7*, 262–64; Schreiner, *New Testament Theology*, 73–75; Wood, "Regathering," 476–80; Holwerda, *Jesus and Israel*, 37–40; Gladd, *From Adam and Israel to the Church*, 78–80; cf. Menninger, *Israel and the Church*, 78–79. Garrett, *Hosea, Joel*, 222, finds, "Prophecy gives us not so much specific predictions but types or patterns by which God works in the world. We need look no further than Hosea 11 to understand that Hosea, too, believed that God followed patterns in working with his people. Here the slavery in Egypt is the pattern for a second period of enslavement in an alien land (v. 5), and the exodus from Egypt is the type for a new exodus (vv. 10–11). Thus the application of typological principles of Hos 11:1 [by Matthew] is in keeping with the nature of prophecy itself and with Hosea's own method." France, *Gospel of Matthew*, 81, rightly views typology with Hos 11:1 in Matt 2:15, but wrongly concludes, "Matthew's christological interpretation consists not of exegesis of what the text quoted meant in its original context, but of a far-reaching theological argument which takes the OT text and locates it within an overarching scheme of fulfillment." France is correct about the larger framework of fulfillment, but as Beale and Garrett have demonstrated, a legitimate typological pattern of sonship within the broader theme of the new exodus expectation means that Matthew's application of Hos 11:1 to Jesus is exegetically defensible.

because Israel was called out of Egypt, though they return to 'Egypt' in exile, the nation will come out again from "Egypt," out of exile. By virtue of its placement in the larger scheme of the book, therefore, the entire chapter orients the rest of the book toward the future.[32]

Additionally, the corporate identification of the people of Israel to an individual messianic representative is connected to the prophecy of the future king of Israel coming out of Egypt (Num 24:7–9, 17–19), which is echoed in Hos 11:10–11 (cf. Num 23:22, 24; 24:8, 9).[33] Beale writes, "The Numbers passages together with Hos. 11:11 are the only places in the OT where there is the combined mention of (1) God bringing Israel 'out of Egypt' and (2) of either the deliverer or the delivered being compared to a lion."[34] According to Hosea, the eschatological exodus of God's son Israel would be accomplished by a messianic Davidic king (Hos 1:10–11; 3:5); a corporate representative identified as God's son elsewhere (2 Sam 7:14; 2 Chr 17:13; 22:10; Pss 2:7; 89:26–27). This individual leader who represents Israel will initiate Israel's restoration from exile in a second exodus. In sum, Richard Hays is correct when he concludes,

> Matthew cannot be unaware of the original contextual meaning of Hosea 11:1 as an expression of God's love for Israel—a love

32. Piotrowski, *Matthew's New David*, 129, emphasis original.

33. Beale, *New Testament Biblical Theology*, 407–10; Beale, "Use of Hosea 11:1," 700–703; Menninger, *Israel and the Church*, 99n88; Garrett, *Hosea, Joel*, 229; cf. France, *Gospel of Matthew*, 80n17. The link between the people of Israel and a representative leader is also found in Hos 1:10–11; cf. Hos 3:5. Interestingly, the corporate identification between an individual son and sons is established by another Matthew allusion to Hosea. In Matt 16:16, Jesus is identified as "the Christ, the Son of the living God" (ESV), which is a close parallel to the "sons of the living God" in Hos 1:10. If so, Peter's confession of Jesus' sonship asserts that "Israel's destiny is fulfilled and summed up in the person of Jesus of Nazareth. Peter's confession indicates that with Jesus comes the fulfillment of Hosea's promise that the living God is acting to restore Israel." Goodwin, "Hosea and 'the Son of the Living God,'" 278.

34. Beale, *New Testament Biblical Theology*, 408. Beale continues by helpfully summarizing that the "overall meaning of Hos. 11 is to indicate that God's deliverance of the Israelites from Egypt, which led to their ungrateful unbelief, is not the final word about God's deliverance of them; though they will be judged, God will deliver them again, even from 'Egypt.' The chapter begins with the exodus from Egypt and ends with the same exodus from Egypt, the former referring to the past event and the latter to a future event." Unfortunately, many works recognize the typological relationship between Israel and Christ in Matthew's use of Hos 11:1 in Matt 2:15, but fail to address the broader context of Hos 11 and the book as a whole, which provides the textual warrant for this typological relationship as well as the grounding for the prospective nature of this typological link. For example, Bandy and Merkle, *Understanding Prophecy*, 79–80; and see the discussion in footnote 30 above.

that persists even through Israel's subsequent unfaithfulness (Hos 11:8-9). Indeed, Matthew's use of the quotation actually depends upon the reader's recognition of the original sense. Note carefully: if Hosea's words ('out of Egypt I called my son') were hermeneutically severed from reference to the original exodus story, the artful literary and theological effect of Matthew's narrative would be stifled.... [That effect is] that Jesus now will carry the destiny of the people Israel, and that the outcome will be the rescue and vindication of Israel, as foreshadowed in the exodus story and brought to fulfillment in the resurrection of Jesus.[35]

Therefore, Matthew's citation of Hos 11:1 with respect to Jesus' flight to Egypt, which can be understood only in light of the broader context of Hos 11, serves two purposes. First, the sonship language—the "son" in Hos 11:1 is Israel, but in Matt 2:15 the "son" is Jesus—and the fact that Hosea 11:1 is situated in the wider prophetic context of a new exodus from "Egypt," means that Israel and Jesus are linked typologically (cf. Jer 31:9; Rom 8:29).[36] Matthew demonstrates that Jesus is the true Israel who recapitulates and embodies Israel's history. Beale explains that Israel, "who came out of Egypt, was not obedient and was judged but would be restored ([Hos] 11:2-11), while the former did what Israel should have done: Jesus came out of Egypt, was perfectly obedient, and did not deserve judgment but suffered it anyway."[37] Second, Matthew informs his readers that this son ushers in

---

35. Hays, *Reading Backwards*, 40-41. As is clear from the citation of Hays, he rightly draws upon the larger context of Hos 11, although he does not make the more comprehensive connections that Beale does. Hays also seems to be inconsistent, for he speaks of the original sense of Hos 11, but earlier he describes Matthew as transfiguring Hosea's text by "reading backwards" (40). However, Beale is on more sure footing in demonstrating that Matthew is elucidating the text by following Hosea's own typological understanding in the immediate context as well as the broader context of the book.

36. Contra Howard, "Use of Hosea 11:1 in Matthew 2:15," 314-28; cf. Feinberg, "Hermeneutics of Discontinuity," 122. Howard's interpretation, typical of the dispensational understanding of typology, rejects the prefiguration intrinsic to typology and instead argues that there is only an "analogical correspondence" between Matt 2:15 and Hos 11:1 ("Use of Hosea 11:1 in Matthew 2:15," 320-25). Interestingly, Howard notes Hos 11:10-11 in conjunction to Hos 11:1, but then posits this eschatological exodus to the restoration of Israel during the millennium. See Beale, "Use of Hosea 11:1," 705n22; and Carson, *Matthew 1-12*, 92.

37. Beale, *New Testament Biblical Theology*, 412. Vlach, *Has the Church Replaced Israel?*, 92, 119, limits the significance of the fulfillment of Hos 11:1 in Matt 2:15 to that of Jesus being the "ultimate Israelite." Vlach fails to grasp the larger context of Hos 11 with respect to Hos 11:1 and the citation of Matt 2:15, and thus completely misses the overtones of new exodus with implications for Israel's restoration. Turner, *Matthew*, 91, rightly finds, "God's special love and covenant loyalty are promised to both the nation

the new exodus, commencing the restoration of Israel. Schreiner writes, "Matthew believed that the return from exile promised in Hosea ultimately became a reality with the true son of Israel, Jesus Christ."[38]

The Gospels further present Jesus as the antitypical Israel and the one who inaugurates Israel's new exodus promises. The prophesied messianic forerunner, John the Baptist, preaches and prepares the way of the Lord, marking the onset of the kingdom in the wilderness.[39] The eschatological Elijah has arrived (Mal 3:1; 4:5; cf. Matt 17:10–13), and Jesus' baptism and the accompanying divine approval (Matt 3:15–17; cf. Mark 1:10–11; Luke 3:21–22) also point to Jesus as the true representative of Israel, the servant of the Lord, and agent of Israel's new exodus.[40] According to Isaiah, Israel's new exodus and restoration would be through water (Isa 11:15;

---

and the kings. For Matthew, these themes are consummated in Jesus, whose individual life is an antitypical microcosm of macrocosmic typological Israel." While recognizing the exodus theme, Turner does not develop the implications. He agrees that there is an antitypical fulfillment in Jesus' recapitulation of redemptive history as the Son goes through a greater exodus (cf. p. 23), but there is no discussion of how Israel's restoration and new exodus is being accomplished through Jesus.

38. Schreiner, *New Testament Theology*, 75. Piotrowski, *Matthew's New David*, 140, writes, "Just as Hosea 11 projects the recreation of Yahweh's exodus people at the end of the exile, by quoting only the *front* end thereof—Hos 11:1, the warrant for the expectation—Matthew has created anticipation for the rest of the gospel that the second exodus, the restoration from exile, is about to begin. Thus, Hos 11:1 functions in Matt 2:15 as it does in its Hosean context, as *preparation* for the *coming* restoration from exile" (emphasis original). Note also Hays, "Canonical Matrix of the Gospels," 65–66. Israel's eschatological future included the nations flowing to Israel. Matthew's genealogy with the mention of gentile women already hinted at Jesus' role extending beyond Israel, but the Magi coming and offering gifts (Matt 2:1–12) is the initial fulfillment of Isa 60:3, 5–6, 10–11, 14. Beale, *New Testament Biblical Theology*, 389; Scobie, "Israel and the Nations," 302–3; Cruise, "'Wealth of the Nations,'" 292–93. For more on how Matt 2 shows Israel's history recapitulated in Jesus with the predominant backdrop of the exodus motif, see Kennedy, *Recapitulation of Israel*, 103–53. Lastly, even though Israel had returned from Babylon and was living in the land, there was an overwhelming sense that their exile had continued under foreign occupation and would not end until God redeemed them by finally dealing with their sin. See Wright, *New Testament and the People of God*, 268–72, 299–301; Ciampa, "History of Redemption," 283–89; Pao, *Acts and the Isaianic New Exodus*, 143–46.

39. See Isa 40:3 in Matt 3:3; and Isa 40:3; Mal 3:1; Exod 23:20 in Mark 1:2–3; and Isa 40:3–5 in Luke 3:4–6. Note also Luke 1:16–17, 76–77 with allusions to Mal 3:1, 4:5–6; and Isa 40:3. These passages are significant for understanding the arrival of Israel's restoration in the gospel of Christ. See Watts, "Mark," 113–20, and Bauckham, "Restoration of Israel in Luke-Acts," 439–48. For the interpretive framework and role of Isa 40:3–5 in Luke-Acts, note especially Pao, *Acts and the Isaianic New Exodus*, 37–69.

40. For further in-depth analysis of Jesus' baptism in relation to Israel, see Holwerda, *Jesus and Israel*, 42–44; Beale, *New Testament Biblical Theology*, 412–17; Kennedy, *Recapitulation of Israel*, 175–84.

42:15; 43:2, 16–17; 44:27–28; 50:2; 51:9–11). With the backdrop of the exodus description of Isa 63:11–15; 64:1 (cf. 1 Cor 10:1–4), where the Spirit brings Israel out of the water and gives them rest, Matt 3:16–17 portrays a greater reenactment: Jesus identifies with his people, goes through the waters, and the Spirit descends upon him.[41] The Spirit descending upon Jesus also evokes messianic prophecies where God places his Spirit upon his chosen servant (see Isa 11:2; 42:1; 61:1; cf. Matt 12:18–21). Further, God's perspective of Jesus in the announcement, "This is my beloved son with whom I am well pleased," (Matt 3:17; cf. Luke 3:22; note also the heavenly voice during Jesus' transfiguration in Matt 17:5; Luke 9:35) recalls several significant OT passages. The pronouncement echoes Isa 42:1 where God promises to place his Spirit upon the servant whom his soul delights, the messianic enthronement psalm of a Davidic king (Ps 2:7: "You are my son, today I have begotten you"), the sonship of Israel, possibly echoing Exod 4:22; Hos 11:1; Jer 31:9 or more likely Jer 38:20 LXX [=Jer 31:20] where Ephraim is called "my beloved son"[42] and possibly Isaac (Gen 22:2, 12).[43] Demanding one specific text over another is unnecessary as taken together the new exodus restoration passage of Isa 42:1 with the figure of the servant of the Lord, the royal enthronement of the king as God's son in Ps 2:7, and the connection to the sonship of Israel all possess an undeniably corporate character that find their fulfillment in the individual, Jesus.[44] The theologi-

---

41. Beale, *New Testament Biblical Theology*, 414–15; Watts, "Mark," 120–22; Kennedy, *Recapitulation of Israel*, 178. Schreiner, *King in His Beauty*, 436, writes that Jesus' "baptism in the waters of the Jordan represents a new exodus . . . and the descent of the dove signifies the onset of new creation (cf. Gen. 1:2; 8:8–12), which fits with Isa. 32:15; 44:3, linking the Spirit to the new creation work of God."

42. Gibbs, "Israel Standing with Israel," 511–26, cites four reasons for finding Jer 38:20 LXX ("A beloved son to me is Ephraim") as a crucial allusion for Matt 3:17: (1) the adjective "beloved" modifying "son" only occurs in the LXX at Jer 38:20 and Gen 22:2, 12, 16; (2) Matthew cites Jer 38:15 LXX in Matt 2:18 and so was well aware of Jer 38; (3) the new exodus theme is prominent in both Jer 38 (see v. 8–9, 31–34) and Matt 3–4; 4) the sonship typology of Israel and Jesus is already present in both Matt 2:15 and 4:1–11 (515–20). In sum, he posits that Isa 42:1 and Jer 38:20 LXX (= Jer 31:20) as the main texts behind Matt 3:17.

43. Davies and Allison, *Matthew 1–7*, 336–41, find Isa 42:1 and Ps 2:7 to be the primary background texts to Matt 3:17, but they suggest that Israel and Isaac could have a secondary typological import. France, *Gospel of Matthew*, 123, thinks the primary allusions are to Isa 42:1 and Gen 22:2, but acknowledges that the parallel account of Jesus' baptism in Mark's and Luke's Gospels readily suggest the echo to Ps 2:7. See the comments on Mark 1:11 in France, *Gospel of Mark*, 80–82, where he argues that Isa 42:1 and Ps 2:7 are the main echoes. For Luke 3:22 and 9:35, Hays, *Reading Backwards*, 60–61, finds that Gen 22, Isa 42:1, and Ps 2:7 are the OT scriptural echoes.

44. See Kynes, *Christology of Solidarity*, 27–28. The servant theme is discussed later in this chapter. Though Ps 2:7 does speak of an individual as the Davidic king, the king

cal implication is that the Father confirms Jesus as the unique Son of God, the true Israel, servant, and king who sums up Israel by recapitulating and embodying the nation in fulfilling the OT prophecies and types that looked forward to him.[45]

The Israel-Christ typology is also evident in the wilderness temptation (Matt 4:1–11; Luke 4:1–13).[46] Having identified with Israel in his baptism, this son is led into the wilderness for forty days to be tempted by Satan, thereby mirroring Israel's wanderings and trials in the wilderness for forty years. As Hans LaRondelle observes, with both the nation of Israel and Jesus,

> a "son of God" was tested ([Exod] 4:22; [Deut] 8:5); both times the testing occurred after their baptism ([Matt] 3:16; [1 Cor]

---

represented the people. While it cannot be explored in detail here, Ps 2 is directly cited in Acts 4:25–26; 13:33; Heb 1:5 and 5:5 (note also Rev 2:26–27; 19:15). The gentiles and the Jews crucifying Jesus (corresponding to the nations plotting against God's anointed Messiah in Ps 2:1–2) and God raising Jesus from the grave in vindication and exaltation (Ps 2:7; cf. Rom 1:4) are typological fulfillments of Ps 2. The coronation of a Davidic king, God's son, is typologically and prophetically fulfilled in Jesus, the true David, who is now enthroned, inheriting the nations and possessing the ends of the earth.

45. Turner, *Power from on High*, 201, writes that Jesus' "endowment [of the Spirit in Luke 3:21–22] would most probably be understood as empowering the messianic son and servant to commence the promised cleansing/restoration of Zion." See also Edwards, *Gospel according to Luke*, 120–21. Likewise, Kennedy, *Recapitulation of Israel*, 184. Turner, *Matthew*, 122, concludes, "In [Matt] 3:17 Jesus is described in terms that clearly represent the Isaianic suffering servant, whom Yahweh has chosen (cf. esp. Isa. 42:1). Related to this is the sonship typology metaphorically applied to Israel as a nation (Exod. 4:22; Jer. 3:19; 31:9, 20; Hos. 11:1) and to David as the ideal king who serves Yahweh (2 Sam. 7:5–16; Pss. 2:7; 89:3, 20, 26–27). The fulfillment of biblical covenantal promises to the nation and to the king is found in Jesus, who recapitulates Israel's history as he sojourns in Egypt and passes through the waters before being tested in the wilderness." Turner's excellent summary highlights typology and the fulfillment of covenantal promises, but how this is reconciled with his progressive dispensationalism is unclear.

46. See France, *Jesus and the Old Testament*, 50–53; Holwerda, *Jesus and Israel*, 44–47; Kennedy, *Recapitulation of Israel*, 184–215; Menninger, *Israel and the Church*, 80–81; LaRondelle, *Israel of God*, 64–65; Kynes, *Christology of Solidarity*, 28–35. There is also the presence of Adam and Moses typology in this passage, see Beale, *New Testament Biblical Theology*, 417–22. Jesus could be presented as the last Adam and true Son who does not succumb to Eden's temptation as Mark 1:13 indicates that after his success in the wilderness wild animals were with him and the angels ministered to him. Such an idea of living with wild animals recalls second-exodus new creation passages of Isaiah (11:6–9; 43:20; 65:25). However, the allusion may be to Isa 35:8–10 and Ps 91:9–13 LXX (cf. Matt 4:5 and Luke 4:9, which explicitly allude to Ps 91 in their accounts of Jesus' temptation). If so, the wild animals are symbolic of hostile forces, but are subjugated now that the kingdom has broken in through Jesus. On this view, see Caneday, "Mark's Provocative Use of Scripture," 19–36.

10:2); and each time there is the temptation to test God whether He will perform a miracle to fulfill His promises ([Deut] 6:16; [Exod] 17:2–7; [Matt] 4:3–7), as well as the test whether Israel will worship God alone ([Deut] 6:13–15; [Matt] 4:10).[47]

Unlike Israel who had failed when faced with hunger and tempted to idolatry, Jesus is the obedient son who specifically answers and thwarts Satan's temptations from Deuteronomy (6:13, 16; 8:3) with each citation coming from Moses' rehearsal of Israel's history of sin and failure.[48] By citing these verses from Deuteronomy, Jesus identifies himself with Israel. Further, Jesus replays Israel's experience in the wilderness, but as the faithful, obedient Son, he emerges victorious, thus signifying Israel's long-hoped for renewal. Max Turner explains, "Essentially this is a story about the beginnings of Israel's restoration, a 'New Exodus' begun in her messianic representative through an ordeal/contest with Satan (in which Jesus emerges as the victorious Isaianic servant-warrior)."[49] Similarly, Mark Strauss states, "As the messianic king and Son of God (2 Sam. 7.14; Ps. 2.7; 89.27; 4QFlor), Jesus represents the nation and fulfills the task of eschatological Israel in the wilderness."[50]

The evaluated texts reveal that Jesus is the antitypical son, the true Israel. The pattern of sonship which began with Adam and continued through Abraham, the nation of Israel, and the Davidic kings, reaches its culmination and fulfillment in Christ. The entailments for the church are significant. Since Christ is the true son, his followers and disciples—the

---

47. LaRondelle, *Israel of God*, 65.

48. Menninger, *Israel and the Church*, 80, writes, "The temptations . . . are all met with OT citations (Deut 8:3; 6:16; 6:13 respectively) that highlight Jesus' victory over the Tempter. Where the nation failed, Jesus succeeds. He is seen here as not only the ideal Israelite but as ideal Israel itself. The Son of God not only reenacts Israel's history, but more importantly, he withstands temptations and anticipates a new people (his followers, namely the true Israel) that will succeed where old Israel failed."

49. Turner, *Power from on High*, 204.

50. Strauss, *Davidic Messiah*, 216. Kennedy's main conclusion in his technical study on Matt 1–4 is that Jesus does not just recapitulate Israel's history but embodies Israel as Son, a role which he must fulfill (Matt 3:15; cf. 1:21), for as "the true Israel, he does everything Israel was to be and do." Kennedy, *Recapitulation of Israel*, 225. The theme of Jesus' obedience is also highlighted in the book of Hebrews. Schreiner, *Hebrews*, 38–39, summarizes, "Hebrews, along with the rest of the NT, sets forth Jesus as the true Israel and the true Davidic king. He was the Son who invariably obeyed, never transgressing the will of the Lord (4:15; 7:26). The Lord promised Israel that his promises to them would be secured through obedience (Gen 18:18–19; cf. Gen 26:5), and Jesus as God's Son learned to obey in his suffering (5:18). . . . Israel was tested in the wilderness and sinned repeatedly, but when Jesus was tested, he didn't fall prey to sin (2:18; 4:15), and thus he was perfected via his sufferings (2:10)." Likewise, Goppelt, *Typos*, 99–100.

church—are now sons of God (see Matt 5:9, 44-45; 13:38; Gal 3:28-29). Those who receive Jesus and believe in him are the only ones who are deemed children of God (John 1:12-13).[51] Other scriptures confirm that the kinship of belonging has been redefined. Paul tells the Galatians that in Christ Jesus they are all sons of God through faith (Gal 3:26). This would be shocking for the Jews because, as Trevor Burke writes,

> [U]nder the old economy only Israel and the Israelites were the "sons of God" (e.g., Exod. 4:22; Deut. 14:1-2; Isa. 1:2-4). But now in the accordance with the purposes of God, the scope of blessing is more far reaching because the Son of God opens up the way for Gentiles to be included and receive this filial status as well.[52]

Additional passages with elements of exodus typology show that in the new covenant age—the era of the Holy Spirit—believers are full sons of God (Gal 4:4-7; Rom 8:14-23). In fact, the adoption includes both Jewish and gentile believers, for prior to the cross both were enslaved (Gal 3:22-25; 4:3; Rom 8:15), but now in the fullness of time (Gal 4:4) the eschatological climax has occurred when God sent his Son in order that all who believe may receive the adoption as sons.[53]

---

51. Dutch Reformed theologian Ridderbos, *Gospel according to John*, 45-46, commenting on John 1:12, writes, "In John being a child is always rooted in a new birth 'of God,' 'of the Spirit,' or 'from above' (cf. vs. 13, 3:3). It denotes a totally new mode of existence, one that belongs to the 'eschatological' renewal of all things by God, which as 'eternal life' has already been initiated by the work of Christ; elsewhere in the New Testament it is as such also often linked with the future ('the revealing of the sons of God,' Ro. 8:19; cf. Col 3:4 but also 1 Jn. 3:2). The privilege of being children of God is special and exclusive. It is not a natural quality . . . nor is it the inalienable right of Israel as 'his own' (cf. 8:42). It is, rather, the gift that is given only to those who believe in the Word."

52. Burke, *Adopted into God's Family*, 115. See also Goldsworthy, *Son of God*, 97-107.

53. Burke, *Adopted into God's Family*, 89 (cf. 86-87), states, "Our adoption as sons, according to Paul, is not our native or natural condition. God's family comprises solely adopted sons and daughters—there are no natural-born sons or daughters in his divine household." See also Schreiner, *Galatians*, 269-72; Byrne, "Sons of God"—"Seed of Abraham," 176-83. The word "adoption" also appears with reference to Israel in Rom 9:4. Many dispensationalists point to Rom 9:4-5 in arguing for the special privilege of Israel. For example, see Vanlaningham, "Jewish People," 121-22. But every single one of the privileges (e.g. adoption, covenants) cited here have already been applied to believing gentiles in Rom 1-8 or elsewhere in Pauline writings. See Chae, *Paul as Apostle*, 227, who finds that "Jews and Gentiles equally share these privileges which previously were exclusively granted to the Jews." Cf. Burke, *Adopted into God's Family*, 168-72.

Israel-Jesus Typology through the Seed Theme

The previous discussion of sonship typology is inseparable from the broader seed theme. Incredibly significant for Jews and their identity is their patrilineal descent from Abraham.[54] How the seed theme is integrated in deriving the Israel-Christ-church relationship is critical for ecclesiology as demonstrated in chapters 3 and 4 with the crucial role of the Abrahamic covenant in covenant and dispensational theologies. Significant for the purposes of this study is Gal 3:16 (cf. 3:19). In the context of combating the claims of Judaizing agitators who sought to compel his primarily gentile readers (cf. Gal 4:8) to be circumcised and abide by the Mosaic Law in order to belong to the people of God, Paul states, "Now the promises were made to Abraham and to his offspring. It does not say, 'And to offsprings,' referring to many, but referring to one, 'And to your offspring,' who is Christ" (ESV). For Paul, Jesus fulfills the Abrahamic covenant as he is the unique, typological seed who receives and achieves all the promises of Abraham.[55] Before unpacking the implications of this verse for theological systems, it is important to provide the background as to how Paul could make this argument in identifying Christ as the true seed of Abraham.

In the Abrahamic covenant, God promises Abraham numerous offspring (Gen 12:2; 13:16; 15:5; 17:2; 22:17; 26:4; 24; 28:14; 32:12; 48:4, 19), land (Gen 12:7; 13:15; 15:18; 17:8; 22:17; 24:7; 26:3; 28:13–14; 35:12; 48:4), and that he would be a channel of blessing to all the families or nations of the earth (Gen 12:3; 17:4–6; 18:18; 22:18; 26:4; 28:14).[56] The programmatic

---

54. For emphasis on Abraham as the father of the Jewish people, see Gen 25:19; 26:15, 24; 28:13; 32:9; 48:15–16; Exod 3:6; Deut 1:8; 6:10; 9:5; 30:20; Josh 24:3; 1 Chron 1:27–28, 34; 16:13. For NT passages, note Acts 3:25, the response of the Jews to Jesus in John 8:33 (cf. 8:39), and Gal 3–4 and Rom 4 where Paul specifically addresses the nature of Abraham's offspring.

55. Gentry and Wellum, *Kingdom through Covenant*, 687–93; 815; Schreiner, *Galatians*, 229–30; Schreiner, *Paul, Apostle of God's Glory*, 79–81; Goppelt, *Typos*, 137–38; Wellum, "Baptism and the Relationship," 133–34; Salter, "Abrahamic Covenant," 42. Though he does not bring typology into the discussion, see also the helpful discussion in Scott, *Adoption as Sons of God*, 180–82. Pyne, "'Seed,'" 215, identifies Paul's reference to Christ as Abraham's seed as typological, but even here the strong sense of Jesus as the fulfillment of the Abrahamic covenant is rejected because promises to ethnic Israel are still future (217). Similarly, Riccardi, "Seed of Abraham," 51–64, also thinks that Christ is the typological seed of Abraham in Gal 3:16 (57, 59–60), but his understanding of typology is truncated, having only correspondence and escalation but not fulfillment as he argues that ethnic Israel still remains the seed of Abraham and will possess the physical, political, and territorial Abrahamic promises in the future. Note also, Moo, *Galatians*, 229–30.

56. For specific treatment of the three core promises to Abraham, see Williamson, "Abraham, Israel and the Church," 99–118. Further, in regard to the "seed" promises,

promises of Gen 12:1–3 are the divine, redemptive response to the dilemma of human sin narrated throughout Gen 3–11.[57]

The promises to Abraham are extended to his seed (Gen 13:15; 17:7–9), but clearly throughout Genesis and the rest of the OT there are important nuances in understanding the heirs of the Abrahamic covenant. First, the "seed" of Abraham refers to his natural and biological offspring, such as Ishmael, Isaac, the sons of Keturah (Gen 25:4), and from Isaac, Esau and Jacob.[58] Nevertheless, not all of the biological offspring of Abraham enjoyed covenant privilege, for Isaac (Gen 17:20; 21:13), not Ishmael, and Jacob (Gen 28:13–14), not Esau, were the *special*, natural seed who received the Abrahamic promises. Clearly the nation of Israel falls into this latter "seed" category as the direct descendants of Jacob, although throughout the OT, foreigners and proselytes could enter into this covenant community through circumcision and submitting to the Mosaic Law.[59]

The Abrahamic covenant passes down to the natural and yet special "seed" who are also to be Abraham's children spiritually in exemplifying a faith like his. It is important to recognize that at one level the nation of Israel did receive the nationalistic promises to Abraham (Gen 12:1–2; 15:5, 18–21; 17:7–8; 22:17; 26:4; 28:14; 32:12). God initially fulfilled his promise that Abraham would become a great nation, for Israel did become as numerous as the stars of heaven (Deut 1:10; 10:22; 28:62; 1 Chr 27:23; Neh 9:23), as numerous as the sand of the sea (1 Kgs 4:20), and as the dust of

---

DeRouchie and Meyer, "Christ or Family as the 'Seed,'" 38, also highlight the promise that Abraham's offspring would possess the gate of his enemies (Gen 22:17; 24:60).

57. Dumbrell, *Covenant and Creation*, 55–64; Dempster, *Dominion and Dynasty*, 75–77; Gentry and Wellum, *Kingdom through Covenant*, 279–80; and Hamilton, "Seed of the Woman," 253–74. Hamilton persuasively argues that the promises of Gen 12:1–3 are a direct answer to the curses of Gen 3:14–19 as the promise of being a great nation answers the curse of Gen 3:16, the promise of land correlates to the curse of the ground and the loss of Eden (Gen 3:17–19, 23), and the blessing to all who bless Abram correspond to the promise of crushing the head of the serpent and ultimate victory (Gen 3:15) (258–61; see also Hamilton, *Typology*, 41). See Wright, *Paul and the Faithfulness of God*, 783–95, who discusses the links between Adam and Abraham, how Abraham and his offspring recapitulate the role of Adam, but also how God will redeem the rest of humanity by undoing the curses through Abraham.

58. For an excellent overview of the "seed" language in the OT, see DeRouchie, "Counting Stars with Abraham," 447–57. See also Reisinger, *Abraham's Four Seeds*, 11–76; Alexander, "Seed," 769–72.

59. DeRouchie, "Counting Stars with Abraham," 455–56; Scobie, "Israel and the Nations," 286–88; Schnabel, "Israel, the People of God," 37–39. See Lev 19:34; Ezek 4:22; cf. Exod 12:49; Lev 24:22; Num 9:14; 15:29, and the examples of Rahab, Ruth, and Uriah the Hittite.

the earth (2 Chr 1:9).⁶⁰ Moreover, there is indication that Israel did possess rest and the land during Joshua's leadership (Josh 11:23; 14:15; 21:44–45; 23:14–15, 43–45) and to a greater degree of fulfillment, during the reign of Solomon as the boundaries of the nation extended to those promised to Abraham (1 Kgs 4:21; cf. 4:24–25; 5:4).⁶¹ Most of the Israelites, however, did not resemble their father Abraham in his faith, obedience, and loyalty and so forfeited their special covenantal status, receiving the covenant curses.⁶² Ultimately, such idolatry at a national level led to the exile of both Israel and Judah (see Lev 26:14–33; Deut 4:27; 28:62–64; 31:17, 29; 32:5, 20; Ps 106:34–43; Jer 9:13–16; Ezek 12:15; 20:23–24). The promise of progeny and land never fully materialized (Isa 48:17–19), but awaited realization under a single messianic leader in the future when those who are "Not My People" would be called "sons of the Living God" and "be like the sand of the sea" (Hos 1:9–11).

From a slightly different angle, the promises to Abraham regarding descendants, land, and blessings for the nations are interwoven and inseparable.⁶³ Abram is promised to be made into a great nation, but when he is renamed *Abraham*, God promises that he would be the father of a multitude of nations (Gen 17:4–5). Even though this latter promise could be fulfilled through Abraham's natural offspring, the reiteration of the Abrahamic promises to Jacob in Gen 35:10–12 brings clarification. Chee-Chiew Lee argues,

> Immediately after God changed Jacob's name to Israel, he declared that "Israel" shall become of "a nation" and "a company of nations." As early as in Genesis, "Israel" as "the people

---

60. Alexander, "Seed," 772; Williamson, "Abraham, Israel and Church," 112; Bandy and Merkle, *Understanding Prophecy*, 98.

61. Clearly the territorial possession during Israel's history fell short of the ideal, see Williamson, "Promise and Fulfilment," 15–34; Martin, *Bound for the Promised Land*, 87–94.

62. Throughout Genesis, "seed" conveys a notion of close resemblance between the producer and the offspring. DeRouchie, "Counting Stars with Abraham," 452; Alexander, "Genealogies, Seed," 260, 265. The storyline of the Bible shows how many of those who were physical descendants of Abraham actually demonstrated that they were of the seed of the serpent, not of the seed of the woman (Gen 3:15). The principle is clearly illustrated in John 8:44. John the Baptist also warned the Jews about presuming upon their patriarchal progenitor (Matt 3:9; Luke 3:8)

63. In other words, the giving of the promises in Gen 12:1–3, the making of the covenant in Gen 15, and the confirmation of the covenant in Gen 17 should be considered a package deal. The nationalistic promises of the Abrahamic covenant serve the larger and more significant universal purposes of blessing all the families of the earth. See Williamson, *Sealed with an Oath*, 84; Bauckham, *Bible and Mission*, 28–32, esp. 30.

of God" is portrayed as consisting of physical descendants of Jacob—the nation of Israel—and a multitude of nations. The nuance between the promise made to Abraham in Gen 17:4–5 and its reiteration to Jacob in Gen 35:10–12 is as follows: while Abraham becoming "the father of many nations" may still be fulfilled through the other physical descendants of Abraham, Jacob becoming "a nation and a company of nations" can only be fulfilled beyond his physical descendants.[64]

Certainly, Paul understood Gen 17:5 (see Rom 4:17–18) to necessarily include gentiles given the context of Rom 4 as the many nations includes those who are reckoned righteous through faith (Rom 4:22–24; cf. Gen 15:6).[65] The inextricable link between the promise of being a great nation and the global promise of all the families of the earth being blessed is further established in how the prophets portray the nations becoming part of end-time Israel. For example, Jer 3:16—4:4 alludes to the Abrahamic promises with respect to Israel's post-exilic restoration.[66] In this passage, Israel has multiplied and increased in the land of their fathers (Jer 3:16, 18; hearkening back to Gen 12:7; 13:14–17; 15:18–21; 26:3–4; 28:13–14; 35:10) and nations comprising of heart-changed people gather together with Israel in a transformed Jerusalem called the "throne of the LORD" (Jer 3:17). Israel's restoration and faithfulness results in the nations declaring themselves blessed (Jer 4:2; cf. Ps 72:17; Isa 2:1–4; 19:24–25; Mic 4:1–3; Zech 8:13, 22–23), which recalls Gen 12:3 and 22:18 as they enjoy salvation under the rule of God. Furthermore, as Jeremiah further explains, part of the means the nations will be blessed is coordinated with heart circumcision (Jer

---

64. Lee, "גים [sic] in Genesis 35:11," 474. See also Gentry and Wellum, *Kingdom through Covenant*, 329–31. Gentry observes that the "company of nations" "cannot refer to the 'tribes' of Israel, for this would not satisfy the Hebrew term *gôyîm*, which refers to the groups of peoples in the world as politically and socially structured entities with government. Nor could it be a reference to the later development when Israel was split into two kingdoms. Two kingdoms are not exactly a company of nations" (330). In light of Gen 35:11, that Abraham would be a father of many nations means that he is "father" in an elected rather than biological sense. See DeRouchie, "Counting Stars with Abraham," 457–59; Alexander, "Royal Expectations," 201.

65. See Stark, "To Your Seed I Will Give . . . : The Land(s)," 11–14. Although not mentioning Gen 35:11, Stark notes that the "nations" (pl.) included in the descendants of Abraham points beyond Israel since the word typically includes one entity outside of Israel. For example, Rebekah's pregnancy features two nations: Israel and Edom (Gen 25:23).

66. Lee, "גים [sic] in Genesis 35:11," 477–78; DeRouchie, "Counting Stars with Abraham," 463; Gentry and Wellum, *Kingdom through Covenant*, 528–31. Wood, "Regathering," 326, notes how Ezek 47:21–23 "grants some form of participation of the Gentiles in the glorious restoration of the Promised Land."

4:3–4). The sign of circumcision within the Abrahamic covenant typologically points to heart circumcision as the prophets anticipate Israel's return from exile and restoration featuring a future covenant community devoted and loyal to Yahweh from the heart (Deut 30:6; Jer 9:25–26; Ezek 44:6–9; cf. 11:16–21; 18:30–32; 36:22–36).[67]

Likewise, the land promise, at first referring to the land of Canaan as the location where Abraham's descendants are to become a great nation, includes a sense of expansion or universalization as the place of blessing for all nations.[68] As discussed, figuratively, Israel did become like the stars of the heavens and as the dust of the earth, but the eschatological nature of these descriptions cannot be ignored as Gen 28:14 strongly suggests that the multiplication of descendants goes beyond the territorial border of Canaan to that of global dimensions: "Your offspring shall be like the dust of the earth, and you shall spread abroad to the west and to the east and to the north and to the south, and in you and your offspring shall all the families of the earth be blessed" (cf. Gen 22:17–18).[69] Further, Isa 54:1–3 alludes back to Sarah and Hagar and echoes Gen 28:14.[70] The offspring of the barren and desolate

---

67. For discussion, see Lemke, "Circumcision of the Heart," 299–319, and Meyer, *End of the Law*, 241–62.

68. Wright, *Old Testament Ethics*, 185 (cf. 187–93). The land promise is theologically linked to the themes of city, inheritance, rest, temple, and God's presence (sacred space). These interconnections are investigated in Walker, *Jesus and the Holy City*. The land is a gift from God (Lev 25:23), the place of blessing, and it is the physical sphere where one lives out their allegiance to the Lord (i.e., the locale of kingdom activity). Contra Grisanti, "Critique of *Kingdom through Covenant*," 129–37. Grisanti fails to fit the nation of Israel as a corporate Adam and completely ignores the many passages in the OT (discussed later in this chapter) that demonstrate that the promised land is expanded as a type of the entire creation. Grisanti's dismissal of edenic terminology for the promised land as merely descriptive (pp. 134–35) means that he fails to link the land to the temple, but he also misses the implications of phrases that invoke the original commission given in Eden (e.g., Ezek 36:10–11, 26–30). See footnote 25 above; cf. Beale and Kim, *God Dwells among Us*, 65–77.

69. See Beale, *New Testament Biblical Theology*, 754. See also Scott, *Paul and the Nations*, 63. Other texts indicating the expansion of the promised land include Gen 26:3–4; Exod 34:24; Num 24:17–18; Deut 19:8–9. Williamson, "Promise and Fulfilment," 22. Based on all these texts, the assertions of Hsieh, "Abraham as 'Heir of the World,'" 99, that "the land promises were always localized to the land of Canaan" and that the promise of an expanded promised land was never revealed to Abraham are groundless and untrue. Hsieh fails to evaluate Gen 22:17–18. Further, if the land promises were always localized, one is left wandering about the claim by the author of Hebrews that Abraham looked to the city built and prepared by God (Heb 11:10, 16). For treatment of the promised land as typological in Heb 4 and 11, see Walker, *Jesus and the Holy City*, 211–13; Church, "'Here We Have No Lasting City,'" 147–57.

70. Beale, *New Testament Biblical Theology*, 755; Motyer, *Prophecy of Isaiah*, 445–46. See also Gentry and Wellum, *Kingdom through Covenant*, 496–97; Scott, *Paul and*

one, historically associated with Sarah, not Hagar, will possess the nations in a manner not suggestive of military conquest but in terms of expanding the family tent. The description of Israel's habitations being stretched out and spreading abroad to the right and the left (Isa 54:2–3) is indicative that the land promise exceeds a specific geographic locale to include the world and cannot be isolated from the promise to bring blessings to the nations (see Pss 2:8; 22:27–28; 47:7–9; 72:8–11; Zeph 3:9–10).[71] Another example where the promises of Abraham come together is likely Isa 51.[72] Theologically, the company of nations that become Abraham's seed coupled with the grandiose numerical imagery of Abraham's offspring ("dust of the earth," "stars of heaven") require that the land extend far beyond Palestine, for the countless numbers of those who possess the faith of father Abraham will not be able to reside in such a narrow strip of land. When the expansion of the land in the restoration promises is coordinated with the depiction of the land as the Garden of Eden (e.g., Isa 51:3; Ezek 36:35) and with how Israel will multiply and be fruitful (Jer 3:16; 23:3; Ezek 36:11), the picture becomes clearer that the Abrahamic promises of being a great nation and possession of the land cannot be disassociated from God's program of blessing the nations and bringing about a new creation.

---

the Nations, 63.

71. DeRouchie, "Counting Stars with Abraham," 470; cf. McComiskey, *Covenants of Promise*, 54. The universalistic element of the land promise also appears in the Psalter, for the description of the recipients who are to inherit the land is cast more broadly than the nation of Israel. In general terms, those who fear Yahweh and are characterized by righteousness and meekness are those who are promised the inheritance of the land (Pss 25:12–13; 37:9, 11, 22, 29, 34; cf. Isa 57:13). Matt 5:5 alludes to Ps 37:11, which confirms the typological nature of the promised land as does several other NT texts: John 15:1–6; Rom 4:13; Eph 6:3; Heb 3:7—4:11; 11:13–16; 13:12–14; 2 Pet 3:13; Rev 21:1—22:5. For discussion of Ps 37 and the promised land, see Beale, *New Testament Biblical Theology*, 756–57; Martin, *Bound for the Promised Land*, 124; LaRondelle, *Israel of God*, 138; Davies and Allison, *Matthew 1–7*, 449–51; and Carson, *Matthew 1–12*, 133–34, 136.

72. Watts, "Echoes from the Past," 495, writes, "It is possible that the movement from Abraham and Sarah to offspring ([Isa 51] v. 2), to restoration of the land (v. 3), and then to justice for the nations (vv. 4–5) is intended not only to invoke the tradition reflected in Gen. 12.1–3 but also its progression: Abram leaves Ur/Haran (Gen. 12.1; Isa. 40–55 just happens to be about an exodus from the same general location), is promised that he will become a great nation and be blessed (v. 2a), and finally is declared to be a blessing for all the peoples on the earth (vv. 2b–3)." Israel's land is again depicted in terms of a restored Eden and garden (Isa 51:3). Also, there are significant points of contact between Isa 51:1–8 and Gal 3:6–9, so Harmon, *She Must and Shall Go Free*, 138–40. That Abraham's seed is now made up of *spiritual* offspring, faithful Jews *and* gentiles (cf. Gal 3:25–29), is only possible because of the work of Christ (Gal 3:13–14), the true seed of Abraham (Gal 3:16).

The brief sketch of the Abrahamic covenant within the OT indicates that the divine promises to Abraham, having nationalistic and universalistic aspects, are packaged together in anticipation of eschatological fulfillment.[73] This understanding of the interwoven nature of the Abrahamic covenant is in sharp contrast to how dispensationalists and covenant theologians understand this programmatic covenant. In sum, Abraham's "seed" expands beyond the natural and yet special offspring of Israel to include a spiritual posterity or "seed" from among the nations, a regenerate people who possess the same faith as Abraham. Even more significant, however, is how the promises are channeled through and crystalized in one, unique, true "seed" of Abraham, a royal deliver.

The narrative of Genesis suggests, and later OT books confirm, that the Abrahamic promises come to fruition through one unique, individual, seed of Abraham. Significantly, in Gen 17:6, 17:16, and 35:11, the promise of kings issuing from Abraham, Sarah, and Jacob are made.[74] Intertwined with these royal promises are the themes of fruitfulness, seed, and land.[75] Within Genesis, these promises of royal offspring look back to Gen 3:15 and forward to Gen 49:8–12, where a king will emerge from Judah who receives the obedience of nations (49:10; cf. Gen 27:29) and whose rule is characterized by prosperity and abundance (49:11). Validation that the Abrahamic promises coalesce in one specific "seed" of Abraham is the usage of the collective singular noun זֶרַע ("seed"). While the term is commonly applied in reference to multiple descendants, the syntactical analyses of Collins and Alexander reveal that the term "seed" is a single individual in Gen 3:15,

---

73. Smith, "Fifth Gospel," 81, writes, "The blessing [of Gen 12:1–3] is for all the clans of the *'adhamah*—the ground that was cursed in Gen 3:17. In sum, the land promised to Abraham was, from the outset, *part of a 'package deal' for the reversal of the curse*. The Promised Land was inseparable from the global goals of the redemptive drama" (emphasis original). See also Bauckham, *Bible and Mission*, 46. Similar to the survey in terms of describing how each strand of the Abrahamic covenant is interwoven is DeRouchie's presentation of a two stage progression. Abraham goes to the land in order to become a great nation, Israel. The first stage is realized by Israel during the era of the Mosaic covenant. The second stage was inaugurated when the representative of Israel, Jesus Christ, the true seed of Abraham, fulfilled the charge to be a blessing (Gen 12:2) by overcoming the curse. He is the instrument of blessing (Gen 12:3) by bringing together Jews and gentiles into one global family. See DeRouchie, "Counting Stars with Abraham," 459–60, 479–80.

74. Diffey, "Royal Promise in Genesis," 313–16. See also Gen 26:3 where Abraham himself is presented as "a prince of God" (ESV).

75. Diffey, "Royal Promise in Genesis," 314. Diffey also observes how in each passage the recipient of the promise is renamed by God. For an overview of messanic hope in Genesis, see Alexander, "Messianic Ideology in Genesis," 19–39. Note also Kaiser, *Messiah in the Old Testament*.

22:17b–18a, and 24:60.⁷⁶ These texts, all closely associated with the Abrahamic covenant, set a trajectory that links the fulfillment of the promises to a single Messianic "seed." Surprisingly, some dispensationalists ignore or neglect how the "seed" theme narrows down to an individual, royal figure.⁷⁷

Subsequent development of the patriarchal promises in the OT connect the Abrahamic covenant to David, but also back to the conditions of Eden and the hopes of overcoming the curse of Gen 3:15. The Balaam oracles recorded in Num 22–24 not only depict Israel in language reminiscent of Eden and the exodus (Num 24:5–6) but reaffirm the Abrahamic promise of blessing and cursing (Num 24:6, 12; 23:8; cf. Gen 12:3), the promise of seed (Num 23:10; cf. Gen 12:2; 13:16; 28:14), and most importantly, Balaam projects the last days when an individual Israelite seed will become exalted, having universal rule, and triumphing over his enemies (Num 24:7–9, 17–19; cf. Gen 12:3; 27:29; 49:9–10).⁷⁸ The organic relationship between the Abrahamic covenant and the Davidic covenant further narrow down the promises to an individual Davidide, for a kingdom will be established for David's "seed" (2 Sam 7:12; 1 Chr 17:11–14; Ps 89:3–4, 28, 36; cf. Ps 132:10–12; Jer 33:21).⁷⁹ The great name and nation promised to Abraham are directed through David (2 Sam 7:9; 1 Chr 17:8; cf. Gen 12:2), as are the promises of place (2 Sam 7:10; cf. Gen 12:7; 15:18; 17:8; Deut 11:24ff). Additionally, the promises of rest from enemies and an established throne coupled with David's assessment of the covenant as being a charter for humanity (2 Sam 7:19b) indicate that a Davidic king will mediate the blessings to the nations and will effect God's rule over the world through his faithfulness as God had commissioned Adam in the garden (cf. Pss 89:23–29; 110:1–7).⁸⁰ The ideal eschatological Davidic king is also directly

---

76. Collins, "Syntactical Note (Genesis 3:15)," 139–48; Alexander, "Further Observations on the Term 'Seed,'" 363–67. Cf. DeRouchie and Meyer, "Christ or Family as the 'Seed,'" 38–40.

77. Feinberg, "Systems of Discontinuity," 72, in his discussion of the multiple sense of "seed" fails to observe that Christ is the true "seed" (Gal 3:16). On the other hand, Vlach, *Has the Church Replaced Israel?*, 151, lists Christ as the unique individual seed of Abraham, but fails to account for the significance of this or the importance of Gal 3:16 in his counter arguments to "supersessionists" (150–51).

78. For more in-depth analysis, see Dempster, *Dominion and Dynasty*, 113–17; Hamilton, "Seed of the Woman," 263–66; Hamilton, *Typology*, 149–52; Beale, *New Testament Biblical Theology*, 99–101.

79. See Gentry and Wellum, *Kingdom through Covenant*, 700–4; Dempster, *Dominion and Dynasty*, 143; Hamilton, "Seed of the Woman," 267–68; Dumbrell, *Covenant and Creation*, 145–51; McComiskey, *Covenants of Promise*, 21–30.

80. On the expression of 2 Sam 7:19b being translated as "and this is the Charter for all mankind, O Lord God!," see Kaiser, "Blessing of David: The Charter for Humanity," 298–318, esp. 310–15. Cf. Gentry and Wellum, *Kingdom through Covenant*, 456–58,

related to the individual "seed" of Abraham in Ps 72 with verse 17 alluding back to the individual "seed" of Gen 22:18 (cf. Gen 12:3).[81] Once again the covenant promises of Abraham—having a great name (Gen 12:2 with Ps 72:17), possessing the land but now in a universalized sense (Gen 15:18 with Ps 72:8; cf. Ps 2:8; Zech 9:10; 14:9),[82] and the blessings of the nations (Gen 12:3 with Ps 72:11, 17)—are brought together as is the promised goal of the "seed" of the woman (Gen 3:15) overcoming the curse (Ps 72:3–4, 9).[83] Other passages point in this direction as well, as "Amos 9:11–15 likewise connects ultimate Davidic vicegerency with Edenic land and abundance, as does Ez 34."[84]

These promises coalesce into the new covenant which has national (Jer 31:36–40; 33:6–16; Ezek 36:24–38; 37:11–28) and international (Isa 42:6; 49:6; 55:3–5; 56:4–8; 66:18–24; Jer 33:9; Ezek 36:36; 37:28) elements that are brought to fulfillment through a Davidic, Abrahamic son (Isa 9:6–7; 11:1–10; Jer 23:5–6; 33:14–26; Ezek 34:23–24; 37:24–28). Gentry and Wellum explain that the new covenant has a universal scope, particularly in Isaiah (42:6; 49:5; 55:3–5; 56:4–8; 66:18–24):

> Isaiah projects the ultimate fulfillment of the divine promises in the new covenant onto an 'ideal Israel,'—a community intimately tied to the servant of the Lord, the Davidic king (who

---

701; Dumbrell, *Covenant and Creation*, 151–52; Routledge, *Old Testament Theology*, 235n28; McComiskey, *Covenants of Promise*, 21–23.

81. Lee, "גים [sic] in Genesis 35:11," 475–77; Gentry and Wellum, *Kingdom through Covenant*, 482–85; cf. Routledge, *Old Testament Theology*, 230, 235; Beetham, "From Creation to New Creation," 248.

82. Beale, *New Testament Biblical Theology*, 754, rightly observes that the description of the end-time Davidic king ruling from sea to sea and from the river to the ends of the earth "is an explicit widening of the original borders of the promised land, which had been set 'from the Red Sea to the sea of the Philistines, and from the wilderness to the River [Euphrates]' (Exod. 23:31). This is summarized in Gen. 15:18 as 'from the river of Egypt as far as the great river, the river Euphrates.' The psalm begins with the 'river' (apparently of Egypt) but substitutes 'the end of the earth' for the 'river Euphrates.' Again, the patriarchal promise related to Israel's land is universalized by the psalm." Cf. Bauckham, *Bible and Mission*, 44. Scott, *Paul and the Nations*, 62–63, notes how the messianic king in the OT was expected to rule the world and so the Abrahamic promise of land expands to include the whole world (he cites particularly from Sir 44:21). According to Scott, this is further illustrated in how Ps 72 shows the universal sovereignty of the king in that he rules over a group of nations (vv. 9–11, 16), which is drawn from the Table of Nations in Gen 10.

83. For the allusions back to Gen 3 in Ps 72, see Hamilton, "Seed of the Woman," 269–70.

84. Beetham, "From Creation to New Creation," 249. See also Hos 2:16—3:5; Jer 30:9.

is true Israel in himself), and located in a rejuvenated new creation (Isa. 65:17; 66:22).[85]

The survey immediately above highlights that the prophetic trajectory of the Abrahamic covenant promises are through the "seed" theme. The "seed" is a typological pattern, possessing a prospective and eschatological orientation that centers in Jesus Christ. The promises to Abraham were passed down to the patriarchs, the nation of Israel, and then to David and the kings, but they culminate, according to the NT, in Jesus since he is the true seed, true Israel, and true David. In returning to Gal 3:16, where Paul confirms Jesus as the typological seed who inherits the promises and in whom they are realized, it is important to note three key features of this text and the passage at large.

First, in the context of showing that the blessings to Israel and the nations have become a reality in Christ (Gal 3:8–9, 14) and that the fulfillment of the Abrahamic covenant means that believers are not under the Mosaic Law (Gal 3:15—4:11), Paul explicitly states the Abrahamic promises were ultimately made to one offspring ($\sigma\pi\acute{\epsilon}\rho\mu\alpha$)—Christ. At the outset, as observed in my survey of the Abrahamic seed theme in the OT, Paul's interpretative move is not allegorization nor a midrashic treatment.[86] The interplay between the plural *seed* and the singular *seed* is present in the Genesis narrative and further, the seed theme narrows down from Abraham to Israel, and then to David in the OT. Paul can emphasize that the Abrahamic promises are to the individual[87] Jesus Christ even as he recognizes the plural sense with his use of this collective noun in Gal 3:29 (cf. Gal 3:7). Nevertheless, there is difficulty with Paul's citation of the OT with the phrase "and to your offspring" (Gal 3:16 ESV). Since the offspring reference is to an individual, Collins, who is followed by dispensationalist Michael Riccardi, argues that Paul is drawing from Gen 22:17–18, one of the passages in the Genesis narrative identified earlier where the term *seed* refers to an individual.[88] Paul's

85. Gentry and Wellum, *Kingdom through Covenant*, 705; cf. Wellum, "Beyond Mere Ecclesiology," 196–97; Williamson, *Sealed with an Oath*, 179–80.

86. Contra, for example, Hester, *Paul's Concept of Inheritance*, 48. See Kagarise, "'Seed' in Galatians 3:16," 67–73, for a helpful defense of the legitimacy of Paul's identifying the Abrahamic *seed* with Christ, though Kagarise fails to note the studies of Collins and Alexander showing the plural and singular aspects of the term. For a survey of interpretations of Paul's use of the OT in Gal 3:16, see Collins, "Galatians 3:16," 76–79.

87. A minority interpretation is that the singular "offspring" refers to one family in Christ and not many families. See Wright, *Climax of the Covenant*, 162–68. While the principle of corporate solidarity is present (Gal 3:14, 26, 28), Wright's interpretation is not sustainable. See the criticisms of DeRouchie and Meyer, "Christ or Family as the 'Seed,'" 36–48; and Windsor, "'Seed,' the 'Many' and the 'One,'" 118–19.

88. Collins, "Galatians 3:16," 84–86; Riccardi, "Seed of Abraham," 56–57; see also

citation cannot be from Gen 22:17-18, however, for the word *and* (καὶ) is part of Paul's citation in Gal 3:16 ("and to your offspring"; καὶ τῷ σπέρματι αὐτοῦ), and it is not conjoined to τῷ σπέρματι αὐτοῦ in the text of Genesis 22:18 (καὶ is separated by the verb and preposition ἐνευλογηθήσονται ἐν in Gen 22:18).[89] The way Paul introduces the phrase in question appears to be a direct citation. Instead of Gen 22:18, Paul is citing from the Septuagint (LXX) of Gen 13:15; 17:8; or 24:7.[90] With the focus on covenant in Gal 3:15 and 17, Gen 17:8 is the most likely source of the citation in Gal 3:16 since both "covenant" and "seed" terms are in the context of Gen 17.[91]

However, if Paul is citing from Gen 17:8, how can he apply this passage where the term *seed* is used in the plural or corporate sense in contrast to other passages where *seed* is singular (as in Gen 3:15; 22:17b-18; and 24:60)? A viable answer is provided by Lionel Windsor.[92] Within the text of

---

August, "Paul's View of Abraham's Faith," 57-60; cf. Steinmann, "Jesus and Possessing the Enemies' Gate," 14n2, 16. For dispensationalists like Riccardi, "Seed of Abraham," 60-62, only the third component of the Abrahamic covenant (spiritual blessings for all the families of the earth) have come to pass, the ethnic and territorial aspects of the Abrahamic covenant are future. According to dispensationalists then, just the particular promise of Gen 12:3 is highlighted in Gal 3 (esp. v. 8). See Saucy, "Israel and the Church," 254; Blaising and Bock, *Progressive Dispensationalism*, 192-93; Ryrie, *Dispensationalism*, 161. Collins, Riccardi, August, and Steinmann, however, miss that the land promise is included in Gen 22:17-18. Right in the middle of this passage where God promises to bless Abraham with offspring as numerous as the stars of the heaven (Gen 22:17, recalling the promise of being a great nation) and that all the nations will be blessed (Gen 22:18, recalling the promise of blessing to all the families of the earth) is the statement that the individual offspring will "possess the gate of his enemies" (Gen 22:17). This phrase clearly reveals that territory is in view. McComiskey, *Covenants of Promise*, 53, writes, "The possession of the gates in Genesis 22:17 is with the promise of land in Genesis 26:2-5. The oath made by God to Abraham after he willing placed his son on the altar . . . is reaffirmed to Isaac in Genesis 26:1-5. In the restatement of the elements of the oath (v. 4) the reference to the 'gates' is replaced by words 'and will give them all these lands' (v. 4)." Therefore, even if Gen 22:17-18 is the background to Gal 3:16, not only is the promised land included, but more, the scope of the promised land is universalized.

89. Schreiner, *Galatians*, 230; Windsor, "'Seed,' the 'Many' and the 'One,'" 250n1; DeRouchie, "Counting Stars with Abraham," 480.

90. Schreiner, *Galatians*, 228, 230; Moo, *Galatians*, 228-29; Windsor, "'Seed,' the 'Many' and the 'One,'" 115, 120-26; Kwon, *Eschatology in Galatians*, 105-6; Williams, "*Promise* in Galatians," 716-17. Kagarise, "'Seed' in Galatians 3:16," 69, thinks that no one particular passage is behind Paul's quotation.

91. Moo, *Galatians*, 228; Harmon, *She Must and Shall Go Free*, 150; cf. Betz, *Galatians*, 156; DeRouchie and Meyer, "Christ or Family as the 'Seed,'" 38. Moo notes that both Gen 15:18 and 17:8 are in Paul's mind since "covenant" and "seed" appear in both contexts, but given that the citation includes "and," Gen 15:18 can be ruled out as the specific source of his citation.

92. Windsor, "'Seed,' the 'Many' and the 'One,'" 120-25.

Gen 17 itself, according to Windsor, there is a distinction between a *plurality* and a *singularity*. The focus of Gen 17:1–6 is on plurality, the "many nations." From Gen 17:7 and following, the more immediate, particular nation of Israel which constitutes Abraham's natural *seed* is brought into focus. It is Abraham's *singular* household (vv. 12–13) and his *singular* people (v. 14) who stand "under Abraham's obligation of circumcision (and, consequently, of law). This obligation is not laid on the future projected 'many' nations of whom Abraham will ultimately be the father."[93] Paul is countering the Judaizers then by showing from Gen 17 itself that his gentile readers are not under the Mosaic Law since the blessing of the nations do not fall under the requirements of circumcision. More importantly, Paul's citation of Gen 17:8 as a reference to Christ leads to the conclusion that the nation of "Israel, the 'seed' which stands under covenantal obligation—is ultimately fulfilled in the person of Christ."[94] The covenant directed to Abraham's offspring in Gen 17:7–14, are promises, according to Paul, that are to one offspring—Christ (cf. Gal 3:19).[95] The typological relationship is apparent, Christ is the true Israel (= true *seed* of Abraham) as Israel's promises and obligations culminate in him.[96] Christ, like Israel, was born under the law (Gal 4:4–5),

---

93. Windsor, "'Seed,' the 'Many' and the 'One,'" 123. Windsor also notes, "Paul refers explicitly to two key terms from his source text: not only the term 'seed' (*sperma*), which denotes singularity, but also the term 'many' (*polys*), which denotes plurality. Although interpreters . . . consistently fail to notice that the equally significant term 'many' also occurs in Gen 17" (122). Harmon, *She Must and Shall Go Free*, 150–51, goes in a different direction in highlighting an Isaac-Christ typological link, for the corporate notion of *seed* narrows down to Isaac (Gen 17:15–19) and so "it is possible that Paul has read the interplay between a singular and plural notion of seed and concluded that a similar phenomenon has taken place in Christ: he is the singular seed through whom the covenant promises are confirmed and extended to his seed." Nevertheless, since the citation is from Gen 17:8, right near the transition point of Gen 17, the solution posed by Windsor is more attractive.

94. Windsor, "'Seed,' the 'Many' and the 'One,'" 123, cf. 125. Kwon, *Eschatology in Galatians*, 122–25, argues unpersuasively that Paul is presenting Christ not as the fulfiller of the Abrahamic promise, but as its original co-recipient. However, Kwon misses the significance that the Abrahamic blessing, the promise of the Spirit, has become a reality in Christ (Gal 3:14; cf. 3:8) and that the law's reign concluded with the coming of the singular offspring for whom the promise was reserved (Gal 3:19). With reference to Gal 3:19, see Schreiner, *Galatians*, 240.

95. The typological relationship between the nation of Israel and Jesus as observed in this study plays out through the principle of corporate solidarity whereby the one represents the many. The Messiah represents the nation, sums up Israel's hopes, and is the ultimate recipient of God's promises to his people. For discussion of corporate solidarity in Gal 3:16, see Kagarise, "'Seed' in Galatians 3:16," 71; Ellis, *Paul's Use of the Old Testament*, 70–73; Longenecker, *Biblical Exegesis*, 106–7, cf. 77; Schreiner, *Galatians*, 229; Johnson, "Pauline Typology," 146–49.

96. Johnson, "Pauline Typology," 186–92, helpfully highlights how the

but this unique Abrahamic *seed* achieves the promises and fulfills the law by his substitutionary death so that Jews and gentiles alike, through redemption, can become the true spiritual *seed* of Abraham, heirs of promise (Gal 3:28–29; cf. Heb 2:10–18, esp. v. 16), and no longer be subject to the Mosaic Law and its obligations.[97]

The typological relationship is further confirmed considering that Gal 3:16 also likely alludes to Isa 41:8 along with Isa 53:10 and 54:3.[98] Isaiah 41:8 describes Israel as the offspring of Abraham and as the Lord's servant, themes which are significant in the latter half of the book (Isa 38–66).[99] As a result of his substitutionary guilt offering, the servant of Isa 53 will see his "offspring" (Isa 53:10; cf. Gal 3:13) and in celebration of this salvation, the offspring of the barren woman will be numerous (Isa 54:1) and inherit the nations (Isa 54:3). As noted previously, the distinguishing characteristics of the servant is that Yahweh placed his Spirit on him (Isa 42:1) and promises to make the servant into a "covenant for the people" (Isa 42:6; 49:8). With the themes of covenant, seed, inheritance, the nations, and the reception of the Holy Spirit present in Gal 3, it is not difficult to see how these Isaiah passages served as a backdrop in Paul's presentation of Christ as the servant who redeems his people (Gal 3:13), the seed who inherits the blessed promise(s) to Abraham (3:16, 18), and how as the true heir and true Israel he shares his sonship and inheritance to all who are united to him by faith (Gal 3:26–29).[100] An entailment of this is that the genealogical principle so critical in covenant theology has come to an end. Isaiah projects, and Paul confirms in Gal 3–4 with the fulfillment wrought in Christ, that the Abrahamic offspring are a people corporately identified with the Messiah,

---

Abraham-Christ typology in Gal 3 has the characteristics of historical correspondence, divinely ordained prefiguration, eschatological intensification, and Christocentric orientation.

97. Burke, *Adopted into God's Family*, 111–20. See also, Holwerda, *Jesus and Israel*, 103 (cf. 32–33), who rightly concludes that Christ is "who represents and defines the authentic covenant lineage. In Christ it has been revealed that the inheritance of the promises is not by law but by promise, that the inheritance is a gift of God's grace (as was Canaan in the Old Testament) to those who believe."

98. Harmon, *She Must and Shall Go Free*, 150–61. Interestingly, Pyne, "'Seed,'" 215, also links Gal 3:16 to Isaiah's Servant Songs, but the theological implications for dispensationalism are not considered.

99. DeRouchie, "Counting Stars with Abraham," 465–74. Not only is there an allusion to Isa 41:8 in Gal 3:16, but the typological relationship between Israel and the community addressed by Hebrews is also observable since Heb 2:10–18, a passage that also focuses on Abraham's offspring, has several elements that link back to Isa 41:8–10.

100. Harmon, *She Must and Shall Go Free*, 158.

the servant's offspring are his via spiritual adoption, not through physical descent, and they are reborn and regenerate (Isa 54:1, 3).[101]

Second, Paul states that it was Abrahamic "promises" (plural) that were (ultimately) spoken to Christ. Paul frequently refers to the "promise" (Gal 3:17, 18, 19, 22, 29; 4:23, 28), and only to "promises" plural in Gal 3:16 and 3:21. Nevertheless, Paul freely oscillates between a singular promise and promises throughout the chapter. The usage of the plural in 3:16 reveals that it is not just Gen 12:3 (the blessings of the nations) in view. David Starling suggests that the promises

> include not only the promise of blessing to the Gentiles but also the promise of the land and the prophetic promises of restoration and the outpouring of the Spirit. All of these promises, it seems, are understood by Paul as constituting a single inheritance, promised by God 'to Abraham and his offspring . . . that is, to one person, Christ.'[102]

In contrast to dispensationalists who assert that only Gen 12:3 is in view, the text indicates that all the Abrahamic covenant promises are included, especially the promise of land (the land is of specific focus in Gen 17:8 that Paul directly cites from in Gal 3:16), which is confirmed in Gal 3:18 where Paul argues that the "inheritance," a term rooted in the OT for the promised land (Gen 15:3–5; 17:8; 22:17; 28:4; Num 26:53–56; Josh 11:23; etc.), is given through promise.[103] As observed, the promised land is a typological pattern, one that Paul confirms in Gal 3 and elsewhere (e.g., Rom 4:13).[104] The land promise anticipates a new transformed universe, an

---

101. DeRouchie, "Counting Stars with Abraham," 483–85. DeRouchie keenly observes, "The 'barren one's' lack of labor and child bearing in Isa 54:1 suggests that *spiritual adoption, not physical birth, would characterize the identity of the new children.* The physical genealogical principle so evident in the Abrahamic and Mosaic covenants does *not* continue once the Abrahamic covenant reaches its fulfillment in the new, for membership is now solely conditioned on *spiritual* rebirth, generated through the sacrificial death of the Servant King (Isa 53:10)" (470–71, emphasis original).

102. Starling, "Yes to All God's Promises," 189; cf. DeRouchie and Meyer, "Christ or Family as the 'Seed,'" 38. On the relationship between the singular "promise" and plural "promises" in Gal 3, Schreiner, *Galatians*, 228n18, rightly observes that the "singular encompasses the totality of the promises made to Abraham." See also Moo, *Galatians*, 228; Longenecker, *Galatians*, 130–31.

103. For treatment that Paul has the promised land in focus in Gal 3:15–18, see Hester, *Paul's Concept of Inheritance*, 76–79; Kwon, *Eschatology in Galatians*, 105–6; Echevarria, *Future Inheritance of Land*, 104–16; Schreiner, *Galatians*, 228n20, 231–32; Moo, *Galatians*, 231; DeRouchie, "Counting Stars with Abraham," 480–81; Williams, "*Promise* in Galatians," 716–20; Byrne, "*Sons of God*"—"*Seed of Abraham*," 159–60; Johnson, "Pauline Typology," 140–43.

104. Hsieh's attempt to interpret that Abraham "would be heir of the world" (ESV)

inheritance of a global kingdom involving a consummated new creation (Rev 21:2-3; cf. Isa 4:5-6; Heb 12:22). The inheritance of land does not await national, ethnic Israel in the future millennium and beyond; rather, the inheritance is enjoyed by all those baptized into Christ, conjoined to him by faith (Gal 3:27-29; cf. 1 Cor 12:13) since all Christians are children of promise, being born through the work of the Holy Spirit (Gal 4:6-7, 28-31).

The third and final point to observe is that the Abrahamic promises, which are ultimately intended for Christ as the singular seed, includes the gift of the Holy Spirit. The promised Holy Spirit (Gal 3:14; cf. Gal 3:2, 5; 4:6) in the OT is inextricably linked to the new covenant and Israel's restoration promises (e.g., Isa 32:15-18; 44:3-5; 59:21; Ezek 36:26-30; 37:1-14; Joel 2:28—3:3; Zech 12:10). Paul's argument in Gal 3:13-14 is that Christ removed the curse of the law so that gentiles may receive the blessing of Abraham, a blessing equivalent to or that includes the promise of the Spirit.[105]

---

as the inheritance of many nations (people, not the promised land as the eschatological world; "Abraham as 'Heir of the World,'" 106-10) does not adequately address that this promise is also to Abraham's offspring ("for the promise to Abraham *and his offspring*," Rom 4:13). Moreover, Hsieh ignores Rom 4:14 where the theme of inheritance is sustained in Paul's argument. In Rom 4:13, Abraham is heir of what Abraham's offspring are also heirs of, but they are heirs not by adherence to the law, but are of the faith of Abraham (Rom 4:14-16). Hsieh's view (also asserted by Blaising, "Premillennial Response," 144-45) fails, for Abraham's offspring (referred to as "heirs") are not inheriting nations in this text, but are heirs of the coming eschatological world of which Paul is directing their hope. For more exegetically satisfying treatments of Rom 4:13, see Stark, "To Your Seed I Will Give . . .: The Land(s)," 12-13; Echevarria, *Future Inheritance of Land*, 141-49. See also, Starling, "Yes to All God's Promises," 194-95, who takes "world" (Rom 4:13) to go beyond any single Abrahamic promise but concludes that Paul rejected a nationalistic view of worldwide Jewish rule and any bounded territorial fulfillment. From a different dispensational perspective, Vanlaningham, "Jewish People," 119-21, recognizes that the land is universalized to the whole world in Rom 4:13, but this blessing is mediated through Israel to the nations. Vanlaningham assumes that the new covenant is still to be instituted to Israel in the future so that Israel will have a mediatorial role to the nations (120). But nowhere in the context of Rom 4 is there a hint of Paul presupposing that Israel must be in the land or that Rom 4:13 describes the end of the process of Israel's restoration. In the context of Rom 4, the offspring of Abraham includes Jews and gentiles who are the heirs of the world; the promise is guaranteed to all his descendants (Rom 4:16). Moreover, every indication throughout Rom 1-8 (e.g., Rom 2:29) is that the promises of the new covenant have already been ushered in. Vanlaningham misses how the Abrahamic promises are fulfilled in Christ and how the blessings to the nations are already occurring through the work of Christ. The future day referred to in Isa 54:1-3 (see p. 119) has come to fruition in Christ (note thematic parallels in Isa 52:13—53:12) as Abraham's fatherhood of the nations is already happening with the expansion of the church, and as also indicated by Paul's citation of Isa 54:1 in Gal 4:27.

105. For the blessing of Abraham being identical to or part of the promise of the

There is no reference to the promise of the Spirit in the Abrahamic narrative in Genesis, but some argue that the promises to Abraham are fulfilled in the one promise of the Spirit.[106] While this latter point is true, Paul links the gift of the Spirit to the promise of Abraham based on Isa 44:3–5, which stands in the background of Gal 3:14.[107] Isaiah 44:3–5 is similar to the other restoration and new covenant prophecies in terms of positing God's future work involving the Spirit, but in this passage alone Yahweh promises to pour out his Spirit on the offspring of servant Israel/Jacob as well as blessings on the servant's descendants (Isa 44:3). Moreover, the context of Isa 44:1–5 is the creation of a new Israel through the inclusion of the nations as the those who tattoo their hands, "belonging to the Lord," and who adopt the name of Jacob or Israel are gentiles (Isa 44:5).[108] The themes of blessing, seed, and Spirit all correlate with the themes of Gal 3. Further, Christ is presented by Paul as servant Israel (see the discussion for this Israel-Christ typological relationship later in this chapter) whose death (Gal 3:13) brings about the Abrahamic blessing to the gentiles, a blessing described as the promise of the Spirit. Harmon aptly summarizes,

> Thus it would appear that Paul understood Isa 44:3–5 to be an expansion of the Abrahamic promise to include the gift of the Spirit, and this link provides him with the necessary premise to link the promise to Abraham, the incorporation of Gentiles,

---

Spirit, see Schreiner, *Galatians*, 218–19; Starling, "Yes to All God's Promises," 189; Longenecker, *Galatians*, 123. Contra Moo, *Galatians*, 216; and Kwon, *Eschatology*, 108–11. Smith, "Fifth Gospel," 89, also observes the importance of Paul identifying the Spirit with the blessing of Abraham in regard to the promised land: "The full impact of this identification emerges when we read Jacob's blessing of Isaac in Genesis 28:1–4: 'May God Almighty . . . give you and your descendants *the blessing of Abraham* so that you may inherit *the land*.' In other words, Paul, by echoing this patriarchal promise, sees the Holy Spirit as the ultimate referent of the land. Intriguingly, he goes on to speak of the '*fruit* of the Spirit' (Gal. 5:22–23), since this abundant fruitfulness is a harvest of virtues akin to the abundant fertility of the land of promise" (emphasis original). The importance of the fruit of the Spirit (Gal 5:22) in regard to Israel's restoration and the new creation prophecies of Isaiah is explored by Beale, *New Testament Biblical Theology*, 583–88.

106. Williams, "*Promise* in Galatians," 712–20. Williams concludes, "The promise of numerous descendants (alluded to at Gal 3:6) and the promise of the world (cf. 3:16) are both, as well, God's promise of the Spirit" (719).

107. See especially Harmon, *She Must and Shall Go Free*, 146–50, for the allusion of Isa 44:3–5 in Gal 3:14. Cf. Schreiner, *Galatians*, 219; Schreiner, *Paul, Apostle of God's Glory*, 78–79; Pyne, "'Seed,'" 219–20. Pyne discusses the Abrahamic blessings in coordination to the restoration and new covenant promises of the Spirit (218–20), but the implications of this to dispensationalism is not addressed.

108. See Gentry, *Biblical Studies*, 26–33, esp. 32–33. The writing on the hands would be acceptable to gentiles, for tattoos are forbidden by the Torah.

and the gift of the Spirit, and do so in the person of Christ, who is the Servant and the promised seed.[109]

Given the background of Isa 44:3–5 in Gal 3:14, as well as the fact that the Abrahamic covenant promises come to fruition in Christ (Gal 3:15–18), the theological implications are significant. OT Israel has not been replaced by a different people, but Israel as a corporate, national entity is summed up in and through Christ. Christ is the antitypical Israel, the Isaianic servant, the true seed of Abraham, who brings forth the restoration promises of Israel including the blessings to the nations promised to Abraham, the outpouring of the Holy Spirit, and the inheritance of the promised land, which is expanded to include the entire world that awaits the new heavens and earth. Accordingly, the new covenant in its entirety has been ratified in Christ, and thus, the so-called spiritual and territorial dimensions of this covenant cannot be separated from each other in the new age of the Spirit.[110] In addition, with the eschatological Spirit and the Abrahamic covenant having come to pass in Christ, although such promises were originally spoken to Israel and Israel's offspring/descendants but with anticipation of non-Jews being joined to Yahweh and Israel (e.g., Isa 44:1–5; 56:8), Paul teaches that the recipient of the restoration promises is the church. The restoration and new covenant promises (Abrahamic blessings, the Holy Spirit, inheritance) according to Gal 3–4 are not just for Jewish believers, but include gentile believers, for they are on equal footing as Abraham's offspring. They now belong to the Lord (Isa 44:5) because they belong to Christ (Gal 3:29).[111]

---

109. Harmon, *She Must and Shall Go Free*, 148.

110. Contra Ware, "New Covenant," 68–97, who splits the spiritual aspects of the new covenant as being implemented "now" or inaugurated in the church from the physical/territorial aspects, which in their entirety are "not yet" fulfilled to the nation of Israel. Besides a questionable understanding of inaugurated eschatology given this split, Ware misses how Israel is typological of an eschatological, restored Israel through Christ, a position that does not entail "a strict identity of Israel and the church" (92). The prophets already depict gentiles among a restored people of God (e.g., Jer 4:2; 12:14–17; 16:14–18), and the NT authors can naturally apply the new covenant promises to the church due to the work of Christ. See Gentry and Wellum, *Kingdom through Covenant*, 528–66; Wellum, "Beyond Mere Ecclesiology," 195–209; DeRouchie, "Is Every Promise 'Yes'?," 34–44; and note also O'Brien, "New Covenant and Its Perfect Mediator," 13–33. O'Brien observes that the new covenant established by Christ relates to the "territorial" promise in Heb 9:15 as the new covenant is connected to the motif of inheritance which is in turn tied to the old covenant land promise. Therefore, Ware also misses the typological nature of the land promise that is now redirected to the church through the new covenant work of Christ.

111. On this point regarding the link between Isa 44:5 and Gal 3:29, see Harmon, *She Must and Shall Go Free*, 149.

CHRIST JESUS, THE TRUE ISRAEL

Israel-Jesus Typology through Other Sonship Links: Jacob and the Son of Man

Based on the seed theme, it should be recognized that Jacob is typological of Christ as well since he is in the line of Abraham and the Abrahamic promises come to him and are channeled through him. The previous survey of the Abrahamic covenant shows how Jacob fits into the storyline of Scripture. Jacob is important to the identity of Israel as the nation derives its name from him and the twelve tribes of Israel spring forth from him. But beside the larger seed motif of which Jacob is a part, Jacob is also associated with Jesus in a way that again sheds light on the larger Israel-Christ relationship.

Although Jacob is not prominent in the NT aside from his patriarchal role alongside Abraham and Isaac, a crucial link between Jesus and Jacob is manifested in the NT. John 1:47–51 alludes back to an important event in the life of Jacob.[112] The first hint of this arises when Jesus says Nathaniel is "an Israelite in whom there is no deceit" (John 1:47), a characterization that hearkens back to Jacob as he is a deceitful character as is also indicated by his name (Gen 27:35–36). More significantly, in John 1:51 Jesus promises his disciples that they "will see heaven opened, and the angels of God ascending and descending on the Son of Man" (ESV).[113] The allusion to Gen 28:12 of Jacob's vision of a ladder with angels ascending and descending is clear.[114] Jacob's vision and the words of the Lord (Gen 28:13–15) make Jacob realize that the Lord is present (Gen 28:16) so that he gives the place the name "house of God" (Bethel) and "gate of heaven" (Gen 28:17). The sanctuary of Bethel as the place where God revealed himself not just points to the tabernacle and temple, but it was also the location where God meets Jacob to extend the Abrahamic promises to him (Gen 35:10–12). Jesus is telling his disciples that just as "angels ascended and descended on Jacob—a sign of God's revelation and reaffirmation of faithfulness to his promises made to Abraham . . . so the disciples are promised further divine confirmation of Jesus' messianic identity."[115] As the Son of Man, Jesus is none other than the distinctly human and yet divine figure of Dan 7:13, but also, this

---

112. For helpful discussion of typology in John's Gospel in relation to OT themes in terms of fulfillment and replacement, see Carson, "John and the Johannine Epistles," 251–56; Morgan, "Fulfillment in the Fourth Gospel," 155–65, esp. 160–65.

113. Dumbrell, "Israel in John's Gospel," 82, notes that the "climactic title Son of Man in 1:51, after the previously confessed titles, Lamb of God, Messiah (1:41), Son of God, King of Israel (1:49), has in mind the Daniel 7 position of the vindication of Israel by humiliation and suffering."

114. For an in depth study of the intertexuality of John 1:51 with Gen 28 along with other interpretative issues, see Kirk, "Heaven Opened," 237–56.

115. Köstenberger, *John*, 85; cf. Ridderbos, *Gospel according to John*, 93–94. See also

new event, God speaking with the Son of Man, fulfills and replaces the old, God speaking with Jacob at Bethel. The initial event, God speaking with Jacob/Israel at Bethel . . . initiates and anticipates a pattern whereby God speaks to his people at the house of God. The culmination of the pattern comes when the Father in heaven speaks to the Son of Man on earth who is both the true Jacob/Israel and the true house of God.[116]

Similarly, Carson notes that in John 1:51, "Jesus is the new Israel. Even the old Bethel, the old 'house of God,' has been superseded. It is no longer *there*, at Bethel, that God reveals himself, but in Jesus."[117]

John can associate the angels descending upon Jacob, or Israel, with the figure of the Son of Man, identified as Jesus, because both are corporate, representative figures[118] or because Jacob's heavenly vision can be associated with the apocalyptic imagery of one like the son of man coming out of heaven (Dan 7:13).[119] Regardless, the implication is that Jacob was the ancestor, progenitor, and representative of the chosen nation, but now a greater Jacob has arrived with Jesus (cf. John 4:5–6 with 4:11–14). Every Jew honored Jacob/Israel as the father of the twelve tribes, but now Jesus

---

Köstenberger, "John," 429–30.

116. Hoskins, *Jesus as the Fulfillment*, 130–31. John 1:51 is one of many passages in John's Gospel (e.g., 1:14; 2:14–22; 4:19–24; 7:1—8:59; 10:22–39; 11:48–52) that present Jesus as the fulfillment and replacement of the tabernacle and temple. For discussions, see Köstenberger, *Theology of John's Gospel*, 422–35; Beale, *Temple and the Church's Mission*, 192–200; McKelvey, *New Temple*, 75–84; Walker, *Jesus and the Holy City*, 163–75; Salier, "Temple," 121–34.

117. Carson, *John*, 164, emphasis original. Dumbrell, "Israel in John's Gospel," 82, makes a key observation of John 1: "Nathanael, prompted by Andrew's recognition of Jesus as Messiah (v. 41), is the true Israelite and he and the community will see in Jesus the locus of the new revelation of God as Jacob did (Gen 28:10–12). Jesus is thus the consummation of all Israel's eschatological hopes."

118. Kirk, "Heaven Opened," 252, finds that "the significance of Jesus's self-identification with Jacob is that it portrays Jesus as the originator of a New Israel. In answer to [the question of the connection between the Jacob-Jesus nexus and the title Son of Man], the title Son of Man carries the New Israel motif to its *telos*—a New Humanity." Beale astutely links Jacob's role back to Adam, for both are to be fruitful and multiply (Gen 35:10) and both have their temple-building commission (Gen 28:13–15). The Son of Man title also refers back to Adam, and thus with reference to John 1:51, Beale, *Temple and the Church's Mission*, 196, writes, "Christ is affirming that he is the true Adam ('Son of Man [Adam])' and true Israel (e.g., Jacob's seed), and along with this, he may also be affirming that he has finally begun to fulfil successfully the commission of Genesis 1:26–28 and to complete Jacob's earlier small-scale building activity by establishing the true temple and increasing its borders throughout the earth."

119. Köstenberger, *John*, 85. Köstenberger also notes that Jesus states that no one has ever gone into heaven except the Son of Man who came from heaven (John 3:13; cf. 6:53–62).

is God's appointed Messiah, the locus of God's revelation and communication.[120] David Kirk aptly surmises in light of John 1:51, "Jesus, in portraying himself in Jacob's place, does not merely have in view the patriarch as an individual. Just as Jacob represents his descendants before the LORD and gives his name Israel to them, Jesus portrays himself as the representative of a new Israel, a new people of God."[121] Kirk also observes that this episode in John's Gospel resonates with the synoptic accounts of Jesus' baptism and the Jacob-Israel servant theme found in Isa 42:1 and elsewhere (cf. Isa 41:8 and 44:1).[122]

The other important feature of John 1:51 is Jesus' identity as the Son of Man. Throughout the Gospels, the Son of Man title is ubiquitously applied to Jesus (about eighty times). The Son of Man figure is more of a prophetic character given the vision of Dan 7 than a typological pattern, though the title taps into the typological persons and roles of Adam and David.[123] Nevertheless, the christological and eschatological aspects of this title and role have significance for ecclesiology in terms of corporate solidarity.[124] The

---

120. Carson, *John*, 164. It is important to highlight that these themes of Jesus as the new Israel and as the fulfillment of the temple in John's Gospel are crucial for ecclesiology and eschatology. For in these capacities, Jesus is the one whose mission is of universal scope as he brings the nations into the people of God (e.g., John 10:16; 11:51–52) and ushers in the restoration promises involving the Holy Spirit with the temple in the midst of the nations. As Salier, "Temple," 132, notes, with Jesus' statement in John 7:37–39 that he is the one from whom living waters will flow, the prophesied role of the temple with respect to the nations is fulfilled as both Zech 14 and Ezek 47 depict water flowing from the temple beyond Israel to the benefit of the nations. Cf. McKelvey, *New Temple*, 188–92; Köstenberger, *Theology of John's Gospel*, 433–34.

121. Kirk, "Heaven Opened," 251. Dumbrell, "Israel in John's Gospel," 83, has a similar conclusion: "There is no mention of the linking ladder at 1:51, but the heavens are open and thus a new phase in salvation history with the choice of the new community which will embody restored Israel has now begun."

122. Kirk, "Heaven Opened," 251–52.

123. Some scholars do consider the Son of Man title in reference to Jesus as typological, so Ellis, *Old Testament in Early Christianity*, 107–8; and Evans and Novakovic, "Typology," 988.

124. See footnote 95 above. Other treatments of the topic of corporate solidarity include Ellis, *Old Testament in Early Christianity*, 110–12; Holwerda, *Jesus and Israel*, 33–34; Beale, *New Testament Biblical Theology*, 179, 192–93; 395; 652; Wright, *Climax of the Covenant*, 41–55; LaRondelle, *Israel of God*, 64–66; Goldsworthy, *Son of God*, 100–102. See also the discussion of corporate solidarity in relation to the title "Son of Man" in Dempster, *Dominion and Dynasty*, 216; and Scobie, *Ways of Our God*, 348–50. Vlach, "What Does Christ as 'True Israel' Mean," 48, argues that in "the corporate solidarity concept, the 'one' represents the 'many'—the one does not substitute the many." Likewise, see Saucy, "Is Christ the Fulfillment of National Israel's Prophesies?," 24; Saucy, "Israel and the Church," 242–43. This dispensational view is a truncated understanding of corporate solidarity and fails to address the nature and significance of what

background of this title is derived from Dan 7:13–14, which presents the Son of Man as both an individual and as a corporate representative of the covenant community.[125] Dempster notes, "the son of man is a distinct individual, yet intimately associated with the saints of the Most High in the same way that the Israelite king is related to his people."[126] The Son of Man in Dan 7 parallels the Davidic rock of Dan 2:31–45 (cf. Ps 80:15–19), and the royal status and dominion also recalls Gen 1:26–28 (cf. Ps 8:4–8), indicating that the Son of Man is the last Adam (also suggested by the juxtaposition of the four savage beasts who represent four kingdoms in opposition to God). The Son of Man is given dominion and a kingdom that will not be destroyed, all of which the saints of the most high will possess (see Dan 7:18, 22, and 27). John links both Jacob and the Son of Man figures in John 1:51, signaling that Jesus is the fulfiller and locus of God's promises as he is the end goal of Jacob's vision but also the end-time king, the Son of Man, who inaugurates the kingdom of God, which is none other than the prophesied kingdom of Israel. As the NT makes clear, the end-time Adam and Israel has arrived in Jesus with the dawning of the eschatological kingdom—the dominion and the glory prophesied in Dan 7:14 has been given to Christ on account of his suffering, death, and ascension (Matt 26:64; John 12:23; Acts 7:55–56; cf. Eph 1:20–23). However, the saints who possess the kingdom, originally Israel in the context of Dan 7:18 (cf. v. 22, 27), are those who are disciples and followers of Christ. The corporate solidarity works in both directions: Christ sums up Israel in himself and receives and fulfills Israel's promises, ushering in the kingdom by exercising Adamic dominion as the true David,

---

Christ accomplishes in being the recipient and fulfiller of Israel's promises. Moreover, Christ does not just represent Israel, but as the antitypical Israel and last Adam, Jesus is the corporate and covenant head of the one people of God in union with him—the church. It is because Christ fulfills Israel's role and promises that the church is the recipient of Israel's promises. Only the new covenant people of God (Jewish and gentile believers) are in union with Christ and share in his accomplished work. Also, corporate solidarity takes its shape from the typological pattern and is not to be pitted against the type-antitype relationship. Contra Vlach, "Have They Found a Better Way?," 17.

125. For discussion of the Son of Man in Dan 7, see Hamilton, *Typology*, 57–60; Beale, *New Testament Biblical Theology*, 191–99, 393–401, 652–53; Routledge, *Old Testament Theology*, 289–91; France, *Jesus and the Old Testament*, 169–71; Dempster, *Dominion and Dynasty*, 215–17; Schreiner, *King in His Beauty*, 437–39; Wright, *Knowing Jesus*, 148–53; Gladd, *From Adam and Israel to the Church*, 68–69, 100.

126. Dempster, *Dominion and Dynasty*, 216. Beale, *New Testament Biblical Theology*, 193, likewise states, "Such [corporate] representation means that what is true of the representative is true of the represented. In the case of Dan. 7, the interpretative section [(v. 15–28)] refers to the Son of Man as the faithful nation Israel, presumably because he as the individual king of Israel representatively sums up the people in himself." On this point, see also Scobie, *Ways of Our God*, 348.

for he is the Son of Man who receives the kingdom (Dan 7:13), and the church is given and possesses the kingdom through Christ since he is the corporate and covenant head of the body of all believers. Christ's people are the restored Israel, the new humanity because their representative king is the last Adam.[127]

Israel-Christ Typological Pattern Evidenced through Servanthood

Clearly the most prominent Israel-Christ typological relationship is observed through the sonship and seed themes. Nevertheless, other titles and roles of Israel also reveal the typological relationship between Israel and Christ. The servant theme, discussed with respect to Jesus' baptism in Matt 3:16-17 and in consideration of the background of Isaiah in Gal 3, having qualities of both prophetic figure and typological import, has its fulfillment in Jesus Christ. In the OT, the notion of servanthood is interwoven with the development of sonship and kingship along with the prophetic and priestly offices.[128] The theme takes on added dimensions in the prophets with the anticipation of a servant who brings about a new world order as his task has national implications for Israel (return from exile, restoration), but more significantly, his work has an international scope in establishing a new covenant and affecting justice and salvation for the nations. The servant ultimately brings about true servants of the Lord via a new exodus,

---

127. Dodd, *According to the Scriptures*, 118, concludes, "The New Testament use of the title 'Son of Man' for Christ results from the individuation of this corporate conception. 'In Christ,' mankind is delivered and exalted by the visitation of God, and becomes a people of the saints of the Most High." Dodd is incorrect in viewing the Son of Man as purely a corporate figure, but his observation that the church's union with the Son of Man means that it is the saints of the Most High (Dan 7:18, 22, 25, 27) is compelling. Gladd, *From Adam and Israel to the Church*, 69, correctly observes, "The victory of the Son of Man leads to the saints' possessing the kingdom (Daniel 7:22). The saints benefit from the triumph of the new Adam.... According to Daniel 7, the triumphant saints have finally appropriated that same rule over God's enemies through the victory of the Son of Man."

128. For a helpful biblical-theological treatment of servanthood, see Dempster, "Servant of the Lord," 128-78. Dempster links servanthood to Adam (Gen 2:5, 15) and traces the theme through Noah, Abraham (Gen 18:3; and note his obedience in Gen 22.16-18), Israel (Exod 7:16, 26; 8:16; 9:1, 13; etc.), Moses (Num 11-12; Deut 34:5), and particularly the supreme role of David as the servant of the Lord (2 Sam 3:18; 7:5, 8; 1 Kgs 11:13; Pss 18:1; 36:1; 89:3, 20; 1 Chr 17:4, 7), along with the future prophesied Davidic servant of the prophets before devoting the focus to Jesus and the NT. Dempster's analysis also shows how the servant theme develops along the covenants culminating in the new covenant and the ideal, perfect servanthood of Jesus Christ. For servant typology, see Evans and Novakovic, "Typology," 988.

an event unlike Israel's exodus and liberation from Egypt. Despite Israel's miraculous redemption from Egypt, Israel failed to live up to the servanthood to which they were called (e.g., Exod 4:23; 19:5–6). The goal of this survey is to explore the identity and task of the servant as presented in the book of Isaiah and demonstrate how Jesus comprehensively fulfills the Isaianic servant role, and show how the church is made up of true, faithful servants who carry on servant Jesus' mission. The servant theme appears in other prophetic texts regarding Israel's restoration (e.g., Ezek 34:23; 37:25; cf. Jer 30:8–10; 33:21–26),[129] but Isaiah's portrayal is the most developed and important.

The Identity and Mission of the Isaianic Servant

At a most fundamental level, a servant is one who is committed and obedient to their master, and who acts on behalf and with the authority of their master.[130] In the latter chapters of Isaiah (38–66),[131] the servant(s) theme is of paramount importance as the eschatological hopes of Israel's restoration—the comfort and consolation of Israel's return from physical and spiritual exile—are bound up with and accomplished through the servant of the Lord and the figure of one who may be called an "Anointed Conqueror" (Isa 59:20–21; 61:1–3).[132]

---

129. Both Ezek 34:23–24 (cf. 34:11–16) and 37:21–28 predict a time when "David my servant" will shepherd and rule over God's people Israel, a restoration granted "to my servant Jacob" (37:25). The appointment of David, the servant and shepherd king, coincides with the restoration of the nation of Israel which is marked by purity, forgiveness of sins, the pouring out of the Spirit, national unity, and the making of a new covenant (e.g., Ezek 37:26). For discussion of how Jesus fulfills Ezekiel's messianic promises (cf. Mic 2:12–13; Isa 40:10–11; 53:5–6) in John 10 with the flock now comprising the church as Jesus' followers, see Köstenberger, *Theology of John's Gospel*, 500–502; Ridderbos, *Gospel according to John*, 359–64; Wood, "Regathering," 646–49.

130. Goldingay, "Servant of Yahweh," 701.

131. Most scholars structure the latter half of the book of Isaiah by sectioning chapters 40–55 together. However, see Motyer, *Prophecy of Isaiah*, 289; Gentry, *Biblical Studies*, 26–27; and Gentry and Wellum, *Kingdom through Covenant*, 491, for grouping together chapters 38–55 under the heading of "Book of the Servant." Webb, "Zion in Transformation," 69–71, lays out how Isa 36–37 are integrally related to what precedes while chapters 38–39 are closely tied to what follows. Chapters 36–39 function as a pivot, a transition from the Assyrian first half of the book to the Babylonian second half.

132. Motyer, *Prophecy of Isaiah*, 15. Motyer also lists Isa 61:10—62:7; 63:1–6 as referring to the "Anointed Conqueror," but these passages are highly debated. Schultz, "King," 160–62, argues against Motyer's identifying the "Anointed Conqueror" with the king, although he does observe that Isa 61 continues the portrayal of the servant. Others consider Isa 61:1–3 as a fifth Servant Song.

The identity of the servant in the four "Servant Songs" has been the subject of much debate and speculation that cannot be explored here.[133] It is clear though, that alongside the servant named Jacob/Israel in Isaiah (41:8, 9; 42:19; 43:10; 44:1-2, 21, 26; 45:4; 48:20), there is another servant, a faithful servant identified as "Israel" (Isa 49:3), who is anointed by the Spirit to deliver Israel and to be a witness to the nations (Isa 42:1-9; 49:1-13; 50:4-11; 52:13—53:12).[134] The servant is the true Israel (Isa 49:3), for he is not characterized as blind and deaf (42:18-19; 43:8) or disobedient (42:23-24) as the nation, nor is he guilty like national Israel, but rather he is faithful and innocent (50:5-9; 53:9).[135] Moreover, the servant of the Servant Songs is described in individualistic terms (e.g., Isa 49:1-2), and he is to restore Israel and the nations (Isa 42:6-7; 49:5-6), ultimately bringing about true freedom from sin through atonement (53:4-6, 8, 10-12), a task Israel could never do for itself.[136] This agent of redemption cannot be the Persian king

---

133. Interpreters have identified the servant as an individual historic person, collectively a reference for Israel, an ideal servant, or a messianic figure. See Scobie, *Ways of Our God*, 407-9. For a thorough presentation of the proposals of the identity of the servant and bibliography, see Wood, "Regathering," 235-37; cf. Goldingay, "Servant of Yahweh," 703-6; Hugenberger, "Servant of the Lord," 106-19.

134. Dempster, "Servant of the Lord," 155. For a helpful discussion of the servant theme in Isaiah, including the theme's significance beyond the context of the Servant Songs, see Harmon, *Servant of the Lord and His Servant People*, 110-42. Scholars typically identify the first two Servant Songs as comprising of Isa 42:1-4 and 49:1-6, but see Williamson, *Sealed with an Oath*, 159n44, as both 42:5-9 and 49:7-13 unpack the servant's work and mission. Lessing, "Isaiah's Servants in Chapters 40-55," 131, argues that the servant of Isa 42:1-4 is the nation of Israel and that the NT use of this passage as applied to Jesus (Matt 12:18-21) is typological. However, such an interpretation fails, for the servant is too ideal a figure and is presented in sharp contrast to Israel, so Webb, *Message of Isaiah*, 170. Webb suggests that if Israel is in this passage, it is in the bruised reed and smoldering wick of v. 3. Aside from Lessing's treatment of Isa 42, there is a typological relationship present because both servants are called *Israel* and share other titles and functions.

135. Watts, "Consolation or Confrontation?," 51, 53; Gentry, "Atonement," 23; Webb, *Message of Isaiah*, 170. Bright, *Kingdom of God*, 150, writes, "The figure of the Servant oscillates between the individual and the group. In many places throughout the book the Servant is merely Israel (e.g., 41:8; 43:10; 44:21; 45:4), so much so that the prophet can call the Servant blind and deaf (42:19)—because that is exactly what Israel has been. In other places, although the Servant is still identified with Israel (e.g., 49:3), it is clear that he is something other than the visible people, because his first duty (49:5) is to lead Israel itself back to its destiny under God. . . . But at all times the Servant is described in individual terms. And it is clear that sometimes this figure overshoots all that Israel, all that the true Israel, all that any individual in Israel ever was, and becomes a description of an ideal figure. He is the coming Redeemer of the true Israel who in his suffering makes the fulfillment of Israel's task possible; he is the central actor in the 'new thing' that is about to take place." See also Gignilliat, "Servant Follower," 109.

136. Gentry and Wellum, *Kingdom through Covenant*, 494-95. See Motyer,

Cyrus (Isa 41:2; 44:24—45:13) even though he is described as a messiah (45:1). Cyrus's mission is limited to ending Israel's physical exile by releasing them from Babylon (48:14).[137]

Only one figure could be identified with and represent the nation and yet be distinct from Israel, the one who can carry out the servant's task including the sacrifice of his life on behalf of the nation, and that is the Davidic king. Numerous reasons have been offered to justify the servant's identity with a royal messiah: the frequency of the description of David as Yahweh's servant (e.g., 2 Sam 7:5, 8, 26), the fact that the expression "my servant" is used of David in Isa 37:35, the resonances of Isa 42:1-6 with the messianic king of Isa 11:1-5 as both are endowed with the Spirit (Isa 11:2; 42:1; cf. 1 Sam 16:13) and have the task of establishing justice (Isa 11:3-4; 42:1, 4), and finally, many royal images emerge in the presentation of the servant (e.g., Isa 49:7; 52:12-15; 53:9 and note 53:2 with 11:1).[138]

Prophecy of Isaiah, 386. Routledge, *Old Testament Theology*, 292, observes that the "relationship between the Servant and the nation may be indicated by different uses of the term 'Israel' in Isaiah 49:1-6. In verse 3 the Servant is identified *as* Israel; however, in verses 5-6 the Servant also has a mission *to* Israel. This is best explained by taking verse 3 to indicate that the Servant is the embodiment of what Israel was intended to be. God called the nation to be his servant. . . . The nation as a whole failed. . . . Nevertheless God's purposes are kept alive through another Servant, who is all that Israel should be, and through whom Israel will be restored" (emphasis original).

137. Watts, "Consolation or Confrontation?," 51–52, observes that servant terminology is not applied to Cyrus, and the characteristics of the servant seem inapplicable to a military and imperial ruler. See also Webb, *Message of Isaiah*, 181–84; Blocher, *Songs of the Servant*, 24–25, 28, 40; Oswalt, *Isaiah 40–66*, 111. Though to be sure, there are a number of verbal affinities between Cyrus and the servant, so Lim, "*Way of the Lord*" in Isaiah, 74–76, but Cyrus's task is purely political while the servant's leadership is political and spiritual (82–83).

138. Many other reasons have been offered as well. See Block, "My Servant David," 43–55; Treat, *Crucified King*, 70–75; Schultz, "King," 154–59; Routledge, *Old Testament Theology*, 293–94; Dempster, "Servant of the Lord," 154–60; Dumbrell, "Role of the Servant," 108; Gentry, "Atonement," 23–24; Wood, "Regathering," 243–49, 252–58. Block, "My Servant David," 45–55, offers compelling reasons undermining Hugenberger's interpretation that the servant in the Servant Songs is a second Moses. Isaiah focuses on the servant motif largely in the second half of the book (the term only appearing in the first half of Isaiah in 20:3; 22:20; 24:2; 37:35) whereas royal imagery abounds in the first half of the book but is not so explicit in the second half. The Davidic monarchy receives attention in the early chapters of Isaiah in order to contrast the failure of the existing kingship, but solidify that God's purposes will be fulfilled (Isa 9:5-6; 11:1-9). In the second half of Isaiah the disobedient nation Israel, the unfaithful servant, receives the focus and this time the contrast is with an obedient, loyal, divine servant. Isaiah demonstrates that the people of Israel and Israel's king have failed, but one individual is both king and servant who will succeed in establishing Israel's restoration and God's worldwide purposes.

Not only is the servant inextricably linked to the king in the early parts of Isaiah, but the portrait of a third figure (Isa 59:20-21; 61:1-6) is presented in a manner that recalls the servant suggesting that they are the same person.[139] There is pause, for this figure is never called a "servant" and scholars have rightly noted that the servant fades into the background in Isa 56-66 as the singular usage of the term never appears after Isa 53. The attention shifts to the "servants" (Isa 54:17; 56:6; 63:17; 65:8-9, 13; 66:14) who carry on the mission of the servant since he has been vindicated— having successfully completed his work he now sees his offspring (53:10).[140] Nevertheless, the verbal associations are compelling, especially in regard to the figure of Isa 61:1-3. The "Anointed Conqueror" and the servant are both endowed with the Spirit (Isa 42:1; 59:21; 61:1; cf. 11:2), proclaim freedom for the captives (42:7; 61:1; cf. 49:9), announce the favor of the Lord (cf. 49:8; 61:2), are characterized by righteousness (53:11; 61:3, 10; 63:1; cf. 9:7; 11:4), and both have a ministry that envelops Israel and the nations (42:1-4; 49:1-6; 52:12—53:12; 59:20-21 with 60:1-22; cf. 62:11-12).

The mission and task of the servant, as already indicated, needs further elucidation. Isaiah 40:1-11 sets the stage for the work of the servant.[141] The prospect of judgment and the Babylonian exile (Isa 39:5-7) will not be final as God promises comfort and consolation for his people (referred to synonymously as *Jerusalem*; Isa 40:2) as the punishment of her sin is pardoned and forgiven (Isa 40:1-2; cf. 49:13). Israel will be reconstituted as the return from exile is depicted as a new exodus (40:3-5).[142] The call for comfort in

---

139. Motyer, *Prophecy of Isaiah*, 13-16, calls this figure the "Anointed Conqueror." Cf. Webb, *Message of Isaiah*, 233-34; Oswalt, *Isaiah 40-66*, 562-63; Pao, *Acts and the Isaianic New Exodus*, 76-77; Beers, *Followers of Jesus*, 44-45. On the other hand, some argue that the speaker of Isa 61 is the offspring of the servant, so Childs, *Isaiah*, 503.

140. Beuken, "Main Theme," 67-87; cf. Dempster, "Servant of the Lord," 159; Harmon, *Servant of the Lord and His Servant People*, 137, 140-42; Beers, *Followers of Jesus*, 41-44; Fantuzzo, "True Israel's 'Mother and Brothers,'" 106-24. The connection between the servants and offspring of the servant is clear, as Beers, *Followers of Jesus*, 43, observes, "After 56:8 the term 'servants' does not appear until 63:17, but the servants are still a significant theme as is seen through the use of the concept זרע ('seed,' 57.3-4; 59.21; 61.9) and צדקה ('righteous[ness]') along with some related forms in 56.1; 57.1, 12; 58.2, 8; 59.4, 9, 14, 16-17; 60.17, 21; 61.3, 10-11; 62.1-2; 63.1, which are closely connected to the servant figure in chs. 40-53. In 56.9—63.16 the righteous (servants) are a focus, for they withstand oppression as the servant's offspring."

141. Besides commentaries, for helpful overviews of Isa 40:1-11, see Pao, *Acts and the Isaianic New Exodus*, 41, 45-51; Dumbrell, *Search for Order*, 111-13; and Webb, *Message of Isaiah*, 161-64.

142. For discussion, see Anderson, "Exodus Typology in Second Isaiah," 177-95. Anderson lists the following texts with second exodus imagery: Isa 40:3-5; 41:17-20; 42:14-16; 43:1-3, 14-21; 48:20-21; 49:8-12; 51:9-10; 52:11-12; 55:11-13. Hugenberger, "Servant of the Lord," 122-24, rightly notes that the new exodus theme is already

verse 1 begins with the preparation of "the way" in the wilderness (40:3-4; cf. Exod 13:21-22; 23:20) and Yahweh's coming is accompanied by the universal revelation and manifestation of his glory to all mankind (Isa 40:5; cf. 42:4, 23; 49:6; 51:4-6; 52:10). This new exodus not only parallels the exodus from Egypt, but eschatological intensification and expectation is illustrated through the language of geographic transformation and the idea that this surpassing redemption involves Israel and the gentiles.[143] Though the people are frail, the new beginning is secured by God's Word (Isa 40:6-8) for God will come in power and with the tenderness of a shepherd as this good news of restoration goes forth from Jerusalem-Zion (40:9-11; cf. 2:3).

The goals of Isa 40:1-11 for the exiles ultimately come to fruition through the servant. Although Cyrus is responsible for the physical restoration (Isa 41:2; 42:18-43:21; 44:24—48:22) as the people return to the promised land so that Jerusalem and the temple can be rebuilt (44:26-28), the second, more vital stage of spiritual restoration is secured through the servant (Isa 49:1—53:12).[144] His multi-faceted accomplishments resound throughout the rest of the book. The servant of the Lord ushers in the rule of God as the presence of the kingdom emerges through his twofold task to Israel and the world. The restoration and redemption of Israel and the nations concentrates in the servant's mission of proclaiming and establishing justice, but specifically in his suffering and death, which achieves a new covenant and implements the new exodus in bringing about a new Zion comprised of loyal servants from all nations.

First, the task of the servant is characterized by the bringing forth of justice and the proclamation of freedom of sin. The message of hope and grace is extended to Israel and the nations, for the servant not only restores Israel in ending her spiritual estrangement from Yahweh, but he is a "light

---

presented throughout Isaiah (4:2-6; 10:24-26; 11:11, 15-16; 35:5-10; 58:8; 60:2, 19; 63) but also adds to Anderson's analysis by noting other texts with exodus themes (Isa 42:13; 44:27; 54:3, 13).

143. Motyer, *Prophecy of Isaiah*, 300, commenting on Isa 40:5, concludes, "Meditation on the exodus developed the thought that it took place not only before the watching world (*all mankind*/'all flesh') but also for the world (Pss 47; 95-100). This suggests taking *see* in the double sense of observing and experiencing" (emphasis original). See also Ninow, *Indicators of Typology*, 171-72.

144. For this breakdown of Israel's restoration in two stages comprising first of a physical return from Babylon to the land accomplished by Cyrus and then a second stage involving spiritual reconciliation, see Gentry and Wellum, *Kingdom through Covenant*, 491-93; Gentry, "Atonement," 21-24; and DeRouchie, "Counting Stars with Abraham," 465. Schultz, "Isaiah," 340, describes Zion's future restoration in three movements: (1) Israel's return to the land through the political deliverer, Cyrus (Isa 40-48); (2) Israel's spiritual restoration through the suffering servant (Isa 49-57); and (3) Zion's glorification by Yahweh and the nations (Isa 58-66).

for the nations" (Isa 42:6; 49:6) such that God's salvation reaches the ends of the earth (Isa 49:6; cf. 51:5; 60:9).[145] The servant is marked by justice and righteousness like the original David (2 Sam 8:15; 1 Chr 18:14), but in a far greater way he will certainly establish judicial order—a broad concept involving the deliverance of Israel, the revelation of God's truth and salvation, and the state of societal wholeness—in the entire world (Isa 42:1-4; 49:4; cf. 9:7; 11:1-5; Jer 23:5; Ps 72:2).[146] Further, the coastal peoples—the remotest parts of the earth—eagerly wait in hope for the servant's instruction or *torah* (Isa 42:4; cf. 42:10-12; 51:5). Such ideas resonate with Isaiah 2:2-4 where Yahweh teaches the gentile pilgrims "his ways" from Zion, thus indicating that the servant's ministry accomplishes the rule and reign of God in the renewed Mount Zion.[147] The servant's establishment of justice coincides with his work of opening blind eyes, freeing prison captives, and releasing those who sit in darkness (42:7; 49:9-10; 61:1). Along the same lines, Isa 61:1-3 interweaves the task of justice with the message of hope in describing the agent of God's eschatological restoration of Israel, revealing that the servant-Messiah is anointed with the Spirit to bring good news to the poor (cf. 40:9; 52:7-12), bind the brokenhearted, proclaim liberty to the captives (cf. Lev 25:9-13), announce the year of the Lord's favor and the day of his vengeance, and comfort those who mourn (cf. Isa 40:1-2; 42:3; 49:13). The clear allusion to the year of Jubilee in the prophet's vision (Isa 61:1-2; see Lev 25:8-55; cf. Isa 49:8-9), which originally was about the release of slaves, debt, and land tenure in the Mosaic Law, typologically points to a greater Jubilee that the Lord's anointed will usher in.[148] The Lord's favor

---

145. Dempster, *Dominion and Dynasty*, 177, observes that Balaam's rising star (Num 24:17) and Abraham's universal blessing (Gen 12:3) have merged and are echoed in Isa 42:6-7 and 49:5-6. See Bird, "'A Light to the Nations,'" 122-31, esp. 124 as Bird notes the link of Isa 42 to Gen 12:3.

146. For discussion of "justice" (מִשְׁפָּט) in Isa 42:1, 3, 4 see Oswalt, *Isaiah 40-66*, 110-11; Dumbrell, *Search for Order*, 115; Dumbrell, "Role of the Servant," 108-9; Webb, *Message of Isaiah*, 171; Köstenberger and O'Brien, *Salvation to the Ends of the Earth*, 46.

147. Köstenberger and O'Brien, *Salvation to the Ends of the Earth*, 47; Dumbrell, "Role of the Servant," 109-10. The theme of *torah* being dispensed from a renewed Zion with justice as a light to the peoples occurs also in Isa 51:3-5, 7.

148. For discussion of the allusion to the year of Jubilee (Lev 25) in Isa 61:1-2, see Bruno, "Jesus Is Our Jubilee," 92-94; Childs, *Isaiah*, 505; Motyer, *Prophecy of Isaiah*, 500. Bruno, "Jesus Is Our Jubilee," 94, rightly notes, "In Isaiah 61, the Jubilee is seen as a pointer to the eschatological restoration of Israel, when all of God's people will be permanently free from their captivity." The typological and eschatological aspects are also discussed by Wright, *Old Testament Ethics*, 205-6, 209-10, although he stresses more the social and economic angles of the Jubilee. Given the new exodus themes in the near context, the liberty from captivity should be understood primarily metaphorically: the Lord's favor foreshadowed in the Jubilee year points to the new age of salvation

goes beyond the grieving Jews in Zion to all of God's people everywhere (Isa 61:2–3).[149] Webb writes, "Through God's grace they become mighty *oaks displaying the LORD's splendour* ([Isa 61:3]), *priests of the Lord engaged in his service* (6a), and eventual inheritors of all things (6b)."[150]

Second, the servant's task involves being "a covenant for the people" (Isa 42:6; cf. 49:8).[151] God's new covenant work is embodied by the servant who is "the agent and guarantor of God's covenant" to all people, not just Israel.[152] Particularly, the covenant is established by the servant's atoning death which brings forgiveness (Isa 53), a connection that is not explicit in Isaiah, but the intersection of the new covenant and the forgiveness of sins is clear elsewhere (Jer 31:34; cf. Zech 9:11). The "covenant of peace" (Isa 54:10) and the "everlasting covenant" (Isa 55:3; cf. 61:8) are also associated with his successful mission, for Isa 54–55 contains the response to, consequences of, and reality of the servant's restoration of Israel delineated in the fourth Servant Song.[153] Furthermore, all of God's promises, including the previous

---

wrought by the atoning work of the suffering servant.

149. Williamson, *Sealed with an Oath*, 162, notes, "The 'double portion' of blessing (Isa. 61:7) answers to the 'double for all her sins' (Isa. 40:2), the restoration in view here clearly transcends national hopes, incorporating 'all who mourn' and not simply 'those who mourn in Zion' (Isa. 61:2–3)." Further, while the accent is on the nation of Israel as the priests and ministers of the Lord who also enjoy the wealth of the nations (Isa 61:6), the presence of foreigners (Isa 61:5) recalls Isa 56:3 where they too participate in the covenant. The priestly role also extends to foreigners in Isa 56:6–7; 66:21. Lastly, the proclamation of hope and liberty to the captives matches the servant's task to the nations (Isa 42:6–7).

150. Webb, *Message of Isaiah*, 235, emphasis original. Elsewhere, Webb astutely observes that the phrase "oaks of righteousness, the planting of the LORD" alludes back to Isa 6:13. The faithful remnant, the eschatological inhabitants of the new Zion, are the final outgrowth, the holy seed, of the stump. Webb, "Zion in Transformation," 83. Beuken, "Main Theme," 71–72, links the phrase back to Isa 60:21. The servants resemble the servant, the promise of a people wholly righteous is fulfilled.

151. There is little significance in identifying the "people" with the nation Israel as suggested by the immediate context of Isa 49:8 because the "people" in Isa 42:6 is Israel and the nations. The phrase "covenant of the people" in Isa 42:6 is in parallelism with the nations/gentiles ("light for the nations") and these are the exact same worldwide people of v. 5. See Williamson, *Sealed with an Oath*, 160n49; Motyer, *Prophecy of Isaiah*, 322; Kaiser, *Mission in the Old Testament*, 60; contra Oswalt, *Isaiah 40–66*, 118.

152. Williamson, *Sealed with an Oath*, 160. See also Childs, *Isaiah*, 326; Webb, *Message of Isaiah*, 172; Peterson, *Transformed by God*, 40.That it is the new covenant in view is established by the fact that this covenant is a future work of the messianic servant. Also, the other references to *covenant* in Isaiah resonate with the new covenant themes of Jeremiah and Ezekiel. See Gentry and Wellum, *Kingdom through Covenant*, 488; Williamson, *Sealed with an Oath*, 158; cf. Oswalt, *Isaiah 40–66*, 438.

153. Williamson, *Sealed with an Oath*, 160–62; Gentry and Wellum, *Kingdom through Covenant*, 494–504. On the relationship of Isa 54–55 with the preceding

covenants, culminate and have their fulfillment in the new covenant of the servant—the climactic covenant of peace (Isa 54:10)—as suggested by the text as verses 1–3 of Isa 54 recalls the Abrahamic covenant, verses 4–8 echo the Mosaic covenant, verses 9–10 bring the Noahic covenant to the fore, and the Davidic covenant is explicitly referenced in Isa 55:3–4.[154] Clearly the servant's new covenant work extends beyond Israel (cf. Jer 33:9, 22; Ezek 36:36; 37:28), for the Abrahamic family tent is expanded (Isa 54:1–3), and the mercies of this future appointed Davidic ruler, brought about by his righteous and obedient acts, means that the new covenant is extended to all as nations come running to him (55:3–5; cf. 11:10–12; 2 Sam 22:44), thus recalling the servant's role to bring light to the nations (cf. Isa 55:1–2).[155] The priestly, new covenant work of the servant (Isa 53) also brings about a covenantal change as the Lord raises up faithful priests beyond the Aaronic priesthood (Isa 61:6) with gentiles becoming priests and Levites (Isa 66:19–21; see Heb 7:11–22; 1 Pet 2:9; Rev 1:6, 5:9–10).[156]

Furthermore, not only is the scope of the new covenant significant in ranging beyond the nation Israel, but so also is the nature of the community who benefit and are transformed by it. First, with the background of the covenant of peace, Isa 54:13 states that all the children of the rebuilt Zion (Isa 54:11–12) will be taught by the Lord.[157] The children are the servant's

---

Servant Song, see Oswald, *Isaiah 40–66*, 413–14; Motyer, *Prophecy of Isaiah*, 443–44. Webb, *Message of Isaiah*, 214, highlights that *peace* is the key that links Isa 54–55 together with Isa 53. The new age of peace has dawned by the sin-bearing atonement of the servant-messiah (Isa 53:5) as the realization of this peace is the reason for the joyful celebration (54:1; 55:12–13).

154. For this observation and conclusion, see Williamson, *Sealed with an Oath*, 161; see also Gentry and Wellum, *Kingdom through Covenant*, 495–500. Isaiah 51 also projects the future salvation as fulfilling the Abrahamic (51:2–3) and Mosaic covenants (51:4–7), and indirectly the Davidic covenant as well given the thematic links of "justice" and "Zion" to a Davidic king. See House, *Old Testament Theology*, 289–90.

155. Dempster, "Servant of the Lord," 160, writes, "By [the perfect Davidic servant-king's] righteous deeds, his mercies, a covenant can be made with everyone, thereby allowing them to experience the benefits of the covenant. This fact fulfils the Davidic hope and, as the text says, this new David continues in the train of David: he is appointed a witness to the peoples to bring light to the nations (55:4–5)." See also Williamson, *Sealed with an Oath*, 179. For understanding the "sure mercies of David" as a subjective genitive, see Dempster, "Servant of the Lord," 159–60; Gentry and Wellum, *Kingdom through Covenant*, 464–75; Gentry, "Rethinking the 'Sure Mercies of David,'" 279–304.

156. See Hamilton, *Typology*, 77–78 for a helpful discussion of the expansion of priesthood beyond the nation of Israel in Isa 61:6 and Isa 66:19–21.

157. Jesus teaches that all who come to him are drawn to him by the Father (John 6:37–45). Jesus paraphrases Isa 54:13 in John 6:45 in support of his claim that those who learn and are taught by the Father come to him. According to Carson, *John*, 293, the "passage [of Isa 54:13] is here applied typologically: in the New Testament the

offspring (Isa 53:10), those counted righteous, and these children are related to the servant as they are described as "servants" (54:17) since they follow in his footsteps in enduring affliction as he did (54:11 with 53:4), but they also enjoy the same vindication that he received (54:17 with 50:8).[158] Everyone in this renewed city of Zion know the Lord, and this matches the new covenant prophecy of Jer 31:33–34 where God writes the law on the hearts of his people as all in this covenant community know him and experience the forgiveness of sin.[159] Moreover, this future covenant community is now marked by covenant faithfulness as Williamson has pointed out from Isa 56:1–8, a passage that explicitly refers to the foreigners as the Lord's "servants" (Isa 56:6):

> This opening pericope (Isa. 56:1–8) addresses the scope of this new covenant community. Clearly it is both inclusive and exclusive; inclusive in that it incorporates foreigners and eunuchs (Isa. 56:3), but exclusive in that the covenant community only includes those who "hold fast to the covenant" (Isa. 56:5–6), which seems to mean maintaining covenant obligations (Isa. 56:1–2). The singling out of sabbath-keeping for particular

---

messianic community and the dawning of the saving reign of God are the typological fulfillments of the restoration of Jerusalem after the Babylonian exile." Cf. Peterson, *Transformed by God*, 179–80.

158. Webb, *Message of Isaiah*, 216; cf. Beers, *Followers of Jesus*, 42.

159. Gentry and Wellum, *Kingdom through Covenant*, 498–99. Significantly, O'Brien, "New Covenant and Its Perfect Mediator," 19, writes, "Jeremiah's prophecy envisages not simply a national knowledge of God, but a personal knowledge.... God promised that *every member of the covenant community would know him directly and personally*, 'from the least of them to the greatest'—the result of his writing his laws on each heart or, as Ezekiel put it, because each would be given a new heart and spirit by God. The expression, 'they shall not teach, each one his neighbour,' is not a rejection of teaching or leadership but a powerful affirmation of the universality of this unmediated knowledge of God. The emphatic words, 'they shall all know me,' demonstrate this" (emphasis added). Against dispensationalism, the "all" of Jer 31:34 who know the Lord, described as the house of Israel and Judah, speaks beyond a reunified northern and southern kingdom and typologically points to the restored remnant which includes representatives of the nations as indicated by the wider context of Jeremiah (3:17; 12:16; 16:19–21). Against covenantalism, the "all" who have knowledge of the Lord includes the whole covenant community and does not await the consummated state or merely refer to the democratization between prophet/priest and people in terms of mediation. The whole faithful remnant will know the Lord because their sins are forgiven, and the NT identifies the church as knowing the Lord, being taught by God, experiencing peace, and receiving forgiveness (see e.g., Heb 10:19–25; 1 Thess 4:9; 1 John 2:20, 27). For other thorough treatments of Jer 31:31–34, see Gentry and Wellum, *Kingdom through Covenant*, 536–563; Wellum, "Beyond Mere Ecclesiology," 196–202; Peterson, *Transformed by God*, 29–35; Shead, "New Covenant and Pauline Hermeneutics," 33–49.

emphasis (cf. Isa. 56:2-3, 6) probably reflects that the root of the matter is a life made up of worship in every part; keeping sabbath is the positive counterpart to avoiding evil, and both are an expression of worship. Thus in answer to the implied question "Who is included in the new covenant community?," this passage answers, "Everyone who gives expression to a genuine relationship with God."[160]

The inclusion of the nations in the covenant community in Isa 56 recalls other OT passages (Isa 19:24-25; 66:19-21; cf. Ps 87; Zech 2:10-12) where the future reconstituted new Israel consists of a remnant "made up of the faithful of Israel . . . as well as those from other nations who have, similarly, put their trust in Israel's God."[161] Lastly, Isaiah communicates that the future coming redeemer, identified as the servant, is the means by which the divine Spirit and word are shared with the repentant in Zion (Isa 59:20-21) and implicitly the worldwide community (Isa 59:19).[162] Motyer explains,

160. Williamson, *Sealed with an Oath*, 163; cf. Gentry and Wellum, *Kingdom through Covenant*, 500-4; Webb, "Zion in Transformation," 79; Routledge, "Replacement or Fulfillment?," 149; Schnabel, "Israel, the People of God," 41. On Isa 56, Beale, *New Testament Biblical Theology*, 659-60, rightly highlights how gentiles and Israelite eunuchs are identified with Israel, participate in temple worship (not possible under the Mosaic covenant), and how the gentile proselytes become ministering priests, a role originally preserved for the tribe of Levi. However, Beale does not address how this universal people who arise out of the eschatological work of the servant are marked by obedience and are clearly faithful covenant keepers (56:4, 6). On the other side, Thomas, "Mission of Israel," 266, wrongly limits the plural "servants" to references of Israel (Isa 54:17; 56:6; 63:17; 65:8-9, 13-15; 66:14). Not only does this not fit the context of Isa 56:6, but the servants and offspring of the servant expand to include all those who belong to him. See Beuken, "Main Theme," 67-87; DeRouchie, "Counting Stars with Abraham," 465-69.

161. Routledge, "Replacement or Fulfillment?," 150, cf. 144-49. For discussion of Isa 19:24-25; 66:19-21; Ps 87; and Zech 2:10-12; see Beale, *New Testament Biblical Theology*, 657-63; Gentry and Wellum, *Kingdom through Covenant*, 505-9, 512-16; Gladd, *From Adam and Israel to the Church*, 53-54, 71-72; cf. Schnabel, "Israel, the People of God," 39-42. In these texts, gentiles are considered true eschatological Israelites. See also the study of Sherwood, *Paul and the Restoration of Humanity*, which examines several texts (e.g., 1 Kgs 8:41-43; Isa 2:2-4; Isa 56-66; Pss 46-48; Zech 8:18-23; Mal 4:1-4; along with Second Temple and Pauline traditions) that reference the Israel-nations unification and look forward to the new creation and the restoration of humanity as the division between Israel and non-Israelites is overcome.

162. Isa 59:20-21 concludes the chapter that is specifically focused on Israel's sin (59:1-8), their confession and repentance (59:9-15a), and their redemption and vindication through God's justice and righteousness (59:15b-20). Motyer, *Prophecy of Isaiah*, 492-93, links the covenant of Isa 59:21 back to the covenants of Isa 42:6; 49:8; 54:10; 55:3. He finds that the recipients of the covenant through the servant are the penitent of Zion, but implicitly the gentiles as well based on Isa 59:19 and given the focus on the nations streaming to Zion in Isa 60. Childs, *Isaiah*, 490, also concludes

"Like the Servant (53:10), those to whom he secures these covenantal blessings are his 'seed.'"[163] The promise of the Holy Spirit with the servant's new covenant work coordinates with other OT texts where the restoration prophecies to Israel underscore the coming of the Spirit (Ezek 36:27; 37:14; 39:29; Zech 4:6; 12:10; Joel 2:28–32; cf. Isa 32:15; 44:3–4).[164] The portrait Isaiah paints is the Messiah reigning over a restored and redeemed Zion community in the new covenant era.

A third and final task associated with the servant, one that is interwoven with the other tasks, is the new exodus deliverance he brings about. Aside from the servant, the central and controlling theme of Isa 40–55 is the new exodus.[165] This second exodus is the eschatological paradigm of redemption (Isa 40:10; 43:1–3; 49:8–12; 51:9–11; 52:10–12), re-creation (Isa 41:17–20; 51:3; 55:12–13), and it is bound up with the pilgrimage theme as the redeemed are gathered to God's holy mountain in Zion (51:11; 52:7–12; 56:6–8; 57:14; 60:4–7; 62:10; 66:20–23; cf. Exod 3:12; 15:17).[166] As

---

regarding Isa 59:21: "The term *covenant* occurs infrequently in Third Isaiah, but in v. 21 seems obviously linked to its programmatic occurrence in 56:5–6, addressed to God's servants who join themselves to him. The effect is to summarize and to interpret the whole section comprising chapters 56–59" (emphasis original).

163. Motyer, *Prophecy of Isaiah*, 493. Likewise, Beuken, "Main Theme," 70, on Isa 59, comments that in "a confession they speak repentantly (from v. 9 on), acknowledge their lack of 'righteousness' (vv. 4, 9, 14) and then, when God's 'righteousness' comes to help (vv. 16f.), they are converted (v. 21). All this happens in terms referring to the servant (cf. v. 9 with 50.10 and v. 21 with 42.1; 51.16)." Also, the reference to "offspring" that goes until the third generation (Isa 59:21) is framed in terms of faithfulness, for these offspring testify to the covenant and share in the Spirit of the Lord.

164. See Routledge, "Spirit and the Future in the Old Testament," 346–67.

165. Watts, "Exodus," 483; Watts, *Isaiah's New Exodus in Mark*, 79–80; and see the sources listed in footnote 142 above.

166. Hamlin, "Deutero-Isaiah's Reinterpretation of the Exodus," 75–80, observes that in the Exodus accounts, the Hebrew word אֶרֶץ ("earth") prominently refers to the promised land, but in Isa 40–55 the term, appearing no less than 40 times, nearly always has a universal sense of the whole created earth (76) which leads to the conclusion that Isaiah "is particularly interested in the restoration of the earth as the living space and place for all nations" (77). Such analysis challenges yet again the dispensational tenet that Israel's restoration as a future event requires the return to the promised land. For example, Vlach, "What Does Christ as 'True Israel' Mean," 50, argues that the servant, Jesus, "will also restore Israel to her land (Isa 49:8)" (cf. Thomas, "Mission of Israel," 267). However, Isa 49:8 is connected to a greater Jubilee in the future ("time of favor"; cf. Isa 61:2–3), but furthermore, the establishment of the land within the immediate context (Isa 49:8–13) hints of something more (vv. 12–13). This text points to a new Joshua who brings about a greater exodus (see Gentry, "Atonement," 38). With this new exodus there is a restructuring of the people of God. As Webb, *Message of Isaiah*, 195, observes, there is a "metamorphosis" of the people of God in Isa 49:7–13: "The accent does not fall on the return of the physical remnant from Babylon, or even on their

Hugenberger has observed, new exodus imagery is found in the immediate contexts of the Servant Songs (Isa 41:17–20; 42:13–16; 48:20–22; 49:8–12; 50:2–3; 52:10–12), which suggests that the presence and task of the future Davidic servant is closely associated with this greater exodus and the goal of God's kingdom reign.[167] But that the suffering servant is the agent of the new exodus is abundantly clear from Isa 52:13—53:12. Like the original exodus, the arm of the Lord (Isa 53:1; 52:10; cf. 40:10–11; 51:9–11; Exod 6:6; 15:6) is the delivering instrument of the people, and this is accomplished by no other than the servant.[168] Moreover, the atoning and sacrificial work of the servant (Isa 53:4–12), which he endures as a silent lamb (53:7), evokes the Passover (Exod 12:3–14), Moses' intercession for Israel's sin (Exod 32:30–34), the Levitical sacrificial system (Lev 5–7), and the annual day of atonement (Lev 16:1–25).[169] The greater exodus accomplished by the suffering servant is not just for the remnant of Israel though. The servant's priestly and substitutionary atoning work encompasses the nations as he sprinkles the nations (Isa 52:15; cf. Exod 29:4; Lev 4:6; 14:7) who are certainly among the "many" (Isa 53:11–12) counted righteous and included in his offspring (53:10).[170] Although the relationship between Israel and the nations in Isa 40–55 is complex, Israel's eschatological restoration reveals that "God will grant foreign nations the status of a 'people of God' when the servant of the Lord accomplishes his will; God will grant everyone who worships him in the last days the full privileges of his people."[171]

---

spiritual restoration to the LORD, but on the mission to the gentiles that will flow from it. The *shout* of praise, then, in verse 13, is the 'Hurrah!' of mission accomplished—a cause of rejoicing to the whole earth. But by the time we reach that point the theme of 'comfort for the people of God' is no longer narrowly on the captives in Babylon. They may be its most immediate point of reference, but it reaches beyond them to embrace all people. And the key to all this is the Servant of the LORD" (emphasis original).

167. Hugenberger, "Servant of the Lord," 126–28. On the relationship between the new exodus and reign of God in Isa 40–55 (cf. Exod 15:1–8; Isa 40:9–11; 52:7), see Treat, *Crucified King*, 76.

168. Watts, "Exodus," 483; Treat, *Crucified King*, 78–79.

169. For discussion, see Gentry, "Atonement," 36; Motyer, *Prophecy of Isaiah*, 422–43; Jeffery et al., *Pierced for Our Transgressions*, 52–61.

170. For further elucidation and rationale as to why the first common plural pronouns in Isa 53 includes an adopted remnant from the nations, see DeRouchie, "Counting Stars with Abraham," 468–69; cf. Gentry, "Atonement," 43. House, *Old Testament Theology*, 290, finds that both nations and Israelites are included in Isa 53 given both are promised light (Isa 9:2–7; 49:6; 50:10–11).

171. Schnabel, "Israel, the People of God," 42. There is significant debate regarding the nations in Isa 40–55. On the one hand there is a universalistic concern for the nations as they enjoy salvation and entry into Zion (Isa 42:10–12; 45:14, 22; 49:6; 51:4–5; 55:5; cf. 56:6–7; 60:3, 6–9; 66:18–19), but on the other hand there is a particularistic

The Isaianic Servant and Mission: Fulfilled in the NT

As the NT makes abundantly clear, Jesus Christ is the prophesied new David and the eschatological servant envisioned in the book of the Isaiah.[172] The portrayal of Jesus as the Isaianic servant permeates throughout the Gospels and the epistles (e.g., Matt 12:18-21; Luke 22:37; Acts 3:13, 26; 8:28-37; 2 Cor 5:14-21; Phil 2:7; 1 Pet 2:21-25; Heb 9:28; Rev 5:6).[173] Yet, Isaiah had presented Israel as God's servant, but the eschatological, messianic servant was also called "Israel" (Isa 49:3), even possessing identical titles and ascriptions of servant Israel.[174] The servant is the embodiment of what Israel was meant to be. The only plausible way to make sense of this is through the principle of corporate solidarity tied to covenantal headship as seen with the cases of sonship, Abraham's true seed, and more broadly through the notion of kingship.[175] Further, even though the Isaianic servant

---

outlook for Israel as the nations are judged or subjugated under Israel (Isa 40:15-17; 41:11-12; 43:3-4; 44:9-20; 45:14; 49:22-26; 51:22-23; cf. 59:18; 60:10-14; 63:3; 66:16). For an overview of the relationship of Israel to the nations in the book of Isaiah, see Oswalt, "Nations in Isaiah," 41-51; Schultz, "Nationalism and Universalism in Isaiah," 122-44; and Watts, *Isaiah's New Exodus in Mark*, 319-22. For specific discussions and proposals for the relationship between Israel and the nations in Isa 40-55, see Winkle, "Relationship of the Nations," 446-58; Grisanti, "Israel's Mission to the Nations in Isaiah 40-55," 39-61; Pao, *Acts and the Isaianic New Exodus*, 218-27; Okoye, *Israel and the Nations*, 129-43; Watts, "Echoes from the Past," 505-8. Gignilliat, "Servant Follower," 107-8, observes, "A web of complexities arises as we deal with nationalism vs. universalism (or universalism vs. particularism) in Isaiah; although, the inherently universalistic outlook of Isaiah 40-66, especially as one enters into the vision of the new heavens and the new earth in Isaiah 65, becomes more persuasive in light of the overall movement of the book."

172. For discussion of the servant theme in the NT, see Dempster, "Servant of the Lord," 165-77; Blocher, *Songs of the Servant*, 9-18; Schreiner, *New Testament Theology*, 265-68, 295-97. See also Routledge, "Replacement or Fulfillment?," 147-51; Bruce, *This Is That*, 83-99.

173. Cf. the previous discussion as Jesus' identity as the servant converges with the theme of sonship and the Abrahamic seed. For the explicit citations of Isa 53 in Luke 22:37; Matt 8:17; John 12:38; Rom 10:16; Acts 8:32-33; and 1 Pet 2:20-25, see Jobes, "'He Bore Our Transgressions,'" 92-105; cf. Litwak, "Use of Quotations from Isaiah 52:13—53:12," 385-94; Stuhlmacher, "Isaiah 53 in the Gospels and Acts," 147-62. For a helpful discussion of the early Christian reading of Isa 40-55 in Phil 2:6-11, the book of Revelation, and the Gospel of John, see Bauckham, *Jesus and the God of Israel*, 33-51. For allusions to the servant narratives (especially Isa 53) in 2 Cor 5:14-21, see Gignilliat, "Servant Follower," 115-21.

174. Kaiser, *Mission in the Old Testament*, 57, lists the individual servant and servant Israel sharing the title of "my chosen" (Isa 42:1 and 41:8-9), and both are called from the womb (49:1 and 44:2, 24; 43:1).

175. For discussion of this point, see Routledge, *Old Testament Theology*, 292; Blocher, *Songs of the Servant*, 40-42; Webb, *Message of Isaiah*, 193-94; Childs, *Isaiah*,

is a prophetic and eschatological figure fulfilled and realized in Christ, a typological pattern is also present. The OT most frequently describes Moses and especially David (and the kings) with servant terminology, but the nation of Israel stands within that trajectory (e.g., Deut 10:12; Luke 1:54) as do the patriarchs (e.g., Gen 26:24; Exod 32:13; Deut 9:27). All of these servants, but particularly Israel given Isaiah's concentration on the nation as the Lord's servant, pointed forward to a faithful, victorious, suffering servant—a servant who would be far greater as he receives divine affirmation, is highly exalted (Isa 52:13), and does the unique work of bearing the sins of others in justifying the many (Isa 53:4-6, 10-12). The prophecy of the servant and the typological pattern of servanthood culminate in Jesus Christ (Acts 3:13, 26; 4:27, 30; cf. Luke 1:69; Heb 3:5-6).

The NT discloses how Jesus carries out the eschatological tasks of the servant as well. The Gospels present the coming of Jesus as the announcement of good news to Israel: in Jesus the forgiveness of sins, the end of exile, the restoration of Israel, and the arrival of the kingdom of God commence. For example, the prologue of the Gospel of Mark (1:1-3) announces the good news (cf. Isa 40:9-11; 52:7; 61:1-2) of Jesus, identifying him as both Christ and Son of God, which evokes royal messianic hopes and telegraphs the onset of the kingdom of God (Mark 1:15).[176] Furthermore, Mark cites Isa 40:3 with a fusion of other texts (Exod 23:20 and Mal 3:1) in verses 2 and 3 that not only highlight the pivotal role of John the Baptist (1:4) in fulfillment of Isaiah's promise of a coming herald who prepares the way of Yahweh in the wilderness, but Mark's citation also introduces God's deliverance of Israel through the power of Jesus. This deliverance is none other than the end of exile through a new exodus whereby God leads his people through the wilderness—their captivity to nations and to sin—back to Zion.[177] Mark's prologue sets the stage in revealing that the Isaianic servant and his work (surveyed earlier in the context of the book of Isaiah) come to fruition in Jesus. The fulfillment of the servant's roles (bringing justice, implementing the new covenant, and accomplishing the new exodus) in Jesus' life and death will be briefly explored.

First, as was sketched earlier, the Isaianic servant has a task of restoring Israel, bringing justice to the nations, and proclaiming the message of salvation. Jesus fulfills the servant's tasks through his ministry of preaching,

---

383-85; Oswald, *Isaiah 40-66*, 291; Moore, "Lucan Great Commission," 59-60; cf. Beale, *New Testament Biblical Theology*, 416.

176. See Vickers, "Mark's Good News of the Kingdom of God," 12-35.

177. Watts, *Isaiah's New Exodus in Mark*, 79-82, 86-90, 134-35; Hays, "Canonical Matrix," 56-58; Hays, *Reading Backwards*, 20-21; Garland, *Theology of Mark's Gospel*, 203-7.

healing, and climactically, in bearing the sins of his people on the cross (Matt 1:21). The Lucan infancy narratives announce that the consolation and restoration of Israel has arrived with the birth of Jesus (Luke 2:25-32; cf. 1:54; Isa 40:1; 49:13; 61:2).[178] His advent is for the glory of Israel and manifests God's salvation in the presence of all peoples (cf. Luke 2:10). The servant's and Israel's commission to the nations (Isa 49:6-9; 42:6-7; cf. 43:10, 12; 44:8) is accomplished by Jesus, for he is the light of the nations according to Luke 2:32 and Acts 26:23 (cf. Luke 1:78-79; John 1:4; 8:12; 9:5; 12:46).[179] Further, Matthew records (4:12-17) that the people dwelling in darkness have seen a great light in fulfillment of Isa 9:1-2 (cf. 42:6) based upon Jesus' preaching the message of the kingdom in Capernaum, the territory of Zebulun and Naphtali. Also, in the context of his healing ministry Matthew cites Isa 42:1-4 in Matt 12:18-21 in terms of fulfillment.[180] The good news that Jesus announces and his accompanying mighty deeds—exorcisms, feedings, and healings (Luke 7:21-23; Matt 11:4-7)—point to the dawning of the new creation, signifying that the promised era of salvation has arrived. This is also seen in Luke's record of Jesus' citation of Isa 61:1-2 and 58:6 in the synagogue at Nazareth (4:16-21) that again points to Israel's restoration and end of spiritual captivity and exile. The audience in the synagogue learns that very day (Luke 4:21) that the prophecy of an anointed servant who is filled with the Spirit to proclaim good news to the poor, liberty to the captives, sight to the blind, and who pronounces the arrival of the eschatological Jubilee year (Luke 4:19; Lev 25:8-10) is coming to pass in the person and work of Jesus.[181] Lastly, the Isaianic servant's task of bringing

---

178. Köstenberger and O'Brien, *Salvation to the Ends of the Earth*, 112-14; cf. Bauckham, "Restoration of Israel," 455-57. Dumbrell, *Search for Order*, 210 (cf. 208-9), commenting on infancy narratives as a prologue to Luke-Acts, writes, "The canticles, the three hymns in Luke 1-2, disclose the theme of the two books: the promise of Israel's restoration is fulfilled in Jesus, the consummation of Old Testament expectations."

179. See Moore, "Lucan Great Commission," 47-48; Beale, *New Testament Biblical Theology*, 683-84; and for a brief discussion of the OT theme and background of light in John's Gospel, see Köstenberger, *Theology of John's Gospel*, 166-67, and Peterson, *Transformed by God*, 172-73. Beers, *Followers of Jesus*, 94-97, also observes how Simeon's comment in Luke 2:34 regarding the rising and fall of many in Israel is tied to the Isaianic servant since he causes division and is rejected by many according to Isa 50 and 53.

180. Dempster, "Servant of the Lord," 167; Schreiner, *New Testament Theology*, 173; Köstenberger and O'Brien, *Salvation to the Ends of the Earth*, 95. For parallels between Jesus' healings and feedings in the Gospel of Mark in relation to Isaiah, see Watts, *Isaiah's New Exodus in Mark*, 169-79.

181. Peterson, *Transformed by God*, 51, writes, "Jesus claims to have been anointed by the Spirit for the prophetic task of announcing the promised restoration of Israel and bringing it into effect." For further discussion on Luke 4:16-21, see Hays, "Liberation of

justice to the nations involved issuing God's instruction or law. The Gospels present Jesus as the new law giver. For instance, Dempster writes,

> The Sermon on the Mount is a new Torah by a new Servant of God who transcends Moses. In effect, Jesus says, "Moses said one thing then, but *I* now say to you . . ." This would suggest a radically new Torah proclaimed by the Servant of Isaiah 42, which will ultimately bring light to the nations.[182]

Second, the servant was prophesied to be a covenant for the people, a covenant that is intertextually linked to the new covenant prophecies of Jer 31 and Ezek 36 and that is implemented through a suffering servant who sprinkles the nations (Isa 52:15; cf. Exod 24:8; Lev 4:6, 17), is pierced for the transgressions of others, bears the iniquities of others by becoming a guilt offering, but who brings healing, peace, and makes the many righteous (Isa 53). According to the NT, the new covenant is ratified by Jesus' death on the cross (Matt 26:28; Mark 14:24; Luke 22:20; Rom 11:27; 1 Cor 11:25; Heb 7:22; 8:6–13; 9:15–18; 10:14–22; 12:24; 13:20). Jesus came to "give his life as a ransom for many" (Mark 10:45; cf. Isa 53:10–12) so that the blood of the covenant (cf. Exod 24:8) is "poured out for many" (Mark 14:24; Matt 26:28; cf. Isa 53:12).[183] Hebrews 9:28 also recalls Isa 53 in the context of the new covenant (Heb 9:15) and with regard to Christ's priestly ministry as the author states that Christ has been offered to bear the sins of many (cf. Isa 53:6, 12 LXX).[184] As the one who embodies the covenant and ratifies it through his atoning death on the cross, there is confirmation yet again that Jesus is the true Israel, the servant *par excellence*.

The servant's role as a covenant for the people (Isa 42:6), as was already discussed, extends beyond national Israel as does those who benefit from his effectual, vicarious, and sacrificial death (52:15—53:12). What Isaiah

---

Israel," 107–9; Dumbrell, *Search for Order*, 211–13; Köstenberger and O'Brien, *Salvation to the Ends of the Earth*, 116–17; Fuller, *Restoration of Israel*, 236–39; Bruno, "Jesus Is Our Jubilee," 95–99; Turner, *Power from on High*, 249–51. The present eschatological fulfillment is highlighted in Luke's narrative (Luke 4:16–30), although the omission of "the day of vengeance" from Isa 61:2b indicates that God's judgment is not yet. On this point, see Schreiner, *New Testament Theology*, 55–56.

182. Dempster, "Servant of the Lord," 166–67, emphasis original.

183. For the influence of Isa 53 on Mark 10:45 and 14:24, see Garland, *Theology of Mark's Gospel*, 174–76, 478; and France, *Gospel of Mark*, 419–21, 571–72. Note also Watts, "Jesus' Death, Isaiah 53, and Mark 10:45," 125–51.

184. For discussion of the background of Isa 53 in Heb 9:28, see O'Brien, *Letter to the Hebrews*, 341; Schreiner, *Hebrews*, 287; and Hahn, "Broken Covenant and the Curse of Death," 433. Hahn also notes the allusions to Isa 53:12 in Heb 9:12, 15, as well as other keyword connections between Isa 53 and Heb 9. See also Hoskins, *That Scripture Might Be Fulfilled*, 134–35.

anticipated receives clarity in the progress of revelation: the "many" whom the servant atones for and the "people" for whom he is a covenant for is the church since Jesus Christ, as the prophesied Isaianic servant and the one who fulfills his eschatological tasks, secures the salvation of those who belong to him. The NT authors understand the new covenant with reference to the messianic community only, those united to Christ by faith, because Isaiah and the other prophets projected a redefined Israel, an eschatological, transnational people of God in coordination with the future coming of the Davidic messiah (e.g., Isa 55:3–5; see the earlier discussion of the nations in Isaiah).

Moreover, the new covenant work of the suffering servant converges with and is inseparable from the themes and typological patterns of the Passover, the sacrificial system, and priesthood (e.g., 1 Cor 5:7; John 1:29, 36; 19:36; 1 Pet 1:19; Heb 5:5–10; 7:12—8:6; 9:11—10:22). The sacrificial observances and the application of the priestly office in the OT were always carried out with reference to the covenant community only (the nation of Israel).[185] Similarly, the servant's atoning work in establishing the new covenant is with respect to only the church since the church is the new covenant community made up of believing Jews and gentiles. Comprised of true disciples of Christ, the church is the sole beneficiary of Christ's sacrificial death and priestly mediation (Eph 5:25; John 17:6–19). The qualitative advance of these typological patterns (Passover, sacrifices, priesthood, tabernacle-temple) is that the atoning death of the servant is far superior than the system established under the old covenant (Heb 7:23–28; 9:11–15; 10:10–12, 14; cf. Rom 8:32–34) because it definitively brings about the forgiveness of sins. Further, Jesus' death ratifies the new covenant completely and effectively which establishes the creation of an expanded covenant community (from national, ethnic Israel to an international, multi-ethnic community—the church) and results in the change to the structure and nature of this new community as all under this new covenant know the Lord, have the forgiveness of sins, and possess the gift of the Holy Spirit.[186] What was anticipated in the OT has been confirmed and brought to completion in the NT. New covenant believers, confident in the finished work of Christ as their great high priest, draw near with true hearts full of assurance, hearts "sprinkled

---

185. See Wellum, "New Covenant Work of Christ," 517–39.

186. For analysis of the new covenant in regard to the shifts in its structure and nature, consult Carson, "Evangelicals, Ecumenism, and the Church," 358–67; Carson, *Showing the Spirit*, 150–58; Wellum, "Beyond Mere Ecclesiology," 195–202; Wellum, "New Covenant Work of Christ," 535–37. Cf. also footnote 159 in this chapter. See especially Peterson, *Transformed by God*, 82–83, on the definitive forgiveness of sins, perfecting a people for himself, in the new covenant sacrifice of Christ.

clean from an evil conscience" and "bodies washed with pure water" (Heb 10:22; cf. Exod 24:6–8; Ezek 36:25; Isa 52:15). The greatness of the suffering servant's atoning sacrificial death entails then an escalation in the people of God. The covenant community under his headship and representation is greater than national Israel in the sense that it is an international community that enjoys the complete forgiveness of sins through Christ's once and for all death, and is characterized entirely by a Spirit-filled, faithful, regenerate people who have circumcised, Torah-inscribed hearts (Rom 2:29; 2 Cor 3:3, 16–18; Col 2:11; Phil 3:3). In sum, Jesus fulfills the servant-Israel's mission by his atoning death (Isa 53; cf. Rom 4:23–25; 8:32; Gal 1:4), a work that brings about the cleansing and restoration of Israel, a restoration that pointed to a renewed eschatological Israel made up of true and faithful servants (e.g., Isa 56:1–8; see further treatment later in this study). Therefore, Jesus does not restore the nation of Israel in order to bless the nations in the future millennium and beyond; he accomplishes this task in his first coming.[187]

Third, Jesus' ministry and atoning death on the cross fulfills Isaiah's prophecy of the new exodus. The journey out of Egypt (Matt 2:15), the baptism of Jesus, the temptation of Jesus in the wilderness, and John the Baptist's role in preparing the way (Luke 3:4–6; cf. Isa 40:3–5), discussed earlier in this chapter, already point to the fact that Israel's promised new exodus is inaugurated by the coming of Jesus. New exodus typology abounds in the NT and cannot be adequately canvassed here, although a few points will suffice.[188] The clearest reference to the fulfillment of new exodus typology is in Luke 9:31 where Moses and Elijah speak to Jesus during the transfiguration regarding his "departure" (ἔξοδον) to be accomplished in Jerusalem, a reference to the redemption brought about by Jesus' death and resurrection.[189] Further, Moses is frequently identified as God's servant in the OT, and in the NT readers receive confirmation that Jesus is the new Moses (John 1:17; 3:14; 6:14; Heb 3:1–6; cf. 12:18–24; cf. Deut 18:15, 18). Indeed, Jesus is greater than Moses and Joshua as he is able to provide new creation rest in bringing his people to a better promised land (Heb 4:1–11, 16, esp. 4:8).[190]

187. Contra Vlach, "What Does Christ as 'True Israel' Mean," 49–50; and Saucy, *Case for Progressive Dispensationalism*, 191.

188. For general treatments, see Watts, "Exodus," 484–87; Routledge, "Exodus and Biblical Theology," 187–209; Patterson and Travers, "Contours of the Exodus Motif," 25–47; Scobie, *Ways of Our God*, 216–17.

189. Watts, *Isaiah's New Exodus in Mark*, 126–27, highlights other exodus parallels in the transfiguration narrative. For the new exodus in Luke-Acts, cf. Pao, *Acts and the Isaianic New Exodus*.

190. For discussion, see Thiessen, "Hebrews and the End of the Exodus," 353–69.

The movement from Mount Sinai to Mount Zion through Christ is manifest (Heb 12:22-24; Gal 4:24-27). Additionally, Jesus is the true Passover lamb who seals Israel's new exodus redemption (John 19:36; cf. 1:29; Exod 12:46; Isa 53:7), he is the true manna from heaven (John 6:30-59; Exod 16; Num 11:8; Ps 78:23-24) who gives life to the world (John 6:33, 51; cf. Isa 49:6), the one who fulfills Israel's exodus feasts (John 7:1-51; 8:12-59) and who is the source of the eschatological waters of the new exodus (John 7:32-38; Exod 17:1-6; cf. Isa 12:3; 44:3; 49:9-11; 55:1-2, 6; 58:11; Ezek 36:25-27; 47:1; Joel 3:18).[191] In sum, Jesus is the Davidic servant who restores Israel through the new exodus he achieves by his mighty deeds (healing those with physical problems, feedings, exorcisms) and by his death and resurrection whereby he ratifies and mediates a new and better covenant (Heb 8).[192]

With the implementation of the new exodus through the agency of Jesus, significant ecclesiological implications result. Israel's identity as a covenant nation was bound up with the exodus from Egypt (e.g., Exod 6:7; 19:5-6; 29:46). In the prophetic writings of Isaiah, the new exodus has a clear eschatological dimension, for the remnant of Israelite exiles are joined

---

191. For a variety of treatments on the new exodus themes and typologies in the Gospel of John, see Köstenberger, *Theology of John's Gospel*, 413-22; cf. 112-13, 163-65; Dennis, *Jesus' Death and the Gathering of True Israel*, 188-220; Dennis, "Presence and Function of Second Exodus-Restoration Imagery," 105-21. In the latter work, Dennis concludes, "Imagery such as the expected 'prophet like Moses' (John 6.14), sign-miracles such as providing bread for the multitude (6.5-11), the crossing of the sea (6.16-21), Jesus' identification with *true* manna ... all combine in this chapter to show that the day of restoration is here and that Jesus the Messiah ... is now leading a second exodus restoration that will lead to eternal life and the restoration of a new community" (121, emphasis original).

192. The typological and prophetic patterns of the Davidic Son, new exodus, and the role of the Isaianic servant converge given the intertexual resonances in Mark 6:34-44. In this narrative, Jesus has compassion on the crowd in the wilderness because they are like sheep without a shepherd (v. 34), evoking Num 27:17 where Moses pleads for a successor and recalling Ezek 34:5 where Ezekiel indicts the false shepherds of Israel. Ezekiel's oracle promised that the solution would be found in one shepherd, the future Davidic servant who shall feed them (cf. the role of the servant in Isa 49:9b-10) and be prince over them (Ezek 34:23-24). Accordingly, Hays, "Canonical Matrix of the Gospels," 61, writes, "When Jesus feeds the multitude in Mk 6, he is not only symbolically re-enacting Moses' manna miracle of the exodus but also prefiguring the restored Davidic kingship promised by Ezekiel's prophecy. The two motifs (exodus and Davidic kingship) should be seen as complementary ... precisely because the new exodus envisioned in the Old Testament ... has as its *telos* the restoration of God's rulership over Israel. Consequently, the Old Testament allusions in Mk 6 lead us to perceive Jesus as a kingly figure who integrates the exodus typology with Ezekiel's vision of a restored kingdom." The only thing to add to Hays's analysis is the theme of servanthood, which is tied to the fact that David is called God's servant in Ezek 34:23 and given that the Isaianic servant is charged with feeding the flock of the new exodus (Isa 49:9-10; cf. Isa 48:21).

with people from among the nations in a future outlook for their collective deliverance, restoration, and return to Zion.[193] Israel has been an unfaithful nation, but the new exodus is grander and better as those who go through this exodus will be a faithful, covenant keeping people, a people truly rescued by God from their captivity to sin. The question that systematic theologians have not addressed then, or given proper attention to is who goes through the new exodus? With the new exodus realized in Christ, those who are redeemed through Christ, the Passover lamb, and brought out of slavery to sin and into the new covenant, deemed sons of God, are those of faith, the church. This typological correspondence from Israel to the church through the new exodus wrought in Christ will also be discussed in chapter 6. However, it is important to observe that the servant-Jesus' task of accomplishing the new exodus is formative for the church just as the exodus was the formative event for the nation of Israel. Not surprisingly, exodus themes appear frequently with reference to the church.[194] There is no mere coincidence that the church is associated as traveling on the "way" or being designated as the "way" (see Exod 13:21–22; 23:20; Isa 40:3; cf. 30:11, 21; 35:8; 42:16; 48:17; 49:11; 57:14; 62:10) in the book of Acts (9:2; 18:25–26; 19:9, 23; 22:4; 24:14, 22), for the church is the reconstituted Israel—God's renewed people who have been liberated from spiritual exile through the Isaianic new exodus that was prepared by John the Baptist and accomplished by Jesus.[195]

---

193. See Routledge, "Exodus and Biblical Theology," 204–5.

194. Acts 2; Rom 8:14–30; 1 Cor 10:1–11; 2 Cor 3:3–18; 6:16; Gal 3–5; Eph 2:11–22; 1 Pet 1:2; 2:4–10; Heb 3:7–19; Rev 1:6; 2:17; 5:6–10; 12:11–17; 15:1–8. See Watts, "Exodus," 485–87. The Isaianic exodus permeates throughout Acts according to Pao, *Acts and the Isaianic New Exodus*. For the intertextual link of being "led by the Spirit" (Rom 8:14) with God's new exodus through the desert through the activity of the Spirit (Isa 63:7–14), along with other echoes such as sonship and "firstborn" (Rom 8:29), see Keesmaat, "Exodus," 29–56.

195. Pao, *Acts and the Isaianic New Exodus*, 59–68, 249; Schnabel, *Acts*, 290; Schreiner, *New Testament Theology*, 695–96. The "way" terminology differentiates true believers in Christ, the church, from opponents. Pao, *Acts and the Isaianic New Exodus*, 68, summarizes, "'The Way' functions as a symbol evoking the transformed foundation story of Israel found in Isaiah 40–55 in the construction of the identity of the community. The symbol signifies the movement's continuity with the past as well as its distinctiveness.... Understanding the 'the Way' as an identity marker helps explain the diverse referents it embodies.... [T]he primary meaning of the term is an ecclesiological one for it is used in the definition of the community as the true heir of the ancestral traditions." The church is the fulfillment of the Isaianic hope then, and correlates with Lim's observation regarding the change from the "way of the Lord" in Isa 40:3 to the "way of my people" in Isa 57:14. Lim, *'Way of the Lord' in Isaiah*, 119, writes that the "very definition of 'my people' has both expanded and contracted since Isa 40:1. In [Isaiah 40–55], God's people comprised all Israel, including those of the

Lastly, one final area needs to be addressed. The textual, epochal, and canonical horizons all point to an integral relationship of Israel—servant—servants. As was briefly discussed, the suffering servant is promised offspring (Isa 53:10),[196] and throughout Isa 54–66 the offspring or servants form a major theme.[197] The movement is from Israel to the one who identifies with and embodies Israel as the servant (Isa 49:3–12) to servants (Isa 54–66). The messianic servant's obedient and righteous activities commissioned by God bring about salvation and restoration for Israel and the nations, producing offspring and servants who carry on his mission. Moreover, the nature of the eschatological servants differs from national Israel, as Fantuzzo writes, "Only those disciples whose turning from transgression demonstrates their solidarity with the righteous servant are true servants of Yahweh ([Isa] 59:20; cf. 49:23; 57:13; 64:3; 65:16). Only they are the 'Redeemed of the LORD' (62:12)."[198] From the perspective of the

---

diaspora. [Isaiah 56–66] broadens this definition such that the foreigner and eunuch are now considered part of God's people who may worship within the house of prayer for all nations (56:1–8)."

196. DeRouchie, "Counting Stars with Abraham," 471, observes four parallels between the work of the suffering servant and the new covenant family of Isa 54 and through the rest of the book: "(1) The 'many' in Isa 52:14–15 and 53:11–12 are the 'many' in the 'miracle family' of Isa 54:1. (2) The servant's 'offspring' in Isa 53:11 are Sarah's 'offspring' in Isa 54:3 who have been expanded by inheriting nations. (3) In Isa 53:11 the 'righteous' servant king makes many 'righteous,' and in Isa 54:14 the redeemed city is established in 'righteousness' (cf. Jer 23:6; 33:16). (4) The 'servant' singular in Isa 52:13 and 53:11 gives rise to 'servants' plural in Isa 54:17 and beyond (cf. Isa 65:8–9, 13–15; 66:14)—servants that explicitly include a remnant from the tribes of Israel (Isa 63:17) *and* the nations (Isa 56:6)" (emphasis original). Paul's explicit citation of Isa 54:1 LXX in Gal 4:27 demonstrates that the church comprises of the children of the barren woman, the gospel produces true offspring and children of promise like Isaac (Gal 4:28). See Schreiner, *Galatians*, 303–4, and Moo, *Galatians*, 305–9. Harmon, *Servant of the Lord and His Servant People*, 137–38, commenting on Isa 54:17, notes, "The various blessings that come to his servant people through work of the servant are summed up as their 'heritage' . . . or their inheritance, language that encompasses the land promise to Abraham but goes far beyond it to express a renewed relationship transcending anything previous."

197. See footnote 140 above and Gignilliat, "Servant Follower," 112–15. Similarly, Seitz, *Figured Out*, 115, writes, "From chapter 54 to 66, the servant is replaced by servants. They share in the servant's affliction, for the sake of God's righteousness. They are the seed of the servant, which was to prosper. . . . [T]he righteous servants of the servant are joined by the nations, and together, as Zion is restored, they take part in God's intended bounty. The joining of the nations to Israel entails their witnessing God's judgment, on his own people and over all creation. . . . Zion's painless birthing of new citizens is emblematic of the new life promised for all God's servants, offspring of Zion. Zion sees seed, and in this way the promises associated with the servant's vindication are made good." Cf. Fantuzzo, "True Israel's 'Mother and Brothers,'" 112–16.

198. Fantuzzo, "True Israel's 'Mother and Brothers,'" 116. Fantuzzo also observes

NT, the servants who are the servant's offspring, continuing the work of the servant, is not national or political Israel but followers of Jesus. The people who continue Jesus' role as God's servants and therefore enjoy the status of God's true, faithful people, are the church. House explains, "Paul viewed the church as the ideal remnant of Jews and Gentiles and cast his own ministry and that of the church in terms of servanthood (cf. Rom 1:1; 9–11; 15:1–2)."[199] A few observations from the NT confirm that the church is the renewed Israel, made-up of the prophesied Isaianic servants, and assumes the role of national Israel.

Israel was to be God's witnesses (Isa 43:10, 12; 44:8) and as observed, the one who *represents* and *is* Israel, the messianic servant, is tasked with being a light to the nations (Isa 42:6; 49:6; cf. 51:4). The servant nation Israel "was called to have a universal role in projecting the covenant God's salvation to the nations, [but] several Christian authors believed that this vocation had subsequently been taken over by Jesus and the church."[200] The church, through Jesus, takes on the role of witnessing and bringing light to the nations. Echoing Isaiah's "light" passages, Matt 5:14 and 5:16 intimate that Jesus' followers are emissaries and heralds of the kingdom of God and like the Isaianic servant they are the "light of the world" (cf. Eph 5:8–9), having the task of making that light shine before others (cf. Phil 2:15).[201] Further, as Thomas Moore has demonstrated, the Lucan great commission (24:46–49) has four aspects that link the disciples' mission to that of the Isaianic servant, Jesus.[202] A transfer of servant motifs to Jesus' followers is unmistakable, for they continue the servant's ministry of proclaiming forgiveness or release from sins (Luke 24:47; cf. 4:18; Isa 61:1) and the designation—"you are witnesses" (24:48)—verbally recalls Israel's role in Isa 43:10, 12; 44:8.[203] The extent of the disciples' mission is to "all the

---

that in the final chapters of Isaiah "[t]here is narrowing: Yahweh will restrict the Israel of God to the offspring of the Servant. Only those whose servanthood indicates their solidarity with the Servant can inhabit holy Zion" (119).

199. House, *Old Testament Theology*, 293.

200. Bird, "'Light to the Nations,'" 123. Bird further avers, "The first Christians came to realize that they had inherited the role of Israel, and that the church was to be what national Israel had failed to be, namely, a light to the nations" (126).

201. Bird, "'Light to the Nations,'" 126. Others note the links to Isa 42:6 and 49:6 in Matt 5:14, see Carson, *Matthew 1–12*, 139–40; France, *Gospel of Matthew*, 175–77.

202. Moore, "Lucan Great Commission," 51–57. See also Beers, *Followers of Jesus*, 113–25, esp. 124–25; Köstenberger and O'Brien, *Salvation to the Ends of the Earth*, 123–27.

203. Moore, "Lucan Great Commission," 53–56. Moore notes, "As 'witnesses,' the disciples were to take up the task of God's servant Israel pictured in Isaiah. Just as Israel was to testify of God's saving acts on behalf of His people (Isa. 43:8–13; 44:6–8), so too

nations" (Luke 24:47), a reference with extensive Isaianic background of the nations streaming to Zion in the last days (Isa 2:2; 66:18–20), worshipping God (56:7), and enjoying salvation which again invokes the messianic servant's role of being a light to the nations so that God's salvation may reach the ends of the earth (49:6). Lastly, the Lucan great commission states that Jesus' followers will be empowered from on high (Luke 24:49), which was fulfilled at Pentecost with the pouring out of the Spirit in Acts 1–2. As Moore has shown, the phrase "from on high" is similar to the wording of Isa 32:15 and is also conceptually linked to Isa 44:3, which was discussed in relation to Gal 3:14. Both of these passages are tied to the eschatological transformation of Israelite society when God would pour out his Spirit, but Luke informs his readers that these prophecies are fulfilled through those who identify with Christ, being in faith union with the Spirit-anointed servant (Isa 42:1; 61:1).

In sum, the disciples continue the ministry of the Isaianic servant as they are commissioned (Matt 28:18–20) as Spirit-empowered servants to be his "witnesses in Jerusalem and in all Judea and Samaria, and to the end of the earth" (Acts 1:8), another verse that evokes Isaianic servant themes (e.g., Isa 49:6; 43:10, 12; 44:8) and shows that Jesus' followers are God's true servants, the people of the new exodus.[204] By Jesus' obedience and vindication through resurrection, all authority in heaven is bestowed upon him (Matt 28:18–20). He commands his servants to make disciples of all nations, to the ends of the earth (Acts 1:8), thus marking the eschatological gathering of the nations to Zion, a reality that pointed to Christ himself (Isa 2:2–5; 45:20–22; 55:5; 56:6–7; Mic 4:1–5; Zech 2:11; 8:20–23; cf. Gal 4:21–31; Heb 12:18, 22–24).[205]

---

the disciples were to testify of God's saving actions in Jesus' death and resurrection" (55).

204. See Moore, "'To the End of the Earth,'" 389–99; Pao, *Acts and the Isaianic New Exodus*, 91–96; Beers, *Followers of Jesus*, 126–33; Köstenberger and O'Brien, *Salvation to the Ends of the Earth*, 129–31; Kaiser, *Mission in the Old Testament*, 62. Turner, *Power from on High*, 300–301, contends that Acts 1:8 has three Isaianic allusions that "unequivocally point in the direction of Israel's restoration. To the circle of disciples falls the vocation of the Isaianic servant, to raise up Jacob and to restore the remnant of Israel. . . . The affirmation 'you will receive power when the Holy Spirit has come upon you' will remind the reader of Lk. 24.49. . . . Lk. 24.49 and Acts 1.8 together evidently rest on Isa. 32.15 (LXX 'until the Spirit from on high comes upon you') which is about the New Exodus restoration of Israel and transformation of her 'wilderness' estate. Similarly, the address 'you shall be my witnesses' takes up Isa. 43.10–12, where restored Israel, 'God's servant,' is given this commission. And thirdly, the task of bearing witness to Jesus 'to the end of the earth' (1.8) is widely recognized to take up the closing line of Isaiah 49.6."

205. Kynes, *Christology of Solidarity*, 182–84, 189–91; Schnabel, "Israel, the People

Moreover, Paul's application of the servant motif to himself and others confirms that the people of God are redefined as the eschatological new Israel, inheriting the mission and role of OT Israel. In Acts 13:47, Paul cites Isa 49:6 and applies the text to himself and Barnabas as a command to be a light for the gentiles. While Jewish evangelism is not rejected, Paul and Barnabas identify with Jesus, the true servant (Acts 3:13, 26; 4:27, 30; 8:32–35), continue his priestly ministry, and are the light of the gentiles by virtue of their preaching Christ.[206] An appropriated or ecclesiological typological pattern is present, again via Christ, in Acts 13:47: the eschatological servant and task is realized in Christ as he brings light to the nations (Luke 2:32; Acts 26:23), and Paul and Barnabas and the church also fulfill this promise of blessing to the nations by virtue of their relationship to Christ.[207] Later, Paul will explain his mission as the continuation of the work of Jesus as the "light" of the suffering and risen messianic servant is proclaimed to the nations through him, for Paul is both a "servant" and a "witness" (Acts 26:13, 16–18, 22–23).[208] Also, it is clear that Paul is a servant of the servant (2 Cor 6:4; Acts 16:17) as he develops the servant and other Isaianic motifs in 2 Cor 5:14–21 before citing Isa 49:8 in 2 Cor 6:2. The implication once again is that Paul identifies with the Isaianic servant of Isa 49 and his priestly, mediatorial role because this work of the servant is typological of Christ's servants. The fulfillment of Israel's restoration has arrived as the day

---

of God," 46–47; Köstenberger and O'Brien, *Salvation to the Ends of the Earth*, 106, 129–31, 135–37. Contra Sailhamer, "Evidence from Isaiah 2," 79–102, as he wrongly argues that Isaiah's vision in Isa 2:1–5 refers to a literal fulfillment in Jerusalem during the millennium of Rev 20.

206. Köstenberger and O'Brien, *Salvation to the Ends of the Earth*, 148–49; and Bird, "'Light to the Nations,'" 127. See also Moore, "Lucan Great Commission," 57–58; Pao, *Acts and the Isaianic New Exodus*, 96–101; Beers, *Followers of Jesus*, 156–57; Thompson, *Acts of the Risen Lord Jesus*, 118–20; Beale, *New Testament Biblical Theology*, 683–84, 713.

207. See Meek, *Gentile Mission in Old Testament Citations in Acts*, 24–55. Meek concludes that Richard Davidson's study of typology (see chapter 2) is helpful in understanding Isa 49:6 in Acts 13:47. Meek particularly develops how Davidson's appropriated or ecclesiological typological fulfillment is at play in this text (51–53). In a similar vein, Moore, "Lucan Great Commission," 60, suggests that the church is not the servant since they continue the ministry of the servant but alternatively, the church may be identified as the Isaianic servant in fulfilling collective aspects since Jesus fulfilled the individual aspects of the servant.

208. Bird, "'Light to the Nations,'" 127–28; and Beers, *Followers of Jesus*, 170–72. Moore, "Lucan Great Commission," 57–58, notes the application of other Isaianic servant language to Paul as he is chosen, suffers, and seeks to open the eyes of the blind in continuing the task of the servant. These characteristics link him to Acts 1:8 and Luke 24:44–47 where Isaianic servant language is appropriated for disciples of Jesus.

of salvation is "now," and the reality of reconciliation and new creation in Christ has come (2 Cor 5:17—6:2; cf. Isa 49:8-13).[209]

Jesus is the Isaianic servant, the true Israel, but servanthood language as well as the servant's prophetic vocation is applied to those who follow and identify with Jesus. The church is where God's true servants are to be found (e.g., Eph 6:6; Phil 1:1; 1 Pet 2:16; Rev 1:1); indeed, Jesus' followers are "sons of light" (John 12:36) since they have come in faith to the one who is the light of the world (John 12:46; cf. 8:12; Isa 42:6; 49:6). The church suffers as the Isaianic servant did (Luke 9:22; cf. Acts 9:16; 14:22; Rom 8:17; 2 Cor 1:5-6; 1 Pet 2:20-24; Rev 6:11), is possessed by the Spirit through the work of the anointed messianic servant, and carries out the servant's ministry in proclaiming the good news (Isa 40:9-11; 52:7; 61:1-2) in his name (Acts 3:16; 5:41), awaiting the vindication (Rev 11:18; 22:1-5) that he received through his obedient life and atoning work on the cross. Fantuzzo observes,

> Jesus is the Servant of the Lord whose mediatorial role inaugurated the eschatological fulfillment of Isaiah's vision. By faith-union with him, servants follow his pattern of Servant-ministry in their ongoing ministry of reconciliation (2 Cor. 5:17-21; cf. Isa. 49:8-13; 65:17; Matt. 5-7; 28:18-20). *From Pentecost to the consummation of the age, this Isaianic vision is fulfilled in the active faith and servanthood of Jesus' disciples.* Consequently, the power to fulfill their calling comes from the redemptive accomplishment of Jesus' messianic suffering and glory, including Pentecost. He is True Israel; in him, servants demonstrate that they are his mother, brothers, and sisters (Matt. 12:49-50).[210]

In Rom 15 Paul confirms that Christ has become a servant of the circumcision, the Jews, on behalf of the truth of God, namely God's covenant faithfulness, in order to confirm the promises to the patriarchs, particularly the promises to Abraham, and so that the gentiles may be included in the people of God in glorifying God for his covenantal mercy (Rom 15:8-9a; cf. 4:9-17).[211] In the supporting catena of scriptural citations (Rom 15:9b-12),

---

209. See Beale, *New Testament Biblical Theology*, 711-16; cf. Gignilliat, "Servant Follower," 115-24. Paul's appropriation of themes from Isa 51-55 in the book of Romans, especially the allusions of the fourth Servant Song (Isa 52:13—53:12), indicates that the larger story of Isa 51-55 was understood by Paul to prefigure his role as apostle and missionary in heralding the gospel to Israel (cf. Isa 52:7) and to the gentiles (cf. Isa 52:15). With the realization of Isaiah's message, Paul understands himself as the servant of the servant.

210. Fantuzzo, "True Israel's 'Mother and Brothers,'" 122, emphasis original.

211. For discussion of Rom 15:7-13, including the difficulty surrounding the syntactical relationship between vv. 8-9, see Moo, "Paul's Universalizing Hermeneutic,"

Paul shows that Christ has fulfilled the covenant promises as Jews and gentiles come together in the church to worship God in joy and peace (cf. Gen 12:3).[212] In particular, Paul's citation of Isa 11:10 LXX (Rom 15:12) announces the eschatological realization of the Jews and gentiles gathering around the Davidic son and servant (cf. Jer 23:5; 33:15). The messianic hope of Isaiah concerning the influx of nations, vindication of Israel, and recovery of the remnant through the second exodus (Isa 11:11–16) has been inaugurated in Christ and is extended through Paul's and the church's mission.[213]

Israel-Christ Typological Pattern Evidenced from the Title *Yeshurun*

A similar theme to the servant typology, but with a slightly different focus, is found in the overflow of blessings described in Paul's eulogy in Eph 1:3–14, a passage reminiscent of the exodus and the new covenant.[214] Ephesians 1:3–6 particularly has lexical and conceptual parallels to Isa 44:1–5: God's election of Israel (vv. 1–2), the future outpouring of the Spirit on his

---

68–70; Sherwood, *Paul and the Restoration of Humanity*, 231–47, esp. 237–39; Wagner, "Christ, Servant of Jew and Gentile," 473–85, esp. 476n18; Chae, *Paul as Apostle*, 51–68; Schreiner, *Romans*, 727–34. Though Paul uses the word διάκονος ("minister" or "servant") to describe Jesus, it is possible Paul is connecting him to the Isaianic servant, so Schreiner, *Romans*, 726n7. Conceptually, the Isaianic servant theme is present given the relationship of Isa 11 with the Servant Songs (discussed previously), which Paul cites just a few verses later (Rom 15:12) and given his quotation of Isa 52:15 in Rom 15:21. Regardless, Paul's description of Christ as "servant" at least highlights his eschatological role as covenant mediator.

212. Discussion of Paul's citations cannot be addressed here, but careful study of Paul's use of Ps 18:49 [17:49 LXX] (or 2 Sam 22:50 LXX), Deut 32:43 LXX, Ps 117:1 [116:1 LXX], and Isa 11:10 LXX indicates, as Hays, *Echoes of Scripture*, 71, explains, that "Paul rests his case on the claim that his churches, in which Gentiles do in fact join Jews in praising God, must be the eschatological fulfillment of the scriptural vision." Cf. Chae, *Paul as Apostle*, 67; and note Sherwood, *Paul and the Restoration of Humanity*, 243.

213. See Schreiner, *Romans*, 729, 733; Hays, *Echoes of Scripture*, 73; Chae, *Paul as Apostle*, 64–65. Contra Saucy, *Case for Progressive Dispensationalism*, 136–38; Hafemann, "Redemption of Israel," 206–13. In contrast, Sherwood, *Paul and the Restoration of Humanity*, 246–47, rightly concludes, "What Paul says of the Roman believers is for him true of all believers, that they are restored Israel and restored humanity. . . . Israel and humanity have been restored, but only insofar as their identity is defined by their relationship to Christ."

214. Starling, "Ephesians and the New Exodus," 142–43, notices how the language of election, adoption, redemption, revelation, and inheritance in Eph 1:3–14 all tie back to the exodus accounts. Cf. Starling, *Not My People*, 186–89.

offspring (v. 3), and God's faithfulness to the Abrahamic promises (vv. 3–5) where gentiles join themselves to Israel.[215] Each of these thematic elements unite in Eph 1:3–6.[216] Paul praises the Father for his blessings, among them being election and adoption which comes by being "in the beloved"—Christ (v. 6). As already seen, Isa 44:1 refers to Israel as God's servant, but Israel is also identified as *Yeshurun* (Isa 44:2; cf. Deut 32:15; 33:5, 26), a term of endearment meaning "upright one," but translated in the LXX of Isa 44:2 as "beloved" ($\dot{\eta}\gamma\alpha\pi\eta\mu\acute{\epsilon}\nu o\varsigma$).[217] This is the exact word Paul uses to identify Jesus Christ, for he is the "beloved" in verse 6. Therefore, given the background of Isa 44:1–5 in Eph 1:3–6, Paul understood Christ to be *Yeshurun*, Israel, and through him, the eschatological presence of the Spirit (Eph 1:3; cf. 1:13–14) and the blessings of the Abrahamic promises have come to fruition. The Ephesian Christians (Jew and gentile) are loved, adopted, and chosen by being united in the "beloved," the true Israel. Paul's

> readers should view their salvation as the fulfillment of the second exodus and new covenant promises of the prophets. Like the promised new covenant of the second exodus—but unlike the scriptural narrations of the original exodus—the deliverance they have experienced is described as being, at its heart, not merely a defeat of hostile powers but a "forgiveness of . . . trespasses." Additional hints are added in Eph 1:13 with references to "the gospel of your salvation" and "the promised Holy Spirit," both of which imply that the prophetic promises of

---

215. Okoye, *Israel and the Nations*, 132, comments, "Isaiah 44:5 is to be interpreted in terms of inclusion of gentiles in 'Israel' and belonging to Yahweh." Likewise, Webb, *Message of Isaiah*, 179–80. Contra, Motyer, *Prophecy of Isaiah*, 342–43, who finds links to Ps 87, but argues that v. 5 refers only to the offspring of Israel/Jacob. Oswalt, *Isaiah 40–66*, 168, thinks v. 5 refers to both groups.

216. The findings of this section are based on the observations and excellent analysis by Greever, "Will the True Israel Stand Up?"

217. Thielman, *Ephesians*, 53–54, writes, "Ancient Jewish literature also speaks of the nation Israel as God's 'beloved' (e.g., Isa. 5:1; Jer. 11:15; 12:7; Bar. 3:36 [3:37 LXX]; Jdt. 9:4), and the LXX translators consistently translated the name 'Jeshurun,' a biblical term of endearment for Israel, with the word 'beloved' (Deut. 32:15; 33:5, 26; Isa. 44:2). . . . Paul's use of the term 'beloved' reflects this same alternation between a chosen and 'beloved' individual and God's chosen and 'beloved' people. He knew the early Christian tradition that Jesus was God's Beloved (Col. 1:13), and he frequently called God's people God's beloved (1 Thess. 1:4; 2 Thess. 2:13; Rom. 9:25; Col. 3:12; Eph. 5:1), sometimes in combination with the claim that God's people are his 'elect' (1 Thess. 1:4). It seems likely, therefore, that when Paul calls Jesus 'the Beloved' in this passage he has in mind Jesus's embodiment within himself of the beloved and elect people of God." See also O'Brien, *Letter to the Ephesians*, 105.

post-exilic restoration of Israel have somehow been proclaimed to and fulfilled among the Gentiles.[218]

While Paul does not elaborate exactly how the promises are being fulfilled in the Eph 1:3–14, the indications are that they have occurred "in Christ" as God's plan is "to unite all things in him" (Eph 1:10 ESV). Through union with Christ, Paul identifies Christians as the "beloved" elsewhere, thus the church is eschatological Israel.[219]

Israel-Christ Typological Pattern Evidenced through Vine Imagery

Finally, another example of the Israel-Christ relationship is found in John 15:1–6. John presents Jesus as the "true vine" who stands over against Israel which is the earthly copy or shadow of the original vine now identified as Jesus.[220] Throughout the OT, the vine as an image of life, fruitfulness, and hope was used to describe the nation Israel.[221] Sadly, although by no fault of the vinedresser (Ezek 17:5–6), the vine produced bad fruit (Isa 5:2; Jer 2:21; Hos 10:1) because Israel swerved from following the Lord. The result of Israel's sin was God's judgment and destruction of his vine (Isa 5:5–7; 16:8, 10; Jer 6:9; 12:10–13; Hos 2:12; Mic 1:6; cf. Zeph 1:13). Nevertheless, covenant curses were forecast to cease as the Lord promised blessing and restoration

---

218. Starling, "Ephesians and the New Exodus," 143. Thielman, *Ephesians*, 82, on Eph 1:13–14 has a similar conclusion: "Here Paul speaks of the fulfillment of the prophetic promise that in the days of Israel's restoration, God's Spirit would dwell among his people (Isa. 32:15; 44:3; Ezek. 11:19; 36:26–27; 37:14; Joel 3:1–2 [2:28–29 Eng.]; cf. Gal. 3:14; Acts 1:4; 2:33). This fulfillment has happened 'in Christ.'" Also embedded within Paul's eschatological blessing is the language of inheritance (Eph 1:11, 13–14; cf. Col 1:12), which again indicates that the promised land is expanded and is given to all believers through the Holy Spirit. See Beale, *New Testament Biblical Theology*, 762–63; Echevarria, *Future Inheritance of Land*, 176–77; Thielman, *Ephesians*, 73.

219. See Rom 9:22–25; 12:19; 16:5, 8, 9, 12; Eph 5:1; Col 3:12; 1 Thess 1:4; 2 Thess 2:13. For discussion of "beloved" with reference to Israel and the church, see Thompson, *Church according to Paul*, 35–36.

220. The adjective "true" with respect to the vine should be understood the same way that Jesus refers to himself as the "true bread" or "true food" or "true drink" in John 6. Jesus is not contrasting himself with false bread or false food or false drink or a false vine (even though Israel was unfaithful as God's vine). Instead, Jesus is the original in comparison to the copies. I owe this insight to Ardel Caneday.

221. See Ps 80:8, 14; Isa 5:1–7; 27:2–6; Jer 2:21; 6:9; 8:13; Ezek 15:1–8; 17:6–8; 19:10–14; Hos 10:1; 14:7; cf. 2 Esdr 5:23 and the associated image of the vineyard (Isa 3:14; 5:1–7; Jer 12:10). Whitacre, "Vine, Fruit of the Vine," 867, observes how the "vine/vineyard is the people of God, planted and cultivated by God for his delight and the produce it should yield." Cf. Burge, "Territorial Religion," 393.

of a healthy, fertile vine (Jer 31:5; 32:15; Amos 9:14; Hos 14:4–9). Also significant for this eschatological projection is Ps 80, especially in the context of the final form of the psalter, where the restoration of the nation of Israel, specifically called a vine (v. 8, 14), is associated with the agency of a royal, messianic figure who is identified as "son of man" (v. 17) and possibly as the "shoot" (v. 15).[222] According to the important study by Andrew Streett,[223] Ps 80 presents the restoration of Israel using vine imagery with motifs of the new exodus and new creation that is especially linked to an eschatological Davidic king.[224] The psalmist laments the destruction of the Israel vine but pleads to God to revive the nation (80:18)—calling for a national restoration and resurrection—through the leadership of a last Adam and Davidic king. This text is likely the most important OT allusion or intertext that backgrounds John 15.[225]

---

222. See Streett, *Vine and the Son of Man*, 37–38. The "branch" or "shoot" of Ps 80:15a is ambiguous, for it could refer to Israel or to a Davidic king (see Isa 11:1; Jer 23:5, 33:15; etc.). The messianic passage, Gen 49:8–12 (cf. vv. 22–26), connects the future king with the vine, but since the king represents the people the reference in Ps 80:15a of a "shoot" or "stalk" is left open.

223. Streett, *Vine and the Son of Man*, 15–47 analyzes Ps 80 within its historical context, but also rightly examines the psalm within the psalter as a unified book (pp. 49–89). Streett rightly places Ps 80 within the setting of Book III and within the psalter as whole given the significance of the five-book division, the groupings of the psalms, the placement of royal and wisdom psalms at the seams of the books, and with how Pss 1–2 and 146–50 serve as the introduction and conclusion to the psalter.

224. Streett, *Vine and the Son of Man*, 26–28, argues that the new exodus motif is present by not just the rehearsal of the exodus event (Ps 80:1, 8; cf. Exod 15:22), but the prayer of v. 14 shares exodus language (Exod 3:7, 16) in calling on God to reenact the exodus (cf. Isa 63:15 where the same phrase "look down from heaven and see" is used in the context of rehearsing the exodus and petitioning God to act once again). Cf. Hays, *Reading Backwards*, 67, as he also recognizes that both Ps 106 and 80 "recall God's deliverance of Israel from Egypt and intercede for a similar renewal of God's saving mercy, in which God will hear the cry of the people and come ('visit') to save them again." Hays finds that God's visitation of Israel has commenced in Jesus as evidenced by the *visitation* language of Luke 1:76 and 7:16. The creation/new creation imagery is present with the vine associated with mountains, cedars, water sources, and having walls like a vineyard or garden (vv. 9–12; cf. the link with Exod 15:17) (see the discussion by Streett, *Vine and the Son of Man*, 28–35). Indications are also present of re-creation through the restoration of Israel in the refrains of vv. 3, 7, and 19. Further, the king (v. 15) is presented as a last Adam who retakes dominion over the beasts that ravaged the vine (see v. 13).

225. Streett, *Vine and the Son of Man*, 213–21. Streett lists the following reasons that the main allusion is to Ps 80 in John 15: "(1) it can account for the identifications of the Son, the Father, and the disciples in the vine image; (2) it possesses some features in common with the Ezekiel passages [15:2; 17:6–9; 19:10–14] that are in play; and (3) it provides a more direct use of the OT than other options" (214). Cf. Dodd, *According to the Scriptures*, 102; Carson, *John*, 513–14; Beasley-Murray, *John*, 272. Even if Ps 80

The prophecy of the restoration of the vine, Israel, through a son of man, the king, is fulfilled in Jesus according to John 15:1, 5.[226] Although John 15 is clearly an allegory (Jesus is the vine; the Father is the vinedresser which implicitly recalls Ps 80:8–9 and 15b; the disciples are the branches), the OT eschatological and restoration implications of the vine imagery cannot be ignored. Jesus' claim to be the "true vine" is another way of saying that he is the true Israel: as the eschatological bearer of Israel's mission, he sums up Israel's purposes as he produces fruit-bearing branches and he commences the anticipated restoration of Israel as the messianic king. Up to this point in John's Gospel, Jesus has "superseded the temple, the Jewish feasts, Moses, and various holy sites; here he supersedes Israel as the very locus of the people of God."[227]

Furthermore, the ecclesiological implications are evident. Based on John 15:1–8, only those who are organically united with the true vine, incorporated as branches bearing fruit, are participants in Jesus, the true Israel. These branches are clearly Jesus' disciples, but ultimately all believers who abide in him through faith (cf. John 14:20). As Andreas Köstenberger rightly observes, the "barely concealed reference to Israel casts Jesus as the true vine, the representative of Israel, and his disciples as the branches,

---

does not serve as the chief background to John 15, the fact that Jesus sums up Israel and fulfills her purposes stands. Ridderbos, *Gospel according to John*, 515, concludes, "The main thing, however, is that Jesus, by calling himself the true vine and, in immediate association therewith, his Father the planter and keeper of the vineyard, applies to himself this redemptive-historical description of the people of God. He thus becomes the one who represents or embodies the people."

226. Köstenberger, *John*, 450. Wenham, *Parables of Jesus*, 200, cited in Streett, *Vine and the Son of Man*, 220, aptly summarizes the significance of Ps 80 for John 15: "The man of the psalm is undoubtedly the king under whom the people will be restored; so we have in Psalm 80 a remarkable combination of ideas that are important for Jesus: the vine, son of God, king and son of man. It is quite possible that the psalm is the background of Jesus' teaching in John 15: he sees the psalmist's prayer being fulfilled in himself—he is the King, 'Son of Man' and Son of God in whom the vine of Israel is being restored."

227. Carson, *John*, 513. Like Carson, Burge, "Territorial Religion," 394, emphasizes the broader themes in John's Gospel, but he also highlights the significance of the promised land in John 15: "Jesus replaces festivals like the Passover (John 6) and institutions like the temple (John 2). . . . He is living bread (6:35), living water (4:10; 7:38), and the light of life (8:12). Jewish ritual sources for these in ceremony and tradition are now obsolete. Now in John 15 we learn that Jesus is the vine, a potent metaphor for Israel itself. He offers what attachment to The Land once promised: rootedness and hope and life. As the final 'I AM' saying, John 15:1 therefore is the culmination of the images paraded throughout the Gospel showing that Jesus replaces what is at the heart of Jewish faith. The Fourth Gospel is transferring spatial, earthbound gifts from God and connecting them to a living person, Jesus Christ." Cf. Martin, *Bound for the Promised Land*, 128–30.

participants in Jesus the 'new' Israel."²²⁸ The same conclusion is also observed by George Beasley-Murray: "That the Vine is *Jesus*, not the Church, is intentional; the Lord is viewed in his representative capacity, the Son of God—Son of Man, who dies and rises that in union with him a renewed people of God might come into being and bring forth fruit."²²⁹ Rather than understanding the church as a replacement of OT Israel, Christ is the one who fulfills Israel's identity and calling, the one who embodies Israel and who is the agent of Israel's restoration in bringing about the renewed, eschatological Israel—the church.²³⁰

---

228. Köstenberger, *Theology of John's Gospel*, 502–3. See also Whitacre, "Vine, Fruit of the Vine," 868.

229. Beasley-Murray, *John*, 272, emphasis original.

230. The vine/vineyard imagery is also present in the parable of the wicked tenants (Matt 21:33–43; Mark 12:1–12; Luke 20:9–18), but this parable is different from John 15 in that the son is distinct from the vineyard, which represents the nation of Israel. Furthermore, Ps 80 does not figure as prominent in the parable of the tenants as this parable is more significantly influenced by Isa 5:1–7 (e.g., Matt 21:33; Mark 12:1) and Ps 118:22–23 (Matt 21:42; Mark 12:10–11). The crux of the parable of the tenants is Jesus' statement in Matt 21:43 that the kingdom of God will be taken from the "vine-growers" or tenant farmers (= Israel's leaders and rulers) and given to a nation who will produce its fruit. Dispensationalists argue that this nation will be a future remnant of eschatological, national Israel and that the passage is really about new leaders for Israel, specifically the twelve apostles. So Blaising and Bock, *Progressive Dispensationalism*, 237–38; Thomas, "Traditional Dispensational View," 95, 105. Nevertheless, the following reasons overrule such an interpretation. First, the immediate context that precipitates the transfer of the kingdom to the singular nation is the death and resurrection of Jesus (see vv. 39–42). It is more natural to understand the church as the "nation" that receives the kingdom of God following Jesus' death and resurrection. Second, the use of Ps 118:22–23 reveals that the rejection of Jesus as the "cornerstone," recalling temple imagery, has only led to him being the chief or foundational cornerstone of the new temple, that is, the new people of God (cf. Matt 16:16–19 and note also 21:12–15, 23–44 as the context of the parable is the temple and the language of 21:44, which also suggests temple imagery; see Beale, *Temple and the Church's Mission*, 183–88). The psalm in its original context refers to Israel or likely a Davidic king and so Israel and David typology are in play. Israel's chief priests, leaders, and all others who reject Jesus are like the nations that surround the nation Israel/Davidic king in Ps 118:10–13. Third and perhaps most importantly, the reference of a singular nation in conjunction with Ps 118:22 appears again in 1 Pet 2:7–9, a passage that clearly refers to the church. Peter is likely reflecting Jesus' teaching from the parable of the tenants. Therefore, the transfer of the kingdom is not from Jews to gentiles, but from OT Israel to a faithful, devoted covenant community—the church. See also Quarles, *Theology of Matthew*, 104; France, "Old Testament Prophecy," 63–64, 68; France, *Gospel of Mark*, 456–64.

CONCLUDING THEOLOGICAL SYNTHESIS

In chapter 2, following the important work of Richard Davidson, typology was shown to be the

> study of the Old Testament salvation historical realities or "types" (persons, events, institutions) which God has specifically designed to correspond to, and predictively prefigure, their intensified antitypical fulfillment aspects (inaugurated, appropriated, consummated) in New Testament salvation history.[231]

Typological patterns belong in the category of indirect prophecy as they develop along the biblical covenants, pointing to and ultimately culminating in Jesus Christ, the primary antitype, with some types having further fulfillment in the church and the consummation.

This chapter has demonstrated that Jesus is the true Israel, the antitypical Israel, because he identifies with Israel, fulfills Israel's roles, vocation, and calling, and more, he brings about Israel's eschatological and restoration promises by inaugurating the kingdom of God and ratifying the new covenant. The Israel-Christ-church typological strands may be summed up as follows:

- ◊ son (Adam, Israel, David) → true Son (Jesus Christ) → sons (church)
- ◊ Abrahamic seeds (Israel) → true Abrahamic Seed (Jesus Christ) → Abrahamic heirs and seed of promise (church)
- ◊ servant-Israel → true servant (Jesus Christ) → servants (church)
- ◊ *Yeshurun* (Israel) → beloved (Christ) → beloved (church)
- ◊ vine (Israel) → true vine (Jesus Christ) → fruitful branches (church)

Furthermore, the Israel-Christ relationship is confirmed through the representative figure of Jacob and the individual and corporate aspects of the prophesied Son of Man. Important throughout this study of the Israel-Christ relationship is how these typological features cannot be abstracted from, but are rather interwoven with, other typological patterns (e.g., the new exodus theme, temple) as well as Israel's prophecies and promises of restoration (messianic and Davidic promises, the new covenant, the Holy Spirit, inheritance of land, nations joining and becoming part of end-time Israel, and the exilic return of a faithful remnant). While space did not permit discussion, even Jesus' resurrection on the third day in accordance to the Scripture (Luke 18:31–33; 24:46; 1 Cor 15:4; cf. Mark 8:31; Luke 24:7,

---

231. Davidson, "Eschatological Hermeneutic," 12; see the references in chapter 2.

21, 25–26), which is likely a reference to Hos 6:2, a passage about Israel's restoration on the third day, demonstrates how Jesus is the antitypical Israel, the agent of Israel's restoration since Israel's destiny is inextricably bound to her messianic representative.[232] Additionally important throughout this study is textual warrant, and this analysis has shown that the Israel-Christ typological pattern has numerous indicators within the OT as well as multiple confirmations in the NT writings. The biblical-theological spade work cultivated throughout this chapter has ramifications for the reigning evangelical systems of theology.

Implications for Dispensational Theology

Dispensationalists reject Israel as a type of Christ and the church, or if they do acknowledge a typological relationship, it is only in the general sense of historical and theological correspondence or analogy because they believe that national, ethnic Israel awaits the fulfillment of OT promises.[233] If the typological relationship is understood such that the shadow points to the reality in the sense that the antitype is the eschatological fulfillment of the type, then Israel is not a type for any variety of dispensationalism. Thus, dispensationalists deny that Jesus is the true, antitypical Israel and rebuff the notion of the church as the eschatologically renewed Israel. As this chapter has sought to demonstrate, the dispensational position is biblically and theologically inaccurate for the following reasons.

First, dispensationalists do not recognize the typological relationship between Israel and Christ, or they redefine the typology in this particular area, because they fail in the task of biblical theology by not being sensitive to the inner textual development of the nation of Israel within the storyline of Scripture. Israel is detached from the sonship, seed, servant, and vine themes in dispensational theology in the sense that these longitudinal themes and Israel's identity and role in conjunction with them are not sufficiently interpreted. Not enough attention is paid to how the nation of Israel

---

232. See Dempster, "From Slight Peg to Cornerstone," 371–409, esp. 407; DeRouchie, "Why the Third Day?," 19–34; LaRondelle, *Israel of God*, 66–68; France, *Jesus and the Old Testament*, 53–55; Walker, *Jesus and the Holy City*, 285. Also, DeRouchie, "Why the Third Day?," 23, commenting on Hos 6:1–3, points out: "Hosea himself appears to make this connection between the one and the many when he relates a plural people with a singular 'Israel,' under whose shadow they will find refuge (Hos 14:4–8 in the Hebrew, seen in the ESV footnotes; cf. Zech 3:7–9). Thus, in Christ's resurrection on the third day, the true Israel in him rises to life."

233. See chapter 4. This point is succinctly summarized by Saucy, "Progressive Dispensational View," 161–62.

within these themes develop along the covenants and intersect with or are enmeshed in eschatological and restoration elements that anticipate and are fulfilled in Jesus Christ and the new covenant age. For example, in the OT new exodus themes converge with the typological patterns of sonship, servanthood, and the vine themes, which in turn climax and culminate in the work of Christ in the NT. However, dispensationalists are either missing or not formulating into their systematic conclusions how the NT presents the new exodus and other restoration prophecies, including new covenant promises, as coming to pass in Jesus, the Davidic king, Isaianic servant, true vine, and true Israel. The nation of Israel needs to be understood in redemptive history with relation to Adam and other corporate, representative figures, such as David and the servant. Also, how the seed theme develops within the OT itself and how the people of God is redefined in the OT with the inclusion of the nations in light of the prophesied new covenant work of the Davidic king and servant are also not given adequate attention in dispensational theology.

Second, and related to the task of biblical theology, is the understanding of the covenants. The Abrahamic covenant promises are treated as unconditional promises to Israel in dispensational thought, but as shown, the Abrahamic promises cannot be isolated from one another as the nationalistic and universalistic aspects are held together in OT prophetic texts. All the Abrahamic promises are fulfilled in Christ (Acts 3:25–26; Rom 4:13–17; 15:8; Gal 3:13–16, 22). Moreover, that the promised land is typological, looking back to Eden and forward to the new heavens and earth, is confirmed by not only textual indications within Genesis itself but in later OT books as well before receiving validation in the NT (e.g., Gal 3:18; Rom 4:13; Matt 5:5; Heb 4:1–11; 11:8–16; 1 Pet 1:4; Eph 1:11; 6:3). Dispensationalists also disassociate the promised land from the themes of rest, inheritance, temple, city, Jubilee, and kingdom, but tracing this theme from the OT and into the NT will not allow for such a conclusion. Similarly, there are no "not-yet" new covenant promises to national Israel awaiting completion in the future. Not only is there no indication in the NT that new covenant promises are still to be fulfilled to national, ethnic Israel in the future, but all the promises and blessings of the new covenant have come through Jesus. It is Jesus who is the covenant for the people, the servant who cuts the covenant through his atoning death, accomplishing a sacrifice that sprinkles the nations and makes the many—Jews and gentiles—righteous in God's sight. Jesus' followers possess all the benefits of the new covenant: the arrival of the prophesied Holy Spirit, which was to coincide with Israel's restoration, forgiveness of sins, being taught by the Lord, the law written

THE ISRAEL-CHRIST-CHURCH RELATIONSHIP

on the heart, and lastly, the inheritance is guaranteed for all new covenant members as well.

Third, the NT use of the OT is an area that has received vast attention in the past fifty or more years. While a difficult subject, the best scholarship has shown that the NT authors do not misread or misappropriate OT passages, but they are sensitive to the original context, and they never cite or allude to the OT in a manner that would contravene the original OT context. In evaluating passages such as Matt 2–4, Gal 3, and John 15, dispensationalists come to different conclusions than those I have presented; however, this is due partly to what I believe is a lack of sensitivity to the theological significance of how the NT authors are citing and alluding to the OT. Progressive dispensationalists are better in this area, but how the apostles cite OT texts regarding Israel and Israel's restoration promises with reference to the fulfillment wrought in Christ and with an orientation to the church is not sufficiently integrated in dispensational thought in general.

Finally, in tracing the Israel-Christ typological pattern through the OT and NT, it has been found that the typological pattern coincides with the principle of corporate solidarity. Jesus is the one who represents the many whereby all of Israel's hopes and promises converge and climax. Dispensationalists redefine corporate solidarity such that Jesus represents Israel but does not fulfill or replace national Israel. Yet, the problem is that the NT authors do not merely identify Jesus with Israel or merely present him as Israel's representative in general, they actually show how Israel's prophecies and the promises to Israel's figureheads or corporate representatives (Abraham, Moses, David, etc.) come to fruition in Christ as he representatively sums up the people in himself. Jesus is the recipient and fulfiller of all the promises. When discussing the principle of corporate solidarity, the eschatological nature of the work of Christ cannot be sidelined, but dispensationalists have failed to contend with this aspect. Moreover, the other side of the corporate solidarity principle has not been given enough attention. Christ sums up the many, but he is now the representative and covenant head of his people—the church. All that is true of Christ is true of his people. Why Jewish Christians would have additional promises or benefits that gentile Christians do not possess is not supported by the NT. Dispensationalists will argue that the NT still presents Israel having a future role as a national political ethnic entity, but chapter 7 will seek to demonstrate that these texts are misconstrued. All believers are united in Christ and are equal sharers in the salvation and all the benefits he secures for them.

Implications for Covenant Theology

The focus of this chapter on the Israel-Christ relationship has more direct application to dispensational theology. After all, most covenant theologians would be in accord with the presentation of Jesus as the true Israel and affirm OT Israel's typological function. Still, in terms of ecclesiology, covenant theologians have not comprehensively understood the place of Christ in putting together the Israel-church relationship. As Graeme Goldsworthy observes, "It has been one of the mistakes of some Reformed theologians to emphasize the role of the church as the new Israel and the new people of God without first highlighting Jesus as the new Israel."[234] The typological pattern is Israel to Christ and then to church, but covenant theology collapses Israel and the church in terms of substitution or direct continuity without fully appreciating that Israel is typologically linked foremost to Christ who brings about, in conjunction with the better covenantal realities he secures, a transformed covenant community united to him by faith. This new covenant community is made up of members who have all experienced the work of the Spirit and enjoy the forgiveness of sins. The eschatological element embedded within the typological pattern means there is an escalation or heightening in the people of God due to the work of Christ. The genealogical principle does not continue straight over into the NT. Isaiah and the NT authors present sonship through the Messiah as being based on spiritual adoption.[235] Abraham's offspring are those of faith and no longer consist of believers and their children.

Second and relatedly, there are other implications for covenant theology in regard to the doctrine of the church. Christ is the typological fulfillment of Israel who brings about Israel's promises, but the inauguration of Israel's restoration poses problems for covenant theology. In the exodus led

---

234. Goldsworthy, *Christ-Centered Biblical Theology*, 31.

235. As White, "Last Adam and His Seed," 70–71, observes, "[C]ontrary to the infant baptist's expectation, but according to Isaiah's prophecy, inclusion within the covenant family can no longer be decided by reference to the genealogical relationship between the covenant family and the covenant head in physical terms. The death and resurrection of Christ, the new covenant mediator, has established the necessity and propriety of reinterpreting the genealogical relationship between the covenant family and the covenant family head in spiritual terms. . . . In the light of the Servant's fulfillment of the covenant in his resurrection, Isaiah summons spiritual Zion, breft [*sic*] of physical children under covenant curse, to rejoice over the multitude of her spiritual children, the fruit of her union with her spiritual husband, the LORD himself (Isa 54:1–5; cf. Deut 30:6). By eschatological correspondence the apostle Paul designates the church collectively as the wife of the Lord of the covenant (Eph 5:22–33) and individually as the children of covenant promise, born to heavenly Jerusalem ('our mother') according to the Spirit (Gal 4:26–31)."

by Moses, the whole covenant community was brought out and delivered from Egypt. In the new exodus, God promises a greater work, the deliverance of sin that brings about regeneration and forgiveness for the exiled Israelite remnant and people who join them from among the nations. The prophets project a covenant community expanding to include gentiles, but more, all of God's people, the entire covenant community, journeys through the new exodus accomplished by the atoning work of the servant. The new exodus, new covenant, and Israel's restoration anticipated a people who would return from exile and would be followers of the Lord, marked by obedience. In short, the prophets anticipated a faithful covenant community, a new covenant community comprised of covenant keepers (see the discussion regarding Isa 56:1–8). Moreover, the priestly work of Christ mediates for the entire covenant community as he intercedes and dies for his people. Baptist ecclesiology can better account for these massively critical areas.

In the next chapter, the Christ-church relationship is investigated through the key theological theme of union with Christ. After the nature of Christ's union with his new covenant people is presented, the relationship between Israel and the church will be examined, including how this typological pattern is refracted through Christ. The contours of this typological relationship will also be explored in terms of Israel's restoration and new exodus promises and how these come over to the church. Conclusions will again be derived and applied to the two dominant theological systems.

Chapter 6

THE ISRAEL-CHURCH RELATIONSHIP VIA CHRIST

Implications for Ecclesiology

THE ARGUMENT OF THIS chapter is two-fold. The Israel-church relationship is *indirect*—the church is the fulfillment of Israel *only* in Christ, the true Israel. Further, the Israel-church relationship is indirect in the sense that it is not a one-to-one correspondence or equivalence; the church is greater than Israel by being a faithful and regenerate people as the eschatological covenant community in union with Christ. Such a formulation is at odds with both covenant theology and dispensationalism. For covenant theology, the danger is that the church is collapsed into Israel because the continuity of the people of God is inescapable given the backdrop of their understanding of the theological construct of covenant. With a covenant of grace framework, one can observe, for example, the many titles and designations of Israel directly applied to the church in the NT[1] and conclude that the relationship is direct or one of fulfillment, but either way, the church is one with Israel and of the same nature in terms of consisting of covenant keepers and breakers. On the other hand, the error of dispensationalism is

---

1. OT designations of Israel applied to the church include, among others, assembly, the people of God, the elect, children of Abraham, the flock of God, circumcision, priesthood, vineyard, and bride/wife. See Minear, *Images of the Church*; Beale, *New Testament Biblical Theology*, 669–79; Wright, "Whole Church," 14–28. Hammett, *Biblical Foundations for Baptist Churches*, 31–49, only gives attention to the images of the church as the people of God, the body of Christ, and as the temple of the Spirit.

to keep Israel and the church so separate such that there are two peoples of God given God's distinct plans for Israel and the church. Alternatively, for dispensationalists who maintain that there is one people of God, the problem remains. How Jewish Christians can be recipients of OT nationalistic promises apart from gentile Christians in a future millennial stage is confounded by the fact that *all* believers' identity is in Christ (Gal 3:26–29; 1 Cor 12:12–13) and *all* the promises and inheritance are theirs through him (Rom 4:12–17; 2 Cor 6:16—7:1; Eph 1:11–23; Heb 9:15) as is fitting for adopted sons of God (Rom 8:15–17; Gal 4:4–7).[2]

Ecclesiology must emerge from Christology: the church is the new, eschatological Israel because Christ, the last Adam, is the new covenant head of his people, the one who reconstitutes the true people of God through his cross. More specifically, it is because Jesus is the antitype of OT Israel that his disciples are deemed the true circumcision (Phil 3:3; Col 2:11), inward Jews (Rom 2:28–29), and Abraham's spiritual seed (Gal 3:7–9; Rom 4:16–18).[3] The redemptive-historical move from Israel to the church is a typological one via Christ. National Israel is the OT type or shadow that pointed forward to Christ, the true Israel, and through Christ, to the church as well. To develop this typological pattern, first the relationship of Christ to his people is considered by exploring individual and corporate union with Christ. Next, specific passages in the NT that confirm the Israel-church typological relationship via Christ will be evaluated.

CHRIST'S UNION WITH HIS PEOPLE: INDIVIDUAL AND CORPORATE

Union with Christ is a gloriously massive subject at the core of Christianity that is focused on the nature of believers being united in, participating and identifying with, and sharing in Christ and his benefits.[4] It is a perennial

---

2. See Starling, "Yes to All God's Promises," 185–204.
3. Ellis, *Paul's Use of the Old Testament*, 132–39.
4. Campbell, *Paul and Union with Christ*, 331–32, highlights the comprehensive nature of the subject: "Salvation, redemption, reconciliation, creation, election, predestination, adoption, sanctification, headship, provision, his death, resurrection, ascension, glorification, self-giving, the gifts of grace, peace, eternal life, the Spirit, spiritual riches and blessings, freedom, and the fulfillment of God's promises are all related to union with Christ." For an overview of the formal concepts or the grammar for talking about union with Christ as objective/subjective/intersubjective and the concepts of union, participation, identification, incorporation, representation, and substitution, see Vanhoozer, "From 'Blessed in Christ,'" 24–26.

subject not just for NT scholars,[5] but systematic theologians concentrate on union with Christ,[6] particularly in regard to the doctrine of salvation, although the topic relates to the role of the Holy Spirit and is crucial for ecclesiology in terms of conceiving of the nature of the church as the new covenant community in Christ. Although not receiving focused attention here, theologians have rightly noted that union with Christ is not exclusively about the salvation wrought by Christ since the person and work of Christ are inseparable just as the benefits of the giver cannot be received apart from the giver himself.[7] For the purposes of exploring the relationship between Christ and the church and how that relates to the Israel-church typology, union with Christ in view of the individual is briefly sketched before illustrating how this matches and correlates with the church's corporate unification with Christ. The NT authors' language of salvation and union with Christ for the individual Christian corresponds with how they describe salvation and union with Christ with reference to the church, the corporate covenant community.[8] Just as individual believers are united to the life, death, and resurrection of Christ, so it is with regard to the church as the church is the community of those identified with Christ. After exploring individual and corporate union with Christ, the implications of the church's union with Christ will be brought to bear on covenant and dispensational theologies.

---

5. Campbell, *Paul and Union with Christ*, 31–58; Macaskill, *Union with Christ*, 17–41; see also Schreiner, *Paul, Apostle of God's Glory*, 156–59.

6. See Murray, *Redemption Accomplished*, 161–73; Hoekema, *Saved by Grace*, 54–67; Demarest, *Cross and Salvation*, 313–44; Ferguson, *Holy Spirit*, 100–13, 144–52; Letham, *Work of Christ*, 75–87; Letham, *Union with Christ*; Horton, *Covenant and Salvation*, 129–52; Horton, *Christian Faith*, 587–619; Johnson, *One with Christ*, 15–57. See also Gaffin, *By Faith, Not by Sight*, 35–41, 58–68. For a helpful overview, see Vanhoozer, "From 'Blessed in Christ,'" 3–33. Note also Calvin, *Institutes of the Christian Religion* 3.1.1, 537–38. For a survey of union with Christ in church history, see Demarest, *Cross and Salvation*, 314–26; Horton, *Christian Faith*, 592–602.

7. Johnson, *One with Christ*, 17–18; cf. 36–38. Letham grounds union with Christ in the incarnation as the Son united himself with a human nature and as the last Adam undoes the damage caused by the first Adam in his active and passive obedience, bringing about salvation for those members of the human race who are in solidarity with him (Letham, *Work of Christ*, 77–79; Letham, *Union with Christ*, 19–43; cf. Ferguson, *Holy Spirit*, 109–10).

8. The idea of correlating individual and corporate union with Christ and how the NT describes these in similar ways is from Stephen Wellum, based upon personal conversations.

Individual Union with Christ

Murray correctly writes,

> Union with Christ is really the central truth of the whole doctrine of salvation not only in its application but also in its once-for-all accomplishment in the finished work of Christ. Indeed, the whole process of salvation has its origin in one phase of union with Christ and salvation has in view the realization of other phases of union with Christ.[9]

The redemption and atonement achieved through the cross have pivotal ramifications for humanity as one is either "in Adam" or he or she is "in Christ" (1 Cor 15:22). Those who are in Christ (which is interchangeable with the expression of Christ being in us[10]) through the supernatural work of the Holy Spirit (believers can also be said to be "in the Spirit" [Rom 8:9–10]) experience new life and have freedom from the consequences of Adam's fall. The breadth and depth of union with Christ are vast, but focus will be given to three areas: the scope of the union, the already-not-yet character of the metaphors for salvation for those united to Christ through the Spirit, and the nature of the union.[11]

The Scope of Union with Christ

First, scholars regularly acknowledge that the scope of union with Christ extends from eternity to eternity: past (election), present (the Spirit's application of Christ's salvific work to believers), and future (glorification and consummation).[12] The span of salvation has its source in the eternal

---

9. Murray, *Redemption Accomplished*, 161.

10. Passages such as Gal 2:20; Col 1:27; Rom 8:10; 2 Cor 13:5; Eph 3:17 speak of Christ dwelling in his people while other texts teach that Christians are in Christ (John 15:4–5, 7; 1 Cor 15:22; 2 Cor 5:17; 12:2; Gal 3:28; Eph 1:4; 2:10; Phil 3:9; 1 Thess 4:16). Some passages have both concepts present (John 6:56; 15:4; 1 John 4:13), which indicate the two ideas are complementary ways of expressing the same reality. See Hoekema, *Saved by Grace*, 54–55; and Demarest, *Cross and Salvation*, 326–27.

11. A study of the prepositions regarding union and participation cannot be treated here. See the surveys by Vanhoozer, "From 'Blessed in Christ,'" 13–16, 28; and Demarest, *Cross and Salvation*, 326. Note also Parsons, "'In Christ' in Paul," 25–44, esp. 25–28; and Son, *Corporate Elements in Pauline Anthropology*, 7–28. Campbell, *Paul and Union with Christ*, 67–266, provides a lengthy exegetical evaluation of the prepositions, but he often treats ἐν Χριστῷ in an instrumental sense and neglects the local sense. See Seifrid, Review of *Paul and Union with Christ*, 262–64.

12. Hoekema, *Saved by Grace*, 55–64; Vanhoozer, "From 'Blessed in Christ,'" 16–19; Johnson, *One with Christ*, 34–40; Gaffin, *By Faith, Not by Sight*, 37–38; Murray,

election of God. God had chosen Abraham and his offspring Israel to be his treasured possession (Deut 7:6-7; 14:2; Isa 41:8), but Paul writes of a sovereignly determined pre-temporal union with Christ "before the foundation of the world" (Eph 1:4; cf. 2 Tim 1:9). God the Father chose Christ from eternity (1 Pet 1:20) and he chose a people from eternity not apart from Christ, but who are *chosen in* Christ. This predetermined oneness and covenantal union with Christ are based upon his redemptive work. Those who have faith in Christ are incorporated into his death and resurrection (Gal 2:20; 1 Cor 15:20; Col 2:12-13; 3:1), and such a union is actualized and experienced when persons come to faith through the indwelling of the Holy Spirit. Finally, while believers share and participate in Christ and his blessings now, the full manifestation and goal of union with Christ is the consummation and eternal glorification in the new heavens and earth (e.g., Phil 3:20-21; Rom 8:17). Before turning to the nature of union with Christ, the present and future dimensions of salvation in Christ need further elaboration.

The Character of Salvation in Christ: Now and Not Yet

The salvation applied to the believers as they are united to Christ is like a multifaceted diamond. Just as a diamond has many faces or aspects, so Christ's salvific work has many dimensions or aspects (regeneration, justification, sanctification, etc.), but they are interwoven into a single, unified whole. These aspects of the application of redemption for those unified with Christ in the Spirit have an eschatological dimension. Ferguson explains, "Those who live in the Spirit, and thus participate in Christ, also live in this world, dominated as it is by the flesh. For that reason, there is always an already/not-yet character to the present experience of salvation."[13] A helpful way of categorizing the present and future dimensions of salvation is offered by Thomas Schreiner and A. B. Caneday. God's work of salvation in Christ may be classified into five metaphors: deliverance, renewal, legal, cultic or transformative, and family.[14]

Redemption Accomplished, 162-65. Ferguson, *Holy Spirit*, 109-11, speaks of three "moments": the eternal, the incarnational, and the existential.

13. Ferguson, *Holy Spirit*, 102. For both the present and future eschatological reality of union with Christ, including the already-not yet of the believer's resurrection, sanctification, and justification, see Gaffin, *By Faith, Not by Sight*, 56-68, 75-108; cf. Letham, *Union with Christ*, 89-90.

14. The discussion that follows is based on the study and observations of Schreiner and Caneday, *Race Set before Us*, 46-86. Also, I am treating the metaphors in a slightly different order than Schreiner and Caneday to generally reflect how the *ordo salutis* is

New life in Christ is portrayed as a deliverance. Schreiner and Caneday find the images of salvation, redemption, and the kingdom of God under the idea of deliverance. Salvation refers to one's rescue from sin and God's wrath, having a background in God's salvation of Israel in Egypt (Exod 14:13; 15:2) and God's promises to save his people in the future kingdom (Isa 35:4; 45:17; 49:6; 52:10; Jer 31:7–9). According to the NT, believers have been rescued (Eph 2:5, 8; Titus 3:5; Rom 8:24), but there is a not yet reality too as believers possess salvation in the future (Matt 10:22; Rom 5:9–10; 13:11–14; 1 Thess 5:8–9; Heb 1:14; 9:28; 1 Pet 1:5). Redemption, likewise, connotes deliverance and signifies liberation, just as the liberation from Egypt typologically anticipates freedom from the power of sin, death, and Satan that believers experience in Christ. Christian redemption is both a present and future reality.[15] The kingdom of God is also a deliverance image since believers are transferred from one realm to another (Col 1:12–13). The kingdom is inaugurated (e.g., Matt 12:28; Luke 17:21) but not yet consummated (Matt 6:10; 26:29; Acts 14:22; 1 Cor 15:50).

NT authors also depict believers united in Christ with renewal metaphors consisting of regeneration, new creation, and resurrection.[16] Regeneration is conceptually linked with new birth (John 3:3; 1:12–13; 1 John 2:29; 3:9; 4:7; 1 Pet 1:3, 23), but the term παλιγγενεσία occurs in the NT in only two places (Titus 3:5; Matt 19:28). For the Christian, regeneration is a past act or reality whereby the Spirit renews a person, bringing them to an initial living union with Christ (cf. Eph 2:4–5). However, Ferguson is correct to note that regeneration does not end where faith begins because Matt 19:28 indicates that the regeneration is fully realized in the consummation.[17] Another renewal metaphor relates to how believers are a new creation (2 Cor 5:17; Gal 6:15) and new persons in Christ (Eph 2:10). Through Christ, the last Adam, believers are already a new creation (Gal 6:14), but the ongoing work of transformation continues as Paul's commands of putting off the old self and putting on the new self (Eph 4:22, 24; Col 3:9–10) demonstrate that a process culminates when believers are fully renewed (1 John 3:2) in a

---

typically presented.

15. Schreiner and Caneday assert that the "promise made to Israel regarding redemption has now been fulfilled in Christ" (*Race Set before Us*, 58). For the realization of redemption in the present, they cite Eph 1:7; Rom 3:24; 1 Cor 1:30; Col 1:14; 1 Pet 1:18–19; Titus 2:4; Heb 9:12. The future reality of redemption is taught in Luke 21:28; Rom 8:23; and Eph 1:13–14.

16. Schreiner and Caneday, *Race Set before Us*, 64–67, also list conversion and eternal life as renewal metaphors that will not be discussed here.

17. Ferguson, *Holy Spirit*, 102–3, 117. Schreiner and Caneday, *Race Set before Us*, 60–61, describe regeneration as an entirely past reality, but they never consider Matt 19:28.

completed new creation (Rev 21:1, 3–4). Last, just as Christ was resurrected, those unified with him will also experience the resurrection of the body in the future (John 5:24–25, 28–29; 1 Cor 15:20–23; Phil 3:11). The emphasis is on the not yet of the resurrection, but Christ is already resurrected and those in him are already raised and seated with him in the heavenly places (Eph 2:6; Col 2:12; 3:1) and now have resurrection power to walk in newness of life (Rom 6:3–5).

The third classification involves the legal or penal realm and includes righteousness/justification and the forgiveness of sins. Debates regarding justification and imputation notwithstanding, justification is still best understood in a forensic sense whereby believers stand right with God as God imputes the righteousness of Christ into their account.[18] Justification is an end-time verdict rendered in the present and righteousness is also an end-time gift granted now. Righteousness awaits the final day of God's declaration (Gal 5:5; Rom 2:13; 3:20), but the saving righteousness of God is a gift now received by faith through the blood of Christ as believers are so identified with Christ that his righteousness becomes theirs (Rom 3:21–24; 5:1–2, 9; 8:1; 1 Cor 1:30; 2 Cor 5:21; Gal 2:16; Phil 3:9; Acts 13:9). Furthermore, the need for the forgiveness of sins conjures the image of God as divine judge with guilty sinners before him (Rom 1:18—3:20; Eph 2:1–3). However, those trusting in Jesus are forgiven (Acts 2:38; 10:43; 13:38) and have this forgiveness in the present (Eph 1:7; Col 1:14; cf. Heb 9:1—10:18), even as believers continue to ask for the forgiveness of their sins (Matt 6:14–15; 1 John 1:8–10).

The fourth metaphor is tied to the OT cultic language associated with the theme of holiness with respect to the temple, God's people Israel who are called to be holy, and ceremonial cleansing. The NT applies such holiness language to believers: those sanctified and called to perfection. At the time of conversion, coincident with faith, repentance, and the baptism of the Spirit (1 Cor 12:13; Rom 6:3–4; Gal 3:26–27), believers are sanctified and designated as saints or holy ones (Rom 1:7; 1 Cor 1:2; Eph 1:1; etc.). Already, believers are definitively holy, set apart, and devoted to the Lord (1 Cor 6:11; Heb 9:13–14; 10:10), but this holiness is to grow progressively (Rom 6:19–22; 1 Thess 4:3–8; 1 Pet 1:15–16). The exhortations to holiness indicate the not yet aspect of sanctification— a not yet realization that awaits the last day when believers will be made holy (1 Thess 5:23–24; Phil 1:6).

---

18. Although the doctrine of the imputation of Christ's righteousness has been challenged, see Vickers, *Jesus' Blood and Righteousness*; Carson, "Vindication of Imputation," 46–78; Horton, *Christian Faith*, 635–42; Campbell, *Paul and Union with Christ*, 399–401.

A fifth set of metaphors are familial. Under the metaphors of family, Schreiner and Caneday identify adoption, inheritance, and reconciliation.[19] Adoption was discussed in chapter 5, but it is important to note that adoption goes back to the nation of Israel (Rom 9:4) and that Paul states that believers in Christ are already adopted (Rom 8:15–17; Gal 4:5; Eph 1:5). The not-yet aspect of adoption is also taught (Rom 8:23). Similarly, those who are in Christ are already children and sons of God (this Israel-church typological relationship will be discussed later) now that the age of fulfillment has arrived (Gal 2:26; 3:7; 3:26; 4:6–7; 4:28; Heb 2:10; 12:5–11) even as there is a future dimension to sonship as well (Matt 5:9; Rom 8:19; Phil 2:15). Inheritance and heirship also evoke familial notions and again goes back to the nation of Israel and the promised land (see chapter 5). According to the NT, this inheritance and status as heirs belong to those who are identified with Christ. Believers are heirs now (Rom 8:17; Gal 3:29; 4:7; Titus 3:7) even as the inheritance of eternal life, the kingdom, and the new heavens and earth are future blessings (e.g., Matt 5:5; 19:29; 25:34; Luke 10:25; 1 Cor 6:9–10; 1 Pet 1:4). Lastly, reconciliation depicts the new relationship God's children now have even though they were estranged from him as enemies (Rom 5:10–11). Through the death of Christ (Col 1:22; 2 Cor 5:18), believers are now reconciled to God.

In summary, the believer's salvation is multifaceted. To use the analogy of Kevin Vanhoozer, salvation is like a single christological coat of many colors.[20] Those who are in Christ possess and share in all that Christ accomplished, participating in his death and resurrection. The inseparable aspects of redemption have an eschatological structure: the blessings are already experienced and they are not yet as the salvation blessings and the full realization of union with Christ await the consummation.

The Nature of Union with Christ

What it means to be united to Christ is a difficult matter and many answers have been provided to unpack the concrete content of this union. Descriptions are necessary even though there is mystery since being one with Christ transcends complete comprehension. Nevertheless, theologians have described union with Christ as Trinitarian as believers have communion and fellowship with the members of the Trinity.[21] Further, the union may be

---

19. Schreiner and Caneday, *Race Set before Us*, 67–71. They also list *children of God* as a familial metaphor.

20. Vanhoozer, "From 'Blessed in Christ,'" 17.

21. Johnson, *One with Christ*, 42–45; Vanhoozer, "From 'Blessed in Christ,'" 26;

described as *spiritual* in that the Holy Spirit is the agent who regenerates and indwells believers and unites them to Christ so that a spiritual relationship is effected as the one in Christ enjoys Christ's presence (John 14:16–20; 1 Cor 6:16–19; 12:13; Rom 8:9–11; 1 John 3:24; 4:13).[22] Being in Christ is also a vital (John 5:26; 11:25; Col 3:3–4), organic (John 15), and comprehensive relationship as the Christian's union is appropriated and lived out through faith.[23] The relationship with Christ is also a mysterious union (Eph 5:32; Col 1:26–27).[24] Particularly important to understanding union with Christ and especially for how the church is conceived of in relation to Christ is the covenantal and eschatological nature of the union.

The familial aspects of union with Christ, such as adoption and the marital motif that describes the church's intimate union with Christ (Rom 7:1–4; 1 Cor 6:15–17; 2 Cor 11:2–3; Eph 5:22–31), the representative characteristics of Christ's mediation, and the atoning death of Christ that brings about the new covenant and the accompanying redemption and salvation, all indicate that union with Christ is foremost covenantal. This is also noticeable in how Paul presents Adam and Christ as covenantal/representative heads in Rom 5:12–21 (cf. 1 Cor 15:21–22); indeed, Adam is a type of the one to come (Christ) in the sense of being the head or representative whose actions effect those in him. Adam's disobedience as the natural and federal head of the human race had the consequences of death, sin, and condemnation for all of humanity and brought about curses and devastation upon the cosmos, ushering in an age marred by sin and death. Except for Jesus, all human beings have a corrupt nature and are polluted by Adam's sin as his guilt is imputed to all (Rom 5:12, 15–19; 1 Cor 15:21–22; Ps 51:5).[25] Sin

---

Campbell, *Paul and Union with Christ*, 363–67, 409; Murray, *Redemption Accomplished*, 171–73; cf. 168–69. Vanhoozer, "From 'Blessed in Christ,'" 27–28, also uses the concepts of *communication* and *communion* to explain the ontological implications of union and participation in Christ. Since the Spirit enables believers to share in the Son's life, love, and fellowship with the Father, so being in Christ means being "communicants" in the triune fellowship. The goal of communication is communion.

22. Murray, *Redemption Accomplished*, 165–66; Demarest, *Cross and Salvation*, 330–31; Ferguson, *Holy Spirit*, 106–7; Campbell, *Paul and Union with Christ*, 360–63. Johnson, *One with Christ*, 43–45, discusses the spiritual union under the Trinitarian heading.

23. Demarest, *The Cross and Salvation*, 331–32; Johnson, *One with Christ*, 45–49. On faith union with Christ, see Hoekema, *Saved by Grace*, 60; Demarest, *Cross and Salvation*, 336–37.

24. Murray, *Redemption Accomplished*, 166–67; Demarest, *Cross and Salvation*, 333; Johnson, *One with Christ*, 49.

25. Of course, Paul's primary purpose in Rom 5:12–21 is not to explain the transmission of sin but the grace and gift of righteousness received through Christ. For discussion of how all become sinners on the basis of Adam's sin with Adam functioning as

and death reign over Adam's descendants, but the second Adam, Christ, inaugurates a new eschatological age of resurrection and life by overcoming Adam's sin so that those conjoined to him by faith have grace and all the blessings outlined with respect to the deliverance, renewal, legal, transformative, and family metaphors (and more, e.g., glorification).[26] Christ is the covenant/federal head of his people, but more precisely, he is the *new* covenant mediator and representative. Union with Christ, being "in Christ," which cannot be disassociated from the gift and ministry of the Holy Spirit, who is also linked to the new covenant promises (Ezek 36:24–27; Joel 2:28–29), must be understood in relation to the new covenant.[27] If one is in Christ, having been transferred from being in Adam to Christ, then one is now a new creation and possesses all the benefits of the new covenant, experiencing these blessings now.

As a final note and as a segue to the church's union with Christ, the covenantal nature of union with Christ corresponds directly with corporate solidarity (the "one" and the "many") and with what some scholars describe as the "incorporative union" of believers in Christ.[28] In chapter 5, the principle of corporate solidarity was discussed in terms of how Jesus Christ identified with Israel and fulfilled Israel's vocation, calling, and promises as Israel's messiah and representative.[29] As Vanhoozer summarizes, "the

---

the representative and head of humanity, see Hoekema, *Created in God's Image*, 148–67; Schreiner, *Romans*, 293–95; cf. Murray, *Imputation of Adam's Sin*, 203–94; Ferguson, *Holy Spirit*, 108–9; Letham, *Work of Christ*, 75–77, 235–36. See also Moo, *Romans*, 351–56. Contra Johnson, *One with Christ*, 62–65; and Campbell, *Paul and Union with Christ*, 343–47. Campbell wrongly reduces the contrasts between Adam and Christ to domains or spheres where they serve as the entry points, and he dismisses the notion of corporate solidarity with Adam and Christ in his study of Rom 5:12–21. For further on the Adam-Christ typology and the role of Adam and Christ as corporate figures, see Son, *Corporate Elements*, 39–65.

26. See Schreiner, *Paul, Apostle of God's Glory*, 152–55.

27. Interestingly, where union with Christ is discussed in relation to covenant (e.g., Vanhoozer, "From 'Blessed in Christ,'" 26–27), the new covenant is seldom referred to, if at all. However, Ferguson, *Holy Spirit*, 106, writes, "At the heart of this new covenant lies the work of Christ through whom renewal and restoration come. New covenant union with God is specifically a union to Christ by the Spirit which brings us the communication of redemptive blessings." In his study, Macaskill, *Union with Christ*, 108–10, 227–29, 297–300, discusses the importance of the new covenant for understanding participation in Christ.

28. See Vanhoozer, "From 'Blessed in Christ,'" 15–16, and the references he cites. Vanhoozer rightly notes that "incorporative union" is not to be confused with earlier proposals regarding "corporate personality" such as those offered by H. Wheeler Robinson. On this point, see also Macaskill, *Union with Christ*, 101–2.

29. Besides the references cited in chapter 5, see also Wright, *Paul and the Faithfulness of God*, 825–35; Schreiner, *Paul, Apostle of God's Glory*, 158–59; and Macaskill,

CHRIST JESUS, THE TRUE ISRAEL

Messiah does what Israel (and Adam) failed to do, and thereby receives the inheritance promised to Adam, Abraham, and David, as does anyone else who is 'in' (i.e., represented by and incorporated into) the Messiah."[30] Stated differently, the relationship between the covenant nation, Israel, and Christ is one of corporate representation that is also of a typological nature. On the other hand, on account of who Christ is and what he accomplishes in ratifying the new covenant and securing redemption, the principle of corporate solidarity takes a different contour with reference to Christ and the NT people of God. All those in Christ share in and possess all the benefits of that union—all that Christ achieved and secured in regard to the promises, resurrection, eternal life, etc.—is theirs since Christ is their covenant head and representative.[31] The incorporative union into Christ is also participation in the new covenant. The relationship formed in/by/through Christ between God and his people after the cross is not a typological one in contrast to the Israel-Christ relationship, but is instead a direct covenantal, vital, organic, and spiritual union.[32] E. Earle Ellis explains that this new covenant corporate solidarity

---

Union with Christ, 126–27. Macaskill rightly connects corporate solidarity to the singular Isaianic servant and the servants, and acknowledges the covenantal framework of the servant's representative role.

30. Vanhoozer, "From 'Blessed in Christ,'" 16.

31. This point regarding union with Christ raises the question of the salvation of OT saints, the faithful remnant of Israel. While OT saints were elected, regenerated by the Spirit, justified by faith, saved on the basis of Christ's future atoning work, and had communion and covenantal union with God, not all of the OT faithful were indwelt by the Spirit. The Spirit did come upon some of the OT saints, but God dwelled among his people through the tabernacle and later, the temple. OT saints trusted in God's promises, and many explicitly looked forward to the Messiah, but the union with Christ that the NT people of God experience is an eschatological reality based on Christ's resurrection and the new covenant and soteriological benefits that appear in these last days (see John 14). Not only does the whole new covenant community experience the circumcision of heart, but all of the NT people of God have greater access to the presence of God through the indwelling Spirit. For a treatment of the variety of positions regarding regeneration and the indwelling presence of the Holy Spirit for OT saints and a defense of the position that each faithful member of Israel was not indwelt by the Spirit but rather that God was *with* or *among* his people, see Hamilton, *God's Indwelling Presence*, 9–56. See also the brief analysis of Cole, *He Who Gives Life*, 143–45.

32. A distinction must be made between the OT people of God and the NT people of God. The church is not ontologically new since God has always called out and saved a people for himself (the elect), but the nature and structure of the people of God has forever changed due to the coming of Christ and his work on the cross which brings about the fulfillment of OT promises and secures greater soteriological blessings. With Christ and the new age he establishes, there is a redemptive-historical shift in the people of God. See Wellum, "Beyond Mere Ecclesiology," 195–96; Wright, "Whole Church," 14; cf. Torrance, *Atonement*, 342. Naturally, dispensationalists and those with

very probably underlies the conviction of the early Christians that those who belong to Christ, Israel's messianic king, constitute *the true Israel*. Consequently, it explains the Christian application to unbelieving Jews of Scriptures originally directed to Gentiles [(Acts 4:25ff.; Rom 8:36, 9:25, 10:13)] and, on the other hand, the application to the church of Scriptures originally directed to the Jewish nation [(2 Cor 6:16ff.; Heb 8:8–12; 1 Pet 2:9)].[33]

Corporate Union with Christ and Its Correlation with Individual Union

The purpose of developing the scope, character, and nature of union with Christ and the soteriological aspects for the believer in Christ is to show that these features and characteristics of the individual believer's union with Christ has direct correlation with the corporate unification of the church with Christ. Individual and corporate union with Christ are presented together in the NT. To establish this link between the individual and the covenant community at large, the points of contact between the aspects of the individual and corporate dimensions of union with Christ will be explored in the same categories of the scope, character, and nature of union with Christ. In discussing the corporate nature of union with Christ, distinctive corporate metaphors of union with Christ (the body of Christ and God's temple) will also be referenced to further unpack the nature of the church in relationship to Christ. The theological entailments and implications of the church's incorporation into Christ for both covenant theology and dispensationalism will then be offered.

Throughout *One with Christ*, Marcus Johnson contends that how one understands the nature of union with Christ determines to a significant degree how one understands the nature of salvation. Further, he suggests, "The same applies to our understanding of the nature of the church. The way we conceive of salvation ought to determine the way in which we conceive of the church, because ecclesiology is simply the robust application of our christology and soteriology."[34] Indeed, the nature of the church is

---

such leanings view the church's inception with the event of Pentecost. See for example, Allison, *Sojourners and Strangers*, 78–82. Covenant theologians, however, typically understand Pentecost as a renewal and stress more the continuity between Israel and the church. See Clowney, *Church*, 53–55; and note also Torrance, *Atonement*, 353–54.

33. Ellis, "How the New Testament Uses the Old," 213 (emphasis original).

34. Johnson, *One with Christ*, 199.

bound up with the person of Christ and the work of salvation he has accomplished. The identity of the church is derived from Jesus Christ, for the church is the community of those who have been united to the life, death, and resurrection of Christ. What is true of the individual's salvation and union with Christ is also true of the community of Christ.

On the relation between individual and corporate union with Christ, Bruce Demarest helpfully observes,

> In certain texts Paul envisaged the intimate relationship of the individual Christian with Christ (2 Cor 5:17; Phil 3:9). In other texts he wrote of the union of multiple believers with Christ, viewed as an aggregate of individuals. In the following Scriptures Paul juxtaposed the many and the one who are in union with Christ (Rom 8:1, cf. v. 2; 1 Cor 1:30, cf. vv. 29, 31; Eph 1:3-4, cf. v. 13; Phil 1:1, 14; 2:1, cf. v. 4; Col. 1:27, cf. v. 28). In still other texts the union envisaged is corporate (1 Cor 15:22; Gal 3:28; Eph 2:13, cf. v. 15). Sometimes Paul contemplated entire churches as being in Christ (and the Father) (Gal 1:22; 1 Thess 1:1; 2:14; 2 Thess 1:1).[35]

Paul discusses the individual Christian's union with Christ but also reflects upon groups of Christians and churches collectively as being in Christ. Given this general contour of Paul's thought, it is helpful to note specifically how the individual and corporate union coincide. This issue will be explored by linking back to the points regarding individual union with Christ.

The Scope of Corporate Union with Christ

First, regarding the scope of union with Christ where a person's union with Christ extends from eternity past to future glorification and is sourced in the election of God, the same principle is observed with respect to the church. In his study of the church in Paul's theology, James Thompson finds that the church of the Thessalonians shared in Israel's identity as the elect and holy but that the christological foundation, their identity in Christ (1 Thess 1:1; 2:14), is what separated them from the synagogue, from gentile outsiders (4:5; also indicating that the gentile Thessalonian believers are part of the

---

35. Demarest, *Cross and Salvation*, 327. See also Parsons, "'In Christ' in Paul," 27. Guthrie, *New Testament Theology*, 651, states, "The same personal emphasis is found when Paul speaks of whole communities being 'in Christ' (cf. 1 Thes. 1:1; Phil. 1:1; 1 Thes. 2:14). What is true of the individual is also true of the community. Indeed it is questionable whether Paul separated the two concepts in his own mind."

people of God whose roots lie in ancient Israel) and is what evoked hostility from outsiders (1:6; 2:14; 3:2–4).[36] The Thessalonian church is loved and chosen by God (1:4), and the deep solidarity of believers with Christ is highlighted as those who are with Christ will be so in the future (4:14, 17; 5:10) even as they are with him in the present (1:1). Thompson explains that Paul affirms, "Both 'we who are alive' (4:17; i.e., those who are in Christ, 1:1) and those who are 'dead in Christ' (4:16) will be 'with him' in the future. The church came into being 'through him' in the past, lives 'in him' in the present, and will be 'with him' in the future."[37] The scope of union with Christ for the individual matches with the scope of union with Christ for the church.

The Corporate Character of Salvation in Christ

The deliverance, renewal, legal, cultic, and family metaphors that characterized the believer's already-not-yet salvation also correlate corporately when considering the church's relationship to Christ. The first metaphor of deliverance consisted of salvation, redemption, and the kingdom of God. These aspects also apply to the church. In Christ, the church is made up of the people who have been saved and will be saved as Paul speaks of God saving "us" in his letters to the churches (e.g., 1 Cor 1:18; Eph 2:5, 8; cf. Rom 8:14; 2 Tim 1:9), and he exhorts the church to godly living as salvation lies ahead (Rom 13:11; cf. 1 Thess 5:8–9). Further, the church is composed collectively of the redeemed through Christ as the personal plural pronouns indicate (see 1 Cor 1:30; Eph 1:7; 1 Pet 1:18–19). With respect to the kingdom, individual believers are transformed from the domain of darkness to the domain of the kingdom, and on the corporate plane, the church may be described as kingdom citizens, subjects of the kingdom.[38]

The renewal metaphors of regeneration, new creation, and resurrection that characterize the believer's union with Christ also apply to the whole church. Those who have received Jesus (John 1:12–13; 1 John 5:4) and conduct themselves in love and righteousness (1 John 2:29; 3:9; 4:7; 5:4, 18) have been born of God. Paul states that the washing of rebirth has happened to "us" (Titus 3:5) as God's regenerating work applies to all of his people. Paul also explicitly describes the church as the people Christ has given himself up for and has cleansed through the washing of water and the

---

36. Thompson, *Church according to Paul*, 47, 54.

37. Thompson, *Church according to Paul*, 55.

38. See Ladd, *Theology of the New Testament*, 109–17; and Allison, *Sojourners and Strangers*, 89–100.

word (Eph 5:26). In addition, while individuals who are in Christ become a new creation (2 Cor 5:17), the language of new creation also applies to believers (Gal 6:15) as the church is the new man or new humanity in Christ (Eph 2:15; cf. v. 10). Similarly, through Christ, the church has resurrection power (Rom 6:4) and is already raised up with Christ and seated with him (Eph 2:6).

The legal metaphors of salvation again are indicative of the parallel nature of individual and corporate union with Christ. Justification and righteousness belong to each individual believer in Christ, and yet these realities are true of the community as Paul tells the church of Rome that "*we* have now been justified by his blood" (Rom 5:9; emphasis added). The righteousness of God is for all who believe (Rom 3:22) as God justifies certain Jews and gentiles by faith (3:30). Regarding forgiveness, Paul's letters to the Ephesians and Colossians refer to how "we" have redemption, the forgiveness of sins (Col 1:14; Eph 1:7). Likewise, the author of Hebrews refers to his recipients as "brothers" who have confidence to enter the holy places by the blood of Jesus with their hearts sprinkled clean and bodies washed, which illustrates how God's people enjoy the forgiveness of sins (Heb 10:19–22). The individual and corporate nature of being in Christ need to be kept together.

The fourth metaphor had to deal with cultic imagery invoking the concept of holiness. While the theme of holiness is of critical importance for individual believers, it is also significant with reference to the church as a whole. Believers are holy and are to grow in holiness, but the church is the temple of God, God's holy nation (see the later discussion of 1 Pet 2:9). Believers are called saints and holy ones, and Paul states that the church in Corinth is "sanctified in Christ Jesus" (1 Cor 1:2).[39] One of the purposes of the cross is that Christ may make the church holy, washing and cleansing her so that she will be presented as a radiant church, without stain or wrinkle, holy and blameless (Eph 5:25–26).

Fifth, individual and corporate union with Christ correlate with regard to the familial metaphors. A Christian is adopted, a child of God, and an heir through Christ. Likewise, the church is the community of believers adopted as children of God who possess the inheritance by being united to Christ. To the saints at Ephesus, Paul says God predestined "us" for adoption through Jesus Christ (Eph 1:5), and Peter tells the churches scattered

---

39. Schnabel, "Community of the Followers of Jesus," 105, asserts, "Paul's theological understanding of the fundamental nature of the church is focused on the phrase 'in Christ.' It is as a result of the person, the life, the death, and the resurrection of Jesus Christ that the Corinthian believers who assemble in the 'church of God' have been 'sanctified' and declared to be 'saints' (1:2)."

in Asia Minor that they have an inheritance kept in heaven for them (1 Pet 1:4). Also, what is true of the individual's reconciliation is true of the church (e.g., Eph 2:16). Torrance writes, "The church is the community of the reconciled, redeemed through the blood of Christ, for in him God has abolished the enmity and sin that estranged us from him."[40]

The Nature of Corporate Union with Christ

As was previously discussed, the nature of union with Christ featured vital, organic, spiritual, and fundamentally covenantal elements. The focus here will be upon the covenantal nature of the union as it pertains to the subject of this study. As far as individual union with Christ, one is either in Adam, or he or she has Christ as their covenant head. The covenantal nature of union with Christ also applies to the church at the corporate level. One passage that not only highlights the corporate nature of new covenant union with Christ but also discusses the unification of Jewish and gentile believers as co-members of God's household, the church, is Eph 2:11–22.[41] This passage is closely related to Eph 2:1–10 both structurally and thematically, but whereas Eph 2:1–10 focused on the believer's union with Christ in his resurrection, ascension, and enthronement as the solution to the predicament of sin, in Eph 2:11–22 the vertical relationship to God continues, but Paul also emphasizes how union with Christ is key in establishing horizontal reconciliation, overcoming the division of Jews and gentiles and demonstrating their joint identity as the new covenant community (God's singular body, household, new humanity, and Spirit-filled new temple).[42] Corporate

---

40. Torrance, *Atonement*, 361.

41. Scholars typically breakdown the structure of Eph 2:11–22 into three parts: the plight of the gentiles and God's response (vv. 11–13), the role of Christ in establishing peace (vv. 14–18), and the gentile membership of God's household (vv. 19–22). So Thielman, *Ephesians*, 148–86; O'Brien, *Letter to the Ephesians*, 182–221; Lincoln, *Ephesians*, 131; Hoehner, *Ephesians*, 351; cf. Yee, *Jews, Gentiles and Ethnic Reconciliation*, 71–72, 127–36, 190. However, others view the present nearness of Eph 2:13 as constituting a separate section or group it with the inclusion of gentiles into the people of God (Eph 2:13–18). See for example, Arnold, *Ephesians*, 148–52. Greever, "Nature of the New Covenant," 73–89, also argues it is likely that Paul has structured this passage so that the plight of the gentiles as strangers to the covenants (Eph 2:11–12) has its solution with gentiles being brought into the covenant of peace (Eph 2:13–18), which is then followed by a discussion of their new identity in Christ as full and equal members of God's people (Eph 2:19–22; see pp. 74–75). Cf. Sherwood, *Paul and the Restoration of Humanity*, 251–52.

42. For a discussion of the relationship between Eph 2:1–10 and 2:11–22, see Thielman, *Ephesians*, 148–49; Arnold, *Ephesians*, 173–75; O'Brien, *Letter to the Ephesians*, 183.

union with Christ (Eph 2:11–22) correlates and is theologically linked to the individual's union with Christ (Paul collectively speaks of a person's salvation and new life in Eph 2:1–10).[43] Concentrating on Eph 2:11–22 more specifically, the aspects of union with Christ in this passage including the corporate images that appear in this text are underscored before exploring the covenantal nature of the union.

The importance of union with Christ in Eph 2:11–22 is crucial. Paul reminds the gentile Christian readers of their past plight and existence as a people separated from Christ, outside of Israel's privileges and covenants, and without God in a hopeless state (Eph 2:11–12). But now gentile believers have been brought near "in Christ" by the means of his blood (Eph 2:13; note also the "in Christ" language in Eph 2:6, 7, 10).[44] Their desperate situation has been dramatically changed as God has incorporated gentiles into Christ, bringing them near to both God and to Israel. Indeed, it is "in himself" (Eph 2:15) that Jews and gentiles are made one, joined together, and it is "through him" (Eph 2:18) that access to God is obtained for all who believe.[45] In removing the enmity of the law of Moses (Eph 2:14–16), both Jews and gentiles are reconciled to God, and both are united together into a new humanity in Christ. Frank Thielman, commenting on verse 15, rightly observes,

> Paul has already used the verb κτίζω (*ktizō*, create) to refer to the individual believer as God's new creation no longer living under the sway of the world, the devil, and the flesh but in the way God originally created human beings to live (2:10; cf. vv. 2–3). Here too Paul has the new creation in mind, but

---

43. Thielman, *Ephesians*, 177, writes that in Eph 2:1–22, "Paul has demonstrated to his Gentile Christian readers the depth of their plight prior to their trust in the gospel at both the individual and corporate levels. Individually, God has rescued them from being led toward his eschatological wrath by the world, its evil prince, and their own sinful tendencies (2:1–3). Corporately, God rescued them from an ethnic hostility that kept them alienated from both the promises of God in the Scriptures and from God himself."

44. Campbell, *Paul and Union with Christ*, 87–88; Arnold, *Ephesians*, 157; and Hoehner, *Ephesians*, 361–62, all argue for the locative sense of "in Christ" for Eph 2:13 instead of the instrumental sense. Thielman, *Ephesians*, 148, rightly observes the same pattern found in Eph 2:1–10 with a description of the human plight without God (vv. 11–12; cf. vv.1–3), an explanation of the divine response to that plight (vv. 13–18; cf. vv. 4–8), and ending with the positive implications of God's response to the plight for the present (vv. 19–22; cf. v. 10).

45. For a discussion of these phrases as they relates to union with Christ, see Campbell, *Paul and Union with Christ*, 178, 262. Cf. Thielman, *Ephesians*, 171, 174.

now conceived as a corporate event, making peace between two estranged groups, Jews and Gentiles.[46]

For Paul, the reality of new creation through union with Christ is true of both the individual believer and the community, the church (cf. also 2 Cor 5:17; Gal 6:15).

Furthermore, two of the common NT images or metaphors for corporate union with Christ appear in this context as well: the body of Christ and the temple.[47] Christ accomplishes reconciliation as both groups are made into *one* entity (Eph 2:14), *one* new man (2:15), and both form *one* body (Eph 2:16), a unified people where peace is established with God and each other.[48] The body imagery is used for the church throughout Ephesians (Eph 1:22–23; 3:6; 4:4, 11–16; 5:23, 29–30) and Paul's other writings (Rom 12:4–5; 1 Cor 10:16–17; 12:12–27). The human body metaphor highlights the organic nature of union with Christ, and in this context the unity of the church is stressed through Christ's reconciling work on the cross as both Jews and gentiles form one body along with the fact that they are fellow citizens and equally members of God's household or family (Eph 2:19; cf. Eph 1:5; 4:6; Gal 6:10).

Additionally, although once aliens and strangers, gentile believers are pieced together with Jewish believers into a single dwelling place, a holy temple "in the Lord" (Eph 2:21). Christ is the one "in whom" (Eph 2:21, 22) the whole temple building is being constructed and grows together.[49] The

---

46. Thielman, *Ephesians*, 170. Sherwood, *Paul and the Restoration of Humanity*, 256, notes that Eph 2:15 shows that the eschatological restored new humanity is Christocentric. For further analysis of the new creation in Christ, see Lincoln, *Ephesians*, 143–44; O'Brien, *Letter to the Ephesians*, 199–200.

47. For discussion of the three prominent images of the church in union with Christ—the body of Christ, the temple of God, and marriage—see Vanhoozer, "From 'Blessed in Christ,'" 20–21; Campbell, *Paul and Union with Christ*, 267–310, 331, 355–56, 373, 381–83; Schreiner, *New Testament Theology*, 714–19, and see 708, 752–53, for the church as the bride of Christ; Thompson, *Church according to Paul*, 66–73, 202–13; Macaskill, *Union with Christ*, 147–71 (although he does not appeal to the imagery of marriage or bride); Son, *Corporate Elements*, 83–111, 121–37; and Fung, "Some Pauline Pictures of the Church," 89–107.

48. Campbell, *Paul and Union with Christ*, 277–78, argues unconvincingly that "in one body" (Eph 2:16) refers to Christ's crucified body, not to the church. Nevertheless, the presence of the adjective "one" strongly suggests that the parallel is to the one entity (Eph 2:14) and the one new man (2:15). Note also Col 3:15. Rightly, Son, *Corporate Elements*, 95–96; Thielman, *Ephesians*, 172; Lincoln, *Ephesians*, 144–45; Arnold, *Ephesians*, 165; Hoehner, *Ephesians*, 382–83; O'Brien, *Letter to the Ephesians*, 201–2; Macaskill, *Union with Christ*, 151; Yee, *Jews, Gentiles and Ethnic Reconciliation*, 171; cf. 175–80.

49. Campbell, *Paul and Union with Christ*, 151, 194, takes the phrases "in the Lord"

mixture of building and organic images (cf. 4:15–16) emerges from the fact that the cornerstone (Christ; 2:20; cf. Isa 28:16), "unites the building because it is organically as well as structurally bound to it."[50] The mixed metaphors not only affirm personal union with Christ as individual stones are added upon the temple building by the Spirit, nor just the union of believers with one another as they are joined and built together, but especially corporate union is highlighted as the whole construction, the church, is organically and structurally united to its cornerstone, Christ.[51] By union with Christ and the filling actualized by the Spirit, the church is God's new temple (cf. 1 Pet 2:5), the eschatological dwelling place of God that is the realization of what the OT Jerusalem temple anticipated. That former place of purification and sacrifice, where God's presence was manifested, the locale where heaven and earth met, was first fulfilled in the incarnation, death, and resurrection of Christ and as Eph 2:21–22 makes clear, it is also fulfilled by those assembled in Christ. One other ecclesiological point may be observed from Paul's corporate temple imagery in Eph 2:20–22. While Paul describes the local church or congregation as the temple of God (1 Cor 3:16–17; 2 Cor 6:16—7:1[52]), here in Ephesians, the church as the "holy temple in the Lord" is not the universal or so-called "invisible" church but is rather a heavenly,

---

and "in whom" (Eph 2:21, 22) as specifying incorporation into Christ. Cf. McKelvey, *New Temple*, 115. Vanhoozer, "From 'Blessed in Christ,'" 20, cleverly points out, "Incorporation into Christ is an ongoing building project, with each living stone sealed—cemented!—by the Spirit to Christ and hence to the rest of the structure."

50. McKelvey, *New Temple*, 116. See also O'Brien, *Letter to the Ephesians*, 219, and Peterson, "New Temple," 170. McKelvey, *New Temple*, 117, also notes that the "statement that the building grows (lit. is growing, i.e., is under construction) into a temple should not be taken to imply that the divine indwelling is a hope that will not be realized till some point in the future when the building is finished. . . . Viewed as the building the church is still under construction; viewed as a temple, however, it is an inhabited dwelling." Beale, *Temple and the Church's Mission*, 263, observes that the growth of the temple occurs also in 1 Cor 3:6–7, 10, 12, 14, and is fitting since the borders of Eden's and subsequent temples were to expand and grow until they reached the ends of the earth with God's presence.

51. See Peterson, "New Temple," 170; cf. 165 Note also Son, *Corporate Elements*, 133, 135–36.

52. While I am not able to develop in detail here, the significance of Paul's use of the array of OT citations and allusions in 2 Cor 6:16–18 (see Lev 26:11–12 and Ezek 37:26–27 for 2 Cor 6:16; Isa 52:11; Ezek 11:17; 20:34, 41 for 2 Cor 6:17; and 2 Sam 7:13–14 for 2 Cor 6:18), especially the prophetic texts which looked forward to Israel's restoration and new temple expectations and the fact that all "these promises" (2 Cor 7:1) are directed to the Corinthian readers, demonstrate that the church is the end-time temple, the beginning fulfillment of the anticipated eschatological, restoration oriented promises concerning the post-exilic temple. See Beale, *Temple and the Church's Mission*, 253–56; DeRouchie, "Is *Every* Promise 'Yes'?," 24–26; and Starling, *Not My People*, 61–106.

eschatological entity.⁵³ Based on their union with the risen and ascended Christ, believers are already seated with Christ in the heavenly sphere (Eph 2:5–6; cf. Col 2:12–13; 3:3), they are the new humanity which entails cosmic proportions (Eph 2:15), they have access to the heavenly Father through Christ (2:18), they are already citizens of the heavenly city-temple (2:19; cf. Phil 3:20; Gal 4:26), and they are unified together in experiencing the dwelling presence (Eph 2:22) of the God in heaven.⁵⁴ The church participates in and manifests the worship of the glorified end-time congregation in the heavenly city (Heb 12:22–24) such that every gathering of the local church "may be regarded as *an earthly expression of the heavenly church*" even as the church anticipates the ultimate reality of the new Jerusalem in the new creation (Rev 21:1–4).⁵⁵ Through union with Christ, "each church is the full manifestation in space and time of the one, true, heavenly, eschatological, new covenant church."⁵⁶

Lastly, Eph 2:11–22 displays corporate union with Christ as comprehensively by nature a new covenant union. Throughout the pericope the problems Paul raises are resolved though union with Christ which is fleshed out in the context of new covenant realities. The plight of the gentiles is covenantal, for they were separated from Israel's messiah, excluded from citizenship with the people of God, strangers to Israel's covenants, and outside of a covenant relationship with God (Eph 2:11–12).⁵⁷ Moreover, the dilemma requires a covenantal solution in that the old covenant with its nationalistic orientation and slave-inducing stipulations not only divided Jews and gentiles (2:13–15) but also estranged both groups from God (2:16–18; cf. 2:3).⁵⁸ It is by the means of Christ's death on the cross (2:13–16), itself a

---

53. O'Brien, *Letter to the Ephesians*, 219–20; O'Brien, "Church as a Heavenly and Eschatological Entity," 101–3; Peterson, "New Temple," 171–72; Carson, "Evangelicals, Ecumenism, and the Church," 365–67; Wellum, "Beyond Mere Ecclesiology," 202–5. Contra Lincoln, *Ephesians*, 156, and McKelvey, *New Temple*, 116, 119, who both think Paul has the universal church in mind in Eph 2:21.

54. See Peterson, "New Temple," 171. Lincoln, *Paradise Now and Not Yet*, 149–50, rightly remarks, "What is of course distinctive about heaven being the place of the Church's life in Paul's thought is that this is totally dependent on his focus on Christ in heaven and the believer's union with him and therefore participation in the life and reign which is his in the heavenlies."

55. Peterson, "New Temple," 172, emphasis original. See also Banks, *Paul's Idea of Community*, 43–51, as he argues that the idea of a "universal church" is not developed in Paul's writings and "various local churches are tangible expressions of the heavenly church" as no suggestion can be found "of a visible, universal church to which local gatherings are related as the part to the whole" (p. 47).

56. Carson, "Evangelicals Ecumenism, and the Church," 366.

57. Greever, "Nature of the New Covenant," 75–77.

58. Greever, "Nature of the New Covenant," 77–79. Lincoln, "Church and Israel,"

new covenant sacrifice, that the whole law-covenant is nullified and put to death so that both gentile and Jewish believers are united into one and are reconciled to God in Christ, having peace. Moreover, the notion of peace is not generic, but is indicative of wholeness, a well-being that is characteristic of a covenant relationship.[59] The repetition and prominence of the theme of peace in Eph 2:14–18 (explicitly mentioned in 2:14, 15, 17)[60] and the modified citation of Isa 57:19 (note also Isa 52:7) in Eph 2:17 (and possible allusions to Isa 57:19 in Eph 2:13 and Isa 9:6 in Eph 2:14) indicates that the Isaianic covenant of peace (i.e., the new covenant; Isa 54:10; cf. 54:13; 55:12; Ezek 37:23–24, 26) which is secured by the suffering servant's death (see esp. Isa 53:5 with 57:19) and the accompanying themes of restoration, new exodus, and the reconstituted and faithful covenant community (including the inclusion of foreign nations) are all soteriological and eschatological realities for Paul that now define and identify Jewish and gentile believers in union with Christ.[61] Further, the mention of the Spirit as the place of

---

613, comments that the author "does not spell out how it is that Israel too was alienated from God and needed reconciliation; but we should probably assume that . . . he believed that the law which separated Israel from the Gentiles had also come to separate Israel from God and to hold her in a state of slavery and condemnation (cf. Gal 3:10–22; 2 Cor 3:7–11; Rom 3:19–20; 7:7–25; 9:30—10:4)." See also, Thielman, *Ephesians*, 172–73; O'Brien, *Letter to the Ephesians*, 202–3.

59. Greever, "Nature of the New Covenant," 80. See also O'Brien, *Letter to the Ephesians*, 193–94.

60. O'Brien, *Letter to the Ephesians*, 193, notes, "Paul employs the term 'peace' four times (vv. 14, 15, 17 [twice]), as well as the related motifs of reconciliation (v. 16), making the two into one (v. 14), creating one new humanity (v. 15), and gaining access to the Father in one Spirit (v. 18)."

61. See Greever, "Nature of the New Covenant," 80–83, and for the elements of Isaiah's new exodus in Eph 2, see Starling, "Ephesians and the New Exodus," 144–48. There are significant interpretative difficulties with Isa 57:19. Some understand the "far" and the "near" to refer to gentiles and Jews, respectively. So Moritz, *Profound Mystery*, 32–34, 45–55; Yee, *Jews, Gentiles and Ethnic Reconciliation*, 180–81; and similarly Thielman, *Ephesians*, 158, 174n33 although he qualifies this position by stating the broader context (Isa 55:5; 56:6–8), not the immediate context of Isa 57, suggests a reference to gentiles is in the background. If this is the case, then Paul's use of Isa 57:19 is straightforward as Isaiah's restoration prophecy of the unification of Israel with other peoples is realized in the gospel. However, many others take the "far" and the "near" to refer to Jews in the dispersion and the "near" to refer to Jews in the land. So Lincoln, *Ephesians*, 146–47; O'Brien, *Letter to the Ephesians*, 207; Arnold, *Ephesians*, 156, 166; Hoehner, *Ephesians*, 386–87; Sherwood, *Paul and the Restoration of Humanity*, 258–59; cf. 116–20; and Starling, *Not My People*, 167–94, esp. 178–79. If the latter interpretation is correct, then the proposal by Starling, *Not My People*, 193 (cf. 201), is attractive since new exodus typology is in play as the gentiles are in solidarity with Jews in their spiritual death such that "Gentiles can find themselves addressed in a promise originally given to exiled Israelites because the predicament of exile which the promises addressed corresponded so precisely with their own predicament as Gentiles, spiritually

access to God (Eph 2:18) and as the means God indwells the church (2:22) is contextually connected to union with Christ. This also reveals that another new covenant reality—the promise of the Spirit (e.g., Ezek 36:26–27; Isa 32:15; 44:3)—is coordinate with the privileged nature of the believers' new situation in Christ.[62] God's eschatological temple now formed via union with Christ (Eph 2:21–22) also reflects the new covenant restoration hopes involving God's residence among his reconstituted people (see Ezek 37:26–28).[63] The establishment of eschatological peace, the inclusion of gentiles into God's new humanity, and the corporate conjoining of Jews and gentiles as God's holy temple all indicate that the OT prophecies involving the end-time gathering of the nations with Israel in unified worship at the Jerusalem temple (Isa 56:3–8; 66:18–20; cf. Isa 2:1–5; Mic 4:1–5) have come to fulfillment through Christ's work on the cross, a realization now occurring for those in solidarity with Christ.[64]

The death of Christ has conferred a new eschatological status upon his followers. Races and ethnicities continue, but the church is the new

---

dead and far off from God." Sherwood, *Paul and the Restoration of Humanity*, 258–59, also finds that the substitution of gentiles for the far-off, distant Israelites in Eph 2:17 "does little violence to the Isaianic source" given that all the parties were at one time removed from God's presence "until [God] actively creates *shalom* between them and himself. Furthermore, the proximity of Israel-nations unification in Eph 2:14b–16 amplifies Isaiah's implicit unification of Israel. . . . Christ is 'our' *shalom* (v. 14a) in that he reconciles believers into the eschatological new humanity of Israel and also reconciles this christocentrically reconstituted Israel to God, with both dimensions being bound up as one act of reconciliation" (emphasis original). Contra Hoehner, *Ephesians*, 387, who argues that Paul implements the imagery of Isa 57:19, but not its meaning.

62. Arnold, *Ephesians*, 163, 167–68, 173; see also Lincoln, *Ephesians*, 149–50, 158–59. Cole, *He Who Gives Life*, 220, describes the Holy Spirit as the designer of the church's unity in Christ. Cole also provides a helpful overview of the Holy Spirit's role in Israel's eschatological hopes in the re-creation of God's people, the outpouring of the Spirit on God's end-time people, and the Spirit's connection to a new creation (pp. 131–41).

63. See Greever, "Nature of the New Covenant," 84. Sherwood, *Paul and the Restoration of Humanity*, 259 observes that in being called God's "holy temple" and "dwelling," the church is not just restored humanity, but evinces restored creation as well.

64. McKelvey, *New Temple*, 111–12; O'Brien, *Letter to the Ephesians*, 212–13, 220; Thielman, *Ephesians*, 184; Beale, *Temple and the Church's Mission*, 260–63; Peterson, "New Temple," 172. Starling, "Ephesians and the New Exodus," 147, asserts, "Sanctuary imagery of these verses [(Eph 2:21–22)] is another echo of the exodus and new exodus narratives of the Old Testament, in which the story of Israel's salvation culminates in them being brought (back) into the sanctuary of the promised land (e.g., Exod 15:17; Ezek 37:26–27; Zech 2:10–12)." For the church's relationship to Israel in Eph 2:11–22, see Lincoln, "Church and Israel," 607–17. Overall, Eph 2:11–22 confirms that the church is the restored, eschatological Israel, the new creation in Christ. See Sherwood, *Paul and the Restoration of Humanity*, 261; Schreiner, *New Testament Theology*, 715–16.

humanity, the one body of Christ, and God's holy temple—his dwelling place—which means that the Jew-gentile divisions and distinctions are past, for the unification of Jews and gentiles through union with Christ means that race "has lost it determinative religious significance (cf. Gal. 3.28; Col. 3.11; Rom. 10.12). What matters now is not whether a person belongs to this race or that but whether or not he is a member of the new society, the people of God who have come into being with the death (and resurrection) of Christ."[65] A person becomes a member of this new society through a covenantal union with Christ and similarly, Eph 2:11–22 also shows that the church is to be understood as the community in new covenant union with Christ.

Theological Synthesis of Christ's Relation to the Church for Systems of Theology

The aim of the first section of this chapter was to examine the Christ-church relationship with concentration upon union with Christ for the purposes of informing the broader topic of the Israel-Christ-church relationship. The union with Christ theme in the NT has many dimensions and here the surface has only been scratched, but observations on the scope, soteriological aspects, and nature of the individual believer's and the church's participation and incorporation into Christ reveal a symmetry. The same truths for the individual believer in their union with Christ also appear with respect to the church. These findings have significant theological import for systems of theology in terms of how they formulate their ecclesiology with respect to union with Christ.

Theological Implications for Dispensationalism

At the center of dispensational thought is the distinction between Israel and the church with OT promises remaining for national Israel. What is not clear is how the church's union with Christ fits within this theological framework. Union with Christ functions as the fulfillment of OT covenantal themes.[66] Israel was God's covenant nation, but now through union with Christ, it is the church, the new covenant community of Jews and gentiles, that is God's holy and covenant nation (1 Pet 2:9). Further, union with Christ is not just soteriological, but eschatological. With the coming of Christ in the

---

65. McKelvey, *New Temple*, 110–11.
66. Ward, "Union of the Believer with Christ," 43–44.

fullness of time and in these last days and based on the salvation and new covenant blessings he has secured through the cross, there is now nothing left outside of Christ—all the OT promises and new covenant benefits are found in Christ and are enjoyed through him. These blessings in him are eschatological, for being adopted in Christ, a son of God through Christ, a co-heir in Christ, a kingdom citizen, possessing salvation as one redeemed and counted righteous in Christ, and being indwelt by the Spirit all carry eschatological overtones now that the new covenant era is manifested. To argue that national Israel will be restored in the future with a unique identity is to miss the point, because the only identity that matters to the NT authors is whether one is identified with Christ and thereby, a member of the church, the body of Christ, God's new temple, and one new humanity. Israel's long anticipated salvation and restoration, including the ingathering of the nations, and Israel's structures (e.g., sacrificial system, temple, priesthood) have all culminated in Israel's antitype, Christ and are now the exclusive benefits of those incorporated into and represented by Christ.

Secondly, union with Christ impinges on the dispensational emphasis placed on the promised land and the notion of a re-built temple in the millennium. Vanhoozer, in his study on union with Christ and topology, concludes that the "church is the place 'in Christ' where all of God's promises are fulfilled."[67] All the important and holy physical places for Israel, specifically, the land, Jerusalem, and the temple, are all typologically fulfilled in Christ and therefore, God no longer resides there but he is now covenantally present wherever the church of Christ may be found. Alistair Donaldson rightly states, "To be *in Christ* is therefore now the 'place' of inheritance and where the blessing of life—i.e., the kingdom of God—are experienced."[68] The blessings once promised through the land are now found in Christ.[69] In addition, the prophetic hopes involving the temple of Jerusalem are fulfilled by Christ and those who are being built into God's holy temple in him (Eph

---

67. Vanhoozer, "Being in Christ," 18. Contra Taylor, "Continuity of the People of God," 13–26. Taylor makes the astonishing claim that the church is God's people through "spiritual union with Jesus Christ as it bears conscious witness to Him. Israel retains its status as the people of God in its physical union with Christ and unconsciously bears testimony to Christ in its history" (25). However, where is this spiritual/physical dichotomy of union with Christ delineated in the NT? Union with Christ and the blessings entailed therein are comprehensively presented in the NT as directed toward those, whether Jews or gentiles, who have faith in Jesus Christ.

68. Donaldson, "Kingdom of God and the Land," 72, emphasis original.

69. Donaldson, "Kingdom of God and the Land," 72–73. See also Burge, *Jesus and the Land*, 55. Davies, *Gospel and the Land*, 217, asserts, "To be 'in Christ'—interpreted in terms of the eschatological 'people of God' and salvation-history or more 'locatively' in terms of the Body of Christ—has replaced being 'in the land' as the ideal life."

2:20–22; 1 Pet 2:4–8). God no longer dwells among his people in a physical structure, rather, eschatological fulfillment has arrived as God dwells within his people through Christ and by the agency of the Spirit. All that the Jerusalem temple looked forward to is now enjoyed in Christ; positing any theological significance for a future temple in Jerusalem is a hermeneutical mistake.

Lastly, the study of corporate union with Christ featured the covenantal unity of the church, especially in consideration of Eph 2:11–22. There are no unique promises or benefits for Jewish believers, for Paul teaches that Jews and gentiles are one body and one new humanity in Christ. Gentiles have been brought near and are now fellow citizens, members of God's household, built together with Jewish believers as God's end-time temple, and fellow heirs and partakers of promise (Eph 3:6). All the blessings and promises of the new covenant brought about through the cross are equally received by Jewish and gentile Christians. Joshua Greever is surely correct when he finds that "Paul's teaching concerning the 'one new man' in Christ suggests there is a *unified people of God* reconstituted along the lines of faith in Christ, as opposed to *distinct peoples of God* within the same covenant community."[70] Jews and gentiles in union with Christ together are the eschatological new humanity in Christ, sharing in the same privileges and responsibility of citizenship (Eph 2:12, 19), having the same identity and function in Christ, and both experience not just the same salvific benefits but equally possess all that was Israel's and more (Eph 2:14–22).[71] Gentiles do not become incorporated into national Israel; more significantly, they are made one with Jewish Christians in the new covenant community, the renewed and eschatological Israel, the people of God in Christ.

---

70. Greever, "Nature of the New Covenant," 86, emphasis original. See also Wellum, "Beyond Mere Ecclesiology," 208–9.

71. Greever, "Nature of the New Covenant," 89n29. Contra Saucy, *Case for Progressive Dispensationalism*, 218, as he wrongly distinguishes Israel's and the church's identity and kingdom function and yet postulates that they share in the same salvation of God and serve in the one kingdom. It is difficult to not view two peoples of God with this formulation. Saucy does an analysis of Eph 2:11–22 (see pp. 158–62), but he does not concentrate on the importance of union with Christ and fails to discuss how the church is the new humanity and the eschatological significance of the Jew-gentile unity, especially as they are the new temple. Hoch, "New Man of Ephesians 2," 98–126, in his treatment of Eph 2:11–22 excludes the eschatological significance of the church as God's new humanity in the fullness of the times (Eph 1:9–10). While Hoch recognizes areas of continuity and discontinuity between Israel and the church (p. 126), he misses how the church transcends both Israel and gentile entities as the eschatological people of God. This is also noticeable in Taylor, "Continuity of the People of God," 14.

Theological Implications for Covenant Theology

Covenant theologians have produced robust theologies of union with Christ. However, the commitment to the covenant of grace framework results in understanding the church as having the same composition as OT Israel, made-up of believers and unbelievers. The corporate images of union with Christ (the church as the body, bride, and temple of Christ) are not neglected in covenant theology, yet, covenant theologians have not adequately considered the correlation of the NT's presentation of individual and corporate union with Christ.[72] The descriptions and language for the individual believer's incorporation into Christ and salvation correspond to how the church is presented in union with Christ. The objective work of the cross applied to the believers is also applied to the whole covenant community. As I have sought to show, the scope, soteriological aspects, and nature of union with Christ with respect to the individual believer categorically matches with how the church is described. Stephen Wellum is correct when he states, "To be 'in Christ' (and thus in the new covenant, a member of his *ekklesia*) means that one is a regenerate believer. The NT knows nothing of one who is 'in Christ' who is not regenerate, effectually called by the Father, born of the Spirit, justified, holy, and awaiting glorification."[73] The NT presents the new covenant people of God as those who are faithful, unified with Christ. Paul did not just contemplate an aggregate of believers as being in Christ, he also asserted that entire churches, local congregations, as being in Christ (1 Cor 1:2; Gal 1:22; Eph 1:1; Phil 1:1; 1 Thess 1:1; 2:14; 2 Thess 1:1).

In considering Eph 2:11–22, the view that the church is a mixed community of covenant keepers and breakers will not stand. As Greever again helpfully points out,

> all members of the new covenant community have been reconciled to God through the death of Christ (2:13, 16). In Paul's theology, to be a member of the new covenant community *is* to be at peace with God, for the covenant is defined as a "covenant of peace." To be a member of this new covenant *is* to be a member of the "one new man," all of whom have put on Christ

---

72. For example, Horton, *Christian Faith*, 587–619, 724–27, 733–37, considers union with Christ and discusses corporate metaphors of union with Christ (bride and body of Christ), but he does not examine the correlation between the believer's union with Christ with the church's union with Christ in the areas I have outlined. Likewise, Berkhof, *Systematic Theology*, 447–53. Murray, *Redemption Accomplished*, 161–73, discusses union of Christ with respect to believers, but his findings are not brought to bear on the nature of the church.

73. Wellum, "Beyond Mere Ecclesiology," 204; see Gentry and Wellum, *Kingdom through Covenant*, 754.

(2:15; cf. 4:22–24). To be part of God's household *is* to be part of God's temple and thus to have unhindered access into his presence by the Spirit (2:18–22; cf. Isa 56:6–7).... Now that the new covenant has dawned in Christ, Paul does not regard Gentiles in the new covenant as truly "uncircumcised" any longer, for the inward circumcision of the heart to which physical circumcision pointed has become a reality for them in the new covenant community (cf. Col 2:11 [and Eph 2:11]).... This community-wide circumcision of the heart *is* the mark of membership in God's people, a people defined not by genealogy and ethnicity but by regenerate hearts.[74]

Moreover, Paul presented the church in Eph 2:11–22 as the body of Christ and as the holy temple, marked by the presence of the Holy Spirit. These images indicate that the new covenant community is made up of believers only, for how can an unbeliever be a member in Christ's body or how can the temple contain stones that are not conjoined to Christ?[75] The church is also God's new humanity, the new creation in Christ, but such a portrayal assumes that the church as a whole consists of people represented by the last and final Adam.

Lastly, appeals to a visible-invisible church distinction are misguided.[76] Certainly there are spurious professions and unbelieving people do gather with God's people for corporate worship, but such is actually irrelevant to the nature of the church since John makes a distinction between those who are "with us" versus those who persevere and show that they were "of us."[77] The presentation of the church in Eph 2:20–22 and in other texts (Col 1:18; Heb 12:22–24) suggests that new covenant congregations, unlike Israel of old, are the extensions and expressions of the one heavenly, eschatological, and spiritual church of Christ. This assumes the church is a regenerate community and that the "visible" local church is not by nature a mixture of believers and unbelievers.[78] In the end, covenant theology fails to integrate the NT's teaching of union with Christ in their doctrine of the nature of the church.

---

74. Greever, "Nature of the New Covenant," 86–87, emphasis original.

75. See Hammett, *Biblical Foundations*, 83.

76. E.g., Berkhof, *Systematic Theology*, 565–67.

77. Carson, "Evangelicals, Ecumenism, and the Church," 373; Wellum, "Beyond Mere Ecclesiology," 205.

78. Carson, "Evangelicals, Ecumenism, and the Church," 366–67; Wellum, "Beyond Mere Ecclesiology," 204–5.

THE CHURCH AS THE RENEWED ISRAEL: THE ISRAEL-CHURCH RELATIONSHIP IN TYPOLOGICAL PERSPECTIVE

In chapter 5, the Israel-Christ typological relationship was evaluated, and in the first part of this chapter the church's relationship to Christ was explored in terms of union with Christ. The last area of inquiry in thinking through the Israel to Christ to church framework is to explore how Israel relates to the church. Through Christ, the bond between OT Israel and the church is typological. Since the typological relationship features correspondence (continuity) but also escalation and eschatological advance (discontinuity), the theological entailment is that the strict continuity between Israel and the church offered by covenant theologians and the strong separation of the two entities which defines dispensationalism are both to be rejected. The typological relationship is through Christ as one must never lose sight of the fact that even though there has always been one people of God ontologically, Christ is the key link in the chain or the hinge upon which there is redemptive historical development and progress as the people of God goes from national Israel to an international, eschatological community of believers in Christ—the church. The burden of this section is to show that the Israel-church relationship is typological in the traditional sense of typology (see chapter 2). Schreiner and Caneday correctly pinpoint the importance of this point:

> We need to recognize the typological relationship between Israel and the church, because the New Testament distinguishes the two as shadow is to reality. According to Paul's theology, Israel was unfaithful and rebellious, but the church is obedient and submissive to Christ (Rom 3:3; 1 Cor 10:1–13; Eph 5:22–33). Israel descended ethnically from Abraham, but all who are in Christ are Abraham's spiritual descendants (Rom 2:25–3:9; Gal 3:29).[79]

In investigating the Israel-church typological relationship via Christ, the focus will be on texts and themes that explicate the nature of the church as the antitype of national Israel and additionally, on passages that have significant implications for understanding the church as the renewed and restored Israel. First, the two passages of Scripture where the Israel-church relationship feature typological correspondences, 1 Pet 2:4–10 and 1 Cor 10:1–13, will be examined. Further, a brief summation of the church as Abraham's true offspring, the children of God, along with the church as

---

79. Schreiner and Caneday, *Race Set before Us*, 225.

God's flock will also indicate the eschatological advance between Israel and the church within a typological structure. Finally, a consideration of Gal 6:16 is offered as this important text, although highly debated and not specifically featuring an Israel-church typology, still links the church to Israel and has implications for the Israel-Christ-church relationship.

Before moving to the Israel-church typology, one noteworthy observation that cannot be developed here is with respect to Jesus' selection of the twelve disciples. It is extremely likely the twelve disciples symbolize the twelve tribes and represent the remnant of Israel, the renewed Israel that is reconstituted around Jesus.[80] The eschatological restoration has begun in embryonic form and the twelve disciples are significant in establishing the nucleus of the restored Israel (Luke 6:12–16; cf. Eph 2:20).[81] Further, although Judas had to be replaced in accordance to Scripture (Acts 1:20; Ps 109:8), the election of Matthias (Acts 1:21–26) does not just complete the circle of the twelve in their capacity as witnesses of Jesus' resurrection, although that is crucial. But Matthias' selection is also necessary in completing the role of the twelve over the eschatological Israel (Luke 22:30) and especially for how Luke unfolds Israel's restoration in Acts. The reestablishing of the representative and symbolic function of the twelve as the core of the restored Israel is critical before the outpouring of the Spirit at Pentecost.[82] The link between the twelve tribes and the twelve apostles is explicit in Rev 21:12–14 where the people of God are presented as complete and finished, depicted as a new Jerusalem with the name of the twelve tribes on the gates and the names of the twelve apostles on the twelve foundations.

---

80. For focused studies on the selection of the twelve disciples as the foundation of an eschatologically restored Israel, see McKnight, "Jesus and the Twelve," 181–214; and Meier, "Jesus, the Twelve and the Restoration of Israel," 365–404, esp. 385–86, 404. See also Bauckham, "Restoration of Israel in Luke-Acts," 469–77; Schreiner, *New Testament Theology*, 680–81, 688; Beale, *New Testament Biblical Theology*, 422, 702; and note Quarles, *Theology of Matthew*, 107–9, on the two references to the lost sheep of Israel (Matt 9:36 and 10:6) and Jesus' appointment of the twelve (Matt 10:1–4).

81. Goppelt, *Typos*, 107–8. Ladd, *Theology of the New Testament*, 107, finds that the "[r]ecognition that the twelve were meant to constitute the nucleus of the true Israel does not exclude the view that the number 12 also involved a claim upon the entire people as Jesus' *qāhāl*. Twelve as a symbolic number looks both backward and forward: backward to the old Israel and forward to the eschatological Israel. . . . By the acted parable of choosing the twelve, Jesus taught that he was raising up a new congregation to displace the nation that was rejecting his message" (emphasis original).

82. See Schreiner, *New Testament Theology*, 688; Pao, *Acts and the Isaianic New Exodus*, 123–27; cf. Jervell, *Luke and the People of God*, 83–89. Fuller, *Restoration of Israel*, 258–61, argues that the rupture of the twelve poses a significant dilemma for Israel's restoration and that Judas' loss is in a sense another phase of exile that needs to be rectified.

The emphasis is on the twelve apostles as the foundation of the church (see Rev 21:19–20). G. K. Beale rightly observes that the apostles as the foundation of the city and the names of the twelve tribes on the gates is the opposite of what one would have expected "since Israel preceded the church in redemptive history. But the reversal figuratively highlights the fact that fulfillment of Israel's promises has finally come in Christ, who together with the apostolic witness to his fulfilling work, forms the foundation of the new temple, the church, which is the new Israel. . . ."[83] Having briefly discussed the movement from Israel to Jesus and his appointment of the twelve disciples as the foundation of the renewed Israel, I turn now to examine the typological relationship between Israel and the church.

First Peter 2:4–10: The Church as the Renewed Israel in Christ

One significant passage that highlights how the church is the antitype of Israel through Jesus is 1 Pet 2:4–10. From the very beginning of the epistle, Peter identifies his primarily gentile audience with language of exile and diaspora, imagery of OT Israel now applied to the eschatological people of God.[84] The prophets anticipated and foresaw the salvation to come in the Christ, and such prophecies not only apply to the church but were specifically intended for the church (1 Pet 1:10–12). In 1 Pet 2:4–10, the identity and function of the church is presented in a way to indicate that the church is the fulfillment of Israel through Christ.[85] Jesus, the resurrected messiah (1

---

83. Beale, *Book of Revelation*, 1070. Mayo, "Those Who Call Themselves Jews," 181, writes that the new Jerusalem "is founded on the twelve apostles illuminates John's intention to identify the city as 'eschatological Israel'—the church. The designation of the twelve gates after the twelve tribes and the foundation stones after the twelve apostles is not intended to communicate a continued distinction between the two, but that the fulfillment of Israel's hope and covenant promises rest on Christ and the testimony of the apostles (cf. Eph 2.20). John has taken Ezekiel's prophecy of a restored Israel and reinterpreted it in light of the redemptive work of the Lamb." See also Schreiner, *New Testament Theology*, 751, 848.

84. First Peter 1:14, 18, 21; 4:2–4, indicate the original readers were predominantly gentile, and yet the exilic language associates them with Israel as does the term *gentiles* which refers to non-Christian outsiders in 1 Pet 2:12, so Bauckham, "James, 1 Peter," 160–61. The majority view is that the recipients of Peter's letter were primarily gentile as the verses cited reference sins and vices typical of gentile pagans. See Schreiner, *1, 2 Peter, Jude*, 38–41; Achtemeier, *1 Peter*, 50–51. Contra Evans, "Israel according to the Book of Hebrews," 140; Vlach, *Has the Church Replaced Israel?*, 147–48. Sibley, "You Talkin' to Me? 1 Peter 2:4–10," 59–75, argues unpersuasively that the original readers were Jewish Christians. Moreover, Sibley's contention that the letter is *exclusively* for Jewish Christians cannot be proven given the geographic designation of the letter.

85. Helyer, *Life and Witness of Peter*, 185, states, "Peter's letter assumes that all who

Pet 1:21; cf. 1:3; 3:18), is the "living stone" and the cornerstone laid in Zion (2:4, 6; cf. Isa 8:14–15; 28:16; Ps 118:22; Matt 21:42–44). Those conjoined to him by faith are the "living stones" of God's "spiritual house" or new temple (cf. 2 Sam 7:13; 1 Kgs 3:2). The church is "being built up"[86] by God (cf. Matt 16:18) for the purpose of serving as priests to offer spiritual sacrifices (1 Pet 2:5; cf. Eph 2:20–22).[87] The implication is that the "temple in Jerusalem is no longer the center of God's purposes; rather, the church of Jesus Christ, composed of believers . . . constitutes the temple of God."[88] Through union with Christ, what is true of Christ (the "living stone," 1 Pet 2:4, the elect and precious cornerstone, v. 6) is true of the church (the "living stones," the building which takes it shape from the cornerstone and forms God's elect race). By being in solidarity with the vindicated and resurrected Lord (vv. 6–7), God's new temple and household of believers takes on Israel's identity and role in a heightened, eschatological sense.[89] Furthermore, the

respond to the gospel of Jesus Christ are now part of the Israel of God (cf. Gal 6:16). But it is a new Israel, a regenerated Israel (Ezek 36:25–27), living under the new covenant (Jer 31:31–34) established 'with the precious blood of Christ, like that of a lamb without defect or blemish' (1 Pet 1:19)."

86. In 1 Pet 2:5, οἰκοδομεῖσθε should be translated as a passive indicative as it is never used as an imperative in the NT and only rarely so in the LXX. See Achtemeier, *1 Peter*, 155; and Schreiner, *1, 2 Peter, Jude*, 106. See also Peterson, "New Temple," 173.

87. For further on the church as the "spiritual house" (1 Pet 2:5) in the sense that the church is where the Holy Spirit dwells and is present, along with the reference of "house" being a description of the church as God's new temple given the context of the "stone" complex, priesthood, and sacrifices, see Achtemeier, *1 Peter*, 155–56, 158–59; Wells, *God's Holy People*, 216–17; Mbuvi, *Temple, Exile and Identity*, 90–95; Davids, *First Epistle of Peter*, 86–87; contra Elliott, *1 Peter*, 414–18, who unpersuasively argues that "house" refers to household or family in 1 Pet 2:5 with no allusion to the temple. The connection of the spiritual house with the temple of Jerusalem is further underscored by 1 Pet 2:6 with the cornerstone being laid in Zion which also conjures up ideas of the temple.

88. Schreiner, *New Testament Theology*, 744. Similarly, France, "First Century Bible Study," 35, writes, "The house of God is no longer a building in Jerusalem, but is made up of living stones who themselves had no part in national Israel, but who through being 'built upon' Jesus have inherited Israel's privileged place as the locus of God's true worship and presence on earth." See also Beale, *New Testament Biblical Theology*, 741, regarding how the building of latter-day temple is tied to restoration promises. Mbuvi, *Temple, Exile and Identity*, 94–95, and Wells, *God's Holy People*, 217, also find typological fulfillment as the OT physical temple pointed to the new eschatological reality, the church. For general discussion of typology in 1 Pet 2:4–10, see Goppelt, *Typos*, 153–55.

89. Peterson, "New Temple," 172, rightly describes the church from this passage in 1 Peter as "the community of all who have come to Christ and fulfil the role of eschatological Israel. . . . [The] locus [of this new people of God] is in heaven because it consists of those who have been brought by faith to the resurrected and exalted Christ (2:4–5; cf. 3:21–22)." Similarly, Elliott, *Elect and the Holy*, 198, writes, "All that has been anticipated aforetime under the Old Dispensation has now reached its culmination in

church is not just the new temple that the OT physical temple foreshadowed but is also the priests who serve and minister in the temple. The church is corporately God's priesthood, and as such the church communicates God's glory to the nations (2:7) and mediates God's blessings in the world (cf. vv. 5, 9) through Jesus Christ.[90]

The theological conclusion to be drawn from 1 Pet 2:4-5 is that while Peter employs OT cultic imagery to describe the church (temple, priesthood, sacrifices) that links the church back to OT Israel, his description of the nature of the new covenant community is markedly different than national Israel. The church consists of believers who have come to Jesus (2:4) and who are "living stones" that are unified together as the eschatological temple, a community who in totality is indwelt by the Spirit (2:5; cf. 1:2; 4:14) and not just comprised of Spirit-filled individuals, and that is uniformly a holy priesthood that offers acceptable spiritual sacrifices through Christ. Such things could not be said of the old covenant community of Israel. The nation of Israel was not a holy priesthood or a spiritual temple and their animal sacrifices were often not accompanied by a whole-hearted devotion or done so in the power of the Spirit. The whole new covenant community is incorporated into Christ with each member being a living stone in the spiritual house. The church is also the holy priesthood "which takes the place of the Levitical priesthood of the old temple."[91] The eschatological advance or heightening characteristic of the Israel-church typology is further elucidated and made explicit in the following verses.

First Peter 2:6-8 reveals how Christ as the divine and eschatological cornerstone divides people into two groups, unbelievers and those who constitute the church, believers. The emphatic contrast between the status of unbelievers and believers is further highlighted as Peter describes the church as God's chosen race, royal priesthood, holy nation, special possession, and the people God has claimed through his remarkable mercy (2:9-10).[92] These titles of the church are characteristic of its present status since

---

the union between the Elect Stone and the Elect Race."

90. The spiritual sacrifices in 1 Pet 2:5 are not just the proclamation of God's excellencies though, for surely spiritual sacrifices entail everything that is pleasing to God in one's conduct and dedication to God by the sanctifying work of the Spirit (cf. Rom 12:1; Heb 9:13-14; 12:28-29; 13:15-16). See Peterson, "New Temple," 174-75; Wells, *God's Holy People*, 219-21; Schreiner, *1, 2 Peter, Jude*, 107-8; Jobes, *1 Peter*, 150-51.

91. France, "First Century Bible Study," 35.

92. For discussion of these OT titles and allusions of Israel and their application to the church, see Carson, "1 Peter," 1030-33; Elliott, *Elect and the Holy*, 38-47; Achtemeier, *1 Peter*, 163-68. In regard to the church being a royal priesthood, Mbuvi, *Temple, Exile and Identity*, 107, observes, "For Ezekiel, the foreigner could not present offerings at the temple nor even serve as a priest [Ezek 44:6-16]. 1 Peter reverses the

the eschatological salvation is already achieved through Jesus Christ (v. 10): "It is Jesus Christ and the bond of faith which determine and acknowledge the eschatological present and the ascription of titles of election."[93] The OT language that Peter alludes to in verses 9 and 10 is from Exod 19:5–6; Isa 43:20–21; and Hos 2:23. Exodus 19:6 is Israel's charter statement when it was constituted as God's people following the exodus and as such features the divine goal of the covenant relationship: if Israel obeys God's covenant then they would be God's treasured possession, a kingdom of priests, and a holy nation. Peter applies these designations to the church because they are the people of the new exodus.[94] The Israel and exodus typology is also evident from Isa 43:20–21 (cf. Isa 43:16–19) as God's chosen race is depicted coming out of the Babylonian exile with overtones of new creation. Regardless of ethnic background, the church is now the true race, the antitypical descendants of Abraham, that God redeems through the lamb of the greater exodus (see 1 Pet 1:19; cf. Isa 53:7; note 1 Pet 1:2 with Exod 24:6–8). Lastly, Peter's use of Hos 2:23 (cf. Hos 1:9–11) in 1 Pet 2:9–10 indicates that God's mercy on the church fulfills Hosea's restoration prophecy. In the context of Hosea, God has disowned Israel because of her idolatry and spiritual adultery. Israel is no longer the covenant people; they are "not my people," becoming just like a gentile nation, cut off from the promises. In Hos 2:23, however, God promises to mercifully restore this faithless, gentile-like nation. According to Peter, the prophecy regarding God's "gentile" people returning and becoming his people once again is understood to be typologically fulfilled as God's mercy is extended to the church, including those who really are gentiles.[95] Throughout this passage, Peter is making it clear

---

edict and without apology regards the Gentile believers as part of the new 'holy' and 'royal' priesthood. Second, we note that 1 Peter does not seem to leave room at all for any other special lineage of priests, Levitical or otherwise. The believers constitute the new priesthood." These changes from the OT administration to the NT arrangement can only be possible in light of the work of Christ.

93. Elliott, *Elect and the Holy*, 47. See also Wells, *God's Holy People*, 221, 224.

94. Bauckham, "James, 1 Peter," 161; Carson, "1 Peter," 1030–31; Schreiner, *New Testament Theology*, 743; cf. Wells, *God's Holy People*, 222; Jobes, *1 Peter*, 158–59.

95. Carson, "1 Peter," 1031–32. Carson helpfully observes, "The logic of the situation—that if the ancient covenant people have become 'Gentiles,' then perhaps God's mercy may extend to those who are (racially) Gentiles—breeds a second line of thought: God's merciful handling of his own 'Gentile' people becomes an action, a pattern, a 'type,' of his handling of even more Gentiles" (p. 1032). See also Jobes, *1 Peter*, 163–64; Schreiner, *1, 2 Peter, Jude*, 114. Bauckham, "James, 1 Peter," 161, also notes that Peter's "image of 'new birth (1.3; 23), effected by God's word which also accomplishes the new Exodus (1 Pet. 1.24–25; Isa 40.7–8), is probably also to be connected with the prophecy of Hosea. This new birth makes those who previously were not God's people 'children of the living God' (Hos 1:10)." The usage of Hos 1:10; 2:23 is also applied by Paul in

that "the privileges belonging to Israel now belong to Christ's church. The church does not replace Israel, but it does fulfill the promises made to Israel; and all those, Jews and Gentiles, who belong to Christ are now part of the new people of God."[96]

The implications of 1 Pet 2:4–10 are significant for systems of theology. For Peter, the church is the eschatological people of God that is inextricably linked to the promises and heritage of OT Israel. A variety of OT typological patterns converge in this passage as Peter teaches that the church is the new temple, the new priesthood, and via the new exodus in Christ (Isa 43:20–21; Hos 2:15, 23; cf. Exod 19:1–6) the church is the fulfillment of OT Israel in being the elect race, holy nation, and the people (λαός; 1 Pet 2:9–10; cf. Deut 4:20; 14:2; Heb 2:7; 4:9) set aside for God's special possession. Further, the church carries out the task that Israel was originally assigned in the aftermath of the Babylonian exile (Isa 43:21): declaring God's praises and his mighty acts of salvation and transformation (1 Pet 2:9). Dispensationalism fails to account for the typological fulfillments presented in this passage. Peter identifies the church as the restored and renewed Israel through Christ. The church is now God's people (2:10) because of their faith union with the eschatological cornerstone that has been laid in Zion (2:6). The privileges and identity of Israel are now the church's in an escalated and heightened sense through the living stone—Jesus Christ—and the salvation

---

Rom 9:23–26. For discussion, see Beale, *New Testament Biblical Theology*, 705–8.

96. Schreiner, *1, 2 Peter, Jude*, 115. Likewise, Wells, *God's Holy People*, 227, concludes, "Not only are Christians given the title λαός ('people'), which previously served as the ethnic (as well as theological) designation for Jewish Israel; they are also termed (far more specifically) a γένος ('race') despite the fact that they are drawn from many nations. This makes the point even more emphatically: that ethnic boundaries are superseded. Prerequisites for belonging to the eschatological λαός are no longer historical or genetic but purely religious: belief in Jesus the Christ." Cf. Goppelt, *Typos*, 140–41, 154–55. Contra, Saucy, *Case for Progressive Dispensationalism*, 205–6, and Glenny, "Israelite Imagery of 1 Peter 2," 156–87. Curiously, Glenny recognizes the typological patterns in 1 Pet 2:4–10, including the element of escalation intrinsic to typological relationships, but he then nullifies this when he concludes that these typological patterns do "not negate the future fulfillment of the national, political, and geographic promises ... made to Israel in these [OT] contexts" (p. 187). If so, Peter's usage of these texts are purely analogical, *not* typological. As I have argued, these OT texts featuring Israel's national/political identity and role which Peter directly applies to the church through Christ are typological because of the fulfillment accomplished by Christ as he establishes the prophesied true temple and executes the new exodus. Glenny is also inconsistent, for Christ can be the final fulfillment of the typological patterns of 1 Pet 2:6–8, but the church is only the initial fulfillment of the pattern described in 1 Pet 2:9–10 (p. 186). This is unconvincing, for if Christ is the end of the road for these typological patterns, why would this not be the case for those conjoined to this eschatological stone, the living stones—the church—in these last times (1 Pet 1:20)?

he has accomplished in the last days (1:20–21).[97] If there were to be a future restoration of national and political Israel, Peter's allusions to key OT structures (temple, priesthood, sacrifices) with reference to being fulfilled with the church as well as Peter's application of Israel's pivotal identity markers to the church renders such a notion to be counterintuitive and unexpected.[98] Peter's understanding of the church as the people of God is emphatically Christocentric and eschatological.

On the other hand, Peter does not just present the church as an equivalence to or in direct continuity with OT Israel as the ecclesiological formulations of covenant theology indicate. Rather, the new covenant community obeys the word by putting on faith in Christ in contrast to those appointed to stumble (2:6–7). Peter's readers are those who have experienced the new birth (1:3, 23) and conversion (2:9; cf. 2:25)[99] in receiving God's mercy in Christ (2:10). Moreover, according to Peter, the new covenant community is comprised of living stones built together as the spiritual house indwelt by the Holy Spirit because they have come to Christ and are conjoined to this living stone as their foundation. Each member of the new covenant community is considered a living stone; the structure of the new temple is not made up of living and dead stones. The escalation and heightening of the typological relationship between Israel and the church is also unavoidable

---

97. Contra Vlach, *Has the Church Replaced Israel?*, 148–50. Vlach's attempts to counter a "supersessionist" reading of 1 Pet 2:9–10 (whereby the church replaces Israel and believing gentiles are identified as "Israel") ultimately fail. Peter's point is not to argue a one-to-one correspondence between Israel and the church, rather, the typological correspondences reveal that the end-time people of God, the church, is not equivalent or equal to national Israel but is the far greater covenant community through union with Christ. Israel's identity markers and titles come over to the church in an escalated sense (a feature indicative of all typological patterns), and once the antitype has arrived, given the eschatological orientation, there is no need to posit a future for national Israel. Vlach's arguments ignore the eschatological significance of the work of Christ and his theological conclusions are not grounded in actual exegesis of 1 Pet 2:4–10.

98. In lieu of his study of 1 Pet 2:4–10, France, "First Century Bible Study," 42–43, observes, "How central to Peter's thinking was the view that the people of God was now, since the coming of Christ, focused not in the national community of Israel but in a reconstituted people of God, drawn from all nations, whose unity was to be found not in political or racial solidarity, but in relationship to Jesus. . . . Some still look for a central place for national Israel in the future outworking of God's purpose, basing their belief not on the teaching of Jesus and his apostles but on elements of Old Testament prophecy interpreted without reference to the New Testament's view that it is in Christ, and derivatively in his people, that those promises have been and continue to be fulfilled."

99. The imagery associated with light and darkness at the end of 1 Pet 2:9 strongly suggests that conversion is in view. See Achtemeier, *1 Peter*, 166–67; Davids, *First Epistle of Peter*, 93; Schreiner, *1, 2 Peter, Jude*, 116.

in this passage of 1 Peter because the church is the restored Israel, for the new covenant community has gone through the new exodus in Christ and thus, in contrast to Israel of old, Peter's readers, and by extension the church, truly are the chosen race, the royal priesthood, the holy nation, and the people of God. While believers need encouragement and are exhorted to contemplate whether they have experienced the kindness of the Lord (1 Pet 2:3), Peter does not present the church as a mixed covenant community but as the new covenant people who belong to Jesus and are joined to him.

First Corinthians 10:1–13: The Typology of Israel's Wilderness Events and the Church as the End-Time People of God

Another passage featuring an Israel-church typological correspondence, or that more specifically discloses that Israel's experiences through the exodus and the wilderness have typological import for the church, is 1 Cor 10:1–13. The passage is challenging, however, and interpreters are divided whether the pericope is strictly paraenesis or combines paraenesis with typology.[100] Further, does the Israel to Christ to church relationship hold if Paul directly corresponds Israel with the church, applying what Richard Hays describes as an ecclesiocentric hermeneutic?[101] In what follows I seek to demonstrate that there is a typological relationship presented between Israel and the church in 1 Cor 10:1–13 that entails both continuity (correspondence) and discontinuity (escalation/heightening) and that this relationship, though not as explicitly Christocentric, hinges upon the person and work of Christ.

---

100. See Davidson, *Typology in Scripture*, 193–94, and the references he lists for each approach. In more recent studies, scholars who identify the presence of some form of typology or elements of typology in Paul's warning to the Corinthians in 10:1–13 include Carson, "Mystery and Fulfillment," 399–400; Hays, *Echoes of Scripture*, 95–102; Vanhoozer and Treier, *Theology and the Mirror of Scripture*, 161–63; Fee, *First Epistle to the Corinthians*, 489–500, 506–7 (Fee views a mixture of type and analogy); Ciampa and Rosner, *First Letter to the Corinthians*, 443–54; note also Goppelt, *Typos*, 144–46, 219–20. On the other hand, Garland, *1 Corinthians*, 447–60, esp. 459, finds only analogies and examples. Similarly, see Willis, *Idol Meat in Corinth*, 125. Dispensationalists generally interpret the passage in terms of analogy and illustration. Covenant theologians seem to acknowledge typological patterns in 1 Cor 10:1–13, so Johnson, *Walking with Jesus*, 59–60; Johnson, "Pauline Typology," 45–56, 68–70, 76–79, 84–89; Vander Hart, "Exodus as Sacrament," 9–46; and more cautiously, Bandstra, "Interpretation in 1 Corinthians 10," 5–21, esp. 15–17.

101. Hays, *Echoes of Scripture*, 84–87, 98, 102, argues that Paul's hermeneutic in 1 Cor 10:1–13 is not Christocentric, but ecclesiocentric, as he "makes the biblical text pass through the filter of his experience of God's action of forming the church" (102).

CHRIST JESUS, THE TRUE ISRAEL

By way of overview, Paul's readers in Corinth are predominantly converted gentiles who were former idolaters (1 Cor 6:9–11; 8:7; 12:2).[102] Turmoil was occurring in the church as Paul addresses issues of factionalism (1:10—4:21), sexual immorality (5:1—7:40), idolatry (8:1—11:1), divisions in regard to corporate worship (11:2—14:40), and confusion regarding the resurrection of the dead (15:1–58).[103] Nevertheless, despite all their problems which incur Paul's exhortations and stern warnings throughout the letter, Paul rebuilds the ecclesial identity, addressing the church in Corinth as "saints," and referring to them as those who are called, sanctified in Christ (1:2), and as those who have experienced conversion (6:11).[104] The Corinthians are the "church of God" (1:2; 10:32; 11:22), God's temple (3:16–17), and the body of Christ (10:17; 11:29; 12:12–26), a community that is one with Christ and that is to display unity and be characterized by holiness through the indwelling presence of the Spirit.[105] "As in the other epistles, Paul's Christology in 1 Corinthians reshapes the concept of the people of God."[106]

First Corinthians 10:1–13 is situated within a larger context where Paul discusses eating food offered to idols and more generally the question of Christian freedom (8:1—11:1). Paul turns from his preceding warning derived from athletic competitions where he provides a vivid illustration of the Corinthians' need for self-control in order to receive the eschatological prize (9:24–27), to a more direct warning based upon Israel's historical failure and apostasy despite their experience of God's deliverance and provision in the exodus and during the wilderness wanderings.[107] Clearly, the main purpose of Paul's warning in this passage is that the Corinthians would heed the pitfalls of Israel's past, persevere in faith, and so avoid idolatry (cf. 10:14).[108] More specifically, the Corinthians are to evade repeating

---

102. See Fee, *First Epistle to the Corinthians*, 4. Hays, *Echoes of Scripture*, 96, commenting on Paul's description of a time when his readers were gentiles (1 Cor 12:1–2), states, "The causal imperfect tense of his description (*ēte*) indicates that Paul thinks of the Corinthian Christians as Gentiles no longer; they have been incorporated into Israel."

103. Garland, *1 Corinthians*, 20–21.

104. Thompson, *Church according to Paul*, 65–66.

105. Thompson, *Church according to Paul*, 66–73. Note also Fee, *First Epistle to the Corinthians*, 19–20. For a succinct list of titles for the congregation in 1 Cor, see Works, *Church in the Wilderness*, 40.

106. Thompson, *Church according to Paul*, 66.

107. For discussion of the immediate context of 1 Cor 10:1–13 with the preceding pericope (9:24–27), see Fee, *First Epistle to the Corinthians*, 486–89; Ciampa and Rosner, *First Letter to the Corinthians*, 443–44; Davidson, *Typology in Scripture*, 203–6.

108. Davidson, *Typology in Scripture*, 204–6, 254; Fee, *First Epistle to the Corinthians*,

Israel's apostasy by resisting what most of the Israelites craved (10:6) and not reenact Israel's evil practices (10:7–10).[109]

Paul's retelling of Israel's redemptive blessings through the exodus and wilderness is designed so that the Corinthians identify with them, observing how they had their own form of "baptism" and "Lord's Supper" (spiritual food and drink), and were related to Christ himself as he was the rock in the wilderness, the source of their nourishment (1 Cor 10:4).[110] One of the keys to the paraenetic warning is the fact that "all" (1 Cor 10:1–4) of the Israelites were delivered and received God's miraculous provisions, but despite these privileges for the entire covenant community, "most of them" (10:5) and "some of them" (10:7–10) were judged and destroyed, failing to enter the promised land.[111] That *all* the ancestors experienced these things mirrors the Corinthians, for they all participated in baptism (1 Cor 1:13) and shared in the Lord's Supper (1 Cor 10:17; cf. 11:17–34).[112] Paul admonishes the Corinthians to not fall (10:12) as most of the Israelites had, for participation in idol feasts, despite experiencing baptism and sharing in the Lord's Supper, can lead to condemnation and failure to enter the eschatological promised land.[113]

486–88. Carson, "Mystery and Fulfillment," 400, writes, "The moral point is obvious: perseverance is required, or these Corinthians who have begun well, like the Israelites of old, may not reach their goal (10:12)."

109. Namely, the Corinthians are to avoid (1) the idolatry the Israelites committed with the golden calf episode (10:7; citing Exod 32:6 LXX; cf. Num 11; 14), (2) the sexual immorality of the Israelites as they had done with the Moabite women (1 Cor 10:8; alluding to Num 25:1–9), (3) the Israelites' testing of Christ by provoking him with complaints of food and water in the wilderness (1 Cor 10:9; alluding to Num 21:5–6; cf. Pss 78:18, 41, 45; 106:14), and (4) the grumbling that characterizes Israel on numerous occasions (1 Cor 10:10; cf. Num 14; 16; Exod 12:23; Ps 106:16–18). For discussion, see Works, *Church in the Wilderness*, 69–78; Ciampa and Rosner, *First Letter to the Corinthians*, 455–64; Fee, *First Epistle to the Corinthians*, 501–6; Garland, *1 Corinthians*, 460–64.

110. Fee, *First Epistle to the Corinthians*, 488; Ciampa and Rosner, *First Letter to the Corinthians*, 444.

111. Fee, *First Epistle to the Corinthians*, 488, 490n449; Ciampa and Rosner, *First Letter to the Corinthians*, 444; Thiselton, *First Epistle to the Corinthians*, 725; Gardner, *Gifts of God*, 115, 118–19.

112. Works, *Church in the Wilderness*, 53.

113. Some interpreters understand the Corinthians to have a misguided, magical view of baptism and the Lord's Supper where they assumed salvation security *ex opere operato*. So Davidson, *Typology in Scripture*, 210; Schreiner, *Paul, Apostle of God's Glory*, 376–77; Fee, *First Epistle to the Corinthians*, 488, 507; Bandstra, "Interpretation in 1 Corinthians 10," 6; Beasley-Murray, *Baptism in the New Testament*, 265. On the other hand, Garland, *1 Corinthians*, 453–54, and Ciampa and Rosner, *First Letter to the Corinthians*, 448–49, think there is no evidence that the Corinthians held to a

Given this summary of 1 Cor 10:1–13, three other exegetical points are necessary. First, in verse 1, Paul describes his readers as "brothers." Despite the perilous warning that Paul is about to issue, he assumes the Corinthians are Christians. Further, the OT covenant people of God are referred to as "our ancestors" which "reflects his understanding that the Corinthians are to understand themselves in the light of the new identity formed through their adoption into the covenant people of God. Even the gentile readers of this letter are now to think of the Israelites of the Exodus as their adopted 'fathers' through their inclusion in the covenant community."[114] The significance of calling Israel "our fathers" is also rightly captured by Gordon Fee, as Paul

> emphasizes at the outset the Corinthians' continuity with what God had done in the past. Since he is writing to a [predominantly] Gentile congregation, this language is sure evidence ... of Paul's understanding of their eschatological existence in Christ (cf. v. 11) as being in true continuity with the past. God's new people are thus God's true Israel, who fulfill the promises made to their fathers.[115]

The church is not only linked to Israel as descendants and heirs, but Israel's exodus, which is the major formative event in Israel's history and that also served as a basis for Israel's restoration hopes in the prophetic books, will "now play a central role in forming the identity not only of Jews but of Gentile believers as well."[116]

---

quasi-magical view of the sacraments as Paul is not correcting misunderstandings of the sacraments but warning of idolatry. Note also Gardner, *Gifts of God*, 117–19; Willis, *Idol Meat in Corinth*, 159–60.

114. Ciampa and Rosner, *First Letter to the Corinthians*, 446. Cf. Garland, *1 Corinthians*, 448–49. Thiselton, *First Epistle to the Corinthians*, 723, translates ἀδελφοί as "my dear fellow Christians."

115. Fee, *First Epistle to the Corinthians*, 490. Hays, *Echoes of Scripture*, 95–97, argues that Paul never uses the expressions "new Israel" or "spiritual Israel" and there is only one Israel, the Israel that has now absorbed gentile Christians. The problem with this analysis, despite the fact that Hays is surely correct that such expressions are not used by Paul, is that it fails to capture the newness associated with Christ and how he reconstitutes the people of God in fulfillment of OT promises. The church is not an enlarged Israel; instead, the church is God's end-time community in Christ (1 Cor 10:11). As Davidson, *Typology in Scripture*, 209, rightly finds, the reference to ancient Israel as "our fathers," "indicates that the Christian church is viewed as existing in continuity with Israel. Indeed, it is the new (eschatological, vs. 11) Israel."

116. Ciampa and Rosner, *First Letter to the Corinthians*, 447. For the importance of the exodus for Israel's identity and how this theme cast their vision for their future restoration, see the discussion in chapter 5, and Keesmaat, "Exodus," 35–37. Note also, Works, *Church in the Wilderness*, 31–40, 51.

Second, Paul recalls (1 Cor 10:1b–2) the exodus event with respect to God's redemptive power and presence in the midst of the Israelites. All of Israel passed through the Red Sea (Exod 14:2–27; Ps 78:13–14; Neh 9:11–12), being guided, protected, and separated from the Egyptians under the theophanic cloud (Exod 14:19–22, 24; cf. 13:21–22; Ps 105:38–39). Being under the cloud and passing through the sea is referred to as a baptism (1 Cor 10:2), paralleling and corresponding to Christian baptism where the convert is immersed under water. Although the Israelites were never wet as they crossed the sea on dry land (Exod 14:22), since the exodus deliverance initiated Israel as God's covenant people, marking their beginning as a redeemed people from the bondage of Egpyt, the correlation with baptism is fitting, for baptism is what initiates and begins the Christian life as one is brought into the new covenant community.[117] To further heighten the correspondence between the Corinthians and Israel, Paul says that all the Israelites were "baptized into Moses" (1 Cor 10:2). This phrase appears nowhere else in Jewish literature, and although several interpretations are offered, the language is likely formulated by Paul to mirror baptism into Christ (Gal 3:27; Rom 6:3; cf. 1 Cor 1:13; 12:13; Matt 28:19).[118] Just as Moses was the covenant mediator and deliverer during Israel's exodus redemption and the one with whom the Israelites identified with, so Christ, the new covenant mediator, is the deliverer that the Corinthians identify with in their baptism. In these two verses, Paul's aim is not to develop a sacramental theology or present the Israelites as if they had their sacramental rites.[119] The reference to being baptized into Moses in the cloud and the sea

117. See Fee, *First Epistle to the Corinthians*, 491; Garland, *1 Corinthians*, 451; Ciampa and Rosner, *First Letter to the Corinthians*, 446. Thiselton, *First Epistle to the Corinthians*, 724, states that because the exodus events "constitute a paradigm of redemption (*from* bondage, *by* God's saving act, *to* a new lifestyle and reality, Exod 14:19–22) Paul finds it appropriate to denote this as a baptismal-like redemptive experience of grace" (emphasis original; bold removed). Bandstra, "Interpretation in 1 Corinthians 10," 8–9 (cf. Vander Hart, "Exodus as Sacrament," 34–35), follows Kline, *By Oath Consigned*, 67–70, in arguing that the "baptism" cannot be by immersion in 1 Cor 10:2, but is instead a fire and water judgment ordeal. However, Malone, *Baptism of Disciples Alone*, 216, explains that the primary sense of baptism, to dip or to immerse, fits best in this context because being immersed into Moses "sustains the idea of the people being put into union with Moses as their mediator and leader (Hebrews 3:2–4, 16), just as Romans 6:3–4 does with Christ." Further, the notion of immersion is also legitimate in the primary sense for Christian initiation as Paul transfers this idea to Israel's crossing of the sea, so Fee, *First Epistle to the Corinthians*, 492n456. Note also Goppelt, *Typos*, 145 and Gardner, *Gifts of God*, 120.

118. Fee, *First Epistle to the Corinthians*, 491; Garland, *1 Corinthians*, 450–51; Willis, *Idol Meat in Corinth*, 129; Ciampa and Rosner, *First Letter to the Corinthians*, 447–48; Works, *Church in the Wilderness*, 56–57; Davidson, *Typology in Scripture*, 214.

119. Rightly, Garland, *1 Corinthians*, 449–52; similarly, Fee, *First Epistle to the*

is intended to highlight that the exodus event formed the new identity of God's covenant people in the saving deliverance through the leadership and covenant mediation of Moses, the passage through the sea separating Israel from Egypt, and the cloud, representing God's presence, faithfully guiding, protecting, redeeming the people, and distinguishing Israel from the nations (Exod 33:15–16; Num 14:13–17). Thus, the Corinthians are warned, for the fathers experienced a symbolic or figurative form of baptism via their exodus, but as Paul shows, Israel's blessings did not prevent them from being seduced into idolatry, resulting in God's judgment (1 Cor 10:5).

A third and final point before addressing the question of typology and arriving at theological conclusions is in regard to verses 3 and 4 where Paul links Israel's feeding on the manna (Exod 16:4, 14–18; Num 11:6–9; Deut 8:3, 16; Pss 78:24; 105:40) and drinking water from the rock (Exod 17:6; cf. Num 20:7–13; Pss 78:15–16; 105:41) with the Lord's Supper (see 1 Cor 10:16–22).[120] The manna and water enjoyed in the wilderness are referred to as "spiritual" food and "spiritual" drink, the reason or explanation (γάρ; 10:4) being that the spiritual drink came from a "spiritual rock." The adjective "spiritual" has received a variety of interpretations, but clearly in the context of the OT narrative, the manna and the water from the rock are supernaturally and miraculously bestowed, of a heavenly or divine origin and source. In addition, the "spiritual" food and drink are associated with the "spiritual" rock—Christ—which suggests they are "spiritual" in not just being supernatural, but in pointing to Christ and having a corresponding typological significance with respect to the Lord's Supper.[121] At issue is not

---

Corinthians, 491–92; Beasley-Murray, *Baptism in the New Testament*, 181–85; Gardner, *Gifts of God*, 117–18.

120. Virtually every commentator agrees that Paul is alluding to the Lord's Supper with the expressions "spiritual food" and "spiritual drink." See Fee, *First Epistle to the Corinthians*, 492–93; Ciampa and Rosner, *First Letter to the Corinthians*, 448–49; Davidson, *Typology in Scripture*, 224; Bandstra, "Interpretation in 1 Corinthians 10," 9; Works, *Church in the Wilderness*, 61–62. Less clear is Thiselton, *First Epistle to the Corinthians*, 726. Ciampa and Rosner, *First Letter to the Corinthians*, 449, assert, "The early church's (and Paul's) understanding of the last supper and the Lord's Supper in terms of the Jewish Passover and the promised second exodus would have made the parallel between the Lord's Supper (see . . . 1 Cor. 11:23–26) and the Israelites' experience in the exodus a natural one for Paul and his readers." This parallel does not establish equivalence, as Garland, *1 Corinthians*, 452, rightly avers that the "'same spiritual bread' and the 'same spiritual drink' do not mean that Paul thinks the Israelites ate the same bread or drank the same drink that Christians eat and drink in the Lord' (*sic*) Supper. . . . The emphasis instead is on the people's unity: they *all* received the *same* spiritual blessings" (emphasis original).

121. See Fee, *First Epistle to the Corinthians*, 493–94, and Garland, *1 Corinthians*, 454–55. For a survey of interpretations of "spiritual" in 1 Cor 10:3–4, see Davidson, *Typology in Scripture*, 225–32, 245–47; Gardner, *Gifts of God*, 136–43; and Willis, *Idol*

the sacramental character of the manna and the water, instead the point is that the spiritual food and drink given by God contrasted with the food that the Israelites actually craved (idolatry) and for Paul, the Corinthians "also knew what it was to partake of spiritual food and drink and were similarly tempted to settle for that which would bring condemnation rather than be content with the food God had provided."[122] Lastly, much ink has been spilt over Paul's contention that the rock that followed the Israelites was Christ, especially given the rabbinic interpretative traditions and legends.[123] In all likelihood, however, Paul is aware that even though the OT does not explicitly mention a rock following the Israelites in the wilderness, the two accounts of water gushing from the miraculous rock at the beginning (Exod 17:1–7) and end (Num 20:2–13) of the wilderness wandering provides this inference.[124] Later biblical texts also suggest that water was provided throughout their wanderings (see Ps 78:15–16; Isa 48:21), but the emphasis is on the fact that God was continuously gracious to the whole covenant community by his recurring provision of water.[125] The main point is the source of Israel's spiritual drink in the desert. For Paul the source is Christ since he associates Christ with the literal rock that accompanied Israel in the wilderness.[126] Given the citation of Deut 32:17 in 1 Cor 10:20, it is not difficult for Christ to be identified as the rock since the God of Israel is ascribed the title "the Rock" in the Song of Moses (Deut 32:4, 15, 18, 30–31;

Meat in Corinth, 130–32.

122. Ciampa and Rosner, *First Letter to the Corinthians*, 449. Likewise, Garland, *1 Corinthians*, 455. See also Fee, *First Epistle to the Corinthians*, 493; contra Davidson, *Typology in Scripture*, 246–47, who argues that ancient Israel received sacramental gifts of the Spirit.

123. For discussion of rabbinic traditions and the legends associated with the rock or well traveling with the Israelites, see Ellis, *Paul's Use of the Old Testament*, 66–70; Enns, "'Moveable Well,'" 23–38; Gardner, *Gifts of God*, 143–48; Thiselton, *First Epistle to the Corinthians*, 727–30; Davidson, *Typology in Scripture*, 233–45; Willis, *Idol Meat in Corinth*, 133–38.

124. So Garland, *1 Corinthians*, 456; cf. Ciampa and Rosner, *First Letter to the Corinthians*, 450; Enns, "'Moveable Well,'" 28–31; Davidson, *Typology in Scripture*, 239. Some scholars also note the ambiguity in regard to the well mentioned in Num 21:16–20, which served as a springboard for the targumic interpretative tradition. For reasons Paul did not appropriate such traditions, see Johnson, "Pauline Typology," 49–50.

125. Gardner, *Gifts of God*, 145–46, and 146n190. In addition, see Davidson, *Typology in Scripture*, 240, as he also lists Deut 8:15–16; Neh 9:15; and Ps 105:41 as texts suggesting continual supply of water.

126. Some commentators argue that the "spiritual rock" is figurative, but Davidson, *Typology in Scripture*, 243–44, is correct that Paul does not shift from the real and concrete food and drink (also described as "spiritual") that the Israelites received in the wilderness to a non-material or figurative rock.

cf. Ps 78:35), another passage that addresses idolatry with the background of God's blessings in the desert.[127] Fee writes,

> That Paul identifies the rock with Christ thus serves his double aim: (1) to emphasize the typological character of Israel's experience, that it was Christ himself that they were being nourished in the wilderness; and (2) thereby also to stress the continuity between Israel and the Corinthians, who by their idolatry are in the process of reenacting Israel's madness and thus are in danger of experiencing similar judgment.[128]

In chapter 2 the nature of typology was delineated as those OT genuinely historical persons, events, and institutions that God had providentially intended to resemble, foreshadow, and prefigure escalated and intensified NT antitypes in and through the person of Jesus Christ. Are elements of 1 Cor 10:1–13 typological, or is Paul finding analogies to serve as illustrations and warnings for the Corinthian church? Clearly, for Paul the historicity of Israel's exodus, reception of manna, water, rock, their rebellion, and judgment (1 Cor 10:5, 7–10) is assumed, otherwise Paul's warning loses its force.[129] It is also obvious that Israel's experience through the exodus and provisions in the wilderness relate to the church as Paul has made it clear that Israel had its redemption, covenant mediator, own form of baptism and spiritual meal, and they too received blessings that were sourced in Christ. OT Israel corresponds to the new, eschatological Israel (1 Cor 10:1, 11). Aside from historical correspondence and parallelism, are these things

---

127. So Ciampa and Rosner, *First Letter to the Corinthians*, 451; Gardner, *Gifts of God*, 146–48; Hays, *Echoes of Scripture*, 94 (although Hays wrongly concludes that Paul takes an imaginative leap in associating Christ with the rock); Garland, *1 Corinthians*, 457–58; Davidson, *Typology in Scripture*, 243. Note also Johnson, "Pauline Typology," 52, who finds "good reason . . . to understand God's provision of food and drink from a rock as provision from the Rock—namely God himself. It is a small step for Paul to appropriate this symbolism by identifying the Rock as Jesus Christ." Some scholars contend that Paul is doing something similar to Philo, linking the rock with the personification of wisdom. See e.g., Banstra, "Interpretation in 1 Corinthians 10," 12–13; Thiselton, *First Epistle to the Corinthians*, 728–29. However, given the allusions to Deut 32, and because 1 Cor 10:9 probably refers to the pre-existent Christ, the notion that Paul is allegorizing in the same manner as Philo is undermined. See further Davidson, *Typology in Scripture*, 242–43; Fee, *First Epistle to the Corinthians*, 495–96.

128. Fee, *First Epistle to the Corinthians*, 496. See Carson, "Mystery and Fulfillment," 409.

129. As Johnson, "Pauline Typology," 46, rightly captures, "Paul argues that since these things happened, the Corinthians ought to be careful to make sure that they do not happen again—to them. Apart from the assumption of historicity the appeal to these specific instances of God's judgment loses its paraenetic force." For further on the historical realities and correspondence, see Davidson, *Typology in Scripture*, 280–81.

prospective in being divinely designed by God, prefiguring an eschatological goal through Christ? Against dispensationalists and other scholars, 1 Cor 10:6 and 11 reveal that Israel's role was typological in two ways: their exodus experience and wilderness blessings, but also in their acts of rebellion.[130] In what follows, the prefiguration, eschatological fulfillment, and Christocentric orientation of these typological patterns are considered.

First, Paul writes that "these things happened as types (τύποι) of us" (1 Cor 10:6). The "these things" (plural) refers to all the content of verses 1–5, not just to the judgment of verse 5.[131] Translating τύποι as "warnings" or "examples" becomes unsatisfactory then, for the exodus deliverance, baptism into Moses, the spiritual food and drink, and the rock are not warnings or examples, rather they establish the historical correspondence between Israel and the church.[132] Similarly, the first clause of 1 Cor 10:11 ("Now these things happened typologically") describes the nature of the events (10:7–10) while the second clause ("and they were written down for our instruction"), just as in verse 6 ("that we might not desire evil as they did"), denotes the purpose of the events as paraenetic warnings.[133] Moreover, that these things are divinely intended prefigurations are established by how Paul states that these things occurred as types/patterns *of us* (10:6) and that these things happened typologically and were written down for our instruction (10:11). In their very occurrence they are types and there is a necessary connection, a providential correspondence, between "our fathers" and "us."[134]

130. Schreiner and Caneday, *Race Set before Us*, 223.

131. Davidson, *Typology in Scripture*, 250–51; Ciampa and Rosner, *First Letter to the Corinthians*, 453; Fee, *First Epistle to the Corinthians*, 499; Garland, *1 Corinthians*, 459; Bandstra, "Interpretation in 1 Corinthians 10," 16. Johnson, "Pauline Typology," 55, astutely observes, "Although some might attempt to limit this reference to the judgment of v. 5, there is no good reason to do so. Paul has grounded his paraenetic point in the salvific correspondence between Israel and the Corinthians (vv. 1–4). It is this salvific continuity which gives the judgment of v. 5 its force."

132. Davidson, *Typology in Scripture*, 251; Johnson, "Pauline Typology," 55–56. Davidson also points out the problem with translating τυπικῶς in 1 Cor 10:11 as "warning" or "example" because in the next clause Paul writes that these things were written for his readers νουθεσίαν, which means "instruction" or "admonition." If τυπικῶς is synonymous with νουθεσίαν, "Paul would then be expressing a tautology ('they happened by way of warning and were written down for our warning')." Davidson, *Typology in Scripture*, 269.

133. On the distinction between the nature and purpose clauses in vv. 6 and 11, see Davidson, *Typology in Scripture*, 270; cf. 254; Johnson, "Pauline Typology," 56.

134. See Johnson, "Pauline Typology," 68–69; Davidson, *Typology in Scripture*, 284–85; Goppelt, *Typos*, 146; Gardner, *Gifts of God*, 112; Ellis, *Paul's Use of the Old Testament*, 127; Schreiner and Caneday, *Race Set before Us*, 223. Carson, "Mystery and Fulfillment," 400, asserts that one "cannot avoid the implications of Paul's insistence that Christ was the rock that followed the Israelites, and that these things 'were written

In their occurrence and in their inscripturation, divine intent is implicitly assumed for these types because the paraenetic purpose is God's, it was by his design that these things happened for the church's instruction so that the church might not desire evil as the Israelites did. Further, that the exodus is a typological pattern of a prophetic and prospective nature is evident from the OT itself (see the discussion of the second exodus in chapter 5). Moses as a typological pattern can also be established as a type although this is not Paul's emphasis here. On the other hand, the foreshadowing aspects of the manna and water, pointing to the Lord's Supper, the rock, pointing to Christ, and Israel's rebellion as a type of eschatological judgment, is less clear from the OT and are probably retrospectively identified by Paul. Nevertheless, the rehearsal of the wilderness events, including many of the elements that Paul highlights, appears in the OT, indicating their critical redemptive historical significance (see Ps 78; Neh 9:9–20; Isa 48:20–21).[135] While Hays is correct that these events prefigured the experience of the church, pointing "toward the present apocalyptic moment," there is no need to regard this as an imaginative device of reading Israel's story or of Paul fancifully reading Christ back into the exodus.[136] With the backdrop of the massive typological pattern of the exodus, there are indications in the textual and epochal horizons in the OT itself that the cloud, the manna, the water from the rock, and the rock pointed beyond themselves to spiritual and heavenly things.

The second aspect, and one that cause interpreters to balk at the presence of typology in 1 Cor 10 is with respect to the eschatological fulfillment intrinsic to the type-antitype relationship. If types are advance presentations designed by God that must have an intensified corresponding realization in the antitypes, then are not the Corinthians presented as reenacting Israel's

---

down *as warnings for us*, on whom the culmination of the ages has come.' The language suggests purpose, ultimately divine purpose; this sounds like some kind or other of typology" (emphasis original). Similarly, Fee, *First Epistle to the Corinthians*, 506, finds that the phrase "were written down as warnings for us" (1 Cor 10:11) indicates "their divinely ordained reason for being in Scripture. In this sentence one captures a sense of Paul's view that both the historical events and the inscripturated narrative are not simply history or isolated texts in Scripture; rather, behind all these things lie the eternal purposes of the living God . . . who therefore has woven the prefiguration into these earlier texts for the sake of God's final eschatological people."

135. Johnson, "Pauline Typology," 71–72, rightly asserts that while types may be noticed only in retrospect, "it is clear that Paul does not understand typology to be merely a matter of retrospective analogy. In both Rom 5 and 1 Cor 10, he asserts that the OT event was divinely intended to present a pattern of that which was still to come. In other words, according to Paul, these OT events 'looked forward' to NT events."

136. Hays, *Echoes of Scripture*, 105, and for Hays' contention of the imaginative device of reading and Paul's fanciful reading of Christ in the exodus, see pp. 95, 97.

failure and so will likewise perish in judgment?[137] Further, Hays argues that unlike the typological patterns unpacked in the letter to the Hebrews, in 1 Cor 10 there is no notion of escalation or heightening and no indication of the antitype fulfilling and annulling the type because the "relation between Israel and the church is one of positive correspondence, not antithesis."[138] Since there are two sets of typological patterns (1 Cor 10:1–4 and 7–10), each need to be evaluated in turn, but first it is necessary to observe that the types Paul discusses have an eschatological oriented fulfillment because these past Israelite experiences happened and were written down for the church, the community upon "whom the end of the ages has come" (1 Cor 10:11).[139] Indeed, "[i]t was understood from the time of the Old Testament prophets that God's eschatological redemption of his people would follow patterns established at the first exodus."[140] The end of the ages, the turning point of redemptive history, has been inaugurated through Jesus Christ's death and resurrection (Gal 4:4; 2 Cor 5:17): "That is what constitutes the typological element in these OT stories; ultimately the whole OT has been pointing toward its eschatological fulfillment in God's new people."[141]

Returning to the eschatological heightening in regard to verses 1–4, it is true that Paul's main purpose is to emphasize the continuity between Israel and the church. Both entities have deliverance through a baptism, a spiritual meal, and additionally, Christ's presence, the source of blessing, is manifested to both. Nevertheless, the covenantal discontinuity implies the eschatological intensification. The Israelites were baptized into Moses, but what this prefigures is baptism into Christ and since Christ is a far superior covenant mediator and representative than Moses (e.g., 2 Cor 3), Christian

---

137. Garland, *1 Corinthians*, 459. Fee, *First Epistle to the Corinthians*, 500, writes, "There seems to be a typological sense to *Israel* and its 'sacraments,' but an analogical sense to the *events* used as warning examples. As typology the passage breaks down precisely at the point of warning" (emphasis original). Cf. Ciampa and Rosner, *First Letter to the Corinthians*, 454.

138. Hays, *Echoes of Scripture*, 97, and see pp. 98–99 for the comparison with Hebrews. Hays further adds, "Here there is no hint that the Christian sacraments are greater or more spiritual than the spiritual food and drink of Israel in the wilderness. . . . There is no hint that the Corinthians' knowledge of God in Christ places them in a better or more secure position, nor that their defiance of God's greater grace will produce a fate still more ghastly. To the contrary . . . the point of Paul's metaphor depends on seeing Israel and the church as pilgrim people who stand in different times, different chapters of the same story, but in identical relation to the same gracious and righteous God" (99).

139. Davidson, *Typology in Scripture*, 281–82; Goppelt, *Typos*, 146; Johnson, "Pauline Typology," 78.

140. Ciampa and Rosner, *First Letter to the Corinthians*, 465.

141. Fee, *First Epistle to the Corinthians*, 507.

baptism far exceeds the Israelites' baptism in the sea and in the cloud.[142] Furthermore, God's gracious provision of manna and water from the rock, even though these were not sacramental in the wilderness context, pointed forward to a better covenant meal that commemorated God's new exodus deliverance and gracious provision in the person and work of Christ.[143] Lastly, although Christ was present in some way with the Israelites as the rock accompanied Israel's wilderness journey, the presence and provision of Christ in the new covenant age is intensified in comparison to what the Israelites experienced in the desert. Again, Paul is not focused on the eschatological heightening in 1 Cor 10:1–4 since he wants the Corinthians to identify with the Israelites and their covenant benefits. But that these things prefigure the deliverance and new covenant blessings for the church at the end of the ages (1 Cor 10:11) is implied. There is an intrinsic eschatological heightening because the deliverance and provisions enjoyed by Israel and the church are not equivalent in every way, for the wilderness events and blessings were shadows and types.

What about Israel's rebellion (1 Cor 10:5, 7–10) and the entailments for the typological escalation and fulfillment? Sometimes typological patterns feature the similarity between the type and the antitype more and at other times, the dissimilarity. For example, Adam is a type of the one to come (Rom 5:14). Adam and Christ are similar in being covenant heads, but the typological pattern is primarily in terms of contrast as Christ is the obedient, divine Son and faithful representative. The salvific continuity between Israel and the church is emphasized in 1 Cor 10:1–4 in order to set-up the basis and potency of the warning so that the Corinthians would not presume they were secure. However, the prefiguring function of Israel's rebellion (1 Cor 10:5, 7–10) is not in terms of similarity as if most of the church will repeat the pattern and fail as most of the old covenant community did with their sinful actions.[144] Instead, Israel's typological role in rebelling against God occurred in history for the purpose of serving as a warning so that God's end-time people (not just the Corinthian church but by extension all believers in Christ) would persevere in faith, not presume upon covenantal privileges, and so not repeat Israel's idolatry (10:6, 12).

142. Johnson, "Pauline Typology," 76–77.

143. Unfortunately, Johnson has difficulty pinpointing the eschatological heightening for vv. 3–4 because he wrongly interprets the wilderness provision as equivalent to the Eucharist. See "Pauline Typology," 77–78. Instead, see Garland, *1 Corinthians*, 452. Elsewhere Jesus teaches that the manna in the wilderness pointed to him as the bread of life (John 6:31–58).

144. Schreiner and Caneday, *Race Set before Us*, 224–25; Davidson, *Typology in Scripture*, 253.

Further, there is also an assurance for the Corinthians, for God is faithful and will provide the way of escape for these temptations (10:13).[145] Since the Corinthian church lives at the end of the ages, possessing the Holy Spirit (6:11; 12:13), the church of God is not destined to have the same fate in the wilderness as the Israelites. In contrast to Hays who argues for a "positive correspondence" between Israel and the church, even though the Corinthian church is at the same critical juncture as Israel, the correspondence is negative or along contrasting lines. In sum, Israel's rebellion does not typologically anticipate the church's failure, for God's people will successfully endure the temptations in the end (10:13) by heeding the warnings of Israel's typological wilderness experiences and by obeying the command to flee idolatry (10:14).[146]

The last area to address regarding the typological considerations of 1 Cor 10 is whether this passage unsettles the Israel-Christ-church framework advanced throughout this study. The pericope seems to unfold a direct correspondence between Israel and the church or suggests that Paul's hermeneutic is ecclesiocentric. The typological patterns in 1 Cor are the OT events surrounding Israel's exodus and wilderness events, but derivatively, a typological link is also present between the nation of Israel and the church (1 Cor 10:1, 11). Christ himself is not the antitype of the typological patterns, but that does not make the typology any less Christocentric.[147] Already in Paul's letter to the Corinthians he has presented Christ as the Passover Lamb of the new exodus (1 Cor 5:7). Now in 1 Cor 10, every typological correspondence recognized by Paul is in some way inextricably linked to Christ. The baptism into Moses implies the baptism into Christ, the spiritual meal in the wilderness points to the Lord's Supper which in turn recalls the gracious provision of the new covenant work of Christ. Moreover, the source of Israel's provision is christologically centered as the pre-existent Christ nourished Israel through the rock. Even Israel's acts of disobedience leading to judgments are oriented toward Christ since Paul says in 1 Cor 10:9 that

---

145. For discussion of God's faithfulness in 1 Corinthians, see Works, *Church in the Wilderness*, 84–88.

146. Schreiner and Caneday, *Race Set before Us*, 226, conclude, "Israel's rebellion is not an example of children to whom God has given spiritual birth and who nonetheless perish eternally. The New Testament writers do not use Israel to show that it is possible for God's spiritually birthed children to apostatize and perish. They appeal to Israel's rebellion to admonish us to be the true people of God that Israel was not. They use Israel to exhort us not to presume upon God's rich provisions and take it for granted that we have inherited privilege."

147. See Johnson, "Pauline Typology," 84–87; and Davidson, *Typology in Scripture*, 282–83. Contra Hays, *Echoes of Scripture*, 101–2.

they were ultimately putting Christ to the test.[148] Further, that these things happened typologically to Israel for the purpose of the church living at the end of the ages (1 Cor 10:11) assumes a redemptive-historical progression, a progression of eschatological fulfillment that can only be associated with Christ. Richard Davidson's analysis is correct: OT types "find their fulfillment in Christ or in the realities of the new covenant related to and brought about by Christ. Christ is presented as the ultimate orientation point of the [types] and their NT fulfillments."[149]

Having evaluated 1 Cor 10:1–13, there are theological conclusions that need to be elucidated for systems of theology. If the above analysis of these verses is correct then dispensationalists are wrong to construe this passage in terms of mere analogy and illustration. These elements are present, of course, but Paul is presenting much more as he is demonstrating that Israel and Israel's experiences were designed by God (prospectively) to typologically anticipate the church and were purposed by God as a warning for the church (10:6). Thus, there is a historical and theological continuation between Israel and the church as Israel's exodus deliverance and wilderness benefits correspond to and foreshadow the church's deliverance and the church's two ordinances. Moreover, that Paul tells his primarily gentile readers that the Israelites were "our fathers" (10:1) proves problematic for dispensationalism given their hermeneutical commitment of separating Israel and the church as distinct peoples or maintaining an exclusive role and function of national Israel in a future millennium and beyond. Based on verse 1, there is more continuity between Israel and the church than dispensationalists are willing to acknowledge as the Corinthian ecclesial identity is shaped by the fact that the Israelites are their ancestors. Another highly significant point is how Paul's teaches that the church is the final eschatological people of God (10:11).[150] The church is in a unique place in

---

148. Some manuscripts for 1 Cor 10:9 read that the Israelites tempted God or the Lord. But "Christ" is the most difficult reading and the most likely original. See Garland, *1 Corinthians*, 470–71.

149. Davidson, *Typology in Scripture*, 417.

150. According to Goppelt, *Theology of the New Testament*, 2:146, the church's typological correspondence to the situation of Israel in the wilderness wanderings signified two things: "a) It signified a salvation-historical correspondence. What was spoken to Israel in the Old Testament as the people of God was now to be connected typologically with the church. It alone was the community that could understand itself as the heir of the Old Testament promises. b) It also signified an eschatological difference. The church was no longer like Israel a people among other peoples; it was not the 'third gender' (*tertium genus*) alongside Jews and Gentiles. Rather the church stood in relationship to all peoples as the eschatological people of God, as the new creation" (emphasis original).

redemptive history, for the nation of Israel did not experience the end of the ages, but now through Christ, Israel and Israel's wilderness experiences prefigured God's climactic work in constituting the church. The movement of redemptive history toward its goal of the salvation of God's end-time people has been inaugurated. If the church is the eschatological and antitypical Israel, God's true temple (1 Cor 3:16–17), how can there be any expectation for a future restoration of national, political Israel?

Finally, there are also theological implications for covenant theology that may be drawn from 1 Cor 10:1–13. First, Paul's point is not to disclose the relationship between faith and baptism or unpack a theology of baptism.[151] Nevertheless, if covenant theologians are to argue for the practice of infant baptism from this passage since all of the Israelites—men, women, and children—were baptized in the cloud and in sea and that this, in turn, is indicative for the new covenant community, then those covenant theologians are obligated to also argue for paedocommunion since *all* of the Israelites ate the spiritual food and drink (10:3–4).[152] But as discussed, this is not Paul's point as the significance that *all* experienced these blessings is that it did not prevent *most* of them from being judged for their evil cravings. A more significant theological entailment for the differences in the covenant communities is the fact that Israel was baptized into Moses whereas the implication is that the church is baptized into Christ. A covenantal shift may be detected then, as Israel's exodus deliverance and baptism into Moses prefigures a covenant community that experiences a greater new exodus deliverance with a baptism into the death and resurrection of the greater covenant mediator, Christ.[153] One other thought is necessary as 1 Cor 10:11 has implications for covenant theology just as it does for dispensationalism. Commenting on this verse in his Westminster Theological Seminary

---

151. Beasley-Murray, *Baptism in the New Testament*, 184–85.

152. See Beasley-Murray, *Baptism in the New Testament*, 183–84; and Crampton, "Sacramental Implications of 1 Cor 10:1–4," 7–39, esp. 23–24, 37. Contra, for example, the implications of infant baptism in the study of Vander Hart, "Exodus as Sacrament," 35–46.

153. Again, Paul's main purpose is to highlight the parallels between the Corinthians and Israel in order to make the point about idolatry. Paul is not elucidating the Israelite's relationship to Moses, but there is a sense of corporate solidarity or unity, the many being saved in the one or through the one. Baptism into Christ is the church's incorporation into Christ, salvation being into his death and resurrection. Similarly, Israel's salvation in the exodus was a baptism into Moses in that "they all participated in the discriminating and saving operation of the cloud and the sea that God accomplished for them by the ministry of Moses." Ridderbos, *Paul*, 405, cf. p. 393. However, the difference is the nature of the mediator and the fact that Israel went through a physical redemption whereas the church goes through a spiritual and effective redemption on account of the work of Christ.

dissertation, H. Wayne Johnson writes, "Paul is referring to the Corinthians as those who stand at the climax of redemptive history. This identification shows that Paul does not view the NT believers only as another Israel or the same Israel, but the eschatologically heightened Israel."[154] Johnson's analysis is correct because as the end-time community, an historical and eschatological progression has occurred with the people of God through Christ. However, Johnson's appropriate identification of the church as not another Israel undercuts the ecclesiology of covenant theology where Israel and the church are held in direct continuity. More specifically, the church is the eschatologically heightened Israel in that it is not a mixed community of covenant keepers and breakers like Israel of old. Paul's warning to the church at Corinth is real, but God provides a way of escape (1 Cor 10:13) and in the age of the Spirit, the church will heed the warnings, flee from idolatry, and not succumb as Israel had in the wilderness.[155] As was mentioned at the outset, Paul describes the church at Corinth as the saints, the called, the body of Christ, and the temple of God. Numerous issues were besetting the Corinthians, but that there was a so-called brother (1 Cor 5) in the community does not demonstrate that the church is by nature a mixed community. Rather, Paul's call for church discipline already presupposes the church to be a pure body of genuine believers.[156]

Other Israel-Church Typological Patterns: The Church as the Children, Flock, and Israel of God

The 1 Pet 2 and 1 Cor 10 texts have already disclosed an Israel-church typology that is refracted through the prism of Christ. Two other typological patterns connecting OT Israel with the church are the sonship themes and from the pastoral imagery, the sheep and flock motif. Considered also within this discussion is Gal 6:16 since this text also bears significantly on the Israel-church relationship.

---

154. Johnson, "Pauline Typology," 78.

155. The purpose of the warning passages in Scripture cannot be evaluated here. The warning passages do not indicate that members of the covenant community can apostasize and fall away; rather, the warnings are a means of salvation that God utilizes to encourage and provoke faith and perseverance. See Schreiner and Caneday, *Race Set before Us*, 142–213; Schreiner, *Run to Win the Prize*; Cowan, "Warning Passages of Hebrews," 189–213.

156. See Hammett, *Biblical Foundations*, 84; cf. 105–7.

The Church as the Seed of Abraham and Children of God

The typological relationship between Israel and the church is primarily visible in the Bible through the sonship theme. In chapter 5, Israel's typological role and identity as God's son and as the offspring of Abraham was demonstrated to be fulfilled in the antitype, Jesus Christ (Matt 1:1, 17; 2:15; 3:15–17; 4:111; Luke 1:55, 72–73; Gal 3:16). The church is now constituted as the children of God (John 1:12; 11:51–52; Rom 8:16–17; 2 Cor 6:16–18; Gal 4:4–7; 1 John 3:2) and the genuine, spiritual seed of Abraham (Rom 4:11–18; Gal 3:7, 26–29; 4:21–31; 1 Pet 3:6; Heb 2:16) because of the work of Christ and the agency of the Holy Spirit. What is true of Christ is true of the church because of covenantal union and corporate solidarity. This section will focus on the church as the spiritual offspring of Abraham. Space does not permit discussion of John 11:47–52, although this important passage refers to Jesus' death as the means of gathering the dispersed children of God into one (see Isa 2:2–4; 56:6–8; 66:18–24; Zech 2:10–12), disclosing that Israel's eschatological restoration typologically began through the effects of Jesus' sacrifice.[157] As the children of God and the spiritual seed of Abraham, the church does not replace Israel nor is it equivalent to Israel;

---

157. On John 11:51–52, Carson, *John*, 422–23, writes, "In a purely Jewish context, 'the scattered children of God' would be understood to refer to the Jews of the diaspora, and would be gathered together in the promised land to share in the kingdom of God (e.g. Is. 43:5; Ezk. 34:12; 36:24ff.). Christians were quick to draw the typological connections: the real children of God are those who receive the incarnate Word and believe in his name (1:12, 13), and if they are dispersed in the world (*cf.* 1 Pet. 1:1) they will be gathered not only at the parousia, but into the one church, the community of the Messiah (*to bring them together and make them one* here seems to refer to the immediate effects of Jesus' death; *cf.* also 17:21)" (emphasis original). See also Ridderbos, *Gospel according to John*, 410–11; Köstenberger, *John*, 353; Beasley-Murray, *John*, 198; Klink, *John*, 514–15; Dennis, "Restoration in John 11,47–52," 57–86. Dennis, *Jesus' Death and the Gathering of True Israel*, 345, concludes, "The 'children of God' for John is a concept that stands for the *totality* of the restored Messianic community and is equivalent to the description 'true Israel.' The 'children of God' is therefore a restoration concept. It was shown that in a number of OT texts the day of restoration is envisioned as a day when Israel would be newly 'begotten' . . . as God's children. This renewed status is often very closely related to the gathering and unification of Israel. Thus, when it is said that the goal of Jesus' mission is to beget 'children of God' (1.12) or to 'gather the children of God' (11.52b), this is another way of saying that the goal of Jesus' mission is to restore Israel to its true identity as the children of YHWH" (emphasis original). Further, Dennis finds that the restoration promise of Israel's dispersion is coming to an end now that the Messiah is bringing about the gathering of the eschatological dispersion, which not only concerns diaspora Israelites but also gentiles (see pp. 347–48). John 11:51–52 is related to John 10:16 (see the next section on the shepherding/flock theme) and ties into the Johannine theme of the children of God as being spiritually born from above (John 1:12; 3:3–7; 8:37–47).

the typological correspondences are prospective and feature eschatological heightening because the end-time people are redefined now that the true Son, seed, and Israel, Jesus Christ has climactically entered into time and space as the incarnate one. Given the treatment of the seed theme in the previous chapter, a briefer analysis is offered here regarding the church as the antitypical and eschatological offspring of Abraham. Two typological strands associated with the Abrahamic covenant may be detected.

First, Abraham is the divinely appointed type of those who are justified by faith.[158] Abraham's faith is not only exemplary as those who believe like he did are reckoned righteous (Gen 15:6; Gal 3:6; Rom 4:3, 22–23), but the prospective and prophetic quality or eschatological orientation of Abraham's justification prior to his circumcision is critical as the Scripture foresaw, according to Paul (Gal 3:8; cf. Rom 4:11–12, 23–24), that God would justify the gentiles apart from works of the law when the gospel was preached in advance that the nations would be blessed in Abraham (Gen 12:3).[159] While the way of salvation is the same for both OT and NT saints in terms of being declared righteous by faith alone, there is an eschatological heightening since OT believers like Abraham looked forward to the culmination of God's promises while NT believers look back in faith to the true seed of Abraham, Jesus Christ, with his death and resurrection as the basis of salvation for all of God's people. Christ is the new covenant mediator and new creation head, the one who fulfills the Abrahamic promises, and his coming is not only eschatological as he is the one whom Abraham ultimately anticipated by faith (John 8:56; Gen 22:17), but Christ also accomplishes the OT prophetic trajectory by producing sons of Abraham who

---

158. Goppelt, *Typos*, 137–38. Moo, *Galatians*, 200, commenting on Gal 3:9, remarks, "Abraham, in this verse at least, is an example of how the promise of blessing is accessed. Yet Abraham's special role in salvation history means that he is not just any example; his response to God's promise is foundational to the fulfillment of God's purposes and becomes a determinative paradigm for those who follow."

159. Goppelt, *Typos*, 137. See also Juncker, "'Children of Promise,'" 131–60. Cf. Hodge, *If Sons, Then Heirs*, 79–91. Schreiner, *Galatians*, 194–95, commenting on Gal 3:8, observes, "As in Rom 4 (cf. Rom 4:2), Gen 15:6 is the foundational text, indicating that Gen 12:3 (and 18:18) must be read through the lens of 15:6. Genesis 12:3 promises that all the nations will be blessed in Abraham, and Paul identifies this promissory word as the gospel proclaimed to Abraham in advance. But it is precisely here that Gen 15:6 plays its axiomatic role, for in giving the promise (12:3) to Abraham, Scripture foresaw that God would declare the Gentiles right in his sight by faith." See also, Hays, *Echoes of Scripture*, 105–11. Hays's appeal to an ecclesiocentric hermeneutic to explain Paul's interpretative moves in Gal 3 is unconvincing. The Galatians' experience of the Spirit and the fulfillment of the justification of the gentiles by faith in becoming Abraham's promised children could only have occurred in lieu of the eschatological fulfillment in Christ.

are no longer merely physical descendants or defined ethnically since they are characteristically empowered by the Spirit and marked by faith as spiritually adopted sons of the Davidic servant and last Adam (Jer 31:33–34; Isa 44:3–5; 52:15; 53:10–12; 54:1–3; 59:20–21; Ezek 36:25–27; 37:14, 22–24; Joel 2:28–32; see also the discussion in chapter 5). In the fullness of time, it is now those who are incorporated into Christ by faith who are true sons of Abraham, blessed with him, and recipients of the Spirit (Gal 3:7, 9, 14; 4:4–7).[160] Paul clearly teaches,

> The bond of kinship established by faith is of such overriding importance that it completely relativizes genetic descent and, at the same time, necessitates a redefinition of the people of God and the basis for membership in that people. Faith like Abraham's is now seen to be the defining characteristic—the sine qua non—of membership in the eschatological people of God.[161]

Therefore, while the whole OT covenant community of Israel consisted of people who were Abraham's physical offspring (clearly there were exceptions such as Rahab, Ruth, Uriah the Hittite, etc.) although not all were Abraham's spiritual offspring,[162] the composition of the eschatological people of God is the exact opposite: many of the members of the new covenant community are not biological descendants of Abraham (gentiles), but every member (Jew and gentile) now exhibits the faith of Abraham (Gal 3:7, 9) and are the spiritual, eschatological seed of Abraham through their covenantal union with Jesus Christ (Gal 3:26–29).[163] Or stated differently,

---

160. Regarding Paul's definition of being descendants of Abraham, Longenecker, *Triumphs*, 132, finds, "It means to be marked out by the same phenomenon of faith that Abraham himself demonstrated. This also provides Paul with the occasion to give an explanation of what it means for the nations to be blessed 'in' (ἐν) him (Gen. 12.3 and 18.18; cited in [Gal] 3.8): it means that their faith, like his, leads to their blessing 'with' or 'alongside' (σύν) him (3.9)."

161. Juncker, "'Children of Promise,'" 134. For a general discussion of gentiles as children of Abraham, see Schreiner, *Paul, Apostle of God's Glory*, 81–83; Bruce, *Time Is Fulfilled*, 64–70.

162. White, "Newness of the New Covenant (Part II)," 88, aptly captures how Israel was a mixed community in stating that it is "clear that for every David there were a dozen Ahabs; for every Josiah a legion of Manassehs. Unfaithfulness, the flaunting of God's law, the rejection of the role of truly being God's people, the rejection of His knowledge, and the experience of His wrath, were the *normative* experiences seen in the Old Covenant" (emphasis original).

163. Longenecker, *Triumphs*, 133, rightly remarks, "By means of their union with Christ (cf. 3.26–28), Christians are joined to the single seed of Abraham and thereby find themselves to be the collective 'descendants of Abraham'. The mechanism in this christological argument is not simply one of similarity of characteristic (i.e., 'faith'), as in 3.6–7, but of incorporation into true Abrahamic descent by means of participation

the shift in the covenant communities from the Abrahamic covenant to the new covenant is from biological descent and physical circumcision to spiritual adoption as sons and heart circumcision (Rom 2:25-29; Gal 4:4-7; Eph 2:11-22; Col 2:11-14).[164] Since Christ is the distinctive and unique seed of Abraham, the blessing of Abraham is now mediated to the church (Gal 3:14, 29) through him.[165] It is this assembly that is *both* Abraham's offspring *and* Christ's offspring (Gal 3:26, 29) and as such, all exemplify the faith of father Abraham, possess the Holy Spirit and bear his regenerating work on their hearts, and all in the new covenant assembly are counted righteous in Christ (Rom 4:9-12, 16-17; Eph 1:5; Isa 53:10-11; 54:1, 3; Jer 31:34).

Alongside the fact that Abraham's paternity is now spiritually delineated so that it is those who have faith like Abraham who are Abraham's true sons, there is a second important typological aspect that Paul highlights: the

---

with Christ." Cf. Hodge, *If Sons, Then Heirs*, 93-107, where she evaluates being "in" Abraham, "in" Isaac, and "in" Christ with respect to descent. Gentiles are incorporated into Christ sharing in the material and qualities of their ancestor, Abraham. For further on the various seeds of Abraham, see Gentry and Wellum, *Kingdom through Covenant*, 691-92, 815-16; and Wellum, "Baptism and the Relationship," 132-37.

164. For further development of this point, see DeRouchie, "Counting Stars with Abraham," 445-85. Juncker, "'Children of Promise,'" 143-44, writes, "Abraham is the spiritual father of two closely related yet distinguishable groups, to whom righteousness is reckoned solely on the basis of faith: Gentiles who believe while in a state of uncircumcision (Rom 4:11); and Jews who not only are circumcised but who also follow in the footsteps of faith that Abraham had while he was uncircumcised (Rom 4:12). The common denominator in both cases is faith—in effect *Gentile* faith (Rom 4:10-12, 16; cf. Gal 2:15-17). It is faith and not genetic descent from Abraham or circumcision or law (Rom 3:21, 4:13) or works of the law (Rom 3:28, 4:2-5) *or anything specifically Jewish* that determines the true nature of Abraham's paternity and the identity of his seed. . . . All who believe are de facto children and seed of Abraham and, as a result, become not only heirs but members of the eschatological people of God" (emphasis original).

165. Longenecker, *Triumphs*, 65-66, is helpful in explaining the significance of union with Christ for Paul's argument regarding sonship in Galatians: "This motif of incorporative location in Christ explains how Paul can claim in 4.4-7 that the Christian has a share in Jesus' own intimate, obedient sonship. In fact, these two passages (3.26-28 and 4.4-7) explain and reinforce each other: Paul can assume in 3.26 that to be 'in Christ Jesus' is to be a son of God since Paul knows Jesus to be the son of God (4.4, 6; cf. 1.16; 2:20); so too Paul can assume in 4.5-7 that redemption involves being adopted as sons into Jesus' sonship since he imagines Christians being united with and incorporated into Christ (3.26-28). Union with Christ, then, is the mechanism whereby believers are incorporated into the sphere of the new creation, the process whereby those enslaved to suprahuman powers become sons of the sovereign God. This union with Christ is said to come 'through faith' in 3.26, and is expanded further in 3.27 by the image of baptism; being baptised *into* Christ (εἰς Χριστόν) facilitates the union between Christ and the Christian. For Paul, baptism represents the believer's transfer from the domination of the power of Sin to the realm of Christ's lordship" (emphasis original).

heirs and recipients of the Abrahamic promises are not granted exclusively to Abraham's physical and spiritual progeny (i.e., believing Jews); rather, they are directed to Christ, the antitypical seed of Abraham, and with the fulfillment in Christ, it is through him that the true heirs and ultimate recipients of the Abrahamic covenant promises are revealed in the church of Jesus Christ (Jew and gentile believers alike). In chapter 5 it was observed that the OT already anticipated nations gathering into the end-time people of God in projecting the fulfillment to the Abrahamic promise of the blessings to the nations, but further, the prophetic outlook indicated that the other Abrahamic covenant promises of a great name, numerous offspring, land, and a royal seed could not be isolated from this promise to the nations since all the Abrahamic promises are interwoven and form a package deal.[166] It is Christ who is the consummate recipient of these promises (Gal 3:16) and as Paul makes plain, the inaugurated realization and fulfillment of the Abrahamic promises, including the land promise, means that the inheritance is enjoyed by all those in union with Christ.[167] Jew and gentile followers of Christ not only enjoy the status as the seed and sons of Abraham, but the privileges of the Abrahamic covenant promises are exclusively theirs through Christ, the one in whom they are baptized into and clothed with (Gal 3:27). As Abraham's offspring and sons then, they are the *heirs* of the Abrahamic promises (Gal 3:29; 4:7).[168] The inheritance bestowed in God's gracious promise is received by faith.

---

166. See chapter 5 footnote 63. See Taylor, "Eschatological Interdependence," 291–316. Taylor rightly finds, "Paul seems to understand the Abrahamic blessing of Genesis 12:1–3 as a unity which would find ultimate fulfilment in Christ, in such a way that the blessing of Israel (Gen. 12:2) and the families of the earth (Gen. 12:3; 18:8) are equally necessary parts of that fulfilment. They would not happen independently but only as parts of the same divine plan, and through the one seed Christ (Gal. 3:16), the Son of God. The promised blessing of Israel awaited the coming of the Messiah, the coming of faith (Gal. 3:23–24), and the blessing of the Gentiles" (313).

167. The issue of *who* receives the inheritance cannot be addressed without also knowing the *content* of the inheritance. As was presented in chapter 5 in the discussion of Gal 3:14–18, the inheritance involves all the Abrahamic promises and especially the promised land now reframed as the eschatological world. For focused studies of inheritance in Gal 3–4, consult Echevarria, *Future Inheritance of Land*, 104–40.

168. Juncker, "'Children of Promise,'" 134, writes, "Alongside of being justified by faith (3:24), being in Christ (3:26, 28), and being sons of God (!) (3:26), being 'Abraham's seed' (3:29) seems almost anticlimactic—that is, unless it is a categorical summary affirmation that all who believe are God's-(polemically redefined) people, who alone possess the aforesaid status and privileges and who alone are the heirs and recipients of God's promises to Abraham. Paul's use of the theologically freighted σπέρμα instead of υἱοί underscores that *when Paul calls believers 'sons of Abraham' he means to say that they are the eschatological people of God*. They are the fulfillment of the 'seed' promises to Abraham and the eschatological recipients ('heirs') of the blessings recounted in the

Moreover, Paul develops the sonship and inheritance themes further in Gal 4:21-31, a passage that climaxes his argument from Gal 3:1.[169] Isaac and Ishmael are also typological figures as Jewish and gentile believers are of the lineage of Isaac, children of promise (Gal 4:28), of the Spirit, liberated in Christ (5:1) while in a surprising eschatological reversal, the Judaizers, and more generally unbelieving Jews, correspond to Ishmael, born according to the flesh, and enslaved to the law along with the city of Jerusalem (4:25, 29-30).[170] By citing Gen 21:10 in Gal 4:30, Paul indicates that the children of the free woman (Sarah; cf. 4:22-23) who also form the new covenant community (cf. Isa 54:1 in Gal 4:27), are the heirs of the Abrahamic promises with Isaac (cf. Rom 9:6-9) while the typological offspring of Hagar, corresponding to Ishmael, the Jewish law-keepers who repudiate Christ, are disinherited.

Two other points may also be derived from in Gal 4:21-31 pertaining to the church as the renewed Israel, citizens of the heavenly, eschatologically restored Jerusalem, and inheritors, like Isaac, of all the Abrahamic promises (note the promises granted to Isaac in Gen 17:19, 21; 26:2-5; cf. Heb 11:9). First, Paul identifies Hagar and her enslaved children with the Mosaic covenant, but Paul never explicitly names the contrasting covenant associated with Sarah (Gal 4:24) and the "Jerusalem above" (4:26). Given

---

OT" (emphasis original). Starling, *Not My People*, 48, rightly states that within Gal 3-4, Paul "pointedly correlates the restoration eschatology of the prophets with the divine promises to Abraham (3:8, 14) and argues that in both cases (3:6-9, 11b) the 'life' and 'righteousness' promised is given not to law-keepers but to 'those who believe' (3:6-9, 11b). Furthermore, because the inheritance of the promise belongs to 'one person . . . Christ' (3:16), it is those 'in Christ' who receive the blessing of Abraham (3:14)—in Christ 'there is no longer Jew or Greek' (3:28)." See also Taylor, "Eschatological Interdependence," 308-9.

169. For the typological aspects of this passage, see Juncker, "'Children of Promise,'" 135-41; Goppelt, *Typos*, 139-40. For the allegorical aspects of Gal 4:21-31, see chapter 2.

170. Although there is debate regarding who specifically Paul indicts by linking Hagar, Sinai, enslaved children, and the Jerusalem of his day, while the Judaizers are in view given the thrust of Paul's arguments throughout the epistle, it is unavoidable that Judaism in general is also in Paul's purview since the charge of slavery upon the present Jerusalem and her children includes non-Christian Jews given the importance of Torah observance for all Jews (which also coincides with how the Judaizers sought to impose the law on the Galatian gentile converts). The present Jerusalem is more broad then, encapsulating Judaism that relies on the law and ignores Christ. Further, in Gal 4:29 Paul refers to the children of the flesh as persecutors which goes beyond the Judaizers, for while they insisted on law observance for the gentiles, there is no evidence they persecuted gentile believers. Instead, it is likely Jewish persecution is what Paul has in view in v. 29. See Moo, *Galatians*, 303-4, 310-11; Schreiner, *Galatians*, 302; Lincoln, *Paradise Now and Not Yet*, 16-17, 28; Walker, *Jesus and the Holy City*, 129; Juncker, "'Children of Promise,'" 138-41.

the references to Sarah and Isaac with the backdrop of the Genesis narrative and the logic of Gal 3:15-18, the Abrahamic covenant is probably the second covenant. Many scholars, however, have argued for good reasons that it is the new covenant that is contrasted with the Mosaic covenant.[171] A decision is difficult; nevertheless, what is noticeable given the elements of Paul's rhetorical arguments within this pericope is that the fulfillment of the Abrahamic covenant has occurred through the establishment of the new covenant in Christ. The citation of Isa 54:1 LXX in Gal 4:27, which supports Paul's assertion that the Jerusalem above is currently the mother of believers (4:26), is a text from Isaiah that immediately follows the description of the new covenant work of the suffering servant (Isa 53; see also Isa 54:10) and projects Jerusalem's/Zion's future restoration.[172] Alluding to Sarah and Hagar (see Gen 11:30; 16:3-4; Isa 51:1-3), the city is symbolized as a barren woman (like Sarah), but she will rejoicingly have more children than the married woman when God intervenes (just as he did with respect to Sarah; cf. Rom 4:17) and renews the city by ending Israel's exile, multiplying her offspring, returning Israel to the land, and so fulfilling the Abrahamic covenant (Isa 54:1-3).[173] This return from exile, the age of the new Jerusalem (Sarah represents the new age; Hagar, Sinai, and the present Jerusalem represent the old age), merge with Abrahamic covenant promises and culminate in God's purposes of the new covenant which for Paul has now commenced in the gospel of Jesus Christ. The entailment is that the

---

171. Those affirming that the Abrahamic covenant, christologically defined, is contrasted with the Mosaic covenant in Gal 4:24, include Moo, *Galatians*, 301; Harmon, *She Must and Shall Go Free*, 174n159; Hays, *Echoes of Scripture*, 114-15; Jobes, "Jerusalem, Our Mother," 316-17; Echevarria, *Future Inheritance of Land*, 136-37; and Wright, *Paul and the Faithfulness of God*, 1139. Others think the new covenant is primarily in view: Schreiner, *Galatians*, 300-301; Longenecker, *Galatians*, 210-11; Seifrid, "Scripture and Identity in Galatians," 111; Lincoln, *Paradise Now and Not Yet*, 16; Willitts, "Isa 54,1 in Gal 4,24b," 199n30, 205-6; and see especially Meyer, *End of the Law*, 122-30.

172. Cf. Isa 1:21-23, 26 [LXX]; 49:13-23; 52:1-10; 54:5-6, 11-14; 66:7-11; Ps 87; Heb 12:22-24; Rev 21:2. For the relationship of Isa 54:1-3 to Isa 53, see Gentry and Wellum, *Kingdom through Covenant*, 496; cf. Moo, *Galatians*, 308. Contra Echevarria, *Future Inheritance of Land*, 136n137 who fails to connect Isa 54:1 to Isa 53 and posits too much of the Abrahamic covenant to the "not yet" of fulfillment. For development, also argued in chapter 5 above, of how the suffering servant's offspring are Abraham's promised offspring with Paul's citation of Isa 54:1, with attention to the larger seed theme of Isa 40-66, see Gignilliat, "Isaiah's Offspring," 205-23.

173. For analyses of Isa 54:1 in Gal 4:27, see Harmon, *She Must and Shall Go Free*, 176-85; Starling, *Not My People*, 23-60; Willitts, "Isa 54,1 in Gal 4,24b," 188-210; De Boer, "Paul's Quotation of Isaiah 54.1," 370-89; Hays, *Echoes of Scripture*, 118-20; and Gignilliat, "Isaiah's Offspring." For an overview of the Zion theme in the book of Isaiah, see Dow, *Images of Zion*, 84-90.

end-time mother Jerusalem is giving birth to children, Jewish and gentile Christians, who are freed from the Mosaic Law and from sin.[174] Furthermore, Paul's reference to being born according to the Holy Spirit in contrast to the flesh in Gal 4:29 not only recalls the deliverance from the present evil age (Gal 1:4) but also points the reader back to Paul's assertion that the blessing of Abraham coincides with the new covenant promise of the Spirit (see Gal 3:14 and the discussion of this verse in chapter 5; cf. 4:6). Further, that Christians are children of the free woman, Sarah, and set free by Christ (Gal 4:30—5:1) also indicates that for Paul, both Abrahamic and new covenants have been fulfilled. Since Christ is the true seed of Abraham, the redeemer of those who were under the law, whose work brings about the promises and blessings of the Abrahamic and new covenants, opening up citizenship in the heavenly Jerusalem, it follows that the inheritors and recipients of these secured blessings are those who have faith in Christ. It is these promised children who are heirs (Gal 4:29) of the eschatological Jerusalem in the renewed cosmos, both now and future. Therefore, Beale rightly concludes,

> Gal. 4:22–27 develops further the contrast between true Israel and false Israel. The true believers in Galatia, 'like Isaac, are children of promise' (v. 28), continuing the typology of Sarah and Isaac in relation to end-time Israel, whom the believing Galatians have begun to form a part in fulfillment of the Isa. 54:1 prophecy. And, as at the time of Ishmael and Isaac, when the one 'born according to the flesh persecuted him born according to the Spirit, so it is now also' (v. 29). This refers to the Christian Judaizers, together with the Judaism they represent, who persecute the true people of God, Christian believers. . . . The church . . . is the true Israel and seed of Abraham (Gal. 3:16, 29) and is beginning to fulfill the Isa. 54:1 restoration prophecy, being identified as spiritual descendants of Isaac and children of the end-time restored Jerusalemite woman (v. 31). Since Christ

---

174. Harmon, *She Must and Shall Go Free*, 183, concludes, "Theologically, Paul uses Isa 54:1 to argue that the fulfillment of the Abrahamic covenant has come in Christ the promised seed, and through his resurrection the new / heavenly Jerusalem has been born and begun to bring forth children (all who belong to Christ by faith)." Moo, *Galatians*, 307, writes, "Here Isaiah combines Abrahamic covenant language with the tradition of the restoration of Zion and return from exile. . . . Paul is convinced, of course, that the 'new Jerusalem,' representing the age to come, has come into being and that it is through the Spirit-empowered preaching of the gospel that this new Jerusalem is being populated." See also Juncker, "'Children of Promise,'" 137. For further on how the Abrahamic covenant becomes merged with the restoration of Zion within the larger context of Isa 54:1, see Harmon, *She Must and Shall Go Free*, 178–79; note also Jobes, "Jerusalem, Our Mother," 307–9.

has already been identified as 'Abraham's seed' (3:16) together with Christians as 'Abraham's seed' (3:29), and since Isa. 54:1 directly follows the great Suffering Servant passage . . . it is likely that Paul sees Christ as the firstborn, end-time Jerusalemite, with whom others can identify and also become new Jerusalem children.[175]

Lastly, a second inference from Paul's instruction regarding the true, spiritual children of the free woman as the heirs of the Abrahamic covenant promises and denizens of heavenly Jerusalem is also warranted.[176] Zion's restoration in the larger context of Isaiah (also confirmed by Paul) not only included gentiles within the exilic return and expansion of the city's children (along with Isa 54:1–3, see 49:6; 56:6–7; 60; 66:18–21), but there were also implications for the geographic hopes (see Isa 54:2) in the age of the new covenant. Whereas in the original context, Isaiah 54:1 refers to the state of Jerusalem, personified as females, at two distinct stages of its history,[177] for Paul, the "present Jerusalem" surprisingly corresponds to Hagar, who is likened to the "one who has a husband" (Isa 54:1; Gal 4:27), and to the Mosaic covenant (Mt Sinai). Paul indicates that the present Jerusalem is actually outside the promised land, in Arabia (Gal 4:25).[178] On the other

---

175. Beale, *New Testament Biblical Theology*, 721–22.

176. While it is not explored in detail here, the vertical dimension of typology is present in this text. The heavenly Jerusalem corresponded to the earthly Jerusalem, but it now corresponds to the church (the inhabitants of the heavenly city), and then culminates into the consummated Jerusalem in the new heavens and earth. Such a notion would be similar to the temple typology, which is presented this way in the book of Hebrews. Dow, *Images of Zion*, 169, notes, "Paul interprets [Isa 54:1] as a prediction that many Gentiles would become citizens of Jerusalem. Clearly, Gentile believers in Christ have not become citizens of the earthly Jerusalem (though perhaps the Judaizers want them to try to be, by being circumcised), but they truly belong to Zion. This must be the heavenly prototype of the earthly city, which remains the true Zion even if the earthly copy has betrayed it and thus has become severed from it. To Paul, Jewish adherence to the Law as something opposed to the message of Jesus has reduced the Jewish earthly city to secular status. It is 'in Arabia' (Gal. 4:25). The promises about Zion in the Old Testament are properly applied to heavenly Jerusalem, of which now it is the church on earth that is the corresponding reality. Thus Zion theology adheres to 'Jerusalem' above and to its citizens, the church, not to earthly Jerusalem (both place and people). This Jerusalem above is opposed to the 'present' Jerusalem, which implies that it is the Jerusalem of the future as well as being the present mother of believers."

177. Moo, *Galatians*, 306; Starling, *Not My People*, 46; Willitts, "Isa 54,1 in Gal 4,24b," 195–97.

178. Lincoln, *Paradise Now and Not Yet*, 15–16, remarks, "To the Judaizers and their sympathizers in the Galatian churches it would have been by no means obvious . . . that Hagar corresponded to the Sinai covenant. In their view the law had been given at Sinai to the descendants of Abraham through Isaac and had nothing to do

hand, according to Paul, the new and heavenly Jerusalem, associated with Sarah as the formerly barren and desolate one, is the restored Jerusalem that has numerous children. Based on these observations, Lincoln pinpoints the ramifications of Paul's teaching in Gal 4:26–27 regarding the heavenly Jerusalem for the inheritance of the promised land:

> The heavenly Jerusalem . . . stands for the new order of salvation bound up with the new age which is accessible now to faith. It is no longer the case that the inheritance promised to the descendants of Abraham is the land of Canaan with its centre in Jerusalem, but now this inheritance (cf. 3:18, 29; 4:1, 7, 30; 5:21) comes to the sons of Abraham by faith and is the new age, the kingdom of God, with its focus as the heavenly Jerusalem.[179]

N. T. Wright also finds from these verses that "Paul sees the Land, and its focal point Jerusalem, as both in theory and in practice relativized by the death and resurrection of the Messiah."[180] For Paul then, the resurrection and exaltation of Christ, the beginning of the new covenant era, means that the restoration promises concerning the earthly Jerusalem, temple, and the promised land take on a heavenly and cosmic dimensions such that the inheritance is no longer focused upon a future, earthly, nationalistic Jerusalem in Palestine, or a physical temple located there, or the land of

---

with Hagar. Thus the further statement with its geographical addition is meant to justify such an unexpected comparison. Hagar can be said to be Sinai because Sinai is in Arabia and Arabia has negative redemptive-historical connotations, since not only associated with the descendants of Hagar and Ishmael but was also outside Palestine, the land of promise." Cf. Schreiner, *Galatians*, 302.

179. Lincoln, *Paradise Now and Not Yet*, 22. Lincoln continues, "Whereas in 2 Baruch and 4 Ezra the heavenly Jerusalem guaranteed that in principle the earthly Jerusalem, whatever its present condition, would eventually fulfil its role in eschatological expectations, here in Galatians 4 there is no such hope for the present Jerusalem, for it is now classed as part of the old age and subject to the forces of that age, the law, sin and death. For Paul the element of continuity with the history of salvation under the old covenant lies not through Jerusalem as such but through Christ and those who by faith in him are children of Sarah through the promise (cf. verses 23, 28, 31)" (22). In a similar manner, see Walker, *Jesus and the Holy City*, 131–32.

180. Wright, "Jerusalem in the New Testament," 69. In another sense, Jerusalem was not entirely relativized by Jesus' death and resurrection because Luke narrates how Israel's restoration occurs in Jerusalem, not Galilee. Fuller, *Restoration of Israel*, 257–58, explains, "Luke cannot have the decisive moment of Israel's restoration take place in Galilee, a place of little importance for Israel's history or future hopes. *In Jerusalem*: the messiah must meet with the core of the re-gathered community; the messiah must make his exit to heaven; the Twelve must be reconstituted; and the Spirit must fall" (emphasis original). See Luke 24:33–36, 45–53; Acts 1–2. It is in Jerusalem then where Luke describes Israel's re-gathering and inaugurated eschatological restoration.

Canaan.¹⁸¹ With Christ exalted in heaven (Eph 1:20), the citizenship of the people of God is the heavenly Jerusalem (Gal 4:26–27; Phil 3:20; Eph 2:6; cf. Heb 12:22–29; Rev 21:2, 10–27) and with Christ as the true temple (see Col 1:19 with Ps 68:16–17) and cornerstone (Eph 2:20–21; cf. 1 Pet 2:6–7), the church and individual Christians are the end-time temple of God (1 Cor 3:16–17; 6:19–20; 2 Cor 6:16–17; Eph 2:19–22; cf. 1 Pet 2:4–5; Rev 21:11), and lastly, as the last Adam and resurrected progenitor of the new creation (1 Cor 15:22–23, 45; Col 1:15, 18), the land promises expand to cover the entire cosmos (Rom 4:13; 8:14–25; cf. Matt 5:5), a theme that also merges with the concept of the heavenly city (Heb 11:8–16; 13:12–14).¹⁸² These realities are not only in keeping with the prophetic anticipations of the OT, but they have come about through the agency of Jesus Christ, and as Paul has demonstrated throughout Gal 3–4 and his other letters, the inheritors and beneficiaries are the people of faith, the church.

---

181. Again, Lincoln, *Paradise Now and Not Yet*, 30, is helpful, for "through the resurrection and exaltation of Christ, the focus of salvation history has moved from earthly to the heavenly realm. For [Paul] the hope of Israel lies not in Jerusalem but in Jesus Christ, the one who fulfils all that Jerusalem dimly foreshadowed in regard to the presence of God with his people. Since Christ is in heaven (cf. for example Phil. 3:20), all that the earthly Jerusalem promised can now be transferred to the reality of the heavenly dimension which Christ has opened up, in fact, to the heavenly Jerusalem. Thus there is an element of continuity in that the name Jerusalem is retained and the significance of that name for the fulfilment of God's promises to Israel still stands in the background, yet what God has accomplished in Christ has radically altered its meaning. The old category has been reinterpreted so that no longer in view is a restored national capital which will be the geographical centre for the ingathering of the nations in the Messianic era but Jerusalem can now designate instead the focal point of the heavenly existence of the new age." Contra Saucy, *Case for Progressive Dispensationalism*, 292–94. Saucy argues that the contrast between the Jerusalem above and present Jerusalem (Gal 4:26) is primarily soteriological and cannot negate the possibility of a future earthly Jerusalem in Paul's eschatology. Certainly there is an eschatological hope when the heavenly Jerusalem emerges in the new heavens and earth (Rev 21:2), but Saucy gives no attention to the link between Gal 4:26 and 27 and fails to analyze the significance of Paul's citation of Isa 54:1, an eschatological and restoration prophecy whereby the earthly Jerusalem is renewed. This text is now being fulfilled with the populating of the heavenly city. While the soteriological differences are crucial, the eschatological aspects are undeniable as Sarah and the heavenly Jerusalem represent the new age of Christ, while Hagar and the Jerusalem below are emblematic of the old age. Finally, Paul's contrast with the "Jerusalem above" with the "present Jerusalem" is fitting because contrasting "the Jerusalem above" with a "Jerusalem below" would undermine the fact that someday the "Jerusalem above" will not be above, but will become spatially located in the new heavens and earth.

182. For the use of Ps 68:16–17 in Col 1:19 with Christ as the temple of divine presence, see Beale, *New Testament Biblical Theology*, 543–44. Beale is also surely right to view all three motifs of Jerusalem, temple, and new creation in 1 Pet 2:4–7 (see p. 768).

In sum, in Gal 4:21–31 Paul "has shown that Christians are the 'children of the free woman,' Sarah, and thus like Isaac are heirs of all the promises that God gave to Isaac and his descendants. Believers can trace their privileged status to both their paternity and their maternity."[183] This is also confirmed in Rom 8:14–25 where the themes of inheritance (which is connected to the promised land; cf. 4:13), new creation, and sonship come together.[184] In a climactic statement, Paul tells his Roman readers that the Spirit bears witness that "we are children of God, and if children, then heirs—heirs of God and fellow heirs with Christ, provided we suffer with him in order that we may also be glorified with him" (Rom 8:16–17 ESV).

The two typological features evaluated in this section were with respect to Abraham's faith which foreshadowed the faith of the eschatological, spiritual offspring of Abraham and the typological pattern also tied to the seed of Abraham which focused upon the identity of the heirs of the Abrahamic promises and the content of that inheritance. With the church as the true Abrahamic sons and thus the renewed Israel via Christ, the implications for ecclesiological proposals are significant. In fact, neither dispensationalists nor covenantalists rightly synthesize the typological aspects concerning Abraham's seed. Dispensationalists do not view all the Abrahamic covenant promises as being directed through Christ to the church, with all members of Abraham's eschatological seed equally sharing that inheritance, while covenant theologians do not sufficiently recognize the national and typological features of the Abrahamic covenant and how in the new age of Christ the Abrahamic seed is no longer manifested by physical lineage but is solely based on conversion and the work of the Spirit. The weaknesses of each system of theology are taken in turn.

---

183. Moo, *Galatians*, 312. Seifrid, "Scripture and Identity in Galatians," 113, similarly writes, "Just as Jews have become 'Gentiles' through transgression of the law, Gentiles have become 'eschatological Jews' not only by virtue of Abraham, their father, but also through this heavenly mother."

184. For the connections between Rom 4:13 and 8:17, see Beale, *New Testament Biblical Theology*, 761–62; and Wright, *Paul and the Faithfulness of God*, 819. In Romans, "heir" occurs only in Rom 4:13–14 and 8:17, and whereas in the former it is Abraham who is heir of the world, in Rom 8:18–23 the heirs are believers who inherit the resurrection of the body in the same manner as Christ's resurrection (8:11) which is also linked to the inheritance of the new creation (8:32; cf. v. 19, 21). For detailed discussion of the inheritance theme in Rom 4:13–25 and Rom 8, see Echevarria, *Future Inheritance of Land*, 141–63. Contra Rudolph, "Zionism in Pauline Literature," 167–94. Rudolph fails to interpret Rom 4:13 within its own wider context, makes no connection to Rom 8:17 (see his discussion on pp. 171–77), and ultimately fails to understand how the Abrahamic covenant is fulfilled in Christ and the new covenant he initiates with the result being that the recipients of these promises are exclusively those in union with Christ by faith.

First, dispensationalists do not properly account for the fact that *all* the spiritual seed of Abraham, Jewish *and* gentile believers in Christ, are heirs of *all* the Abrahamic promises that are ultimately Christ's (Gal 3:16, 18; cf. Eph 3:6; see also the discussion in chapter 5). Gentile Christians are not just recipients of salvific benefits as if only the Abrahamic promise of the blessing to the nations (Gen 12:3) was fulfilled. On the contrary, all believers are like Isaac (Gal 4:28) in being children of promise, Sarah's offspring, but more, they are also the heirs of the Abrahamic covenant promises just as Isaac was (Gal 4:30–31; cf. 3:29; 4:7). Second, attempts by dispensationalists and Christian Zionists to argue that Gal 3:28 does not erase ethnic and national identities just as unity in Christ does not obliterate sexual identity ("neither male nor female") in advancing a nationalistic particularity for Israel are well wide of the mark.[185] Of course Paul does not deteriorate ethnic or sexual distinctions in the unity of Christ given his other writings. But the issue is whether there are certain Christians (i.e., Jewish believers) who receive exclusive benefits based upon the Abrahamic promises that are not privy to other believers (gentiles). To take the matter in a different, hypothetical direction, would anyone say that male Christians are more entitled as heirs to the promises than female Christians? Of course not. But just because there are ethnic or sexual distinctions in the church does not entail or logically mean that Jewish believers receive promises and benefits that gentiles do not. The point is that union with Christ ensures the equal status and privileges of all believers, for all believers possess all the benefits of Christ (cf. Rom 8:15–17, 32), being coheirs to the promises of Abraham, including the land.[186] Third, as I have noted both in chapter 5 and in this section, not only are the Abrahamic covenant promises fulfilled in Christ, but the new covenant and restoration elements (e.g., experience of the Holy Spirit [cf. Isa 44:3–5], inheritance, citizenship in the heavenly Jerusalem in fulfillment of Isa 54:1) within the context of Paul's description of the eschatological seed of Abraham in Gal 3–4 means that Jews and gentiles incorporated into the singular seed, Christ, are the genuine, legitimate Abrahamic offspring and true sons of God and therefore, are the renewed,

---

185. See Blaising, "Biblical Hermeneutics," 87–88; Rudolph, "Zionism in Pauline Literature," 180–81.

186. Schreiner, *Galatians*, 258, writes, "As coheirs of the promise of Abraham, Jews are not superior to Gentiles, those who are free are not more important than slaves, and men are not worth more than women. All those who are united to Christ are equal members of Abraham's family." Social distinctions may not be erased, but distinct promises and blessings for national Israel is not what Paul teaches. In fact, quite the opposite; anyone in Christ receives the Abrahamic promises. Cf. Moo, *Galatians*, 254–55.

antitypical Israel.[187] Starling suggests that Paul's arguments about the promises and inheritance in Gal 3–4 supports his

> emphatic assertion of the full inclusion of Gentile believers—apart from the law and irrespective of their uncircumcision—among the justified people of God and the heirs of his promises. All that was promised—blessing, land, life, righteousness, the Spirit—is inherited 'through faith in Christ Jesus' and given 'to those who believe' (3:22).[188]

Just as the fulfillment of the Abrahamic promises in the unique, antitypical seed of Christ and for those in solidarity with him—the church—poses challenges for the dispensational scheme, so it does for covenant theology. Recalling the prototypical role of Abraham's faith and how OT prophetic texts projected a faithful, eschatological, Abrahamic, and messianic offspring based on the work of Abraham's true royal seed (Christ), it is also observable that for Paul, the only Abrahamic offspring that is to be accounted for in the new covenant era are those who possess faith. As Martin Salter rightly observes,

> Now Christ has come and fulfilled the covenant requirements and exhausted the covenant curses the promise to Abraham is fulfilled. As a consequence new covenant members find themselves connected to Abraham *through* Christ. The spiritual adoption into Abraham's family is by virtue of faith in Christ. There is no connection to Abraham other than *via* Christ, by faith. Christ's covenantal mediatorship means covenantal infidelity is now impossible because in him the requirements are met and the curses exhausted.[189]

Or, as Jason DeRouchie observes,

> All members in the new covenant are identified with Christ in the heavenly realms (Eph 2:5–6; Col 2:12–13; 3:3); they are children of 'the Jerusalem above' (Gal 4:26, 31; cf. Heb 12:22–24), meaning that, regardless of one's original heritage, all have new

---

187. Contra Feinberg, "Systems of Discontinuity," 71–73; Saucy, *Case for Progressive Dispensationalism*, 49–50, 155–57, 200; Vlach, *Has the Church Replaced Israel?*, 150–51; Riccardi, "Seed of Abraham," 51–64.

188. Starling, "Yes to All God's Promises," 189. For an overview of Jesus as the seed of Abraham and inheritor of the promised land with the church as the redefined eschatological covenant people who through incorporation into Christ are also the seed and inheritors of the land, see Isaac, *From Land to Lands*, 231–70.

189. Salter, "Abrahamic Covenant," 43, emphasis original.

birth certificates declaring, 'This one was born there'—in Zion (Psalm 87).[190]

Indeed, Gal 3-4 is crucial for understanding the nature of the new covenant community because when Paul addresses justification by faith, the nature of Abrahamic sonship, and more generally the relationship between the Abrahamic and Mosaic covenants, he locates these ideas within a nexus of new covenant themes and realities: the reception of the Spirit by faith, the significance of Christ as the antitypical Abrahamic seed, the fulfiller of the Mosaic Law, and redeemer, and the topic of union with Christ which is also covenantal. Paul demonstrates that those who are justified by faith, recipients of the Holy Spirit, and who constitute the true, children of Abraham in the new age are only those who are united to Christ by faith. The new covenant community is exclusively the spiritual seed of Abraham and that relationship is not through physical descent, Torah observance, or circumcision, but through union with Christ. Therefore, the genealogical principle and the dual aspect of the covenant so crucial for covenant theologians in their defense of paedobaptism has come to an end with the arrival of Christ on the scene and the fulfillment he has actualized.[191]

The Church as the Flock of God

The flock and sheep imagery provides another point of contact between OT Israel and the church. The metaphor of a flock is a common designation for

---

190. DeRouchie, "Counting Stars with Abraham," 483.

191. Wellum, "Baptism and the Relationship," 132-61; Salter, "Abrahamic Covenant," 42-49. Contra, e.g., Horton, *Christian Faith*, 794-98; Venema, "Covenant Theology and Baptism," 201-29; and Gibson, "On Abraham, Covenant, and the Theology of Paedobaptism," 14-34. Gibson agrees that Gal 3:16 indicates that Christ is the fulfillment of the Abrahamic covenant, but he also argues that this was a covenant of grace with Christ; Abraham's covenant was also Christ's covenant as Christ not only fulfills it but receives it (see pp. 16-21). Of course, Abraham is in a salvific sense an offspring of Christ in that his salvation was ultimately won by Christ, but here Gibson ignores the redemptive historical argument that Paul is making as Paul specifically says that the promise was to Abraham and his offspring, Christ. By already identifying Christ as the offspring, he is not arguing for a covenant of grace with its foundation in Christ well before Abraham because the term *offspring* already signifies a chronological movement, for Abraham's offspring can only come after Abraham himself. Likewise, in Gal 3:19, a verse Gibson ignores, Paul makes the point that the law was in place until the offspring should come to whom the promise had been made. To argue that the genealogical principle is constant throughout the storyline of the Bible, as Gibson does, is to diminish the typological patterns, covenantal shifts, and prophetic texts that state otherwise. In the end, Gibson forces the text of Gal 3:16 into his preconceived notion of the covenant of grace.

the nation of Israel in the OT (e.g., Pss 77:20; 78:52-55; 80:1; Isa 40:9-11; cf. Num 27:17; 2 Sam 5:2). The shepherd and flock imagery also appears in prophetic texts where God himself will gather the scattered remnant of his flock and directly shepherd them, and intriguingly, a Davidic messiah is also charged with shepherding God's people (Jer 23:1-6; 31:10-12; Ezek 34:7-16, 22-25; 37:24-28; Mic 5:2-4). In the NT, the sheep and flock imagery is applied to the church and these motifs belong inseparably to the image of the shepherd: the flock is in the possession of God with Christ as the appointed shepherd (see Heb 13:20; 1 Pet 2:25; 5:2-4; cf. Acts 20:28).[192] Covenant and kingdom motifs additionally merge with the flock and sheep imagery as the kingdom is granted to the little flock (Luke 12:32) and the shepherd is bound to his sheep via the blood of the eternal new covenant (Heb 13:20).[193] Here again we see that identifiers for Israel (flock, sheep) are applied to the church, but not in a direct or equivalent manner as the coming of Jesus Christ, the messianic shepherd, means that the new covenant people of God are reoriented and cultivated around him and his sacrificial work. For my purposes, the fulfillment in Christ of the eschatological, restoration hopes of a Davidic shepherd-king who will gather and unite the people of Israel is important in establishing the church as God's true flock. These facets emerge in John 10.

Jesus is described as the good shepherd in John 10, and those whom he lays down his life for and who listen to his voice are his followers, the sheep (10:11, 14-16; cf. 10:2-4). The shepherding motif in this discourse evokes the prophecy of Ezek 34 where Israel's shepherds or religious leaders are indicted for failing to care for God's sheep (cf. Isa 56:9-12; Jer 23:1-4; Zech 11). The ultimate solution for God's people Israel is that God himself and his servant David will shepherd and rescue the sheep and the flock (Ezek 34:10-16, 23-25). The coming of a future Davidic shepherd-king coincides with the making of a covenant peace and the overcoming of the curse as God's sheep will dwell securely in the land with the banishment of wild beasts (Ezek 34:25). "The same themes – God's servant David ruling over his people in the constraints of a new covenant, 'a covenant of peace,' and 'an everlasting covenant', and serving as their shepherd – recur in Ezekiel 37"[194] where the miracle of the revivification of the dry bones appears. In John 10 Jesus is presented in one sense the divine shepherd but also the

---

192. Minear, *Images of the Church*, 84-85.
193. Minear, *Images of the Church*, 85.
194. Carson, *John*, 381.

antitypical and prophesied shepherd in the line of David. He is the gate as his sheep "will go in and out and find pasture" (John 10:9).[195]

Moreover, Jesus knows his own and those who refuse to follow him are not part of his messianic flock (10:26), a notion that reflects how earlier Jesus declared that unbelieving Jews were not of God (8:42-47).[196] A new development occurs in verse 16 with other sheep not of this original sheep fold or pen being gathered by Jesus.[197] These other sheep also respond to his voice so that altogether, all of Jesus' sheep become one flock with one shepherd, which is an allusion to Ezek 34:23-24 and 37:24.[198] The other sheep not of this sheep fold, referring back to John 10:1-5 where Jesus leads his sheep out of the pen or courtyard of Judaism, are believers from the gentile realm (cf. John 11:51-52).[199] The composition of the messianic sheep extends beyond the national and ethnic boundaries of Israel and all together they form one flock (Ezek 37:15-28; Isa 56:3-8; Mic 2:12; cf. Eph 2:11-22; 4:3-6).[200] "While Ezekiel 34 . . . refers to the unification of Israel and Judah (v. 22), Jesus extends the scope of the passage to include both Jews and Gentiles in the new messianic community, the church."[201] The whole point then, with the typological implications, is rightly captured by D. A. Carson:

---

195. Köstenberger, *John*, 304, comments on this phrase: "Jesus' language here [of going in and out] (a Semitism) echoes covenant terminology, especially Deuteronomic blessings for obedience (cf. Deut. 28:6; cf. Ps. 121:8). It is also reminiscent of Moses' description of Joshua (LXX: Ἰησοῦς, *Iēsous*), who led Israel into the promised land (Num. 27:16-17). . . . The pasture imagery is also found in OT references to Israel's final restoration (Isa. 49:9-10) and deliverance from the nations (Ezek. 34:12-15)."

196. Hays, *Echoes of Scripture in the Gospels*, 340; Köstenberger, *Theology of John's Gospel*, 502.

197. For a thorough analysis of John 10:16, see Köstenberger, "Jesus the Good Shepherd," 67-96.

198. See Hays, *Echoes of Scripture in the Gospels*, 340-41; Köstenberger, *Theology of John's Gospel*, 501; Ridderbos, *Gospel according to John*, 363. Jesus' death will draw all kinds of people to himself (John 12:32) and so the Greeks who seek to follow Jesus (12:20-23) would be considered among the "other sheep" who hear Jesus' voice, so Hays, *Echoes of Scripture in the Gospels*, 342.

199. Carson, *John*, 388; Köstenberger, *Theology of John's Gospel*, 502n182; Klink, *John*, 465-66, 515. Ridderbos, *Gospel according to John*, 363, says that the sheep fold "represents the whole of historic Israel." See also the discussion of Pancaro, "Relationship of the Church to Israel," 396-405, esp. 397-98, 403-4.

200. Köstenberger, *John*, 307. In a comment that could have implications for older forms of dispensationalism, Beasley-Murray, *John*, 171, states, "The sheep of the different folds are not to remain in their separateness, but 'they become one flock,' under the care of the one Shepherd. Their unity is the fruit of his solitary sacrifice (vv 15, 17-18) and his unique relation to God and man (vv 14-15a) as the Pauline epistles joyfully proclaim (Rom 5:12-21; 2 Cor 5:14-21; Eph 2:11-18)."

201. Köstenberger, "Jesus the Good Shepherd," 77-78. Similarly, see Klink, *John*,

[W]hen Jesus proclaims himself the good shepherd (John 10), the reader cannot forget that in the OT Yahweh (Ezek. 34:11) or the messiah (Ezek. 34:23) is the shepherd who cares for his flock: Jesus identifies his ministry with theirs, and the appropriation of Ezekiel 34 is fairly direct. But the entailment, for the church, is that it is the new messianic community that 'fulfills' Israel's role in the Ezekiel passage; and that connexion is unavoidably typological, and bound up with the replacement of the type.[202]

As the antitypical flock of Ezekiel's vision with the messianic Davidic shepherd as their good shepherd, Christ's sheep form the eschatological people of God. The church is composed of Jesus' disciples who are unified in their allegiance to the shepherd (they hear his voice and know him; John 10:14–16; cf. Gal 3:26–29) and as the Gospel of John unpacks throughout, Christ's sheep are the recipients of the covenant of peace that is ratified by the shepherd who lays down his life for them at the cross.

Two brief ecclesiological implications may be drawn from the typological pattern of the sheep and flock motifs. First, regarding dispensationalism and other like-minded Christian Zionists, the NT appropriation of the sheep and flock motif with reference to the church not only links OT Israel to the church, but presents the church itself as the eschatological flock of God. Further, the prophecies regarding God restoring his flock, Israel under a royal, Davidic shepherd has come to fruition in Jesus Christ, but this singular restored flock now consists of not only faithful Jews but also gentiles. There is one flock with one shepherd, but the notion that certain sheep in this flock (Jews) are to be granted particular promises (e.g., land, nationalistic reign) in the future cuts against the fact that already in John 10 Israel's restoration as the flock under the Davidic shepherd is expanded to include gentiles who share equally in the benefits of the good shepherd, Jesus.

---

466. For further on the gathering of the flock as a restoration image in John 10:16 with reference to 1 Enoch 90:33, see Pate et al., *Story of Israel*, 174–75.

202. Carson, "John and the Johannine Epistles," 255. For further on shepherd typology, see Goppelt, *Typos*, 88–89, 109. Köstenberger, "Jesus the Good Shepherd," 88–89, adds, "In light of passages such as Isa 56:3–8, a subtle but nonetheless very significant paradigm shift becomes apparent. While the 'other sheep' who believe in Jesus the Messiah are, in a sense, considered to be part of 'the dispersed of Israel,' the unbelieving Jews are shown to be beyond the pale of God's 'flock.' Jesus' coming can thus be said to have functioned as a catalyst for surfacing the 'true Israel of God.' . . . No longer is it possible to claim being a 'Jew' without believing in the Jewish Messiah. . . . On the other hand, if a non-Jew believes in Jesus the Messiah, he is showing himself to be part of God's 'flock.' . . . While the basic flock is still Israel, Jesus affirms that other dispersed people are gathered to Israel. By redefining 'Israel' as all those who believe in the Messiah, the Lord abolishes the notion of any 'Israel' apart from faith in the Messiah."

Second, while the flock of Israel in the OT consisted of a mixed community of faithful and unfaithful people, the one flock that Jesus is shepherd overhear his voice and are secured by the fact that the shepherd lays down his life *for the sheep* (John 10:11–18; cf. 1 Pet 2:24–25). Here the ideas of effectual calling and Christ's particular, atoning, substitutionary death on the cross go hand in hand with the nature of the flock he gathers together. The church as the flock of God is a regenerate, faithful community because it consists of only those who have heard Jesus' voice, follow him, and who are granted eternal life through his work on the cross (see John 10:27–29). In contrast to the ecclesiology of covenant theology then, the NT's presentation of the church as the flock of God differs from the depiction of the flock under the old covenant precisely due to the arrival of the messianic shepherd and because of the effective work he has accomplished on behalf of his sheep. The church in its entirety is regenerate for God's new covenant flock is the faithful remnant, the sheep that are gathered together and led by Jesus.

Galatians 6:16: The Identity of the Israel of God

The typological relationship between Israel and the church has been established in the preceding discussion. However, one key text that receives much attention in consideration of the church as the renewed or eschatological Israel is Gal 6:15–16. Although this passage does not disclose or explicate an explicit Israel-church typological relationship, it is vitally important, nevertheless, as it directly bears on the Israel-church relationship via Christ and has implications for both dispensationalism and covenant theology. Paul writes: "For neither circumcision counts for anything, nor uncircumcision, but a new creation. And as for all who walk by this rule, peace and mercy be upon them, and [καὶ] upon the Israel of God" (ESV). The interpretation of verse 16 is widely debated. There are three views for the identity of the "Israel of God."

Two of the positions can be treated together since they are united in concluding that the "Israel of God" is not a reference for the church.[203] First, some scholars and dispensationalists interpret the "Israel of God" as a reference to Christian Jews or Israelites who have received Christ as their

---

203. For example, Johnson, "Paul and 'Israel of God,'" 181–96, surveys the three views and seems to only rule out the view that interprets the "Israel of God" is the church. Likewise, Saucy, "Israel and the Church," 245–48, holds that Paul's "Israel of God" phrase is a reference to either Jews who were walking according to Paul's rule (and so Christian Jews) or to ethnic Jews destined for eschatological salvation (see pp. 247–48).

Messiah.²⁰⁴ A second position is similar in that the "Israel of God" is a reference for Jews, but differs in that the reference is to ethnic Israel in general and not specifically Jewish Christians.²⁰⁵ Either way, Gal 6:16 has two groups in view because the third καὶ in the verse should be rendered as a normal copulative, not as an unusual explicative, such that the translation is "and."²⁰⁶ Moreover, if Paul had intended to equate the "Israel of God" with those "who walk by this rule" he would have omitted καὶ since it would be unnecessary.²⁰⁷ A second reason that the "Israel of God" does not refer to the church is because Paul's usage of the word *Israel* refers only to the nation or a portion of the nation in every other occurrence in the NT.²⁰⁸ Finally, a third reason for understanding the "Israel of God" as a distinct group of ethnic Jews (whether as Jewish Christians or ethnic Jews who will be saved at Christ's return) is that such a phrase accords well with the purpose and context of the epistle as a whole.²⁰⁹ Paul defends his gospel of salvation by

---

204. Vlach, *Has the Church Replaced Israel?*, 143–45; Das, *Paul and the Jews*, 44–46; Betz, *Galatians*, 320–23; Pratt, "'Israel of God' in Gal 6:16," 66–75.

205. Allison, *Sojourners and Strangers*, 83–86; Bruce, *Galatians*, 275; Eastman, "Israel and the Mercy of God," 367–95; Richardson, *Israel in the Apostolic Church*, 74–84. For Richardson, the "Israel of God" refers to those Israelites who will receive the gospel of Christ. These Israelites are not yet part of the church, and so Paul prays for blessing upon both the church and a part of the nation of Israel who will eventually believe (82–83).

206. Saucy, "Israel and the Church," 246; Vlach, *Has the Church Replaced Israel?*, 143–44; Johnson, "Paul and 'The Israel of God,'" 191–94.

207. Das, *Paul and the Jews*, 45; Johnson, "Paul and 'The Israel of God,'" 188.

208. Saucy, "Israel and the Church," 246; Allison, *Sojourners and Strangers*, 85; Vlach, *Has the Church Replaced Israel?*, 144–45; Johnson, "Paul and 'The Israel of God,'" 190; Pratt, "'Israel of God' in Gal 6:16," 70–71. See also Das, *Paul and the Jews*, 46n74.

209. Saucy, "Israel and the Church," 246. Both the positions that argue that the "Israel of God" reference is to a distinct group of ethnic Jews contend that their position best accords with the context of the whole letter to the Galatians. For example, regarding the position that the reference is to Jewish Christians, Vlach, *Has the Church Replaced Israel?*, 144, argues, "Paul is defending the concept of salvation by grace through faith against the error of the Judaizers who held that circumcision contributed to salvation. In doing this, Paul singles out Christian Jews in Galatia who correctly believed the gospel of grace and did not follow the error of the Judaizers." Cf. Das, *Paul and the Jews*, 45–46; Johnson, "Paul and 'The Israel of God,'" 185. On the other hand, Allison, *Sojourners and Strangers*, 84, describes this position as unlikely: "The idea [that the expression 'Israel of God' refers to Jewish believers] would cut across the grain of the entire letter and its theme of Jews and Gentiles together in Christ (e.g., Gal. 3:26–29). Moreover, it would contradict Paul's belittling of the distinction between circumcision and uncircumcision (e.g., 5:6), the very point that has led him to frame the rule of Galatians 6:16." Instead, Allison thinks Paul has in mind Jews in general and that this view is a fitting conclusion to Paul's letter because he has been critical of the Jews, rebuked Peter and other Jewish believers, taught that the Mosaic Law was fulfilled,

faith apart from the works of the Law. Yet Paul argues that the one gospel which unites Jew and gentile (Gal 3:29) still "manifests itself in a distinct mission to Jews as Jews and in a mission to Gentiles as Gentiles (2:7)."[210] Thus, Paul still distinguishes between Jew and gentile. As a result, the "Israel of God" now redefines Israel as those Jews who believe or will believe in Paul's gospel in contrast to those Judaizing opponents who preach "another gospel" that calls for the gentiles to obey the Law (Gal 1:8–9; 2:4–5).

Proponents of these two views that understand the "Israel of God" as a designation for ethnic Jews have offered many strong arguments. The seemingly ambiguous phrase in Paul's conditional blessing, however, should be interpreted to refer to the entire Galatian church (including gentile Christians) for the following four reasons.

First, G. K. Beale has shown that the common meaning for καί must not be assumed as an appositional or explicative sense is possible via the rule of maximal redundancy.[211] Since Paul uses καί in an epexegetical or explicative elsewhere, the infrequency of such use is not sufficient grounds to rule out a potential usage in Gal 6:16. Further, other scholars have also observed that syntax, grammar, and word order alone is not determinative of the "Israel of God" referent.[212] Context is the ultimate determiner

---

identified Jews who want to be under the law with Hagar and slavery (Gal 4:21–31), and he has emphasized that circumcision counts for nothing. Allison, *Sojourners and Strangers*, 85, continues, "Such strong criticism, he fears, could be misunderstood to be a scathing indictment of the Jewish people—not what Paul intends to communicate. Appropriately, he prays for divine blessing both for the church—'all who walk by this rule'—as well as for 'the Israel of God.'" One wonders if Allison's position suffers from the same problem he leveled against the Jewish Christian view.

210. Das, *Paul and the Jews*, 45. Similarly, Saucy, "Israel and the Church," 246–47.

211. Beale, "Peace and Mercy," 206–7; Beale, *New Testament Biblical Theology*, 722–24; cf. Ray, "Identity of the 'Israel of God,'" 105–14. Beale describes the rule of maximal redundancy: "One should opt for a meaning 'which contributes the least new information to the total context.'" Both Beale and Ray appeal to the linguistic studies of Kermit Titrud. See also Cowan, "Context Is Everything," 81 and 84n21. Köstenberger, "Identity of the ΙΣΡΑΗΛ ΤΟΥ ΘΕΟΥ," 13, opts for the ascensive understanding of the conjunction: "Even upon the Israel of God" as he thinks those who walk according to Paul's rule are Galatian Christians while Paul's reference to the "Israel of God" is broadened as a reference to Christians in general.

212. Schreiner, *Galatians*, 381–82; Moo, *Galatians*, 400–403; Köstenberger, "Identity of the ΙΣΡΑΗΛ ΤΟΥ ΘΕΟΥ," 13; Cowan, "Context Is Everything," 80. Moo, *Galatians*, 401–2, admits that the syntax favors the conjunctive usage of the καί or an adverbial usage modifying a second prepositional phrase dependent upon "mercy": "Peace be upon them and mercy *also* upon the Israel of God." But the ambiguity concerning the syntax means that it is context that matters most. Eastman, "Israel and the Mercy of God," 372–73, follows Richardson in seeing two distinct blessings or separate benedictions (or really a benediction followed by a prayer for God's mercy on Israel) as "mercy" is extended to the "Israel of God" as an independent clause: "And mercy be

of meaning and therefore, what really matters for the identification of the "Israel of God" is the overall context of Galatians.

The most important factor for interpreting the "Israel of God" as the church is the entire message to the Galatians. Galatians 6:16 needs to be placed within the whole letter and evaluated with attention to its immediate context (Gal 6:11–18). With respect to the whole letter a number of observations are important. Paul's benediction parallels the curse pronounced in the letter's opening (Gal 1:8–9). Those who preach a gospel contrary to the one Paul preached are cursed, but the blessing is upon all who follow Paul's gospel and like Paul, boast in the cross of Christ (Gal 6:14).[213] The benediction is for those who walk according to the rule of the new creation (Gal 6:15–16), a walk that corresponds to those who keep in step with the Spirit (Gal 5:25), and that undoubtedly characterizes the church. More importantly, as was explored in the last chapter, Paul presents Jesus as the ultimate Abrahamic offspring (Gal 3:16), the one who receives all the promises of Abraham and fulfills the Mosaic Law. The old barriers separating Jews and gentiles—circumcision and the Mosaic Law—are removed as the true children of Abraham are now defined by those who are united to Christ by faith and thus share in his sonship and inheritance (Gal 3:7, 14, 26–29; 4:4–7).[214]

---

even upon the Israel of God." The problem with Eastman's view is that the second καί must function disjunctively in introducing a separate blessing (or prayer) to a different entity, but Paul could have used δέ or ἀλλά to indicate this disjunction (on this point, see Köstenberger, "Identity of the ΙΣΡΑΗΛ ΤΟΥ ΘΕΟΥ," 13). Or, Paul could have removed the third καί altogether to express the separate benedictions (so Wright, *Paul and the Faithfulness of God*, 1149). A second problem with Eastman's proposal, along with other proposals where the "Israel of God" is interpreted as a reference generally for Jews, is the difficulty with the genitive *of God*. Eastman argues that instead of using "Israel of God" as a reference for the church, Paul would have used the phrase "Israel of Christ or Israel according to promise" and that the genitive has an authorial or possessive force as empirical Israel owes its existence to God and belongs to God (see "Israel and the Mercy of God," 385–90). This fails to convince, however, for Eastman does not consider the immediate context (see below) of Gal 6:11–18 or really the cumulative thrust of the whole letter. More specifically, it is unlikely Paul would be referring to an Israel according to the flesh as if they were *of God* when throughout his letter all references to God are bound up with Messiah or his people (Gal 1:13; 2:19–21; 3:20–21; 4:7–9). See Wright, *Paul and the Faithfulness of God*, 1147, and note his critique of Eastman's approach on 1150n436, n437.

213. Vickers, "Who Is the 'Israel of God,'" 6; Cowan, "Context Is Everything," 78; cf. Schreiner, *Galatians*, 381. Ray, "Identity of the 'Israel of God,'" 113, similarly thinks Gal 1:8–9 is bookended by the blessing of 6:16.

214. For an overview of the epistle, see Köstenberger, "Identity of the ΙΣΡΑΗΛ ΤΟΥ ΘΕΟΥ," 4–11, and Ray, "Identity of the 'Israel of God,'" 108–14. For discussion of how the whole letter presents Jew and gentile believers in Christ as Abraham's family, such that the church is the eschatological people of God, the "Israel of God," see Vickers, "Who Is the 'Israel of God,'" 6–8; Moo, *Galatians*, 403; Schreiner, *Galatians*,

The ethnic distinction between Jew and gentile is removed (Gal 3:28) as both have a common lineage to Abraham by belonging to Christ (Gal 3:29). The Galatian Christians (both Jew and gentile) are Sarah's eschatological children; they are the covenant people, the end-time Israel. Their mother is the "Jerusalem above" (Gal 4:26) since they are children of promise like Isaac (4:28). It is the agitators or Judaizers who are of the lineage of Hagar in persecuting the true people of God, Christian believers.

This last point concerning the Judaizers is also important for considering the immediate context of Gal 6:16, for the benediction is also a summary statement of the epistle which has featured an anti-Judaizing stance throughout. A careful study of the closing of Paul's epistle to the Galatians, 6:11–18, provides the hermeneutical key for unlocking Paul's primary intentions for writing.[215] Paul concludes the letter by recapitulating the main themes, the primary one being the cross of Christ that distinguishes him from his opponents.[216] Paul's opponents are motivated to boast in the circumcision of the Galatians in order to avoid the persecution of the cross (Gal 6:12–13) while Paul only boasts in the cross (6:14) and willingly accepts the persecution associated with Jesus (6:17).[217] The opponents compel the Galatians to be circumcised (6:12, 13), but Paul asserts that circumcision does not matter because of the cross (6:15; see 2:21; 5:2–12). Lastly, the Judaizers live in the "world" (6:14) or realm where life is lived under the law (3:23; 4:21; 5:1), under control of the flesh (5:13–17), and where rigid distinctions are maintained (see 3:28).[218] On the other hand, Paul and followers of Jesus live in the inaugurated "new creation" (6:15; cf. 5:6; 1 Cor 7:19) having been delivered from the present evil age (Gal 1:4) and now experience a foretaste of the cosmic transformation that will be consummated upon the Israel of

---

382–83; Cowan, "Context Is Everything," 80–81; Beale, "Peace and Mercy," 215–17.

215. Weima, "Gal. 6:11–18," 90–107. See also Wright, *Paul and the Faithfulness of God*, 1142–45; Harmon, *She Must and Shall Go Free*, 313–14; Longenecker, *Galatians*, 286–89; Beale, "Peace and Mercy," 219–22.

216. Weima, "Gal. 6:11–18," 92–94.

217. Weima, "Gal. 6:11–18," 94–100. Historical reconstruction indicates that Jewish zealot activity was strong. Ibid., 97. Wright, *Paul and the Faithfulness of God*, 1145, forcibly argues the importance of Gal 6:17 within the final paragraph and how it impinges on interpreting verse 16: "[Verse 17] offers a strong and again ironic and polemical reinforcement of 6.15, where neither circumcision nor uncircumcision matters: the marks of persecution which Paul bears, the sign of his sharing of the Messiah's sufferings, are the only physical marks which mean anything, and anyone who tries to say otherwise is 'making trouble' for him. And the earlier parts of the paragraph, 6.11–15, tell the same story, in the same tone. If we are to read the last phrase of verse 16 in any other sense we would be, in effect, treating it as a strange aside. . . ."

218. Weima, "Gal. 6:11–18," 101.

CHRIST JESUS, THE TRUE ISRAEL

God at the eschaton (Rom 8:19–22).[219] There is freedom under the lordship of Jesus (see 2:19–20; 4:8–11; 5:24). The centrality of the cross that breaks down the distinctions between Jew and gentile and that establishes the eschatological inclusion of gentiles into God's people with the dawning of the new creation (Gal 6:15) along with the other elements of the final paragraph (6:11–18) strongly suggests that the peace and mercy benediction is not addressed to those who follow Paul's gospel and to a separate "Israel of God," but to all believers in Christ.[220] The eschatological people of God are defined by their union with Christ (Gal 2:20; 3:14, 22, 26–28; 5:6), but for Paul to smuggle into his benediction a distinct blessing for an Israel separate from the church or for a subset of the church (Jewish Christians) is to counteract the argument of his whole epistle where Jew/gentile distinctions and barriers have been erased in Christ.[221] Aaron Sherwood helpfully observes that

> Paul's central concern for the letter over the nature of God's people ... culminates in a veritable instance of Israel-nations unification, as the ἔθνη audience are definitively and christocentrically re-identified as Ἰσραὴλ τοῦ θεοῦ. For Paul, the Christ-event and its result of the restoration of humanity are at once a sweeping invasion of God's eschatological, cosmic reign and at

---

219. For the concept of "new creation" within an eschatological matrix involving individual conversion (anthropology), the new community, and the transformation of the cosmos inaugurated through the death and resurrection of Christ, see Moo, *Galatians*, 397–98; Moo, "Creation and New Creation," 39–60; Jackson, *New Creation in Paul's Letters*. Harmon, *She Must and Shall Go Free*, 230–35, finds crucifixion/resurrection, the restoration of Jerusalem, and the gift of the Spirit are related to the concept of new creation and permeate throughout Galatians, having Isaianic roots as well as being connected to the new creation language associated with the Isaianic servant.

220. Moo, *Galatians*, 403, aptly captures the point of Paul's benediction: "In verses 14–16 Paul sets forth the vision that should exercise controlling influence over believers in Christ. [They] (1) have been definitely removed from the controlling influence of this world; (2) participate in the new creation, God's (ultimately cosmic) restoration project; and (3) belong to God's people, now redefined around Jesus the Messiah. Everything, Paul is saying, has been reconstituted in light of the cross, and believers must live out this fundamental, world-changing reality (v. 16a)."

221. See Sherwood, *Paul and the Restoration of Humanity*, 228; Vickers, "Who Is the 'Israel of God,'" 8; Moo, *Galatians*, 403; Schreiner, *Galatians*, 383; Wright, *Paul and the Faithfulness of God*, 1151; Cowan, "Context Is Everything," 81; Longenecker, *Galatians*, 298; Jackson, *New Creation in Paul's Letters*, 111–13; Köstenberger, "Identity of the ΙΣΡΑΗΛ ΤΟΥ ΘΕΟΥ," 15–17. Longenecker, *Galatians*, 298–99, and Weima, "Gal. 6:11–18," 105, suggest that the "Israel of God" phrase could also have been a self-designation for Paul's opponents, but Paul transforms and applies the phrase to refer to those who are already the "Israel of God" by faith *in* Christ. Köstenberger, "Identity of the ΙΣΡΑΗΛ ΤΟΥ ΘΕΟΥ," 14, finds this hypothesis unconvincing since the division is not between a non-messianic Judaism and a messianic Judaism, but the conflict is between Jews who purported to be Christians and gentile Christians.

the same time—without an excluded middle—the *telos* of God's scriptural, covenantal objective for Israel.[222]

Third, the phrase *Israel of God* is unique in that it appears nowhere else in the NT or in Second Temple Jewish writings,[223] but as was discussed in the chapter 5, there are many other titles, metaphors, and imagery for Israel's identity that are directly applied to Christ and the church. Further, the concept of an Israel distinguished from national/ethnic Israel appears elsewhere in Paul's writings (Rom 9:6; 1 Cor 10:18) as does a distinction between ethnic and spiritual Israel (Rom 2:28–29; Phil 3:3).[224] Paul also calls the Galatian believers "sons of God" (Gal 3:26) which is essentially a synonym for Israel.[225] While not decisive itself in interpreting Gal 6:16, this observation evaporates any objection that the term "Israel" can never be used to refer to the church.

Finally, Paul's benediction should be viewed within the background of Isa 54:10 LXX, a verse that has the combined uses of "peace" and "mercy" within the new creation context (Isa 54:11–12) at the time of Israel's restoration.[226] All three of these elements appear in Gal 6:15–16. Moreover, Paul

---

222. Sherwood, *Paul and the Restoration of Humanity*, 229, emphasis original.

223. Köstenberger, "Identity of the ἸΣΡΑΗΛ ΤΟΥ ΘΕΟΥ," 14; Longenecker, *Galatians*, 299. It is also important that Paul's reference is to the Israel *of God*. According to Köstenberger, "Identity of the ἸΣΡΑΗΛ ΤΟΥ ΘΕΟΥ," 14–15, "similar genitive qualifiers are found in Galatians elsewhere: in 1:13, where the reference is made to 'the church of God' . . . and in 6:2, where Paul refers to 'the Law of Christ.' . . . Thus the reference to 'the Israel of God' may well connote a similar use of the genitive, and perhaps a similar reapplication of familiar terminology as in the case of 'the Law of Christ.'" Cf. Jackson, *New Creation in Paul's Letters*, 112. Wright, *Paul and the Faithfulness of God*, 1144, also notes the importance of Gal 1:13 to interpreting 6:16, but adds that the only other occurrence of "church of God" is in 1 Cor 10:32, where Paul explicitly distinguishes the church from Jews and Greeks, which comports well with Gal 1:13 and the message of the letter as a whole.

224. See Wright, *Paul and the Faithfulness of God*, 1146–48, 1148n425; Schreiner, *Galatians*, 382; Moo, *Galatians*, 402–3; Cowan, "Context Is Everything," 80. Note also Vickers, "Who Is the 'Israel of God,'" 8–9, and Schreiner, "Church as the New Israel," 17–38, esp. 17–24. Even if Rom 9–11 posits a future for ethnic Israel, it does not mean Gal 6:16 should be interpreted based on this passage; each setting needs to be considered on its own. Contra Eastman, "Israel and the Mercy of God," 367–95. Rightly, Köstenberger, "Identity of the ἸΣΡΑΗΛ ΤΟΥ ΘΕΟΥ," 14; Sherwood, *Paul and the Restoration of Humanity*, 228–29.

225. Moo, *Galatians*, 250, notes that "sons of God" language was appropriated by Jews in Paul's day that typically focused on the eschatological gathering of God's people (Jub 1:24–25; Sir 36:17; 3 Macc 6:28; 4 Ezra 6:55–59; Pss Sol 17:26–27). Cf. Byrne, "Sons of God"—"Seed of Abraham," 62–63.

226. Beale, "Peace and Mercy," 210–211; see also Harmon, *She Must and Shall Go Free*, 236–38.

would have had Isa 54 in mind since he already quoted Isa 54:1 in Gal 4:27, and he drew upon the new creation prophecies of Isa 43:19 and Isa 65:17 in 2 Cor 5:17.[227] Within the background of Isa 54 LXX, gentiles experience the new creation restoration by identifying with the God of Israel; however, Paul understands the beginning of the fulfillment of Isaiah's prophecy to have occurred for the gentiles and Jews who identify with Jesus, the true Israel.[228] Matthew Harmon helpfully summarizes:

> By pronouncing a blessing upon God's people (Jew and Gentile in Christ) from the language of a restoration promise, Paul prays that the Galatians would experience the reality of the restoration that Christ the Isaianic Servant has already accomplished on their behalf at the cross. Referring to believers as the Israel of God signals that Paul has redefined the people of God around the Christ-event, which inaugurated the new creation and unleashed the eschatological Spirit. Since the redemption accomplished by Christ is at once the restoration of Jerusalem (Gal 4:26–28) and the inauguration of the new creation (Gal 6:15), it is only appropriate that Paul prays for God's redeemed people, the Israel of God, to experience the eschatological peace brought about by God's mercy (Gal 6:16).[229]

Based on the above analysis, Gal 6:16b should be translated as "peace and mercy be upon them, *that is*, upon the Israel of God" or "peace and mercy be upon them, *even* upon the Israel of God." The significance of this designation within the larger message of Galatians is vitally important for systems of theology. The church *is* the Israel of God, and Paul labors throughout his letter to characterize the people redefined around Jesus: the eschatological people of God have freedom from the power of the old age (the Law, the flesh, and the world), are filled and directed by the eschatological Spirit (the Spirit mediating Christ's presence, empowering God's people for service and righteous living), are part of the new creation (the transformation encompassing the anthropological, ecclesiological, and the cosmological spheres), and the church is granted the promise of

---

227. Beale, "Peace and Mercy," 210, 216. Harmon, *She Must and Shall Go Free*, 234–35, notes that the restoration of Jerusalem and the new creation motifs are connected in Isa 65:17–25, which in turn tie back to Isa 54:1–17 where Jerusalem's restoration is the result of the Servant's work (Isa 53). These themes all appear in Galatians. For discussion of new creation in Isa 65:17 and 66:22, see Jackson, *New Creation in Paul's Letters*, 17–32. Jackson also finds the Isaianic new creation themes present in Gal 6:15–16 (see p. 113).

228. Beale, "Peace and Mercy," 217–18.

229. Harmon, *She Must and Shall Go Free*, 237–38.

eschatological peace.²³⁰ In contrast to all forms of dispensationalism, the church can be directly linked to OT Israel and further, the eschatological realities bound up with the Christ and his new covenant work mean there is nothing left for Israel's national restoration. The Israel-church relationship is typological. The Jerusalem above and the new creation are present now and the children of promise, the Israel of God, consist of Jews and gentiles united and conjoined together in Christ.²³¹

On the other hand, Paul does not simply equate the church with OT Israel or make them equivalent in Gal 6:16 or throughout his epistle. In contrast to covenant theology, the church is on a greater plane than national Israel, again given the escalated soteriological and eschatological realities that Paul has unpacked in his letter. Despite all the problems the Galatians were facing (e.g., Gal 1:6–9; 3:1–4; 4:9–11; 5:2–4, 15), Paul's opponents, the Judaizers, are never considered part of the covenant community, instead they are outsiders along with the "false brothers" Paul encountered in Jerusalem (Gal 2:4). The Galatians are warned by Paul that rejecting the gospel leads to final judgment and he exhorts them to live by faith and walk by the Spirit, and yet Paul calls his readers "brothers" (Gal 1:11; 3:15; 4:12, 28, 31; 5:11, 13; 6:1, 18), and as discussed above, he identifies Abraham's true offspring as those who have faith like Abraham (Gal 3:7, 9, 26–29). The "Israel of God" is the new covenant community, the people Paul associates with the new creation, and the people who have been baptized into Christ and have put on Christ (Gal 3:27).²³² In a situation where Judaizers were advocating gentiles to be circumcised and follow the Mosaic Law, Paul does not argue against circumcision by appealing to baptism as the replacement for the initiation rite into the new covenant community.²³³ Instead, he contrasts circumcision with faith. Entry into the new age of the last Adam as Abrahamic sons is by faith (Gal 3:26) which is also accompanied by being born according to the Spirit (4:29). Baptism appropriately signifies

---

230. These features are summarized by Harmon, *She Must and Shall Go Free*, 238–48.

231. Sherwood, *Paul and the Restoration of Humanity*, 231, finds that in Gal 6:11–16, "Paul summarizes his argument by configuring his audience's christocentric identity in terms of the restoration of creation as well as that of Israel and humanity, namely, the Gentile audience themselves. That is, that the capstone of Galatians is the fact that they are Israel (through [faith]) means that the eschatological New Creation has been inaugurated by and in their very experience of being believers. Or put another way, the coming of the New Creation reciprocally enables and is proven by the audience's being God's righteous people."

232. On Gal 3:27, see Schreiner, *Galatians*, 256–57; Moo, *Galatians*, 251–52; Longenecker, *Galatians*, 154–56; and Beasley-Murray, *Baptism in the New Testament*, 146–51.

233. Schreiner, *Galatians*, 256; cf. Salter, "Abrahamic Covenant," 44.

incorporation into Christ and participation with Christ (union with Christ) since baptism encapsulates the entire conversion experience (faith, repentance, the gift of the Spirit) and vividly displays this union as immersion into water symbolizes how the Christian is plunged into Christ's death and then is brought up out of the water in symbolizing their resurrection with Christ (cf. Rom 6:3–6). Those baptized into Christ (Gal 3:27), an act that symbolized conversion and indicative of faith (Gal 3:26), have crucified the old self and are clothed with Christ. The whole new covenant community is characterized by union with Christ.

SUMMARY: THE CHURCH AS ISRAEL'S ANTITYPE IN CHRIST

Based on the preceding analysis, there is confirmation that the nation of Israel is a typological pattern. Through the chief antitype, Christ, the new covenant community is also Israel's antitype. Israel's experiences (1 Cor 10:1–11), structures (kingdom, temple, priesthood) and core identity as God's chosen race, Abraham's seed, and as God's flock were all advance presentations of the eschatological Israel of God (Gal 6:16). The church is the restored flock of God, the true seed of Abraham (Gal 3–4; Rom 4), the new temple, the people of the new exodus, the ultimate chosen race, royal priesthood (Exod 19:6; 1 Pet 2:9; cf. Rev 1:4), and holy nation. Although outside the scope of this study, the book of Revelation also affirms this thesis. Revelation deals with the end in terms of final salvation and judgment, and yet the book provides no clear evidence of a future for national, ethnic Israel. In fact, it is the church of God, those who put their trust in Christ, the lamb of God, who are vindicated in John's apocalyptic vision. Already from the very beginning of John's address to the seven churches facing Roman imperialism (Rev 1:4, 11; 2:1—3:22), John communicates that the church is the renewed, eschatological Israel.[234] Further, Philip Mayo's monograph on John's view of Judaism and the church examines the synagogue of Satan accusations (Rev 2:9; 3:9), the 144,000 and the multitude of Rev 7:1–17, the two witnesses (11:1–13), the heavenly woman (12:1–17), and the new Jerusalem (21:1—22:5). The conclusion Mayo draws is that John perceives the church as God's new spiritual Israel.[235] Mayo finds that the church

---

234. See Schreiner, *New Testament Theology*, 749–53. Schreiner helpfully observes that John addresses particular churches but he is also intending his writings for all the churches (Rev 2:7, 11, 17, 29; 3:6, 13, 22). See also Tabb, *All Things New*, 102–8.

235. Mayo, "*Those Who Call Themselves Jews*," 199–204. For studies of the church in the book of Revelation, see Mangina, "God, Israel, and Ecclesia in the Apocalypse,"

is not Israel's replacement but its fulfillment. The church is both Israel and the nations as one people of God; however, it is not Israel ethnically but spiritually. Thus John freely appropriates Jewish national and cultic symbols for the church. He also appropriates as Jewish covenant promises and eschatological hopes and believes them fulfilled in and on behalf of the followers of the Lamb—the church. John has altered his understanding of a "true Jew" by not only broadening its scope beyond ethnic boundaries but also by redefining it theologically. Spiritual faithfulness is now the mark of a "true Jew," which implies keeping the commandments of God and holding the testimony of Jesus (12.17).[236]

John's presentation of the church in Revelation is in accord with the conclusions I have drawn from other, more explicit texts. The church is the eschatological Israel (contra dispensationalism) and is comprehensively a faithful community through Christ (contra covenant theology).

In the next chapter, passages that appear to undermine my proposal as defeaters for the Israel-Christ-church relationship are briefly examined. For example, Rom 11, appealed to by dispensationalists, is taken to indicate a future for national, political Israel, but this will be shown to be a misinterpretation. This passage does not nullify the Israel to church typological pattern.

85–103; Pattemore, *People of God*; Tabb, *All Things New*, 89–111.

236. Mayo, "Those Who Call Themselves Jews," 202. Pattemore, *People of God*, 216, is also helpful as he concludes, "[A]s Israel's story was a story with a direction from captivity to the Promised Land, so the story of the new people of God can be told in colours not only of the original Exodus from Egypt, but even more of the New Exodus from Babylon. This journey occupies the whole of the book, and their destiny is thus described in terms of a New Jerusalem, the dwelling place of God. More intimate is their relationship with their Messiah, the Lamb. *Revelation's ecclesiology is crucially dependent on its christology.* Drawing on and extending the individual-corporate relationship between Daniel's 'one like a son of man' and 'the holy ones of the most high,' John's portraits of the people of God show them as close companions of the Lamb, members of the messianic army" (emphasis added).

CHAPTER 7

CHALLENGING TEXTS FOR PROGRESSIVE COVENANTALISM

Overcoming Potential Defeaters

THROUGHOUT THIS STUDY, IT has been the contention that to understand the canonical development of the people of God through the plotline of Scripture is to rightly account for how national Israel pointed forward to and relates to Christ first before turning to the question of the Israel-church relationship. Specifically, the nation of Israel needs to be recognized as a typological pattern culminating in Christ as the primary antitype, and consequentially, the church is the secondary antitype of Israel through union with Christ. Chapter 5 sought to show the biblical data for confirming Israel as a type with Christ as the antitype and in the last chapter, the scriptural warrant for the Israel-church typology was offered. Nevertheless, if there were NT texts affirming a future role for not just the Jewish people, but specifically for national, political Israel, then it would be the case that OT national Israel is not a type but only an analogy of Christ and the church. For example, Michael Vlach avers in his critical review of *Kingdom through Covenant* that even though the "'antitype negates type' approach may apply in some cases, it does not work in regard to Israel and Jesus."[1] In this chapter I will briefly highlight key texts (Matt 19:28; Luke 13:34–35; 21:24; Acts 1:6–8; 3:17–21; Rom 11) that are appealed to as defeaters to the progressive covenantal view of the Israel-Christ-church typological relationship,

---

1. Vlach, "Have They Found a Better Way?," 16.

CHALLENGING TEXTS FOR PROGRESSIVE COVENANTALISM

primarily appealed to by dispensationalists, and demonstrate that these do not upset the thesis offered throughout this study.

MATTHEW 19:28 (AND LUKE 22:30)

Concerning this text, Vlach writes that "Jesus is referring to the relevance of Israel in the *eschaton*. When the renewal of the cosmos ('regeneration') occurs and Jesus sits on His glorious throne (i.e., Davidic throne), the restored twelve tribes of Israel will be ruled by the twelve apostles. In this case the ultimate Israelite, Jesus, predicts a future existence for the tribes of Israel."[2] This interpretation is problematic, however. The "regeneration" spoken of here is the eschatological new age, connoting the renewed creation—the consummation of God's work beginning at creation.[3] Therefore, the dispensational approach would have to assume that the twelve apostles are ruling over the twelve tribes of national Israel in the eternal state. Where does the church fit with this perspective? As was discussed in the previous chapter with respect to Rev 21:12-14, the names of the twelve tribes and twelve apostles listed on the gates and the foundations of the new Jerusalem in the new heaven and earth are bound up with imagery of the church. The twelve apostles represent the renewed, eschatological Israel, the church. The immediate context of Matt 19:28 is about being a disciple of Jesus (Matt 19:27-31). The point of Matt 19:28 is that the twelve disciples are Jesus' followers, sharing in his eschatological judgement. According to I. Howard Marshall, Matt 19:28 (and Luke 22:29-30)

> probably refers to the Twelve sharing in judgment on the unbelieving people of Israel in association with Jesus rather than to some kind of rule over a reconstituted ethnic Israel. The language is symbolical, but the symbolism points to some kind of community which corresponds to the twelve tribes of Israel. Jesus is saying in the strongest way possible that the old Israel is coming under judgment, and that the judgment will be in the hands of those who have been called by him as his close disciples. The implication is that there will be what we may call a new Israel.[4]

---

2. Vlach, "Have They Found a Better Way?," 13, emphasis original. See also Vlach, *Has the Church Replaced Israel?*, 182-85; Saucy, *Case for Progressive Dispensationalism*, 267-69; Blaising and Bock, *Progressive Dispensationalism*, 238.

3. Pennington, "Heaven, Earth, and a New Genesis," 40-43.

4. Marshall, "Church," 123. See also, Schreiner, *New Testament Theology*, 681.

Additionally, the allusion to Dan 7:22, 29 is crucial. In "Daniel 7 it is *Israel* ('the saints of the Most High') who receives the kingdom and rules over the *nations*, whereas Jesus asserts that it will be the *twelve disciples* who will judge the *twelve tribes of Israel*. This transfer highlights the role of the disciples for the spiritual state and the eschatological fate of Israel."[5]

LUKE 13:34–35 (AND MATT 23:37–39)

Another passage cited by dispensationalists that teaches a future day when the inhabitants of Jerusalem will respond positively to their Messiah and thus indicates that Israel's temporary judgement will give way to Israel's national restoration is Luke 13:34–35 (cf. Matt 23:37–39).[6] Jesus' use of Ps 118:26 with its joyful context of deliverance in Luke 13:35 (cf. Matt 23:39) reveals that the desolation of Jerusalem and the temple is not final, but a repentant Israel will bless the one who comes in the name of the Lord at the time of their restoration which coincides with the future parousia.[7]

Nevertheless, the interpretative difficulties surrounding Luke 13:35, particularly the phrase "you will not see me until you say, 'Blessed is he who comes in the name of the Lord!'" (ESV), should temper the dispensational assertion that this affirms a restoration of national Israel. The appearance of Ps 118:26 in Luke 13:35 as a reference to the parousia of Christ is not

---

5. Schnabel, "Israel, the People of God," 45, emphasis original. Cf. France, "Old Testament Prophecy," 70. For more on the allusion to Dan 7 in Matt 19:28, see France, *Jesus and the Old Testament*, 65–66, 143. Note also, Jervell, *Theology of the Acts of the Apostles*, 81–82. Edwards, *Gospel according to Luke*, 635–36, commenting on Luke 22:30, states, "The call and formation of the apostolic college is not an epilogue to the story of Israel, but the completion of the foreordained messianic task of Jesus. The church is not a scissors-and-paste remedy when Israel failed to receive its Messiah, but the rightful consummation of the work of God in Israel. The church does not replace or nullify the history of Israel; it fulfills the purpose for which Israel was created."

6. Vlach, *Has the Church Replaced Israel?*, 185–90; Bock, "Restoration of Israel," 172–73; Bock, "Israel in Luke-Acts," 108–9; Bock, *Proclamation from Prophecy and Pattern*, 117–21; Saucy, *Case for Progressive Dispensationalism*, 264–66.

7. Vlach, *Has the Church Replaced Israel?*, 187–88. Bock notes that the language of the house being desolate and empty alludes to Jer 12:7; 22:5, and the reference to the house in Luke 13:35 is not the temple, but refers to the fact that Israel's "abandoning exile has come." Bock, "Israel in Luke-Acts," 108–9, and Bock, "Restoration of Israel," 172. Bock is correct regarding the allusions to Jer 22:5 and 12:7, but Edwards, *Gospel according to Luke*, 408, finds that the "distinction between 'your' and 'house' (v. 35), however, may imply a more precise interdiction on the temple (or Jerusalem itself), thus corroborating the similar prophecy of the destruction of both temple and Jerusalem in 19:41–44 and 21:20." See also Walker, *Jesus and the Holy City*, 61–62, for reasons that the "house" includes the temple.

so clear as Luke places Jesus' lament before his entry into Jerusalem, in the midst of his travel narrative. Since Luke cites Ps 118:26 again in Luke 19:38, the reference in Luke 13:35 could be in regard to Jesus' anticipated entry into Jerusalem.[8] However, a clear reference to the parousia is intended in Matt 23:37–39 since that appears after the triumphal entry. Accepting Jesus' comments as pertaining to his second coming does not resolve the matter, though, for two reasons.

First, will the acknowledgement of the one coming in the name of the Lord be willing or compelled?[9] Dispensationalists understand Luke 13:35 as the joyful exaltation of Israel, but the lament of Luke 13:34–35 is in the context of the announcement of judgment, suggesting that the acknowledgement of Jesus could be reluctant.[10] If so, Israel's national restoration or conversion is not in view. Jesus' proclamation says nothing explicitly about the fate of those who greet Jesus with these words. Instead, the one who will come will function as judge (cf. Luke 19:27) and exclude "from participation in eschatological salvation members of Israel who have already refused to acknowledge the earthly Jesus as the Messiah"[11] (Luke 13:23–30; 14:24; Acts 3:23).

Second, not only is the nature of the recognition of Jesus as the messiah questionable, but so is the identity of those who make the statement. A positive, rejoiceful response at or preceding the parousia may not be indicative of the nation of Israel, but given the parallel account of the triumphal entry, since it is the disciples of Jesus who utter the words of Ps 118:26 in Luke 19:38, it could be that it is Jesus' followers who respond to Jesus' return in Luke 13:35.[12] More importantly, even if Luke 13:35 refers to Jerusalem's jubilant welcoming of Jesus at or just before the parousia, "Luke would clearly have connected this [city's] restoration with the confession of Jesus' lordship.... Even on this interpretation the verse does not speak of a political [or national] restoration of Jerusalem [or Israel] within the ordinary course of history."[13]

---

8. Pao and Schnabel, "Luke," 338; Carroll, *Response to the End of History*, 162.

9. See Dow, *Images of Zion*, 144. She notes that commentators are divided on the matter.

10. Walker, *Jesus and the Holy City*, 62, 99; Edwards, *Gospel according to Luke*, 408; LaRondelle, *Israel of God*, 160–64, esp. 163–64.

11. Wolter, "Israel's Future and the Delay of the Parousia," 309.

12. Liefield and Pao, *Luke*, 240.

13. Walker, *Jesus and the Holy City*, 100. Chance, *Jerusalem, the Temple*, 130–32, argues that the fulfillment of Luke 13:35 for Israel precedes the parousia, but Chance discusses this in terms of the redemption of Jews and does not make the case for a restoration of national Israel from this text. Instead of the speculative interpretation

LUKE 21:24

Both Vlach and Darrell Bock, like their approach to Luke 13:35, place emphasis on the "until" of Luke 21:24. According to them and other dispensationalists, the trampling of Jerusalem under the dominating control of the gentiles is of a limited duration ("the times of the gentiles") and a subsequent period will come when Israel's judgment will end, and Israel's national restoration and prominent role among the nations will then occur (cf. Rom 11:25–26).[14] Once again, however, the theological freight that dispensationalists load onto Luke 21:24 will not bear the weight. Luke 21:24 is a difficult verse to interpret and two points need to be made.

First, some have argued the fulfillment of the "times of the Gentiles" addresses the physical destruction of Jerusalem or the period during which the Romans occupied and controlled the city (language alluded to in Dan 8:13).[15] Parallel passages in Matt 24:22 and Mark 13:20 regarding "those days" being cut short for the sake of the elect offers support for this view as the onslaught of Jerusalem will have a short duration. Further, the verses

---

offered by dispensationalists on Luke 13:34–35 and Matt 23:37–39, the clearer passages on this topic need to be heeded. Dow, *Images of Zion*, 238–39, correctly summarizes, "In the Gospels, the earthly city of Jerusalem forfeits its link with the glorious eschatological city of the prophets by its rejection of Jesus (e.g. Lk. 13.34–35; 19.41). Instead, it falls into the old pattern of sinful Jerusalem denounced by the prophets (Lk. 21.22). ... The Old Testament prophecies of the restoration of Zion and the Temple are applied to the resurrection of Jesus (e.g. Jn 2.21; 12.32), the formation of the church (Acts 15.14–18; Heb. 12.22), and the heavenly hope of believers in Jesus (e.g. Gal. 4.26; Heb. 13.14). Earthly Jerusalem is no longer necessary for worship (Jn 4.21). Instead, earthly Jerusalem is going to be destroyed (Lk. 19.41–44). Zion theology is applied to Jesus and to the church and its glorious eschatological future. The Gospels show Jesus giving an opportunity to Jerusalem to receive her King and accept his purifying work (Mt. 21.1–17 par). But these overtures are rejected (Mt. 21.15, 23; Lk. 13.34). Jesus then predicts divine abandonment (Mt. 23.37–39; Lk. 13.35) and destruction (Mt. 24.1–2; Mk 13.2–4; Lk. 19.43–44) of the Temple and city. Jesus is depicted as the new locus of God's presence with his people (Mt. 1.22; 18.20; 28.20), the object of the pilgrimage of the nations (Mt. 28.19; Jn 12.31), and his resurrection inaugurates the restoration of Israel and Jerusalem (Mt. 26.61; Jn 2.19–21)."

14. Vlach, *Has the Church Replaced Israel?*, 195–97, and Vlach, "Have They Found a Better Way?," 20; Bock, "Israel in Luke-Acts," 109–10; Bock, "Restoration of Israel," 173; Saucy, *Case for Progressive Dispensationalism*, 266–67; Helyer, "Luke and the Restoration of Israel," 325; and cf. Chance, *Jerusalem, the Temple*, 134–38, though he offers some qualifications. Note also Kinzer, "Zionism in Luke-Acts," 150–51. For a dispensational discussion of Luke 21:24 and how it might fit into the tribulation up through the second advent of Christ, see Pentecost, *Things to Come*, 213, 314–16.

15. Reicke, "Synoptic Prophecies and the Destruction of Jerusalem," 121–34, 127; and Walker, *Jesus and the Holy City*, 100, 101n67. France, "Old Testament Prophecy," 75, also lists this as an interpretative option.

directly preceding Luke 21:24 (v. 20–23) are all related to the complex of events that occurred in AD 70 when the temple was destroyed, and Jerusalem was laid siege by the Romans.

On the other hand, other scholars interpret the "times of the gentiles" as being "fulfilled" with the second coming of Jesus given that the following verses speak of the Son of Man coming in a cloud with power and glory (Luke 24:25–27).[16] Going in this direction could suggest a link to Paul's statement in Rom 11:25 regarding the full number of the gentiles coming in.[17] But even if this interpretation is correct, R. T. France rightly argues,

> There is nothing in Luke 21 to suggest what will happen to Jerusalem when the "times of the Gentiles" are over, and the total lack of any other suggestion in Jesus' teaching, or indeed the whole New Testament, of a political and territorial restoration of the Jews must surely make us cautious in assuming such an implication here.... It is perhaps more likely that no sequel to the "times of the Gentiles" is envisaged other than the ultimate consummation.[18]

In summary, Luke 21:24 cannot be pressed to affirm a future restoration of Jerusalem or the nation of Israel. The use of the word "until" does not necessarily mean that there will be a change or reversal in the previous circumstance.[19] Luke 13:35 and 21:24

---

16. Schnabel, *40 Questions about the End Times*, 133. See also LaRondelle, *Israel of God in Prophecy*, 164–67, and Carroll, *Response to the End of History*, 163. Edwards, *Gospel according to Luke*, 606, seems to go in the direction that the "times of the Gentiles" goes until the second coming of Christ, but he is more general in this assessment, drawing attention to the salvation of the gentiles in redemptive history: "Luke's emphatic threefold inclusion of Gentiles in v. 24, and especially the final proleptic reminder, 'until the times of the Gentiles are fulfilled,' assures readers that the fall of Jerusalem is not the miscarriage of the divine purpose, but a fulfillment of the divine purpose for the salvation of Gentiles. The fall of Jerusalem necessitates the extension of the promise to Israel to the nations. 'God's salvation has been sent to the Gentiles, and they will listen' (Acts 28:28)."

17. Liefield and Pao, *Luke*, 307. LaRondelle, *Israel of God in Prophecy*, 166, acknowledges the connection between Luke 21:24 with Rom 11:25–26 but criticizes this position since Rom 11 is about Israel's spiritual return to God through gospel faith whereas Luke 21:24 is specifically political.

18. France, "Old Testament Prophecy," 75–76. See also Dow, *Images of Zion*, 152.

19. Hendriksen, *Israel in Prophecy*, 28, argues that the conjunction *until* in Luke 21:24 does not necessarily mean that the exact opposite, which was described in preceding part of the sentence, will occur, but only that Jerusalem will be in the condition of being trampled underfoot and that such will not cease but will last continually *until* Christ's second coming. See also LaRondelle, *Israel of God in Prophecy*, 167, as he notes the usage of "until" in Rev 2:10, 25, 26; 1 Cor 15:25 all employ the word (*archi*) but

provide the most slender of foundations on which to build a Lukan doctrine of Jerusalem's subsequent "restoration." In both, the interpretation is partly dependent on what is meant by the ambiguous words translated "until" (ἕως in 13:35; ἄχρι οὗ in 21:24); and neither text explicitly invokes the concept of "restoration" or similar ideas. A few verses later Jesus speaks to his followers of "*your* redemption" (21:28) in apparent contradistinction to any supposed "redemption" of Jerusalem. Above all, the over-riding context of both these verses is the judgment that awaits the city.[20]

Therefore, the dispensational appeal to these texts for a future nationalistic role for Israel make the argument assuming already what the argument sets out to prove. In other words, the dispensational position must be presupposed for these passages to fit within their framework. On the other hand, the points raised regarding these Lucan passages indicate that these passages do not necessarily support a political, nationalistic role of Israel in the future, especially given the interpretative ambiguity.

ACTS 1:6–8

Another critical text and potential defeater for identifying national Israel as a typological pattern is Acts 1:6–7. For dispensationalists and Christian Zionists, this passage supports the necessity of a future restoration of Israel.[21] They advance that the apostles' question regarding the timing of the restoration of the kingdom to Israel was not misguided. Rather, the apostles rightly anticipated national Israel's restoration and Jesus' response in verses 7 and 8 did not correct or rebuke such a notion of geopolitical restoration because he only refused to affirm the timing of the kingdom. A few key points mitigate against the dispensational conclusion, however.

The disciples' question and Jesus' response in Acts 1:6–8 has received differing interpretations. In contrast to the dispensational view, some

---

without any notion of a change to the previous situation taking place.

20. Walker, *Jesus and the Holy City*, 101, emphasis original. France, "Old Testament Prophecy, 76; and Schnabel, *40 Questions about the End Times*, 134, both articulate similar conclusions.

21. Vlach, *Has the Church Replaced Israel?*, 190–92; Vlach, "Have They Found a Better Way?," 13–14; Bock, "Israel in Luke-Acts," 111–12; Bock, "Restoration of Israel," 174–75; Saucy, *Case for Progressive Dispensationalism*, 268–71; Blaising and Bock, *Progressive Dispensationalism*, 180, 237, 240; Helyer, "Luke and the Restoration of Israel," 326–27; Kinzer, "Zionism and Luke-Acts," 162–64; cf. Chance, *Jerusalem, the Temple*, 133.

scholars think that Jesus rebukes or at least corrects the disciples since their question displays a misplaced sociopolitical and territorial expectation for the national restoration of Israel.[22] For this interpretation and the one offered by dispensationalists there is a disconnect because Jesus either changes the topic or he does not directly answer their question: Jesus "talks of the church age while implicitly postponing a restoration of Israel to the future, or he talks of a universal mission empowered by the Holy Spirit in contrast to the disciples' focus on purely national and political concerns for ethnic Israel."[23] Nevertheless, a third, and better approach is tendered that acknowledges that the disciples were not mistaken in asking the question and that Jesus answers their question in affirming and explaining that Israel's kingdom hopes, the reality of restoration, commences with the arrival of the Spirit and the disciples' mission in this program (Acts 1:7–8).[24] The immediate context indicates the disciples question naturally arises based on Jesus' teaching concerning the kingdom (1:3–5) and the fulfillment of Israel's restoration is inaugurated based upon Jesus' answer (1:7–8) as well as the unfolding narrative of the book.

First, the disciples' question regarding the timing of when Jesus himself will restore the kingdom is appropriate given the setting of the previous verses. For forty days the resurrected Jesus has been instructing them concerning the kingdom (Acts 1:3), and he commands them not to depart Jerusalem but wait for the promise of the Father—the Holy Spirit (1:4–5).[25] The teaching of the kingdom, the disciples' anticipated reception of the eschatological gift of the Spirit as the promise of the Father, particularly in Jerusalem, the locus of many OT prophetic hopes, would have fostered the eschatological anticipation of Israel's restoration.[26] Moreover, the mention of John the Baptist recalls his role in forecasting that the coming messiah

---

22. See Stott, *Message of Acts*, 40–42; Burge, *Jesus and the Land*, 60–61; Storms, *Kingdom Come*, 283–88; Robertson, *Israel of God*, 129–37. Walker, *Jesus and the Holy City*, 292–93, also thinks the disciples were assuming a political solution for the nation of Israel.

23. Thompson, *Acts of the Risen Lord Jesus*, 105.

24. Thompson, *Acts of the Risen Lord Jesus*, 103–8; Peterson, *Acts of the Apostles*, 108–11; Schnabel, *Acts*, 75–78. See also Maston, "How Wrong Were the Disciples," 169–78; Pao, *Acts and the Isaianic New Exodus*, 95–96, 229; Fuller, *Restoration of Israel*, 258–59; Turner, *Power from on High*, 297–302.

25. Thompson, *Acts of the Risen Lord*, 104, 106; Peterson, *Acts of the Apostles*, 108.

26. For the OT restoration hopes for Israel, see Isa 1:26; 2:2–4; 9:7; Jer 16:14–15; 23:5–8; 33:15–17; Ezek 34–37; Hos 3:5; 11:11; Amos 9:11–15; Zech 9:9–10. For the importance of Jerusalem in Israel's future restoration, see Isa 40:1–2; 65:18–25; Zech 8; Mic 4:2. See Fuller, *Restoration of Israel*, 257–58, on the importance of Jerusalem in Acts 1–2 with respect to Israel's restoration. Cf. Peterson, *Acts of the Apostles*, 107.

would baptize in the Spirit (Luke 3:16), and the announcement that John's promise of the Spirit would be poured upon them in only a few days (Acts 1:5) provide additional rationale for why the disciples would inquire into Israel's restoration "at this time" (1:6).[27]

Therefore, the disciples' question regarding the restoration of the kingdom to Israel is not inappropriate, but the problem with the dispensational interpretation and the other common interpretation that Jesus rebuked or corrected the disciples for failing to understand the nature of the kingdom is that they both wrongly assume that the disciples' question regarding the kingdom was narrowly nationalistic, political, and territorial.[28] The kingdom the disciples refer to is not to a separate program for Israel. Instead, the kingdom to Israel is the same kingdom described throughout the Gospel of Luke (and in the other Gospels) that is both a present and future reality as God's sovereign rule and reign is manifested among his people through the coming of king Christ (Luke 4:23; 8:1, 10; 9:23–27; 12:31–32; 13:23–30; 17:20–21; 18:16–30; 21:31) and the work he accomplishes, including the forgiveness of sins and the miraculous deeds of healing (Luke 10:9; 11:20).[29] Such kingdom hopes had a national dimension (Isa 49:6–7; Dan 7:14, 27; cf. Luke 1:32–33, 46–55, 67–79; 2:29–32, 38), but the restoration hopes of Israel also included the participation of the nations in the kingdom (e.g., Isa 2:2–4; Mic 4:1–5).[30] The kingdom is also territorial or spatial as God's reign also includes a realm, for God's rule over and through Israel pointed to his rule over the whole earth (e.g., Pss 2; 47).[31] While these points are not made explicit since Luke only generally references Jesus speaking about the kingdom for forty days, the importance of the Holy Spirit for Israel's kingdom restoration hopes (Joel 2:28–32; Isa 32:15; 44:3; Ezek 11:19–20; 36:25–27) is made plain in Acts 1:4–5 and had to have had implications for the disciples, steeped as they were in the OT, and their question of the timing of Israel's kingdom restoration. Jesus' response to the disciples adds further clarity for the timing of the kingdom.

In Acts 1:7–8 Jesus provides an answer that addresses both the timing of the kingdom and the disciples' role in the restoration of the kingdom to Israel. Jesus does correct the disciples in that they are not to concern

---

27. Schnabel, *Acts*, 76; Peterson, *Acts of the Apostles*, 107–8. The conjunction οὖν ("therefore") in Acts 1:6 links the disciples' question directly with the previous verses (1:3–5). Rightly, Thompson, *Acts of the Risen Lord*, 104.

28. See Maston, "How Wrong Were the Disciples," 170–77.

29. Schnabel, *Acts*, 73; Peterson, *Acts of the Apostles*, 105. Both commentators note the importance of the kingdom of God in Acts (8:12; 14:22; 19:8; 20:25; 28:23, 31).

30. Maston, "How Wrong Were the Disciples," 176–77.

31. Maston, "How Wrong Were the Disciples," 171–73.

themselves with the chronological details of Israel's kingdom restoration, for the times and seasons—the specifics of the restoration from its beginning to the consummation—belong to sovereign authority of the Father (Acts 1:7; cf. Matt 24:36; Mark 13:32).[32] In another sense though, Jesus does provide an answer on the timing as well as the task of the disciples in Israel's restoration in Acts 1:8. The beginning of Israel's restoration occurs with the arrival and power of the Holy Spirit and will continue through the disciples' missionary activity. The appearance of the Holy Spirit not only recalls Jesus' teaching in Acts 1:5 but invokes new covenant prophecies and the Isaianic new exodus as Israel's new age restoration would be marked by the pouring out of the Spirit "from on high" (Isa 32:15; 44:3–5; cf. Luke 24:49).[33] Further, the Spirit's empowering work helps Jesus' disciples to be his witnesses which alludes to Isa 43:10, 12 where Isaiah envisages a reversal to Israel's blindness (Isa 42:18–25) as the renewed people of God in the new age will be so transformed that they will become witnesses of God's salvation.[34] Jesus also tells his disciples that they will be his witnesses even "to the end of the earth" (Acts 1:8) which continues the theme of Isaiah's new exodus as the phrase reflects Isa 49:6 (cf. Acts 13:47) where the messianic servant restores the tribes of Judah and is a light to the nations so that God's salvation goes to the gentiles.[35] The salvation of the gentiles can happen when God "restores the tribes of Judah." It is important then, to also observe that Jesus' reply does not leave Israel out. Alan Thompson observes:

> When Jesus refers to Jerusalem as well as to "all Judea and Samaria," he is of course referring to Israel. Jerusalem was the religious capital of Israel, and the phrase "all Judea and Samaria" was representative of the southern and northern kingdoms of

---

32. Schnabel, *Acts*, 77; Peterson, *Acts of the Apostles*, 110. Cf. Storms, *Kingdom Come*, 285; Robertson, *Israel of God*, 132; Thompson, *Acts of the Risen Lord*, 105.

33. Thompson, *Acts of the Risen Lord*, 106–7; Turner, *Power from on High*, 300; Pao, *Acts and the Isaianic New Exodus*, 92–93; Peterson, *Acts of the Apostles*, 110–11; Schreiner, *New Testament Theology*, 104; Storms, *Kingdom Come*, 287. Pao, "Jesus's Ascension," 144, writes that the context of Isa 32 "depicts the arrival of the Spirit that brings to an end the desolation of Judah when God begins to restore his people."

34. Thompson, *Acts of the Risen Lord*, 107; Turner, *Power from on High*, 300–301; Pao, *Acts and the Isaianic New Exodus*, 93; Peterson, *Acts of the Apostles*, 111–12; Schnabel, *Acts*, 78; Storms, *Kingdom Come*, 287–88; Pao, "Jesus's Ascension," 144.

35. Thompson, *Acts of the Risen Lord*, 107; Turner, *Power from on High*, 300–301; Pao, *Acts and the Isaianic New Exodus*, 94–95; Peterson, *Acts of the Apostles*, 112–13; Schnabel, *Acts*, 79; Storms, *Kingdom Come*, 288. Carroll, *Response to the End of History*, 125, in reference to Acts 1:7–8, asserts that the "restoration of the kingdom to Israel will include participation of the nations. The subsequent narrative makes clear that Gentiles will come to enjoy the realization of the 'hope of Israel.'"

Israel respectively. In the light of the division of Israel almost from the outset of its history under kings ... and the prophetic hopes found in passages such as Ezekiel 37 for a united Israel, any talk of restoration would have to include some reference to the division between north and south known throughout much of Israel's history.[36]

Therefore, with the eschatological presence of the Holy Spirit, the witnessing prerogative of the renewed Israel, and the fact that salvation is coming upon Jerusalem, going out to Judea and Samaria indicating a restoration and reconstitution of geographical Israel (cf. Acts 8:1–25) and then proceeding forth to the outcasts (Acts 8:26–40; cf. Isa 56:3, 5) and the gentiles (Acts 10), all cumulatively demonstrate that Jesus is in fact not postponing Israel's restoration. Indeed, through Jesus the fulfillment of Israel's restoration is inaugurated, the kingdom has arrived, and the outworking of this kingdom restoration grows through the mission of the church. The later narrative of Acts confirms that Israel's restoration is being fulfilled as the Holy Spirit descends at Pentecost (Acts 2:1–11), Jesus is enthroned and rules as the Davidic king (Acts 2:22–36; 13:32–37; 15:13–18), and the twelve apostles represent the nucleus of the restored Israel (Acts 1:15–22; note Acts 2:9–11 with Isa 43:5–7).[37] Based on these points the dispensational interpretation of Acts 1:6–8 should be rejected.

ACTS 3:17–21

Related to Acts 1:6 given the presence of the word *restoration* and the reference to "times" and "time" (cf. Acts 1:7) is Acts 3:19–21, a text that

---

36. Thompson, *Acts of the Risen Lord*, 106. Pao, *Acts and the Isaianic New Exodus*, 94–95, 127, also points out that the three categories—(1) the city of Jerusalem, (2) the two regions of Judea and Samaria, and (3) the whole inhabited world (gentiles)—are "theopolitical" and not merely geographic markers. Pao, *Acts and the Isaianic New Exodus*, 95, writes, "Taken together, then, the three categories correspond to three stages of the Isaianic New Exodus which signifies the arrival of the new era: (1) the dawn of the salvation upon Jerusalem; (2) the reconstitution and reunification of Israel; and finally (3) the inclusion of the Gentiles within the people of God." Elsewhere Pao, "Jesus's Ascension," 145, writes: "The three parts of Acts 1:8 therefore point to the fulfillment of God's promises to Israel: salvation will come to Jerusalem, and God will then restore his divided people before the Gentiles can join this restored people of God."

37. According to Peterson, *Transformed by God*, 61, Israel's "end-time restoration begins with the pouring out of the promised Spirit and the bringing of God's salvation, first to Israel and then 'to the ends of the earth' (Isa. 49:6; 42:6–7). It is consummated when Jesus returns (Acts 1:11; 3:20–21)." See Peterson pp. 62–63 for a discussion on the subsequent narratives of Acts that validate this interpretation.

dispensationalists also consider as an affirmation of the physical and spiritual future blessings for national Israel.[38] Similar to Acts 1:6, dispensationalists consider Peter's message of repentance to the Jews involves a hope for Israel's full restoration including the restoration of the promised land (e.g., Jer 16:15; 24:6). The "times of refreshing" (Acts 3:20), or Israel's restoration and eschatological redemption, is connected to Jesus' future coming.

The dispensational approach to Acts 3:20-21 is problematic, however. First, in regard to the "times of refreshing," David Peterson points out that this phrase and the following clause ("that he may send the Messiah") in verse 20 are not complementary statements about the same event; rather, "the argument of vv. 19-21 is cumulative, implying that these seasons of refreshment occur in an intervening period, before Christ's return and the consummation of God's plan in a renewed creation. . . ."[39] In addition, Peter's mention that the prophets spoke about "these days" (Acts 3:24), the present epoch of salvation, confirms that the "times" of refreshment "are not a future event but the present reality of God's restoration of Israel through Jesus, the Messiah."[40] More importantly, however, Acts 3:19-20 is parallel to Peter's response to the Jews at Pentecost in Acts 2:38.[41] Repentance demonstrated through baptism, forgiveness of sins, and the reception of the gift of the Holy Spirit in Acts 2:38 is structurally similar to Acts 3:19-20 where repentance, the wiping away of sins, and times of refreshing are mentioned. Pao also notes that the "times of refreshment" is best understood as a reference to the descent of the Holy Spirit (Isa 32:15; cf. Acts 1:8) and refers to

---

38. See the discussion in Bock, "Reign of the Lord Christ," 56–57; Bock, "Israel in Luke-Acts," 112; and Bock, "Restoration of Israel," 175; Saucy, *Case for Progressive Dispensationalism*, 271; Blaising and Bock, *Progressive Dispensationalism*, 189, 268; Helyer, "Luke and the Restoration of Israel," 327–28.

39. Peterson, *Acts of the Apostles*, 180. Turner, *Power from on High*, 308–9, helpfully describes the sequence of Acts 3:19–25.

40. Schnabel, *Acts*, 215. See also Pao, *Acts and the Isaianic New Exodus*, 133–34. Pao states, "Those who insist that the phrase 'times of refreshing' can only point to the future event of Jesus' return fail to take note of the plural form of the word 'times' (καιροί), one that commonly refers to a period of time. This duration of time should not simply be conflated with the return of Jesus as referred to in the second part of the verse (3:20b). This period of time should rather be interpreted together with the previous phrase in which repentance becomes the way to participate in the community of the Spirit (vs 19)" (p. 134). See also Turner, *Power from on High*, 309; Carroll, *Response to the End of History*, 143–44; Bayer, "Christ-Centered Eschatology," 236–50, esp 245–47.

41. Pao, *Acts and the Isaianic New Exodus*, 133; Schnabel, *Acts*, 215; Peterson, *Acts of the Apostles*, 181; Thompson, *Acts of the Risen Lord*, 157. Pao, *Acts and the Isaianic New Exodus*, 132–33, also points out the significance of Isa 32:15, particularly the translation of Symmachus, for Acts 3:20 as well.

the period when the Spirit is among his people.⁴² Given these observations then, the times of refreshing must do with the relief that comes from having sins removed, a refreshment that is present now that the new covenant has arrived in Christ. It is the period marked by the bestowal of the Holy Spirit on God's people as the Spirit brings about this refreshing.⁴³

Next, the time of universal restoration or "times" (χρόνων) of restoration of all things in Acts 3:21 is parallel to the "times of refreshing" (3:20) and to "these days" (3:24) and thus indicates that the restoration Peter speaks of is not exclusively future.⁴⁴ The restoration is of course closely associated with Jesus' return and the consummation of God's new creation, but the restoration includes present events prior to this end-time climax. Already in the book of Acts the restoration of Israel (1:6) begins with the pouring out of the Spirit and the proclamation of the gospel (Acts 2), is further illustrated with the healing of the lame man (Acts 3), a miracle also anticipating the renewal of the whole creation (Isa 35:1–10; 65:17–25; Ezek 47:1–12), and Peter also teaches that the messianic restoration of Israel leads to the blessings of all the nations through the seed of Abraham (Acts 3:25–26).⁴⁵ According to Max Turner Acts 3:19–26 pictures the restoration of Israel first, leading to blessings for the nations.

> Nevertheless, these promises to Israel are only to be realized in the church; for they depend upon repentance and acceptance of the messiah's teaching. To make this point as sharply as possible, Peter invokes the prophet-like Moses Christology [(Acts 3:22–23)]. As the word of God given through Moses was constitutive for Israel of old, so now the messianic word of the prophet-like-Moses is constitutive for the 'Israel of fulfilment'—those who do not accept his teaching are cut off from 'the people (of God)'.⁴⁶

Therefore, Acts 3:19–20, like Acts 1:6, is misunderstood by dispensationalists. Such passages cannot be used to rule out the identification of national, OT Israel as a type of Christ and the church. In fact, quite the opposite is the case. These passages actually indicate that Israel's restoration has

---

42. Pao, "Jesus's Ascension," 151.

43. Schnabel, *Acts*, 215.

44. Pao, *Acts and the Isaianic New Exodus*, 134–35; Schnabel, *Acts*, 216; Peterson, *Acts of the Apostles*, 182; Bayer, "Christ-Centered Eschatology," 247–48; Turner, *Power from on High*, 309n112; Thompson, *Acts of the Risen Lord*, 108n14; Pao, "Jesus's Ascension," 151–52.

45. See Peterson, *Acts of the Apostles*, 182; Peterson, *Transformed by God*, 68; Schnabel, *Acts*, 216.

46. Turner, *Power from on High*, 310–11.

commenced through Christ and that Israel's restoration is ongoing through the presence and mission of the renewed Israel, the church, through the descent, presence, and experience of the eschatological Spirit.

ROMANS 11

Probably the most critical passage for Paul's conception of the future of Israel is Rom 11. For dispensationalists, this is a crux text in establishing their view that there is a future salvation for ethnic Jews, but also a future restoration of national Israel.[47] The amount of research on Rom 11, especially the meaning of the phrase "all Israel will be saved" (Rom 11:26), is staggering, and no attempt will be offered here to analyze this passage and defend a position.[48] Instead, the main argument put forward by dispensationalists that Rom 11 affirms a national, political restoration for Israel will be evaluated

47. Some studies by dispensationalists focus on Rom 11 to prove that there is a future salvation for ethnic Israel. See Hoehner, "Israel in Romans 9–11," 145–67; Johnson, "Evidence from Romans 9–11," 199–23, esp. 211–19; Gromacki, "Israel: Her Past, Present, and Future," 47–76. However, many nondispensationalists can affirm that Rom 11:26 refers to the future salvation of ethnic Israel at or just before Christ's return. For example, note Ladd, "Israel and the Church," 206–13. Some covenant theologians affirm this view as well. See chapter 3 footnote 80. More important is how dispensationalists argue for not just a future salvation but a restoration of national Israel from Rom 11. On this particular point, consult Vlach, *Has the Church Replaced Israel?*, 160–62, 171–72, 180–81; Vlach, "Non-Typological Future-Mass-Conversion View," 25, 36–37, 41–43, 47–61, 65–71; Saucy, "Does the Apostle Paul Reverse the Prophetic Tradition," 66–90; Saucy, *Case for Progressive Dispensationalism*, 250–63; Vanlaningham, "Jewish People," 122–23, 126–27; Blaising, "Biblical Hermeneutics," 96–97.

48. Four main views on Rom 11:26 are offered and defended in the literature (the descriptors are from Zoccali, referenced later): the "ecclesiological" view ("all Israel" refers to the church), the "total national elect" or Jewish remnant view (the elect or believing remnant of Jews saved throughout the present age), the "eschatological miracle" or ethnic national view (the whole nation of Israel will turn to Christ after the ingathering of the gentiles at the parousia), and the "two-covenant" view ("all Israel" refers to the historic nation of Israel that is saved regardless of having faith in Christ). For a detailed survey of these various approaches to Rom 11:26, see Zoccali, "'And So All Israel Will Be Saved,'" 289–318. For surveys of the main positions and defense of the majority view that the nation of Israel will be saved *en masse* at Christ's return, see Goodrich, "Until the Fullness of the Gentiles Come In," 5–32; Meyer, *End of the Law*, 188–94; and Waymeyer, "Dual Status of Israel in Romans 11:28," 57–71. For a brief overview of the three main views and defense of the "total national elect" view, see Merkle, "Romans 11 and the Future of Ethnic Israel," 709–21. Cf. Merkle, "Typological Non-Future-Mass-Conversion View," 161–208. See also Gathercole, "Locating Christ and Israel," 131–36, esp. 135 for "all Israel" referring to all Jews who embrace the gospel throughout the last days. For another overview of the positions, but a defense of the "ecclesiological" perspective, see Staples, "What Do the Gentiles Have to Do with 'All Israel'?," 371–90.

since such would defeat the notion of national Israel as a type fulfilled in Christ and the church. A future mass ingathering of Jews at the parousia does not pose a problem for the thesis offered in this study because the church is a Jew-gentile entity composed of Christ followers, and the claim is that it is specifically the OT nation of Israel that is typological. Secondly, one other defeater text from Rom 11 will be evaluated, but this time from a covenant theologian as the implication he draws from Paul's teaching has direct import for the nature of the new covenant community and has implications for how the church should be understood as Israel's antitype.

The crucial argument from Rom 11 offered by dispensational scholars that would overturn viewing OT Israel as a type derives from Rom 11:26–27.[49] They contend that with Rom 11:26 teaching a future salvation for Israel, Paul's immediate citation of Isa 59:20–21 and 27:9 (Rom 11:26–27) means that Israel's future salvation is linked to the new covenant promises that coordinate Israel's forgiveness with the restoration of Israel (cf. Isa 60:1–4; Jer 31:31–40), a restoration that includes the inheritance of the promised land.[50] Such a conclusion resonates with how dispensationalists understand the new covenant (see chapter 4) either in terms of being inaugurated (progressive dispensationalism) or with the church having only an indirect relationship to the new covenant since the fullness of the new covenant awaits national Israel (more traditional forms of dispensationalism).

---

49. For analysis and critique on the dispensational interpretations of Rom 11, see Lucas, "Dispensational Appeal to Romans 11," 235–53. Some dispensationalists put forward a second argument from Rom 11 to show Paul anticipated Israel's full restoration. Based on the sequence described in Rom 11:12 and 11:15, some dispensationalists argue that Paul did not reverse the dominant OT prophecy whereby nations would come to salvation in the aftermath of Israel's salvation and restoration. See Saucy, "Does the Apostle Paul Reverse the Prophetic Tradition," 67, 79–85; Saucy, *Case for Progressive Dispensationalism*, 259–61; Vanlaningham, "Jewish People," 122–23. According to Saucy, there is a minor prophetic theme where gentiles would be saved while Israel was disobedient (Deut 32:21; Isa 65:1; Mal 1:11), and therefore, in conjunction with the *a fortiori* arguments of Rom 11:12, 15, Israel's rebellion climaxing in the rejection of Christ leads to salvation going out to gentiles in this present age, which is then followed by a third stage where national Israel will be restored at the return of Christ, and a fourth stage will emerge where the nations are saved as they witness Israel's glorification and come to worship along with the restored Israel. See Saucy, "Does the Apostle Paul Reverse the Prophetic Tradition," 70–74. However, Lucas, "Dispensational Appeal," 245–51, has demonstrated that this dispensational argument founders on a number of points. First, this dispensational argument means they have two different understandings of "fullness" (Rom 11:12, 25) for Israel and the gentiles. Second, dispensationalists fail to observe how Israel's restoration has commenced following Christ's first coming.

50. See Vlach, *Has the Church Replaced Israel?*, 162, 181; Vlach, "Non-Typological Future-Mass-Conversion View," 48–59, 63–79; Saucy, "Does the Apostle Paul Reverse the Prophetic Tradition," 86; Blaising, "Biblical Hermeneutics," 97; Blaising and Bock, *Progressive Dispensationalism*, 270; Vanlaningham, "Jewish People," 126–27.

In evaluating the dispensational claim that the citation of Isa 59:20–21 and 27:9 in Rom 11:26–27 invokes new covenant restoration promises for Israel's future, two points are necessary in demonstrating that this is a spurious argument. First, it is more likely that Paul's citation of Isa 59:20–21 and 27:9 refers not to Christ's second coming but to what he accomplished in his first coming. In the original context of Isa 59:20–21, a text that was shown to correspond to the work of the servant in chapter 5 above, the redeemer comes to Zion (i.e., the people of Israel; cf. Rom 9:33) to turn away their transgression and to make a covenant with them which involves the conferral of the Spirit upon them (cf. Joel 2:28–29).[51] The fulfillment of the elements of this new covenant prophecy occurred with the coming of Christ and the aftermath of the cross. In fact, the broader themes of Isa 59:19–21, including the fear of the name of the Lord, the Lord's coming as a rushing stream and wind, the redeemer coming to Zion, the repentance of Jews/Jacob, and the reception of the covenant promise of the Spirit have all been demonstrated to appear in the early chapters of Acts, especially Acts 2.[52] Even the modifications Paul has made to Isa 59:20–21 support the conclusion that Rom 11:26b–27 is about the benefits of the new covenant already achieved by Christ. Instead of the redeemer coming to Zion (Isa 59:20), Paul writes that the redeemer will come "from Zion." The change in the wording reminds the readers that Christ came from Israel bringing salvation to all, including gentiles, but also for the Jews in banishing ungodliness from Jacob.[53] Further, although Paul does not continue citing Isa 59:21 with the

---

51. Peterson, *Transformed by God*, 131, notes, "Although the heavenly Jerusalem is mentioned in Galatians 4:26 (cf. Heb. 12:22; Rev. 3:12; 21:2), 'Zion' and 'Jacob' are literary variants for 'Israel' in Isaiah 59:20 and should be understood that way in Romans 11:26." See also Bruno, "Deliverer from Zion," 126–28, and Kirk, "Why Does the Deliverer Come?," 81–99, esp. 90–91, for additional reasons for why "Zion" in Rom 11:26 is not referring to the heavenly Jerusalem but is instead a metonymy for the earthly Jerusalem or people of Israel. Contra Zaspel and Hamilton, "Typological Future-Mass-Conversion View," 115, 120.

52. See Ruthven, "'This Is My Covenant with Them': Isaiah 59.19–21 (Part I)," 32–47; and Ruthven, "'This Is My Covenant with Them': Isaiah 59.19–21 (Part II)," 219–37.

53. See Kirk, "Why Does the Deliverer Come?," 96–97. Chae, *Paul as Apostle*, 278, finds that Paul's substitution "probably indicates that he undermines the notion that the Deliverer comes on the sole and special behalf of the Jews. The LXX text has already modified the original Hebrew text with a more nationalistic connotation: not merely the Redeemer will 'come to Zion . . . ' but will come *for the sake of* Zion. . . . But for Paul he is coming *from* Zion (ἐκ Σιών). The ἐκ Σιών indicates more than the origin of the Deliverer, or the place of Christ's resurrection, or that the Messiah comes *out of* Zion (i.e., David's city) and brings salvation *to* Israel. Paul seems to indicate also that the Redeemer comes *from* Zion (thus Israel will benefit first, of course) and goes *out for others outside* Israel" (emphasis original). Cf. Wright, *Paul and the Faithfulness of God*, 1248–52. For other treatments of Rom 11:26–27 as a reference to Christ's first coming,

reference to the Spirit, his allusion to Isa 27:9 with the removal of sin is no less than a new covenant reality accomplished by the death and resurrection of Christ.[54] Rather than viewing Israel's new covenant promises and restoration in a futuristic setting, Rom 11:26–27 as well as other NT texts that refer to or imply the new covenant (2 Cor 3; Heb 8–9; Rom 1–8) demonstrate that the new covenant and Israel's restoration are already inaugurated. Even if this interpretation is incorrect and Rom 11:26–27 does refer to the future coming of Christ, it does not necessarily entail the dispensational view, for Paul focuses on Israel's salvation (v. 26a), the removal of ungodliness and sins from Israel (vv. 26–27), which means soteriology is what is emphasized and nothing explicit is affirmed by Paul about a nationalistic restoration.[55]

A second point with respect to the dispensational interpretation of Rom 11:26–27 relates to their asymmetrical understanding of the new covenant in general. It is illegitimate to parcel out the new covenant into spiritual and physical aspects with the soteriological blessings having both present and future fulfillment while the material blessings are completely future, awaiting the return of Christ and directed to national Israel.[56] Throughout this study the ratification of the new covenant through Christ has been highlighted. Christ did not just fulfill part of the new covenant, he has initiated the entire new covenant, including the material or physical promises as they are taken up into such themes as inheritance, new creation, and new temple. Christ has inaugurated the land promise by introducing the new

---

see Das, *Paul and the Jews*, 109–11; and Hvalvik, "'Sonderweg' for Israel," 87–107, esp. 91–95; and Gathercole, "Locating Christ and Israel," 137–38. Gathercole thinks it is fitting that the redeemer comes ἐκ Σιών as the headquarters of Israel because in the beginning of Paul's argument in Rom 9:4–5 Christ came *from* the Israelites and in the very beginning of the epistle, Paul defines Christ as descending *from* David according to the flesh (Rom 1:3). See also the helpful interaction of the three positions represented by N. T. Wright, J. Ross Wagner, and Robert Jewett in Whittle, *Covenant Renewal*, 58–75.

54. Peterson, *Transformed by God*, 132, observes that the "[a]ddition of the words 'when I take away their sins' [(Isa 27:9)] brings Paul's citation more closely in line with the specific predictions of Jer 31:31–34. Paul adapts Isaiah's prediction to express more emphatically the sequence of thought in Jeremiah's oracle: God 'will banish ungodliness from Jacob' when he takes away their sins. Since the death of Christ has achieved the promised redemption (Rom. 3:21–26) and made possible a definitive forgiveness of sin (4:5–8), what is needed now is a softening of hearts to believe this message and confess Jesus as Lord (10:8–13)."

55. For example, Stanley, "'Redeemer Will Come ἐκ Σιών,'" 118–42, points out that Paul's concern for Israel in Romans is with respect to their salvation and especially in Rom 11 Paul looks forward to Israel's salvation as their attitude toward the gospel will one day change (see pp. 138–42).

56. See Lucas, "Dispensational Appeal to Romans 11," 240–42.

creation by his physical resurrection,[57] and God's covenantal presence is no longer confined to a place in Palestine or to a temple structure, but God's rule and presence is extended throughout the world in God's new temple, the church. All the new covenant promises are now exclusively enjoyed by those in union with Christ. Vlach writes, astoundingly, that the "supersessionist" view of the incorporation of a future *en masse* salvation of ethnic Jews into the church (Rom 11:25) is problematic because "there will be no special role or function for Israel apart from the church."[58] But Vlach fails to understand that salvation and the enjoyment of the new covenant benefits both now and in the future can only be found in Christ, and if one is in union with Christ, he or she, Jew or gentile, is automatically a member of his people, the church. Vlach wrongly conceives of the church as the "new covenant community of believing Jews and Gentiles *in this age*. . . ."[59] But the church is the end time people of God as I have demonstrated throughout this work and there is no evidence of the church standing alongside national Israel following the second coming of Christ. In sum, there is no evidence from Rom 11:26–27 that proves there will be a future national restoration of Israel or that Israel will receive a distinct aspect of the new covenant or exclusive blessings apart from the gentiles in the future age.[60]

Lastly, from an entirely different standpoint, covenant theologian Michael Horton also appeals to Rom 11 in a manner that would challenge the nature of the new covenant community and the sense in which the church is the antitype of Israel as has been advocated in this study. Horton writes that it is "true [that] in the new covenant as in the old that not all physical descendants of the covenant community are living branches of the Vine (Ro 9:6; 11:6–24). In this covenant there are some who belong outwardly to Christ's visible body but do not actually trust Christ. . . . [B]ranches that do not bear fruit are broken off by Christ (Jn 15:2; Ro 11:1–30)."[61] It is evident that Horton is drawing a significant theological conclusion from Rom 11 and particularly from the imagery of the olive tree (11:16–24). However, the conclusion Horton draws is unacceptable because he is pushing the tree (and vine) imagery too far. The olive tree image is used as an illustration so that gentiles would not take pride over unbelieving Jews, the natural branches that have been broken off. Instead, they are to stand firm in faith, and have a sense of fear in not presuming upon God's grace. The olive tree represents

---

57. Beale, *New Testament Biblical Theology*, 751.
58. Vlach, *Has the Church Replaced Israel?*, 161.
59. Vlach, "Non-Typological Future-Mass-Conversion View," 70 (emphasis added).
60. Lucas, "Dispensational Appeal to Romans 11," 242.
61. Horton, *Christian Faith*, 616.

the people of God, and just as gentiles become a part of the people of God through faith, Jews, despite their historical privileges and pedigree, can be excluded from the people of God because of their unbelief. As Fred Malone finds, the "issue in Romans 11 is not that of an individual being a New Covenant member who has been broken off as a covenant breaker. Rather, Paul speaks of faith, not ethnic origin, as the prerequisite of being engrafted into the root in the New Covenant era, whether Jew or Gentile."[62] The olive tree imagery can be no more applied to the issue of covenant breakers than it can be applied to apostate Christians who lose their salvation by falling from grace.

SUMMARY

In chapter 5 the focus was upon national Israel as a type of Jesus Christ. As the antitype, Israel's identity, roles, and calling culminate in Christ and are fulfilled in him. In chapter 6, both the Christ-church relationship and the Israel-church relationship—centered in and through Christ—was examined. The church's relationship to Christ is not a typological one but is marked by covenantal union and representation. The church's union with Christ is eschatological and parallel to the individual believer's union with Christ. Next, a variety of NT texts confirm that OT Israel is typological of the church but typological only through Christ and his work. The typological relationship shows not only a close correspondence to national Israel but also an escalation and heightening so that the church is not equivalent or directly continuous with Israel but is instead the renewed, eschatological Israel. Finally, NT texts employed as defeaters were examined. Analysis of these texts did not nullify the conclusion that OT Israel is a typological pattern.

Concentrating on the church's union with Christ and the church as the antitype of Israel has led to the unavoidable conclusion that both dispensational and covenant theology have not fully integrated these areas into their respective ecclesiology. By union with Christ and given the eschatological entailments of the church as the antitype of Israel, the church consists of members of the new covenant community, a regenerate people. God's new temple and new humanity is marked by faith and the indwelling presence of the Holy Spirit. Covenant theologians do not accept this conclusion however, because they are too committed to the notion of *covenant* as a theological construct. The commitment to the covenant of grace framework results in the theological entailment that the church is of the same nature as OT

---

62. Malone, *Baptism of Disciples Alone*, 99.

Israel. Likewise, dispensationalism and its varieties have not integrated the theological implications of union with Christ into their ecclesiology. National Israel or Jewish Christians still have certain blessings that await them in the future. But union with Christ establishes that gentiles are on equal footing with Jewish believers and that all the inheritance and promises are bestowed to them as well. Moreover, just like other OT types, Israel is a type and shadow of Christ and the church. The church is the renewed, antitypical Israel, and as such, Israel's prophecies and promises are translated to Christ and through Christ to the church. The dispensational distinction between Israel and the church is unwarranted.

Chapter 8

CONCLUSION

THE PURPOSE OF THIS study is to unpack the nature of the Israel-Christ-church relationship through the canon of Scripture and apply the resulting theological conclusions to the reigning systems of evangelical theology: covenant and dispensational theology. Particularly vital for ecclesiological formulation is the subject of typology and the interpretative challenges associated with types. Nevertheless, this study concluded that neither covenant theology or dispensationalism has rightly put together the Israel-Christ-church relationship and this problem may be pinpointed in how they misunderstand typology (dispensationalism) or are inconsistent in delineating the significance of the type-antitype relationship (covenant theology).

Given the focus on typology, chapter 2 delineated the nature and characteristics of typology. Typology was distinguished from allegory and typology was found to involve historical correspondences between OT persons, events, and institutions that are prospective and God-ordained, pointing to greater, eschatological events that come to fruition in or through Christ. The textual warrant for identifying types was also presented in order to confirm that typological patterns are open to verification.

Chapters 3 and 4 laid down the hermeneutics of covenant and dispensational theology. The theological constructs and hermeneutics that drive these systems were presented with particular focus on how the Israel-church relationship is formulated and how they understand typological patterns. Dispensationalists recognize Israel as a type of Christ and the church in only an illustrative or analogical way, or alternatively, they outright reject that Israel can be a type. Covenant theologians recognize Israel as a type of Christ and the church, but then problems emerge given their commitment to the covenant of grace framework. They understand the church to be one with Israel and characterized by the same nature as Israel, a mixed community of covenant keepers and breakers. With this scheme is difficult to see how the typological elements of escalation and fulfillment are present given the essential equivalence of Israel and the church.

In chapter 5, the exegetical and biblical-theological arguments were presented in order to show that Jesus Christ is the antitype of OT Israel. Christ may be considered, then, the true Israel since Israel's identity, roles, vocation, prophecies, and promises are fulfilled in him. While Jews retain an ethnic status in the NT, dispensationalists have incorrectly posited a future restoration for national Israel. They have failed to observe how the biblical-theological data demonstrates how Israel's identity markers, vocation as a covenant people, and restoration promises are ultimately centered in Jesus. The typological relations explored in chapter 5 reveal that the Israel-Christ-church relationship may be summed up as follows:

- ◊ son (Adam, Israel, David) → true Son (Jesus Christ) → sons (church)
- ◊ Abrahamic seeds (Israel) → true Abrahamic seed (Jesus Christ) → Abrahamic heirs and seed of promise (church)
- ◊ servant-Israel → true servant (Jesus Christ) → servants (church)
- ◊ *Yeshurun* (Israel) → beloved (Christ) → beloved (church)
- ◊ vine (Israel) → true vine (Jesus Christ) → fruitful branches (church)

The typology involving the sonship and Abrahamic seed themes pose difficulties for covenant theology since the analysis reveals that the genealogical principle is no longer operative. The whole new covenant community now consists of genuine sons of God and faithful offspring of Abraham. Moreover, the elucidated Israel-Christ typology poses challenges to dispensationalism by showing how Jesus fulfills the roles and vocation of national Israel. While the term *Israel* is not applied to Christ in the NT, Israel's titles, metaphors, and imagery, all embedded within the covenant structures of the Bible are applied and reach culmination in Jesus Christ. Israel's promises and prophesied restoration have been inaugurated by Christ and as such, are channeled through him to his new covenant people, the church.

Concentration on the two final areas of the Israel-Christ-church relationship were the topic of chapter 6. The church's relationship with Christ is a covenantal union that mirrors the individual believer's union with Christ. Also, the church's relationship to Israel was demonstrated to be typological. Both union with Christ and the church as the antitype of Israel pose significant dilemmas for dispensationalism given their commitment to the Israel-church distinction. The same conclusions were also drawn with respect to covenant theology since the church's union with Christ and the church as antitypical, renewed Israel means that new covenant community is not of the same nature of OT Israel but is instead a community of faith that marks all of its members.

Chapter 7 briefly surveyed some of the favorite texts that dispensationalists appeal to defend their system. However, as I have sought to show, these passages do not ultimately demand the dispensational scheme.

If covenant and dispensational theologies have not rightly formulated the biblical-theological development of the people of God and how Israel functions as a type, what can offer a more biblical proposal? The progressive covenantalism framework advanced by Stephen Wellum and Peter Gentry serves as a via media to dispensational and covenant theology and is more faithful to the contours of the Bible's storyline with respect to the people of God. Progressive covenantalism understands national Israel as a typological pattern not unlike other OT persons, institutions, and events. God used a corporate Adam, the Israelite nation, to point to a greater son, Jesus, and to a faithful community, the church. Israel is related to the church secondarily as the typological relationship is directed through Christ. Since Christ is the antitypical and true Israel, the agent of restoration who brings to fruition Israel's promises and fulfills the covenants, the church, through him, is the one and only new covenant community (Jer 31:26–40; Ezek 36:22–36). All followers of Jesus have direct knowledge of the Lord, being taught by God (cf. Isa 54:3; John 6:45; 1 Thess 4:9; 1 John 2:20, 27), possessing the gift of the eschatological Holy Spirit with the law written on the heart, and they look back to the finality of the forgiveness of sins through the cross (Jer 31:31–34). These new covenant promises, like the typological aspects of national Israel, are channeled through Christ to God's end-time people—the church—which is comprised of Jew and gentile alike. Thus, the church does not replace or absorb OT Israel; rather, Israel was a type of Jesus and derivatively, of a new and regenerate covenant community. In this way, the Israel-Christ-church relationship in typological and redemptive-historical perspective avoids the direct unification of Israel and the church as promulgated in covenant theology, while also evading the significant separation of Israel and the church with each having distinct plans or promises as portrayed in dispensational theology.

BIBLIOGRAPHY

Achtemeier, Elizabeth R. "Typology." In *The Interpreter's Dictionary of the Bible, Supplementary Volume,* edited by G. Buttrick. Nashville: Abingdon, 1976.

Achtemeier, Paul J. *1 Peter.* Hermeneia. Minneapolis: Fortress, 1996.

Alexander, Ralph H. "A New Covenant—An Eternal People (Jeremiah 31)." In *Israel, the Land and the People: An Evangelical Affirmation of God's Promises,* edited by H. Wayne House, 169–206. Grand Rapids: Kregel, 1998.

Alexander, T. Desmond. *From Eden to the New Jerusalem: Exploring God's Plan for Life on Earth.* Nottingham, UK: InterVarsity, 2008.

———. "Further Observations on the Term 'Seed' in Genesis." *TynBul* 48 (1997) 363–67.

———. "Genealogies, Seed and the Compositional Unity of Genesis." *TynBul* 44 (1993) 255–70.

———. "Messianic Ideology in the Book of Genesis." In *The Lord's Anointed: Interpretation of Old Testament Messianic Texts,* edited by Philip E. Satterthwaite, et al., 19–39. Grand Rapids: Baker, 1995.

———. "Royal Expectations in Genesis to Kings: Their Importance for Biblical Theology." *TynBul* 49 (1998) 191–212.

———. "Seed." In *NDBT,* edited by T. Desmond Alexander and Brian S. Rosner, 769–73. Downers Grove: InterVarsity, 2000.

Allen, R. Michael. *Reformed Theology.* New York: T & T Clark, 2010.

Allis, Oswald T. *Prophecy and the Church.* Philadelphia: P & R, 1945.

Allison, Gregg R. *Historical Theology: An Introduction to Christian Doctrine.* Grand Rapids: Zondervan, 2011.

———. *Sojourners and Strangers: The Doctrine of the Church.* Foundations of Evangelical Theology. Wheaton, IL: Crossway, 2012.

Alsup, John E. "Typology." In *ABD,* edited by David Noel Freedman, 682–85. New York: Doubleday, 1992.

Anderson, Bernhard W. "Exodus Typology in Second Isaiah." In *Israel's Prophetic Heritage: Essays in Honor of James Muilenburg,* edited by Bernhard W. Anderson and Walter Harrelson, 177–95. New York: Harper & Brothers, 1962.

Arnold, Clinton E. *Ephesians.* ZECNT. Grand Rapids: Zondervan, 2010.

Ateek, Naim. "The Earth Is the Lord's: Land, Theology, and the Bible." *Mishkan* 27 (1997) 75–80.

BIBLIOGRAPHY

Auerbach, Erich. "Figura." In *Scenes from the Drama of European Literature*, Theory and History of Literature 9, translated by Ralph Manheim, 11–76. Minneapolis: University of Minnesota Press, 1984.

August, Jared M. "Paul's View of Abraham's Faith: Genesis 22:18 in Galatians 3." *BibSac* 176 (2019) 51–61.

Ayres, Lewis. *Nicaea and Its Legacy: An Approach to Fourth Century Trinitarian Theology*. New York: Oxford University Press, 2004.

Bailey, Mark L. "Dispensational Definitions of the Kingdom." In *Integrity of Heart, Skillfulness of Hands: Biblical and Leadership Studies in Honor of Donald K. Campbell*, edited by Charles H. Dyer and Roy B. Zuck, 201–21. Grand Rapids: Baker, 1994.

Baker, Bruce A. "Is Progressive Dispensationalism Really Dispensational?" In *Progressive Dispensationalism: An Analysis of the Movement and Defense of Traditional Dispensationalism*, edited by Ron J. Bigalke Jr., 343–75. Lanham, MD: University Press of America, 2005.

Baker, David L. *Two Testaments, One Bible*. 3rd ed. Downers Grove: InterVarsity, 2010.

———. "Typology and the Christian Use of the Old Testament." *SJT* 29 (1976) 137–57.

Bandstra, Andrew J. "Interpretation in 1 Corinthians 10:1–11." *CTJ* 6 (1971) 5–21.

Bandy, Alan S., and Benjamin L. Merkle. *Understanding Prophecy: A Biblical-Theological Approach*. Grand Rapids: Kregel, 2015.

Banks, Robert. *Paul's Idea of Community: The Early House Churches in their Historical Setting*. Grand Rapids: Eerdmans, 1980.

Barker, Kenneth L. "The Scope and Center of Old and New Testament Theology and Hope." In *Dispensationalism, Israel and the Church: The Search for Definition*, edited by Craig A. Blaising and Darrell L. Bock, 293–328. Grand Rapids: Zondervan, 1992.

Barr, James. "Biblical Theology." In *The Interpreter's Dictionary of the Bible*, Supplementary Volume. Edited by G. Buttrick. Nashville: Abingdon, 1976.

———. *Old and New Interpretation: A Study of the Two Testaments*. London: SCM, 1966.

———. *The Semantics of Biblical Language*. London: SCM, 1961.

Bartholomew, Craig G. "Covenant and Creation: Covenant Overload or Covenantal Deconstruction." *CTJ* 30 (1995) 11–33.

Bartholomew, Craig G., and Michael W. Goheen. *The Drama of Scripture: Finding Our Place in the Biblical Story*. Grand Rapids: Baker, 2004.

Bass, Clarence B. *Backgrounds to Dispensationalism: Its Historical Genesis and Ecclesiastical Implications*. Grand Rapids: Eerdmans, 1960.

Bateman, Herbert W., IV. "Dispensationalism Tomorrow." In *Three Central Issues in Contemporary Dispensationalism*, edited by Herbert W. Bateman IV, 307–17. Grand Rapids: Kregel, 1999.

———. "Dispensationalism Yesterday and Today." In *Three Central Issues in Contemporary Dispensationalism*, edited by Herbert W. Bateman IV, 21–60. Grand Rapids: Kregel, 1999.

Bauckham, Richard. *Bible and Mission: Christian Witness in a Postmodern World*. Grand Rapids: Baker, 2003.

———. "James, 1 Peter, Jude, and 2 Peter." In *A Vision for the Church: Studies in Early Christian Ecclesiology in Honour of J. P. M. Sweet*, edited by Marcus Bockmuehl and Michael B. Thompson, 160–61. Edinburgh: T&T Clark, 1997.

———. *Jesus and the God of Israel: God Crucified and Other Studies on the New Testament's Christology of Divine Identity.* Grand Rapids: Eerdmans, 2009.

———. "The Restoration of Israel in Luke-Acts." In *Restoration: Old Testament, Jewish, and Christian Perspectives*, edited by James M. Scott, 435–87. JSJSup 72. Leiden: Brill, 2001.

Bauer, Walter. *A Greek-English Lexicon of the New Testament and Other Early Christian Literature.* Edited and translated by William F. Arndt et al. 3rd ed. Chicago: University of Chicago Press, 2000.

Bavinck, Herman. *Reformed Dogmatics.* Edited by John Bolt. Translated by John Vriend. 4 vols. Grand Rapids: Baker Academic, 2003–2008.

Bayer, Hans F. "Christ-Centered Eschatology in Acts 3:17–26." In *Jesus of Nazareth: Lord and Christ: Essays on the Historical Jesus and New Testament Christology*, edited by Joel B. Green and Max Turner, 236–50. Grand Rapids: Eerdmans, 1994.

Beach, J. Mark. *Christ and the Covenant: Francis Turretin's Federal Theology as a Defense of the Doctrine of Grace.* Göttingen, Germany: Vandenhoeck & Ruprecht, 2007.

Beacham, Roy E. "The Church Has No Legal Relationship to or Participation in the New Covenant." In *Dispensational Understanding of the New Covenant: Three Views*, edited by Michael Stallard, 117–19. Schaumburg, IL: Regular Baptist, 2012.

Beale, G. K. *The Book of Revelation.* NIGTC. Grand Rapids: Eerdmans, 1999.

———. "Did Jesus and His Followers Preach the Right Doctrine from the Wrong Texts? An Examination of the Presuppositions of Jesus' and the Apostles' Exegetical Method." In *The Right Doctrine from the Wrong Texts?*, edited by G. K. Beale, 387–404. Grand Rapids: Baker, 1994.

———. *The Erosion of Inerrancy in Evangelicalism: Responding to New Challenges to Biblical Authority.* Grand Rapids: Baker, 2008.

———. "Finding Christ in the Old Testament." *JETS* 63 (2020) 25–50.

———. *Handbook on the New Testament Use of the Old Testament: Exegesis and Interpretation.* Grand Rapids: Baker, 2012.

———. *A New Testament Biblical Theology: The Unfolding of the Old Testament in the New.* Grand Rapids: Baker, 2011.

———. "The Peace and Mercy Upon the Israel of God: Old Testament Background of Galatians 6,16b." *Biblica* 80 (1999) 204–23.

———. *The Temple and the Church's Mission: A Biblical Theology of the Dwelling Place of God.* NSBT 17. Downers Grove: InterVarsity, 2004.

———. "The Use of Hosea 11:1 in Matthew 2:15: One More Time." *JETS* 55 (2012) 697–715.

Beale, G. K., and Benjamin L. Gladd. *Hidden but Now Revealed: A Biblical Theology of Mystery.* Downers Grove: InterVarsity, 2014.

Beale, G. K., and Mitchell Kim. *God Dwells among Us: Expanding Eden to the Ends of the Earth.* Downers Grove: InterVarsity, 2014.

Beasley-Murray, George. R. *Baptism in the New Testament.* Exeter: Paternoster, 1972. Reprint, Eugene, OR: Wipf & Stock, 2006.

———. *John.* WBC, vol. 36. 2nd ed. Nashville: Thomas Nelson, 1999.

Beers, Holly. *The Followers of Jesus as the 'Servant': Luke's Model from Isaiah for the Disciples in Luke-Acts.* LNTS 535. London: Bloomsbury T & T Clark, 2015.

Beetham, Christopher A. "From Creation to New Creation: The Biblical Epic of King, Human Vicegerency, and Kingdom." In *From Creation to New Creation: Biblical*

Theology and Exegesis, edited by Daniel M. Gurtner and Benjamin L. Gladd, 237–54. Peabody, MA: Hendrickson, 2013.

Beisner, E. Calvin, ed. *The Auburn Avenue Theology, Pros and Cons: Debating the Federal Vision.* Fort Lauderdale, FL: Knox Theological Seminary, 2004.

Benware, Paul N. *Understanding End Times Prophecy.* Rev. ed. Chicago: Moody, 2006.

Berkhof, Louis. *Principles of Interpretation.* 2nd ed. Grand Rapids: Baker, 1952.

———. *Systematic Theology.* Rev. ed. Grand Rapids: Eerdmans, 1996.

Berkouwer, G. C. *Sin.* Studies in Dogmatics. Translated by Philip C. Holtrop. Grand Rapids: Eerdmans, 1971.

Betz, Hans Dieter. *Galatians.* Hermeneia. Philadelphia: Fortress, 1979.

Beuken, W. A. M. "The Main Theme of Trito-Isaiah: 'The Servants of YHWH.'" *JSOT* 47 (1990) 67–87.

Bigalke, Ron J., Jr. "The Abrahamic Covenant." In *Progressive Dispensationalism: An Analysis of the Movement and Defense of Traditional Dispensationalism*, edited by Ron J. Bigalke Jr., 39–84. Lanham, MD: University Press of America, 2005.

———, ed. *Progressive Dispensationalism: An Analysis of the Movement and Defense of Traditional Dispensationalism.* Lanham, MD: University Press of America, 2005.

Bigalke, Ron J., Jr., and Mal Couch. "The Relationship between Covenants and Dispensations." In *Progressive Dispensationalism: An Analysis of the Movement and Defense of Traditional Dispensationalism*, edited by Ron J. Bigalke Jr., 17–38. Lanham, MD: University Press of America, 2005.

Bigalke, Ron J., Jr., and George A. Gunn. "Contingency of the Davidic Reign in Peter's Pentecost Sermon." In *Progressive Dispensationalism: An Analysis of the Movement and Defense of Traditional Dispensationalism*, edited by Ron J. Bigalke Jr., 179–204. Lanham, MD: University Press of America, 2005.

Bigalke, Ron J., Jr., and Thomas D. Ice. "History of Dispensationalism." In *Progressive Dispensationalism: An Analysis of the Movement and Defense of Traditional Dispensationalism*, edited by Ron J. Bigalke Jr., xvii–xlii. Lanham, MD: University Press of America, 2005.

Bird, Chad L. "Typological Interpretation within the Old Testament: Melchizedekian Typology." *CJ* 26 (2000) 36–52.

Bird, Michael F. "'A Light to the Nations' (Isaiah 42:6 and 49:6): Inter-Textuality and Mission Theology in the Early Church." *RTR* 65 (2006) 122–31.

———. "New Testament Theology Re-Loaded: Integrating Biblical Theology and Christian Origins." *TynBul* 60 (2009) 265–91.

Blackburn, Earl M., ed. *Covenant Theology: A Baptist Distinctive.* Birmingham, AL: Solid Ground Christian, 2013.

Blaising, Craig A. "Biblical Hermeneutics: How Are We to Interpret the Relation Between the Tanak and the New Testament on This Question?" In *The New Christian Zionism: Fresh Perspectives on Israel and the Land*, edited by Gerald R. McDermott, 79–105. Downers Grove: InterVarsity, 2016.

———. "A Case for the Pretribulation Rapture." In *Three Views on the Rapture: Pretribulation, Prewrath, or Posttribulation*, edited by Alan Hultberg, 25–73. 2nd ed. Grand Rapids: Zondervan, 2010.

———. "Contemporary Dispensationalism." *SWJT* 36 (1994) 5–13.

———. "A Critique of Gentry and Wellum's *Kingdom through Covenant*: A Hermeneutical-Theological Response." *MSJ* 26 (2015) 111–27.

———. "Development of Dispensationalism by Contemporary Dispensationalists: Part 2 of Developing Dispensationalism." *BibSac* 145 (1988) 254–80.

———. "Dispensationalism: The Search for Definition." In *Dispensationalism, Israel and the Church: The Search for Definition*, edited by Craig A. Blaising and Darrell L. Bock, 13–34. Grand Rapids: Zondervan, 1992.

———. "Doctrinal Development in Orthodoxy: Part 1 of Developing Dispensationalism." *BibSac* 145 (1988) 133–40.

———. "The Future of Israel as a Theological Question." *JETS* (2001) 435–50.

———. "God's Plan for History: The Consummation." In *Dispensationalism and the History of Redemption: A Developing and Diverse Tradition*, edited by D. Jeffrey Bingham and Glenn R. Kreider, 195–218. Chicago: Moody, 2015

———. "A Premillennial Response." In *Three Views on the Millennium and Beyond*, edited by Darrell L. Bock, 143–53. Grand Rapids: Zondervan, 1999.

———. "Typology and the Nature of the Church." Paper presented at the annual meeting of the National Evangelical Theological Society, San Diego, November 19, 2014.

Blaising, Craig A., and Darrell L. Bock. "Dispensationalism, Israel and the Church: Assessment and Dialogue." In *Dispensationalism, Israel and the Church: The Search for Definition*, edited by Craig A. Blaising and Darrell L. Bock, 378–84. Grand Rapids: Zondervan, 1992.

———, eds. *Dispensationalism, Israel and the Church: The Search for Definition*. Grand Rapids: Zondervan, 1992.

———. *Progressive Dispensationalism*. Grand Rapids: Baker, 1993.

Blocher, Henri. "Old Covenant, New Covenant." In *Always Reforming: Explorations in Systematic Theology*, edited by A. T. B. McGowan, 240–70. Downers Grove: InterVarsity, 2006.

———. *Songs of the Servant: Isaiah's Good News*. London: InterVarsity, 1975. Reprint, Vancouver: Regent College, 2005.

Block, Daniel I. "Eden: A Temple? A Reassessment of the Biblical Evidence." In *From Creation to New Creation: Biblical Theology and Exegesis*, edited by Daniel M. Gurtner and Benjamin L. Gladd, 3–29. Peabody, MA: Hendrickson, 2013.

———. "My Servant David: Ancient Israel's Vision of the Messiah." In *Israel's Messiah in the Bible and the Dead Sea Scrolls*, edited by Richard S. Hess and M. Daniel Carroll R., 17–56. Grand Rapids: Baker, 2003.

Bock, Darrell L. "Covenants in Progressive Dispensationalism." In *Three Central Issues in Contemporary Dispensationalism*, edited by Herbert W. Bateman IV, 169–223. Grand Rapids: Kregel, 1999.

———. "Current Messianic Activity and OT Davidic Promise: Dispensationalism, Hermeneutics, and NT Fulfillment." *TrinJ* 15 (1994) 55–87.

———. "Evangelicals and the Use of the Old Testament in the New." *BibSac* 142 (1985) 209–23, 306–19.

———. "Hermeneutics of Progressive Dispensationalism." In *Three Central Issues in Contemporary Dispensationalism*, edited by Herbert W. Bateman IV, 85–118. Grand Rapids: Kregel, 1999.

———. "Israel in Luke-Acts." In *The People, the Land, and the Future of Israel: Israel and the Jewish People in the Plan of God*, edited by Darrell L. Bock and Mitch Glaser, 103–15. Grand Rapids: Kregel, 2014.

———. *Proclamation from Prophecy and Pattern: Lucan Old Testament Christology.* JSNTSup 12. Sheffield: JSOT, 1987.

———. "The Reign of the Lord Christ." In *Dispensationalism, Israel and the Church: The Search for Definition*, edited by Craig A. Blaising and Darrell L. Bock, 37–67. Grand Rapids: Zondervan, 1992.

———. "The Restoration of Israel in Luke-Acts." In *Introduction to Messianic Judaism: Its Ecclesial Context and Biblical Foundations*, edited by David Rudolph and Joel Willitts, 168–77. Grand Rapids: Zondervan, 2013.

———. "Scripture Citing Scripture: Use of the Old Testament in the New." In *Interpreting the New Testament Text: Introduction to the Art and Science of Exegesis*, edited by Darrell L. Bock and Buist M. Fanning, 255–76. Wheaton, IL: Crossway, 2006.

———. "Single Meaning, Multiple Contexts and Referents: The New Testament's Legitimate, Accurate, and Multifaceted Use of the Old." In *Three Views on the New Testament Use of the Old Testament*, edited by Kenneth Berding and Jonathan Lunde, 105–51. Grand Rapids: Zondervan, 2008.

———. "The Son of David and the Saints' Task: The Hermeneutics of Initial Fulfillment." *BibSac* 150 (1993) 440–57.

———. "Why I Am a Dispensationalist with a Small 'd.'" *JETS* 41 (1998) 383–96.

Boersma, Hans. *Nouvelle Théologie and Sacramental Ontology: A Return to Mystery.* Oxford: Oxford University Press, 2009.

Bolt, John. "Why the Covenant of Works Is a Necessary Doctrine: Revisiting the Objections to a Venerable Reformed Doctrine." In *By Faith Alone: Answering the Challenges to the Doctrine of Justification*, edited by Gary L. W. Johnson and Guy P. Waters, 171–89. Wheaton, IL: Crossway, 2006.

Booth, Robert R. *Children of Promise: The Biblical Case for Infant Baptism.* Phillipsburg, NJ: P & R, 1995.

Borg, Michael. "The New Covenant (Jeremiah 31:31–34)." *PRJ* 6 (2014) 16–34.

Boyarin, Daniel. "Origen as Theorist of Allegory: Alexandrian Contexts." In *The Cambridge Companion to Allegory*, edited by Rita T. Copeland and Peter T. Struck, 39–54. New York: Cambridge University Press, 2010.

Brack, Jonathan M., and Jared S. Oliphint. "Questioning the Progress in Progressive Covenantalism: A Review of Gentry and Wellum's *Kingdom through Covenant*." *WTJ* 76 (2014) 189–217.

Brand, Chad O., and Tom Pratt Jr. "The Progressive Covenantal View." In *Perspectives on Israel and the Church: 4 Views*, edited by Chad O. Brand, 231–80. Nashville: B & H, 2015.

Bright, John. *The Kingdom of God.* Nashville: Abingdon, 1953.

Bromiley, Geoffrey W. *Children of Promise: The Case for Baptizing Infants.* Grand Rapids: Eerdmans, 1979.

Brown, Justin Michael. "Is Typology an Interpretative Method?" M. Th. thesis, Master's Seminary, 2014.

Brown, Michael G., and Zach Keele. *Sacred Bond: Covenant Theology Explored.* Grandville, MI: Reformed Fellowship, 2012.

Brown, Raymond E. "Hermeneutics." In *The Jerome Biblical Commentary*, edited by Raymond E. Brown et al., 605–23. Englewood Cliffs, NJ: Prentice Hall, 1968.

———. "The Problems of *Sensus Plenior*." *Ephemerides Theologicae Lovanienses* 43 (1967) 460–69.

———. *The Sensus Plenior of Sacred Scripture*. Baltimore: St. Mary's University, 1955.
Bruce, F. F. *Galatians*. NIGTC. Grand Rapids: Eerdmans, 1982.
———. *This Is That: The New Testament Development of Some Old Testament Themes*. Exeter: Paternoster, 1968.
———. *The Time Is Fulfilled: Five Aspects of Fulfilment of the Old Testament in the New*. The Moore College Lectures. Exeter: Paternoster, 1978.
Brumm, Ursula. *American Thought and Religious Typology*. New Brunswick, NJ: Rutgers University Press, 1970.
Bruno, Christopher R. "Review of *Kingdom through Covenant*, by Peter J. Gentry and Stephen J. Wellum." *Themelios* 37 (2012) 503–5.
———. "The Deliverer from Zion: The Source(s) and Function of Paul's Citation in Romans 11:26–27." *TynBul* 59 (2008) 119–34.
———. "'Jesus Is Our Jubilee' ... But How? The OT Background and Lukan Fulfillment of the Ethics of Jubilee." *JETS* 53 (2010) 81–101.
Burge, Gary M. *Jesus and the Land: The New Testament Challenge to "Holy Land" Theology*. Grand Rapids: Baker, 2010.
———. "Territorial Religion, Johannine Christology, and the Vineyard of John 15." In *Jesus of Nazareth: Lord and Christ; Essays on the Historical Jesus and New Testament Christology*, edited by Joel B. Green and Max Turner, 384–96. Grand Rapids: Eerdmans, 1994.
Burke, Trevor J. *Adopted into God's Family: Exploring a Pauline Metaphor*. NSBT 22. Downers Grove: InterVarsity, 2006.
Burns, J. Lanier. "Israel and the Church of a Progressive Dispensationalist." In *Three Central Issues in Contemporary Dispensationalism*, edited by Herbert W. Bateman IV, 263–303. Grand Rapids: Kregel, 1999.
Byrne, Brendan. *"Sons of God"—"Seed of Abraham:" A Study of the Idea of Sonship of God of All Christians in Paul against the Jewish Background*. Analecta Biblica 83. Rome: Pontifical Biblical Institute, 1979.
Calvin, John. *Institutes of the Christian Religion*. Edited by John T. Neil. Translated by Ford Lewis Battles. Library of Christian Classics 20–21. Louisville: Westminster John Knox, 1960.
Campbell, Constantine R. *Paul and Union with Christ: An Exegetical and Theological Study*. Grand Rapids: Zondervan, 2012.
Campbell, Donald K. "The Church in God's Prophetic Program." In *Essays in Honor of J. Dwight Pentecost*, edited by Stanley D. Toussaint and Charles H. Dryer, 149–61. Chicago: Moody, 1986.
———. "The Interpretation of Types." *BibSac* 112 (1955) 248–55.
———, ed. *Walvoord: A Tribute*. Chicago: Moody, 1982.
Caneday, A. B. "Biblical Types: Revelation Concealed in Plain Sight to be Disclosed—'These Things Occurred Typologically to Them and Were Written Down for Our Admonition.'" In *God's Glory Revealed in Christ: Essays on Biblical Theology in Honor of Thomas R. Schreiner*, edited by Denny Burk et al., 135–55. Nashville: B & H Academic, 2019.
———. "Christ as Paul's Bifocal Optic for Reading the Hebrew Scriptures: Mystery and Fulfillment in the Letter to the Romans." Paper presented at the annual meeting of the National Evangelical Theological Society, Lisle, IL, November 17–19, 1994.
———. "Covenant Lineage Allegorically Prefigured: 'Which Things Are Written Allegorically' (Galatians 4:21–31)." *SBJT* 14 (2010) 50–77.

———. "God's Parabolic Design for Israel's Tabernacle: A Cluster of Earthly Shadows of Heavenly Realities." *SBJT* 24 (2020) 103–24.

———. "Mark's Provocative Use of Scripture in Narration: 'He Was with the Wild Animals and Angels Ministered to Him.'" *BBR* 9 (1999) 19–36.

———. "The Muzzled Ox and the Abused Apostle: Deut 25:4 in 1 Cor 9:9." Paper presented at the annual meeting of the Society of Biblical Literature, St. Paul, March 31, 2006.

Carroll, John T. *Response to the End of History: Eschatology and Situation in Luke-Acts*. Society of Biblical Literature Dissertation Series 92. Atlanta: Scholars, 1988.

Carson, D. A. *The Collected Writings on Scripture*. Wheaton, IL: Crossway, 2010.

———. "Evangelicals, Ecumenism, and the Church." In *Evangelicals, Ecumenism and the Church*, edited by Kenneth S. Kantzer and Carl F. H. Henry, 347–85. Grand Rapids: Zondervan, 1990.

———. *Exegetical Fallacies*. 2nd ed. Grand Rapids: Baker, 1996.

———. "1 Peter." In *Commentary on the New Testament Use of the Old Testament*, edited by G. K. Beale and D. A. Carson, 1015–45. Grand Rapids: Baker, 2007.

———. *The Gagging of God: Christianity Confronts Pluralism*. Grand Rapids: Zondervan, 1996.

———. *The Gospel according to John*. PNTC. Grand Rapids: Eerdmans, 1991.

———. "John and the Johannine Epistles." In *It Is Written: Scripture Citing Scripture: Essays in Honour of Barnabas Lindars*, edited by D. A. Carson and H. G. M. Williamson, 245–64. Cambridge: Cambridge University Press, 1988

———. *Matthew 1–12*. In vol. 1 of *The Expositor's Bible Commentary*. Edited by Frank E. Gaebelein, 1–300. Grand Rapids: Zondervan, 1995.

———. "Mystery and Fulfillment: Toward a More Comprehensive Paradigm of Paul's Understanding of the Old and the New." In *The Paradoxes of Paul*, vol. 2 of *Justification and Variegated Nomism*, edited by D. A. Carson et al., 393–436. Grand Rapids: Baker, 2004.

———. *Showing the Spirit: A Theological Exposition of 1 Corinthians 12–14*. Grand Rapids: Baker, 1987.

———. "Systematic Theology and Biblical Theology." In *NDBT*, edited by T. Desmond Alexander and Brian S. Rosner, 89–104. Downers Grove: InterVarsity, 2000.

———. "Theological Interpretation of Scripture: Yes, But . . ." In *Theological Commentary: Evangelical Perspectives*, edited by R. Michael Allen, 187–207. London: T & T Clark, 2011.

———. "The Vindication of Imputation: On Fields of Discourse and Semantic Fields." In *Justification: What's at Stake in the Current Debates*, edited by Mark Husbands and Daniel J. Treier, 47–78. Downers Grove: InterVarsity, 2004.

Carter, Craig A. *Interpreting Scripture with the Great Tradition: Recovering the Genius of Premodern Exegesis*. Grand Rapids: Baker Academic, 2018.

Chae, Daniel Jong Sang. *Paul as Apostle to the Gentiles: His Apostolic Self-Awareness and its Influence on the Soteriological Argument in Romans*. Paternoster Biblical and Theological Monographs. Carlisle, UK: Paternoster, 1997.

Chance, J. Bradley. *Jerusalem, the Temple, and the New Age in Luke-Acts*. Macon, GA: Mercer University Press, 1988.

Chantry, Walter J. "The Covenants of Works and of Grace." In *Covenant Theology: A Baptist Distinctive*, edited by Earl M. Blackburn, 89–110. Birmingham, AL: Solid Ground Christian, 2013.

Chapman, Colin. *Whose Promised Land? The Continuing Crisis over Israel and Palestine.* Grand Rapids: Baker, 2002.

Charity, A. C. *Events and their Afterlife: The Dialetics of Christian Typology in the Bible and Dante.* Cambridge, UK: Cambridge University Press, 1966.

Chase, Mitchell L. *40 Questions about Typology and Allegory.* Grand Rapids: Kregel Academic, 2020.

Childs, Brevard S. "Allegory and Typology within Biblical Interpretation." In *The Bible as Christian Scripture: The Work of Brevard S. Childs*, edited by Christopher R. Seitz and Kent Harold Richards, 299–310. Atlanta: Society of Biblical Literature, 2013.

———. *Isaiah: A Commentary.* OTL. Louisville: Westminster John Knox, 2001.

Church, Philip A. F. "Dispensational Christian Zionism: A Strange but Acceptable Aberration or a Deviant Heresy?" *WTJ* 71 (2009) 375–98.

———. "'Here We Have No Lasting City' (Heb 13:14): The Promised Land in the Letter to the Hebrews." In *The Gospel and the Land of Promise: Christian Approaches to the Land of the Bible*, edited by Philip Church et al., 45–57. Eugene, OR: Pickwick, 2011.

Ciampa, Roy E. "The History of Redemption." In *Central Themes in Biblical Theology: Mapping Unity in Diversity*, edited by Scott J. Hafemann and Paul R. House, 254–308. Grand Rapids: Baker, 2007.

Ciampa, Roy E., and Brian S. Rosner. "I Corinthians." In *Commentary on the New Testament Use of the Old Testament*, edited by G. K. Beale and D. A. Carson, 695–752. Grand Rapids: Baker, 2007.

———. *The First Letter to the Corinthians.* PNTC. Grand Rapids: Eerdmans, 2010.

Clark, R. Scott. "Christ and Covenant: Federal Theology in Orthoxdoxy." In *A Companion to Reformed Orthodoxy*, edited by Herman J. Selderhuis, 403–28. Boston: Brill, 2013.

Clowney, Edmund P. *The Church.* Contours of Christian Theology. Downers Grove: InterVarsity 1995.

———. "The Final Temple." *WTJ* 35 (1972) 156–89.

———. "Interpreting the Biblical Models of the Church: A Hermeneutical Deepening of Ecclesiology." In *Biblical Interpretation and the Church: The Problem of Contextualization*, edited by D. A. Carson, 64–109. Nashville: Thomas Nelson, 1984. Reprint, Eugene, OR: Wipf and Stock, 2002.

———. "The New Israel." In *A Guide to Biblical Prophecy*, edited by Carl Edwin Armerding and W. Ward Gasque, 207–20. Peabody, MA: Hendrickson, 1989.

———. *Preaching and Biblical Theology.* Phillipsburg, NJ: P & R, 1979.

Cocceius, Johannes. *The Doctrine of the Covenant and Testament of God.* Classic Reformed Theology 3. Edited by Casey Carmichael. Grand Rapids: Reformation Heritage, 2016.

Cole, Graham A. *He Who Gives Life: The Doctrine of the Holy Spirit.* Wheaton, IL: Crossway, 2007.

Collins, C. John. "Galatians 3:16: What Kind of Exegete was Paul?" *TynBul* 54 (2003) 75–86.

———. *Genesis 1–4: A Linguistic, Literary, and Theological Commentary.* Phillipsburg, NJ: P & R, 2006.

———. "What Does Baptism Do For Anyone? Part I." *Presbyterion* 38 (2012) 1–33.

———. "What Does Baptism Do For Anyone? Part II." *Presbyterion* 38 (2012) 74–98.

Collins, Jack. "A Syntactical Note (Genesis 3:15): Is the Woman's Seed Singular or Plural?" *TynBul* 48 (1997) 139–48.

Compton, Jared M. "Shared Intentions? Reflections on Inspiration and Interpretation in Light of Scripture's Dual Authorship." *Themelios* 33 (2008) 23–33.

Compton, R. Bruce. "Dispensationalism, the Church, and the New Covenant." *DBSJ* 8 (2003) 3–48.

Cone, Christopher, ed. *An Introduction to the New Covenant*. Hurst, TX: Tyndale Seminary Press, 2013.

———. "Dispensational Definition & Division Revisited." In *Dispensationalism Tomorrow & Beyond: A Theological Collection in Honor of Charles C. Ryrie*, edited by Christopher Cone, 145–63. Fort Worth, TX: Tyndale Seminary, 2008.

———. "Hermeneutical Ramifications of Applying the New Covenant to the Church: An Appeal to Consistency." *Journal of Dispensational Theology* 13 (2009) 5–22.

Cosgrove, Charles H. "The Law Has Given Sarah No Children (Gal. 4:21–30)." *NovT* 29 (1987) 219–35.

Couch, Mal. "Dispensational Hermeneutics and the Doctrine of Ecclesiology." In *A Biblical Theology of the Church*, edited by Mal Couch, 13–28. Grand Rapids: Kregel, 1999.

Cowan, Christopher W. "Context Is Everything: 'The Israel of God' in Galatians 6:16." *SBJT* 14 (2010) 78–85.

———. "The Warning Passages of Hebrews and the New Covenant Community." In *Progressive Covenantalism: Charting a Course between Dispensational and Covenant Theologies*, edited by Stephen J. Wellum and Brent E. Parker, 189–213. Nashville: B & H, 2016.

Cragoe, Thomas H. "The Davidic Covenant." In *Progressive Dispensationalism: An Analysis of the Movement and Defense of Traditional Dispensationalism*, edited by Ron J. Bigalke Jr., 99–134. Lanham, MD: University Press of America, 2005.

Crampton, W. G. "The Sacramental Implications of 1 Corinthians 10:1–4: A Confessional Study of Baptism and the Lord's Supper." *RBTR* 7 (2010) 7–39.

Cruise, Charles E. "The 'Wealth of the Nations:' A Study in the Intertextuality of Isaiah 60:5, 11." *JETS* 58 (2015) 283–97.

Currid, John D. "Recognition and Use of Typology in Preaching." *RTR* 53 (1994) 115–29.

Dalrymple, Rob. *Understanding Eschatology: Why It Matters*. Eugene, OR: Wipf & Stock, 2013.

Daniélou, Jean. *From Shadows to Reality: Studies in the Biblical Typology of the Fathers*. Translated by Wulstan Hibberd. London: Burns and Oates, 1960.

Das, A. Andrew. *Paul and the Jews*. Library of Pauline Studies. Peabody, MA: Hendrickson, 2003.

Davids, Peter H. *The First Epistle of Peter*. NICNT. Grand Rapids: Eerdmans, 1990.

Davidson, Richard M. "The Eschatological Hermeneutic of Biblical Typology." *TheoRhēma* 6 (2011) 5–48.

———. "The Nature [and Identity] of Biblical Typology—Crucial Issues." Paper presented at the annual meeting of the Midwest Evangelical Theological Society, St. Paul, MN, March 14, 2003.

———. *Typology in Scripture: A Study of Hermeneutical ΤΥΠΟΣ Structures*. Andrews University Seminary Doctoral Dissertation Series 2. Berrien Springs, MI: Andrews University Press, 1981.

Davies, W. D. *The Gospel and the Land: Early Christianity and Jewish Territorial Doctrine*. Berkeley: University of California Press, 1974. Reprint, Sheffield: JSOT, 1994.

Davies, W. D., and D. C. Allison. *Matthew 1–7*. ICC 1. New York: T & T Clark, 1988. Reprint, 2006.

Davis, John P. "Who Are the Heirs of the Abrahamic Covenant?" *ERT* 29 (2005) 149–63.

Davis, Thomas M. "The Traditions of Puritan Typology." In *Typology and Early American Literature*, edited by Sacvan Bercovitch, 11–46. Amherst: University of Massachusetts Press, 1972.

Dawson, John David. *Christian Figural Reading and the Fashioning of Identity*. Berkeley: University of California Press, 2002.

De Boer, Martinus C. "Paul's Quotation of Isaiah 54.1 in Galatians." *NTS* 50 (2004) 370–89.

De Lubac, Henri. *Theological Fragments*. Translated by Rebecca Howell Balinski. San Francisco: Ignatius, 1989.

Decker, Rodney J. "The Church Has a Direct Relationship to the New Covenant." In *Dispensational Understanding of the New Covenant: Three Views*, edited by Michael Stallard, 194–222. Schaumburg, IL: Regular Baptist, 2012.

———. "The Church's Relationship to the New Covenant." *BibSac* 152 (1995) 290–305, 431–56.

Demarest, Bruce. *The Cross and Salvation: The Doctrine of Salvation*. Foundations of Evangelical Theology. Wheaton, IL: Crossway, 1997.

Dempster, Stephen G. *Dominion and Dynasty: A Theology of the Hebrew Bible*. NSBT 15. Downers Grove: InterVarsity, 2003.

———. "The Servant of the Lord." In *Central Themes in Biblical Theology: Mapping Unity in Diversity*, edited by Scott J. Hafemann and Paul R. House, 128–78. Grand Rapids: Baker, 2007.

———. "From Slight Peg to Cornerstone to Capstone: The Resurrection of Christ on 'the Third Day' according to the Scriptures." *WTJ* 76 (2014) 371–409.

Denault, Pascal. *The Distinctiveness of Baptist Covenant Theology: A Comparison Between Seventeenth-Century Particular Baptist and Paedobaptist Federalism*. Birmingham, AL: Solid Ground Christian, 2013.

Dennis, John A. *Jesus' Death and the Gathering of True Israel: The Johannine Appropriation of Restoration Theology in Light of John 11.47–52*. WUNT 2/217. Tübingen: Mohr Siebeck, 2006.

———. "The Presence and Function of Second Exodus-Restoration Imagery in John 6." *Studien zum Neuen Testament und Seiner Umwelt* 30 (2015) 105–21.

———. "Restoration in John 11,47–52: Reading the Key Motifs in Their Jewish Context." *Ephemerides Theologicae Lovanienses* 81 (2005) 57–86.

DeRouchie, Jason S. "Counting Stars with Abraham and the Prophets: New Covenant Ecclesiology in OT Perspective." *JETS* 58 (2015) 445–85.

———. "Is *Every* Promise 'Yes'? Old Testament Promises and the Christian." *Themelios* 42 (2017) 16–45.

———. "Why the Third Day? The Promise of Resurrection in All of Scripture." *Midwestern Journal of Theology* 20 (2021) 19–34.

DeRouchie, Jason S., and Jason C. Meyer. "Christ or Family as the 'Seed' of Promise? An Evaluation of N. T. Wright on Galatians 3:16." *SBJT* 14 (2010) 36–48.

DeRouchie, Jason S., et al. *40 Questions about Biblical Theology*. Grand Rapids: Kregel Academic, 2020.

DeWitt, Dale S. *Dispensational Theology in America During the Twentieth Century: Theological Development and Cultural Context*. Grand Rapids: Grace Bible College, 2002.

Di Mattei, Steven. "Paul's Allegory of the Two Covenants (Gal 4.21–31) in Light of First-Century Hellenistic Rhetoric and Jewish Hermeneutics." *NTS* 52 (2006) 102–22.

Diffey, Daniel S. "The Royal Promise in Genesis: The Often Underestimated Importance of Genesis 17:6, 17:16, and 35:11." *TynBul* 62 (2011) 313–16.

Dockery, David S. *Biblical Interpretation Then and Now: Contemporary Hermeneutics in the Light of the Early Church*. Grand Rapids: Baker, 1992.

———. "Typological Exegesis: Moving beyond Abuse and Neglect." In *Reclaiming the Prophetic Mantle: Preaching the Old Testament Faithfully*, edited by George L. Klein, 167–78. Nashville: Broadman, 1992.

Dodd, C. H. *According to the Scriptures: The Sub-Structure of New Testament Theology*. London: James Nisbet & Co, 1952. Reprint, London: Fontana, 1965.

Donaldson, Alistair W. *The Last Days of Dispensationalism: A Scholarly Critique of Popular Misconceptions*. Eugene, OR: Wipf & Stock, 2011.

Donaldson, Alistair. "The Kingdom of God and the Land: The New Testament Fulfillment of an Old Testament Theme." In *The Gospel and the Land of Promise: Christian Approaches to the Land of the Bible*, edited by Philip Church et al., 58–74. Eugene, OR: Pickwick, 2011.

Dow, Lois K. Fuller. *Images of Zion: Biblical Antecedents for the New Jerusalem*. New Testament Monographs 26. Sheffield: Sheffield Phoenix, 2010.

Drane, John W. "Typology." *EvQ* 50 (1978) 195–210.

Duguid, Iain M. "Israel." In *Dictionary of the Old Testament Prophets*. Edited by Mark J. Boda and J. Gordon McConville. Downers Grove: InterVarsity, 2012.

Dumbrell, William J. *Covenant and Creation: A Theology of Old Testament Covenants*. Carlisle, UK: Paternoster, 1997.

———. "Israel in John's Gospel." In *In the Fullness of Time: Biblical Studies in Honour of Archbishop Donald Robinson*, edited by David Peterson and John Pryor, 79–94. Homebush West, Australia: Lancer, 1992.

———. "The Role of the Servant in Isaiah 40–55." *RTR* 48 (1989) 105–13.

———. *The Search for Order: Biblical Eschatology in Focus*. Grand Rapids: Baker, 1994.

Dunn, Matthew W. I. "Raymond Brown and the *Sensus Plenior* Interpretation of the Bible." *Studies in Religion* 36 (2007) 531–51.

Eastman, Susan Grove. "Israel and the Mercy of God: A Re-Reading of Galatians 6.16 and Romans 9–11." *NTS* 56 (2010) 367–95.

Echevarria, Miguel G., Jr. *The Future Inheritance of Land in the Pauline Epistles*. Eugene, OR: Pickwick, 2019.

Edwards, James R. *The Gospel according to Luke*. PNTC. Grand Rapids: Eerdmans, 2015.

Eichrodt, Walther. "Is Typological Exegesis an Appropriate Method?" Translated by James Luther Mays. In *Essays on Old Testament Hermeneutics*, edited by Claus Westermann, 224–45. Richmond, VA: John Knox, 1963.

Elliot, Mark W. "Allegory." In *The New Interpreter's Dictionary of the Bible*. Vol. 1. Nashville: Abingdon, 2006.

Elliott, John H. *The Elect and the Holy: An Exegetical Examination of 1 Peter 2:4–10 and the Phrase* βασίλειον ἱεράτευμα. NovTSup 12. Leiden, Netherlands: Brill, 1966. Reprint, Eugene OR: Wipf & Stock, 2005.

———. *1 Peter*. Anchor Bible, vol. 37b. New York: Doubleday, 2000.

Ellis, E. Earle. "How the New Testament Uses the Old." In *New Testament Interpretation: Essays on Principles and Methods*, edited by I. Howard Marshall, 199–219. Exeter: Paternoster, 1979.

———. *The Old Testament in Early Christianity: Canon and Interpretation in the Light of Modern Research*. WUNT 54. Tübingen, Germany: Mohr Siebeck, 1991.

———. *Paul's Use of the Old Testament*. Grand Rapids: Eerdmans, 1957.

Emadi, Samuel. "Covenant, Typology, and the Story of Joseph." *TynBul* 69 (2018) 1–24.

Emerson, Matthew Y. "Arbitrary Allegory, Typical Typology, or Intertextual Interpretation? Paul's Use of the Pentateuch in Galatians 4:21–31." *BTB* 43 (2013) 14–22.

Enns, Peter. "Fuller Meaning, Single Goal: A Christotelic Approach to the New Testament Use of the Old in Its First-Century Interpretative Environment." In *Three Views on the New Testament Use of the Old Testament*, edited by Kenneth Berding and Jonathan Lunde, 167–217. Grand Rapids: Zondervan, 2008.

———. *Inspiration and Incarnation: Evangelicals and the Problem of the Old Testament*. Grand Rapids: Baker, 2005.

———. "The 'Moveable Well' in 1 Cor 10:4: An Extrabiblical Tradition in an Apostolic Text." *BBR* 6 (1996) 23–38.

Essex, Keith H. "The Abrahamic Covenant." *MSJ* 10 (1999) 191–212.

Estelle, Bryan D. "The Covenant of Works in Moses and Paul." In *Covenant, Justification, and Pastoral Theology: Essays by the Faculty of Westminster Seminary California*, edited by R. Scott Clark, 89–135. Phillipsburg, NJ: P & R, 2007.

Evans, Craig A. "Israel according to the Book of Hebrews and the General Epistles." In *The People, the Land, and the Future of Israel: Israel and the Jewish People in the Plan of God*, edited by Darrell L. Bock and Mitch Glaser, 133–46. Grand Rapids: Kregel, 2014.

Evans, C. A., and Lidija Novakovic. "Typology." In *Dictionary of Jesus and the Gospels*, 2nd ed. Edited by Joel B. Green et al. Downers Grove: InterVarsity, 2013.

Fackre, Gabriel J. *Ecumenical Faith in Evangelical Perspective*. Grand Rapids: Eerdmans, 1993.

Fairbairn, Patrick. *The Interpretation of Prophecy*. 2nd ed. Suffolk, UK: St Edmundsbury Press, 1865. Reprint, Edinburgh: Banner of Truth, 1993.

———. *Typology of Scripture*. 2 vols. in 1. New York: Funk & Wagnalls, 1900. Reprint, Grand Rapids: Kregel, 1989.

Fantuzzo, Christopher J. "True Israel's 'Mother and Brothers:' Reflections on the Servants and Servanthood in Isaiah." In *Eyes to See, Ears to Hear: Essays in Memory of J. Alan Groves*, edited by Peter Enns et al., 106–24. Phillipsburg, NJ: P & R, 2010.

Fee, Gordon D. *The First Epistle to the Corinthians*. NICNT. Rev. ed. Grand Rapids: Eerdmans, 2014.

Feinberg, John S. "Dispensationalism and Support for the State of Israel." In *The Land Cries Out: Theology of the Land in the Israeli-Palestinian Context*, edited by Salim J. Munayer and Lisa Loden, 104–31. Eugene, OR: Cascade, 2012.

———. "Israel in the Land as an Eschatological Necessity?" In *The People, the Land, and the Future of Israel: Israel and the Jewish People in the Plan of God*, edited by Darrell L. Bock and Mitch Glaser, 183–94. Grand Rapids: Kregel, 2014.

———. "Systems of Discontinuity." In *Continuity and Discontinuity: Perspectives on the Relationship between the Old and New Testaments*, edited by John S. Feinberg, 63–86. Wheaton, IL: Crossway, 1988.

Feinberg, Paul D. "The Hermeneutics of Discontinuity." In *Continuity and Discontinuity: Perspectives on the Relationship between the Old and New Testaments*, edited by John S. Feinberg, 109–28. Wheaton, IL: Crossway, 1988.

Ferguson, Sinclair B. *The Holy Spirit*. Contours of Christian Theology. Downers Grove: InterVarsity, 1996.

Fesko, J. V. "Calvin and Witsius on the Mosaic Covenant." In *The Law is Not of Faith: Essays on Works and Grace in the Mosaic Covenant*, edited by Bryan D. Estelle et al., 25–43. Phillipsburg, NJ: P & R, 2009.

———. *Last Things First: Unlocking Genesis 1–3 with the Christ of Eschatology*. Fearn, Scotland: Christian Focus, 2007.

———. *The Trinity and the Covenant of Redemption*. Fearn, Scotland: Mentor, 2016.

Fishbane, Michael. *Biblical Interpretation in Ancient Israel*. New York: Oxford University Press, 1985.

Foulkes, Francis. "The Acts of God: A Study of the Basis of Typology in the Old Testament." In *The Right Doctrine from the Wrong Texts?*, edited by G. K. Beale, 342–71. Grand Rapids: Baker, 1994.

Fowl, Stephen E., ed. *The Theological Interpretation of Scripture: Classic and Contemporary Readings*. Oxford: Blackwell, 1997.

———. "Who Can Read Abraham's Story? Allegory and Interpretative Power in Galatians." *JSNT* 55 (1994) 77–95.

Frame, John M. *The Doctrine of the Knowledge of God*. Phillipsburg, NJ: P & R, 1987.

———. *Systematic Theology: An Introduction to Christian Belief*. Phillipsburg, NJ: P & R, 2013.

France, R. T. "First Century Bible Study: Old Testament Motifs in 1 Peter 2:4–10." *JEPTA* 28 (1998) 26–48.

———. "The Formula Quotations of Matthew 2 and the Problem of Communication." *NTS* 27 (1981) 233–51.

———. *The Gospel of Mark*. NIGTC. Grand Rapids: Eerdmans, 2002.

———. *The Gospel of Matthew*. NICNT. Grand Rapids: Eerdmans, 2007.

———. *Jesus and the Old Testament: His Application of Old Testament Passages to Himself and His Mission*. Vancouver: Regent College Publishing, 1998.

———. "Old Testament Prophecy and the Future of Israel." *TynBul* 26 (1975) 53–78.

Freedman, David Noel. "Divine Commitment and Human Obligation: The Covenant Theme." *Int* 18 (1964) 419–31.

Frei, Hans W. *The Eclipse of Biblical Narrative: A Study in Eighteenth and Nineteenth Century Hermenutics*. New Haven, CT: Yale University Press, 1974.

Fritsch, Charles T. "To 'Antitypon." In *Studia Biblica et Semitica*. Wageningen, The Netherlands: H. Veenman, 1966.

———. "Biblical Typology." *BibSac* 104 (1947) 87–100, 214–22.

Fruchtenbaum, Arnold G. "Israel and the Church." In *Issues in Dispensationalism*, edited by Wesley R. Willis and John R. Master, 113–30. Chicago: Moody, 1994.

———. *Israelology: The Missing Link in Systematic Theology*. Rev. ed. Tustin, CA: Ariel Ministries, 1993.
Frye, Northrop. *The Great Code: The Bible and Literature*. New York: Harcourt Brace Jovanovich, 1982.
Fuller, Daniel. *Gospel and Law: Contrast or Continuum?* Grand Rapids: Eerdmans, 1980.
Fuller, Michael E. *The Restoration of Israel: Israel's Re-Gathering and the Fate of the Nations in Early Jewish Literature and Luke-Acts*. BZNW 138. Berlin: Walter de Gruyter, 2006.
Fung, Ronald Y. K. "Some Pauline Pictures of the Church." *EvQ* 43 (1981) 89–107.
Gaffin, Richard B., Jr. *By Faith, Not by Sight: Paul and the Order of Salvation*. Waynesboro, GA: Paternoster, 2006.
———. "Pentecost: Before and After." *Kerux* 10 (1995) 3–24.
———. "Systematic Theology and Biblical Theology." *WTJ* 38 (1976) 281–99.
Gamble, Richard C. "The Relationship between Biblical Theology and Systematic Theology." In *Always Reforming: Explorations in Systematic Theology*, edited by A. T. B. McGowan, 211–39. Downers Grove: InterVarsity, 2006.
Gardner, Paul Douglas. *The Gifts of God and the Authentication of a Christian: An Exegetical Study of 1 Corinthians 8—11:1*. Lanham, MD: University Press of America, 1994.
Garland, David E. *1 Corinthians*. BECNT. Grand Rapids: Baker, 2003.
———. *A Theology of Mark's Gospel: Good News about Jesus the Messiah, the Son of God*. BTNT. Grand Rapids: Zondervan, 2015.
Garrett, Duane A. *Hosea, Joel*. NAC, vol. 19b. Nashville: B & H, 1997.
Gathercole, Simon. "Locating Christ and Israel in Romans 9–11." In *God and Israel: Providence and Purpose in Romans 9–11*, edited by Todd D. Still, 115–39. Waco, TX: Baylor University Press, 2017.
Gentry, Peter J. "The Atonement in Isaiah's Fourth Servant Song (Isaiah 52:13—53:12)." *SBJT* 11 (2007) 20–47.
———. *Biblical Studies*, Vol. 1. Peterborough, Canada: H&E Academic, 2020.
———. "Rethinking the 'Sure Mercies of David' in Isaiah 55:3." *WTJ* 69 (2007) 279–304.
———. "The Significance of Covenants in Biblical Theology." *SBJT* 20 (2016) 9–33.
Gentry, Peter J., and Stephen J. Wellum. *Kingdom through Covenant: A Biblical-Theological Understanding of the Covenants*. 2nd ed. Wheaton, IL: Crossway, 2018.
Gerstner, John A. *Wrongly Dividing the Word of Truth: A Critique of Dispensationalism*. 2nd ed. Morgan, PA: Soli Deo Gloria, 2000.
Gibbs, Jeffrey A. "Israel Standing with Israel: The Baptism of Jesus in Matthew's Gospel (Matt 3:13–17)." *CBQ* 64 (2002) 511–26.
Gibson, David. "'Fathers of Faith, My Fathers Now!' On Abraham, Covenant, and the Theology of Paedobaptism." *Themelios* 40 (2015) 14–34.
———. "Sacramental Supersessionism Revisited: A Response to Martin Salter on the Relationship between Circumcision and Baptism." *Themelios* 37 (2012) 191–208.
Gignilliat, Mark. "Isaiah's Offspring: Paul's Isaiah 54:1 Quotation in Galatians 4:27." *BBR* 23 (2015) 205–23.
———. "Paul, Allegory, and the Plain Sense of Scripture: Galatians 4:21–31." *JTI* 2 (2008) 135–46.

———. "A Servant Follower of the Servant: Paul's Eschatological Reading of Isaiah 40–66 in 2 Corinthians 5:14—6:10." *HBT* 26 (2004) 98–124.
Gladd, Benjamin L. *From Adam and Israel to the Church: A Biblical Theology of the People of God*. Downers Grove: InterVarsity, 2019.
Glenny, W. Edward. "The Divine Meaning of Scripture: Explanations and Limitations." *JETS* 38 (1995) 481–500
———. "The Israelite Imagery of 1 Peter 2." In *Dispensationalism, Israel and the Church: The Search for Definition*, edited by Craig A. Blaising and Darrell L. Bock, 156–87. Grand Rapids: Zondervan, 1992.
———. "Typology: A Summary of the Present Evangelical Discussion." *JETS* 40 (1997) 627–38.
Golding, Peter. *Covenant Theology: The Key of Theology in Reformed Thought and Tradition*. Fearn, Scotland: Christian Focus, 2004.
Goldingay, John. "Servant of Yahweh." In *Dictionary of the Old Testament Prophets*. Edited by Mark J. Boda and J. Gordon McConville. Downers Grove: InterVarsity, 2012.
Goldsworthy, Graeme. *Christ-Centered Biblical Theology: Hermeneutical Foundations and Principles*. Downers Grove: InterVarsity, 2012.
———. *Christ-Centered Hermeneutics: Foundations and Principles of Evangelical Interpretation*. Downers Grove: InterVarsity, 2006.
———. "Kingdom of God." In *NDBT*, edited by T. Desmond Alexander and Brian S. Rosner, 615–20. Downers Grove: InterVarsity, 2000.
———. *The Son of God and the New Creation*. Short Studies in Biblical Theology. Wheaton, IL: Crossway, 2015.
Goodrich, John K. "Until the Fullness of the Gentiles Come In: A Critical Review of Recent Scholarship on the Salvation of 'All Israel' (Romans 11:26)." *Journal for the Study of Paul and His Letters* 6 (2016) 5–32.
Goodwin, Mark J. "Hosea and 'the Son of the Living God' in Matthew 16:16b." *CBQ* 67 (2005) 265–83.
Goppelt, Leonhard. "τύπος." In *TDNT*, edited by Gerhard Kittel and Gerhard Friedrich, translated by Geoffrey W. Bromiley, 8:246–59. Grand Rapids: Eerdmans, 1974.
———. *Typos: The Typological Interpretation of the Old Testament in the New*. Translated by Donald H. Madvig. Grand Rapids: Eerdmans, 1982.
———. *The Variety and Unity of the Apostolic Witness to Christ*. Vol. 2 of *Theology of the New Testament*. Edited by Jürgen Roloff. Translated by John E. Alsup. Grand Rapids: Eerdmans, 1982.
Goulder, M. D. *Type and History in Acts*. London: SPCK, 1964.
Green, Bradley G., ed. *Shapers of Christian Orthodoxy: Engaging Early and Medieval Theologians*. Downers Grove: InterVarsity, 2010.
Green, Joel B. "Practicing the Gospel in a Post-Critical World: The Promise of Theological Exegesis." *JETS* 47 (2004) 387–97.
Greever, Joshua M. "The Nature of the New Covenant: A Case Study in Ephesians 2:11–22." *SBJT* 20 (2016) 73–89.
———. "Will the True Israel Stand Up? Jesus as the True Israel in Ephesians 1:3–6." Paper presented at the meetings of the National Evangelical Theological Society, Baltimore, November 19, 2013.
Greidanus, Sidney. *Preaching Christ from the Old Testament: A Contemporary Hermeneutical Method*. Grand Rapids: Eerdmans, 1999.

Grenz, Stanley J. *The Millennial Maze: Sorting Out Evangelical Options.* Downers Grove: InterVarsity, 1992.
Grenz, Stanley, and John Franke. *Beyond Foundationalism: Shaping Theology in a Postmodern Context.* Louisville: Westminster John Knox, 2000.
Grindheim, Sigurd. "What the OT Prophets Did Not Know: The Mystery of the Church in Eph 3,2–13." *Biblica* 80 (2003) 531–53.
Grisanti, Michael. "A Critique of Gentry and Wellum's *Kingdom through Covenant*: An Old Testament Perspective." *MSJ* 26 (2015) 129–37.
———. "The Davidic Covenant." *MSJ* 10 (1999) 233–50.
———. "Israel's Mission to the Nations in Isaiah 40–55: An Update." *MSJ* 9 (1998) 39–61.
Gromacki, Gary. "The Fulfillment of the Abrahamic Covenant." *JMT* 18 (2014) 77–119.
Gromacki, Robert. "Israel: Her Past, Present, and Future in Romans 9–11." *JMT* 18 (2014) 47–76.
Gundry, Stanley N. "Typology as a Means of Interpretation: Past and Present." *JETS* 12 (1969) 233–40.
Guthrie, Donald. *New Testament Theology.* Leicester: InterVarsity, 1981.
Hafemann, Scott J. "The Covenant Relationship." In *Central Themes in Biblical Theology: Mapping Unity in Diversity*, edited by Scott J. Hafemann and Paul R. House, 20–65. Grand Rapids: Baker, 2007.
———. "The Redemption of Israel for the Sake of the Gentiles." In *Introduction to Messianic Judaism: Its Ecclesial Context and Biblical Foundations*, edited by David Rudolph and Joel Willitts, 206–13. Grand Rapids: Zondervan, 2013.
Hahn, Scott W. "A Broken Covenant and the Curse of Death: A Study of Hebrews 9:15–22." *CBQ* 66 (2004) 416–36.
———. *Kingship by Covenant: A Canonical Approach to the Fulfillment of God's Saving Promises.* London: Yale University Press, 2009.
Hamilton, James M., Jr. *God's Indwelling Presence: The Holy Spirit in the Old and New Testaments.* NACSBT. Nashville: B & H, 2006.
———. "The Seed of the Woman and the Blessing of Abraham." *TynBul* 58 (2007) 253–74.
———. "The Typology of David's Rise to Power: Messianic Patterns in the Book of Samuel." *SBJT* 16 (2012) 4–25.
———. *Typology—Understanding the Bible's Promise-Shaped Patterns.* Grand Rapids: Zondervan, 2022.
———. "'The Virgin Will Conceive': Typological Fulfillment in Matthew 1:18–23." In *Built upon the Rock: Studies in the Gospel of Matthew*, edited by John Nolland and Dan Gurtner, 228–47. Grand Rapids: Eerdmans, 2008.
Hamlin, E. John. "Deutero-Isaiah's Reinterpretation of the Exodus in the Babylonian Twilight." *Proceedings* 11 (1991) 75–80.
Hammett, John S. *Biblical Foundations for Baptist Churches: A Contemporary Ecclesiology.* Grand Rapids: Kregel, 2005.
Hanson, A. T. *Jesus Christ in the Old Testament.* London: SPCK, 1965.
Harless, Hal. *How Firm a Foundation: The Dispensations in the Light of the Divine Covenants.* Society of Biblical Literature 63. New York: Peter Lang, 2004.
Harmon, Matthew S. "Allegory, Typology, or Something Else? Revisiting Galatians 4:21—5:1." In *Studies in Paul's Letters: A Festschrift for Douglas J. Moo*, edited by Jay E. Smith and Matthew Harmon, 144–58. Grand Rapids: Zondervan, 2014.

———. *The Servant of the Lord and His Servant People: Tracing a Biblical Theme through the Canon*. NSBT 54. Downers Grove: InterVarsity, 2020.

———. *She Must and Shall Go Free: Paul's Isaianic Gospel in Galatians*. BZNW 168. Berlin: Walter de Gruyter, 2010.

Harris, Dana M. "Typological Trajectories in the Epistle to the Hebrews." In *Interpreting the Old Testament Theologically: Essays in Honor of Willem A. VanGemeren*, edited by Andrew T. Abernethy, 280–92. Grand Rapids: Zondervan, 2018.

Hart, John F., ed. *Evidence for the Rapture: A Biblical Case for Pretribulationalism*. Chicago: Moody, 2015.

Hart, Trevor. "Systematic—In What Sense?" In *Out of Egypt: Biblical Theology and Biblical Interpretation*. Vol. 5. Scripture and Hermeneutics Series, edited by Craig Bartholomew et al., 341–51. Grand Rapids: Zondervan, 2004.

Harvey, Graham. *The True Israel: Uses of the Names Jew, Hebrew and Israel in Ancient Jewish and Early Christian Literature*. Leiden, Netherlands: Brill, 1996.

Hasel, Gerhard F. "The Nature of Biblical Theology: Recent Trends and Issues." *AUSS* 32 (1994) 203–15.

Haykin, Michael G. *Rediscovering the Church Fathers: Who They Were and How They Shaped the Church*. Wheaton, IL: Crossway, 2011.

Hays, Richard B. "The Canonical Matrix of the Gospels." In *The Cambridge Companion to the Gospels*, edited by Stephen C. Barton, 53–75. Cambridge: Cambridge University Press, 2006.

———. *Echoes of Scripture in the Gospels*. Waco, TX: Baylor University Press, 2016.

———. *Echoes of Scripture in the Letters of Paul*. New Haven, CT: Yale University Press, 1989.

———. "Figural Exegesis and the Retrospective Re-cognition of Israel's Story." *BBR* 29 (2019) 32–48.

———. "The Liberation of Israel in Luke-Acts: Intertextual Narration as Countercultural Practice." In *Reading the Bible Intertextually*, edited by Richard B. Hays et al., 101–17. Waco, TX: Baylor University Press, 2009.

———. *Reading Backwards: Figural Christology and the Fourfold Gospel Witness*. Waco, TX: Baylor University Press, 2014.

Helyer, Larry R. *The Life and Witness of Peter*. Downers Grove: InterVarsity, 2012.

———. "Luke and the Restoration of Israel." *JETS* 36 (1993) 317–329.

———. *The Witness of Jesus, Paul and John: An Exploration in Biblical Theology*. Downers Grove: InterVarsity, 2008.

Hendriksen, William. *Israel in Prophecy*. Grand Rapids: Baker, 1968.

Hester, James D. *Paul's Concept of Inheritance: A Contribution to the Understanding of Heilsgeschichte*. Scottish Journal of Theology Occasional Papers 14. Edinburgh: Oliver and Boyd, 1968.

Hoch, Carl B., Jr. *All Things New: The Significance of Newness for Biblical Theology*. Grand Rapids: Baker, 1995.

———. "The New Man of Ephesians 2." In *Dispensationalism, Israel and the Church: The Search for Definition*, edited by Craig A. Blaising and Darrell L. Bock, 98–126. Grand Rapids: Zondervan, 1992.

Hodge, Caroline Johnson. *If Sons, Then Heirs: A Study of Kinship and Ethnicity in the Letters of Paul*. Oxford: Oxford University Press, 2007.

Hodge, Charles. *Systematic Theology*. Grand Rapids: Eerdmans, 1982.

Hoehner, Harold W. *Ephesians: An Exegetical Commentary*. Grand Rapids: Baker, 2002.

———. "Israel in Romans 9–11." In *Israel, the Land and the People: An Evangelical Affirmation of God's Promises*, edited by H. Wayne House, 145–67. Grand Rapids: Kregel, 1998.

Hoekema, Anthony A. *The Bible and the Future*. Grand Rapids: Eerdmans, 1979.

———. *Created in God's Image*. Grand Rapids: Eerdmans, 1986.

———. *Saved by Grace*. Grand Rapids: Eerdmans, 1989.

Holsteen, Nathan D. "The Hermeneutic of Dispensationalism." In *Dispensationalism and the History of Redemption: A Developing and Diverse Tradition*, edited by D. Jeffrey Bingham and Glenn R. Kreider, 101–21. Chicago: Moody, 2015.

Holwerda, David E. *Jesus and Israel: One Covenant or Two?* Grand Rapids: Eerdmans, 1995.

Horton, Michael S. *The Christian Faith: A Systematic Theology for Pilgrims on the Way*. Grand Rapids: Zondervan, 2011.

———. *Covenant and Eschatology: The Divine Drama*. Louisville: Westminster John Knox, 2006.

———. *Covenant and Salvation: Union with Christ*. Louisville: Westminster John Knox, 2007.

———. *Introducing Covenant Theology*. Grand Rapids: Baker, 2006.

Hoskins, Paul M. "Deliverance from Death by the True Passover Lamb: A Significant Aspect of the Fulfillment of the Passover in the Gospel of John." *JETS* 52 (2009) 285–99.

———. *Jesus as the Fulfillment of the Temple in the Gospel of John*. Paternoster Biblical Monographs. Eugene, OR: Wipf and Stock, 2006.

———. *That Scripture Might Be Fulfilled: Typology and the Death of Christ*. LaVergne, TN: Xulon, 2009.

House, Paul R. *Old Testament Theology*. Downers Grove: InterVarsity, 1998.

House, H. Wayne. "The Church's Appropriation of Israel's Blessings." In *Israel, The Land and the People: An Evangelical Affirmation of God's Promises*, edited by H. Wayne House, 77–110. Grand Rapids: Kregel, 1998.

———. "The Future of National Israel." *BibSac* 166 (2009) 463–81.

———. "Traditional Dispensationalism and the Millennium." *CTR* 11 (2013) 3–27.

Howard, Tracy L. "The Use of Hosea 11:1 in Matthew 2:15: An Alternative Solution." *BibSac* 143 (1986) 314–28.

Hsieh, Nelson S. "Abraham as 'Heir of the World': Does Romans 4:13 Expand the Old Testament Abrahamic Land Promises?" *MSJ* 26 (2015) 95–110.

Hugenberger, G. P. "Introductory Notes on Typology." In *The Right Doctrine from the Wrong Texts?*, edited by G. K. Beale, 331–41. Grand Rapids: Baker, 1994.

———. *Marriage as a Covenant: Biblical Law and Ethics as Developed from Malachi*. Grand Rapids: Baker, 1998.

———. "The Servant of the Lord in the 'Servant Songs' of Isaiah: A Second Moses Figure." In *The Lord's Anointed: Interpretation of Old Testament Messianic Texts*, edited by Philip E. Satterthwaite et al., 105–40. Grand Rapids: Baker, 1995.

Hullinger, Jerry M. "The Function of the Millennial Sacrifices in Ezekiel's Temple, Part 1." *BibSac* 167 (2010) 40–57.

———. "The Function of the Millennial Sacrifices in Ezekiel's Temple, Part 2." *BibSac* 167 (2010) 166–79.

———. "The Realization of Ezekiel's Temple." In *Dispensationalism Tomorrow & Beyond: A Theological Collection in Honor of Charles C. Ryrie*, edited by Christopher Cone, 375–95. Fort Worth, TX: Tyndale Seminary, 2008.

Hummel, Horace D. "The Old Testament Basis of Typological Interpretation." *BR* 9 (1964) 38–50.

Hvalvik, Reidar. "A 'Sonderweg' for Israel: A Critical Examination of a Current Interpretation of Romans 11.25–27." *JSNT* 38 (1990) 87–107.

Ice, Thomas D. "Dispensational Hermeneutics." In *Issues in Dispensationalism*, edited by Wesley R. Willis and John R. Master, 29–49. Chicago: Moody, 1994.

Instone-Brewer, David. "Paul's Literal Interpretation of 'Do Not Muzzle the Ox.'" In *The Trustworthiness of God: Perspectives on the Nature of Scripture*, edited by Paul Helm and Carl R. Trueman, 139–53. Grand Rapids: Eerdmans, 2002.

Isaac, Munther. *From Land to Lands, from Eden to the Renewed Earth: A Christ-Centered Biblical Theology of the Promised Land*. Carlisle, UK: Langham Monographs, 2015.

Jackson, T. Ryan. *New Creation in Paul's Letters: A Study of the Historical and Social Setting of a Pauline Concept*. WUNT 2/272. Tübingen, Germany: Mohr Siebeck, 2010.

Jeffery, Steve, et al. *Pierced for Our Transgressions: Rediscovering the Glory of Penal Substitution*. Wheaton, IL: Crossway, 2007.

Jervell, Jacob. *Luke and the People of God: A New Look at Luke-Acts*. Minneapolis: Augsburg, 1972.

———. *The Theology of the Acts of the Apostles*. Cambridge: Cambridge University Press, 1996.

Jewett, Paul K. "Concerning the Allegorical Interpretation of Scripture." *WTJ* 17 (1954) 1–20.

———. *Infant Baptism & the Covenant of Grace*. Grand Rapids: Eerdmans, 1978.

Jobes, Karen H. *1 Peter*. BECNT. Grand Rapids: Baker, 2005.

———. "'He Bore Our Transgressions:' Apostolic Reflections on Isaiah 53." In *Eyes to See, Ears to Hear: Essays in Memory of J. Alan Groves*, edited by Peter Enns et al., 92–105. Phillipsburg, NJ: P & R, 2010.

———. "Jerusalem, Our Mother: Metalepsis and Intertextuality in Galatians 4:21–31." *WTJ* 55 (1993) 299–320.

Johnson, Dennis E. *Him We Proclaim: Preaching Christ from All the Scripture*. Phillipsburg, NJ: P & R, 2007.

———. *Walking with Jesus through His Word: Discovering Christ in All of Scriptures*. Phillipsburg, NJ: P & R, 2015.

Johnson, Elliott E. "The Church Has an Indirect Relationship to the New Covenant." In *Dispensational Understanding of the New Covenant: Three Views*, edited by Michael Stallard, 164–75. Schaumburg, IL: Regular Baptist, 2012.

———. "Covenants in Traditional Dispensationalism." In *Three Central Issues in Contemporary Dispensationalism*, edited by Herbert W. Bateman IV, 121–68. Grand Rapids: Kregel, 1999.

———. "Prophetic Fulfillment: The Already and Not Yet." In *Issues in Dispensationalism*, edited by Wesley R. Willis and John R. Master, 183–201. Chicago: Moody, 1994.

———. "A Traditional Dispensational Hermeneutic." In *Three Central Issues in Contemporary Dispensationalism*, edited by Herbert W. Bateman IV, 63–84. Grand Rapids: Kregel, 1999.

Johnson, H. Wayne. "The Pauline Typology of Abraham in Galatians 3." Ph.D. diss., Westminster Theological Seminary, 1993.

Johnson, Jeffrey D. *The Kingdom of God: A Baptist Expression of Covenant and Biblical Theology*. Conway, AR: Free Grace, 2014.

Johnson, Marcus Peter. *One with Christ: An Evangelical Theology of Salvation*. Wheaton, IL: Crossway, 2013.

Johnson, S. Lewis. "Evidence from Romans 9–11." In *A Case for Premillennialism: A New Consensus*, edited by Donald K. Campbell and Jeffrey L. Townsend, 199–23. Chicago: Moody, 1992.

———. *The Old Testament in the New: An Argument for Biblical Inspiration*. Grand Rapids: Zondervan, 1980.

———. "Paul and 'The Israel of God': An Exegetical and Eschatological Case-Study." In *Essays in Honor of J. Dwight Pentecost*, edited by Stanley D. Toussaint and Charles H. Dryer, 181–96. Chicago: Moody, 1986.

Johnston, Philip, and Peter Walker, eds. *The Land of Promise: Biblical, Theological and Contemporary Perspectives*. Downers Grove: InterVarsity, 2000.

Juncker, Günther H. "'Children of Promise': Spiritual Paternity and Patriarch Typology in Galatians and Romans." *BBR* 17 (2007) 131–60.

Kagarise, Robby J. "The 'Seed' in Galatians 3:16—A Window to Paul's Thinking." *EJ* 18 (2000) 67–73.

Kaiser, Walter C., Jr. "An Assessment of 'Replacement Theology:' The Relationship between the Israel of the Abrahamic-Davidic Covenant and the Christian Church." *Mishkan* 21 (1994) 9–20.

———. "The Blessing of David: The Charter for Humanity." In *The Law and the Prophets: Old Testament Studies Prepared in Honor of Oswald Thompson Allis*, edited by John H. Skilton, 298–318. Nutley, NJ: P & R, 1974).

———. "The Land of Israel and the Future Return (Zechariah 10:6–12)." In *Israel, the Land and the People: An Evangelical Affirmation of God's Promises*, edited by H. Wayne House, 209–27. Grand Rapids: Kregel, 1998.

———. *The Messiah in the Old Testament*. Grand Rapids: Zondervan, 1995.

———. *Mission in the Old Testament: Israel as a Light to the Nations*. 2nd ed. Grand Rapids: Baker, 2012.

———. "Single Meaning, Unified Referents: Accurate and Authoritative Citations of the Old Testament by the New Testament." In *Three Views on the New Testament Use of the Old Testament*, edited by Kenneth Berding and Jonathan Lunde, 45–89. Grand Rapids: Zondervan, 2008.

———. *The Uses of the Old Testament in the New*. Chicago: Moody, 1985.

Kaiser, Walter C., Jr., and Moisés Silva. *Introduction to Biblical Hermeneutics: The Search for Meaning*. Rev. ed. Grand Rapids: Zondervan, 2007.

Karlberg, Mark W. *Covenant Theology in Reformed Perspective: Collected Essays and Book Reviews in Historical, Biblical, and Systematic Theology*. Eugene, OR: Wipf and Stock, 2000.

———. "Israel and the Eschaton." *WTJ* 52 (1990) 117–30.

———. "Legitimate Discontinuities between the Testaments." *JETS* 28 (1985) 9–20.

———. "The Significance of Israel in Biblical Typology." *JETS* 31 (1988) 257–69.

Karleen, Paul S. "Understanding Covenant Theologians: A Study in Presuppositions." *GTJ* 10 (1989) 125–38.

Katanacho, Yohanna. *The Land of Christ: A Palestinian Cry.* Eugene, OR: Pickwick, 2013.
Keesmaat, Sylvia C. "Exodus and the Intertextual Transformation of Tradition in Romans 8.14–30." *JSNT* 54 (1994) 29–56.
Kennedy, Joel. *The Recapitulation of Israel: Use of Israel's History in Matthew 1:1—4:11.* WUNT 2/257. Tübingen, Germany: Mohr Siebeck, 2008.
Kinzer, Mark S. "Zionism in Luke-Acts: Do the People of Israel and the Land of Israel Persist as Abiding Concerns in Luke's Two Volumes?" In *The New Christian Zionism: Fresh Perspectives on Israel and the Land*, edited by Gerald R. McDermott, 141–65. Downers Grove: InterVarsity, 2016.
Kirk, David R. "Heaven Opened: Intertextuality and Meaning in John 1:51." *TynBul* 63 (2012) 237–56.
Kirk, J. R. Daniel. "Conceptualising Fulfillment in Matthew." *TynBul* 59 (2008) 77–98.
———. "Why Does the Deliverer Come ἐκ Σιών (Romans 11.26)?" *JSNT* 33 (2010) 81–99.
Kline, Meredith G. *By Oath Consigned: A Reinterpretation of the Covenant Signs of Circumcision and Baptism.* Grand Rapids: Eerdmans, 1968.
———. *Kingdom Prologue: Genesis Foundations for a Covenantal Worldview.* Eugene, OR: Wipf & Stock, 2006.
Klink, Edward W., III. *John.* ZECNT. Grand Rapids: Zondervan, 2016.
Klooster, Fred H. "The Biblical Method of Salvation: A Case for Continuity." In *Continuity and Discontinuity: Perspectives on the Relationship between the Old and New Testaments*, edited by John S. Feinberg, 131–60. Wheaton, IL: Crossway, 1988.
Kloosterman, Nelson D. "The Use of Typology in Post-Canonical Salvation History: An Orientation to Jonathan Edwards' *A History of the Work of Redemption*." *MAJT* 14 (2003) 59–96.
Knoppers, Gary N. "Ancient Near Eastern Royal Grants and the Davidic Covenant: A Parallel?" *JAOS* 116 (1996) 670–97.
Köstenberger, Andreas J. "The Identity of the ΙΣΡΑΗΛ ΤΟΥ ΘΕΟΥ (Israel of God) in Galatians 6:16." *Faith & Mission* 19 (2001) 3–24.
———. "Jesus the Good Shepherd Who Will Also Bring Other Sheep (John 10:16): The Old Testament Background of a Familiar Metaphor." *BBR* 12 (2002) 67–96.
———. *John.* BECNT. Grand Rapids: Baker, 2004.
———. "John." In *Commentary on the New Testament Use of the Old Testament*, edited by G. K. Beale and D. A. Carson, 415–512. Grand Rapids: Baker, 2007.
———. "The Present and Future of Biblical Theology." *SWJT* 56 (2013) 3–25.
———. *A Theology of John's Gospel and Letters.* BTNT. Grand Rapids: Zondervan, 2009.
Köstenberger, Andreas J., and Peter T. O'Brien. *Salvation to the Ends of the Earth: A Biblical Theology of Mission.* NSBT 11. Downers Grove: InterVarsity, 2001.
Kreider, Glenn R. "What Is Dispensationalism? A Proposal." In *Dispensationalism and the History of Redemption: A Developing and Diverse Tradition*, edited by D. Jeffrey Bingham and Glenn R. Kreider, 15–46. Chicago: Moody, 2015.
Kwon, Yon-Gyong. *Eschatology in Galatians: Rethinking Paul's Response to the Crisis in Galatians.* WUNT 2/183. Tübingen, Germany: Mohr Siebeck, 2004.
Kynes, William L. *A Christology of Solidarity: Jesus as the Representative of His People in Matthew.* Lanham, MD: University Press of America, 1991.

Ladd, George Eldon. "Historic Premillennialism." In *The Meaning of the Millennium: Four Views*, edited by Robert G. Clouse, 18–29. Downers Grove: InterVarsity, 1977.

———. "Israel and the Church." *EvQ* 36 (1964) 206–13.

———. *The Presence of the Future: The Eschatology of Biblical Realism*. Rev. ed. Grand Rapids: Eerdmans, 1974.

———. *A Theology of the New Testament*. Rev. ed. Grand Rapids: Eerdmans, 1993.

Lampe, G. W. H. "The Reasonableness of Typology." In *Essays on Typology*. Studies in Biblical Theology 22. Naperville, IL: Alec R. Allenson, 1957.

———. "Typological Exegesis." *Theology* 56 (1953) 201–8.

Lampe, G. W. H., and K. J. Woollcombe. *Essays on Typology*. Studies in Biblical Theology 22. Naperville, IL: Alec R. Allenson, 1957.

LaRondelle, Hans K. *The Israel of God in Prophecy: Principles of Interpretation*. Berrien Springs, MI: Andrews University Press, 1983.

———. *Our Creator Redeemer: An Introduction to Biblical Covenant Theology*. Berrien Springs, MI: Andrews University Press, 2005.

Lee, Chee-Chiew. "גוים [sic] in Genesis 35:11 and the Abrahamic Promise of Blessings for the Nations." *JETS* 52 (2009) 467–82.

Legarth, Peter V. "Typology and Its Theological Basis." *EJT* 5 (1996) 143–55.

Leithart, Peter J. *Deep Exegesis: The Mystery of Reading Scripture*. Waco, TX: Baylor University Press, 2009.

Lemke, Werner E. "Circumcision of the Heart: The Journey of a Biblical Metaphor." In *A God So Near: Essays on Old Testament Theology in Honor of Patrick D. Miller*, edited by Brent A. Strawn and Nancy R. Bowen, 299–319. Winona Lake, IN: Eisenbrauns, 2003.

Lessing, R. Reed. "Isaiah's Servants in Chapters 40–55: Clearing up the Confusion." *CJ* 37 (2011) 130–34.

Letham, Robert. "'Not a Covenant of Works in Disguise' (Herman Bavinck): The Place of the Mosaic Covenant in Redemptive History." *MAJT* 24 (2013) 143–77.

———. *Union with Christ: In Scripture, History, and Theology*. Phillipsburg, NJ: P & R, 2011.

———. *The Work of Christ*. Contours of Christian Theology. Downers Grove: InterVarsity, 1993.

Levering, Matthew. "Readings on the Rock: Typological Exegesis in Contemporary Scholarship." *Modern Theology* 28 (2012) 707–31.

Liefield, Walter L., and David W. Pao. *Luke*. In vol. 10 of *The Expositor's Bible Commentary*. Rev ed. Edited by Tremper Longman III and David E. Garland, 19–355. Grand Rapids: Zondervan, 2007.

Lightner, Robert. "Covenantism and Dispensationalism." *JMT* 3 (1999) 62–74.

Lim, Bo H. *The 'Way of the Lord' in the Book of Isaiah*. LHB/OTS 522. New York: T & T Clark, 2010.

Lincoln, Andrew T. "The Church and Israel in Ephesians 2." *CBQ* 49 (1987) 605–24.

———. *Ephesians*. WBC, vol. 42. Dallas: Word, 1990.

———. *Paradise Now and Not Yet: Studies in the Role of the Heavenly Dimension in Paul's Thought with Special Reference to His Eschatology*. SNTSMS 43. Cambridge: Cambridge University Press, 1981.

Lindsey, Hal. *The Late Great Plant Earth*. Grand Rapids: Zondervan, 1970.

Lints, Richard. *The Fabric of Theology: A Prolegomenon to Evangelical Theology.* Grand Rapids: Eerdmans, 1993.

Lioy, Dan. "Progressive Covenantalism as an Integrating Motif of Scripture." *Conspectus* 1 (2006) 81–107.

Litwak, Kenneth D. "The Use of Quotations from Isaiah 52:13—53:12 in the New Testament." *JETS* 26 (1983) 385–94.

Loden, Lisa, Peter Walker, and Michael Wood, eds. *The Bible and the Land: An Encounter.* Jerusalem: Musalaha, 2000.

Longenecker, Bruce. *The Triumphs of Abraham's God: The Transformation of Identity in Galatians.* Edinburgh: T & T Clark, 1998.

Longenecker, Richard N. *Biblical Exegesis in the Apostolic Period.* 2nd ed. Grand Rapids: Eerdmans, 1999.

———. *Galatians.* WBC, vol. 41. Nashville: Thomas Nelson, 1990.

Louth, Andrew. *Discerning the Mystery: An Essay on the Nature of Theology.* New York: Oxford University Press, 1983.

Lucas, Richard J. "The Dispensational Appeal to Romans 11 and the Nature of Israel's Future Salvation." In *Progressive Covenantalism: Charting a Course between Dispensational and Covenantal Theologies,* edited by Stephen J. Wellum and Brent E. Parker, 235–53. Nashville: B & H, 2016.

Macaskill, Grant. *Union with Christ in the New Testament.* Oxford: Oxford University Press, 2013.

Malone, Fred A. *The Baptism of Disciples Alone: A Covenantal Argument for Credobaptism versus Paedobaptism.* 2nd ed. Cape Coral, FL: Founders, 2007.

Mangina, Joseph L. "God, Israel, and Ecclesia in the Apocalypse." In *Revelation and the Politics of Apocalyptic Interpretation,* edited by Richard B. Hays and Stefan Alkier, 85–103. Waco, TX: Baylor University Press, 2012.

Mappes, David, and H. Wayne House. "A Biblical and Theological Discussion of Traditional Dispensational Premillennialism." *JMT* 17 (2013) 5–56.

Markus, R. A. "Presuppositions of the Typological Approach to Scripture." *CQR* 158 (1957) 442–51.

Marsh, Cory M. "A Dynamic Relationship: Christ, the Covenants, and Israel." *MSJ* 30 (2019) 257–75.

Marsh, Herbert. *Lectures on the Criticism and Interpretation of the Bible.* London: J. G. & F. Rivington, 1838.

Marshall, I. Howard. "Church." In *Dictionary of Jesus and the Gospels.* Edited by Joel B. Green, Scot McKnight, and I. Howard Marshall. Downers Grove: InterVarsity, 1992.

Martens, Peter W. "Origen against History? Reconsidering the Critique of Allegory." *Modern Theology* 28 (2012) 635–56.

———. "Revisiting the Allegory/Typology Distinction: The Case of Origen." *Journal of Early Christian Studies* 16 (2008) 283–317.

Martin, Oren R. *Bound for the Promised Land: The Land Promise in God's Redemptive Plan.* NSBT 34. Downers Grove: InterVarsity, 2015.

Master, John R. "The New Covenant." In *Issues in Dispensationalism,* edited by Wesley R. Willis and John R. Master, 93–110. Chicago: Moody, 1994.

Maston, Jason. "How Wrong Were the Disciples about the Kingdom? Thoughts on Acts 1:6." *Expository Times* 126 (2015) 169–78.

BIBLIOGRAPHY

Mathison, Keith A. *Dispensationalism: Rightly Dividing the People of God?* Phillipsburg, NJ: P & R, 1995.

Mayo, Philip L. *"Those Who Call Themselves Jews": The Church and Judaism in the Apocalypse of John.* Princeton Theological Monograph Series 60. Eugene, OR: Pickwick, 2006.

Mbuvi, Andrew M. *Temple, Exile and Identity in 1 Peter.* LNTS 345. New York: T & T Clark, 2007.

McCartney, Dan, and Charles Clayton. *Let the Reader Understand: A Guide to Interpreting and Applying the Bible.* 2nd ed. Phillipsburg, NJ: P & R, 2002.

McComiskey, Thomas Edward. *The Covenants of Promise: A Theology of the Old Testaments Covenants.* Grand Rapids: Eerdmans, 1985.

McGowan, A. T. B. *Adam, Christ and Covenant: Exploring Headship Theology.* London: InterVarsity, 2016.

McKay, David. *The Bond of Love: Covenant Theology and the Contemporary World.* Fearn, Scotland: Christian Focus, 2001.

McKelvey, R. J. *The New Temple: The Church in the New Testament.* Oxford Theological Monographs. Oxford: Oxford University Press, 1969.

———. "Temple." In *NDBT*, edited by T. Desmond Alexander and Brian S. Rosner, 806–11. Downers Grove: InterVarsity, 2000.

McKnight, Scot. "Jesus and the Twelve." In *Key Events in the Life of the Historical Jesus: A Collaborative Exploration of Context and Coherence*, edited by Darrell L. Bock and Robert L. Webb, 181–214. Grand Rapids: Eerdmans, 2010.

McManigal, Daniel. *Encountering Christ in the Covenants: An Introduction to Covenant Theology.* West Linn, OR: Monergism, 201.

Meadors, Gary T., ed. *Four Views on Moving beyond the Bible to Theology.* Grand Rapids: Zondervan, 2009.

Meek, James A. *The Gentile Mission in Old Testament Citations in Acts: Text, Hermeneutic and Purpose.* LNTS 385. New York: T & T Clark, 2008.

———. "Toward a Biblical Typology." M.Th. thesis, Westminster Theological Seminary, 1981.

Meier, John P. "Jesus, the Twelve and the Restoration of Israel." In *Restoration: Old Testament, Jewish, and Christian Perspectives*, edited by James M. Scott, 365–404. JSJSup 72. Leiden, Netherlands: Brill, 2001.

Menninger, Richard E. *Israel and the Church in the Gospel of Matthew.* American University Studies 7. Theology and Religion. Vol. 162. New York: Peter Lang, 1994.

Merkle, Benjamin L. *Discontinuity to Continuity: A Survey of Dispensational & Covenant Theologies.* Bellingham, WA: Lexham, 2020.

———. "Old Testament Restoration Prophecies Regarding the Nation of Israel: Literal or Symbolic?" *SBJT* 14 (2010) 14–25.

———. "Romans 11 and the Future of Ethnic Israel." *JETS* 43 (2000) 709–21.

———. "A Typological Non-Future-Mass-Conversion View." In *Three Views on Israel and the Church: Perspectives on Romans 9-11*, edited by Jared Compton and Andrew David Naselli, 161–208. Grand Rapids: Kregel, 2018.

Merrill, Eugene H. *Everlasting Dominion: A Theology of the Old Testament.* Nashville: B & H, 2006.

Meyer, Jason C. *The End of the Law: Mosaic Covenant in Pauline Theology.* NACSBT. Nashville: B & H, 2009.

Minear, Paul S. *Images of the Church in the New Testament*. Philadelphia: Westminster Press, 1960. Reprint, Louisville: Westminster John Knox, 2004.

Moberly, R. W. L. "What Is Theological Interpretation of Scripture?" *JTI* 3 (2009) 161–78.

Moo, Douglas J. "Creation and New Creation." *BBR* 20 (2010) 39–60.

———. *The Letter to the Romans*. NICNT. 2nd ed. Grand Rapids: Eerdmans, 2018.

———. *Galatians*. BECNT. Grand Rapids: Baker, 2013.

———. "Paul's Universalizing Hermeneutic." *SBJT* 11 (2007) 62–90.

———. "The Problem of *Sensus Plenior*." In *Hermeneutics, Authority, and Canon*, edited by D. A. Carson and John D. Woodbridge, 179–211. Grand Rapids: Zondervan, 1986.

Moo, Douglas J., and Andrew David Naselli, "The Problem of the New Testament's Use of the Old Testament." In *The Enduring Authority of the Christian Scriptures*, edited by D. A. Carson, 702–46. Grand Rapids: Eerdmans, 2016.

Moore, Russell D. *The Kingdom of Christ: The New Evangelical Perspective*. Wheaton, IL: Crossway, 2004.

Moore, Thomas S. "'To the End of the Earth:' The Geographical and Ethnic Universalism of Acts 1:8 in Light of Isaianic Influence on Luke." *JETS* 40 (1997) 389–99.

———. "The Lucan Great Commission and the Isaianic Servant." *BibSac* 154 (1997) 47–60.

Morgan, Christopher W., and Robert A. Peterson, eds. *The Kingdom of God*. Wheaton, IL: Crossway, 2012.

Moritz, Thorsten. *A Profound Mystery: The Use of the OT in Ephesians*. NovTSup 85. Leiden, Netherlands: Brill, 1996.

Motyer, J. Alec. *The Prophecy of Isaiah: An Introduction and Commentary*. Downers Grove: InterVarsity, 1993.

Motyer, Stephen. "Israel, New." In *Evangelical Dictionary of Theology*. 2nd ed. Edited by Walter A. Elwell. Grand Rapids: Baker, 2001.

Muller, Richard A. *Holy Scripture: The Cognitive Foundation of Theology*. Vol. 2. *Post Reformation Reformed Dogmatics: The Rise and Development of Reformed Orthodoxy, ca. 1520 to ca. 1725*. 2nd ed. Grand Rapids: Baker, 2003.

Munayer, Salim J., and Lisa Loden, eds. *The Land Cries Out: Theology of the Land in the Israeli-Palestinian Context*. Eugene, OR: Cascade, 2012.

Murray, John. *Collected Writings of John Murray*. 4 Vols. Carlisle, PA: Banner of Truth, 1982.

———. *The Covenant of Grace: A Biblico-Theological Study*. London: Tyndale, 1953. Reprint, Phillipsburg, NJ: P & R, 1988.

———. *Redemption Accomplished and Applied*. Grand Rapids: Eerdmans, 1955.

Naselli, Andrew David. "D. A. Carson's Theological Method." *SBET* 29 (2011) 245–74.

———. *From Typology to Doxology: Paul's Use of Isaiah and Job in Romans 11:34–35*. Eugene, OR: Pickwick, 2012.

Neill, Jeffrey D. "The Newness of the New Covenant." In *The Case for Covenantal Infant Baptism*, edited by Gregg Strawbridge, 127–55. Phillipsburg, NJ: P & R, 2003.

Nichols, Stephen J. "The Dispensational View of the Davidic Kingdom: A Response to Progressive Dispensationalism." *MSJ* 7 (1996) 213–39.

Nicole, Roger R. "Patrick Fairbairn and Biblical Hermeneutics as Related to the Quotations of the Old Testament in the New." In *Hermeneutics, Inerrancy, and the*

Bible, edited by Earl D. Radmacher and Robert D. Preus, 765–76. Grand Rapids: Zondervan, 1984.

Niehaus, Jeffrey J. "An Argument against Theologically Constructed Covenants." *JETS* 50 (2007) 259–73.

Ninow, Friedbert. *Indicators of Typology Within the Old Testament: The Exodus Motif.* Friedensauer Schriftenreihe: Reihe I, Theologie, Band 4. Berlin: Peter Lang, 2001.

O'Brien, P. T. "The Church as a Heavenly and Eschatological Entity." In *The Church in the Bible and the World: An International Study*, edited by D. A. Carson, 88–119. Grand Rapids: Baker, 1987. Reprint, Eugene, OR: Wipf and Stock, 2002.

———. *The Letter to the Ephesians*. PNTC. Grand Rapids: Eerdmans, 1999.

———. *The Letter to the Hebrews*. PNTC. Grand Rapids: Eerdmans, 2010.

———. "The New Covenant and Its Perfect Mediator." In *The Perfect Saviour: Key Themes in Hebrews*, edited by Jonathan Griffiths, 13–33. Nottingham, UK: InterVarsity, 2012.

O'Keefe, John J., and R. R. Reno. *Sanctified Vision: An Introduction to Early Christian Interpretation of the Bible*. Baltimore: Johns Hopkins University, 2005.

Okoye, James Chukwuma. *Israel and the Nations: A Mission Theology of the Old Testament*. Maryknoll, NY: Orbis, 2006.

Olsen, Glenn W. "Allegory, Typology, and Symbol: The *Sensus Spiritalis*, Part I: Definitions and Earliest History." *Communio: International Catholic Review* 4 (1977) 161–89.

———. "Allegory, Typology, and Symbol: The *Sensus Spiritalis*, Part II: Early Church through Origen." *Communio: International Catholic Review* 4 (1977) 357–84.

Orlinsky, Harry M. "The Biblical Concept of the Land of Israel: Cornerstone of the Covenant between God and Israel." In *The Land of Israel: Jewish Perspectives*, edited by Lawrence A. Hoffman, 27–64. Notre Dame: University of Notre Dame Press, 1986.

Osborne, Grant R. "Type; Typology." In *ISBE*. Edited by Geoffrey W. Bromiley. Rev. ed. Grand Rapids: Eerdmans, 1988.

Oss, Douglas A. "Canon as Context: The Function of *Sensus Plenior* in Evangelical Hermeneutics." *GTJ* 9 (1988) 105–27.

Oswalt, John N. *The Book of Isaiah: Chapters 40–66*. NICOT. Grand Rapids: Eerdmans, 1998.

———. "The Nations in Isaiah: Friend or Foe; Servant or Partner." *BBR* 16 (2006) 41–51.

Ounsworth, Richard. *Joshua Typology in the New Testament*. WUNT 2/328. Tübingen, Germany: Mohr Siebeck, 2012.

Packer, J. I. "Biblical Authority, Hermeneutics and Inerrancy." In *Jerusalem and Athens: Critical Discussions on the Theology and Apologetics of Cornelius Van Til*, edited by E. R. Geehan, 141–53. Nutley, NJ: P & R, 1971.

———. "An Evangelical View of Progressive Revelation." In *Evangelical Roots: A Tribute to Wilbur Smith*, edited by Kenneth S. Kantzer, 143–58. Nashville: Thomas Nelson, 1978.

———. "Infallible Scripture and the Role of Hermeneutics." In *Scripture and Truth*, edited by D. A. Carson and John D. Woodbridge, 321–56. Grand Rapids: Baker, 1992.

Pancaro, Severino. "The Relationship of the Church to Israel in the Gospel of St John." *NTS* 21 (1975) 396–405.

Pao, David W. *Acts and the Isaianic New Exodus*. Biblical Studies Library. Grand Rapids: Baker, 2002.

———. "Jesus's Ascension and the Lukan Account of the Restoration of Israel." In *Ascent into Heaven in Luke-Acts: New Explorations of Luke's Narrative Hinge*, edited by David K. Bryan and David W. Pao, 137–55. Minneapolis: Fortress, 2016.

Pao, David W., and Eckhard J. Schnabel. "Luke." In *Commentary on the New Testament Use of the Old Testament*, edited by G. K. Beale and D. A. Carson, 251–414. Grand Rapids: Baker, 2007.

Parle, Joseph. *Dispensational Development and Departure: Comparing Classical, Essentialist, and Progressive Dispensational Models*. Lee's Summit, MO: Exegetica, 2020.

Parsons, Michael. "'In Christ' in Paul." *Vox Evangelica* 18 (1988) 25–44.

Pate, C. Marvin, et al., *The Story of Israel: A Biblical Theology*. Downers Grove: InterVarsity, 2004.

Pattemore, Stephen. *The People of God in the Apocalypse: Discourse, Structure, and Exegesis*. SNTSMS 128. Cambridge: Cambridge University Press, 2004.

Patterson, Richard D., and Michael Travers. "Contours of the Exodus Motif in Jesus' Earthly Ministry." *WTJ* 66 (2004) 25–47.

Pennington, Jonathan T. "Heaven, Earth, and a New Genesis: Theological Cosmology in Matthew." In *Cosmology and New Testament Theology*, edited by Jonathan T. Pennington and Sean M. McDonough, 28–44. LNTS 355. New York: T & T Clark, 2008.

Pentecost, J. Dwight. *Things to Come: A Study in Biblical Eschatology*. Findlay, OH: Dunham, 1958.

———. *Thy Kingdom Come: Tracing God's Program and Covenant Promises throughout History*. Grand Rapids: Kregel, 1995.

Perriman, Andrew C. "Typology in Paul." *Theology* 90 (1987) 200–6.

Peterson, David G. *The Acts of the Apostles*. PNTC. Grand Rapids: Eerdmans, 2009.

———. "The New Temple: Christology and Ecclesiology in Ephesians and 1 Peter." In *Heaven on Earth: The Temple in Biblical Theology*, edited by T. D. Alexander and Simon Gathercole, 161–76. Carlisle, UK: Paternoster, 2004.

———. *Transformed by God: New Covenant Life and Ministry*. Nottingham, UK: InterVarsity, 2012.

Pettegrew, Larry D. "The New Covenant." *MSJ* 10 (1999) 251–70.

Philpot, Joshua. "See the True and Better Adam: Typology and Human Origins." *Bulletin of Ecclesial Theology* 5 (2018) 79–103.

———. "Was Joseph a Type of Daniel? Typological Correspondence in Genesis 37–50 and Daniel 1–6." *JETS* 61 (2018) 681–96.

Piotrowski, Nicholas G. *Matthew's New David at the End of Exile: A Socio-Rhetorical Study of Scriptural Quotations*. NovTSup 170. Leiden, Netherlands: Brill, 2016.

Piotrowski, Nicholas G., with Ryan Johnson. "One Spirit, One Body, One Temple: Paul's Corporate Temple Language in 1 Corinthians 6." *JETS* 65 (2022) 733–52.

Porter, Stanley E. "What Is Theological Interpretation of Scripture, and Is It Hermeneutically Robust Enough for the Task to Which It Has Been Appointed?" In *Horizons in Hermeneutics: A Festschrift in Honor of Anthony C. Thiselton*, edited by Stanley E. Porter and Matthew R. Malcom, 234–67. Grand Rapids: Eerdmans, 2013.

Powers, Philip E. "Prefigurement and the Hermeneutics of Prophetic Typology." Ph.D. diss., Dallas Theological Seminary, 1995.
Poythress, Vern Sheridan. "Divine Meaning of Scripture." *WTJ* 48 (1986) 241–79.
———. *Understanding Dispensationalists*. 2nd ed. Phillipsburg, NJ: P & R, 1994.
Pratt, Jonathan. "The 'Israel of God' in Galatians 6:16." *DBSJ* 23 (2018) 59–75.
Pratt, Richard L., Jr. "Infant Baptism in the New Covenant." In *The Case for Covenantal Infant Baptism*, edited by Gregg Strawbridge, 156–74. Phillipsburg, NJ: P & R, 2003.
———. "To the Jew First: A Reformed Perspective." In *To the Jew First: The Case for Jewish Evangelism in Scripture and History*, edited by Darrell L. Bock and Mitch Glaser, 168–88. Grand Rapids: Kregel, 2008.
Provan, Iain. *The Reformation and the Right Reading of Scripture*. Waco, TX: Baylor University Press, 2017.
Puckett, David L. *John Calvin's Exegesis of the Old Testament*. Louisville: Westminster John Knox, 1995.
Pugh, T. Maurice. "Dispensationalism and Views of Redemptive History." In *Dispensationalism and the History of Redemption: A Developing and Diverse Tradition*, edited by D. Jeffrey Bingham and Glenn R. Kreider, 219–48. Chicago: Moody, 2015.
Pyne, Robert A. "The 'Seed,' the Spirit, and the Blessing of Abraham." *BibSac* 152 (1995) 211–22.
Quarles, Charles L. *A Theology of Matthew: Jesus Revealed as Deliverer, King, and Incarnate Creator*. Explorations in Biblical Theology. Phillipsburg, NJ: P & R, 2013.
Ramm, Bernard. *Protestant Biblical Interpretation: A Textbook of Hermeneutics*. 3rd ed. Grand Rapids: Baker, 1970.
Ray, Charles A., Jr. "The Identity of the 'Israel of God.'" *The Theological Educator* 50 (1994) 105–14.
Reicke, Bo. "Synoptic Prophecies and the Destruction of Jerusalem." In *Studies in New Testament and Early Christian Literature: Essays in Honor of Allen P. Wikgren*, edited by David E. Aune, 121–34. NovTSup 33. Leiden, Netherlands: E. J. Brill, 1972.
Reisinger, John G. *Abraham's Four Seeds*. Frederick, MD: New Covenant Media, 1998.
Renihan, Samuel. *The Mystery of Christ, His Covenant, and His Kingdom*. Cape Coral, FL: Founders, 2019.
Reno, R. R. "From Letter to Spirit." *IJST* 13 (2011) 463–74.
Reventlow, Henning Graf. *Problems of Biblical Theology in the Twentieth Century*. Translated by John Bowden. Philadelphia: Fortress, 1986.
Reymond, Robert L. "The Traditional Covenantal View." In *Perspectives on Israel and the Church: 4 Views*, edited by Chad Brand, 17–68. Nashville: B & H, 2015.
———. *A New Systematic Theology of the Christian Faith*. 2nd ed. Nashville: Thomas Nelson 1998.
Ribbens, Benjamin J. "Typology of Types: Typology in Dialogue." *JTI* 5 (2011) 81–95.
Riccardi, Michael. "The Seed of Abraham: A Theological Analysis of Galatians 3 and Its Implications for Israel." *MSJ* 25 (2014) 51–64.
Richardson, Peter. *Israel in the Apostolic Church*. SNTSMS 10. Cambridge: Cambridge University Press, 1969.
Ridderbos, Herman N. *The Gospel according to John: A Theological Commentary*. Translated by John Vriend. Grand Rapids: Eerdmans, 1997.

———. *Paul: An Outline of His Theology*. Translated by John Richard De Witt. Grand Rapids: Eerdmans, 1975.

Riddlebarger, Kim. *A Case for Amillennialism: Understanding the End Times*. Grand Rapids: Baker, 2003.

Roberts, Vaughan. *God's Big Picture: Tracing the Storyline of the Bible*. Downers Grove: InterVarsity, 2002.

Robertson, O. Palmer. *The Christ of the Covenants*. Phillipsburg, NJ: P & R, 1980.

———. *The Christ of the Prophets*. Phillipsburg, NJ: P & R, 2004.

———. "The Hermeneutics of Continuity." In *Continuity and Discontinuity: Perspectives on the Relationship between the Old and New Testaments*, edited by John S. Feinberg, 89–108. Wheaton, IL: Crossway, 1988.

———. "Is There a Distinctive Future for Ethnic Israel in Romans 11?" In *Perspectives on Evangelical Theology*, edited by Kenneth S. Kanzer and Stanley N. Gundry, 209–27. Grand Rapids: Baker, 1979.

———. *The Israel of God: Yesterday, Today, and Tomorrow*. Phillipsburg, NJ: P & R, 2000.

———. "The Outlook for Biblical Theology." In *Toward a Theology for the Future*, edited by David F. Wells and Clark H. Pinnock, 65–91. Carol Stream, IL: Creation House, 1971.

Roehrs, Walter R. "The Typological Use of the Old Testament in the New Testament." *CJ* 10 (1984) 204–16.

Rogers, Cleon L., Jr. "The Davidic Covenant in Acts-Revelation." *BibSac* 151 (1994) 71–84.

———. "The Davidic Covenant in the Gospels." *BibSac* 150 (1993) 458–78.

Rosner, Brian S. "Biblical Theology." In *NDBT*, edited by T. Desmond Alexander and Brian S. Rosner, 3–11. Downers Grove: InterVarsity, 2000.

Routledge, Robin. "The Exodus and Biblical Theology." In *Reverberations of the Exodus in Scripture*, edited by R. Michael Fox, 187–209. Eugene, OR: Pickwick, 2014.

———. *Old Testament Theology: A Thematic Approach*. Downers Grove: InterVarsity, 2008.

———. "Replacement or Fulfillment? Re-Applying Old Testament Designations of Israel to the Church." *STR* 4 (2013) 137–54.

———. "The Spirit and the Future in the Old Testament: Restoration and Renewal." In *Presence, Power and Promise: The Role of the Spirit of God in the Old Testament*, edited by David G. Firth and Paul D. Wegner, 346–67. Downers Grove: InterVarsity, 2011.

Rudolph, David. "Zionism in Pauline Literature: Does Paul Eliminate Particularity for Israel and the Land in His Portrayal of Salvation Available for All the World?" In *The New Christian Zionism: Fresh Perspectives on Israel and the Land*, edited by Gerald R. McDermott, 167–94. Downers Grove: InterVarsity, 2016.

Ruthven, Jon. "'This Is My Covenant with Them': Isaiah 59.19–21 as the Programmatic Prophecy of the New Covenant in the Acts of the Apostles (Part I)." *Journal of Pentecostal Theology* 17 (2008) 32 47.

———. "'This Is My Covenant with Them': Isaiah 59.19–21 as the Programmatic Prophecy of the New Covenant in the Acts of the Apostles (Part II)." *Journal of Pentecostal Theology* 17 (2008) 219–37.

Ryrie, Charles C. *Dispensationalism*. Rev. ed. Chicago: Moody, 2007.

———. "Update on Dispensationalism." In *Issues in Dispensationalism*, edited by Wesley R. Willis and John R. Master, 15–28. Chicago: Moody, 1994.

Sailhamer, John H. "Evidence from Isaiah 2." In *A Case for Premillennialism: A New Consensus*, edited by Donald K. Campbell and Jeffrey L. Townsend, 79–102. Chicago: Moody, 1992.

Salier, Bill. "The Temple in the Gospel according to John." In *Heaven on Earth: The Temple in Biblical Theology*, edited by T. Desmond Alexander and Simon Gathercole, 121–34. Carlisle, UK: Paternoster, 2004.

Salter, Martin. "The Abrahamic Covenant in Reformed Baptist Perspective." *Themelios* 40 (2015) 35–49.

Sanders, E. P. *Paul and Palestinian Judaism*. Minneapolis: Fortress, 1977.

Saucy, Mark R. "Israel as a Necessary Theme in Biblical Theology." In *The People, the Land, and the Future of Israel: Israel and the Jewish People in the Plan of God*, edited by Darrell L. Bock and Mitch Glaser, 169–81. Grand Rapids: Kregel, 2014.

———. *The Kingdom of God in the Teaching of Jesus in 20th Century Theology*. Dallas: Word, 1997.

Saucy, Robert L. *The Case for Progressive Dispensationalism: The Interface Between Dispensational and Non-Dispensational Theology*. Grand Rapids: Zondervan, 1993.

———. "The Church as the Mystery of God." In *Dispensationalism, Israel and the Church: The Search for Definition*, edited by Craig A. Blaising and Darrell L. Bock, 127–55. Grand Rapids: Zondervan, 1992.

———. "Contemporary Dispensational Thought." *Theological Students Fellowship Bulletin* 7 (1984) 10–11.

———. "Does the Apostle Paul Reverse the Prophetic Tradition of the Salvation of Israel and the Nations?" In *Building on the Foundations of Evangelical Theology: Essays in Honor of John S. Feinberg*, edited by Gregg R. Allison and Stephen J. Wellum, 66–90. Wheaton, IL: Crossway, 2015.

———. "Is Christ the Fulfillment of National Israel's Prophesies? Yes and No!" *MSJ* 28 (2017) 17–39.

———. "Israel and the Church: A Case for Discontinuity." In *Continuity and Discontinuity: Perspectives on the Relationship between the Old and New Testaments*, edited by John S. Feinberg, 239–59. Wheaton, IL: Crossway, 1988.

———. "The Progressive Dispensational View." In *Perspectives on Israel and the Church: 4 Views*, edited by Chad O. Brand, 155–208. Nashville: B & H, 2015.

Scacewater, Todd A. "The Predictive Nature of Typology in John 12:37–43." *WTJ* 75 (2013) 129–43.

Schnabel, Eckhard J. *Acts*. ZECNT. Grand Rapids: Zondervan, 2012.

———. "The Community of the Followers of Jesus in 1 Corinthians." In *The New Testament Church: The Challenge of Developing Ecclesiologies*, edited by John P. Harrison and James D. Dvorak, 103–29. McMaster Biblical Studies Series 1. Eugene, OR: Pickwick, 2012.

———. *40 Questions about the End Times*. Grand Rapids: Kregel Academic, 2011.

———. "Israel, the People of God, and the Nations." *JETS* 45 (2002) 35–57.

Schodde, G. H. "Allegory." In *ISBE*. Edited by Geoffrey W. Bromiley. Rev. ed. Grand Rapids: Eerdmans, 1979

Schreiner, Thomas R. "The Church as the New Israel and the Future of Ethnic Israel in Paul." *Studia Biblica et Theologica* 13 (1983) 17–38.

———. *1, 2 Peter, Jude*. NAC, vol. 37. Nashville: B & H, 2003.
———. *Galatians*. ZECNT. Grand Rapids: Zondervan, 2010.
———. *Hebrews*. Evangelical Biblical Theology Commentary. Bellingham, WA: Lexham, 2020.
———. *The King in His Beauty: A Biblical Theology of the Old and New Testament*. Grand Rapids: Baker, 2013.
———. *New Testament Theology: Magnifying God in Christ*. Grand Rapids: Baker, 2008.
———. *Paul, Apostle of God's Glory in Christ A Pauline Theology*. Downers Grove: InterVarsity, 2001.
———. *Romans*. BECNT. 2nd ed. Grand Rapids: Baker, 2018.
———. *Run to Win the Prize: Perseverance in the New Testament*. Wheaton, IL: Crossway, 2010.
Schreiner, Thomas R., and Ardel B. Caneday. *The Race Set before Us: A Biblical Theology of Perseverance and Assurance*. Downers Grove: InterVarsity, 2001.
Schrock, David. "What Designates a Valid Type? A Christotelic, Covenantal Proposal." *STR* 5 (2014) 3–26.
Schultz, Richard L. "Isaiah, Book of." In *DTIB*, edited by Kevin J. Vanhoozer, 336–44. Grand Rapids: Baker, 2005.
———. "The King in the Book of Isaiah." In *The Lord's Anointed: Interpretation of Old Testament Messianic Texts*, edited by Philip E. Satterthwaite et al., 141–65. Grand Rapids: Baker, 1995.
———. "Nationalism and Universalism in Isaiah." In *Interpreting Isaiah: Issues and Approaches*, edited by David G. Firth and H. G. M. Williamson, 122–44. Downers Grove: InterVarsity, 2009.
Scobie, Charles H. H. "The Challenge of Biblical Theology." *TynBul* 42 (1991) 31–61.
———. "Israel and the Nations: An Essay in Biblical Theology." *TynBul* 43 (1994) 283–305.
———. *The Ways of Our God: An Approach to Biblical Theology*. Grand Rapids: Eerdmans, 2003.
Scott, James M. *Adoption as Sons of God: An Exegetical Investigation into the Background of ΥΙΟΘΕΣΙΑ in the Pauline Corpus*. WUNT 2/48. Tübingen, Germany: Mohr, 1992.
———. *Paul and the Nations: The Old Testament and Jewish Background of Paul's Mission to the Nations with Special Reference to the Destination of Galatians*. WUNT 84. Tübingen, Germany: Mohr Siebeck, 1995.
Seifrid, Mark. Review of *Paul and Union with Christ: An Exegetical and Theological Study* by Constantine R. Campbell. *Themelios* 38 (2013) 262–64.
———. "Scripture and Identity in Galatians." In *All That the Prophets Have Declared: The Appropriation of Scripture in the Emergence of Christianity*, edited by Matthew R. Malcolm, 95–114. Crownhill, UK: Paternoster, 2015.
Seitz, Christopher R. *Figured Out: Typology and Providence in Christian Scripture*. Louisville: Westminster John Knox, 2001.
Shead, Andrew G. "The New Covenant and Pauline Hermeneutics." In *The Gospel to the Nations: Perspectives on Paul's Mission*, edited by Peter Bolt and Mark Thompson, 33–49. Downers Grove: InterVarsity, 2000.

Sherwood, Aaron. *Paul and the Restoration of Humanity in Light of Ancient Jewish Traditions*. Ancient Judaism and Early Christianity 82. Leiden, Netherlands: Brill, 2013.

Sibley, Jim R. "You Talkin' to Me? 1 Peter 2:4–10 and a Theology of Israel." *SWJT* 59 (2016) 59–75.

Silva, Moisés. "Galatians." In *Commentary on the New Testament Use of the Old Testament*, edited by G. K. Beale and D. A. Carson, 785–812. Grand Rapids: Baker, 2007.

———. "Has the Church Misread the Bible?" In *Foundations of Contemporary Interpretation*. Edited by Moisés Silva. Grand Rapids: Zondervan, 1996.

Sizer, Stephen. *Christian Zionism: Road-Map to Armageddon?* Leicester, UK: InterVarsity, 2004.

Smith, Adrian T. "The Fifth Gospel." In *Eyes to See, Ears to Hear: Essays in Memory of J. Alan Groves*, edited by Peter Enns, Douglas J. Green, and Michael B. Kelly, 77–91. Phillipsburg, NJ: P & R, 2010.

Smith, Gary V. "Structure and Purpose in Genesis 1–11." *JETS* 20 (1977) 307–19.

Son, Sang-Won (Aaron). *Corporate Elements in Pauline Anthropology: A Study of Selected Terms, Idioms, and Concepts in the Light of Paul's Usage and Background*. Analecta Biblica 148. Rome: Editrice Pontificio Istituto Biblico, 2001.

Soulen, R. Kendall. *The God of Israel and Christian Theology*. Minneapolis: Fortress, 1996.

Stackhouse, John G., Jr., ed. *Evangelical Futures: A Conversation on Theological Method*. Grand Rapids: Baker, 2000.

Stallard, Michael, ed. *Dispensational Understanding of the New Covenant: Three Views*. Schaumburg, IL: Regular Baptist, 2012.

———. "Literal Interpretation, Theological Method, and the Essence of Dispensationalism." *JMT* 1 (1997) 5–36.

Stanley, Christopher D. "'The Redeemer Will Come ἐκ Σιών': Romans 11.26–27 Revisited." In *Paul and the Scriptures of Israel*, edited by Craig A. Evans and James A. Sanders, 118–41. JSNTSup 83. Sheffield: JSOT, 1993.

Stanley, Walter D. "Wood, Sand and Stars: Structure and Theology in Gn 22:1–19." *TJT* 3 (1987) 301–30.

Staples, Jason A. "What Do the Gentiles Have to Do with 'All Israel'? A Fresh Look at Romans 11:25–27." *JBL* 130 (2011) 371–90.

Stark, J. David. "To Your Seed I Will Give . . . : The Land(s) Promised to Abraham in Genesis and Second Temple Judaism." *BBR* 30 (2020) 1–21.

Starling, David. "Ephesians and the Hermeneutics of the New Exodus." In *Reverberations of the Exodus in Scripture*, edited by R. Michael Fox, 139–59. Eugene, OR: Pickwick, 2014.

———. "Justified Allegory: Scripture, Rhetoric, and Reason in Galatians 4:21—5:1." *JTI* 9 (2015) 227–45.

———. *Not My People: Gentiles as Exiles in Pauline Hermeneutics*. BZNW 184. Berlin: Walter de Gruyter, 2011.

———. "The Yes to All God's Promises: Jesus, Israel and the Promises of God in Paul's Letters." *RTR* 71 (2012) 185–204.

Steinmann, Andrew E. "Jesus and Possessing the Enemies' Gate (Genesis 22:17–18; 24:60)." *BibSac* 174 (2017) 13–21.

Stek, John H. "Biblical Typology Yesterday and Today." *CTJ* 5 (1970) 133–62.

———. "'Covenant' Overload in Reformed Theology." *CTJ* 29 (1994) 12–41.
Storer, Kevin. "Theological Interpretation and the Spiritual Sense of Scripture: Henri de Lubac's Retrieval of a Christological Hermeneutic of Presence." *JTI* 7 (2013) 79–96.
Storms, Sam. *Kingdom Come: The Amillennial Alternative*. Fearn, Scotland: Christian Focus, 2013.
Stott, John R. W. *The Message of Acts: The Spirit, the Church, and the World*. The Bible Speaks Today. Downers Grove: InterVarsity, 1990.
Strauss, Mark L. *The Davidic Messiah in Luke-Acts: The Promise and its Fulfillment in Lukan Christology*. JSNTSup 110. Sheffield: Sheffield Academic, 1995.
Strawbridge, Gregg, ed. *The Case for Covenant Communion*. Monroe, LA: Athanasius, 2006.
Streett, Andrew. *The Vine and the Son of Man: Eschatological Interpretation of Psalm 80 in Early Judaism*. Minneapolis: Fortress, 2014.
Streett, Daniel R. "As It Was in the Days of Noah: The Prophets' Typological Interpretation of Noah's Flood." *CTR* 5 (2007) 33–51.
Strimple, Robert B. "Amillennialism." In *Three Views of the Millennium and Beyond*, edited by Darrell L. Bock, 83–129. Grand Rapids: Zondervan, 1999.
Stuhlmacher, Peter. "Isaiah 53 in the Gospels and Acts." In *The Suffering Servant: Isaiah 53 in Jewish and Christian Sources*, edited by Bernd Janowski and Peter Stuhlmacher, 147–62. Translated by Daniel P. Bailey. Grand Rapids: Eerdmans, 2004.
Svigel, Michael J. "The History of Dispensationalism in Seven Eras." In *Dispensationalism and the History of Redemption: A Developing and Diverse Tradition*, edited by D. Jeffrey Bingham and Glenn R. Kreider, 69–100. Chicago: Moody, 2015.
Tabb, Brian J. *All Things New: Revelation as Canonical Capstone*. NSBT 48. Downers Grove: InterVarsity, 2019.
———. "Johannine Fulfillment of Scripture: Continuity and Escalation." *BBR* 21 (2011) 495–505.
Tan, Paul Lee. "Symbols and Types in Prophecy." In *An Introduction to Classical Evangelical Hermeneutics: A Guide to History and Practice of Biblical Interpretation*, edited by Mal Couch, 71–84. Grand Rapids: Kregel, 2000.
Taylor, Howard. "The Continuity of the People of God in Old and New Testaments." *SBET* 3 (1985) 13–26.
Taylor, John W. "The Eschatological Interdependence of Jews and Gentiles in Galatians." *TynBul* 63 (2012) 291–316.
Terry, Milton S. *Biblical Hermeneutics: A Treatise on the Interpretation of the Old and New Testaments*. Rev. ed. New York: Methodist Book Concern, 1911.
Thielman, Frank S. *Ephesians*. BECNT. Grand Rapids: Baker, 2010.
Thiessen, Matthew. "Hebrews and the End of the Exodus." *NovT* 49 (2007) 353–69.
Thiselton, Anthony C. *First Corinthians: A Shorter Exegetical and Pastoral Commentary*. Grand Rapids: Eerdmans, 2006.
———. *The First Epistle to the Corinthians: A Commentary on the Greek Text*. NIGTC. Grand Rapids: Eerdmans, 2000.
———. *Hermeneutics: An Introduction*. Grand Rapids: Eerdmans, 2009.
Thomas, Robert L. "The Hermeneutics of Progressive Dispensationalism." *MSJ* 6 (1995) 79–95.

———. "The Mission of Israel and of the Messiah in the Plan of God." In *Israel, the Land and the People: An Evangelical Affirmation of God's Promises*, edited by H. Wayne House, 261–80. Grand Rapids: Kregel, 1998.

———. "The New Testament Use of the Old Testament." In *Dispensationalism Tomorrow & Beyond: A Theological Collection in Honor of Charles C. Ryrie*, edited by Christopher Cone, 165–88. Fort Worth, TX: Tyndale Seminary, 2008.

———. "The Traditional Dispensational View." In *Perspectives on Israel and the Church: 4 Views*, edited by Chad O. Brand, 87–136. Nashville: B & H, 2015.

Thompson, Alan J. *The Acts of the Risen Lord Jesus: Luke's Account of God's Unfolding Plan*. NSBT 27. Downers Grove: InterVarsity, 2011.

Thompson, James W. *The Church according to Paul: Rediscovering the Community Conformed to Christ*. Grand Rapids: Baker, 2014.

Thorsell, Paul R. "The Spirit in the Present Age: Preliminary Fulfillment of the Predicted New Covenant according to Paul." *JETS* 41 (1998) 397–413.

Tidball, Derek. *The Message of the Cross: Wisdom Unsearchable, Love Indestructible*. The Bible Speaks Today. Leicester, UK: InterVarsity, 2001.

Torrance, Thomas F. *Atonement: The Person and Work of Christ*. Edited by Robert T. Walker. Downers Grove: InterVarsity, 2009.

Toussaint, Stanley D. "A Biblical Defense of Dispensationalism." In *Walvoord: A Tribute*, edited by Donald K. Campbell, 81–91. Chicago: Moody, 1982,

———. "Israel and the Church of a Traditional Dispensationalist." In *Three Central Issues in Contemporary Dispensationalism*, edited by Herbert W. Bateman IV, 227–62. Grand Rapids: Kregel, 1999.

Toussaint, Stanley D., and Jay A. Quine. "No, Not Yet: The Contingency of God's Promised Kingdom." *BibSac* 164 (2007) 131–47.

Townsend, Jeffrey L. "Fulfillment of the Land Promise in the Old Testament." *BibSac* 142 (1985) 320–37.

Treat, Jeremy R. *The Crucified King: Atonement and Kingdom in Biblical and Systematic Theology*. Grand Rapids: Zondervan, 2014.

Treier, Daniel J. *Introducing Theological Interpretation of Scripture*. Grand Rapids: Baker, 2008.

———. "Pursuing Wisdom: (Back) Toward Evangelical Spiritual Exegesis." *Crux* 48 (2012) 17–26.

———. "The Superiority of Pre-Critical Exegesis? Sic et Non." *TrinJ* 24 (2003) 77–103.

Trimm, Charlie. "Evangelicals, Theology, and Biblical Interpretation: Reflections on the Theological Interpretation of Scripture." *BBR* 20 (2010) 311–30.

Turner, David L. "'Dubious Evangelicalism?' A Response to John Gerstner's Critique of Dispensationalism." *GTJ* 12 (1991) 263–77.

———. *Matthew*. BECNT. Grand Rapids: Baker, 2008.

———. "Matthew among the Dispensationalists." *JETS* 53 (2010) 697–716.

Turner, Max. *Power from on High: The Spirit in Israel's Restoration and Witness in Luke-Acts*. Journal of Pentecostal Theology Supplement Series 9. Sheffield: Sheffield Academic, 1996.

Turretin, Francis. *Institutes of Elenctic Theology*. Edited by James T. Dennison Jr. Translated by George Musgrave Giger. 3 Vols. Phillipsburg, NJ: P & R, 1992–1997.

Van Groningen, Gerard. *Messianic Revelation in the Old Testament*. Grand Rapids: Baker, 1990.

Vander Hart, Mark D. "The Exodus as Sacrament: The Cloud, the Sea, and Moses Revisited." *MAJT* 12 (2001) 9–46.
VanDrunen, David, and R. Scott Clark. "The Covenant before the Covenants." In *Covenant, Justification, and Pastoral Theology: Essays by the Faculty of Westminster Seminary California*, edited by R. Scott Clark, 167–96. Phillipsburg, NJ: P & R, 2007.
VanGemeren, Willem A. "Israel as the Hermeneutical Crux in Interpretation and Prophecy." *WTJ* 45 (1983) 132–44.
———. "Israel as the Hermeneutical Crux in Interpretation and Prophecy (II)." *WTJ* 46 (1984) 254–97.
Vanhoozer, Kevin J. "Ascending the Mountain, Singing the Rock: Biblical Interpretation Earthed, Typed, and Transfigured." *Modern Theology* 28 (2012) 781–803.
———. "Being in Christ: Ontology, Topology, and the Church as Eutopic Theater." *CTR* 13 (2015) 3–21.
———. "From 'Blessed in Christ' to 'Being in Christ': The State of Union and the Place of Participation in Paul's Discourse, New Testament Exegesis, and Systematic Theology Today." In *"In Christ" in Paul: Explorations in Paul's Theology of Union and Participation*, edited by Michael J. Thate et al., 3–33. WUNT 2/384. Tübingen, Germany: Mohr Siebeck, 2014.
———. *The Drama of Doctrine: A Canonical Linguistic Approach to Christian Theology.* Louisville: Westminster John Knox, 2005.
———. "'Exegesis I Know, and Theology I Know, but Who are You?' Acts 19 and the Theological Interpretation of Scripture." In *Theological Theology: Essays in Honour of John Webster*, edited by R. David Nelson et al., 289–306. London: Bloomsbury T&T Clark, 2015.
———. "Intention/Intentional Fallacy." In *DTIB*, edited by Kevin J. Vanhoozer, 327–30. Grand Rapids: Baker, 2005.
———. *Is There a Meaning in This Text? The Bible, the Reader, and the Morality of Literary Knowledge.* Grand Rapids: Zondervan, 1998.
———. "Systematic Theology." In *New Dictionary of Theology: Historic and Systematic.* 2nd ed. Edited by Martin Davie et al. Downers Grove: InterVarsity, 2016.
Vanhoozer, Kevin J., and Daniel J. Treier. *Theology and the Mirror of Scripture: A Mere Evangelical Account.* Downers Grove: InterVarsity, 2015.
Vanlaningham, Michael G. "The Jewish People according to the Book of Romans." In *The People, the Land and the Future of Israel: Israel and the Jewish People in the Plan of God*, edited by Darrell L. Bock and Mitch Glaser, 117–31. Grand Rapids: Kregel, 2014.
Van Winkle, D. W. "The Relationship of the Nations to Yahweh and to Israel in Isaiah XL–LV." *VT* 35 (1985) 446–58.
Venema, Cornelis P. *Children at the Lord's Table?* Grand Rapids: Reformation Heritage, 2009.
———. "Covenant Theology and Baptism." In *The Case for Covenantal Infant Baptism*, edited by Gregg Strawbridge, 201–29. Phillipsburg, NJ: P & R, 2003.
———. "The Mosaic Covenant: A 'Republication' of the Covenant of Works? A Review Article: *The Law is Not of Faith: Essays on Works and Grace in the Mosaic Covenant*." *MAJT* 21 (2010) 35–101.
———. *The Promise of the Future.* Carlisle, PA: Banner of Truth, 2000.

———. "'In This Way All Israel Will Be Saved:' A Study of Romans 11:26." *MAJT* 22 (2011) 19–40.
Verbruggen, Jan L. "Of Muzzles and Oxen: Deuteronomy 25:5 and 1 Corinthians 9:9." *JETS* 49 (2006) 699–711.
Vickers, Brian J. *Jesus' Blood and Righteousness: Paul's Theology of Imputation*. Wheaton, IL: Crossway, 2006.
———. "Mark's Good News of the Kingdom of God." *SBJT* 8 (2004) 12–35.
———. "Who Is the 'Israel of God' (Galatians 6:16)?" *Eusebeia* 6 (2006) 5–10.
Vlach, Michael J. *Has the Church Replaced Israel? A Theological Evaluation*. Nashville: B & H, 2010.
———. "Have They Found a Better Way? An Analysis of Gentry and Wellum's *Kingdom through Covenant*." *MSJ* 24 (2013) 5–24.
———. "A Non-Typological Future-Mass-Conversion View." In *Three Views on Israel and the Church: Perspectives on Romans 9–11*, edited by Jared Compton and Andrew David Naselli, 21–73. Grand Rapids: Kregel, 2018.
———. "Various Forms of Replacement Theology." *MSJ* 20 (2009) 57–69.
———. "What Does Christ as 'True Israel' Mean for the Nation Israel? A Critique of the Non-Dispensational Understanding." *MSJ* 21 (2012) 43–54.
———. "What Is Dispensationalism?" In *Christ's Prophetic Plans: A Futuristic Premillennial Primer*, edited by John MacArthur and Richard Mayhue, 19–38. Chicago: Moody, 2012.
———. "What Is Dispensationalism Not?" In *Christ's Prophetic Plans: A Futuristic Premillennial Primer*, edited by John MacArthur and Richard Mayhue, 39–58. Chicago: Moody, 2012.
von Rad, Gerhard. *Old Testament Theology*, vol. 2, *The Theology of Israel's Prophetic Traditions*. Translated D. M. G. Stalker. Edinburgh: Oliver and Boyd, 1965.
———. "Typological Interpretation of the Old Testament." Translated by John Bright. *Int* 15 (1961) 174–92
Voorwinde, Stephen. "How Jewish Is *Israel* in the New Testament?" *RTR* 67 (2008) 61–90.
Vos, Geerhardus. *Biblical Theology: Old and New Testaments*. Grand Rapids: Eerdmans, 1948. Reprint, Edinburgh: Banner of Truth, 2004.
———. "The Doctrine of the Covenant in Reformed Theology." In *Redemptive History and Biblical Interpretation: The Shorter Writings of Geerhardus Vos*, edited by Richard B. Gaffin Jr., 234–67. Phillipsburg, NJ: P & R, 1980.
———. "The Idea of Biblical Theology as a Science and a Theological Discipline." In *Redemptive History and Biblical Interpretation: The Shorter Writings of Geerhardus Vos*, edited by Richard B. Gaffin Jr., 3–24. Phillipsburg, NJ: P & R, 1980.
———. *Reformed Dogmatics*. Edited and translated by Richard B. Gaffin Jr. Vol. 2, *Anthropology*. Bellingham, WA: Lexham, 2013.
———. *The Teaching of the Epistle to the Hebrews*. Grand Rapids: Eerdmans, 1956.
Wagner, J. Ross. "The Christ, Servant of Jew and Gentile: A Fresh Approach to Romans 15:8–9." *JBL* 116 (1997) 473–85.
Walker, Peter W. L. *Jesus and the Holy City: New Testament Perspectives on Jerusalem*. Grand Rapids: Eerdmans, 1996.
Waltke, Bruce K. "Kingdom Promises as Spiritual." In *Continuity and Discontinuity: Perspectives on the Relationship between the Old and New Testaments*, edited by John S. Feinberg, 263–87. Wheaton, IL: Crossway, 1988.

———. *An Old Testament Theology: An Exegetical, Canonical, and Thematic Approach.* Grand Rapids: Zondervan, 2007.

———. "The Phenomenon of Conditionality within Unconditional Covenants." In *Israel's Apostasy and Restoration*, edited by Avraham Gileadi, 123–39. Grand Rapids: Baker, 1988.

Walvoord, John F. "Biblical Kingdoms Compared and Contrasted." In *Issues in Dispensationalism*, edited by Wesley R. Willis and John R. Master, 75–91. Chicago: Moody, 1994.

———. "Christological Typology." *BibSac* 105 (1948) 286–96.

———. "Christological Typology." *BibSac* 106 (1949) 27–33.

———. "Does the Church Fulfill Israel's Program?" *BibSac* 137 (1980) 17–31, 118–24, 212–22.

———. *The Millennial Kingdom: A Basic Text in Premillennial Theology.* Findlay, OH: Dunham, 1959. Reprint, Grand Rapids: Zondervan, 1983.

———. "The New Covenant." In *Integrity of Heart, Skillfulness of Hands: Biblical and Leadership Studies in Honor of Donald K. Campbell*, edited by Charles H. Dyer and Roy B. Zuck, 186–200. Grand Rapids: Baker, 1994.

Ward, Rowland S. *God and Adam: Reformed Theology and the Creation Covenant.* Wantirna, Australia: New Melbourne, 2003.

Ward, Tim. "The Union of the Believer with Christ in Paul." In *In Christ Alone: Perspectives on Union with Christ*, edited by Stephen Clark and Matthew Evans, 39–66. Fearn, Scotland: Mentor, 2016.

Ware, Bruce A. "The New Covenant and the People(s) of God." In *Dispensationalism, Israel and the Church: The Search for Definition*, edited by Craig A. Blaising and Darrell L. Bock, 68–97. Grand Rapids: Zondervan, 1992.

Waters, Guy, and Ligon Duncan, eds. *Children and the Lord's Supper.* Fearn, Scotland: Christian Focus, 2011.

Watts, Rikki E. "Consolation or Confrontation? Isaiah 40–55 and the Delay of the New Exodus." *TynBul* 41 (1990) 31–59.

———. "Echoes from the Past: Israel's Ancient Traditions and the Destiny of the Nations in Isaiah 40–55." *JSOT* 28 (2004) 481–508.

———. "Exodus." In *NDBT*, edited by T. Desmond Alexander and Brian S. Rosner, 478–87. Downers Grove: InterVarsity, 2000.

———. *Isaiah's New Exodus in Mark.* Biblical Studies Library. Grand Rapids: Baker, 2000.

———. "Jesus' Death, Isaiah 53, and Mark 10:45: A Crux Revisited." In *Jesus and the Suffering Servant: Isaiah 53 and Christian Origins*, edited by William H. Bellinger Jr., and William R. Farmer, 125–51. Harrisburg, PA: Trinity Press, 1998.

———. "Mark." In *Commentary on the New Testament Use of the Old Testament*, edited by G. K. Beale and D. A. Carson, 111–249. Grand Rapids: Baker, 2007.

Waymeyer, Matt. "The Dual Status of Israel in Romans 11:28." *MSJ* 16 (2005) 57–71.

Webb, Barry G. *The Message of Isaiah: On Eagle's Wings.* The Bible Speaks Today. Downers Grove: InterVarsity, 1996.

———. "Zion in Transformation: A Literary Approach to Isaiah." In *The Bible in Three Dimensions: Essays in Celebration of Forty Years of Biblical Studies in the University of Sheffield*, edited by David J. A. Clines et al., 65–84. JSOTSup 87. Sheffield: JSOT, 1990.

Weber, Timothy P. "Dispensational and Historic Premillennialism as Popular Millennialist Movements." In *A Case for Historic Premillennialism: An Alternative to 'Left Behind' Eschatology*, edited by Craig L. Blomberg and Sung Wook Chung, 1–22. Grand Rapids: Baker, 2009.

Webster, John. "What Makes Theology Theological?" *Journal of Analytic Theology* 3 (2015) 17–28.

Weima, Jeffrey A. D. "Gal. 6:11–18: A Hermeneutical Key to the Galatian Letter." *CTJ* 28 (1993) 90–107.

Weinfeld, M. "The Covenant of Grant in the Old Testament and in the Ancient Near East." *JAOS* 90 (1970) 184–203.

Wells, Mary Jo Bailey. *God's Holy People: A Theme in Biblical Theology*. JSOTSup 305. Sheffield: Sheffield Academic, 2000.

Wells, Tom, and Fred G. Zaspel. *New Covenant Theology*. Frederick, MD: New Covenant Media, 2002.

Wellum, Stephen J. "Baptism and the Relationship between the Covenants." In *Believer's Baptism: Sign of the New Covenant in Christ*, edited by Thomas R. Schreiner and Shawn D. Wright, 97–161. NACSBT. Nashville: B & H, 2006.

———. "Beyond Mere Ecclesiology: The Church as God's New Covenant Community." In *The Community of Jesus: A Theology of the Church*, edited by Kendell H. Easley and Christopher W. Morgan, 183–212. Nashville: B & H, 2013.

———. "The New Covenant Work of Christ: Priesthood, Atonement, and Intercession." In *From Heaven He Came and Sought Her: Definite Atonement in Historical, Biblical, Theological, and Pastoral Perspective*, edited by David Gibson and Jonathan Gibson, 517–39. Wheaton, IL: Crossway, 2013.

Wellum, Stephen J. and Brent E. Parker, eds. *Progressive Covenantalism: Charting a Course between Dispensational and Covenant Theologies*. Nashville: B & H, 2016.

Wenham, David. *The Parables of Jesus*. Downers Grove: InterVarsity, 1989.

Wenham, Gordon J. "Sanctuary Symbolism in the Garden of Eden Story." In *"I Studied Inscriptions from the Flood": Ancient Near Eastern, Literary, and Linguistic Approaches to Genesis 1–11*, edited by Richard S. Hess and David Toshio Tsumura, 399–404. Winona Lake, IN: Eisenbrauns, 1994.

Wenkel, David H. "The Most Simple and Comprehensive Script for the Theo-Drama of Scripture: Three Acts or Four Acts?" *SBET* 30 (2012) 78–90.

Whitacre, R. A. "Vine, Fruit of the Vine." In *Dictionary of Jesus and the Gospels*. Edited by Joel B. Green et al. Downers Grove: InterVarsity, 1992.

Whitcomb, John C. "Christ's Atonement and Animal Sacrifices in Israel." *GTJ* 6 (1985) 201–17.

White, A. Blake. *The Newness of the New Covenant*. Frederick, MD: New Covenant Media, 2007.

———. *What Is New Covenant Theology? An Introduction*. Frederick, MD: New Covenant Media, 2012.

White, James R. "The Newness of the New Covenant (Part I)." *RBTR* 1 (2004) 144–68.

———. "The Newness of the New Covenant (Part II)." *RBTR* 2 (2005) 83–104.

White, R. Fowler. "The Last Adam and His Seed: An Exercise in Theological Preemption." *TrinJ* 6 (1985) 60–73.

Whitman, Jon. *Allegory: The Dynamics of an Ancient and Medieval Technique*. Oxford: Clarendon, 1987.

Whittle, Sarah. *Covenant Renewal and the Consecration of the Gentiles in Romans.* SNTSMS 161. New York: Cambridge University Press, 2015.

Wilken, Robert Louis. "In Defense of Allegory." *Modern Theology* 14 (1998) 197–212.

Williams, Michael D. *Far as the Curse Is Found: The Covenant Story of Redemption.* Phillipsburg, NJ: P & R, 2005.

———. "Systematic Theology as a Biblical Discipline." In *All for Jesus: A Celebration of the 50th Anniversary of Covenant Theological Seminary*, edited by Robert A. Peterson and Sean Michael Lucas, 167–96. Fearn, Scotland: Christian Focus, 2006.

Williams, Sam K. "*Promise* in Galatians: A Reading of Paul's Reading of Scripture." *JBL* 107 (1988) 709–20.

Williamson, Paul R. "Abraham, Israel and the Church." *EvQ* 72 (2000) 99–118.

Williamson, Paul R. "Covenant." In *NDBT*, edited by T. Desmond Alexander and Brian S. Rosner, 419–29. Downers Grove: InterVarsity, 2000.

———. "The *Pactum Salutis*: A Scriptural Concept or Scholastic Mythology?" *TynBul* 69 (2018) 259–81.

———. "Promise and Fulfilment: The Territorial Inheritance." In *The Land of Promise: Biblical, Theological and Contemporary Perspectives*, edited by Philip Johnston and Peter Walker, 15–34. Downers Grove: InterVarsity, 2000.

———. *Sealed with an Oath: Covenant in God's Unfolding Purpose.* NSBT 23. Downers Grove: InterVarsity, 2007.

Willis, Wendell Lee. *Idol Meat in Corinth: The Pauline Argument in 1 Corinthians 8 and 10.* Society of Biblical Literature Dissertation Series 68. Chico, CA: Scholars, 1985.

Willitts, Joel. "Isa 54,1 in Gal 4,24b: Reading Genesis in Light of Isaiah." *ZNW* 96 (2005) 188–210.

Wilson, Allistair I. "Luke and the New Covenant: Zechariah's Prophecy as a Test Case." In *The God of Covenant: Biblical, Theological and Contemporary Perspectives*, edited by Jamie A. Grand and Alistair I. Wilson, 156–77. Leicester, UK: InterVarsity, 2005.

Wilson, Douglas. *"Reformed" Is Not Enough: Recovering the Objectivity of the Covenant.* Moscow, ID: Canon, 2002.

Windsor, Lionel. "The 'Seed,' the 'Many' and the 'One' in Galatians 3:16: Paul's Reading of Genesis 17 and its Significance for Gentiles." In *All that the Prophets Have Declared: The Appropriation of Scripture in the Emergence of Christianity*, edited by Matthew R. Malcolm, 115–26. Crownhill, UK: Paternoster, 2015.

Witsius, Herman. *The Economy of the Covenants between God and Man: Comprehending a Complete Body of Divinity.* Translated by William Crookshank. London: R. Baynes, 1822. Reprint, Grand Rapids: Reformation Heritage, 2010.

Wolff, Hans Walter. "The Hermeneutics of the Old Testament." Translated by Keith Crim. In *Essays on Old Testament Hermeneutics*, edited by Claus Westermann, 160–99. Richmond, VA: John Knox, 1963.

Wolter, Michael. "Israel's Future and the Delay of the Parousia, according to Luke." In *Jesus and the Heritage of Israel: Luke's Narrative Claim upon Israel's Legacy*, edited by David P. Moessner, 307–24. Harrisburg, PA: Trinity Press International, 1999.

Wood, Thomas R. "The Regathering of the People of God: An Investigation into the New Testament's Appropriation of the Old Testament Prophecies Concerning the Regathering of Israel." Ph.D. diss., Trinity International University, 2006.

Woollcombe, K. J. "The Biblical Origins and Patristic Development of Typology." In *Essays on Typology*. Studies in Biblical Theology 22. Naperville, IL: Alec R. Allenson, 1957.

Works, Carla Swafford. *The Church in the Wilderness: Paul's Use of Exodus Traditions in 1 Corinthians*. WUNT 2/379. Tübingen, Germany: Mohr Siebeck, 2014.

Woudstra, Marten H. "Israel and the Church: A Case for Continuity." In *Continuity and Discontinuity: Perspectives on the Relationship between the Old and New Testaments*, edited by John S. Feinberg, 221–38. Wheaton, IL: Crossway, 1988.

Wright, Christopher J. H. *Knowing Jesus through the Old Testament*. Downers Grove: InterVarsity, 1992.

———. *Old Testament Ethics for the People of God*. Downers Grove: InterVarsity, 2004.

———. "The Whole Church—A Brief Biblical Survey." *ERT* 34 (2010) 14–28.

Wright, N. T. *The Climax of the Covenant: Christ and the Law in Pauline Theology*. Minneapolis: Fortress, 1992.

———. "Jerusalem in the New Testament." In *Jerusalem Past and Present in the Purposes of God*, edited by P. W. L Walker, 53–77. 2nd ed. Grand Rapids: Baker, 1994.

———. *New Testament and the People of God*, Vol. 1. Christian Origins and the Question of God. Minneapolis: Fortress, 1992.

———. *Paul and the Faithfulness of God*. Book 2. Vol. 4. Christian Origins and the Question of God. Minneapolis: Fortress, 2013.

———. *What Saint Paul Really Said: Was Paul of Tarsus the Real Founder of Christianity*. Grand Rapids: Eerdmans, 1996.

Yee, Tet-Lim N. *Jews, Gentiles and Ethnic Reconciliation: Paul's Jewish Identity and Ephesians*. SNTSMS 130. Cambridge: Cambridge University Press, 2005.

Yoshikawa, Scott T. "The Prototypical Use of the Noahic Flood in the New Testament." Ph.D. diss., Trinity Evangelical Divinity School, 2004.

Young, Frances M. "Alexandrian and Antiochene Exegesis." In *A History of Biblical Interpretation*. Vol. 1. *The Ancient Period*, edited by Alan J. Hauser and Duane F. Watson, 334–54. Grand Rapids: Eerdmans, 2003.

———. "Allegory and the Ethics of Reading." In *The Open Text: New Directions for Biblical Study?* Edited by Francis Watson, 103–20. London: SCM, 1993.

———. *Biblical Exegesis and the Formation of Christian Culture*. Cambridge: Cambridge University Press, 1997.

———. "Typology." In *Crossing the Boundaries: Essays in Biblical Interpretation in Honour of Michael D. Goulder*, edited by Stanley E. Porter et al., 29–48. Leiden: Brill, 1994.

Zaspel, Fred G., and James M. Hamilton, Jr. "A Typological Future-Mass-Conversion View." In *Three Views on Israel and the Church: Perspectives on Romans 9-11*, edited by Jared Compton and Andrew David Naselli, 97–140. Grand Rapids: Kregel, 2018.

Zens, Jon. "Is There a 'Covenant of Grace?'" *Baptist Reformation Review* 6 (1977) 43–53.

Zoccali, Christopher. "'And So All Israel Will Be Saved': Competing Interpretations of Romans 11.26 in Pauline Scholarship." *JSNT* 30 (2008) 289–318.

Zorn, Raymond O. *Christ Triumphant: Biblical Perspectives on His Church and Kingdom*. Rev. ed. Edinburgh: Banner of Truth Trust, 1997.

Zuck, Roy B. *Basic Bible Interpretation: A Practical Guide to Discovering Biblical Truth*. Colorado Springs: Victor, 1991.

Author Index

Achtemeier, Elizabeth R., 26n31, 44n79
Achtemeier, Paul J., 265n84, 266n86, 266n87, 267n92, 270n99
Alexander, Ralph H., 145n115
Alexander, T. Desmond, 166n25, 166n28, 178n58, 179n60, 179n62, 180n64, 183, 183n75, 184n76, 186n86
Allis, Oswald T., 15, 15n1, 62n130, 102n60
Allison, D. C., 71n152, 167n29, 169n31, 173n43, 182n71, 306n205, 306nn208–209, 307n209
Allison, Gregg R., 18n6, 120n17, 144n109, 247n32, 249n38
Alsup, John E., 18n6, 44n79
Alva McClain, 133n62
Anderson, Bernhard W., 69n148, 203n142
Arnold, Clinton E., 251nn41–42, 252n44, 256n61, 257n62
Auerbach, Erich, 18n5
August, Jared M., 187n88
Ayers, Lewis, 19n8

Bailey, Mark L., 130n55, 132n61, 132n62, 133n64
Baker, Bruce A., 28n34, 31n42, 33n49, 44n80, 46n85, 46n88, 49n96, 49n99, 50, 58n118, 60n123, 66, 67, 67n140, 68n146, 76, 129n50, 133n63, 150n130, 154n145
Ball, John, 87, 87n21

Bandstra, Andrew J., 271n100, 273n113, 275n117, 276n120, 278n127, 279n131
Bandy, Alan S., 170n34, 179n60
Banks, Robert, 255n55
Barker, Kenneth L., 117n11
Barr, James, 18n7, 21n15, 29n37, 46n87
Bartholomew, Craig G., 11n29, 82n7
Bass, Clarence B., 115n1, 118n12, 120n20, 133n64
Bateman, Herbert W., IV, 115n1, 118n12, 119n16, 121n21, 121n22, 121n23, 122n30
Bauckham, Richard, 172n39, 179n63, 183n73, 185n82, 211n173, 213n178, 264n80, 265n84, 268nn94–95
Bavinck, Herman, 75n163, 83n9, 85n15, 85n16, 86n18, 88n24, 91n28, 91n29, 93n32, 95n36, 96n39, 96n40, 96n42, 97, 97n43, 98n48, 99n49, 100n53, 106, 106n80
Bayer, Hans F., 327n40, 328n44
Beach, J. Mark, 87n21
Beacham, Roy E., 144n110, 145n113
Beale, G. K., 11n29, 12n32, 26, 26nn30–31, 31n42, 33n49, 37n60, 44n80, 46n89, 48n94, 50–51, 50n101, 56n115, 58n120, 59n121, 63n132, 65n136, 67n140, 68, 68n146, 70, 70nn150–151, 71, 71nn153–154, 75n161, 77n166, 77n167, 95n36,

AUTHOR INDEX

(G. K. Beale continued)
98n48, 100n54, 100n56, 101n56, 101n60, 104, 105n74, 105n75, 105n78, 108n85, 109n89, 110n89, 110n90, 111n92, 112n95, 113n98, 137n79, 147n121, 160n7, 165nn24–25, 166n25, 169n31, 170, 170nn33–34, 171, 171nn35–37, 172n38, 172n40, 173n41, 174n46, 181n68, 181nn69–70, 182n71, 184n78, 185n82, 192n105, 195n116, 195n118, 196n124, 197nn125–126, 208nn160–161, 212n175, 213n179, 222n206, 223n209, 226n218, 229n230, 236n1, 254n50, 254n52, 257n64, 264n80, 265, 265n83, 266n88, 269n95, 295n175, 297n182, 298n184, 307, 307n211, 309n214, 311n226, 312nn227–228, 333n57

Beasley-Murray, George R., 227n225, 229, 229n228, 273n113, 276n119, 285nn151–152, 287n157, 303n200, 313n232

Beers, Holly, 202nn139–140, 207n158, 213n179, 220n202, 221n204, 222n206, 222n208

Beetham, Christopher A., 165n23, 185n81, 185n84

Beisner, E. Calvin, 81n5

Benware, Paul N., 117n10, 124n33, 128n46, 132n62, 133n67, 134n70, 138n84, 139n88, 140n91, 141nn94–96, 142n98, 144n109, 145n114

Berkhof, Louis, 1n1, 23n20, 68n146, 81n4, 83n9, 84n15, 86, 86n17, 89n24, 91n28, 93n30, 93n32, 94, 94n33, 94n34, 94n35, 95n36, 95n37, 96n39, 96n40, 96n42, 97n43, 98, 98n47, 98n48, 100n53, 102n61, 102n63, 104, 105n74, 105n75, 105n78, 106, 106n80, 261n72, 262n76

Berkouwer, G. C., 84n12

Betz, Hans Dieter, 187n91, 306n204

Beuken, W. A. M., 202n140, 205n150, 208n160, 209n163

Bigalke, Ron J., Jr., 115n1, 116, 116n7, 117n8, 119n15, 126n40, 133n65, 138n84, 139n88, 140, 140nn90–91, 140n93, 148n124, 149n127, 151n133

Bird, Michael F., 8n19, 69n148, 204n145, 220nn200–201, 222n205, 222n208

Blackburn, Earl M., 81n6

Blaising, Craig A., 2n3, 115n1, 115n2, 116n4, 116n6, 116n7, 117n8, 117n10, 117n11, 119n14, 120, 120n17, 120n19, 121–22, 121n21, 121n22, 121n23, 122, 122n25, 123n30, 123n32, 124n35, 124n36, 125, 125n39, 126, 126n39, 126n40, 126n41, 128n47, 129, 129n48, 129n50, 129n51, 130, 130nn52–53, 131n56, 131n58, 132n59, 132n62, 135nn73–74, 135n74, 136n76, 136n77, 137, 137n80, 138n82, 139nn86–89, 140nn92–93, 141nn94–96, 142n97, 143, 143nn103–105, 143n107, 144n109, 146, 146nn117–118, 147n121, 149n125, 151n135, 152n139, 153–54, 153n142, 153nn143–144, 154n145, 158n2, 163n15, 187n88, 191n104, 229n230, 299n185, 317n2, 322n21, 327n38, 329n47, 330n50

Blocher, Henri, 85n16, 211n172, 211n175

Block, Daniel I., 166n25, 201n138

Bock, Darrell L., 2n3, 48n94, 50n101, 74n161, 75n161, 78n169, 116n4, 116n6, 117n8, 117n10, 117n11, 120, 120n17, 120n19, 121n22, 121n23, 122, 122n25, 124n35, 125, 125n39, 126, 126n40, 126n41, 128n47, 129, 129n48, 129nn49–50, 129n51, 130, 130nn52–53, 131n55, 131n56, 131n57, 131n58, 132nn59–60, 132n62, 135, 135n73, 135n74,

136n75, 136n76, 136nn77–78, 136n79, 137, 137n80, 138n82, 138n84, 139nn86–89, 140nn92–93, 141nn94–96, 142n97, 143, 143nn103–105, 143n106, 143n107, 143n108, 144n109, 146, 146n116, 146nn117–118, 146n119, 147n121, 149n125, 151, 151nn135–136, 152, 152n137, 152n138, 152n139, 152n140, 152n141, 153n141, 153n142, 154, 187n88, 229n230, 317n2, 318nn6–7, 320, 320n14, 322n21, 327n38, 330n50
Boersma, Hans, 21n16
Bolt, John, 84n14
Booth, Robert R., 95n36, 98n48, 111n92
Borg, Michael, 95n37
Boyarin, Daniel, 30n41
Brack, Jonathan M., 111n93
Brand, Chad O., 7n17, 159n6
Bright, John, 99n49, 200n135
Bromiley, Geoffrey W., 94n35
Brown, Justin Michael, 150n130, 150n131, 151n132
Brown, Michael G., 81n4, 82, 83n10, 84n15, 87n20, 88n22, 91n28, 92, 92n30, 94n35, 95n37
Brown, Raymond E., 75n163, 76n163, 78n170
Bruce, F. F., 160n8, 166n27, 211n172, 289n161, 306n205
Brumm, Ursula, 26n31, 28n34, 103n69
Bruno, Christopher R., 162n13, 204n148, 214n181, 331n51
Bullinger, Heinrich, 93n31
Bunyan, John, 23
Burge, Gary M., 158n3, 160n7, 226n221, 228n227, 259n69, 323n22
Burke, Trevor J., 176, 176nn52–53, 189n97
Burns, J. Lanier, 123n33, 136n76
Byrne, Brendan, 176n53, 190n103, 311n225

Calvin, John, 42, 42n76, 93n32, 238n6
Campbell, Constantine R., 237n4, 238n5, 239n11, 242n18, 244nn21–22, 245n25, 252nn44–45, 253nn47–48
Campbell, Donald K., 133n67, 148n124
Caneday, Ardel B., 25n27, 29n39, 33, 33n49, 34n50, 36, 36n57, 37n60, 37n61, 38, 38nn63–64, 39, 39nn65–67, 40n68, 40n71, 48n92, 53nn106–107, 54n108, 66nn137–138, 74nn160–161, 174n46, 226n220, 240, 240n14, 241, 241nn15–17, 243, 243n19, 263, 263n79, 279n130, 279n134, 282n144, 283n146, 286n155
Carroll, John T., 319n8, 321n16, 325n35, 327n40
Carson, D. A., 8n19, 10n26, 11n29, 11n30, 22n19, 30n41, 32n46, 32n48, 41n74, 44n79, 45n82, 47n91, 48n94, 50n102, 51n102, 54n108, 55n111, 55n113, 60n123, 64n135, 65n136, 66n139, 71n152, 150n130, 161n10, 164n18, 169n31, 171n36, 182n71, 194n112, 195, 195n117, 196n120, 206n157, 215n186, 220n201, 227n225, 228n227, 242n18, 255n53, 255n56, 262n77, 267n92, 268nn94–95, 271, 273n108, 278n128, 279n134, 287n157, 302n194, 303, 303n199, 304n202
Carter, Craig A., 19n8, 42n74, 42n76
Chae, Daniel Jong Sang, 176n53, 224nn211–213, 331n53
Chafer, Lewis Sperry, 116n2, 126, 149n125
Chance, J. Bradley, 320n14, 322n21
Chantry, Walter J., 94n32
Chapman, Colin, 158n3
Charity, A. C., 27n32
Chase, Mitchell, 32n45, 33n49, 47n91, 52n104, 72n155, 73n156

Childs, Brevard S., 18n6, 20n11, 202n139, 205n152, 208n162, 211n175
Church, Philip A. F., 158n3, 181n69
Ciampa, Roy E., 11n29, 37n58, 172n38, 271n100, 272n107, 273nn109–111, 273n113, 274n114, 274n116, 275nn117–118, 276n120, 277n122, 277n124, 278n127, 279n131, 281n137, 281n140
Clark, R. Scott, 80, 80n2, 81n3, 81n4, 87n20
Clayton, Charles, 23n20, 44n79, 48n94, 77n166, 105n74
Clowney, Edmund P., 1n1, 10n28, 63n132, 95n37, 98n48, 100n53, 101n57, 104, 104n71, 105n74, 105n78, 107, 107n83, 108n86, 110, 110n91, 111n92, 247n32
Cocceius, Johannes, 67, 84n14, 85n15, 91n28, 103
Cole, Graham A., 24n26, 246n31, 257n62
Collins, C. John, 82n7, 82n9, 111n92, 186, 186n86, 186n88, 187n88
Collins, Jack, 183, 184n76
Compton, Jared M., 76n164, 77n167, 144n109, 144nn111–112, 145nn113–114
Cone, Christopher, 116n6, 117n10, 118n12, 121n21, 144n109, 144n111, 145nn113–114
Cosgrove, Charles H., 38n62
Couch, Mal, 116, 116n4, 116n7, 117n8, 127n42, 134n70
Cowan, Christopher, 286n155, 307n212, 308n213, 309n214, 310n221, 311n224
Cragoe, Thomas H., 141n94, 141n96, 142nn98–99, 142n101
Crampton, W. G., 285n152
Cruise, Charles E., 172n38
Currid, John D., 28n34, 31n42, 33n49, 35n55, 47n91, 48n94, 104, 105n74, 105n78

Dabney, R. L., 85n16

Dalrymple, Rob, 63n132
Daniélou, Jean, 18n6, 21n16, 32nn45–47, 76n163
Darby, John Nelson, 115, 115n1, 121, 126, 131n55
Das, A. Andrew, 306n204, 306nn207–209, 307n210, 332n53
Davids, Peter H., 266n87, 270n99
Davidson, Richard M., 4n12, 4n13, 7, 12n32, 24n26, 25n28–29, 28, 28nn34–35, 29, 33n49, 44nn79–80, 44n80, 45n81, 45n83, 46n88, 48n94, 53, 53n107, 54n108, 56nn114–115, 56n115, 58n120, 59n122, 60–61, 60n125, 61nn126–127, 63, 67n142, 69n149, 70, 70n150, 103n66, 150n130, 222n207, 230, 230n231, 271, 272nn107–108, 273n113, 274n115, 275n118, 276nn120–121, 277nn122–126, 278n127, 278n129, 279nn131–134, 281n139, 282n144, 283n147, 284, 284n149
Davies, W. D., 71n152, 71n153, 167n29, 169n31, 173n43, 182n71, 259n69
Davis, Thomas M., 101n58, 103n69
Dawson, John David, 17n5, 23n23
De Boer, Martinus C., 38n62, 293n173
De Lubac, Henri, 19n8, 21n16
Decker, Rodney J., 144n109, 144n111, 145n114
Demarest, Bruce, 238n6, 239nn10–11, 244nn22–24, 248, 248n35
Dempster, Stephen G., 165n22, 178n57, 184nn78–79, 196n124, 197, 197nn125–126, 198n128, 200n134, 201n138, 202n140, 204n145, 206n155, 211n172, 213n180, 214, 214n182, 231n232
Denault, Pascal, 81n6, 87n21, 93n32, 95n36, 96n42, 97n45
Dennis, John A., 217n191, 287n157
DeRouchie, Jason S., 9n21, 52n104, 69n147, 69n149, 178n56, 178nn58–59, 179n62, 180n66,

182n71, 183n73, 184n76,
186n87, 187n89, 187n91,
189n99, 190n101, 190n102,
190n103, 193n110, 203n144,
208n160, 210n170, 219n196,
231n232, 254n52, 290n164, 300,
301n190
DeWitt, Dale S., 120n20, 122n27,
133n65, 133n67, 134nn69–70,
139n86
Di Mattei, Steven, 37n61, 38n62,
39n64
Diffey, Daniel S., 183nn74–75
Dockery, David S., 3, 3n8, 18n6
Dodd, C. H., 161n11, 198n127,
227n225
Donaldson, Alistair W., 108n85,
117n9, 121n24, 122n24, 158n5,
162, 162n12, 259nn68–69
Dow, Louis K. Fuller, 293n173,
295n176, 319n9, 320n13, 321n18
Drane, John W., 30n41, 53n107
Duguid, Iain M., 164n20
Dumbrell, William J., 82n7, 83n9,
84n14, 108n85, 178n57, 184n79,
185n80, 194n113, 195n117,
196n121, 201n138, 202n141,
204nn146–147, 213n178,
214n181
Duncan, Ligon, 110n91
Dunn, James, 81n5
Dunn, Matthew W. I., 78n170

Eastman, Susan Grove, 306n205,
307n212, 308n212, 311n224
Echevarria, Miguel G., Jr., 38n62,
190n103, 191n104, 226n218,
291n167, 293n171, 293n172
Edwards, James R., 174n45, 318n5,
318n7, 319n10, 321n16
Edwards, Jonathan, 103
Eichrodt, Walther, 24n26, 26n31,
49n96
Elliot, Mark W., 21n14, 23n21
Elliott, John H., 266n87, 266n89,
267n92, 268n93
Ellis, E. Earle, 15n2, 28n34, 38n62,
44n79, 47, 47n90, 188n95,

196n121, 237n3, 246, 247n33,
277n123, 279n134
Emadi, Samuel, 72n155
Emerson, Matthew Y., 38n64, 39n64,
39n67
Enns, Peter, 59n121, 75n161, 75n162,
277nn123–124
Essex, Keith H., 138n84, 139n86
Estelle, Bryan D., 84n14
Evans, C. A., 29n37, 30n40, 196n123,
198n128, 265n84

Fackre, Gabriel J., 158n2
Fairbairn, Patrick, 23n22, 26n31,
47n90, 48n94, 67n142, 68n145,
69n147, 99n52, 101n60, 102n61,
103–4, 103n64, 103n65, 103n66,
104n70, 107n81, 148, 150n130,
160, 160n9
Fantuzzo, Christopher J., 202n140,
219, 219nn197–198, 223n210
Fee, Gordon D., 271n100, 272n102,
272n105, 272nn107–108,
273nn109–111, 273n113,
274, 274n115, 275nn117–119,
276nn120–121, 277n122, 278,
278n128, 279n131, 280n134,
281n137, 281n141
Feinberg, John S., 2, 2n6, 116n5,
118n12, 120, 120n18, 121n21,
121n24, 122, 122n30, 124n33,
125, 139n86, 148n125, 149n129,
150nn130–131, 151n133, 158n3,
184n77, 300n187
Feinberg, Paul D., 124n37, 127n44,
128n45, 148n124, 149, 149n126,
150n130, 150n132, 151n133,
171n36
Ferguson, Sinclair B., 238nn6–7,
240n12, 241, 241n17, 244n22,
245n25, 245n27
Fesko, J. V., 81n4, 83n9, 87n20,
165n25
Fishbane, Michael, 29n38, 69n148
Foulkes, Francis, 38n62, 44n79,
46n85, 49n99, 50n99, 56n115
Fowl, Stephen E., 17n4, 23n23, 38n62
Frame, John M., 10, 10n26, 89n24

France, R. T., 31n43, 33n49, 44n80, 46n85, 46n88, 49nn96–97, 49n99, 50, 66, 67n140, 76, 76n165, 99n49, 169n31, 173n43, 174n46, 197n125, 214n183, 220n201, 229n230, 231n232, 266n88, 267n91, 270n98, 318n5, 320n15, 321, 321n18, 322n20
Franke, John, 8n18
Freedman, David Noel, 82n8
Frei, Hans W., 17n5, 31n43, 43, 43n77
Fritsch, Charles T., 24, 25nn27–28, 26n31, 28n34, 47n90, 53n107, 57, 58n118, 66n139, 111n92
Fruchtenbaum, Arnold G., 62n129, 116n4, 124n33, 128n45, 132n62, 134n69, 141n94, 144n111
Frye, Northrop, 23n23, 46n88
Fuller, Daniel, 85n16, 168n29, 214n181, 264n82, 323n24, 323n26
Fuller, Michael E., 296n180
Fung, Ronald Y. K., 161n10, 253n47

Gaffin, Richard B., Jr., 8n19, 98n46, 238n6, 239n12, 240n13
Gamble, Richard C., 8n19
Gardner, Paul Douglas, 275n117, 276n119, 276n121, 277n123, 277n125, 278n127, 279n134
Garland, David E., 37n58, 212n177, 214n183, 271n100, 272n103, 273n109, 273n111, 273n113, 274n113, 274n114, 275nn117–119, 276nn120–121, 277n122, 277n124, 278n127, 279n131, 281n137, 282n143, 284n148
Garrett, Duane A., 169n31, 170n33
Gathercole, Simon, 329n48, 332n53
Gentry, Peter J., 2n4, 5n15, 6n17, 7n17, 8n19, 9n20, 10n24, 11n29, 11n30, 12n31, 26n31, 30n41, 44n79, 47n91, 56n115, 58n119, 60n124, 61n128, 64n135, 66n137, 67n143, 73n156, 77n166, 77n167, 82n8, 84n14, 95n36, 97n45, 113n99, 113n100, 123n30, 153n144, 159n6, 165n24, 177n55, 178n57, 180n64, 180n66, 181n70, 184n79, 184n80, 185n81, 186n85, 192n108, 193n110, 199n131, 200n135, 200n136, 201n138, 203n144, 205nn152–153, 205nn154–155, 207n159, 208nn160–161, 209n166, 210nn169–170, 261n73, 290n163, 293n172, 338
Gerhard, J., 27n32
Gerstner, John A., 158n5
Gibbs, Jeffrey A., 173n42
Gibson, David, 111n92, 111n93, 301n191
Gignilliat, Mark, 20n11, 20n12, 200n135, 211n171, 211n173, 219n197, 223n209, 293nn172–173
Gladd, Benjamin L., 63n132, 65n136, 95n37, 137n79, 161n10, 164n20, 166nn25–26, 169n31, 197n125, 198n127, 208n161
Glenny, W. Edward, 2, 2n5, 3, 3n9, 4n14, 76n163, 77n166, 77n168, 104n72, 106n79, 148n123, 149n125, 151n134, 152n139, 269n96
Goheen, Michael W., 11n29
Golding, Peter, 84n12, 91n28, 94n33, 96n40, 96n41, 96n42
Goldingay, John, 165n22, 199n130, 200n133
Goldsworthy, Graeme, 3n11, 8n19, 9n22, 11n29, 16n3, 18n6, 45n82, 58n120, 67n143, 73n156, 95n37, 104n72, 160n8, 176n52, 196n124, 234, 234n234
Goodrich, John K., 329n48
Goodwin, Mark J., 170n33
Goppelt, Leonhard, 3n11, 15, 15n2, 23n23, 24n26, 27n32, 28, 28n34, 33n49, 38n62, 44n79, 47n90, 48n94, 56n115, 59n121, 73n157, 150n130, 175n50, 177n55, 264n81, 266n88, 269n96, 271n100, 275n117, 279n134, 281n139, 284n150,

288nn158–159, 292n169, 304n202
Goulder, M. D., 44n80, 45n84
Green, Bradley G., 41n72
Green, Joel B., 17n4
Greever, Joshua M., 225n216, 251n41, 255nn57–58, 256n59, 256n61, 257n63, 260, 260nn70–71, 262n74
Greidanus, Sidney, 47n89, 50, 50n100, 73n157, 74n158, 105n74
Grenz, Stanley J., 8n18, 116n4, 118n12, 119n14, 128n46
Grindheim, Sigurd, 137n79
Grisanti, Michael, 141n94, 181n68, 211n171
Gromacki, Gary, 138n84, 139n87, 139n88, 140n93, 329n47
Groningen, Gerald Van, 72n155, 103n64
Grudem, Wayne A., 77n166
Gundry, Stanley N., 3n11, 4n13, 15n2, 35n53, 104n71
Gunn, George A., 133n65
Guthrie, Donald, 248n35

Hafemann, Scott J., 11n29, 84n14, 224n213
Hahn, Scott W., 82n8, 214n184
Hamilton, James M., 15n2, 30n40, 33n49, 50n100, 62n131, 69n147, 70n150, 72n155, 165n24, 166n26, 166n28, 169n30, 178n57, 184nn78–79, 185n83, 197n125, 206n156, 246n31, 331n51
Hamlin, E. John, 209n166
Hammett, John S., 236n1, 262n75, 286n156
Hanson, A. T., 16n2
Harless, Hal, 123n30, 137n82, 138n84, 139n87, 140n91, 141nn94–95, 142n98, 144n109, 145n114
Harmon, Matthew S., 38n62, 39n65, 40n67, 40n71, 182n72, 187n91, 188n93, 189n98, 189n100, 192 192n107, 193n109, 193n111,

200n134, 202n140, 219n196, 293n171, 293n173, 294n174, 309n215, 310n219, 311n226, 312, 312n227, 312n229, 313n230
Harris, Dana M., 44n79, 58n120, 69n148
Hart, Trevor, 9n20, 119n14
Harvey, Graham, 164n19
Hasel, Gerhard F., 8n19
Haykin, Michael G., 41n72
Hays, Richard B., 18n5, 21n15, 26n30, 38n62, 49, 49n95, 49n98, 50n100, 71n152, 76n165, 168n29, 170, 171n35, 172n38, 173n43, 212n177, 213n181, 217n192, 224nn212–213, 227n224, 271nn100–101, 272n102, 274n115, 278n127, 280n136, 281, 281n138, 283n147, 288n159, 293n171, 293n173, 303n196, 303n198
Helyer, Larry R., 115n1, 117n10, 126n39, 129n48, 135n74, 265n85, 320n14, 322n21, 327n38
Hendriksen, William, 101n60, 106, 106n80, 321n19
Hester, James D., 186n86, 190n103
Hoch, Carl B., Jr., 135, 136n76, 136n77, 136n78, 144n109, 260n71
Hodge, Charles, 84–85, 84n15, 85n16, 86, 86n17, 88n22, 91n28, 92n29, 93n30, 94n35, 95n36, 95n37, 98n48, 101n58, 288n159, 290n163
Hoehner, Harold W., 251n41, 252n44, 253n48, 256n61, 257n61
Hoekema, Anthony A., 61n128, 62n130, 83, 83nn11–12, 84n13, 98n48, 101n56, 101n60, 105n77, 106, 106n80, 112n94, 238n6, 239n10, 239n12, 244n23, 245n25
Holsteen, Nathan D., 122, 122nn27–28, 129n48
Holwerda, David E., 63n132, 71n153, 98n48, 105n77, 106, 106n80, 108n85, 110n90, 112n95,

(David E. Holwerda continued)
    164n19, 169n31, 172n40,
    189n97, 196n124
Horton, Michael S., 1n1, 8n18, 10n27,
    80n1, 83n9, 83n10, 84n14,
    85n16, 87n20, 88n22, 89n25,
    90n27, 94n34, 96n39, 97, 97n44,
    98n48, 99n50, 100n53, 100n54,
    101n57, 108n85, 110n90,
    112n96, 113n98, 238n6, 242n18,
    261n72, 301n191, 333, 333n61
Hoskins, Paul M., 23n22, 29n38,
    33n49, 44nn79–80, 44n80,
    45n83, 47n90, 48n94, 52n104,
    56n115, 56n116, 57n117,
    63n132, 64n134, 75n161,
    77n166, 77n167, 78n171,
    150n130, 195n116, 214n184
House, H. Wayne, 123n33, 126,
    126n40, 127, 127n42, 127n43,
    127n44, 128n45, 133, 133n63,
    133n66, 134n68, 158n2,
    205n154, 210n170, 220n199
Howard, Tracy L., 171n36
Hsieh, Nelson S., 181n69,
    190–191n104
Hugenberger, G. P., 44n79, 67n143,
    68, 68n144, 82n7, 83n10,
    104n71, 105n75, 105n78,
    200n133, 210, 210n167
Hullinger, Jerry M., 62n129, 128n46
Hummel, Horace D., 26n31, 69n148
Hvalvik, Reidar, 332n53

Ice, Thomas D., 115n1, 119n15,
    122n26, 126, 128n45
Instone-Brewer, 36n58
Isaac, Munther, 300n188

Jackson, T. Ryan, 310n219, 310n221,
    311n223, 312n227
Jeffery, Steve, 210n169
Jenkins, Jerry B., 1n2
Jervell, Jacob, 264n82, 318n5
Jewett, Paul K., 22n17, 110n91
Jewett, Robert, 332n53
Jobes, Karen H., 39n65, 40, 40n70,
    268nn94–95, 293n171, 294n174

Johnson, Dennis E., 26n31, 47n90,
    53n107, 72n155, 102n61,
    105n74, 108n86, 271n100
Johnson, Elliott E., 122n26, 126,
    126n40, 127n42, 127n44,
    133n63, 136n75, 139n86,
    139n89, 140n90, 141nn94–95,
    142nn98–99, 142n101, 142n102,
    144n109, 145n114
Johnson, H. Wayne, 28, 28nn35–36,
    29, 29n37, 44n80, 52n105,
    53n107, 105n74, 188nn95–96,
    190n103, 208n135, 271n100,
    277n124, 278n127, 278n129,
    279nn131–134, 280n135,
    281n139, 282nn142–143,
    283n147, 286, 286n154
Johnson, Jeffrey D., 81n6, 89n25
Johnson, Marcus Peter, 238nn6–7,
    239n12, 243n21, 244nn22–24,
    245n25, 247, 247n34
Johnson, S. Lewis, 3n11, 36n56,
    75n161, 76, 76n165, 78n169,
    305n203, 306nn206–209,
    329n47
Johnston, Philip, 71n153
Jordan, James, 67, 67n143
Juncker, Günther H., 288n159,
    289n161, 290n164, 291n168,
    292nn169–170, 294n174

Kagarise, Robby J., 186n86, 187n90,
    188n95
Kaiser, Walter C., Jr., 4n13, 18n6,
    23n20, 26n31, 35n53, 37n60,
    45n82, 53n107, 75n161, 139n89,
    158n2, 163n15, 183n75, 184n80,
    205n151, 211n174, 221n204
Karlberg, Mark W., 3, 3n7, 87n20,
    93n31, 98n46, 99n49, 104,
    104n73, 105n74, 105n76, 106,
    107n81
Karleen, Paul S., 158n5
Katanacho, Yohanna, 164n19
Keele, Zach, 81n4, 82, 83n10, 84n15,
    87n20, 88n22, 91n28, 92, 92n30,
    94n35, 95n37
Keesmaat, Sylvia, 218n194, 274n116

Kennedy, Joel, 167n29, 172n38, 172n40, 173n41, 174n45, 174n46, 175n50
Kim, Mitchell, 63n132, 181n68
Kinzer, Mark S., 320n14, 322n21
Kirk, David R., 194n114, 195n118, 196, 196nn121–122, 331n51, 331n53
Kirk, J. R. Daniel, 169n30
Kline, Meredith G., 83n9, 87n20, 88n22, 90n27, 95n37, 275n117
Klink, Edward W., III, 287n157, 303n199, 303n201
Klooster, Fred H., 83n12, 84n13, 98n46
Kloosterman, Nelson D., 103n68
Knoppers, Gary N., 138n85
Köstenberger, Andreas J., 8n19, 54n110, 55n112, 194n115, 195n115, 195n116, 195n119, 196n120, 199n129, 204nn146–147, 213n178, 213n179, 213n180, 214n181, 217n191, 220n202, 221n204, 222nn205–206, 228, 228n226, 229n228, 287n157, 303n195, 303n196, 303n197, 303nn198–199, 303n200, 303n201, 304n202, 307nn211–212, 308n212, 308n214, 310n221, 311nn223–224
Kreider, Glenn R., 116n4, 116n6, 117n8, 117n11, 119n14
Kümmel, W. G., 15n2
Kwon, Yon-Goyong, 187n90, 188n94, 190n103, 192n105
Kynes, William L., 161, 161n11, 173n44, 174n46, 221n205

Ladd, George Eldon, 7n17, 16n3, 61n128, 122n24, 132, 157n1, 249n38, 264n81, 329n47
LaHaye, Tim, 1n2
Lampe, G. W. H., 18n6, 44n80, 46n85, 46n88, 66n137
LaRondelle, Hans K., 16n2, 23n22, 23n25, 25n28, 30, 30n40, 33n49, 48n94, 50n99, 59n121, 73n157, 81n5, 99n49, 104n72, 142n100, 148n123, 155n146, 164n20, 174, 174n46, 175n47, 182n71, 196n124, 231n232, 319n10, 321nn16–17, 321n19
Lee, Chee-Chiew, 180n64, 180n66, 185n81
Legarth, Peter V., 3n11, 45n81, 48n94, 68n145
Leithart, Peter J., 17n4, 34n50, 67, 67n143, 73n158, 75, 75n162, 81n5
Lemke, Warner E., 181n67
Lessing, R. Reed, 200n134
Letham, Robert, 80, 80n2, 86–87, 86nn18–19, 87n20, 87n21, 88n24, 89, 90n26, 238nn6–7, 240n13, 245n25
Levering, Matthew, 34n50
Liefield, Walter L., 319n12, 321n17
Lightner, Robert, 117n8
Lim, Bo H., 218n195
Lincoln, Andrew T., 38n62, 251n41, 253n46, 253n48, 255n53, 255n54, 256n61, 257n62, 257n64, 292n170, 293n171, 295n178, 296n179, 297n181
Lindsey, Hal, 1n2
Lints, Richard, 3n11, 8n18, 10n26, 10n28, 11n30, 31n42, 47n91, 48n94, 57, 57n117, 58n118, 104, 104n73, 105n74, 105n75
Lioy, Dan, 6n17
Litwak, Kenneth D., 211n173
Loden, Lisa, 158n4
Longenecker, Richard N., 37, 37n59, 38n62, 75n161, 188n95, 190n102, 192n105, 289n160, 289n163, 290n165, 293n171, 309n215, 310n221, 311n223, 313n232
Louth, Andrew, 19n8, 20n11
Lucas, Richard J., 146n119, 147n121, 330n49, 332n56, 333n60
Lusk, Richard, 81n5

Macaskill, Grant, 238n5, 245nn27–29, 246n29, 253nn47–48

Malone, Fred A., 275n117, 334, 334n62
Mangina, Joseph L., 314n235
Mappes, David, 126, 126n40, 127, 127n42, 127n43, 127n44, 128n45, 133, 133n66, 134n68
Markus, R. A., 3n11, 31n42, 33n49, 48n94
Marsh, Herbert, 68, 68n145, 138n82, 138n84, 145n113, 168n29
Marshall, I. Howard, 317n4
Martens, Peter W., 18n5, 18n6, 18n7, 21n14, 27n32, 32n48
Martin, Oren R., 71n153, 179n61, 182n71, 228n227
Master, John R., 144n109, 144n112, 145n113
Maston, Jason, 323n24, 324n28, 324nn30-31
Mathison, Keith A., 107n83, 109n88, 122n24, 158n5
Mayo, Philip L., 265n83, 314, 314n235, 315n236
Mbuvi, Andrew M., 266nn87-88, 267n92
McCartney, Dan, 23n20, 44n79, 48n94, 77n166, 105n74
McClain, Alva, 126
McComiskey, Thomas Edward, 83n9, 101n58, 182n71, 184n79, 185n80, 187n88
McGowan, A. T. B., 81n5, 83n12
McKay, David, 83n10, 85n16, 100n53, 100n54, 102n62
McKelvey, R. J., 63n132, 195n116, 196n120, 254nn49-50, 255n53, 257n64, 258n65
McKnight, Scot, 264n80
McManigal, Daniel, 83n10, 88n22, 95n36, 95n37
Meek, James A., 44n79, 46n86, 222n207
Meier, John P., 264n80
Menninger, Richard E., 167n29, 169n31, 170n33, 174n46, 175n48
Merkle, Benjamin L., 6n17, 44n79, 62n131, 81n3, 98n48, 104n72, 130n52, 137n81, 148n123, 170n34, 179n60, 329n48
Merrill, Eugene H., 138n82, 141n94, 144n109
Meyer, Jason C., 38n62, 178n56, 181n67, 184n76, 186n87, 187n91, 190n102, 293n171, 329n48
Minear, Paul S., 100n55, 236n1, 302nn192-193
Moberly, R. W. L., 17n4
Moo, Douglas J., 4, 4n13, 18n6, 23n23, 31n42, 38n62, 40n69, 48, 48n93, 50n99, 52n104, 52n105, 58n120, 60n123, 75n161, 75n163, 76n163, 77n166, 77n167, 77n168, 177n55, 187nn90-91, 190n102, 192n105, 219n196, 223n211, 245n25, 288n158, 292n170, 293n171, 293n172, 294n174, 295n177, 298n183, 299n186, 307n212, 308n214, 310nn219-221, 311nn224-225, 313n232
Moore, Russell D., 5n15, 132n59, 143n106, 157n1
Moore, Thomas S., 212n175, 213n179, 220, 220nn202-203, 221, 221n204, 222nn206-208
Morgan, Christopher W., 16n3, 194n112
Moritz, Thorsten, 256n61
Motyer, Stephen, 161n11, 181n70, 199nn131-132, 200n136, 202n139, 203n143, 204n148, 205n151, 205n153, 208, 208n162, 209n163, 210n169, 225n215
Muller, Richard A., 42n75
Munayer, Salim, 158n4
Murray, John, 9, 9n23, 83, 83n9, 83n12, 85n16, 91n28, 93n32, 94n33, 94n35, 95n36, 96n39, 114, 114n101, 238n6, 239, 239n9, 239n12, 244nn21-22, 244n24, 245n25, 261n72

AUTHOR INDEX

Naselli, Andrew David, 8n18, 9n21, 48n94, 52n104, 58n120, 60n123, 69n147, 69n149, 75n161, 75n163, 76n163, 77n166, 77n168
Neill, Jeffrey D., 95n36
Nichols, Stephen J., 119n15, 133n64
Nicole, Roger R., 31n42, 103n64
Niehaus, Jeffrey J., 82n7
Ninow, Friedbert, 2n5, 12n32, 23n22, 44n80, 48n94, 67n142, 69n148, 103n66, 104n70, 104n71, 104n72, 148n123, 150n130, 203n143
Novakovic, Lidija, 29n37, 30n40, 69n149, 196n123, 198n128

O'Brien, P. T., 161n10, 193n110, 204nn146–147, 207n159, 213n178, 213n180, 214n181, 214n184, 220n202, 221n204, 222nn205–206, 225n217, 251nn41–42, 253n46, 254n50, 255n53, 256nn58–61, 257n64
O'Keefe, John J., 17, 17n4, 17n5, 23n21, 32n48, 34n50
Okoye, James Chukwuma, 211n171, 225n215
Oliphant, Jared S., 111n93
Olsen, Glenn W., 19n8, 21n15
Orlinsky, Harry M., 158n4
Osborne, Grant R., 31n42, 44n79, 50n100
Oss, Douglas A., 75n161, 77n168
Oswalt, John N., 201n137, 202n139, 204n146, 205n151, 205n152, 211n171, 212n175
Ounsworth, Richard, 25nn27–28, 26n31, 27–28, 27n33, 28nn34–35, 35, 35nn52–53, 45n81, 47n91
Owen, John, 87n21

Packer, J. J., 9n22, 76n164, 78n169
Pancaro, Severino, 303n199
Pao, David W., 168n29, 172n39, 202n139, 202n141, 211n171, 216n189, 218n195, 221n204, 222n206, 264n82, 319n8, 319n12, 321n17, 323n24, 325nn33–35, 326n36, 327, 327nn40–41, 328n42, 328n44
Parker, Brent E., 6n17
Parle, Joseph, 116n2, 117n10, 121n22, 149n125
Parsons, Michael, 239n11, 248n35
Pate, C. Marvin, 304n201
Pattemore, Stephen, 315nn235–236
Patterson, Richard D., 216n188
Pennington, Jonathan T., 317n3
Pentecost, J. Dwight, 62n129, 117n10, 123n33, 126, 132n62, 133n65, 134n70, 137n81, 138n83, 138n84, 139n86, 139n87, 139n88, 139n89, 140nn90–91, 141n94, 141nn95–96, 141n97, 142nn98–99, 144n109, 145n114, 148n124, 149n126, 320n14
Perriman, Andrew C., 53n107
Peterson, David G., 205n152, 207n157, 207n159, 213n179, 213n181, 215n186, 254n50–51, 255nn53–55, 257n64, 266n86, 266n89, 267n90, 323nn24–25, 323n26, 324n27, 324n29, 325nn32–35, 326n37, 327, 327n39, 327n41, 328nn44–45, 331n51, 332n54
Peterson, Robert A., 16n3
Pettegrew, Larry D., 144n109, 145n115
Philpot, Joshua, 45n83, 58n120, 72n155
Piotrowski, Nicholas G., 63n133, 169, 170n32, 172n38
Porter, Stanley E., 22n19
Powers, Philip E., 152n141, 153n141
Poythress, Vern Sheriden, 3n7, 29n37, 75n161, 76n164, 77n168, 104, 108n86, 118n12, 121n24, 130n54
Pratt, Jonathan, 306n204, 306n208
Pratt, Richard L., Jr., 96n41, 99n50, 109n88, 112n95
Pratt, Tom Jr., 7n17, 159n6
Provan, Iain, 42n74
Puckett, David L., 42n76
Pugh, T. Maurice, 116n6, 117n8, 123n32

Pyne, Robert A., 177n55, 189n98, 192n107

Quarles, Charles L., 229n230, 264n80
Quine, Jay A., 133n65

Ramm, Bernard, 23n20, 23n22, 23n24, 31n42, 34n51, 48n94, 73n157
Ray, Charles A., Jr., 307n211, 308nn213–214
Reicke, Bo, 320n15
Reisinger, John G., 7n17, 178n58
Renihan, Samuel, 74n159, 81n6, 94n32
Reno, R. R., 17, 17n4, 17n5, 21n16, 23n21, 32n48, 34n50
Reventlow, Henning Graf, 3n11, 16n2, 69n148
Reymond, Robert L., 85n16, 86, 86n17, 91n28, 92n29, 94, 94n33, 98n48, 100n53, 100n54, 105n77, 106n80, 113n97
Ribbens, Benjamin J., 4n12, 20, 20n12, 35, 41n73
Riccardi, Michael, 177n55, 186, 186n88, 187n88, 300n187
Richardson, Peter, 136n78, 163n15, 306n205, 307n212
Ridderbos, Herman N., 98n48, 100n54, 100n55, 101, 101n57, 101n59, 176n51, 194n115, 199n129, 228n225, 285n153, 287n157, 303n198, 303n199
Riddlebarger, Kim, 101n60, 105n77, 106, 106n80, 108n85
Robertson, O. Palmer, 8n19, 26n31, 81n4, 82n8, 89n24, 90n26, 93n30, 93n32, 95n36, 95n37, 98n48, 100n56, 102n62, 105n74, 105n77, 106, 106n80, 107, 107n83, 107n84, 111n93, 112n95, 323n22, 325n32
Robinson, H. Wheeler, 245n28
Roehrs, Walter R., 26n31, 38n62, 53, 54n108
Rogers, Cleon L., Jr., 141n94, 142nn99–100

Rosner, Brian S., 8n19, 9, 9n21, 37n58, 271n100, 272n107, 273nn109–111, 273n113, 274n114, 274n116, 275nn117–118, 276n120, 277n122, 277n124, 278n127, 279n131, 281n137, 281n140
Routledge, Robin, 185n80, 185n81, 197n125, 201n136, 201n138, 208nn160–161, 209n164, 211n172, 211n175, 216n188, 218n193
Rudolph, David, 298n184, 299n185
Ruthven, Jon, 331n52
Ryrie, Charles C., 2n3, 115n1, 115n2, 116n4, 116n6, 116n7, 117n8, 118n12, 118n13, 119, 119n14, 119n15, 120n17, 121, 121n21, 122, 122n24, 123, 123n33, 124n35, 125, 126, 126n40, 127n42, 128n45, 129n50, 132n61, 132n62, 133n63, 133nn66–67, 134, 134nn69–70, 136n79, 139n88, 142n101, 144n109, 144n112, 149n125

Sailer, Bill, 195n116, 196n120
Sailhamer, John H., 222n205
Salter, Martin, 177n55, 300, 300n189, 301n191, 313n233
Sanders, E. P., 81n5
Saucy, Mark R., 131n58, 132n59
Saucy, Robert L., 2n3, 115n1, 119n14, 120n17, 121n24, 123nn32–33, 124n34, 124n36, 126, 130n51, 130n52, 131, 131nn56–57, 132n60, 135nn72–74, 136n76, 136nn77–79, 137n81, 138n82, 138n84, 139nn87–89, 140nn92–93, 141nn94–97, 143n103, 143n106, 144n109, 145, 146n119, 146nn146–118, 147, 148n122, 163n15, 187n88, 196n124, 216n187, 224n213, 231n233, 260n71, 269n96, 297n181, 300n187, 305n203, 306n205, 306nn208–209,

307n210, 317n2, 318n6, 322n21, 327n38, 329n47, 330nn49–50
Scacewater, Todd A., 54nn109–110, 55nn111–113
Schnabel, Eckhard J., 168n29, 178n59, 208nn160–161, 210n171, 218n195, 221n205, 250n39, 318n5, 319n8, 321n16, 322n20, 323n24, 324n27, 324n29, 325n32, 325nn34–35, 327nn40–41, 328nn43–44
Schodde, G. H., 23n21, 23n22, 23nn24–25, 34, 34n51
Schreiner, Thomas R., 9n20, 16n3, 38n62, 52, 52n105, 53n107, 56n115, 59n122, 160n9, 164n19, 169n31, 172n38, 173n41, 175n50, 176n53, 177n55, 187nn89–90, 188nn94–95, 190n102, 192n105, 192n107, 197n125, 211n172, 213n180, 214n181, 214n184, 218n195, 219n196, 224n211, 224n213, 238n5, 240, 240n14, 241, 241nn15–17, 243, 243n19, 245n25, 245n26, 245n29, 253n47, 257n64, 263, 263n79, 264n80, 264n82, 265n83, 265n84, 266n86, 266n88, 267n90, 268n94, 268n95, 269n96, 270n99, 273n113, 279n130, 279n134, 282n144, 283n146, 286n155, 288n159, 289n161, 292n170, 293n171, 296n178, 299n186, 307n212, 308nn213–214, 310n221, 311n224, 313nn232–233, 314n234, 317n4, 325n33
Schrock, David, 73n156
Schultz, Richard L., 199n132, 201n138, 203n144, 211n171
Scobie, Charles H. H., 8n19, 9n20, 164n20, 172n38, 178n59, 196n124, 197n126, 200n133, 216n188
Scofield, C. I., 115, 117, 117n10, 121
Scott, James M., 177n55, 181n69, 181n70, 185n82

Seifrid, Mark, 239n11, 293n171
Seitz, Christopher, 17n5, 219n197
Shead, Andrew G., 207n159
Sherwood, Aaron, 208n161, 224nn211–212, 224n213, 251n41, 253n46, 256n61, 257n61, 257nn63–64, 310, 310n221, 311n222, 313n231
Sibley, Jim R., 265n84
Silva, Moisés, 18n6, 23n20, 31n43, 38n62, 45n82
Sizer, Stephen, 158n3
Smith, Adrian T., 183n73, 192n105
Smith, Gary V., 84n14, 165n24
Son, Sang-Won, 239n11, 245n25, 253nn47–48, 254n51
Soulen, R. Kendall, 158n2
Stackhouse, John G., 8n18
Stallard, Michael, 121n22, 122n29, 123n30, 126, 144n109, 144n111
Stanley, Walter D., 74n158, 332n55
Staples, Jason A., 329n48
Stark, J. David, 180n65, 191n104
Starling, David, 40n71, 190n102, 191n104, 192n105, 224n214, 226n218, 237n2, 254n52, 256n61, 257n64, 292n168, 293n173, 295n177, 300, 300n188
Steinmann, Andrew E., 187n88
Stek, John H., 45n83, 46n86, 46n87, 57n117, 82, 82n7, 83n9, 83n12, 103n64, 104, 104n70, 105n74
Storer, Kevin, 21n16
Storms, Sam, 99n50, 323n22, 325nn32–35
Stott, John R. W., 323n22
Strauss, Mark L., 168n29, 175, 175n50
Strawbridge, Gregg, 110n91
Streett, Andrew, 227, 227nn222–225, 228n226
Streett, Daniel R., 69n148
Strimple, Robert B., 101n60, 105n77, 106n80, 108n85
Stuhlmacher, Peter, 211n173
Svigel, Michael J., 115n1, 119, 119n16

Tabb, Brian J., 54n109, 55n111, 314n234, 315n235

AUTHOR INDEX

Tan, Paul Lee, 148nn124–125, 149, 149nn126–128
Taylor, Howard, 259n67, 260n71
Taylor, John W., 291n166, 292n168
Terry, Milton S., 24n26, 47n90
Thielman, Frank S., 225n217, 226n218, 251nn41–42, 252, 252nn43–45, 253n46, 253n48, 256n58, 256n61, 257n64
Thiessen, Matthew, 216n190
Thiselton, Anthony C., 23n22, 23n23, 23nn24–25, 31n44, 273n111, 274n114, 275n117, 276n120, 277n123, 278n127
Thomas, Robert L., 119n15, 122n26, 126, 126n40, 127n43, 127n44, 128n45, 129n49, 139n89, 208n160, 209n166, 229n230
Thompson, Alan J., 222n206, 323nn23–25, 324n27, 325, 325nn32–35, 326n36, 327n41, 328n44
Thompson, James W., 226n219, 248, 249, 249nn36–37, 253n47, 272nn104–106
Thorsell, Paul R., 144n109, 144n112, 146n119
Tidball, Derek, 73n158
Titrud, Kermit, 307n211
Torrance, Thomas F., 246n32, 247n32, 251, 251n40
Toussaint, Stanley D., 116n4, 116n6, 117n10, 132n62, 133n62, 133n65
Townsend, Jeffrey R., 139n89
Travers, Michael, 216n188
Treat, Jeremy R., 201n138, 210nn167–168
Treier, Daniel J., 17n4, 17n5, 20, 20nn12–13, 21n16, 22n18, 271n100
Trimm, Charlie, 22n19
Turner, Max, 131n58, 133n65, 158n5, 171n37, 172n37, 174n45, 175, 175n49, 214n181, 221n204, 323n24, 325nn33–35, 327nn39–40, 328, 328n44, 328n46

Turretin, Francis, 83n9, 87, 87n21, 91n28, 93, 93n30, 93n31, 93n32, 95n36, 95n37, 96n39

Vander Hart, Mark D., 271n100, 275n117, 285n152
VanDrunen, David, 81n4
VanGemeren, Willem A., 99n52, 106n80
Vanhoozer, Kevin J., 8n18, 10n26, 12n31, 17n4, 18n5, 23n21, 26n30, 30n41, 31, 31n43, 34n51, 35, 35n54, 41n74, 42n76, 43n77, 77n168, 104n73, 237n4, 238n6, 239nn11–12, 243, 243nn20–21, 244n21, 245nn27–28, 246n30, 253n47, 254nn49–50, 259, 259n67, 271n100
Vanlaningham, Michael G., 176n53, 191n104, 329n47, 330nn49–50
Venema, Cornelis P., 87n20, 88, 88n24, 89n25, 90n26, 90n27, 93n32, 96n39, 98n48, 101n56, 105n74, 105n75, 106, 106n80, 107n82, 110n91, 301n191
Verbruggen, Jan L., 36, 36n56, 37n60
Vickers, Brian J., 212n176, 242n18, 308nn213–214, 310n221, 311n224
Vlach, Michael J., 2n3, 116n5, 118n12, 120n18, 120n19, 122, 123nn30–31, 124, 124n33, 124n36, 125, 125n38, 134n71, 146nn118–119, 148n122, 150nn131–132, 151n133, 158n2, 163n14, 171n37, 184n77, 196n124, 197n124, 209n166, 216n187, 265n84, 270n97, 300n187, 306n204, 306n205, 306nn208–209, 316, 316n1, 317, 317n2, 318nn6–7, 319n13, 320, 320n14, 322n21, 329n47, 330n50, 333, 333n58, 333n59
von Rad, Gerhard, 44n80, 45n84, 46nn86–88, 46n87, 49n96, 57n117, 67n140
Voorwinde, Stephen, 163, 163n16, 164, 164nn17–18

AUTHOR INDEX

Vos, Geerhardus, 8n19, 9, 9n20, 25n28, 48n94, 58n118, 68n146, 85n16, 87n21, 92n29, 95n37, 104, 105n74, 105n78

Wagner, J. Ross, 224n211, 332n53
Walker, Peter, 71n153, 181nn68–69, 195n116, 231n232, 292n170, 296n179, 318n7, 319n10, 319n13, 320n15, 322n20, 323n22
Waltke, Bruce K., 48n94, 75n161, 82n8, 98n49, 104, 104n72, 105n74, 105n76, 105n77, 107, 107n82, 112n95, 165n24
Walvoord, John F., 123n33, 126, 132n62, 133n66, 134n70, 137n81, 138n82, 138n84, 139n86, 139nn88–89, 140n90, 141n94, 142n98, 142n100, 142n102, 144n109, 144n112, 148nn124–125, 149n125, 150n130, 151n132
Ward, Roland S., 83n9, 86n17, 87n21, 258n66
Ware, Bruce A., 126, 132n59, 144n109, 146nn117–120, 193n110
Waters, Guy, 110n91
Watts, Rikki E., 172n39, 173n41, 182n72, 200n135, 201n137, 209n165, 210n168, 211n171, 212n177, 213n180, 214n183, 216n188, 216n189, 218n194
Waymeyer, Matt, 329n48
Webb, Barry G., 199n131, 200n134, 201n137, 202n139, 202n141, 204n146, 205n150, 205n153, 207n158, 208n160, 209n166, 211n175, 225n215
Weber, Timothy P., 115n1, 116n2, 116n3
Webster, John, 8n18
Weima, Jeffrey A. D., 100n56, 309nn215–218, 310n221
Weinfeld, M., 82n8, 138n84
Wells, Tom, 7n17, 266nn87–88, 267n90, 268nn93–94, 269n96

Wellum, Stephen J., 2n4, 5n15, 6n17, 7n17, 8n19, 9n20, 10n24, 11n29, 11n30, 12n31, 26n31, 30n41, 44n79, 47n91, 52n104, 56n115, 58n119, 60n124, 61n128, 64n135, 66n137, 73n156, 77n166, 77n167, 82n8, 84n14, 95n36, 96n39, 97n45, 111n92, 113n99, 113n100, 123n30, 153n144, 159, 159n6, 161n10, 165n24, 177n55, 178n57, 180n64, 180n66, 181n70, 184n79, 184n80, 185n81, 186n85, 193n110, 199n131, 200n136, 203n144, 205nn152–153, 205nn154–155, 207n159, 208nn160–161, 215n185, 215n186, 246n32, 255n53, 260n70, 261, 261n73, 262n77, 290n163, 293n172, 301n191, 338
Wenham, David, 228n226
Wenkel, David H., 11n29
Whitacre, R. A., 226n221, 229n228
Whitcomb, John C., 62n129
White, A. Blake, 7n17, 95n36
White, R. Fowler, 111n93, 234n235, 289n162
Whitman, Jon, 23n22
Whittle, Sarah, 332n53
Wilken, Robert Louis, 20, 21, 21n14, 21n16, 22n17, 23n21, 36
Williams, Michael D., 10n25, 77n168, 82, 82n9, 95n36, 99n50, 100, 100n53, 100n54, 101n57, 108n85, 108n87
Williams, Sam K., 187n90, 190n103, 192n106
Williamson, Paul R., 60n124, 81n4, 82, 82n7, 83n9, 83n11, 84n13, 177n56, 179n60, 179n61, 179n63, 181n69, 186n85, 200n134, 205n149, 205nn151–153, 206nn154–155, 207, 208n160
Willis, Wendell Lee, 271n100, 274n113, 275n118, 276n121, 277n123

Willitts, Joel, 40n69, 293n171, 293n173, 295n177
Wilson, Allistair I., 168n29
Wilson, Douglas, 81n5
Windsor, Lionel, 186n87, 187, 187nn89–90, 187n92, 188, 188nn93–94
Winkle, 211n171
Witsius, Herman, 67n143, 81n4, 85n15, 86n17, 91n28, 93n30, 93n31, 93n32, 95n36, 95n37, 96n39, 103, 103n67, 106, 106n80
Wolff, Hans Walter, 44n80, 46n88
Wolter, Michael, 319n11
Wood, Thomas R., 166n25, 169n31, 180n66, 199n129, 200n133, 201n138
Woollcombe, K. J., 18n6, 28n34, 28n35, 31n42, 43n78, 44n80, 46n85
Woolsey, Andrew A., 80n2
Works, Carla Swafford, 272n105, 273n109, 273n112, 274n116, 275n118, 276n120, 283n145
Woudstra, Martin H., 1n1, 98n48, 100n53, 100n54, 101n56, 102n61
Wright, Christopher J. H., 46n85, 46n88, 83n11, 165n22, 181n68, 197n125, 204n148, 236n1, 246n32
Wright, N. T., 11n29, 81n5, 106n80, 158n3, 160n7, 165n24, 168n29, 172n38, 178n57, 186n87, 196n124, 245n29, 293n171, 296, 296n180, 298n184, 308n212, 309n215, 309n217, 310n221, 311nn223–224, 331n53, 332n53

Yee, Tet-Lim N., 251n41, 253n48, 256n61
Yoshikawa, Scott T., 23n22, 26n31, 45n81, 59n122, 66n138
Young, Frances M., 18, 18n7, 19, 19n8, 19n9, 20, 20n11, 23n21, 26–27, 27n32, 31n44, 34n50, 41n72, 44n80

Zaspel, Fred G., 7n17, 331n51
Zens, Jon, 113n99
Zoccali, Christopher, 329n48
Zorn, Raymond O., 99n49, 99n51, 100n53
Zuck, Roy B., 128n45, 148, 148nn124–125, 149, 149n125, 149nn126–127

Scripture Index

OLD TESTAMENT

Genesis

	38n64, 39n64, 40, 70, 84, 178, 183, 183n75, 232, 293
1–2	52n105, 84
1:2	173n41
1–3	72
1:26–28	195n118, 197
2:4	168n29
2:5	198n128
2:10	175n50
2:15	198n128
2:15–17	84
2:16	138n82
2:17	85, 138n82
2:18	175n50
2:24	20
3	91, 185n83
3:1–19	138n82
3:8	166n25
3–11	178
3:14–19	178n57
3:15	52n105, 57, 70, 91, 92, 93, 166, 178n57, 179n62, 183, 184, 185, 187
3:16	177n55, 178n57, 187, 187n88
3:17	39n64, 183n73
3:17–19	178n57
3:20	39n64
3:23	178n57
4:15	175n50
5:1 LXX	168n29
5:1–2	72
5:18	175n50
6:9	92
6:17–18	84
6:18	83
7:1	92
8:8–12	173n41
9:8–17	84
9:9	92
9:26–27	92
11:30	293
12	164
12:1	182n72
12:1–2	178
12:1–3	94n33, 178, 178n57, 179n63, 182n72, 183n73, 291n166
12:2	141n97, 142n97, 146, 177, 183n73, 184, 185, 291n166
12:3	142n97, 146, 177, 180, 183n73, 184, 185, 187n88, 190, 204n145, 224, 288, 288n159, 289n160, 291n166, 299
12:7	142n97, 177, 180, 184
13:10	166n25
13:14–16	94n33
13:14–17	180
13:15	139, 177, 178, 187
13:16	177, 184
14	51, 71
14:18–20	40n68
15	164, 179n63

SCRIPTURE INDEX

(Genesis continued)

15:1–21	138
15:3–5	190
15:5	177, 178
15:6	180, 288, 288n159
15:18	177, 184, 185, 185n82, 187n91
15:18–21	94n33, 180
16:3–4	293
16:9	39n64
16–17	38n62, 38n64
16–21	38, 40n67
17	164, 179n63, 187, 188, 188n93
17:1	89n24
17:1–6	188
17:1–16	94n33
17:2	165, 177
17:4–5	179, 180
17:4–6	177
17:5	180
17:6	142n97, 183
17:7	92, 139, 188
17:7–8	178
17:7–9	178
17:7–14	188
17:8	177, 184, 187, 187n91, 188, 188n93, 190
17:12–13	188
17:13	139
17:14	188
17:15–19	188n93
17:16	142n97, 183
17:17b–18a	184
17:19	139, 292
17:20	178
17:21	292
18:3	198n128
18:8	291n166
18:18	177, 288n159, 289n160
18:18–19	175n50
18–21	178
20:7	72
21	38n64
21:10	38n62, 292
21:13	178
22	73, 173n43
22:2	173, 173n42, 173n43
22:12	173, 173n42
22:16	173n42
22:16–18	94n33, 198n128
22:17	177, 178, 178n56, 187n88, 190, 288
22:17–18	181, 181n69, 186, 187, 187n88
22:17b–18	187
22:18	177, 180, 185, 187, 187n88
24:7	177, 187
24:60	178n56, 184, 187
25:4	178
25:19	177n54
26:1–5	187n88
26:2–5	187n88, 292
26:3	177
26:3 ESV	183n74
26:3–4	180, 181n69
26:4	177, 178, 187n88
26:5	175n50
26:15	177n54
26:24	177, 177n54, 212
27:29	183, 184
27:35–36	194
28	194n114
28:3	165
28:4	190
28:10–12	195n117
28:12	194
28:13	177n54
28:13–14	177, 178, 180
28:13–15	194, 195n118
28:14	177, 178, 181, 184
28:16	194
28:17	194
32:9	177n54
32:12	177, 178
32:28	164
35:10	180, 195n118
35:10–12	179, 180, 194
35:11	165, 180n64, 180n65, 183
35:12	177
47:27	165
48:3–4	165
48:4	177
48:15–16	177n54
48:19	177
49:8–12	183, 227n222

SCRIPTURE INDEX

49:9–10	184
49:10	183
49:11	183
49:22–26	227n222

Exodus

	39n64
1:7	165
3:6	177n54
3:12	209
3:15	92
4:22	165, 169, 173, 174, 174n45, 176
4:23	165, 199
6:6	54, 210
6:7	217
7:16	164, 198n128
7:26	198n128
8:16	198n128
9:1	198n128
9:13	198n128
12:3–14	210
12:23	273n109
12:46	217
12:49	178n59
13:5	165n25
13:21–22	203, 218, 275
14:2–27	275
14:13	241
14:19–22	275, 275n117
14:22	275
14:24	275
15:1–8	210n167
15:2	241
15:6	210
15:14–17	70
15:15–17	166n26
15:17	209, 227n224, 257n64
15:22	227n224
16	217
16:4	276
16:14–18	276
17:1–6	217
17:1–7	277
17:2–7	175
17:6	276
17:8–13	32
19:4	164
19:5	88, 92, 111n93
19:5–6	199, 217, 268
19:6	164, 268, 314
19:7–8	88
20:12	88
23:20	172n39, 203, 212, 218
23:31	185n82
24:6–8	216, 268
24:8	214
24:40	24
29:4	210
29:46	217
32:6 LXX	273n109
32:13	212
32:30–34	210
33:15–16	276
34:24	181n69

Leviticus

4:6	210, 214
4:17	214
5–7	210
14:7	210
16	64n135
16:1–25	210
18:5	86, 88
18:25–28	112
18:26–28	88
19:34	178n59
20:22	88
24:22	178n59
25	204n148
25:8–10	213
25:8–55	204
25:9–13	204
25:23	181n68
26	166n25
26:9	165
26:11–12	254n52
26:12	166n25
26:14–26	112
26:14–33	179

399

Numbers

	39n64
9:14	178n59
11	273n109
11:6–9	276
11:8	217
11–12	198n128
11:27–29	109
14	273n109
14:13–17	276
15:49	178n59
16	273n109
20:2–13	277
20:7–13	276
21:5–6	273n109
21:16–20	277n124
22–24	184
23:8	184
23:10	184
23:22	170
23–24	70
23:24	170
24:5–6	184
24:6	184
24:7–9	170, 184
24:8	170
24:9	170
24:12	184
24:17	204n145
24:17–18	181n69
24:17–19	170, 184
25:1–9	273n109
26:53–56	190
27:16–18	72
27:17	217n192, 302

Deuteronomy

	175
1:8	177n54
1:10	178
4:10	100
4:20	269
4:25–31	112
4:27	179
4:37	164
4:39	164
6:10	177n54
6:13	175, 175n48
6:13–15	175
6:16	175, 175n48
7:6	164
7:6–7	240
7:7	164
7:8	164
7:13	165
8:3	175, 175n48, 276
8:5	174
8:7–10	166n25
8:15–16	277n125
8:16	276
9:5	177n54
9:10	100
9:27	212
10:4	100
10:12	212
10:15	164
10:22	178
11:8–17	166n25
11:24ff	184
14:1	165
14:1–2	176
14:2	240, 269
18:15	216
18:15–18	70
18:18	216
19:8–9	181n69
24–25	36, 36n56
25	36
25:1–3	36
25:4	36, 37
28:6	303n195
28:15–68	112
28:62	178
28:62–64	179
29:2–4	54
29:13	92
30:6	181, 234n235
30:9	165
30:20	177n54
31:17	179
31:29	179
32:4	277
32:5	179
32:15	225, 225n217, 277

32:17	277
32:18	277
32:20	179
32:21	330n49
32:30–31	277
32:43 LXX	224n212
33:5	225, 225n217
33:26	225, 225n217
34:5	198n128

Joshua

6:22	32n47
11:23	179, 190
14:15	179
21:44–45	179
23:14–15	179
23:43–45	179
24:3	177n54

1 Samuel

2:27–35	62n131
16:13	201

2 Samuel

	201
3:18	198n128
5:2	302
6:14	166n27
6:17–18	166n27
7	141, 143
7:5	198n128, 201
7:5–16	174n45
7:8	198n128
7:9	141n97, 184
7:10	142n97, 184
7:12	184
7:12–16	142n97
7:13	266
7:13–14	254n52
7:14	92, 170, 175
7:19b	184, 184n80
7:26	200
7:29	142n97
8:15	204
8:18	166n27
22:44	206
22:50 LXX	224n212
23:1–7	166n27

1 Kings

3:2	266
4:20	178
4:21	179
4:24–25	179
5:4	179
8:41–43	208n161
11:13	198n128

1 Chronicles

1:27–28	177n54
1:34	177n54
16:13	177n54
16:16–17	139
17	141
17:4	198n128
17:7	198n128
17:8	184
17:11–14	184
18:14	204
27:23	178

2 Chronicles

1:9	179
17:13	170
22:10	170

Nehemiah

9:9–20	280
9:10	54
9:11–12	275
9:15	277n125
9:23	178
9:26	54

Job

	70n149
38–41	69n149, 70n149
41	69n149
41:3a	69n149

Psalms

	164
1–2	227n223
2	70, 71, 72, 174n46, 324
2:1–2	174n46
2:7	170, 173, 173n43, 173n44, 174n45, 174n46, 175
2:8	182, 185
2:27–28	182
8	167
8:4–8	52n105, 72, 197
16	142n100
17:49 LXX	224n212
18:1	198n128
18:49	224n212
22	166n27
25:12–13	182n71
36:1	198n128
37	71, 182n71
37:9	182n71
37:11	182n71
37:22	182n71
37:29	182n71
37:34	182n71
46–48	208n161
47	203n143, 324
47:7–9	182
51:5	244
68:16–17	297, 297n182
72	71, 185n82, 185n83
72:2	204
72:3–4	185
72:8	185
72:8–11	182
72:9	185
72:9–11	185n82
72:11	185
72:16	185n82
72:17	142n97, 180, 185
77:20	165, 302
78	280
78:13–14	275
78:15–16	276, 277
78:18	273n109
78:23–24	217
78:24	276
78:35	278
78:41	273n109
78:45	273n109
78:52–55	302
80	227, 227n223, 227n224, 227n225, 228n226, 229n230
80:1	227n224, 302
80:3	227n224
80:7	227n224
80:8	165, 226n221, 227, 227n224
80:8–9	228
80:8–15	23
80:13	227n224
80:14	226n221, 227
80:15	227, 227n224
80:15–19	197
80:15a	227n222
80:15b	228
80:18	227
80:19	227n224
80:51a	227n222
87	208, 225n215, 293n172, 301
89:3	174n45, 198n128
89:3–4	184
89:20	174n45, 198n128
89:23–29	184
89:26–27	170, 174n45
89:27	175
89:28	184
89:36	184
91	174n46
91:9–13 LXX	174n46
95	152
95–100	203n143
100:3	165
105:6	164
105:9	72
105:9–10	139
105:12–15	72
105:38–39	275
105:40	276
105:41	276, 277n125

106	227n224	5:1–7	165, 226n221, 229n230
106:14	273n109	5:2	226
106:16–18	273n109	5:5–7	226
106:34–43	179	6:9–10	54
107:38	165	6:10	54, 54n110, 55n111
109:8	264	6:13	205n150
110	51, 71, 142n100, 143	8:14–15	266
110:1–7	184	9:1–2	213
110:4	40n68	9:2–7	201n170
116:1 LXX	224n212	9:5–6	70, 201n138
117:1	224n212	9:6	256
118:10–13	229n230	9:6–7	185
118:19–27	63	9:7	202, 204, 323n26
118:22	229n230, 266	10:24–26	203n142
118:22–23	229n230	11	224n211
118:26	318, 319	11:1	201, 227n222
121:8	303n195	11:1–5	70, 201, 204
132	142n100, 143	11:1–9	201n138
132:10–12	184	11:1–10	185
146–150	227n223	11:2	173, 201, 202
		11:3–4	201
		11:4	202
		11:6–9	174n46

Ecclesiastes

12:3–7	23

Isaiah

	152, 172, 211, 211n171, 212, 213n180, 217, 220n198
1:2	165
1:2–4	176
1:4	165
1:21–23 LXX	293n172
1:26	323n26
1:26 LXX	293n172
2:1–4	180
2:1–5	222n205, 257
2:2	221
2:2–4	204, 208n161, 287, 323n26, 324
2:2–5	221
2:3	203
2:4	136
3:14	226n221
4:2–6	203n142
4:5–6	191
5:1	225n217

11:10 LXX	224, 224n212
11:10–12	206
11:10–16	164n21
11:11	203n142
11:11–16	224
11:15	172
11:15–16	203n142
12:3	217
12:3–4	136
16:8	226
16:10	226
19:24–25	180, 208
20:3	201n138
22:20	201n138
24:2	201n138
24:18	71
24:20	201n138
27:2–6	165, 226n221
27:9	330, 331, 332, 332n54
28:2	71
28:16	254, 266
30:11	218
30:21	218
32:15	173n41, 209, 221, 226n218, 257, 324, 325, 327, 327n41

SCRIPTURE INDEX

(Isaiah continued)		
32:15 LXX	221n204	
32:15–18	191	
35:1–10	328	
35:4	241	
35:5–10	203n142	
35:8	218	
35:8–10	174n46	
36–37	199n131	
36–39	199n131	
37:35	201, 201n138	
38–39	199n131	
38–55	199n131	
38–66	189, 199	
39:5–7	202	
40	69n149, 70n149	
40:1	203, 213, 218n195	
40:1–2	202, 204, 323n26	
40:1–11	202, 202n141, 203	
40:2	202, 205n149	
40:3	172n39, 212, 218, 218n195	
40:3–4	203	
40:3–5	172n39, 202, 202n142, 216	
40:3–11	164n21	
40:5	203, 203n143	
40:6–8	203	
40:7–8	268n95	
40:9	204	
40:9–11	203, 210n167, 212, 223, 302	
40:10	209	
40:10–11	199n129, 210	
40:11	165	
40:13	69n149	
40:15–17	211n171	
40–48	203n144	
40–55	182n72, 199n131, 209, 209n166, 210, 210n167, 210n171, 211n171, 211n173, 218n195	
40–66	211n171, 293n172	
41:2	201, 203	
41:8	164, 189, 189n99, 196, 200, 200n135, 240	
41:8–9	211n174	
41:8–10	189n99	
41:9	200	
41:11–12	211n171	
41:17–20	202n142, 209, 210
42	200n134, 204n145, 214
42:1	173, 173n42, 173n43, 174n45, 189, 196, 201, 202, 204n146, 209n163, 211n174, 221
42:1–4	200n134, 202, 204, 213
42:1–6	201
42:1–9	200
42:3	200n134, 204, 204n146
42:4	201, 203, 204, 204n146
42:5	205n151
42:5–9	200n134
42:6	136, 185, 189, 204, 205, 205n151, 208n162, 213, 214, 220, 220n201, 223
42:6–7	200, 204n145, 205n149, 213, 326n37
42:7	202, 204
42:10–12	204, 210n171
42:13	203n142
42:13–16	210
42:14–16	202n142
42:15	173
42:16	218
42:18–19	200
42:18—42:21	203
42:19	200, 200n135
42:23	203
42:23–24	200
43:1	211n174
43:1–3	202n142, 209
43:2	71, 173
43:3–4	211n171
43:5	287n157
43:5–7	326
43:8	200
43:8–12	164n21
43:8–13	220n203
43:10	200, 200n135, 213, 220, 221, 325
43:10–12	221n204
43:12	213, 220, 221, 325
43:14–21	202n142
43:16–17	173
43:16–19	268
43:18–25	325
43:19	312

SCRIPTURE INDEX

43:20	174n46
43:20–21	268, 269
43:21	269
44:1	196, 225
44:1–2	200, 224
44:1–5	192, 193, 224, 225
44:2	211n174, 225, 225n217
44:3	173n41, 192, 217, 221, 225, 226n218, 257, 324
44:3–4	209
44:3–5	191, 192, 192n107, 193, 225, 289, 299, 325
44:5	192, 193, 193n111, 225n215
44:6–8	220n203
44:8	213, 220, 221
44:9–20	211n171
44:21	200, 200n135
44:24	211n174
44:24—45:13	201
44:24—48:22	203
44:26	200
44:26–28	203
44:27	203n142
44:27–28	173
45:1	201
45:4	200, 200n135
45:14	210n171, 211n171
45:17	241
45:20–22	221
45:22	210n171
48:14	201
48:17	218
48:17–19	179
48:20	200
48:20–21	202n142, 280
48:20–22	210
48:21	217n192, 277
49	222
49:1	211n174
49:1–2	200
49:1–6	200n134, 201n136, 202
49:1–13	200
49:1—53:12	203
49:3	200, 200n135, 201n136, 211
49:3–12	219
49:4	204
49:5	185, 200n135
49:5–6	200, 204n145
49:6	136, 166n25, 185, 201n170, 203, 204, 210n171, 217, 220, 220n201, 221, 221n204, 222, 222n207, 223, 241, 295, 325, 326n37
49:6–7	324
49:6–9	213
49:7	201
49:7–13	200n134, 209n166
49:8	189, 202, 205, 205n151, 208n162, 209n166, 222
49:8–9	204
49:8–12	202n142, 209, 210
49:8–13	209n166, 223
49:9	202
49:9–10	204, 217n192, 303n195
49:9–11	217
49:9b–10	217n192
49:11	218
49:12–13	209n166
49:13	202, 204, 210n166, 213
49:13–23	293n172
49:22–26	211n171
49:23	219
49–57	203n144
50	213n179
50:2	173
50:2–3	210
50:4–11	200
50:5–9	200
50:8	207
50:10	209n163
50:10–11	201n170
50:21	209n163
51	182, 206n154
51:1–3	293
51:1–8	182n72
51:1—52:15	164n21
51:2	164, 182n72
51:2–3	71, 206n154
51:2a	182n72
51:2b–3	182n72
51:3	166n25, 182, 182n72, 209
51:3–5	204n147
51:4	220
51:4–5	182n72, 210n171
51:4–6	203
51:4–7	206n154

SCRIPTURE INDEX

(Isaiah continued)

51:5	204
51:7	204n147
51:9–10	202n142
51:9–11	173, 209, 210
51:11	209
51:16	209n163
51:22–23	211n171
51–55	223n209
52:1–10	293n172
52:7	210n167, 212, 223, 223n209, 256
52:7–12	204, 209
52:10	203, 210, 241
52:10–12	209, 210
52:11	254n52
52:11–12	202n142
52:12–15	201
52:12—53:12	202
52:13	212, 219n196
52:13—53:12	191n104, 200, 210, 223n209
52:14–15	219n196
52:15	210, 214, 216, 223n209, 224n211, 289
52:15—53:12	214
53	54n110, 62, 64n135, 189, 201n170, 202, 205, 206, 206n153, 211n173, 213n179, 214, 214n183, 214n184, 216, 293, 293n172, 312n227
53:1	54, 54n110, 55, 210
53:2	201
53:4	207
53:4–6	200, 212
53:4–8	55
53:4–12	210
53:5	206n153, 256
53:5–6	199n129
53:6 LXX	214
53:7	210, 217, 268
53:8	200
53:9	200, 201
53:10	189, 190n101, 202, 207, 209, 210, 219
53:10–11	111, 290
53:10–12	200, 212, 214, 289
53:11	202, 219n196
53:11–12	210, 219n196
53:12	214, 214n184
53:12 LXX	214
54	219n196, 312
54 LXX	312
54:1	38n62, 38n64, 39n65, 40, 40n68, 111, 189, 190, 190n101, 191n104, 206n153, 219n196, 290, 292, 293n172, 293n173, 294, 294n174, 295, 295n176, 297n181, 299, 312
54:1 LXX	219n196, 293
54:1–3	181, 191n104, 206, 289, 293, 293n172, 295
54:1–5	234n235
54:1–17	312n227
54:2	295
54:2–3	182
54:3	111, 189, 190, 203n142, 219n196, 290, 338
54:4–8	206
54:5	165
54:5–6	293n172
54:5–8	100
54:8–9	71
54:9–10	206
54:10	205, 206, 208n162, 256, 293
54:10 LXX	311
54:11	207
54:11–12	206, 311
54:11–14	293n172
54:13	60, 102n63, 203n142, 206, 206n157, 256
54:14	219n196
54:17	202, 207, 208n160, 219n196
54–55	205, 205n153, 206n153
54–66	219, 219n197
55:1–2	206, 217
55:3	205, 208n162
55:3–4	206
55:3–5	146, 185, 206, 215
55:4–5	206n155
55:5	210n171, 221, 256n61
55:6	217
55:11–13	202n142
55:12	256
55:12–13	206n153, 209

SCRIPTURE INDEX

56	208, 208n160	59:21	191, 202, 202n140, 208n162, 209n162, 209n163, 331
56:1	202n140		
56:1–2	207		
56:1–8	207, 216, 219n195, 235	60	208n162, 295
56:2–3	208	60:1–4	330
56:3	205n149, 207, 326	60:1–22	202
56:3–8	257, 303, 304n202	60:2	203n142
56:4	208n160	60:3	210n171
56:4–8	185	60:4–7	209
56:5	326	60:6–9	210n171
56:5–6	207, 209n162	60:9	204
56:6	202, 207, 208, 208n160	60:10–14	211n171
56:6–7	205n149, 210n171, 221, 262, 295	60:17	202n140
		60:19	203n142
56:6–8	209, 256n61, 287	60:21	202n140, 205n150
56:7	221	61	202n139, 204n148
56:8	193	61:1	173, 202, 204, 220, 221
56:9–12	302	61:1–2	204, 204n148, 212, 213, 223
56:19–21	208	61:1–3	199, 199n132, 202, 204
56–59	209n162	61:1–6	202
56–66	202, 208n161, 219n195	61:2	202, 213
57	256n61	61:2–3	205, 205n149, 209n166
57:1	202n140	61:2b	214n181
57:3–4	202n140	61:3	202, 202n140, 205
57:12	202n140	61:5	205n149
57:13	182n71, 219	61:6	62n131, 102n63, 206, 206n156
57:14	209, 218, 218n195		
57:19	256, 256n61, 257n61	61:6a	205
58:2	202n140	61:6b	205
58:6	213	61:7	205n149
58:8	202n140, 203n142	61:8	205
58:11	217	61:9	202n140
58–66	203n144	61:10	202
59	209n163	61:10–11	202n140
59:1–8	208n162	61:10—62:7	199n132
59:4	202n140, 209n163	62:1–2	202n140
59:9	202n140, 209n163	62:4–7	209
59:9–15a	208n162	62:5	100
59:14	202n140, 209n163	62:10	209, 218
59:15b–20	208n162	62:11–12	202
59:16–17	202n140	62:12	219
59:16f	209n163	63	203n142
59:18	211n171	63:1	202, 202n140
59:19	208, 208n162	63:1–6	199n132
59:19–21	331	63:3	211n171
59:20	219, 331, 331n51	63:7–14	218n194
59:20–21	199, 202, 208, 208n162, 289, 330, 331	63:11–15	173
		63:15	227n224

SCRIPTURE INDEX

(Isaiah continued)

63:17	202, 202n140, 208n160
64:1	173
64:1–3	164n21
64:3	219
65	211n171
65:1	330n49
65:6	219n196
65:8–9	202, 208n160, 219n196
65:13	202
65:13–15	208n160, 219n196
65:16	219
65:17	186, 219n196, 223, 312, 312n227
65:17–25	312n227, 328
65:18–25	323n26
65:25	174n46
65–66	151
66:7–11	293n172
66:14	202, 208n160, 219n196
66:16	211n171
66:18–19	210n171
66:18–20	221, 257
66:18–21	295
66:18–24	185, 287
66:19–21	62n131, 206, 206n156
66:20–23	209
66:21	205n149
66:22	186
76	209n166
77	209n166

Jeremiah

	205n152
2:2	47n89, 100, 165
2:21	165, 226, 226n221
3:16	102n63, 180, 182
3:16—4:4	180
3:17	180, 207n159
3:18	180
3:19	174n45
4:2	180, 193n110
4:3–4	180–81
6:9	226, 226n221
8:13	226n221
9:13–16	179
9:25–26	181
11:15	225n217
12:7	225n217, 318n7
12:10	226n221
12:10–11	165
12:10–13	226
12:14–17	193n110
12:16	207n159
16:14–15	164n21, 323n26
16:14–18	193n110
16:15	327
16:19–21	207n159
22:5	318n7
23:1–4	302
23:1–6	302
23:3	182
23:5	70, 204, 224, 227n222
23:5–6	185
23:5–8	164n21, 323n26
23:6	219n196
24:6	327
30:8–10	199
30:9	185n84
30:10	165
31	214
31:5	227
31:7–9	241
31:9	171, 173, 174n45
31:10–12	302
31:15	70–71
31:15–20	71
31:20	165, 174n45
31:26–40	338
31:28–34	111
31:29–40	60
31:31–34	71, 102n63, 207n159, 266n85, 332n54, 338
31:31–40	330
31:32	165
31:33	92
31:33–34	207, 289
31:34	60
31–34	71
31:34	205, 207n159, 290
31:36–40	185
32:15	227
32:36–44	111n93
32:37	111n93
32:38	111n93

408

SCRIPTURE INDEX

32:39	111n93
32:40	107, 111n93
32:42–44	111n93
33:6–16	185
33:9	185, 206
33:14–26	62n131, 185
33:15	224, 227n222
33:15–17	323n26
33:16	219n196
33:21	184
33:21–26	199
33:22	206
33:24	164
33:26	164
38:8–9	173n42
38:15 LXX	173n42
38:20 LXX (31:20)	173, 173n42
38:31–34	173n42
46:27–28	165
50:5	107

Ezekiel

	205n152
4:22	178n59
11:15–20	164n21
11:16–21	181
11:17	254n52
11:19	226n218
11:19–20	324
12:15	179
15:1–8	165, 226n221
15:21–22	227n225
16	165
16:60	107
17:1–10	23
17:5–6	226
17:6–8	226n221
17:6–9	227n225
18:30–32	181
19:10–14	165, 226n221, 227n225
20:23–24	179
20:34	254n52
20:41	254n52
34	165, 185, 302, 304
34:5	217n192
34:7–16	302
34:10–16	302
34:11	304
34:11–16	199n129
34:12	287n157
34:12–15	303n195
34:22	303
34:22–25	302
34:23	70, 199, 217n192, 304
34:23–24	185, 199n129, 217n192, 303
34:23–25	302
34:25	302
34–37	323n26
36	214
36:10–11	181n68
36:11	182
36:22–36	181, 338
36:24–27	245
36:24–38	60, 185
36:24ff	287n157
36:25	216
36:25–27	109, 217, 266n85, 289, 324
36:26–27	226n218, 257
36:26–30	181n68, 191
36:27	209
36:35	71, 166n25, 182
36:36	185, 206
37	302, 326
37:1–14	191
37:11–28	185
37:14	147n121, 209, 226n218, 289
37:15–28	303
37:21–28	199n129
37:22–24	289
37:23–24	256
37:24	70, 303
37:24–28	185, 302
37:25	199, 199n129
37:26	107, 199n129, 256
37:26–27	254n52, 257n64
37:26–28	257
37:28	185, 206
39:29	209
40–48	62n131
44:6–9	181
44:6–16	267n92
47	196n120

(Ezekiel continued)

47:1	217
47:1–12	62, 71, 166n25, 328
47:12	166n25
47:21–23	180n66

Daniel

2:31–45	197
2:34–35	63
7	194n113, 196, 197, 198n127, 318, 318n5
7:13	194, 195, 198
7:13–14	52n105, 72, 197
7:14	197, 324
7:15–28	197n126
7:18	197, 198n127
7:22	197, 198n127, 318
7:25	198n127
7:27	197, 198n127, 324
7:29	318
8:13	320
9:26	71
12:6–9	77n166

Hosea

	169, 170, 268
1–3	165
1:9–11	179, 268
1:10	165, 170n33, 268n95
1:10–11	170, 170n33
2:12	226
2:14–15	164n21
2:14–20	47n89
2:15	269
2:16—3:5	185n84
2:23	268, 268n95, 269
3:5	70, 170, 170n33, 323n26
6:1–3	231n232
6:2	231
10:1	226, 226n221
10:1–2	165
11	169, 169n30, 169n31, 170n34, 171, 171n35, 172n38
11:1	51n102, 150, 152, 165, 168, 169, 169n30, 169n31, 170, 170n34, 171, 171n36, 171n37, 172n38, 173, 174n45
11:2–11	171
11:5	169, 169n31
11:8–9	171
11:10–11	169, 169n31, 170, 171n36
11:11	169, 170, 323n26
14:2	102n63
14:4–8	231n232
14:4–9	227
14:7	165, 226n221

Joel

2:3	71, 166n25
2:28—3:3	191
2:28–29	226n218, 245, 331
2:28–32	109, 209, 289, 324
3:1–2	226n218
3:18	62, 217

Amos

9:11	70
9:11–12	102, 102n62
9:11–15	185, 323n26
9:14	227

Jonah

2:2	70
2:6	70

Micah

1:6	226
2:12	303
2:12–13	199n129
4:1–3	180
4:1–5	221, 257, 324
4:2	323n26
4:3	136
4:6–7	164n21
5:2–4	302
6:6–8	102n63
7:15–20	164n21
7:18–20	164

Zephaniah

1:13	226
3:9–10	182

Zechariah

2:10–12	208, 257n64, 287
2:11	221
3:7–9	231n232
4:6	209
6:9–15	62n131
8	323n26
8:3	70
8:13	180
8:18–23	208n161
8:20–23	221
8:22–23	180
9:9–10	136, 323n26
9:10	185
9:11	205
10:6–12	164n21
11	302
12:10	191, 209
13:1	62
14	196n120
14:8	62
14:8–11	71
14:9	185

Malachi

1:11	330n49
3:1	172, 172n39, 212
4:1–4	208n161
4:5	172
4:5–6	172n39

DEUTEROCANONICAL BOOKS

Baruch

3:36	225n217
3:37 LXX	225n217

2 Esdras

5:23	226n221

4 Ezra

6:55–59	311n225

Jubilees

1:24–25	311n225

Judith

9:4	225n217

3 Maccabees

6:28	311n225

Sirach

36:17	311n225
44:21	185n82

PSEUDEPIGRAPHA (OLD TESTAMENT)

1 Enoch

90:33	304n201

Psalms of Solomon

17:26–27	311n225

SCRIPTURE INDEX

DEAD SEA SCROLLS

4QFlor 175

ANCIENT JEWISH WRITERS

Philo 32, 32n46, 40

RABBINIC WORKS

Talmud 36n58
Mishnah 36n58

Targums 36n58

NEW TESTAMENT

Matthew
 168n30, 171, 172n37, 172n38
1:1 168n29, 287
1:1–17 167
1–4 175n50
1:21 175n50, 213
1:22 168n30, 320n13
2 172n38
2:1–12 172n38
2–4 232
2:5 168n30
2:15 29, 51n102, 150, 152, 168, 168n30, 169n30, 169n31, 170n34, 171, 171n36, 171n37, 172n38, 173n42, 216, 287
2:17 168n30
2:17–18 71
2:18 173n42
2:23 168n30
3:3 172n39
3–4 173n42
3:9 179n62
3:15 175n50
3:15–17 172, 287
3:16 174
3:16–17 173, 198
3:17 173, 173n42, 173n43, 174n45
4:1–11 29, 173n42, 174
4:3–7 175
4:5 174n46
4:10 175
4:11 287
4:12–17 213
4:14 168n30
5:5 182n71, 232, 243, 297
5–7 223
5:9 176, 243
5:14 220, 220n201
5:16 220
5:44–45 176
6:10 241
6:14–15 242
8:17 168n30, 211n173
9:36 264n80
10:1–4 264n80
10:6 264n80
10:22 241

11:4–7	213
12	56
12:6	56, 62
12:17	168n30
12:18–21	173, 200n134, 211, 213
12:28	241
12:39–42	29
12:41	56
12:42	56
12:49–50	223
13:35	168n30
13:38	176
15:13	107
16:16 ESV	170n33
16:16–19	229n230
17:5	173
17:10–13	172
18:20	320n13
19:27–31	317
19:28	241, 241n17, 316, 317, 318n5
19:29	243
21:1–17	320n13
21:4	168n30
21:12–15	229n230
21:15	320n13
21:23	320n13
21:23–44	229n230
21:33	229n230
21:33–43	229n230
21:39–42	229n230
21:42	229n230
21:42–44	63, 266
21:43	102n63, 229n230
21:44	229n230
22:1–14	23
23:37–39	318, 320n13
23:39	318
24:1–2	320n13
24:22	320
24:36	325
25:34	243
25:37–39	319
26:28	214
26:29	241
26:61	320n13
26:64	197
27:9	168n30
27:51–53	62
28:18–20	168n29, 221, 223
28:19	275, 320n13
28:20	320n13

Mark

	212, 213n180
1:1–3	212
1:2	212
1:2–3	172n39
1:3	212
1:4	212
1:10–11	172
1:11	173n43
1:13	174n46
1:15	212
2:18–20	100
6	217n192
6:34	217n192
6:34–44	217n192
8:31	230
10:45	214, 214n183
12:1	229n230
12:1–9	107
12:1–12	229n230
12:10–11	229n230
13:2–4	320n13
13:20	320
13:32	325
14:24	214, 214n183
14:58	62

Luke

	324
1	168n29
1–2	213n178
1:16–17	172n39
1:32–33	167, 324
1:46–55	324
1:54	212, 213
1:54–55	167
1:55	287
1:67–79	167, 324
1:69	212
1:72–73	287
1:76	227n224

SCRIPTURE INDEX

(Luke continued)

1:76–77	172n39
1:78–79	213
2:10	213
2:25–32	213
2:29–32	167, 324
2:32	213, 222
2:38	167, 324
3:4–6	172n39, 216
3:8	179n62
3:16	324
3:21–22	172, 174n45
3:22	173, 173n43
3:38	165
4:1–13	174
4:9	174n46
4:16–21	213, 213n181
4:16–30	214n181
4:18	220
4:19	213
4:21	213
4:23	324
6:12–16	264
7:9–12	227n224
7:16	227n224
7:21–23	213
8:1	324
8:10	324
9:22	223
9:23–27	324
9:35	173, 173n43
10:25	243
11:47	54
12:31–32	324
12:32	100, 302
13:23–30	319, 324
13:34	320n13
13:34–35	316, 318, 319, 320n13
13:35	318, 318n7, 319, 319n13, 320n13, 321, 322
14:24	319
15:8–13	167
17:20–21	324
17:21	241
18:16–30	324
18:31–33	230
19:27	319
19:38	319
19:41	320n13
19:41–44	318n7, 320n13
19:43–44	320n13
20:9–18	229n230
21	321
21:20	318n7
21:20–23	321
21:22	320n13
21:24	316, 320, 320n14, 321, 321n16, 321n17, 321n19, 322
21:28	241n15, 322
21:31	324
22:15–18	62n131
22:20	60, 214
22:29–30	317
22:30	264, 317, 318n5
22:37	211, 211n173
24:7	230–31
24:21	230–31
24:25–26	230–31
24:25–27	321
24:27	15
24:33–36	296n180
24:44	15
24:44–47	222n208
24:45–53	296n180
24:46	230
24:46–49	220
24:47	220, 221
24:48	220
24:49	221, 221n204, 325

John

	211n173, 217n191, 304
1	195n117
1:4	213
1:9	58n119
1:12	176n51, 287, 287n157
1:12–13	176, 241, 249
1:13	176n51, 287n157
1:14	62, 195n116
1:17	216
1:29	61, 215, 217
1:36	61, 215
1:41	194n113, 195n117
1:47	194

SCRIPTURE INDEX

1:47–51	194	8:33	177n54
1:49	194n113	8:37–47	287n157
1:51	62, 194n114, 195, 195n116, 195n118, 196, 196n121	8:39	177n54
		8:42–47	303
1:51 ESV	194	8:44	179n62
2	228n227	8:56	288
2:14–22	62, 195n116	9:5	213
2:19–21	320n13	10	199n129, 302, 304
2:21	320n13	10:1–5	303
3:3	176n51, 241	10:1–8	100
3:3–7	287n157	10:1–16	23
3:10–11	65n136	10:2–4	302
3:13	195n119	10:9	303
3:14	216	10:11	302
4:5–6	195	10:11–18	305
4:10	228n227	10:14–15a	303n200
4:11–14	195	10:14–16	302, 304
4:19–24	195n116	10:15	303n200
4:20–24	62	10:16	196n120, 287n157, 303, 303n196, 304n201
4:21	320n13		
5:24–25	242	10:17–18	303n200
5:26	244	10:22–39	195n116
5:28–29	242	10:26	303
5:39	15	10:27–29	305
5:39–40	65n136	11:25	244
6	226n220	11:47–52	287
6:5–11	217n191	11:48–52	195n116
6:14	216, 217n191	11:51–52	196n120, 287, 287n157, 303
6:16–21	217n191		
6:30–59	217	11:52b	287n157
6:31–58	282n143	12:20–23	303n196
6:32	29, 29n38, 58n119	12:23	197
6:32–50	56	12:31	320n13
6:33	217	12:32	303n196, 320n13
6:35	228n227	12:36	223
6:37–45	206n157	12:37	54
6:45	60, 206n157, 338	12:37–43	29, 54, 55, 56
6:51	217	12:38	54, 55, 55n111, 211n173
6:53–62	195n119	12:39	55, 55n111
6:56	239n20	12:39–40	55
7:1—8:59	195n116	12:40	54
7:1–51	217	12:46	213, 223
7:28–39	109	14	246
7:32–38	217	14:16	244
7:37–39	62–63, 196n120	14:20	228
7:38	228n227	15	100, 227, 227n225, 228, 228n225, 228n226,
8:12	213, 223, 228n227		
8:12–59	217		

SCRIPTURE INDEX

(John continued)

	228n227, 229n230, 232, 244
15:1	29, 228, 228n227
15:1–6	182n71, 226
15:1–8	228
15:2	333
15:4	239n20
15:4–5	239n20
15:5	228
15:7	239n20
17:6–19	215
17:21	287n157
19:36	215, 217
20:25	28

Acts

	326, 328, 331
1–2	221, 296n180, 323n26
1:3	323
1:3–5	323, 324n27
1:4	226n218
1:4–5	323, 324
1:5	324, 325
1:6	324, 324n27, 326, 327, 328
1:6–7	322
1:6–8	316, 322, 326
1:7	322, 325, 326
1:7–8	323, 324, 325n35
1:8	221, 221n204, 222n208, 322, 325, 327
1:11	326n37
1:15–22	326
1:20	264
1:21–26	264
2	109, 142n100, 143, 218n194, 328, 331
2:1–11	326
2:9–11	326
2:14–36	142
2:16–17	59
2:22–36	326
2:24–36	167
2:29–36	102n63
2:30	166n27
2:33	226n218
2:38	242, 327

3	328
3:13	211, 212, 222
3:17–21	316, 326
3:19	327n40
3:19–20	327, 328
3:19–21	327
3:19–26	328
3:20	327, 327n41, 328
3:20–21	326n37, 327
3:21	328
3:22–23	328
3:23	319
3:24	327, 328
3:25	177n54
3:25–26	232, 328
3:26	211, 212, 222
4:25–26	174n46
4:25ff	247
4:27	212, 222
4:30	212, 222
7	72n155
7:38	100
7:43	28
7:44	24, 28
7:52	54
7:55–56	197
8:1–25	326
8:12	324n29
8:26–40	326
8:28–37	211
8:32–33	211n173
8:32–35	222
9:2	218
9:16	223
10	326
10:43	242
13:9	242
13:32–37	167, 326
13:33	174n46
13:38	242
13:47	222, 222n207, 325
14:22	223, 241, 324n29
15	102
15:13–18	326
15:14–18	102n63, 320n13
15:15–18	102n62
16:17	222
18:25–26	218

SCRIPTURE INDEX

19:8	324n29
19:9	218
19:23	218
20:25	28n36, 324n29
20:28	302
22:4	218
24:14	218
24:22	218
26:13	222
26:16–18	222
26:22–23	222
26:23	213, 222
28:23	324n29
28:28	321n16
28:31	324n29

Romans

1:1	220
1:2	65
1:3	332n53
1:3–4	167
1:4	174n46
1:7	242
1–8	176n53, 191n104, 332
1:18—3:20	242
2:6–14	86
2:13	242
2:25—3:9	263
2:25–29	290
2:28–29	100, 237, 311
2:29	191n104, 216
3:3	263
3:19–20	256n58
3:20	242
3:21	65, 94n35, 290n164
3:21–24	242
3:21–26	58, 58n119, 332n54
3:22	250
3:24	241n15
3:28	290n164
3:30	250
4	53, 177n54, 180, 191n104, 314
4:2–5	290n164
4:3	288
4:5–8	332n54
4:9–12	290
4:9–17	223
4:10–12	290n164
4:11	290n164
4:11–12	288
4:11–18	287
4:12	290n164
4:12–17	237
4:13	101, 182n71, 190, 191n104, 232, 290n164, 297, 298n184
4:13–14	298n184
4:13–17	232
4:13–25	298n184
4:14	191n104
4:14–16	191n104
4:16	100, 191n104, 290n164
4:16–17	290
4:16–18	237
4:17	293
4:17–18	180
4:21–31	292
4:22–23	288
4:22–24	180
4:23–24	288
4:23–25	216
5	61, 280n135
5:1–2	242
5:2	101
5:9	242, 250
5:9–10	241
5:10–11	243
5:12	56, 244
5:12–19	53
5:12–21	52n105, 84, 167, 244, 244n25, 245n25, 303n200
5:14	24n26, 28, 52, 282
5:15–19	244
6:3	275
6:3–4	242, 275n117
6:3–5	59, 242
6:3–6	314
6:4	250
6:17	28n36
6:19–22	242
7:1–4	244
7:7–25	256n58
8	298n184

SCRIPTURE INDEX

(Romans continued)

8:1	242, 248
8:2	248
8:3	61
8:9–10	239
8:9–11	109, 244
8:10	239n20
8:11	298n184
8:14	218n194, 249
8:14–23	176
8:14–25	297, 298
8:14–30	218n194
8:14ff	101
8:15	176
8:15–17	237, 243, 299
8:16–17	287
8:16–17 ESV	298
8:17	101, 223, 240, 243, 298n184
8:18–23	298n184
8:19	176n51, 243, 298n184
8:19–22	310
8:20	84
8:21	101, 298n184
8:23	146, 241n15, 243
8:24	241
8:29	171, 218n194
8:32	73, 216, 298n184, 299
8:32–34	215
8:36	247
8:42	176n51
9:4	101, 113, 176n53, 243
9:4–5	176n53, 332n53
9:6	311, 333
9:6–9	292
9–11	69n149, 70n149, 106, 220, 311n224
9:22–25	226n219
9:23–26	269n95
9:25	102n63, 225n217, 247
9:26	102n63
9:27	100
9:30—10:4	256n58
9:33	331
10:5	86
10:8–13	332n54
10:12	258
10:13	247
10:16	211n173
11	99, 315, 316, 321n17, 329, 329n47, 330, 330n49, 332n55, 333, 334
11:1–30	333
11:5–7	100
11:6–24	333
11:12	330n49
11:15	330n49
11:16–24	333
11:25	65n136, 321, 330n49, 333
11:25–26	320, 321n17
11:25–27	146
11:26	106n80, 329, 329n48, 330, 331n51
11:26–27	330, 331, 331n53, 332, 333
11:26a	332
11:26b–27	331
11:27	214
11:28	100
11:34–35	69n149, 70n149
12:1	267n90
12:4–5	253
12:19	226n219
13:11	249
13:11–14	241
15	223
15:1–2	220
15:4	47
15:7–13	223n211
15:8	65, 232
15:8–9	223n211
15:8–9a	223
15:9b–12	223
15:12	224, 224n211
15:16	61
16:5	226n219
16:8	226n219
16:9	226n219
16:12	226n219
16:25	65n136
16:25–27	65

1 Corinthians

53n107, 272, 272n105, 283, 283n145

SCRIPTURE INDEX

1:2	242, 250, 250n39, 261, 272		272n107, 274, 278, 284, 285
1:10—4:21	272	10:1b-2	275
1:13	273, 275	10:2	174-75, 275
1:18	249	10:3	276
1:29	248	10:3-4	276n121, 282n143, 285
1:30	241n15, 242, 248, 249	10:4	59n122, 64n135, 273, 276
1:31	248	10:5	273, 276, 278, 279, 279n131, 282
2:1	65n136		
2:1-10	65n136	10:6	24n26, 28, 52, 56, 279, 279n133, 282, 284
2:7	65n136		
3:6-7	254n50	10:7	273n109
3:10	254n50	10:7-10	273, 278, 279, 281, 282
3:12	254n50	10:8	273n109
3:14	254n50	10:9	273n109, 278n127, 283, 284n148
3:16-17	63, 254, 272, 285, 297		
4:1	65n136	10:10	273n109
5	286	10:11	24n26, 28, 47, 52, 56, 59n122, 135n72, 161n10, 274, 274n115, 278, 279, 279n132, 279n133, 280n134, 281, 282, 283, 284, 285
5:1—7:40	272		
5:6-8	61		
5:7	56, 215, 283		
5:7-8	64n135		
5:7b	29	10:12	53n107, 273, 273n108, 282
6:9	101	10:13	283, 286
6:9-10	243	10:14	272, 283
6:9-11	272	10:16-17	253
6:10	101	10:16-22	276
6:11	242, 272, 283	10:17	272, 273
6:15-17	244	10:18	311
6:16-19	244	10:20	277
6:19	63, 63n133	10:32	272, 311n223
6:19-20	297	11:2—14:40	272
7:19	309	11:17-34	273
8:1—11:1	272	11:22	272
8:7	272	11:23-26	276n120
9	21n15	11:25	60, 144, 214
9:9	37	11:26	62n131
9:9-10	21, 36	11:29	272
9:9-11	36, 37	12:1-2	272n102
9:17	116	12:2	272
9:24-27	272, 272n107	12:12-13	237
10	52, 59n122, 61, 280, 280n135, 281, 283, 286	12:12-26	272
		12:12-27	253
10:1	274, 278, 283, 284	12:13	191, 242, 244, 275, 283
10:1-4	173, 273, 279n131, 281, 282	13:2	65n136
10:1-11	20, 100, 218n194, 314	14:2	65n136
10:1-13	53, 152, 153n141, 263, 271, 271n100, 272,	15:1-58	272
		15:4	230

(1 Corinthians continued)

15:20	240
15:20–22	52
15:20–23	84, 242
15:21–22	29, 167, 244
15:22	239, 239n20, 248
15:22–23	297
15:25	321n19
15:45	297
15:45–49	29, 52, 84, 167
15:50	101, 241
15:51	65n136

2 Corinthians

1:5–6	223
1:20	60
3	60, 281, 332
3:3	216
3:3–18	218n194
3:6	144
3:7–11	256n58
3:7ff	101
3:11	62n131
3:16–18	216
3:18	101
5:14–21	211, 211n173, 222, 303n200
5:17	161, 239n20, 241, 248, 250, 253, 281, 312
5:17—6:2	223
5:17–21	223
5:18	243
5:21	242
6:2	222
6:4	222
6:16	63, 218n194, 254n52
6:16—7:1	237, 254
6:16–17	297
6:16–18	254n52, 287
6:16ff	247
6:17	254n52
6:18	254n52
7:1	254n52
11:2	47n89, 100
11:2–3	244
12:2	239n20
13:5	239n20

Galatians

	290n165
1:4	216, 294, 309
1:6–9	313
1:8–9	307, 308
1:11	313
1:13	308n212, 311n223
1:16	290n165
1:22	248, 261
2:4	313
2:4–5	307
2:7	307
2:15–17	290n164
2:16	242
2:19–20	310
2:19–21	308n212
2:20	239n20, 240, 290n165, 310
2:21	309
2:26	243
3	140, 187n88, 189, 189n96, 189n98, 190, 192, 198, 232
3:1	292
3:1–4	313
3:2	191
3–4	177n54, 189, 193, 291n167, 292n168, 297, 299, 300, 301, 314
3:5	191
3–5	218n194
3:6	192n106, 288
3:6–7	289n163
3:6–9	182n72, 292n168
3:7	186, 243, 287, 289, 308, 313
3:7–9	237
3:8	54, 65, 187n88, 188n94, 288, 288n159, 289n160, 292n168
3:8–9	186
3:9	288n158, 289, 289n160, 313
3:10–22	256n58
3:11b	292n168
3:12	86
3:13	189, 192
3:13–14	182n72, 191
3:13–16	232
3:13–28	94n35

SCRIPTURE INDEX

3:14	186, 186n87, 188n94, 191, 192, 192n107, 193, 221, 226n218, 289, 290, 292n168, 294, 308, 310	4:4	176, 281, 290n165
		4:4–5	188
		4:4–7	176, 237, 287, 289, 290, 290n165, 308
3:14–18	291n167	4:5	243
3:15	187, 313	4:5–7	290n165
3:15—4:11	186	4:6	191, 290n165, 294
3:15–18	193, 293	4:6–7	191, 243
3:16	72, 167, 177, 177n55, 182n72, 184n77, 186, 186n86, 188n95, 189, 189n99, 190, 287, 291, 291n166, 292n168, 294, 295, 299, 301n191, 308	4:7	101, 243, 291, 296, 299
		4:7–9	308n212
		4:8	177
		4:8–11	310
		4:9–11	313
		4:12	313
3:16 ESV	186	4:13	298
3:17	187, 190	4:21	39n66, 309
3:18	189, 190, 232, 296, 299	4:21–31	20, 21, 36, 37, 38, 38n62, 40, 40n68, 221, 287, 292, 292n169, 298, 307n209
3:19	177, 188, 188n94, 190, 301n191		
3:20–21	308n212		
3:21	190	4:22	39n66, 296n179
3:22	190, 232, 300, 310	4:22–23	38, 292
3:22–25	176	4:22–27	294
3:23	309	4:23	190, 296n179
3:23—4:7	89n25	4:24	21n14, 21n15, 37, 39n66, 113, 292, 293n171
3:23–24	291n166		
3:24	291n168	4:24–27	40n68, 217
3:25–29	182n72	4:25	292, 295, 295n176
3:26	176, 186n87, 243, 290, 290n165, 291n168, 311, 313, 314	4:26	111, 255, 292, 293, 297n181, 300, 309, 320n13, 331n51
3:26–27	242	4:26–27	296, 297
3:26–28	289n163, 290n165, 310	4:26–28	312
3:26–29	189, 237, 287, 289, 304, 306n209, 308, 313	4:26–31	234n235
		4:27	38n64, 39n66, 191n104, 219n196, 292, 293, 293n173, 295, 297n181, 312
3:27	275, 290n165, 291, 313, 313n232, 314		
3:27–29	191	4:28	190, 219n196, 243, 292, 294, 296n179, 299, 309, 313
3:28	186n87, 239n20, 248, 258, 291n168, 292n168, 299, 309		
3:28–29	176, 189	4:28–30	38
3:29	100, 101, 186, 190, 193, 193n111, 243, 263, 290, 291, 291n168, 294, 295, 296, 299, 307, 309	4:28–31	191
		4:29	292n170, 294, 313
		4:29–30	292
		4:30	39n66, 292, 296
4	21n15, 296n179	4:30—5:1	294
4:1	296	4:30–31	299
4:3	176		

SCRIPTURE INDEX

(Galatians continued)

4:31	111, 294, 296n179, 300, 313
4:41–31	37
5:1	292, 309
5:2–4	313
5:2–12	309
5:5	242
5:6	306n209, 309, 310
5:11	313
5:13	313
5:13–17	309
5:15	313
5:21	101, 296
5:22	192n105
5:22–23	192n105
5:24	310
5:25	308
6:1	313
6:2	311n223
6:10	253
6:11–15	309n217
6:11–18	308, 308n212, 309, 310
6:12	309
6:12–13	309
6:13	309
6:14	241, 308, 309
6:14–16	310n230
6:15	161, 241, 250, 253, 309, 309n217, 310, 312
6:15–16	305, 308, 311, 312n227
6:16	100, 164, 264, 266n85, 286, 305, 306, 306n209, 307, 308, 309, 309n217, 311, 312, 313, 314
6:16a	310n230
6:16b	312
6:17	309, 309n217
6:18	313

Ephesians

1:1	242, 261
1:3	225
1:3–4	248
1:3–6	224, 225
1:3–13	224n214
1:3–14	224, 226
1:4	100, 239n20, 240
1:5	101, 243, 250, 253, 290
1:6	225
1:7	241n15, 242, 249, 250
1:9	65n136
1:9–10	260n71
1:10	116, 160n8
1:10 ESV	226
1:11	226n218, 232
1:11–23	237
1:13	225, 248
1:13–14	109, 136, 225, 226n218, 241n15
1:20	297
1:20–23	197
1:22–23	253
2:1–3	242, 252n43, 252n44
2:1–10	251, 251n42, 252, 252n44
2:1–22	252n43
2:2–3	252
2:3	255
2:4–5	241
2:4–8	252n44
2:5	241, 249
2:5–6	111, 161n10, 255, 300
2:6	242, 250, 252, 297
2:7	252
2:8	241, 249
2:10	239n20, 241, 250, 252, 252n44
2:11	262
2:11–12	251n41, 252, 252n44, 255
2:11–13	251n41
2:11–18	303n200
2:11–22	102, 218n194, 251, 251n41, 251n42, 252, 255, 257n64, 258, 260, 260n71, 261, 262, 290, 303
2:12	113, 260
2:13	248, 251n41, 252, 252n44, 256, 261
2:13–15	255
2:13–16	255
2:13–18	251n41, 252n44
2:14	253, 253n48, 256, 256n60
2:14–16	252
2:14–18	251n41, 256
2:14–22	260
2:14a	257n61

2:14b–16	257n61
2:15	161, 248, 250, 252, 253, 253n48, 255, 256, 256n60, 262
2:16	251, 253, 256n60, 261
2:16–18	255
2:17	256, 256n60, 257n61
2:18	252, 255, 256n60, 257
2:18–22	262
2:19	253, 255, 260
2:19–22	63, 251n41, 252n44, 297
2:20	254, 264, 265n83
2:20–21	297
2:20–22	254, 259–60, 262, 266
2:21	253, 254n49, 255n53
2:21–22	254, 257, 257n64
2:22	253, 254n49, 255, 257
3:2	116
3:3–4	65n136
3:3–6	136
3:6	136n79, 137n79, 253, 260, 299
3:6–9	136n79
3:9	65n136
3:17	239n20
4:3–6	303
4:4	253
4:6	253
4:11–16	253
4:15–16	254
4:22	241
4:22–24	262
4:24	241
5:1	225n217, 226n219
5:8–9	220
5:22–31	244
5:22–33	234n235, 263
5:23	253
5:25	215
5:25–26	250
5:26	250
5:28–32	20
5:29–30	253
5:32	47n89, 65n136, 244
6:1–11	23
6:3	182n71, 232
6:6	223
6:19	65n136

Philippians

1:1	223, 248, 248n35, 261
1:6	242
1:14	248
2:1	248
2:4	248
2:6–11	211n173
2:7	211
2:15	220, 243
3:3	100, 111, 216, 237, 311
3:9	239n20, 242, 248
3:11	242
3:17	28, 28n36
3:19	101
3:20	255, 297, 297n181
3:20–21	240

Colossians

1:2	101
1:12	226n218
1:12–13	241
1:12–14	161n10
1:13	225n217
1:14	241n15, 242, 250
1:15	297
1:18	262, 297
1:19	297, 297n182
1:22	243
1:25	116
1:26–27	65n136, 244
1:27	239n20, 248
1:28	248
2:2	65n136
2:11	100, 216, 237, 262
2:11–14	290
2:12	59, 242
2:12–13	111, 240, 255, 300
2:16–17	29
2:17	29n38, 56, 58n119, 74
3:1	240, 242
3:3	161n10, 255, 300
3:3–4	244
3:4	176n51
3:9–10	241
3:11	258
3:12	225n217, 226n219

(Colossians continued)

3:15	253n48
4:3	65n136

1 Thessalonians

1:1	248, 248n35, 249, 261
1:4	225n217, 226n219
1:6	249
1:7	28n36
2:14	248, 248n35, 249, 261
2:15	54
3:2–4	249
4:3–8	242
4:5	248
4:9	60, 207n159, 338
4:14	249
4:16	239n20, 249
4:17	249
5:8–9	241, 249
5:10	249
5:23–24	242

2 Thessalonians

1:1	248, 261
2:7	65n136
2:13	225n217, 226n219
3:9	28n36

1 Timothy

1:4	116
3:9	65n136
3:16	65n136
4:12	28n36

2 Timothy

1:9	240, 249
1:9–10	59n122

Titus

2:4	241n15
3:4–7	111
3:5	241, 249

3:7	243

Hebrews

	56n115, 113n98, 281
1:1–14	167
1:2	59
1:5	174n46
1:14	241
2:5–18	167
2:6–8	52n105
2:7	269
2:10	243
2:10–18	189, 189n99
2:15–18	84
2:16	189, 287
3:1–6	216
3:2–4	275n117
3–4	29, 113n98, 152
3:5–6	212
3:7—4:11	182n71
3:7–19	218n194
3:16	275n117
4	181n69
4:1–11	97, 216, 232
4:8	216
4:9	269
4:15	175n50
4:16	216
5:5	167, 174n46
5:5–10	215
7	29, 51
7:1–10	40n68
7:11–12	62n131
7:11–22	206
7:12—8:6	215
7:18	107
7:22	214
7:23–28	215
7:26	175n50
8	92, 217
8:1–13	107
8:2	58n119
8:5	24, 24n26, 25, 28, 54n108, 74
8:6–13	62n131, 214
8:7–13	113
8:8–12	247

8:8–13	102n63	13:15–16	267n90
8–9	332	13:20	214, 302
8–10	60, 64n135		
8:13	89n25	## 1 John	
9	214n184		
9:1—10:18	242	1:8–10	242
9:9	29n38	2:20	60, 207n159, 338
9–10	61, 62n131	2:27	60, 207n159, 338
9:11—10:22	215	2:29	241, 249
9:11–15	215	3:2	176n51, 241, 287
9:12	214n184, 241n15	3:9	241, 249
9:13–14	242, 267n90	3:24	244
9:15	193n110, 214, 214n184, 237	4:7	241, 249
9:15–18	214	4:13	239n20, 244
9:22–25	24	5:4	249
9:24	24n26, 25, 28, 54n108, 58n119	5:18	249
9:28	211, 214, 214n184, 241	## 1 Peter	
10	29		
10:1	56, 58n119, 74		267n92, 268n92, 271
10:10	242	1:1	287n157
10:10–12	215	1:2	218n194, 267, 268
10:14	215	1:3	241, 266, 268n95, 270
10:14–22	214	1:4	232, 243, 251
10:19–22	62, 250	1:5	241
10:19–25	207n159	1:10–12	51, 77, 77n166, 265
10:22	216	1:11	77n166
11	181n69	1:12	77n166
11:8–16	232, 297	1:14	265n84
11:9	292	1:15–16	242
11:10	181n69	1:18	265n84
11:10 ESV	90	1:18–19	61, 241n15, 249
11:13–16	182n71	1:19	215, 266n85, 268
11:16	181n69	1:20	240, 269n96
11:40 NIV	74	1:20–21	270
12:5–11	243	1:21	265–66, 265n84
12:18	221	1:23	241, 268n95, 270
12:18–24	216	1:24–25	268n95
12:18–28	100	2	286
12:22	191, 320n13, 331n51	2:4	266, 267
12:22–24	161n10, 217, 221, 255, 262, 293n172, 300	2:4–5	266n89, 267, 297
		2:4–7	297n182
12:22–29	297	2:4–8	260
12:24	214	2:4–10	29, 63, 218n194, 263, 265, 266n88, 269, 269n96, 270n97, 270n98
12:28–29	267n90		
13:12–14	182n71, 297		
13:14	161n10, 320n13	2:5	61, 254, 266, 266n86, 266n87, 267, 267n90
13:15	61		

425

SCRIPTURE INDEX

(1 Peter continued)

2:6	266, 266n87, 269
2:6–7	266, 270, 297
2:6–8	267, 269n96
2:7	267
2:7–9	229n230
2:9	100, 102n63, 135n72, 206, 247, 250, 258, 267, 268, 269, 270, 314
2:9–10	153n141, 267, 268, 269, 269n96, 270n97
2:10	268, 269, 270
2:12	265n84
2:16	223
2:20–24	223
2:20–25	211n173
2:21–25	211
2:24–25	305
2:25	270, 302
3:6	287
3:18	266
3:18–22	59
3:21	24n26, 28, 54n108
3:21–22	266n89
4:2–4	265n84
4:14	267
5:2–4	302

2 Peter

3:6–7	61
3:13	182n71

Revelation

	91, 211n173, 314
1:1	223
1:4	314
1:4–6	135n72
1:6	100, 102n63, 206, 218n194
1:11	314
2:1—3:22	314
2:7	314n234
2:9	314
2:10	321n19
2:11	314n234
2:17	218n194, 314n234
2:25	321n19
2:26	321n19
2:26–27	174n46
2:29	314n234
3:6	314n234
3:9	314
3:12	331n51
3:13	314n234
3:22	314n234
5:6	211
5:6–10	61, 218n194
5:9–10	135n72, 206
5:10	102n63
6:11	223
7:1–17	314
7:4	164
11:1–13	314
11:18	223
12:1–17	314
12:11–17	218n194
12:17	315
13:8	61
15:1–8	218n194
19:7–9	62n131
19:15	174n46
20	222n205
20:4–6	123
21:1	242
21:1–4	255
21:1—22:5	182n71, 314
21:2	293n172, 297, 297n181, 331n51
21:2–3	191
21:3–4	242
21:10–27	297
21:11	297
21:12	164
21:12–14	264, 317
21:19–20	265
21:22	63
22:1–5	223

EARLY CHRISTIAN WRITINGS

Clement of Alexandria — 32

Cyril of Jerusalem — 31–32

Irenaeus of Smyrna — 32, 32n47

John Chrysostom — 32

Justin — 32

Melito of Sardis

Peri Pascha — 18

Origen of Alexandria — 18, 21, 32, 40

Tertullian — 31, 32

www.ingramcontent.com/pod-product-compliance
Lightning Source LLC
Chambersburg PA
CBHW071225290426
44108CB00013B/1288